The Gardener's Book of Sources

The Gardener's Book of Sources

William Bryant Logan

A ROUNDTABLE PRESS BOOK

Viking

To my parents, who made me wonder

A ROUNDTABLE PRESS BOOK
Directors: Susan E. Meyer, Marsha Melnick
Managing Editor: Marguerite Ross
Research Assistant: Martha Richheimer
Design: Betty Binns Graphics, Inc.
Illustration: Sandra Forrest
Art Production: Carol L. Fitschen

VIKING
Viking Penguin Inc., 40 West 23rd Street, New
York, New York 10010, U.S.A.

Penguin Books Ltd, 27 Wrights Lane, London
W8 5TZ (Publishing & Editorial), and
Harmondsworth, Middlesex, England
(Distribution & Warehouse)

Penguin Books Australia Ltd, Ringwood,
Victoria, Australia

Penguin Books Canada Limited, 2801 John
Street, Markham, Ontario, Canada L3R 1B4

Penguin Books (N.Z.) Ltd, 182-190 Wairau
Road, Auckland 10, New Zealand

First published in simultaneous hardcover
and paperback editions by Viking Penguin
Inc. 1988
Published simultaneously in Canada

Copyright © 1988 Roundtable Press, Inc.

All rights reserved.

Grateful acknowledgment is made for
permission to reprint excerpts from the
following copyrighted material:
The Gardener's Year, by Karel Capek.
Copyright © 1984 University of Wisconsin
Press.
The Little Bulbs, by Elizabeth Lawrence.
Copyright © 1986 Duke University Press.
The History of Gardens, by Christopher
Thacker. Copyright © 1979 The University of
California Press.
Plants, Man and Life by Edgar Anderson.
Copyright © 1967 The University of
California Press.
*A Field Guide to the Wildflowers of
Northeastern and North Central North America*,
Roger Tory Peterson and Margaret McKenny.
Copyright © 1974 Houghton Mifflin
Company.
V. Sackville-West's Garden Book, by Vita
Sackville-West. Copyright © 1983 Atheneum
Publishers.

Library of Congress Cataloging in
Publication Data
Logan, William Bryant. The gardener's book
of sources. 1. Gardening—United States—
Directories. 2. Gardening—Bibliography.
3. Gardening—Directories.
4. Gardening—Equipment and
supplies—Directories. 5. Horticultural
literature. I. Title.
[SB450.943.U6L64 1988b]
 635′.025′73   87-40306
ISBN 0-670-81223-4

Printed in the United States of America by
Kingsport Press, Inc., Kingsport, Tennessee
Set in Bembo Medium and Gill Sans Light

Contents

Introduction

My earliest memory of well-being is owed to the garden. I must have been about three years old. We lived in the Mojave Desert and kept a garden in the yard. I can still smell the acrid tomato vines. I see my father clipping several ripe tomatoes and passing them through the open kitchen window to my mother, who immediately washed them in the sink and set them on the sill. It wasn't that I loved tomatoes so much. More moving to me was the astounding fact that, holding the fruits, my parents' hands seemed pinker.

Many years later, I finally came on a satisfying explanation for the power of this memory. In a brilliant essay called "Nearer than Eden," John Brinckerhoff Jackson remarked that gardening satisfies the aspirations of ordinary existence, of work shared with family or friends. Our gardens are not so important for what they do to the world, as for the way in which they vivify our relationships. Maybe this is why gardeners are so generous, why the best of them are such great correspondents, readers, and explorers. Again and again in the course of research for this book, I have found that the best garden writers—people like Elizabeth Lawrence, Vita Sackville-West, Celia Thaxter, and Karel Capek—bring their friends, their reading and their own experience into their work in a way that the finest novelist might envy. Surprisingly enough, the same turned out to be true for most of the nurserypeople and garden-club writers who appear in this book. Gardening, it seems, is the art of daily life.

The Gardener's Book of Sources has two purposes. The first is to put you in contact with the companies, books, magazines, and individuals who can give you what you need for virtually any sort of gardening. There are well over 1000 resources listed here, drawn not only from the U.S. and Canada, but from around the world. I had hoped to be comprehensive, but I was obliged to settle for listing the best and most unusual resources in the gardening world. A Hindu proverb says that within every grain of sand in the Ganges lies another Ganges. The same goes for garden suppliers and publications. Every one you look at suggests dozens more you simply have to get. I hope, then, that this book will not only provide you with what you immediately need, but start you on that endless chain of delightful research.

The book's second purpose is to focus on gardening as a human pursuit. Wherever possible, I have classified nurseries, books, magazines, designers, clubs, and suppliers according to what they offer *and* to their attitudes towards gardening. In practical terms, this should give you a better idea of what you are getting into when you use the resource. Also, I hope, it will delight you as it did me. There are few things more charming than coming upon an article in a gesneriads magazine that begins, "As everyone knows . . .", only to complete the paragraph with a precise disquisition on the discovery of the African violet, containing arcana that only the obsessed or in-love could suppose were common knowledge. The most pleasurable thing about writing this book was discovering the character of the gardeners and suppliers whose work it describes.

Acknowledgments are due to the many sources who responded to my queries—by letter, on the phone, or in person—with generous information. In many respects, I have simply been their scribe, though all mistakes, of course, are mine. Also, some resources that I wanted to list could not be included because they did not respond to queries, because I could not find their current addresses, or because, in the case of publications, they had gone out of print. (A few out-of-print titles appear, simply because they seem worth the trouble of tracking down, at the library or from a specialty bookseller.) Then too, space and time limitations forced me to leave out some items that, in an ideal world, I would have included.

Special thanks are owed to the editors at Roundtable Press. Susan Meyer, Marsha Melnick, and Meg Ross were remarkably diligent and understanding. It was a pleasure to work with people whose main goal was to make the best book possible. Thanks, too, to the library staff of The New York Botanical Garden, who cheerfully put up with the weeks during which I laid siege to their collection. Finally, my thanks to Constance Sayre, who acquired this book for Viking Penguin, and to Dan Frank, who thoughtfully edited it.

Here are a few hints for using *The Gardener's Book of Sources.* We have made our best efforts to assure that all addresses are correct; we apologize for any inadvertent errors and hope that you will bring them to our attention. Also, it may happen that some addresses will have changed since the time of this writing; in that case, the post office will generally inform you of the new address. Prices, too, may have changed before you read this, but they were the exact prices current at the time of writing. To avoid repetition, we have listed publishers' addresses at the back of the book. If the volume you are looking for is not available from a local bookseller, you can send for it directly.

A few abbreviations appear consistently in the book. Here is what they mean. SASE stands for self-addressed stamped envelope. Some nurseries ask that you send a SASE in exchange for their catalogue. Ppd. means post paid—that shipping charges were included in the price quoted. GBS stands for *The Gardener's Book of Sources.* I have used the abbreviation to avoid writing out the entire name when making cross-references.

Lately, I have begun gardening with my own young son, preparing the soil in city tree pits, pruning, and caring for a community-garden greenhouse. Mainly, though, I have been tied to the word processor, a fact that both my son and wife have patiently borne. Now that it is done, I hope we will make use of the book, and go out and get our hands dirty.

William Bryant Logan

Annotated Contents

The sources listed below are organized according to specialized areas of interest. Within each chapter these sources appear in alphabetical order, where they can be easily located. Specific page numbers for each source can also be found in the general index on page 259.

1 General Sources

GARDENING FOR LOVE
GREEN THOUGHTS: A WRITER IN THE GARDEN
HOME GROUND
ONWARD AND UPWARD IN THE GARDEN
PLANTS, MAN AND LIFE
PLANTS OF THE BIBLE

How-To

THE AUDUBON SOCIETY GUIDE TO ATTRACTING BIRDS
THE AVANT GARDENER
THE COMPLETE URBAN GARDENER
COUNTRY WISDOM BULLETINS
EARTHWORMS FOR GARDENERS AND FISHERMEN
THE ENCYCLOPEDIA OF ORGANIC GARDENING
GENERAL GARDENING ENCYCLOPEDIAS (3)
FLOWER AND GARDEN
GARDEN

GARDEN BOOK SERIES (5)
GARDENING THROUGH THE YEAR
GROWING AND SAVING VEGETABLE SEEDS
GURNEY'S GARDENING NEWS
HARROWSMITH
HORTICULTURE
HORTIDEAS
MOON SIGNS GARDENING DATES
THE MOTHER EARTH NEWS PRESENTS AN ARRAY OF GARDENS
THE OLD FARMER'S ALMANAC
PARK'S SUCCESS WITH BULBS
PARK'S SUCESS WITH SEEDS
PLANT PROPAGATION
PLANTS OF THE BIBLE
READER'S DIGEST ILLUSTRATED GUIDE TO GARDENING
RODALE'S ORGANIC GARDENING
SEAWEED IN AGRICULTURE AND HORTICULTURE
THE SMALLHOLDER
SUNSET
SUNSET NEW WESTERN GARDEN BOOK

THE VICTORY GARDEN SERIES (4)
THE VIRGINIA MASTER GARDENER HANDBOOK
THE WHOLE EARTH REVIEW
THE WISLEY BOOK OF GARDENING

Pests and Diseases

THE GARDENER'S BUG BOOK
GROWER'S WEED IDENTIFICATION HANDBOOK
A GUIDE TO SAFE PEST CONTROL AROUND THE HOME
INSECT IDENTIFICATION HANDBOOK
THE ORTHO PROBLEM SOLVER
PLANT HEALTH HANDBOOK
RODALE'S COLOR HANDBOOK OF GARDEN INSECTS
WEEDS OF THE NORTH CENTRAL STATES
WESTCOTT'S PLANT DISEASE HANDBOOK, 4TH ED.

2 *Annuals and Perennials* 52

Alpine and Rock Gardens

ALPINE GARDEN SOCIETY
AMERICAN ROCK GARDEN SOCIETY
BLUESTONE PERENNIALS
CARROLL GARDENS
CHADWELL HIMALAYAN PLANT SEED
KLAUS R. JELITTO
THE MACDONALD ENCYCLOPEDIA OF ALPINE FLOWERS
MAVER NURSERY
NATURE'S GARDEN
OWL RIDGE ALPINES
RICE CREEK GARDENS
ROCK GARDENING
ROCK GARDENS
SCOTTISH ROCK GARDEN CLUB
SEEDALP
WHITE FLOWER FARM

Annuals

THE COUNTRY GARDEN
THE FRAGRANT PATH
THE MOTHER EARTH NEWS A-TO-Z FLOWER GARDEN FAVORITES

Aquatics

HERMITAGE GARDENS
HORTICO
HORTICULTURAL SYSTEMS
LILYPONS WATER GARDENS
MOORE WATER GARDENS

PARADISE WATER GARDENS
RICE CREEK GARDEN
WILLIAM TRICKER, INC.
VAN NESS WATER GARDENS
THE WATER LILY SOCIETY
WATER LILY WORLD

Spring and Fall Bulbs

AMERICAN DAFFODIL SOCIETY
C. A. CRUICKSHANK, INC.
THE DAFFODIL MART
DUTCH GARDENS
HOLBROOK FARM & NURSERY
THE LITTLE BULBS
JOHN D. LYON, INC.
MCCLURE & ZIMMERMAN
MESSELAAR BULB CO.
GRANT MITSCH NOVELTY DAFFODILS
ROYAL GARDENS
SPRING HILL NURSERIES
TYTY PLANTATION
VELDHEER TULIP GARDENS
WHITE FLOWER FARM

Chrysanthemums

HUFF'S GARDENS
THON'S GARDEN MUMS
WHITE FLOWER FARM

Clematis

FISKE'S CLEMATIS NURSERY
THE D. S. GEORGE NURSERIES

MAROUSHEK GARDENS
WAYSIDE GARDENS
WHITE FLOWER FARM

Coleus

COLOR FARM

Cyclamen

MONTROSE NURSERY

Dahlias

AMERICAN DAHLIA SOCIETY
FERNCLIFF GARDENS
GLADSIDE GARDENS
LEGG DAHLIA GARDENS
SWAN ISLAND DAHLIAS
WHITE FLOWER FARM

Dianthus

ALLWOOD BROS.
BLUESTONE PERENNIALS

Day Lilies

BORBELETA GARDENS
BUSSE GARDENS
CAPRICE FARM NURSERY
ENGLERTH GARDENS
HOMESTEAD DIVISION OF SUNNYBROOK FARMS
HORTICO
JERNIGAN GARDENS

KLEHM NURSERY
LOUISIANA NURSERY
SEAWRIGHT GARDENS
SHADY OAKS NURSERY
ANDRÉ VIETTE FARM & NURSERY
WHITE FLOWER FARM
WILDWOOD FARM

Ferns

AMERICAN FERN SOCIETY
FANCY FRONDS
FERN GROWER'S MANUAL
FERNS TO KNOW & GROW
A FIELD MANUAL OF THE FERNS & FERN-ALLIES OF THE UNITED STATES AND CANADA
FOLIAGE GARDENS
SHADY OAKS NURSERY
WHITE FLOWER FARM
WILDWOOD FARM

Flower and Gardening Reference

AMERICAN HORTICULTURAL SOCIETY
THE COMPLETE SHADE GARDENER
FLOWER DICTIONARIES (10)
THE FRAGRANT GARDEN
GARDENING WITH PERENNIALS
THE LITTLE BULBS
THE MACDONALD ENCYCLOPEDIA OF ALPINE FLOWERS
THE MOTHER EARTH NEWS A-TO-Z FLOWER GARDEN FAVORITES
THE PERENNIAL GARDEN
PERENNIALS FOR YOUR GARDEN
RIGHT PLANT, RIGHT PLACE
ROCK GARDENING
ROCK GARDENS
SEQUENCE OF BLOOM OF PERENNIALS, BIENNIALS, AND BULBS
THAXTER, CELIA (2)
WHITE FLOWER FARM

Geraniums and Pelargoniums

INTERNATIONAL GERANIUM SOCIETY
MERRY GARDENS

Gladiolus

FERNCLIFF GARDENS
GLADSIDE GARDENS
PLEASANT VALLEY GLADS

Ornamental Grasses

KURT BLUEMEL, INC.
CARROLL GARDENS
THE CROWNSVILLE NURSERY
HORTICO

MAVER NURSERY
RICE CREEK GARDENS
ANDRÉ VIETTE FARM & NURSERY
WILDWOOD FARM

Ground Covers

ANGLEWOOD NURSERIES
GILSON GARDENS
GROUNDCOVERS IN THE LANDSCAPE
HOMESTEAD DIVISION OF SUNNYBROOK FARMS
MERRY GARDENS
PEEKSKILL NURSERIES
PRENTISS COURT GROUND COVERS
RICE CREEK GARDENS
SHADY OAKS NURSERY

Hosta

BUSSE GARDENS
CAPRICE FARM NURSERY
ENGLERTH GARDENS
FAIRWAY ENTERPRISES
HAUSER'S SUPERIOR VIEW FARM
HILDENBRANDT'S IRIS GARDENS
HOMESTEAD DIVISION OF SUNNYBROOK FARMS
JERNIGAN GARDENS
KLEHM NURSERY
MAROUSHEK GARDENS
SAVORY'S GREENHOUSES AND GARDENS
SHADY OAKS NURSERY
ANDRÉ VIETTE FARM & NURSERY
WHITE FLOWER FARM

Iris

AMERICAN IRIS SOCIETY
BAY VIEW GARDENS
BORBELETA GARDENS
BUSSE GARDENS
CAPRICE FARM NURSERY
C. A. CRUICKSHANK, INC.
ENGLERTH GARDENS
FERNCLIFF GARDENS
HILDENBRANDT'S IRIS GARDENS
HORTICO
JERNIGAN GARDENS
KLEHM NURSERY
LAURIE'S GARDEN
LOUISIANA NURSERY
MISSION BELL GARDENS
ROYAL GARDENS
SCHREINER'S GARDEN
ANDRÉ VIETTE FARM & NURSERY
WHITE FLOWER FARM
GILBERT H. WILD & SONS

Lilies

BORBELETA GARDENS
NORTH AMERICAN LILY SOCIETY
REX BULB FARMS
WHITE FLOWER FARM

Nerines

NERINE NURSERIES

Peonies

AMERICAN PEONY SOCIETY
BUSSE GARDENS
CAPRICE FARM NURSERY
FERNCLIFF GARDENS
HILDENBRANDT'S IRIS GARDENS
KLEHM NURSERY
DAVID REATH NURSERY
ANDRÉ VIETTE FARM & NURSERY
WHITE FLOWER FARM
GILBERT H. WILD & SONS

Perennials Nurseries and Topics

BLACKMORE & LANGDON
KURT BLUEMEL, INC.
BLUESTONE PERENNIALS
BUSSE GARDENS
CARROLL GARDENS
CLIFFORD'S PERENNIAL & VINE
THE COUNTRY GARDEN
C. A. CRUICKSHANK, INC.
THE FRAGRANT PATH
GARDENING WITH PERENNIALS
GILSON GARDENS
HAUSER'S SUPERIOR VIEW FARM
HOLBROOK FARM & NURSERY
HORTICO
KLAUS R. JELITTO
KLEHM NURSERY
MAVER NURSERY
MILAEGER'S GARDENS
MONTROSE NURSERY
NATURE'S GARDEN
THE PERENNIAL GARDEN
PERENNIALS FOR YOUR GARDEN
ROYAL GARDENS
SEEDALP
SHADY OAKS NURSERY
SPRING HILL NURSERIES
ANDRÉ VIETTE FARM & NURSERY
WAYSIDE GARDENS
WHITE FLOWER FARM
WILDWOOD FARM

Oriental Poppies

C. A. CRUICKSHANK, INC.
HILDENBRANDT'S IRIS GARDENS
MOHN'S, INC.
ANDRÉ VIETTE FARM & NURSERY

Primulas

BLACKMORE & LANGDON
CHEHALIS RARE PLANT NURSERY
MAROUSHEK GARDENS

Azaleas and Rhododendrons

AMERICAN RHODODENDRON SOCIETY
AZALEA SOCIETY OF AMERICA
BOVEES NURSERY
CAMELLIA FOREST NURSERY
CARLSON'S GARDENS
GIRARD NURSERIES
GREER GARDENS
HOW TO IDENTIFY RHODODENDRON & AZALEA PROBLEMS
NUCCIO'S NURSERIES
WESTON NURSERIES
WOODLAND NURSERIES

Bonsai

AMERICAN BONSAI SOCIETY
BRUSSEL'S BONSAI NURSERY
GIRARD NURSERIES
GREER GARDENS
HORTICA GARDENS
INTERNATIONAL BONSAI ARBORETUM
MATSU-MOMIJI NURSERY
SHANTI BITHI BONSAI

Camellias

AMERICAN CAMELLIA SOCIETY
CAMELLIA FOREST NURSERY
NUCCIO'S NURSERIES

Dwarf Conifers

BOVEES NURSERY
DILATUSH NURSERY
FOXBOROUGH NURSERY
GIRARD NURSERIES
GREER GARDENS
MICHAEL & JANET L. KRISTICK
MATSU-MOMIJI NURSERY
STONEHURST RARE PLANTS
VINELAND NURSERIES

Fruit, General

ADAMS COUNTY NURSERY
AMES' ORCHARD AND NURSERY
BEAR CREEK NURSERY
BURNT RIDGE NURSERY
CALIFORNIA NURSERY COMPANY
CONVERSE NURSERY
CUMBERLAND VALLEY NURSERIES
EDIBLE LANDSCAPING

FEDCO TREES
FOWLER NURSERIES
GOLDEN BOUGH TREE FARM
GREENMANTLE NURSERY
GROOTENDORST NURSERIES
HARMONY FARM SUPPLY
JOHNSON NURSERY
V. KRAUS NURSERY
LAKESHORE TREE FARMS
MAY NURSERY COMPANY
J. E. MILLER NURSERIES
NEW YORK STATE FRUIT TESTING COOPERATIVE ASSOCIATION
SUNSWEET FRUIT & BULB NURSERY
MAUDE WALKER
WAYNESBORO NURSERIES
WESTON NURSERIES
WOMACK'S NURSERY COMPANY
ZILKE BROTHERS NURSERY

Fruit, Heirloom and Unusual

APPLESOURCE
BEAR CREEK NURSERY
CALIFORNIA RARE FRUIT GROWERS
CONVERSE NURSERY
ECOLOGICAL FRUIT PRODUCTION IN THE NORTH
FEDCO TREES
FRIENDS OF THE TREES SOCIETY
THE FRUITION PROJECT
GREENMANTLE NURSERY
HARMONY FARM SUPPLY
HIDDEN SPRINGS NURSERY
JOHNSON NURSERY
LAWSON'S NURSERY
LIVING TREE CENTRE
MAVER NURSERY
J. E. MILLER NURSERIES
NORTH AMERICAN FRUIT EXPLORERS
OLD FASHION APPLE TREES
RAINTREE NURSERY
SOUTHMEADOW FRUIT GARDENS
TOLLGATE GARDEN NURSERY
TRIPPLE BROOK FARM
WORCESTER COUNTY HORTICULTURAL SOCIETY

Heaths and Heathers

HEATHS & HEATHERS
VINELAND NURSERIES

Japanese Maples

GREER GARDENS
HUGHES NURSERY
MICHAEL & JANET L. KRISTICK

MAPLEWOOD SEED CO.
MATSU-MOMIJI NURSERY
STONEHURST RARE PLANTS

Kalmia

CARLSON'S GARDENS
FOXBOROUGH NURSERY
GOSSLER FARMS NURSERY

Lilacs

CARLSON'S GARDENS
HEARD GARDENS
WOODLAND NURSERIES

Magnolias

GOSSLER FARMS NURSERY

Nuts

THE BOOK OF EDIBLE NUTS
CASCADE FORESTRY SERVICE
CUMBERLAND VALLEY NURSERIES
EARL DOUGLASS
FEDCO TREES
FOWLER NURSERIES
GOLDEN BOUGH TREE FARM
GRIMO NUT NURSERY
HALL CREEK NURSERY
JOHNSON NURSERY
LAWSON'S NURSERY
MAVER NURSERY
MAY NURSERY COMPANY
J. E. MILLER NURSERIES
NOLIN RIVER NUT TREE NURSERY
NORTHERN NUT GROWERS ASSOCIATION
RAINTREE NURSERY
SUNSWEET FRUIT & BULB NURSERY
MAUDE WALKER
WAYNESBORO NURSERIES
WESTON NURSERIES
WOMACK'S NURSERY CO.

Ornamental, General

APPALACHIAN GARDENS
BOVEES NURSERY
DUTCH MOUNTAIN NURSERY
EISLER NURSERIES
FOXBOROUGH NURSERY
GIRARD NURSERIES
GOLDEN BOUGH TREE FARM

GOSSLER FARMS NURSERY
GREER GARDENS
HILLIER NURSERIES
HORTICO
INTERNATIONAL OLEANDER SOCIETY
V. KRAUS NURSERIES
LAKE COUNTY NURSERY
LAKESHORE TREE FARMS
MAVER NURSERY
J. E. MILLER NURSERIES
VALLEY NURSERY
WAYNESBORO NURSERIES
WESTON NURSERIES
WHITMAN FARMS
WOMACK'S NURSERY COMPANY
WOODLAND NURSERIES
ZILKE BROTHERS NURSERY

Reference

THE HUNDRED FINEST TREES AND SHRUBS FOR
TEMPERATE CLIMATES
LANDSCAPE PLANTS IN DESIGN
MANUAL OF WOODY LANDSCAPE PLANTS
THE MORTON ARBORETUM
NURSERY SOURCE MANUAL

ORNAMENTAL AND SHADE TREES FOR UTAH
PRUNING
PRUNING SIMPLIFIED
SHRUBS AND VINES FOR AMERICAN GARDENS
THE SHRUB IDENTIFICATION BOOK
SHRUBS IN THE LANDSCAPE
THE TREE IDENTIFICATION BOOK
TREES FOR AMERICAN GARDENS
TREES FOR EVERY PURPOSE
TREES OF NORTH AMERICA AND EUROPE
WINTER GUIDES (2)

Shade

CASCADE FORESTRY SERVICE
DUTCH MOUNTAIN NURSERY
ECCLES NURSERIES
EISLER NURSERIES
FRIENDS OF THE TREES SOCIETY
GOLDEN BOUGH TREE FARM
HILLIER NURSERIES
HORTICO
INTERNATIONAL FOREST SEED CO.
V. KRAUS NURSERIES
LAKESHORE TREE FARMS
MAVER NURSERY

J. E. MILLER NURSERIES
MUSSER FORESTS
RAINTREE NURSERY
DEAN SWIFT SEED CO.
TRIPPLE BROOK FARM
VALLEY NURSERY
WAYNESBORO NURSERIES
WESTON NURSERIES
WHITMAN FARMS
WOODLAND NURSERIES

West/South Coastal Zones

CALIFORNIA NURSERY COMPANY
ENDANGERED SPECIES
HARMONY FARM SUPPLY
HIDDEN SPRINGS NURSERY
HOWLETT'S COASTAL ZONE NURSERY
RAINTREE NURSERY
STEVE RAY'S BAMBOO GARDENS
SUNSET NURSERY
SUNSWEET FRUIT & BULB NURSERY
MAUDE WALKER

4 *Wildflowers and Native Plants*

California Natives

EARTHSIDE NATURE CENTER
FLOWERING PLANTS IN THE LANDSCAPE
GROWING CALIFORNIA NATIVE PLANTS
LARNER SEEDS
LAS PILITAS NURSERY
NATIVE SONS
THE THEODORE PAYNE FOUNDATION
SELECTED CALIFORNIA NATIVE PLANTS WITH
COMMERCIAL SOURCES
WEBER NATIVE PLANT NURSERY
YERBA BUENA NURSERY

General

APPALACHIAN WILDFLOWER NURSERY
APPLEWOOD SEED CO.
BOEHLKE'S WOODLAND GARDENS
GREEN DRAGONS AND DOLL'S EYES
GROW NATIVE SHRUBS IN YOUR GARDEN
LARNER SEEDS
MOON MOUNTAIN WILDFLOWERS
NATIVE SEEDS, INC.
ORCHID GARDENS
PAINTED MEADOWS SEED CO.
PASSIFLORA
CLYDE ROBIN SEED COMPANY
VERMONT WILDFLOWER FARM
THE WILD GARDEN

Prairie

RICHARD, JAMES, AND KATHERINE CLINEBELL
GRASSES: AN IDENTIFICATION GUIDE
HOME GROWN PRAIRIES
DAVID KROPP
LA FAYETTE HOME NURSERY
LITTLE VALLEY FARM
MIDWEST WILDFLOWERS
THE MORTON ARBORETUM
THE NATURAL GARDEN
PRAIRIE MOON NURSERY
PRAIRIE NURSERY
PRAIRIE PROPAGATION HANDBOOK
TEXAS NATIVES (4)
WINDRIFT PRAIRIE SHOP & NURSERY

Reference

THE AUDUBON SOCIETY NATURE GUIDES (7)
DIRECTORY TO RESOURCES ON WILDFLOWER
PROPAGATION
THE EARTH MANUAL
FIELD GUIDES (7)
FLOWERING PLANTS IN THE LANDSCAPE
A GARDEN OF WILDFLOWERS
GRASSES: AN INDENTIFICATION GUIDE
GROW NATIVE SHRUBS IN YOUR GARDEN
GROWING AND PROPAGATING WILDFLOWERS
GROWING WILDFLOWERS: A GARDENER'S GUIDE

GROWING WOODLAND PLANTS
LANDSCAPING WITH NATIVE PLANTS
THE NATIONAL WILDFLOWER RESEARCH CENTER
NATURAL LANDSCAPING
NATURE'S DESIGN
NEW ENGLAND WILDFLOWER SOCIETY
BOOKS (4)
THE NEW WILDFLOWERS & HOW TO GROW THEM
THE ROOT BOOK
SEED IDENTIFICATION MANUAL
SOURCES OF NATIVE SEEDS AND PLANTS
WILDFLOWER

Southeastern Natives

NATURAL GARDENS
NORTH CAROLINA NATIVE PLANT PROPAGATION
HANDBOOK
WOODLANDERS

Southwestern Natives

BERNARDO BEACH NATIVE PLANT FARM
DESERT PLANTS
FJELLGARDEN
HUBBS BROS. SEED
PLANTS OF THE SOUTHWEST
SOUTHWESTERN NATIVE SEEDS
TEXAS NATIVES (4)
WILDLAND & NATIVE SEEDS FOUNDATION

U.S. Natives

NEW ENGLAND WILDFLOWER SOCIETY BOOKS (4)
ORCHID GARDENS

Western Natives

FOREST FARM
A GUIDE TO MOUNTAIN FLOWERS

JEWELS OF THE PLAINS
LANDSCAPE PLANTS FROM UTAH'S MOUNTAINS
LARNER SEEDS
NATIVE TREES OF THE INTERMOUNTAIN REGION
SISKIYOU RARE PLANT NURSERY

Woodland Natives

ARTHUR EAMES ALLGROVE
RICHARD, JAMES, AND KATHERINE CLINEBELL

GARDENS OF THE BLUE RIDGE
GRIFFEY'S NURSERY
GROWING WOODLAND PLANTS
LA FAYETTE HOME NURSERY
LITTLE VALLEY FARM
MIDWEST WILDFLOWERS
NEW ENGLAND WILDFLOWER SOCIETY BOOKS (4)
THE ROOT BOOK
SISKIYOU RARE PLANT NURSERY
THE WILDFLOWER SOURCE
WILDGINGER WOODLANDS

5 *Vegetables and Herbs*   *125*

Berries and Grapes

AHRENS STRAWBERRY NURSERY
ALLEN COMPANY
BOSTON MOUNTAIN NURSERIES
BRITTINGHAM PLANT FARMS
BUNTING'S NURSERIES
HARTMANN'S PLANTATIONS
ISON'S NURSERIES
WM. KROHNE PLANT FARMS
MAKIELSKI BERRY NURSERY
REDWOOD CITY SEED CO.
SQUARE ROOT NURSERY

Chili Peppers

HORTICULTURAL ENTERPRISES
NATIVE SEEDS/SEARCH

Green Manure

ARKANSAS VALLEY SEED CO.
BOUNTIFUL GARDENS
LOCKHART SEEDS
MOOSE TUBERS

Herbs

AMERICAN MEDICINAL PLANTS
ANCIENT HERBS IN THE J. PAUL GETTY MUSEUM GARDEN
BARNEY'S GINSENG PATCH
BOUNTIFUL GARDENS
COMPANION PLANTS
CAPRILANDS HERB FARM
CULPEPER'S COLOR HERBAL
GARDENING WITH HERBS
THE HEIRLOOM GARDEN
HERB AND AILMENT CROSS REFERENCE CHART

THE HERB BASKET
THE HERB GARDEN
AN HERB GARDEN COMPANION
HERB GARDEN DESIGN
THE HERB GARDENER'S RESOURCE GUIDE
HERB GATHERING, INC.
THE HERB QUARTERLY
HIDDEN SPRINGS NURSERY
HORTICULTURAL ENTERPRISES
LE JARDIN DU GOURMET
LE MARCHÉ SEEDS INTERNATIONAL
LOST PRAIRIE HERB FARM
MEDICINES FROM THE EARTH
THE MEDIEVAL HEALTH HANDBOOK
A MODERN HERBAL
OLD-TIME HERBS FOR NORTHERN GARDENS
PARK'S SUCCESS WITH HERBS
PEACE SEEDS
READER'S DIGEST MAGIC AND MEDICINE PLANTS
REDWOOD CITY SEED COMPANY
OTTO RICHTER AND SONS LTD.
THE ROSEMARY HOUSE
SEEDS BLUM
SOUTHERN EXPOSURE SEED EXCHANGE
SUNNYBROOK FARMS
TAYLOR'S HERB GARDEN
TERRITORIAL SEED CO.
WYRTTUN WARD
WELL-SWEEP HERB FARM

How-To

BEGINNING HYDROPONICS
BETTER VEGETABLE GARDENS THE CHINESE WAY
THE COMMUNITY GARDEN BOOK
THE COMPLETE BOOK OF EDIBLE LANDSCAPING
THE GARDENER'S HANDBOOK OF EDIBLE PLANTS
GARDENING FOR ALL SEASONS
GARDENING: THE COMPLETE GUIDE TO GROWING AMERICA'S FAVORITE FRUITS AND VEGETABLES
GARDEN WAY'S JOY OF GARDENING
GOOD & WILD
THE HOME VEGETABLE GARDEN

HOW TO GROW MORE VEGETABLES (THAN YOU EVER THOUGHT POSSIBLE ON LESS LAND THAN YOU CAN IMAGINE)
INSECT DISEASES IN THE HOME VEGETABLE GARDEN
THE KIMBERTON HILLS AGRICULTURAL CALENDAR
LIVING OFF THE LAND
THE MOTHER EARTH NEWS
NO-DIG, NO-WEED GARDENING
THE SEED FINDER
SQUARE FOOT GARDENING
VEGETABLE GROWING HANDBOOK
YOUR NUTRITIOUS GARDEN

Mushrooms

FAR WEST FUNGI
THE MUSHROOM CULTIVATOR
MUSHROOMPEOPLE

Oriental Vegetables

KITAZAWA SEED CO.
TSANG AND MA
DR. YOO FARM

Societies

AMERICAN GOURD SOCIETY
BIODYNAMIC FARMING & GARDENING ASSOCIATION
NATIONAL COLONIAL FARM
NATIONAL GARDENING ASSOCIATION
NATIVE SEEDS/SEARCH
PERMACULTURE INSTITUTE OF NORTH AMERICA

Sweet Potatoes

FRED'S PLANT FARM
MARGRAVE PLANT COMPANY

Tomato Specialists

M. HOLMES QUISENBERRY
SIBERIA SEEDS
TOMATO GROWER'S SUPPLY CO.
THE TOMATO SEED CO.

Vegetables, General

BECKER'S SEED POTATOES
GIANT WATERMELONS
JOHNNY'S SELECTED SEEDS
JOHNSON SEED CO.
LAGOMARSINO SEEDS
D. LANDRETH SEED CO.
LOCKHART SEEDS
MOUNTAIN SEED & NURSERY
TERRITORIAL SEED CO.

WILLHITE SEED CO.
WILTON'S ORGANIC POTATOES

Vegetables, Gourmet

THE COOK'S GARDEN
HERB GATHERING, INC.
LE JARDIN DU GOURMET
LE MARCHÉ SEEDS INTERNATIONAL
SHEPHERD'S GARDEN SEEDS

Vegetables, Heirloom

BOUNTIFUL GARDENS
BUTTERBROOKE FARM
CORNS
ELYSIAN HILLS
G. SEED CO.
THE GARDEN SEED INVENTORY

HEIRLOOM VEGETABLE GARDEN
KALMIA FARM
KUSA RESEARCH FOUNDATION
JOHNNY'S SELECTED SEEDS
JOHNSON SEED CO.
D. LANDRETH SEED CO.
MOOSE TUBERS
NATIONAL COLONIAL FARM
NATIVE SEEDS/SEARCH
NEW ROOTS FOR AGRICULTURE
THE ONE-STRAW REVOLUTION
PEACE SEEDS
REDWOOD CITY SEED COMPANY
SEED SAVERS EXCHANGE
SEED SAVING TECHNIQUES OF THE NATIONAL
COLONIAL FARM
SEEDS BLUM
SHAKER SEED INDUSTRY
SOUTHERN EXPOSURE SEED EXCHANGE
THE SUNFLOWER
THE VEGETABLE GARDEN

6 Cacti and Succulents   148

ABBEY GARDENS
ALTMAN SPECIALTY PLANTS
AZTEKAKTI
BOOJUM UNLIMITED
BRITISH CACTUS & SUCCULENTS SOCIETY
CACTI AND SUCCULENTS FOR THE AMATEUR
THE CACTUS & SUCCULENT SOCIETY OF
AMERICA
CACTUS BY DODIE
THE CACTUS PRIMER
CALIFORNIA EPI CENTER
CHRISTA'S CACTUS

COUNTRY COTTAGE
ENCYCLOPEDIAS (2)
THE ENCYCLOPEDIA OF CACTI
PHYLLIS FLECHSIG CACTI & SUCCULENTS
GRIGSBY CACTUS GARDENS
INTERMOUNTAIN CACTUS
K&L CACTUS & SUCCULENT NURSERY
KIRKPATRICK'S
GERHARD KOHRES
LEXICON OF SUCCULENT PLANTS
MESA GARDEN
NEW MEXICO CACTUS RESEARCH

POPULAR EXOTIC CACTI IN COLOR
RAINBOW GARDENS NURSERY AND BOOKSHOP
RED'S RHODIES & ALPINE GARDENS
JIM & IRENE RUSS, QUALITY PLANTS
SHEIN'S CACTUS
SINGER'S GROWING THINGS
SOUTHWEST SEEDS
ED STORMS, INC.
SUNNYVALE CACTUS
SWAKAROO NURSERY
ROY YOUNG SEEDS

7 Roses   156

Floribunda

ALL-AMERICA ROSE SELECTIONS
A BOOK OF ROSES
GREENMANTLE NURSERY
HISTORICAL ROSES
JACKSON & PERKINS CO.
ROSE ACRES
ROSES BY FRED EDMUNDS
ROSEWAY NURSERIES
SPRING HILL NURSERIES
STOCKING ROSE NURSERY
THOMASVILLE NURSERIES

Hybrid Teas and Grandifloras

ALL-AMERICA ROSE SELECTIONS
A BOOK OF ROSES
CLASSIC ROSES
GREENMANTLE NURSERY
HISTORICAL ROSES
JACKSON & PERKINS CO.
ROSE ACRES
ROSES BY FRED EDMUNDS
ROSEWAY NURSERIES

STOCKING ROSE NURSERY
THOMASVILLE NURSERIES

Miniatures

ALL-AMERICA ROSE SELECTIONS
MINI-ROSES
NOR'EAST MINIATURE ROSES
PIXIE TREASURES MINIATURE ROSES
SEQUOIA NURSERY—MOORE MINIATURE ROSES

Tropical Foliage and Flowering Plants

ALBERTS & MERKEL BROS.
JOHN BRUDY EXOTICS
DOW SEEDS HAWAII
ENDANGERED SPECIES
EXOTICA
EXOTIC PLANT MANUAL
FAIRCHILD TROPICAL GARDEN
FOX ORCHIDS
GARDEN OF DELIGHTS

GLASSHOUSE WORKS
JERRY HORNE
C. W. HOSKING—EXOTIC SEED
IMPORTER/EXPORTER
INTERNATIONAL AROID SOCIETY
INTERNATIONAL TROPICAL FERN SOCIETY
KARTUZ GREENHOUSES
LOGEE'S GREENHOUSES
LOUISIANA NURSERY
TROPICA
WILSON PLANT SALES
GUY WRINKLE/EXOTIC PLANTS

Tropical Fruits

THE BANANA TREE
GARDEN OF DELIGHTS
GARDEN WORLD
GLASSHOUSE WORKS
C. W. HOSKING—EXOTIC SEED
IMPORTER/EXPORTER
WM. O. LESSARD
LOGEE'S GREENHOUSES
LOUISIANA NURSERY
SANTA BARBARA SEEDS
WILSON PLANT SALES

9 Tools and Supplies

Beekeeping

A. I. ROOT CO.

Bonsai Tools

THE BONSAI FARM

Carts, Seeders, Spreaders

CART WAREHOUSE
EARTHWAY PRODUCTS
GARDEN WAY MANUFACTURING CO.
HOMESTEAD CARTS
A. M. LEONARD, INC.
PEACEFUL VALLEY FARM SUPPLY
RADIO STEEL & MANUFACTURING CO.
SPECIALTY MANUFACTURING CO.
TSI CO.

Containers

HUBBARD FOLDING BOX CO.
MOLDED FIBER GLASS TRAY CO.
WELLS & WADE

Drip Irrigation

DRIP IRRIGATION GARDEN
HARMONY FARM SUPPLY
INTERNATIONAL IRRIGATION SYSTEMS
RAINDRIP, INC.
TRICKLE SOAK SYSTEMS
URBAN FARMER STORE

Fences and Barriers

DARE PRODUCTS
A. M. LEONARD, INC.
RINGER RESEARCH

Fertilizers, General

BRIGHTON BY-PRODUCTS CO.
DODE'S GARDENS
JOHNSON'S INDUSTRIAL SUPPLY CO.

Fertilizers, Organic

GREEN EARTH ORGANICS
GRO-TEK
GROWING CRAZY
HARMONY FARM SUPPLY
NATURAL GARDENING RESEARCH CENTER
NECESSARY TRADING COMPANY
NORTH AMERICAN KELP
OHIO EARTH FOOD
PEACEFUL VALLEY FARM SUPPLY
PLANTJOY
RINGER RESEARCH

Flower Arranging Supplies

DOROTHY BIDDLE SERVICE
THE KETH CO.

Garden Tools

BRAMEN CO.
BRIGHTON BY-PRODUCTS
CLAPPER'S

FANNO SAW WORKS
GARDENER'S EDEN
GARDENER'S SUPPLY CO.
GOLDBLATT TOOLS
GOSERUD PRODUCTS
GREEN EARTH ORGANICS
GREEN RIVER TOOLS
GRO-TEK
HARMONY FARM SUPPLY
THE JAPAN WOODWORKER
JOHNSON'S INDUSTRIAL SUPPLY CO.
KEMP CO.
THE KINSMAN CO.
A. M. LEONARD, INC.
LITTLE WONDER
MERIDIAN EQUIPMENT CORPORATION
WALTER F. NICKE
NORTHERN WIRE PRODUCTS
PEACEFUL VALLEY FARM SUPPLY
RINGER RESEARCH
SCOVIL HOE CO.
ALLEN SIMPSON MARKETING DESIGN LTD.
SMITH & HAWKEN
SNOW & NEALLEY
SURVIVAL EQUIPMENT CO.
TSI CO.
WILSON SAFETY PRODUCTS

Greenhouse Supplies

BRAMEN CO.
CHARLEY'S GREENHOUSE SUPPLIES
EQUIPMENT CONSULTANTS AND SALES
E.C. GEIGER
GROW-N-ENERGY
GRO-TEK
A. M. LEONARD, INC.
MEMORY METALS
OFE INTERNATIONAL
TROPICAL PLANT PRODUCTS
YONAH MANUFACTURING CO.

Hydroponics

APPLIED HYDROPONICS OF CANADA
HYDRO-GARDENS, INC.
HYDROPONIC SOCIETY OF AMERICA

Integrated Pest Management

COMMON SENSE PEST CONTROL QUARTERLY
GREAT LAKES IPM
INTRODUCTION TO INTEGRATED PEST
MANAGEMENT

Pest Control, Organic

BENEFICIAL INSECTARY
BETTER YIELD INSECTS
FOOTHILL AGRICULTURAL RESEARCH

GREEN EARTH ORGANICS
GRO-TEK
GROWING CRAZY
HARMONY FARM SUPPLY
KING'S NATURAL PEST CONTROL
NATURAL GARDENING RESEARCH CENTER
NATURAL PEST CONTROLS
NECESSARY TRADING COMPANY
OHIO EARTH FOOD
PEACEFUL VALLEY FARM SUPPLY
REUTER LABORATORIES
RINCON-VITOVA INSECTARIES
RINGER RESEARCH
UNIQUE INSECT CONTROL

Soil Tests

LAMOTTE CHEMICAL PRODUCTS CO.
LUSTER LEAF PRODUCTS
MICRO ESSENTIAL LABORATORY

Tillers

BCS MOSA, INC.
GARDEN WAY MANUFACTURING CO.
MAINLINE NORTH AMERICA
MANTIS MANUFACTURING CO.

Watering Devices

CLAPPER'S
THE DRAMM CO.
GARDENER'S SUPPLY CO.
HARMONY FARM SUPPLY
PROEN PRODUCTS CO.
RAIN BIRD NATIONAL SALES
RL CORPORATION
H. B. SHERMAN MANUFACTURING CO.
SMITH & HAWKEN
SPECIALTY MANUFACTURING CO.

10 Furniture and Ornament 198

Birdbaths

ASCOT DESIGNS
CARRUTH STUDIO
GARDEN CONCEPTS COLLECTION
THE HOUSE OF BOUGHS

Bird Feeders

BIRD 'N HAND
DUNCRAFT
GARDEN CONCEPTS COLLECTION
THE HOUSE OF BOUGHS
HYDE BIRD FEEDER CO.
WILD BIRD SUPPLIES

Birdhouses

MR. BIRDHOUSE
HEATH MANUFACTURING CO.
SMITH & HAWKEN
WILD BIRD SUPPLIES

Bridges

BOW HOUSE
THE HOUSE OF BOUGHS
NAMPARA GARDENS

Columns

COLUMBINE
GARDEN CONCEPTS COLLECTION
THE LONDON ARCHITECTURAL SALVAGE AND
SUPPLY CO.
MARY ROEHM

Finials, Urns and Balustrades

ASCOT DESIGNS
CROWTHER OF SYON LODGE
THE HOUSE OF BOUGHS
KUMA ENTERPRISES
THE LONDON ARCHITECTURAL SALVAGE AND
SUPPLY CO.
SCULPTURE DESIGN IMPORTS

Fountains and Wellheads

ASCOT DESIGNS
ROBERT COMPTON LTD.
CROWTHER OF SYON LODGE
ERKINS STUDIOS
FLORENTINE CRAFTSMEN
GARDEN CONCEPTS COLLECTION
THE LONDON ARCHITECTURAL SALVAGE AND
SUPPLY CO.
SCULPTURE DESIGN IMPORTS
STRASSACKER BRONZE

Furniture

ASCOT DESIGNS
BACKHOUSE, INC.
BENCH MANUFACTURING CO.
CHARLESTON BATTERY BENCH
CLAPPER'S
CROWTHER OF SYON LODGE
COUNTRY CASUAL
CYPRESS STREET CENTER
ERKINS STUDIO
FLORENTINE CRAFTSMEN
GARDEN APPOINTMENTS
GARDEN CONCEPTS COLLECTION
GARDENER'S EDEN
THE HOUSE OF BOUGHS
SUE FISHER KING
KUMA ENTERPRISES
LIVE OAK RAILROAD CO.
THE LONDON ARCHITECTURAL SALVAGE AND
SUPPLY CO.
DANIEL MACK RUSTIC FURNISHINGS
NAMPARA GARDENS
PARK PLACE
THE PLOW & HEARTH
THE ROCKER SHOP
REED BROS.
SCULPTURE DESIGN IMPORTS
SMITH & HAWKEN
SUMMIT FURNITURE
WALPOLE WOODWORKERS
WILLSBORO WOOD PRODUCTS
DAN WILSON & CO.
WOOD CLASSICS

Garden Structures

BOW HOUSE
CASSIDY BROS. FORGE
DALTON PAVILIONS
FLORENTINE CRAFTSMEN
GARDEN CONCEPTS COLLECTION
THE HOUSE OF BOUGHS
SUE FISHER KING
THE LONDON ARCHITECTURAL SALVAGE AND
SUPPLY CO.
MACHIN DESIGNS
SAN FRANCISCO VICTORIANA
SHAKERTOWN
SUN DESIGNS
VIXEN HILL MANUFACTURING CO.

Greenhouses

EVERLITE GREENHOUSES
GOTHIC ARCH GREENHOUSES
THE HOUSE OF BOUGHS
JANCO GREENHOUSES
MACHIN DESIGNS
NORTHERN GREENHOUSE SALES
SANTA BARBARA GREENHOUSES
STURDI-BUILT MANUFACTURING CO.
SUNCRAFT
SUNGLO SOLAR GREENHOUSES

Lighting

GARDENER'S EDEN
GENIE HOUSE
GREENLEE LANDSCAPE LIGHTING
HERITAGE LANTERNS
IDAHO WOOD
KIM LIGHTING
POPOVITCH ASSOCIATES
MARK SHEEHAN
STRASSACKER BRONZE

Ornamental Metalwork

AXELSSON METAL DESIGNS
JOSEPH A. BONIFAS
CASSIDY BROS. FORGE
CROWTHER OF SYON LODGE
GARDEN CONCEPTS COLLECTION
GARDEN IRON
THE HOUSE OF BOUGHS
THE LONDON ARCHITECTURAL SALVAGE AND
SUPPLY CO.
LYNN H. POULTER
ROBINSON IRON CORPORATION

SCHWARTZ'S FORGE & METALWORKS
MARK SHEEHAN
TOM TORRENS: SCULPTURE DESIGN
ROBERT WALSH

Paving

ASCOT DESIGNS
BOMANITE CORPORATION
CAL-GA-CRETE INDUSTRIES
CONCRETE PAVING STONES
COUNTRY FLOORS
HILLTOP SLATE CO.
HUNTINGTON PACIFIC CERAMICS
INTERNATIONAL AMERICAN CERAMICS
THE LONDON ARCHITECTURAL SALVAGE AND
SUPPLY CO.
ROMAFLEX, INC.
SUMMITVILLE TILES

Planters and Containers

BONSAI CREATIONS
ROBERT COMPTON, LTD.
ERKINS STUDIOS
FLORENTINE CRAFTSMEN
FOSTER-KEVILL
GARDEN CONCEPTS COLLECTION
GARDENER'S EDEN
ANNE GOLDMAN
HEATH MANUFACTURING CO.
HERITAGE ARTS
THE HOUSE OF BOUGHS
INTERNATIONAL BONSAI CONTAINERS
JACKALOPE
SUE FISHER KING
THE LONDON ARCHITECTURAL SALVAGE AND
SUPPLY CO.
NORSTAD POTTERY
SCULPTURE DESIGN IMPORTS
WEST RINDGE BASKETS
DAN WILSON & CO.
WINTERTHUR'S GIFT AND GARDEN SAMPLER
ZANESVILLE STONEWARE CO.

Play Equipment

CHILD LIFE PLAY SPECIALTIES
WOODPLAY

Sculpture

PETER BRAMHALL
CARRUTH STUDIO

CROWTHER OF SYON LODGE
ERKINS STUDIOS
FIVE ARTISTS AT NOAA
FLORENTINE CRAFTSMEN
BARBARA GRYGUTIS
THE HOUSE OF BOUGHS
JACKALOPE
THE LONDON ARCHITECTURAL SALVAGE AND
SUPPLY CO.
ROB MACCONNELL
ROBERT MIHALY
CHARLES C. PARKS
ROSS L. PEACOCK MADISON AVENUE GALLERY
SCULPTURE CAST
MARK SHEEHAN
STRASSACKER BRONZE
TOM TORRENS: SCULPTURE DESIGN
DAVID TRESIZE
MARIAN J. VIEUX
WINTERTHUR'S GIFT AND GARDEN SAMPLER

Stained Glass

THOMAS MEYERS STUDIO

Sundials

ASCOT DESIGNS
CASSIDY BROS. FORGE
KATHLEEN CERVENY
FLORENTINE CRAFTSMEN
REPLOGLE GLOBES

Tiles

KATHLEEN CERVENY
COUNTRY FLOORS
ROBERT MIHALY
SUMMITVILLE TILES

Topiary Frames and Treillage

ASCOT DESIGNS
CASSIDY BROS. FORGE
EXOTIC BLOSSOMS
GARDEN IRON
MACHIN DESIGNS
TOPIARY, INC.
VINE ARTS

NEW YORK COOPERATIVE EXTENSION SERVICE
PLIMOTH PLANTATION
RHODE ISLAND COOPERATIVE EXTENSION
SERVICE
VERMONT COOPERATIVE EXTENSION SERVICE

Reference

THE LIVING HISTORY SOURCEBOOK

Southeast

ALABAMA COOPERATIVE EXTENSION SERVICE
ARKANSAS COOPERATIVE EXTENSION SERVICE
THE BLUE RIDGE FARM MUSEUM
FLORIDA COOPERATIVE EXTENSION SERVICE
GEORGIA COOPERATIVE EXTENSION SERVICE
KENTUCKY COOPERATIVE EXTENSION SERVICE
MISSISSIPPI COOPERATIVE EXTENSION SERVICE
MONTICELLO
MOUNT VERNON
TENNESSEE COOPERATIVE EXTENSION SERVICE

VIRGINIA COOPERATIVE EXTENSION SERVICE
THE VIRGINIA GARDENER

Southwest

ARIZONA COOPERATIVE EXTENSION SERVICE
JOURDAN-BACHMAN PIONEER FARM
NEW MEXICO COOPERATIVE EXTENSION SERVICE
TAYLOR PUBLISHING COMPANY
TEXAS GARDENER

13 Sources of Sources

249

AGACCESS
THE AMERICAN BOTANIST, BOOKSELLERS
ANCHOR & DOLPHIN BOOKS
WARREN F. BRODERICK—BOOKS
CAPABILITY'S BOOKS
EARTHWORM BUYER'S GUIDE
THE ESSENTIAL WHOLE EARTH CATALOGUE

GARDENING BY MAIL
HONINGKLIP NURSERIES
HURLEY BOOKS
ISBS, INC.
LANDSCAPE BOOKS
LLOYDS OF KEW
PLANT SCIENCES DATA CENTER

POMONA BOOK EXCHANGE
SECOND LIFE BOOKS
JANE SUTLEY HORTICULTURAL BOOKS
TIMBER PRESS
GARY WAYNER, BOOKSELLER
ELISABETH WOODBURN

1 General Sources

Abundant Life Seed Foundation

PO Box 772
Port Townsend, WA 98368

- *Nonprofit organization offering seed for open-pollinated vegetables, native and naturalized trees and shrubs, wildflowers, herbs, and garden flowers; mail-order books.*
- *40-page catalogue, quarterly newsletter; $4–10 annual membership, according to ability to pay; any seed order will bring following year's catalogue.*

The Abundant Life catalogue is a whole ethos contained in 40 pages. Foundation director Forest Shomer is something of a cross between a hippie and a Franciscan, a mix that makes for the finest and oddest list of organic growing and natural lifestyle books I've seen. Among the many listings are a complete set of Rudolf Steiner biodynamic farming lectures, an 1855 oration given by a Seattle Indian chief, a number of excellent choices for garden design and seed propagation, and important anthropological volumes such as *Corn Among the Indians of the Upper Missouri*. In general, the seed list is less

startling than one would expect. A number of the vegetables are the generally available types, but Shomer has selected those that do well in the Pacific Northwest. The herb selection, on the other hand, is truly outstanding, and the list is strong in heirloom beans, corn, and early lettuces and tomatoes. Among the trees and shrubs are a few native berry plants of unusual interest.

> As soon as spring is in the air Mr. Krippendorf and I begin an antiphonal chorus, like two frogs in neighboring ponds: What have you in bloom, I ask, and he answers from Ohio that there are hellebores in the woods, and crocuses and snowdrops and winter aconite. Then I tell him that in North Carolina the early daffodils are out but that the aconites are gone and the crocuses past their best.
>
> —ELIZABETH LAWRENCE, FROM *THE LITTLE BULBS: A TALE OF TWO GARDENS* (1986)

Agway

PO Box 4741
Syracuse, NY 13221

- *Farmers' cooperative offering seed for vegetables, mainly annual flowers, and lawn grass to the home gardener in the Northeast; pesticides and fertilizers.*
- *26-page vegetable and flower catalogue, approx. 88 color illustrations, free; "Agway Lawn and Garden Guides," "Guide to Starting Seeds Indoors," "Pocket Guide to Quick Lawn Weed Identification," and periodical* Lawn and Garden Adviser, *free to customers.*

Agway is a good place to start for Northeastern gardeners. The planting guides and growing tips offered in the flower-and-vegetable catalogue are good for beginners. All major types of vegetables and annual flowers appear, though the veggies list has a far wider choice of varieties within a species than does the flower list. The little garden guides and advisers are meant to sell Agway products, but they do provide information. The seed-starter's guide is useful and uncomplicated. Agway is also a good source of lawn seed. Mixes for the home are listed in the catalogue.

Alberta Nurseries & Seeds Ltd.

Box 20
Bowden, Alberta
CANADA T0M 0K0

- *Flower and vegetable seed, bulbs, trees, shrubs, perennial plants, lawn grass, tools, and supplies.*
- *52-page catalogue, approx. 233 color illustrations, free in Canada, $2.00 in U.S.*

Offering one of the finest general garden catalogues in Canada, Alberta Nurseries has been at work since 1922. The list is good for all seeds and plants, with vegetable selections keyed for earliness. Cultural instructions are lacking. Though most varieties are offered elsewhere, there are enough strengths here to warrant a look, even if you don't live in the region. Aside from the unusual native saskatoon, there is a good group of flowering kales, a selection of 4 old roses (Hansa, Persian Yellow, Prairie Dawn, and Adelaide Hoodless), and a garden lupine that is less imperious than the Russell hybrids.

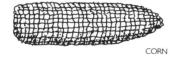
CORN

Allen, Sterling & Lothrop

191 U.S. Route 1
Falmouth, ME 04105

- *Vegetable, flower, and lawn seed; tools and supplies.*
- *52-page catalogue, a few illustrations, free.*

The firm does a big rack and wholesale business in its local area, so the list is fairly predictable. However, its seed prices are by and large lower than those of the bigger companies. A few selections are very good; lawn seed, peas, and corn. If you love the taste of Seneca sweet corn, AS&L has 5 varieties, with novelties like Golden Midget (3-foot-high plants). Cultural instructions are good for veggies, absent for flowers. The list of ornamentals is strong on annuals, weak on perennials. AS&L is also a fine source of cover crops and fertilizers for organic gardeners.

American Community Gardening Association

c/o Chicago Botanic Garden
PO Box 400
Glencoe, IL 60022

- *Nonprofit association dedicated to growth of community gardening.*

Most city dwellers should be able to find out about local community gardening resources by calling a city agency. If you can't, or if you want more detailed information to help you get started, you might try contacting this association. It is the national society for professionals in the field, but it can certainly point you in the right direction for your area, and its journal may offer useful resources.

American Horticultural Society

PO Box 0105
Mount Vernon, VA 22121

- *Nonprofit association dedicated to general gardening for the advanced amateur.*
- *44-page bimonthly* American Horticulturist, *many color illustrations; bimonthly* American Horticulturist News Edition, *some illustrations; annual free seed distribution; garden information service; seed exchange via magazines; discount on garden books; annual membership $20.00, 2 years $35.00.*

The AHS covers the map in gardening, though it tends to focus most of its interest on ornamentals and garden design for the upper-middle-brow amateur. Articles are generally by topflight garden writers and experts like Pamela Harper, best known for her astonishing photo collection, and Frederick McGourty, who used to run the Brooklyn Botanic Garden's publications. Book-review sections in both publications are very good, the News Edition even including reviews of outstanding plant society and cooperative extension publications. (Many of the books can be bought at a member's discount.) Members' want lists appear in the News Edition as well, and all members receive the association's seed-distribution list in January. The society recently began doing its own very handsome Endangered Wildflowers Calendar. Members get it for a $.70 discount, at $6.25.

The Amicus Journal

122 E. 42nd Street
Room 4500
New York, NY 10168

- *Variable-length, nonprofit quarterly of the National Resources Defense Council (NRDC), many illustrations, annual subscription $8.00, annual membership $10.00.*

What is a blatantly ecological publication doing in a garden book? Well, maybe you live over an aquifer that's drying up, or maybe you garden near Atlantic City, on the edge of the Pine Barrens, and you would like to have the Barrens remain there. Whatever your excuse, you may be interested in this very committed journal, which frequently features articles on forest preservation, water resources, soil conservation, and the like. Its tone can be preachy, but it frequently gets excellent writers, like Robert Boyle on acid rain. The book reviews are a useful culling of topical and armchair naturalist's volumes. I could do without the poems.

Archia's Seed Store

PO Box 109
Sedalia, MO 65301

- *Seeds and plants for vegetables, field crops, lawn grass, berries, and flowers; bulbs; garden and greenhouse tools and supplies; bee supplies.*
- *32-page catalogue, more than 100 illustrations, free.*

Here's a regional catalogue for Missouri. The flower list is pretty insignificant, but the veggies selection is strong in all of the common varieties. Archia's has kept a number of open-pollinated corns in its list, and it features several tomatoes developed at the University of Missouri. There are 5 different varieties of popcorn. A few open-pollinated strains survive among the other vegetables as well. You can find a good selection of farm seed for green manuring here, plus a range of lawn grass. The supplies section is comprehensive for pesticides and fertilizers.

ORCHID

The Audubon Society Guide to Attracting Birds

by Stephen W. Kress
Scribner's

- *377 pages, many illustrations, $24.95.*

Here is a terrific book for the gardener/bird-fancier, including suggestions for everything short of smearing suet on your arms. There are excellent regional plant lists, detailing the species best suited both for ornament and for attracting members of the feathered tribe. Information on how to build nesting and feeding structures is first-rate, including a few helpful (and hilarious) pages of squirrel deterrents.

The Avant Gardener

PO Box 489
New York, NY 10028

- *Horticultural newsletter.*
- *8-page monthly newsletter, annual subscription $15.00.*

The Powells, who publish these newsletters, must spend their lives buried in books, catalogues, and magazines. They appear to know everything that is going on in ornamental and edible gardening just as it is happening— and sometimes before it happens. A recent issue has an article introducing the just-released "Oregon Rainbow" Iceland poppies, and another on the jostaberry, a soon-to-be-available cross between a black currant and gooseberry. Almost every issue has some valuable suggestions for dealing with pests, without the use of chemical insecticides whenever possible. Often, a whole issue will be devoted to a single theme, such as ornamental grasses or dwarf conifers. The articles are concise and informative, and will list sources of the plant material, product, or service described. For my money, this is the best newsletter in the field.

Biology of Plants

by Peter H. Raven
Worth Publishers

- *775 pages, many illustrations, $39.95.*

Raven is the director of the Missouri Botanical Garden (see page 242) and one of the leading botanists in America. He writes drily but clearly, packing more information into an already large book than most people could digest in a lifetime. Still, if you are interested in plants—any kind of plants—you can peck away at this tome until you grow too old to lift it, finding the how-come behind all the how-to you have gotten elsewhere.

A man who builds a rock garden feels himself to be a Cyclops when he, so to speak, with elemental power, piles stone upon stone, creates hills and dales, transports mountains and erects rocky cliffs. Later, when with aching back he has finished his gigantic masterpiece, he finds that it looks rather different from the romantic mountain which he had in mind; and it seems to be only a heap of rubble and stones. But don't worry; in a year these stones will change into a most beautiful bed, sparkling with tiny flowers, and grown over with nice green cushions; and your pleasure will be great. I tell you, make a rock garden.

—KAREL CAPEK, FROM *THE GARDENER'S YEAR* (1929)

Bioshelters, Ocean Arks, City Farming

by Nancy Jack Todd and John Todd
Sierra Club Books

- *210 pages, some illustrations, $10.95 pbk.*

Here is a popular ecological design book from two founders of the New Alchemy Institute (see page 130). Some of the discussion centers on large-scale community design and on things like the Todds' own project for revolutionizing the Guyanese fishing industry. The gardener will be most pleased with the suggestions for bioshelters, solar greenhouses that make use of ingenious water containers as sources of fish, warmth, and fertilizer. This is also a place to find out more about such visionary projects as Lindisfarne, Arcosanti, and the New Alchemy Institute itself.

Botanical Dictionaries

A Dictionary of Botany

by R. John Little and C. Eugene Jones
Van Nostrand Reinhold

- *400 pages, some illustrations, $28.95 hc. $14.95 pbk. Both out of print.*

Longman Illustrated Dictionary of Botany

by Andrew Sugden
Longman Group Ltd.
Burnt Hill, Harlow
Essex
UNITED KINGDOM

- *192 pages, many color illustrations, $7.95.*

The Penguin Dictionary of Botany

Edited by Stephen Blackmore and Elizabeth Toothill
Viking Penguin

- *391 pages, a few illustrations, $7.95 pbk.*

When I first bought a botanical dictionary, it was to help me understand plant genetics. The Little and Jones dictionary had all the words I needed to understand, but the definitions were too brief and technical for someone as ignorant as myself. The Blackmore & Toothill volume, on the other hand, not only had longer and more comprehensible definitions, but it provided cross-references to the definitions of technical words appearing within each definition. You can use the volume to learn more about growth, morphology, plant families, plant nutrition, and even things like antitranspirants, growth inhibitors, and pesticides. It's a hard-to-beat dictionary. (Incidentally, its hardcover version is published by Facts on File as *The Facts on File Dictionary of Botany;* it sells for $21.95.)

My one complaint about Blackmore & Toothill is its few and poor illustrations, a matter I thought par-ticularly galling when I was trying to figure out how genes assort themselves. I didn't know then about the *Longman Illustrated Dictionary.* Though it is less comprehensive than the others, it is marvelously illustrated in colors so bright you can't miss some pesky gene crossing over in the 8th row. There are only 1,200 terms in it, each briefly defined, but the pictures make up for the concise text. Also, it is divided into chapters like "chemistry," "genetics," "reproduction," and "fruits and seeds," so you get a sort of short visual primer in each subject, without having to wander around the whole book looking for the cross-references.

W. Atlee Burpee Co.

300 Park Avenue
Warminster, PA 18974

- *Vegetable and flower seed, nursery stock for trees and shrubs, perennial plants, roots, and bulbs; tools and equipment.*
- *192-page catalogue, more than 950 color illustrations, free.*

Burpee's address is graven on the memories of many thousand gardeners. If you are a defender of open-pollinated vegetables, you will complain about Burpee's countless hybrids; if you love catalogues, you will lament the fact that Burpee has changed to a cheaper paper that makes its lovely illustrations a little muddy. Still, hardly anyone fails to look at the Burpee list. Burpee's breeders have invented everything from the Big Boy tomato to a better marigold, and the name Fordhook—so often found even on frozen vegetables as a guarantee of quality—refers to Burpee's famous Fordhook farm. Furthermore, the firm is so large that it is able to stock an unusually full line of trees, shrubs, bulbs, and perennial plants, as well as seed. You could buy roses or strawberries from Burpee, with no need to look further. Whatever other cata-logues you use, don't fail to look at Burpee's at least for melons, beans, lettuce, peas, radishes, squash, and tomatoes. The only real trouble with the catalogue is that the cultural instructions can be sketchy, but you can send for free booklets on the culture of most crops. If I were alone on a desert island with nothing but a post office and I could have but one catalogue, I am not sure that I wouldn't choose Stokes over Burpee, but I would try to hide Burpee away in my luggage somewhere.

But only the little-known god Priapus seems to have had definite responsibility for gardens. The principal centre for his worship was at Lampsacus, on the Hellespont. The son of Aphrodite, the goddess of love, whose flower is the rose and whose fruit is the apple, and Dionysus, Priapus is a god both of fertility and of the garden. Images of him show him to be ugly, small in stature, but with enormous genitals, and carrying a sickle or a pruning-knife.

—CHRISTOPHER THACKER, FROM *THE HISTORY OF GARDENS* (1979)

D. V. Burrell Seed Growers Co.

405 N. Main
Rocky Ford, CO 81067

- *Vegetable and flower seed.*
- *96-page catalogue, approx. 107 illustrations, free.*

This firm is first and foremost for commercial growers, but it offers small, inexpensive seed packets to the home gardener as well. There is little surprising in the catalogue, though there are a number of vegetable varieties developed in and for the Intermountain West. Rocky Ford has been an important breeding ground for melons, so Burrell's list for these is unusually strong and well worth looking at.

The Complete Urban Gardener

by Joan Puma
Harper & Row

■ *392 pages, some illustrations, a few in color, $14.95 pbk.*

The title is misleading. The book is really about container gardening on rooftops and terraces. It *is* a decent compendium of information for container gardeners, including nice selections of appropriate trees and shrubs and flowers and vegetables, plus the usual information on pruning, propagation, and the like. Surprisingly, however, it is not very revealing about the specific problems of city rooftops and terraces, particularly with regard to such matters as weight of soil, difficulties with wind and desiccation, and problems with the landlord. Not that it doesn't mention these issues; I would simply have wished for a more lively and detailed coverage of them, with some examples. Among the color photos, for instance, is a lovely shot of a water garden, but the book gives little idea as to just how I could get such a thing safely onto my roof or terrace.

Comstock, Ferre & Co.

263 Main Street
Wethersfield, CT 06109

■ *Vegetable and flower seed.*
■ *36-page catalogue, approx. 90 illustrations, free.*

This firm traces its origins back to the beginning of the 19th century. As you might expect, it has remained loyal to some open-pollinated vegetable favorites, to a large selection of herbs, and to old-fashioned flowers like marigolds, heliotropes, and pansies. For the rest, the list is thorough, if unremarkable, and the instructions for growing vegetables are good. Comstock, Ferre's store is worth a visit, not only for all the nursery goodies you can buy there, but because the surviving buildings are like a history of the American seed trade.

Country Wisdom Bulletins

Garden Way Publishing

■ *32 pages each, some illustrations, $1.95 each.*

Garden Way publishes lots of little booklets about every subject the edibles gardener or homesteader might be interested in. You can get the basics here on everything from raising livestock, to building fences, to growing tomatoes, to getting the chimney clean. Depth of coverage is not the selling point of these bulletins, but they are good, cheap introductions.

Crosman Seed Corporation

500 W. Commercial Street
PO Box 110
East Rochester, NY 14445

■ *Seed for vegetables and mainly annual flowers.*
■ *2-page list, free.*

Crosman is the venerable source of a whole lot of package seed for the retail garden-center trade. Its list is not rich in rarities, but it is a little broader than one might expect. Home gardeners must order a minimum of $3.00, but the packets are very reasonably priced, most at $.59 each. (This is the same Crosman that sells air rifles and BB guns, a line it developed out of its research into seed-packaging machinery!)

Culture and Horticulture

by Wolf D. Storl
Biodynamic Farming & Gardening Association
PO Box 550
Kimberton, PA 19442

■ *435 pages, a few illustrations, $10.00.*

Storl is an intelligent writer and convert to Rudolf Steiner's biodynamic gardening methods. His book is subtitled "A Philosophy of Gardening," which lets you know that his is the zeal of a convert. Still, this is a fine introduction to this semimystical end of organic gardening and farming. Steiner was a pioneer in the use of organics, and his reasons for recommending them hark back to everything from medieval cosmology, to

ZUCCHINI

astrology, to the Doctrine of Signatures. If nothing else, Storl has done an admirable job not only of summarizing Steiner's ideas, but of showing how they have been applied by both Steiner's various followers and organic gardeners in general. The suggestion, basic to Steiner, that a healthy society has a healthy relationship to the earth, is powerful. It goes a long way toward helping even us skeptics get through the various cosmic forces and relationships that he and his disciples believe in. If you have the slightest interest in biodynamics, here is the book to start with.

DeGiorgi Co.

PO Box 413
Council Bluffs, IA 51502

- *Seed for annual and perennial flowers, vegetables, herbs, and ornamental grasses; scythes and grass hooks.*
- *114-page catalogue, approx. 250 illustrations, $1.00.*

This is the most refreshing general seed catalogue I've seen. Although it lacks the pretty illustrations of a Burpee or a Park, its descriptions and cultural instructions are excellent for both vegetables and flowers, with emphasis on culture in the prairie states. The list contains many of the varieties to be found in the all-color catalogues, together with distinctive selections in most categories. The grasses and rock-garden perennials are very strong; so is cabbage. The thoughtful glossary of Latin names with their English translations is a nice touch, as are the fine, traditional European scythes and hooks.

Dominion Seed House

115 Guelph Street
Georgetown, Ontario
CANADA L7G 4A2

- *Seed, bulbs, and plants for vegetables, berries, annual and perennial flowers, shrubs, and houseplants; tools and supplies. Canadian orders only.*
- *86-page catalogue, more than 600 color illustrations, free.*

Dominion is a full-service mail-order house. It's too bad that gardeners in the northern tier of the United States are not able to order from its list because the selection is quite good, particularly in very early vegetables. Dominion culls the new releases from Burpee and Harris for some of its varieties, but there are also a goodly number of specialties, including some seldom-seen types like an early white okra, a big, long-picking green

bean called Burly, a whole group of baby carrots, a serpentine cucumber, a yellow ground cherry, a much earlier than normal salsify, and a cantaloupe relative called the vine peach. Corn and tomato selections are large, including many Illinis for the former and many subarctics for the latter. Here too is a source of the tomato variety called Sweet 100, a very early pole or trellis plant that bears 300–500 cherry-sized fruits per plant. Dominion also offers a little plastic jacket to slip over your tomatoes, improving fruit set and ripening in cooler areas. A multiplier onion is also offered here, as are an unusually large variety of potato eyes. The flower list is serviceable, strongest in azaleas, marigolds, and zinnias, though offering pretty good coverage throughout; some perennials come as plants. Gladiolus, day lily, and dahlia bulbs are all very strong, including quite a selection of cactus dahlias. I'm partial to them, and I find Dominion's lilac-tipped white "Veritable" dahlia a knockout. The tool-and-supply list is very extensive; much is sensible high-quality material, including a quick-couple hose system and a nice-looking set of Canadian-made hand tools. The charts provided as planting guides for both veggies and flowers are about the best I've seen.

Earthworms for Gardeners and Fishermen

Distributed by ISBS, Inc.
5602 N.E. Hassalo Street
Portland, OR 97213

- *15 pages, some illustrations, $1.75.*

This very engaging and useful little pamphlet from Australia offers a little essay on what earthworms do for the soil, a funny section on what they like and don't like (this includes cau-

tions on pesticides), instructions for growing your own earthworms, a little biology of the creatures, and, last but not least, a recipe for Earthworm Omelette and another for Applesauce Surprise Cake. You can guess the surprise.

The Ecologist

Worthyvale Manor Farm
Camelford, Cornwall
ENGLAND PL32 9TT

- *Variable-length bimonthly, some illustrations, annual subscription $20.00.*

This is Britain's leading ecological journal. The articles cover the whole field, and they are generally well documented and eminently readable.

Ecology

by Paul Colinvaux
John Wiley & Sons

- *725 pages, many illustrations, $32.95.*

Here is the best textbook on the science of ecology that you are likely to find. It is a stimulating antidote to the soft-headed, mystical versions of the science that are all too appealing and all too dogmatic. Colinvaux's history of ecological thinking shows that there is considerable diversity of opinion among serious ecologists themselves, and his analysis of the state of the science will help anyone interested in the subject to flesh out his or her emotional commitment with a balanced and intelligent body of knowledge.

> Ancient books teach that the smell of many plants, rosemary among them, strengthens the memory. . . .
>
> —LOUISE BEEBE WILDER, FROM *THE FRAGRANT GARDEN* (1936)

Ecology of Compost

by Daniel L. Dindal
State University of New York
College of Environmental Science and Forestry
Syracuse, NY 13210

- *12 pages, a few illustrations, $.25.*

A brief, cheap, and useful guide to making a compost pile. If you haven't learned already, Dindal will help you.

CALLA LILY

The Encyclopedia of Organic Gardening

Rodale Press

- *1,236 pages, many illustrations, $24.95.*

This is most comprehensive for edible and other economic plants, but there are a fair number of entries on ornamentals (even houseplants) as well. Everywhere, the style is informal but accurate and informative. This is not a place to find out about the latest and greatest cultivars of any species, but it is a fine source for learning about effectively planting and using the species in the garden. As you expect, the entries reflect Rodale's philosophy: "Carson, Rachel" is an admiring biography, while "Fertilizers, Chemical" is positively combative. The information on organic soil amendments and cultural insect control is especially wide-ranging.

Encyclopedias, General Garden

Wyman's Gardening Encyclopedia

by Donald Wyman
Macmillan

- *1,221 pages, some illustrations, $50.00.*

America's Garden Book

by James and Louise Bush-Brown
Scribner's

- *819 pages, some illustrations, $27.50*

Taylor's Encyclopedia of Gardening, Horticulture, and Landscape Design

Edited by Norman Taylor
Houghton Mifflin

- *1,329 pages, some illustrations, a few in color, $27.95.*

These are the big 3 general gardening books in North America. Each covers ornamentals, vegetables, garden styles, and so on. I was all set to review Taylor glowingly when the publisher informed me that it would probably be going out of print. Horrors. Of our 3 general garden encyclopedias, it is easily my favorite, because it considers physiography and design more thoroughly than the others. There are entries for every state in the Union, with comments on climate, geography, soils, and the plants that are native to or do best there. Reading these, you get a very good feeling for why your neighborhood looks the way it does. Taylor also seems to think that design is as important as planting, so there are extensive separate entries for things like arbors and bog gardening, whereas Wyman simply considers these briefly under more general headings. Furthermore, Taylor is everywhere lively and sugges-

tive. About actinidias, he writes, "handsome foliage and ability to cover completely arbors and trellises," where Wyman simply comments, "One should have a good reason for planting them in the garden." Now there's nothing wrong with a difference of opinion, but if Wyman thinks there's any good reason for planting them, he ought to tell us. Similarly, Taylor warns against the water plantain, as a possible water garden pest, but Wyman simply describes it without comment.

Not that Wyman is not a fine and useful book. It is just more listy and dry. Indeed, it is superior to Taylor when it comes to evaluating cultivars and varieties for their garden value, simply because it lists more of them. There are also very good lists of plants with certain virtues or characteristics, like fine autumn color. There are, of course, entries on design, but they appear under broad heads like "water gardening" or "garden structures."

Both the above volumes are extremely comprehensive—even for botanical terms and pesticides. The same can be said for *America's Garden Book*, though this is more an encyclopedia in disguise. Where the others are organized alphabetically, it is organized by broad topics like "terraces and patios," "lawns," "the home swimming pool," "trees," and "prairie and meadow." Frankly, I think the alphabetical format is easier to use, but maybe it's just force of habit on my part. Much space is devoted to detailed consideration of design elements. I found it dry but informative, with perhaps slightly narrower coverage than Taylor. It was particularly nice to see the chapters devoted to "special habitats," like prairie, woodland, water, and rock gardens. The listings of individual plants are, if anything, even better than Wyman's, including "cultivars of merit" selected by a consulting team from the New York Botanical Garden and detailed notes on virtually everything.

Henry Field Seed and Nursery Co.

Shenandoah, IA 51602

■ *Seed and plants for annuals, perennials, vegetables, fruit and nut trees, grasses, berries, landscape trees and shrubs, and hedges; tools and supplies.*
■ *96-page catalogue, more than 1,000 color illustrations, free.*

Field has everything, especially when it comes to vegetables, berries, and fruit and nut trees. Emphasis is on latest varieties, though some old open-pollinated types survive, particularly among the corn. The tone is folksy, and the pictures are appetizing. Each catalogue offers special sales on selected flowers and vegetables.

 The love of dirt is among the earliest of passions, as it is the latest.
—CHARLES DUDLEY WARNER, IN *MY SUMMER IN THE GARDEN* (1870)

Flower and Garden

4251 Pennsylvania Avenue
Kansas City, MO 64111

■ *64-page bimonthly magazine, many color illustrations, annual subscription $6.00*

The magazine appeals intelligently to middle American taste. Articles tell you what to use with rocks on your property, to drape over a wall, or the like. Most features in each issue introduce plants that may be well known to very serious gardeners, but not to the rest of us. A recent issue had surveys of liriope, buddleia, love-lies-bleeding, the Jerusalem artichoke, and pak-choi. Garden tips like "Keeping Glads Straight" and "Shear Your Candytufts" are scattered through the pages. Regional editors report on what to do in any season for all regions of the U.S.

Flowers and Fruit

by Colette
Farrar Straus & Giroux

■ *163 pages, $14.95.*

The brief pieces that make up *Flowers and Fruit* are gathered from various pieces of Colette's nonfiction, but they all show her real genius for investing objects with an emotional character, largely by dint of relating them to her immediate surroundings, her memories, and her formidable store of metaphors. Many of the writings are about specific flowers, drawn from texts she did for a volume of fine flower prints. I like best the memory essays, her reflections on the flowers she sees when she walks through Paris, or the memoir of her childhood gardens in "Flora and Pomona." The book is a lovely tribute to plants and provides a fine glimpse of the France Colette loved.

Friends of the Earth

550 7th Street S.E.
Washington, DC 20003

■ *Nonprofit organization dedicated to advocacy on environmental issues.*
■ *Variable-length, bimonthly tabloid Not Man Apart, some illustrations, annual membership $25.00*

FOE has always been a politically active group. Recently it moved its headquarters to Washington from San Francisco, perhaps a symbol of its focus on legislative issues. The tabloid is therefore full of political and legislative news, but it has not given up on the feature articles that explore the organization's favored topics. A recent issue, for example, had an article by Wes Jackson on the need to revitalize not the family farm, but the whole culture of the rural community. Acid rain and pesticides are two hot issues with FOE, so the paper is a good place to keep abreast of them.

Garden Book Series

Brooklyn Botanic Garden

1000 Washington Avenue
Brooklyn, NY 11225

HP Books

575 E. Drive Road
Tucson, AZ 85703

Ortho Books

Chevron Chemical Co.
Consumer Products Division
575 Market Street
San Francisco, CA 94105

Sunset Books

Lane Publishing Co.
Willow & Middlefield Roads
Menlo Park, CA 94025

Time–Life Series

American Horticultural Society
PO Box 0105
Mount Vernon, VA 22121

Each of these series numbers at least 2 dozen titles. Each of them has a volume to cover any general garden subject you wish to be introduced to. Though the overall high quality of all the series will be found to vary from volume to volume, each series has its particular virtues.

The Brooklyn Botanic Garden series is unique among them. It has more volumes on a wider variety of topics, and each is composed of topical essays, usually by acknowledged experts in the field. Where most of the series try to offer a wide, if not deep, introduction to each of the fields, the BBG books offer deeper stabs into individual topics within the larger subject area. You can read the BBG books through, while you will tend to flip through the others for useful advice. Take a subject like low-maintenance gardening, for example. Where the Ortho volume offers a general introduction to the design and planting of low-maintenance gardens—with a fine plant list and good color pictures—the BBG book delves into specific topics—including some that Ortho barely broaches, like prairie gardening and container gardening in flue tiles. It has nothing like Ortho's plant dictionary, though. Generally, then, you may find that the BBG volumes will be the second volume you buy on the subject, once you have gotten your introduction and are developing a deep interest in the field. Having said this, I still think you ought to compare on a specific topic before buying. On azaleas and rhododendrons, for instance, the BBG has both a fine general introduction for every region and deep articles, such as one on the rare Georgia ericaceous plant *Elliottia.*

HP Books is a relative latecomer to the garden-series game, but it has made up for lost time. It tries to combine the virtues of other series, matching the good writing of a Time-

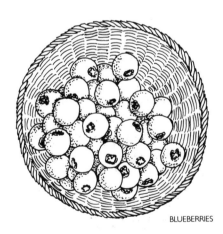

BLUEBERRIES

Life volume with the pretty color photographs of the Ortho series, and putting out its volumes at a price to compete with Ortho and Sunset. A few of the recent volumes are so copious and good-looking that they are beyond introductions to their fields.

Look especially at Derek Fell's *Annuals, Trees and Shrubs* and *Vegetables,* and at Pamela Harper's *Perennials.* (In all 4, HP has made use of both the writing and photographic talents of the authors.)

The Ortho series must have caused a lot of consternation at Sunset when the first volumes appeared. Where Sunset had always depended on black-and-white line drawings and photographs, offering excellent information at a very low price, Ortho reasoned that the public would pay slightly more for high-quality text *and* color illustration. The Ortho books are perhaps the prettiest of all the series—well organized, attractively designed, and with lots of nice photos. Charts and plant dictionaries are always useful and easy to read, and landscape plans are colorful and dramatic. I generally find the quality of the writing less satisfactory. It is indeed informative, but I could do without some of the cutesy and condescending introductory chapters.

Sunset Books must have the sense that the field has become much more crowded now than when it first entered the market. Its books have made some concessions to the rage for color, offering color-illustrated sections in their new editions, but the focus is still on fine information in a strictly-adhered-to 96 pages, at a low price. Sunset's books are not, by and large, meant only for the West, and wherever you live, they are worth comparing with those of other series before you buy. Where Sunset has the most resources and expertise—with the deck-and-patio style it did so much to make popular in the West—its volumes are often your best choice. It is interesting to compare HP of Tucson and Sunset of the San Francisco Bay area: at first glance, HP's *Plants for Dry Climates* is the choice over Sunset's *Desert Gardening.* The photographs are prettier, the region covered is slightly broader,

and fine consideration is given to habitat and elevation. On second glance, however, the choice isn't so obvious.

> It is time to think in different terms and consider possible and pleasant ways of bringing into our modest landscape some of the magic of the alpine and saxatile plants.
> —H. LINCOLN FOSTER, FROM *ROCK GARDENING* (1982)

If you are just planting in an existing garden, the color illustrations in the HP book may tip the scales in its favor—despite Sunset's better organization, which separates out the lists of natives, exotics, and cacti and succulents—but if you are designing a garden from scratch, go with Sunset. The great variety of arid-land garden design it presents is far superior to HP's suggestions, even though its illustrations are mainly black-and-white.

The Time-Life series is the only one to be sold in hardcover. At first, it was available mainly through the giant firm's mail-order sales, but the books were so good that they sold well through bookstores as well. Part of the reason was the series' use of authors like James Crockett and Donald Wyman; another was the skill with which Time-Life carefully fashions its books for nationwide relevance. Another plus, for those of us who like flower painting, was the choice of color paintings, instead of photographs, for the plant dictionaries, though color photographs and charts in the design and hands-on sections are also appealing. The original series is now out of print, but the American Horticultural Society is presently updating the series and rereleasing it under the society's imprint.

Garden

The Garden Society
New York Botanical Garden
Bronx, NY 10458

- *32-page bimonthly magazine, many color illustrations, annual subscription $12.00. Free to members of the following organizations: Atlanta Botanical Garden; Boerner Botanical Gardens of Milwaukee County, Wisconsin; Bok Tower Gardens; California Arboretum Foundation; Chicago Horticultural Society; Crosby Arboretum; Horticultural Society of New York; Horticultural Society of the Indianapolis Museum of Art; The Inniswood Society, Columbus & Franklin Counties, Ohio; Memphis Botanic Garden Foundation; New York Botanical Garden; Queens Botanical Garden; and University of British Columbia Botanical Garden.*

This is an attractive magazine. I sometimes feel it is a bit thin, but things I have read in it are always popping to mind. Published at the New York Botanical Garden, it is a refreshing change from the countless hands-on gardening magazines. When articles concern the culture of a given plant, it is usually a particularly interesting or neglected one—like the native pawpaw—and the writer usually provides a good deal more than planting tips. There are numerous features on garden history, popular botany, and ecological issues. Every once in awhile, the editors indulge in a theme issue. A recent one, about city gardening, qualifies as a brief handbook for community gardeners.

The Gardener's Bug Book

by Cynthia Wescott
Doubleday

- *689 pages, some illustrations, a few in color, $19.95.*

Insect friends as well as enemies appear here—in great numbers, as befits the insect realm. There are 1,900 bugs discussed in this standard refer-

ence work, along with about 700 species of their leafy prey. (Cross-listing allows you to search from bug to prey or vice versa.) Wescott is a thorough writer, with a bit of verve. She tells us the source, looks, life cycle, and favorite food of each of the garden friends or foes, in language that will not offend a nonscientist. Suggestions for pest control are usually chemical in nature. Generally speaking, the *Ortho Problem Solver* (see page 42) is more usefully illustrated, but I wouldn't want to miss the horrifyingly lovely color illustrations in Wescott, which show lurid bugs in the process of disfiguring their hosts.

The Gardener's Year

by Karel Capek
University of Wisconsin Press

- *160 pages, some crazy illustrations, $7.95.*

If you don't already have this book or if you don't go out and get it, there is something the matter with you. It is the funniest, wisest, sweetest disquisition on the actual practice of gardening that I have ever read. It was written back in the late 1920s by the great Czech playwright Capek, better known, perhaps, for having coined the term "robot." The book pretends to follow you, the gardener, through the year, admonishing and instructing you as it goes. In fact, it is the most wonderful compilation of crazy lists of bugs, soils, seeds, and the like; of portraits of cactus maniacs, rock-garden loons, and nefarious vacationers who leave you to care for their gardens; of struggles with hoses and tools and beds; and of genuine aphorisms to live by. Here is a sample: "No pudding could be more complicated than the preparation of a garden soil; as far as I have been able to find out, dung, manure, guano, leafmould, sods, humus, sand, straw, lime, kainit, Thomas's powder, baby's powder,

saltpetre, horn, phosphates, droppings, cow dung, ashes, peat, compost, water, beer, knocked-out pipes, burnt matches, dead cats, and many other substances are added. All this is continually mixed, stirred in, and flavoured. . . ." Read it.

Gardenimport

PO Box 760
Thornhill, Ontario
CANADA L3T 4A5

- *Bulbs, seeds, and plants for annuals, perennials, and vegetables; tools.*
- *30–48-page catalogues, spring and fall; approx. 60–75 illustrations each, many in color; annual subscription $2.00.*

Gardenimport shops where royalty does: its bulb grower is supplier to the Queen of the Netherlands, and it features a select flower and vegetable seed list drawn from the catalogue of Sutton Seeds (see page 48), purveyors to Her Majesty Queen Elizabeth II and the Queen Mother. Bulb and seed lists are both fine, the former a bit broader than the latter. Along with loads of the usual spring- and fall-flowering bulbs, the firm offers about 80 varieties of the less common bulbs, 40 choices among irises, and a good dozen peonies. Lily lovers may be pleased or terrified, according to their preferences, by the gigantic orange Thunderbolt variety, which can grow 7 feet high. Unfortunately, Gardenimport has had to select from the Sutton catalogue, instead of offering it whole. Sutton specialties like cyclamen and sweet peas are represented here, but one wishes the list were larger throughout. The firm is willing to import special orders from Sutton, so a serious gardener might get the Sutton catalogue and order via Gardenimport. For people interested in trying British and European varieties of the common vegetable types, the company offers seed for a number of interesting ones, particularly broad beans and cabbages. Prices are given in Canadian dollars, making this a very easy-to-use catalogue for Canadian gardeners. Americans, unless obsessed with Sutton offerings, may do as well to order from the New Jersey–based branch of the English firm Thompson and Morgan (see page 48), which is strong in the same sort of British favorites as Sutton. Both, for example, have the quilled Radio calendula, a flower that appears to have been electrocuted. A real surprise in this catalogue, however, is the very nice list of woodland plants for wild gardens.

Gardening for Love

by Elizabeth Lawrence
Duke University Press

- *238 pages, $15.95.*

When Elizabeth Lawrence's friend Eudora Welty first put her onto the *Mississippi Market Bulletin*, Lawrence began an affair with the rural journal that lasted for decades. Essentially, market bulletins were bulletin boards, by means of which the men sold livestock and crop seed, while the women sold flower seed and bulbs. "Like Eudora Welty's novels," writes Lawrence, "the market bulletins are a social history of the Deep South." It was Lawrence's idea to make a book about the bulletins, including much of her voluminous correspondence with the farm women whose seed she sent for; this book is Lawrence's lively and moving "social history," much as she would have published it herself. We hear a lot about the virtues of rural culture these days, but seldom from an observer so sane, loving, and articulate as Lawrence. The book is a remarkable document as well as a useful volume for Southern gardeners who want to grow old-fashioned plants.

Gardening Through the Year

by Hazel Evans
Harper & Row

- *192 pages, many color illustrations, $10.95 pbk.*

As the handsome design and illustrations immediately show, this is another nice-looking garden book imported from England. It takes a month-by-month approach to both ornamental and vegetable gardens, like James Crockett's *Victory Garden* (see page 49). Unfortunately, however, since this book was made for the British market, its timing is off for most of the colder parts of the U.S. People in California, the Pacific Northwest and the South will be able to follow along pretty well, but others have to use the valuable suggestions at times other than those advised. The illustrations are particularly good for suggested garden plans—especially one for a cottage garden—and tasks like making a topiary frame or blanching endives, better explained with pictures than with words alone.

Gardens of North America and Hawaii: A Traveler's Guide

by Irene and Walter Jacob
Timber Press

- *368 pages, a few illustrations, $24.95.*

Here's the most complete and up-to-date guide now available to the public gardens of the U.S. and Canada. Descriptions are brief, but all the vital statistics are here, together with a clever shorthand that helps you gauge what plants and features are to be found in each. There are arboreta, botanic and historic gardens, conservatories, and even a list of annual open-house tours in some areas.

Gaze Seed Co.

PO Box 640
St. John's, Newfoundland
CANADA A1C 5K8

- *Seed and bulbs for vegetables, lawn grass, and annual and perennial flowers; plants for ornamental trees, shrubs, and roses; tools and supplies.*
- *42-page catalogue, more than 150 illustrations, free.*

This is a down-home catalogue for people in Newfoundland and Labrador. There is nothing surprising in it, but it has good coverage of all the major varieties. There are a surprising number of roses, mostly hybrid teas and floribundas, with some shrub roses and polyanthas thrown in. Almost half the catalogue is devoted to tools and supplies, including a lovely one-wheeled hand plow, a potato hook with good long forks, a grass hook, and a blueberry rake.

The Green Guerrillas

625 Broadway
New York, NY 10012

- *Nonprofit organization devoted to urban and community gardening in the New York City area. Annual membership $10.00.*

This aptly named group has been known to toss wildflower bombs into vacant lots, and, in the bad old days, they might simply occupy a vacant lot, turning it into a garden. Mainly, the "guerrillas" provide technical assistance to urban gardeners, give away plants to community garden groups, and offer urban gardening workshops. For New York community gardeners, they are an important resource, and they might well serve as a model for groups starting elsewhere. Their 8-page quarterly newsletter focuses on New York news and information, but it contains generally useful and inspiring reports as well.

Green Thoughts: A Writer in the Garden

by Eleanor Perenyi
Random House

- *289 pages, $5.95 pbk.*

Each of the good women authors who has written on gardening and gardens seems to draw from a common stock of knowledge, experience, and taste, but each retains a characteristic tone of her own. You imagine Vita Sackville-West always rushing off to try something new and always eager to tell you her results; Colette adds a whiff of allure to whatever she describes; Katharine White is quietly witty, with a healthy sense of her own limits and a genuine affection for almost everything. When you read Perenyi, you feel that she is always lying in wait to ambush you with an opinion or a bit of arcana. When she is conveying knowledge, she is fine indeed. In this very miscellaneous A-to-Z collection of her garden musings, she provides a spirited defense and a brief anatomy of organic gardening; explains economic botany and puts us onto Oakes Ames, its finest scholar; tells how she smuggled home and grew some lovely French potatoes; reflects on blue flowers, suggesting favorites and meditating on the class-consciousness of gardeners; discovers for us the ancient Mediterranean gardens of Adonis; and quite a lot more. Her opinions, however, are less gen-

erous. She begins a disquisition on the artichoke only to end by pouncing on the poor Jerusalem artichoke, which she regards as insipid and ineradicable. Likewise, I was irritated by her comparatively long article dismissing the rock gardens of the Western world. Still, she belongs on the short list of garden writers to read.

Grower's Weed Identification Handbook

California Cooperative Extension Service
University of California
6701 San Pablo Avenue
Oakland, CA 94608

- *231-pages in looseleaf binder, all color illustrations, $55.00; additional packets of 16 sheets each, $4.25.*

It's a lot of money to pay, and it is geared specifically to California, but since most weeds are cosmopolitan, let me mention this book anyway. The pictures are fantastic, showing not only whole plants but nutlets, roots, and stems as well. Each sheet also contains a nice natural history of the culprit on the back. Unfortunately, it gives no advice on how to control the weeds. If you are really wild about weed identification, however, I can't think of a better resource.

Growing and Saving Vegetable Seeds

by Marc Rogers
Garden Way Publishing

- *140 pages, some illustrations, $7.95 pbk.*

Here is a good, broad introduction to seed-saving techniques. Along with instructions for preventing cross-pollination and for cleaning and storing seed, there is also enough on the biology of seeds to help you understand why you are doing what you do.

A Guide to Safe Pest Control Around the Home

Cornell Miscellaneous Bulletin 74
New York State College of
Agriculture and Life Sciences
7 Research Park
Cornell University
Ithaca, NY 14850

- *60-page book, some color illustrations, $2.50.*

Here is a very fine guide to the use of pesticides, both organic and chemical, in the garden. Not only does it provide clear color pictures of the common plant predators and their effects on their prey, but it also contains exhaustive lists of houseplants, outdoor annuals and perennials, ornamental trees and shrubs, fruit trees and vines, and vegetables. Each entry describes the pests that attack the given plant and offers pesticide solutions, together with spray schedules where appropriate. There is even a 2-page chart at the front of the book to help you select the kind of sprayer best suited to the variety of uses you may have for it. The emphasis is admittedly on chemical pesticides, so organic gardeners will avoid the book, though the listings also provide nonspray suggestions for limiting the spread of pests.

Gurney's Gardening News

Gurney Seed & Nursery Co.
110 Capitol
Yankton, SD 57079

- *32-page bimonthly tabloid, many illustrations, annual subscription $5.95.*

This publication comes from Gurney's Seed & Nursery (see following entry), and is considerably more valuable than one might expect. Of course, the company does blow its

BIRDHOUSE

own trumpet a bit, and some articles are tendentious. For example, in a recent article on the virtues of hybrid vegetables, the author cited exclusively the advice of a prominent hybridizer. What he said is true enough—many hybrids *are* more vigorous and generally better plants than nonhybrids—but his advice not to bother with saving hybrid seed might be mistaken by some as advice not to save seed at all. One could have wished for a better-balanced article. Still, the magazine is generally serious, and the quality of its tips and suggestions is good. Issues may be devoted to regional round-ups or to special subjects like growing vegetables off the ground. There are always odd little features like an article on moon-sign planting and another entitled "200 Species of Spider Mites Spell Trouble." The bulk of most issues is dedicated to vegetable growing, but there are some ideas for growing flowers as well.

Gurney's Seed & Nursery Co.

110 Capitol
Yankton, SD 57079

- *Seed and plants for annual and perennial flowers, vegetables, fruit and nut trees, grasses, berries, landscape trees and shrubs, and hedges; tools and supplies.*
- *66-page catalogue, more than 1,250 color illustrations, free.*

If Henry Field has everything, Gurney's has everything and more—about 4,000 varieties, in fact. The larger Gurney's catalogue is mainly accounted for by the varieties the firm has thrown in to accommodate Northern climates, including a nice selection of subzero roses and a number of Gurney's own vegetable, fruit, and berry introductions. The folksy tone and the scrumptious look of the catalogue resemble those of Field's, as do the periodic special sales. This is not so surprising when you consider

that both companies are now owned by the giant Amfac corporation. Gurney's has the better planting charts and cultural hints; they are among the best and easiest to use that I've seen.

 THE CHRONICLES OF A VERY SMALL POND

Part I: Starting From Scratch
by Susan Hesselgesser

After discovering a charming little corner in our backyard, I approached my generous and completely unsuspecting husband with the idea of a lily pond. Little did we know that we were about to start an adventure of near epic proportions—comedy, tragedy, success, failure, birth and death—all in that 120 square foot space.
—FROM *THE WATER LILY JOURNAL* (1985)

Harris Seeds

3670 Buffalo Road
Rochester, NY 14624

- *Seed for vegetables, annual and perennial flowers, and lawn grass; tools and supplies.*
- *98-page catalogue, more than 550 color illustrations, free.*

There aren't many people left in the home-garden trade who do their own breeding work; Harris is one of the few and, for vegetables, one of the best. Hybridizing and selection create strains that ripen early and are more uniform and/or more disease-resistant. The Harris cucumbers, tomatoes, eggplants, and sweet corns have a high reputation. Recent introductions include an Oriental eggplant called Little Fingers and 2 very early white sweet corns, Quicksilver and Silverado. The whole veggies list is worth a look, not only for what it of-

fers but for some very good planting tips, like this one for deterring cutworms: "Plant a 4–5″ nail right alongside each transplant (touching the stem). Cutworms wrap their bodies around the plant and the nail bothers them." Harris breeders are also at work on flowers. The list gives a very good choice of varieties for all the annuals, a somewhat more limited selection for perennials. They have a couple of nice pastel-colored salvia and one that is, yecchh, purple. The tools and supplies list is getting high-tech: there is a watering computer and one of those interesting cold frames whose springs sense the temperature, opening or closing the frame accordingly!

Harrowsmith

Camden House Publishing
Camden East, Ontario
CANADA K0K 1J0

The Creamery
Charlotte, VT 05445

- *Variable-length bimonthly, many color illustrations, annual subscription $15.00 Canada, $18.00 U.S.*

Long the leading garden magazine in Canada, *Harrowsmith* recently started an edition for the U.S. market as well. It's a sort of *Country Journal* with a more strictly garden focus. The writing is unusually good, with essays on country living by the likes of Joyce Maynard, profiles of farm towns, and reports of a seed saver who actually tried to save seeds. The emphasis sways somewhat toward the edible end of the garden, but there is fair coverage of ornamentals, too. Every season, the magazine evaluates the new crop of vegetables and ornamentals from the major seed houses. A nice feature called "Sourcebank" reports on new garden ideas from companies and experiment stations.

H. G. Hastings Co.

PO Box 4274
Atlanta, GA 30302

- *Seed and a few plants for vegetables and flowers; plants for roses, ornamental trees and shrubs, fruit and nut trees, and vines; supplies.*
- *64-page catalogue, more than 300 color illustrations, free.*

Most of what you will find in this fine and extensive regional catalogue is by no means unique to Hastings, but everything has been selected for Southern growing conditions—a matter of no small consequence when it comes to fruiting plants. Here, too, you'll find some unusual stuff for warmer climates or Southern tastes, like jicama, 2 kinds of peanuts, a remarkable page full of cream and crowder peas, and 9 varieties of okra (including a red and a white one). The choice of fruiting trees, bushes, and vines is very wide, notably for blueberries and grapes. This is the best Southern catalogue I have seen.

High Altitude Gardens

PO Box 4238
Ketchum, ID 83340

- *Seed for wildflowers, native grass, and vegetables; tools, supplies, books, and organic fertilizers and pest controls.*
- *78-page catalogue, approx. 30 illustrations, $2.00.*

This young, bioregional seed company is trying to be a full-service seed house for the Intermountain states. If you are tired of petunias and salvia and the latest Burpee tomato and would like to make a garden in harmony with your region's natural flora, this is a fine place to turn. The wildflower and grass lists are exceptional. Many of the species offered consist of seed collected in Idaho's mountains, so the list is by no means just the usual suspects. The text itself is thorough and often entertaining, as in the

entry for *Arnica cordifolia,* which not only extols the plant's beauty but suggests using a tea made of it to soothe aching feet. Proprietor Bill McDorman has also come up with a nice way of packaging wildflower mixes: they are determined according to the species actually growing together in a given place—along the Salmon River or the Oregon Trail, for example. McDorman's vegetable list looks for the most part like a standard company list minus all the hybrids. (Tomatoes are an exception: a number of unusual varieties appear here.) He believes in gardening with strictly open-pollinated types, and he has selected among them for earliness, making the list a good place for short-season growers to look and equally good for people in warmer climates who may want to grow a second season of vegetables in the fall. Plants are unusually well described, including charts showing optimum temperatures for germination. McDorman

OKRA

has also been very creative in grouping types together in garden collections, offered for sale as a group. You can choose among harsh-climate, salad-garden, medicinal-herb, tea-herb, insect-repellent, and several other collections. The herb list itself is reasonably comprehensive, and plants as well as seed are offered. The tools and supplies section is brief but choice, including a pot called "Wall o' Water" that surrounds your plants with 3 gallons of insulating water, making it possible to set them outside earlier. Books are selected largely from the ecologically correct literature on gardening. Not many seed companies have a heading in their

book list called "Philosophy and Politics." In short, this is one of the finest general catalogues I have seen. McDorman has even created 3 "educational series" collections—one for wild edibles, one for wild medicinals, and one for poisonous plants.

Home Ground

by Allen Lacy
Farrar Straus & Giroux

- *259 pages, $14.95.*

Farther Afield

by Allen Lacy
Farrar Straus & Giroux

- *286 pages, $16.95.*

Allen Lacy started gardening as a child, after he bit his teacher's leg and was forced to do penance in an iris garden. Later, he became a professor of philosophy. I don't know whether it's his humble horticultural beginnings or his philosophical training that has done it, but Lacy has developed a wonderful, informal style for writing personal essays on gardening and sense of place. Whether his topic is a garden catalogue, a plant he loves or hates, a garden book, or a gardener he has met, he gives you the feeling that he is sharing his discoveries in a casual conversation. Take for example the hilarious piece called "Onopordiums: Formidable Friends." He has a problem, it seems, with the kids who cut through the flower bed at the edge of his corner lot, seeking a shortcut to the local video-game parlor. He tries a low fence, but it doesn't work. The fence maker suggests barbed wire, electric fencing, or sharpened bamboo sticks. ("I may be grumpy, but I don't hate children," remarks Lacy.) He settles on planting Scotch thistles, which do the trick just fine. (They are not so invasive as you might think, he reports, and may do well as a small but formidable barrier.) Lacy usually disclaims any special horticultural knowledge, admitting at one point that his wife does a lot of the garden work while he "gardens at the typewriter," but each of his essays has at least one piece of useful knowledge.

Horticulture

755 Boylston Street
Boston, MA 02116

- *Variable-length monthly, many color illustrations, annual subscription $18.00, 2 years $32.00.*

Vegetables get into *Horticulture,* but ornamentals are the focus. The writing here is generally first-rate— among the best in the business. Roger Swain writes a monthly column, and people like Allen Lacy frequently contribute. You will find articles on every subject from a great horticultural bookseller, to the training of climbing roses, to fragrant plants for the home. There are periodic reviews of new cultivars, and a source list at the back of each issue tells where to get all the plants discussed in that issue. The illustrations are of very high quality.

HortIdeas

Route 1
Box 302
Gravel Switch, KY 40328

- *Variable-length monthly, annual subscription $10.00.*

HortIdeas is frequently compared with the *Avant Gardener,* perhaps because both are small newsletters that do an exceptionally fine job of keeping their readers up to the minute. There is, however, a big difference in focus. Though *HortIdeas* does not exclude ornamentals, its coverage is weighted toward edibles. Further-

more, it typically presents summaries, book reviews, and articles derived from the more technical journals in horticulture, so that in a given issue, you may find such topics as "seed germination of fire-following herbs" and "cyanide in lima beans." In 1986, the newsletter devoted 2 issues to the proceedings of the International Horticultural Congress. Regardless, it does make for fascinating reading, and you definitely don't have to be a pro to get a lot of benefit from it. *HortIdeas* probably packs more information into every issue than does the *Avant Gardener,* though this means that the reader must wade a little more to find what he or she is looking for. The wading is worthwhile.

> Gardeners of all ages, I find, are much more eager to plant flowers than to take care of them afterward. This must be the reason for the popularity of little bulbs. Once planted in a soil and situation that satisfy their requirements they can be forgotten until they begin to bloom.
>
> —ELIZABETH LAWRENCE, FROM *THE LITTLE BULBS: A TALE OF TWO GARDENS* (1986)

Hortus Third

by L. H. Bailey and E. Z. Bailey and the staff of the Liberty Hyde Bailey Hortorium, Cornell University
Macmillan

- *1,290 pages, some illustrations, $125.00.*

Hortus, the standard American botanical reference work, modestly subtitles itself "A Concise Dictionary of Plants Cultivated in the United States and Canada." Well, compared to the 10-volume *New York Botanical Garden Illustrated Encyclopedia of Horticulture* or the 4-volume *Royal Horticultural Society Dictionary of Garden-*

ing, I suppose that *Hortus* is concise. Nonetheless, if you opened it and hollowed it out, your cat could sleep comfortably inside. The comparative briefness and astonishing range of *Hortus* is a real advantage in some respects, since here is a book that authoritatively lists almost any plant you will ever think of growing and one that, if you save your pennies, you can conceive of someday owning. The disadvantage of its conciseness is that the entries on individual plants are often written entirely in "Botanese," which takes some getting used to. Furthermore, *Hortus* will not give you the range of cultural information that the N.Y. Bot's tomes will. Still, it is a wonderful thing. It is too seldom pointed out that the book, aside from its thousands of genus and species entries, contains numerous and very well written entries about all the common fruits and vegetables and about all kinds of ornamental gardening. The little essays are very readable and do a commendable job of briefly laying out the subject. The common-names index is also useful for finding the plants whose Latin monikers have escaped you.

How Plants Get Their Names

by L. H. Bailey
Dover

- *181 pages, a few illustrations, $3.95 pbk.*

If Latin nomenclature bothers you, this book might change your mind. The great horticulturist Liberty Hyde Bailey begins by describing a Jerusalem cherry and, before you know it, you find yourself interested in all kinds of unpronounceable names and their provenance. There is a useful dictionary of Latin names with translations at the back of the book, so you can learn why a plant might be called something as strange as *marmoratus.*

How to Identify Plants

by H. D. Harrington and L. W. Durrell
Harper & Row

- *203 pages, many illustrations, $7.95.*

Glaucous and glabrous, sciliate and scabrous, cordate and palmate, thryses and umbels: the botanical reference works that use such terms will often append a brief key to them, but the explanations are sometimes as abstruse as the words themselves. Here is a book with simple illustrations and clear definitions to tell you what most of the terms you encounter really mean.

PALM LEAF

J. L. Hudson, Seedsman

PO Box 1058
Redwood City, CA 94064

- *Seed for flowers, shrubs, trees, herbs, and vegetables.*
- *104-page catalogue, approx. 134 illustrations, $1.00.*

Hudson inherited the worldwide seed collection of Harry E. Saier, a collection that once numbered 18,000 varieties. Hudson has nowhere near that number, but his catalogue is still very impressive. There are rarities and wildlings galore here, especially among the flowers and shrubs. Particularly interesting is a selection of vegetables and herbs gathered from the Zapotec Indians of Mexico. Many common varieties are also included here, and the cultural instructions are generally very good. Still, since Hudson cannot do germination tests on everything he's got and since some of the plants are difficult to grow under the best of circumstances, this is a catalogue best suited to the serious, experimental gardener. However, it is such good reading that it is hard to resist the temptation to suggest that everyone send for it.

Ed Hume Seeds

PO Box 1450
Kent, WA 98032

- *Seeds and bulbs for vegetables and annual and perennial flowers; books and videos.*
- *24-page catalogue, 5 illustrations, free.*

The list contains the usual varieties, but selected for cool-weather growing in the Pacific Northwest. According to Hume, the seeds are also popular for fall crops in hot-season areas. There are a few local university releases included, and Hume is also a source for the prolific Sweet 100 cherry tomato and a similar tomato called Sweetie. The dahlia selection is very good. Ed runs a regional gardening show, and he offers his gardening book, as well as a few basic pamphlets and a moon-signs planting calendar for the Northwest gardener. Videos from his programs are also for sale. In general, this is a first rate source for those who garden in cooler climates.

Insect Identification Handbook

University of California Cooperative
Extension Service
6701 San Pablo Avenue
Oakland, CA 94608

- *22 sheets in looseleaf binder, all color illustrations, $6.50; 7-sheet supplement, $2.50.*

Like the *Grower's Weed Identification Handbook* (see page 32), this is a publication directed at Californians, but its illustrations and its comments on pests are so good that I could not resist including it. Illustrations not only show egg, larval, and adult stages of the beasts, but also show the effect of the critters on their favorite prey. An advantage to this book, as opposed to the weed book, is that it also suggests the best means for controlling the pest.

Island Seed Mail Order

PO Box 4278
Station A
Victoria, British Columbia
CANADA V8X 3X8

- *Seed for vegetables and flowers.*
- *80-page catalogue, 12 illustrations, $2.00.*

Island has an excellent, basic list for the Pacific Northwest, well set up for the beginning gardener. Cultural instructions are good for both vegetables and flowers. Among the tomatoes are 2 bred at Island for the local climate, and there is an intriguing list of Swiss alpines for the rock garden. Island has gone the meadow-in-a-can people one better, with its Gold Medal Box, a complete vegetable and flower garden-in-a-box.

Kester Wild Game Food Nurseries

PO Box V
Omro, WI 54963

- *Seed and bulbs for aquatic and perennial land plants favored as food and cover by game birds, game fish, and land animals.*
- *38-page catalogue, approx. 50 illustrations, $2.00.*

As proprietors of the oldest game-food nursery in the country, the Kesters turn out a very fine catalogue of aquatics, legumes, and grain crops for birds, fish, and animals. The planting instructions are not only complete, they are the stuff of a bird lover's dreams. With respect to Sago pondweed for example, they write: "If the water level drops low enough, then all puddle type ducks and also geese and swans glut themselves on the tubers." Or consider this recommendation for wild celery: "Canvasbacks, Redheads, Bluebills, Mallards, etc., darken the sky over the Wild Celery beds." Well, it does sound a little ominous. Nonhunters may well want to consider this list for naturalized ponds, streams, and pasture areas. It includes some fair ornamentals, like arrowhead *(Sagittaria latifolia)*. The Indians ate the tubers, and the Kesters will send you instructions for eating it, if you wish. There is also a nice group of native and showy water lilies, cattails, pickerel plant, and water iris. Kester's is a source of agrotricum, a perennial cross of wheat and tall wheatgrass, and of an excellent selection of millets, sorghums, and buckwheats. The proprietors make an impassioned plea for sportsmen as the most faithful conservationists, and in their favor, it might be pointed out that much of what they offer is the sort of stuff now gaining favor among ecology and sustainable-agriculture people. One piece of advice in the catalogue belongs in the enough-said category. It is titled "To Produce More Rabbits." Apparently, the only animals the Kesters do not like are carp, which wreak havoc among their water plants and compete with game fish.

Krider Nurseries

Box 29
Middlebury, IN 46540

■ *Plants for roses, ornamental trees and shrubs, fruit trees, berries, vines, ground covers, bulbs, and perennial flowers.*
■ *16-page catalogue, approx. 69 illustrations, some in color, free.*

Krider's is a lovely, intelligent catalogue. It has not tried to cover as much as big Midwestern firms like Field and Gurney, but what it does cover, it covers very well. The rose selection is first-rate—as good as or better than that offered by many rose specialists. It includes not only hybrid teas and floribundas, but a few hybrid perpetuals, polyanthas, and species roses as well. Trees and shrubs are also excellent, covering a wider range than the firm's main

competitors. This is a terrific place to find street trees, beeches, and unusual ornamental shrubs. The lists of fruit trees, berries, vines, ground covers, bulbs, and perennials are basic and selective.

Lakeland Nursery Sales

Unique Merchandise Mart
Building 1
Hanover, PA 17333

■ *Seeds, bulbs, and plants for fruits, vegetables, ornamental trees and shrubs, and annual and perennial flowers; supplies and gadgets.*
■ *32-page catalogue, more than 175 color illustrations, free.*

When a plantsperson complains of a nursery naming a common plant with an uncommon name just to sell it, this may be the nursery they are talking about. Still, the catalogue is so entertaining that you can hardly hold nomenclature against the place. Among its gadgets is a windmill that thumps the ground to scare moles, and it offers mole plant *(Euphorbia lathyrus)* under the name "Gopher

 Hybrid Teas
ADMIRAL RODNEY— When you're scarfing up trophies and ribbons with this fragrant, two-toned pink, you'll think you have the world by the tail. The form is outstanding and the blooms set off by dark green, glossy foliage. But you'll quickly let go when you watch it defoliate with rust, and realize that only one of the three crops of bloom it produces per season is worth a hoot. Surprisingly hardy. "M". Basildon Rose Gardens, 1973.

—FROM ROSES BY FRED EDMUNDS, INC. 1986 CATALOGUE

Purge," complete with an illustration of a belly-up gopher, apparently done in the style of Henri Rousseau. On the same page, a concerned-looking doctor offers you comfrey for anything that ails you. This is a catalogue with a lot of names in quotes, like the Blueberry "Tree," an ordinary blueberry trained to tree form. It is also a catalogue of monsters, including a 6-ear sweet corn, a dogwood that blooms in 3 colors on a single tree, and 3 of the nicest ugly roses I've ever seen (a black one, a green one, and a lavender one). Every plant is described with superlatives, even crown vetch, which they call "the world's most spectacular ground cover." The list of flowering shrubs is pretty good, and there are some intriguing oddities that most people will grow in pots: what they call the "Chocolate Pudding Tree" and list by the wrong species name is really sapote, a Mexican tree of the persimmon genus, and they also list jojoba ("a real conversation piece!"). As one might expect, their cultural descriptions are sanguine, which may lead you to be cautious in ordering from them, but they have a fair guarantee, so it might be worth a shot.

Orol Ledden & Sons

PO Box 7
Sewell, NJ 08080

■ *Seeds and bulbs for vegetables, lawn grass, field grass, and flowers; supplies and tools.*
■ *36-page catalogue, approx. 50 illustrations, a few in color, free.*

This is a good, basic list of both veggies and flowers, some of the veggies specially selected for the Northeast. The vegetable planting chart is unusually thorough. Selections for pasture and lawn grass are good. A few interesting heirlooms have crept in among the edibles, including the Jenny Lind melon.

Lexington Gardens

93 Hancock Street
Lexington, MA 02173

- *Plants, seeds, and bulbs for everything outdoors and indoors; tools and supplies.*
- *36-page catalogue and map to get you there, free.*

Lexington does no mail order, but it is such a fine garden center and so convenient to many New England gardeners that it ought not to be left out. You can find more than 1,000 varieties of garden plants here. Selections are very broad in every category except vegetables, and are particularly good for trees and wildflowers. A good percentage of the available cultivars for modern roses, azaleas, and rhododendrons are also offered. The perennials selections are excellent. If you find yourself forever complaining about the limited choices at your local garden center, visit Lexington.

HIBISCUS

Liberty Seed Co.

PO Box 806
New Philadelphia, OH 44663

- *Seed for vegetables and flowers.*
- *56-page catalogue, approx. 175 illustrations, some in color, free.*

Liberty's good, basic selections are intended to be grown in the Northeastern quarter of the United States, excluding the far north. A few gourmet varieties—including baby beans and carrots and a French leek—appear among the otherwise standard list, but the best things in the catalogue are the full and very clear cultural instructions for vegetables.

The Lives of Plants

by Doris M. Stone
Scribner's

- *256 pages, some illustrations, $15.95.*

Here is a well-written introduction to plant biology, complete with a set of simple experiments you can do while you're reading it. It is detailed enough to use as a textbook, but lively and clear enough for a general reader.

Louisiana Nursery

Route 7
Box 43
Opelousas, LA 70570

- *Plants for magnolias, other trees and shrubs, perennials, fruit trees, ornamental grasses, pot plants, and vines.*
- *64-page "Magnolias and Other Garden Aristocrats" catalogue, $3.50.*

If you don't know what you are looking for, this catalogue is liable to be confusing. Endless varieties are offered, with virtually no information on hardiness or final size of plants. If you do know what you're looking for, are particular about what you get, and are willing to pay a steep price for it, then do look at this catalogue *at least* for the following: the massive list of magnolias and magnolia relatives, including all major hybrid groups; a list of ornamental trees featuring many Southern specialties, plus good selections of hardy trees like ginkgo and tulip tree; a fine group of shrubs and vines of all sorts, with particularly good choices among illicium, oleander, bougainvillea, and wisteria; large selections of elephant's-ears, azaleas, angel's-trumpet, bamboo, sedums, succulents, bananas, and palms; a lot of perennial lilyturf and ground covers; an herb list strong in Southern plants like yerba mate, Texas purple sage, and cassava; specialty lists of hibiscus, jasmines, gin-

ger lilies, crape myrtles, and water lilies; and excellent fruit tree and berry choices for the South.

McConnell Nurseries

Port Burwell, Ontario
CANADA N0J 1T0

- *Plants and bulbs for flowers, roses, ornamental trees and shrubs, and fruiting trees, shrubs, and vines.*
- *72-page catalogue, more than 350 color illustrations, free.*

This is one of those colorful catalogues whose pictures practically obscure the text, so it gives the impression of a tremendous grab bag. That's just what it is, but the catalogue is surprisingly thorough and full of excellent cultivar selections for the North. There are a few wildflowers and native ferns scattered amongst the flowers. One of these is the pink lady's-slipper orchid; I wonder what it's like and whether it will grow and flower for us. Among the roses are a half-dozen Brownell sub-zero varieties and a few good choices for hedging. All in all, it's a nice catalogue for browsing.

McFayden Seeds

PO Box 1800
Brandon, Manitoba
CANADA R7A 6N4

- *Seed, plants, and bulbs for vegetables and ornamentals; supplies and books.*
- *Variable-length spring and fall catalogues, many color illustrations, free.*

McFayden offers good color catalogues of the usual varieties, selected for Canadian gardeners. Growing guides are thoughtfully arranged in charts that include notes on winter protection. For those with plans for a potable harvest, you will find among the list a page of wine-and beer-making supplies.

Major Howell's International Seed Collection

Fire Thorn
6 Oxshott Way
Cobham, Surrey
ENGLAND KT11 2RT

- *Seed-distribution service.*
- *Annual subscription, $3.00.*

Here is one of the great grab bags of the horticultural world. Major Howell collects all kinds of seed, mainly from botanical gardens, and offers a huge distribution list of about 5,000 species. Your subscription will bring you the list. A lot of this stuff is not commercially available. Take a chance?

Man and Nature, or Physical Geography as Modified by Human Action

by George Perkins Marsh
Harvard University Press

- *472 pages, $8.95 pbk.*

This is a classic of American ecological thinking, predating the latest rage for the subject by more than a century. Perkins opens with some still-relevant chapters on the effects on plant and animal communities of the migration of peoples and the establishment of agriculture. The bulk of the book focuses on forest conservation—a matter in which Marsh was deeply involved at the practical level—with pioneering chapters on soil erosion and desertification. Before you get all hot and bothered over the latest bioregional, ecotopic fantasy, go read this very convincing and unhysterical cornerstone of the whole ecological movement.

Another eye-opening title on a similar topic, Paul Shepard's *Man in The Landscape* was published during the late 1960s and may now be out of print. It is worth looking for. The book is so wide-ranging—it covers topics from the origins of the human eye, to the history of gardens, to fertility goddesses, to national parks, to patterns of settlement in the ancient and modern worlds—that it can't help being uneven, but Shepard's idiosyncratic approach often breaks open our ordinary way of looking at the nature/culture question. Even if you are not so committed a conservationist as he seems to be, he will make you think. His writing is astonishing, as for example in this consideration of our eyes: "If the traveler looks ahead, the point of fixation on the horizon becomes a germinating bud of landscape, from which the world dilates as he approaches." What a wonderful description of our pleasure in landscape!

OSOME MUSTARD SPINACH

Earl May Seed & Nursery Co.

208 N. Elm Street
Shenandoah, IA 51603

- *Seed, bulbs, and plants for vegetables, flowers, fruit trees, berries, landscape trees and shrubs, vines, hedges, etc.; tools and supplies.*
- *80-page spring catalogue, more than 600 color illustrations, free; 32-page fall catalogue, approx. 150 color illustrations, free.*

May is another of the big, dependable Midwestern companies, like Field and Gurney. Its list is slightly smaller than the others', but the catalogue features everything that most gardeners will want. It is extremely well organized and illustrated. Among the vegetables, the onions, corn, and tomatoes include some distinctive selections. The catalogue offers a few interesting prairie grasses, most of them contained in a very nice prairie-in-a-sack collection. May is also a source of some of the less-often-seen shrub roses. Cultural instructions are good for vegetables, and the firm will send its customers free any of its helpful pamphlets on planting and growing most of the things it sells. The fall catalogue has a basic selection of bulbs, plus a few peonies. The best thing about it is the bulb-planting chart, which shows prettily and at a glance when each sort of bulb blooms and how tall it grows. I cut it out for my scrapbook.

Mellingers

2310 W. South Range Road
North Lima, OH 44452

- *Seeds, bulbs, plants, and grafted stock for fruits, nuts, vegetables, berries, annual and perennial flowers, lawn grass, exotics, and ornamental trees and shrubs; many books, tools, gadgets, and supplies.*
- *112-page catalogue, many illustrations, some in color, free; 32-page fall catalogue, many illustrations, free.*

Leave Mellingers' catalogues in the bathroom and you will wonder at the long absences of your family and friends. There is hardly any item for home horticulture that cannot be found here, be it plants, seeds, tools, cooking gadgets, organic and chemical pest controls, deer repellents, cover crops, wildflowers, fertilizers, garden wheelbarrows for children, or plastic birds. Despite its comprehensive index, this is a book you will probably just wander around in. The fall catalogue is much briefer, but that is like saying Chicago is smaller than New York. It features on its cover just the things you might be looking for, like antidesiccants by the pint, quart, or gallon. In both catalogues, most of the firm's lists are good to very good, and the book lists are excellent. Just get them.

Men's Garden Clubs of America

5560 Merle Hay Road
PO Box 241
Johnston, IA 50131

■ *Nonprofit organization with 170 affiliated clubs nationwide; annual membership $10.00, including bimonthly* The Gardener *and periodical newsletter.*

An organization of good fellows, as useful for their intentions as for their knowledge, the MGCA runs programs for the disturbed and the disabled, for kids, and for civic beautification. The bulk of the magazine is filled with comments from regional editors, whose contributions vary from reports on recommended varieties for local planting to some very charming epistles.

RED-HOT POKER

The Meyer Seed Co.

600 S. Caroline Street
Baltimore, MD 21231

■ *Seed and bulbs for vegetables, flowers, pasture grass, and lawn grass; tools and supplies.*
■ *50-page catalogue, more than 200 illustrations, a few in color, free.*

Another good company serving a limited region, Meyer specializes in the area extending from Baltimore through Washington, D.C., and north-

ern Virginia. The list includes all of the usual suspects, with a planting guide that tells when to plant in this region. The selection of tools is unusually broad.

Moon Signs Gardening Dates

by Ed Hume
Ed Hume Seeds
PO Box 1450
Kent, WA 98032

■ *Annual 23-page moon-signs planting calendar, $1.00.*

For Northwestern gardeners who want to plant and care for vegetables and flowers according to the zodiac and the phases of the moon, here is a complete little pamphlet that tells you just what to do. Hume is not totally convinced that the method works. In fact, he encourages responses from gardeners who use the calendar so he can learn if it does. Regardless, it will give you something to do in the garden every day of the year, though when an instruction commands you to "destroy blackberries," you may wonder how to do it.

The Mother Earth News Presents an Array of Gardens

The Mother Earth News
PO Box 70
Hendersonville, NC 28791

■ *176-page magazine-format book, many illustrations, some in color; $3.95.*

Mother Earth's series of magazinelike garden books—others are reviewed in the appropriate sections throughout this book—are admirable in that they seriously try to get as much information as possible into a cheap 176-page volume. The result is a miscellaneous mix of articles, some quite

good and some reflecting the time and money limits imposed on a publication that sells at such a reasonable price. This volume offers at least 2 or 3 articles, most written from a personal perspective, on such topics as historical gardening, container gardening, edible landscaping, wild gardening, and rock gardening. At the back of the book is a very interesting group of articles on gardening for profit. The usefulness of the individual pieces varies: one article on moss gardening was first-rate, while one about a natives garden was plain wrong. I don't think it's wrong to collect the plants of common wildflowers in your area, but this piece suggested collecting things like yellow lady's-slipper and showy orchis—plants that are scarce enough to warrant your not uprooting them to take home. Still, this is a good volume for the bathroom, where you can flip through the pages reading an article per sitting, until you have found what you can use.

North American Horticulture: A Reference Guide

Scribner's

■ *367 pages, $50.00.*

The best one-stop source for address references in the world of horticulture. You should use it in the library. It contains information on the following: national associations, plant societies, research institutions, garden clubs, conservation organizations, state horticultural societies, nomenclature-registration authorities, cooperative extension services, colleges, libraries, herbariums, public gardens and arboretums, museums, historical and estate gardens, community garden programs, test gardens, flower shows, and even cemeteries!

North Star

Sandy Olson
Box 1655 A
RFD 1
Burnham, ME 04922

- Seed and plant search service for annual and perennial flowers, native plants, vegetables, fruit and nut trees, ferns, grasses, roses, bulbs, and even some tropicals.
- First request $5.00, additional requests $2.50 each; special services available; can import plants on your behalf.

Sandy Olson has more than 100,000 plant names, together with world-wide sources for the plants, filed on a computer. If you are looking for a plant you can't find elsewhere, give Olson a try. If the search is not fruitful, you will pay only a $2.00 handling charge, or you may opt for a special search via contacts in the plant world instead of via microchip in the data base.

The Old Farmer's Almanac

by Robert B. Thomas
Yankee Publishing Inc.

- 232-page almanac, some illustrations, $2.25.

Almanacs are books that try to tie their whole universe together using the stars, the seasons, and the days as string. The *OFA* is their granddaddy in the U.S., having been published since 1792. Though the number of people who actually use it for weather forecasts and planting guidelines must have declined dramatically since then—after all, all the astronomical calculations are for Boston, and it is a little confusing to use the conversion charts for elsewhere—I can't help thinking that the *OFA* serves its primary function even better than it did when it was more readily useful. The weather forecast for the year is one continuous doggerel rhyme that runs down a narrow column beside the dates, making a simple calendar into a sort of poetic weather recipe. The little vignettes in the monthly Farmer's Calendar section are, to my mind, slightly too folksy in tone, though often funny and moving. Separate articles may be about anything from cures for the toothache, to the policy problems of a president, to the grid team system of the great 19th-century surveys and its effect on the Midwestern mind. My favorite part is the daily calendars themselves, in which appear all kinds of statistics on famous births, deaths, and events, plus a sprinkling of adages. One month notes both the birth of St. Francis of Assisi and the day Colonel Yeager broke the sound barrier; in another, we learn that Willie Shoemaker and Emily Brontë were born on succeeding dates; skunks are said to mate on the day following "Daniel Webster's great speech." Throughout, you discover things like when Congressional sessions were first televised, when the rubber heel was patented, when tea is ripe in China, when Ansel Adams was born, when we first sent advisers to Vietnam (1950), when the first asphalt pavement was laid, when Jane Addams was born, and when the rhinoceros was first seen in New York. Each of these notes could be a subject for the day's meditation, and together they are something like the dots that, could we only connect them, would show what American culture is about.

Onward and Upward in the Garden

by Katharine S. White
Farrar Straus & Giroux

362 pages, $6.95 pbk.

This book is a collection of pieces on gardening that Katharine White wrote for *The New Yorker* from the late 1950s through the 1960s. In the main, these were reviews of catalogues and books. Today, many of those she discussed are either out of business or out of print. (A helpful index at the back of this book tells you what has become of each item she mentions.) Regardless, this is one of my all-time favorite gardening books, not least because it taught me how to enjoy garden catalogues. "Reading this literature," she writes, "is unlike any other reading experience. Too much goes on at once. I read for news, for driblets of knowledge, for aesthetic pleasure, and at the same time I am planning the future, and so I read in

DAISIES

dream." *Onward and Upward* has just the same virtues. White was a charming and modest writer, making us take her likes and dislikes more seriously than we might were she merely enthusiastic or carping. Though many of the releases she describes are no longer new or unusual, her comments can easily be read forward to our latest bright monsters (what she called "blobs of bloom") or modest successes. She reminds us of any number of books that, though they are now out of print, are worth looking for. Then, too, there are her memories of gardening and of flowers, like the following: "Goldenrod has many unusual uses. It can be made into a crown of gold for a Harvest Queen or a necklace for a child. Sewn into a white bedsheet, it makes excellent cloth of gold. I lay under just such a sumptuous covering one summer day in my early teens when there was a regatta on Lake Chocorua. . . . My sisters and I began the day by gathering bucketfuls of goldenrod, which my aunt spent the morning stitching onto a sheet in an intricate pattern—no stems or leaves showing, only the plumy golden blooms."

Orion Nature Quarterly

136 E. 64th Street
New York, NY 10021

- *64-page quarterly magazine, many color and black-and-white illustrations; annual subscription $12.00.*

If you have been reading too many politically oriented ecology magazines, *Orion* is a refreshing change. Its articles are generally exploratory or appreciative, not combative, and the quality of the illustrations is very fine. The editors have a talent for finding material to reprint, including, in recent issues, an essay on herb gardening by the great naturalist Henry Beston, a survey of American landscape and gardening by historian-geographer John Stilgoe, and a piece about W. H. Hudson's children's book recalling his life on the Pampas. It is also a good idea, it seems to me, that each issue focuses on a theme, like landscape, horticulture, insects, wildlife management, architecture and environment, or rhythm in nature. The best way into *Orion* for the gardener may be to purchase a back issue of the Spring 1985 edition. It is devoted entirely to gardening, including new or reprinted essays by Beston and Stilgoe, Tamara Thornton, the fine young landscape architect Michael Van Valkenburgh, and Carolyn Jabs. I have only 2 complaints about the magazine: first, the original articles and book reviews can be too academic in tone, and second, the focus on nature sets up what I think is a false dichotomy between civilization on the one hand and nature on the other. Writers and editors too glibly toss off jibes at the shopping mall and the roadside. Someone said that the rabid medievalists should be sent to live in the Middle Ages; maybe all the rabid naturalists should be sent straight away to live in a tree-bark hut. In spite of these criticisms, I'd certainly recommend *Orion*.

The Ortho Problem Solver

Ortho Information Services
575 Market Street
San Francisco, CA 94105

- *1,022 pages, many color illustrations, $179.75.*

Look for this in libraries. Garden centers also often keep a copy, which they may let you use for your reference. The tome is dedicated to the cooperative extension services, as well it should be, since it resembles a gigantic coop exension bulletin. The index alone runs 218 pages! All in all, it is a remarkably well-illustrated and completely cross-referenced guide to any kind of weed, pest, or disease that might attack any ornamental or edible plant in your garden. You can start with the plant and work toward the problem, or vice versa. As you might expect, the solutions offered are usually pesticides or herbicides, often Ortho products.

Richard Owen Nursery

2300 E. Lincoln Street
Bloomington, IL 61701

- *Plants for trees and shrubs, perennials, berries, fruit trees, ferns, roses, a few grasses, and a few vegetables; tools and supplies.*
- *48-page catalogue, approx. 200 color illustrations, free.*

Owen's catalogue is not as extensive as those from the biggest Midwestern companies, but its coverage is pretty good, and the firm seems to have gone out of its way to bring in a few less common items. The selection of Marhigo iris is nice. There is a red hydrangea, should you want such a thing, a good group of subzero roses, a hideous standard rose concocted of both Peace and Chrysler Imperial, a heath for ground cover, some trailing lantana, tree peonies, and a few odd Japanese orchids.

Pacific Horticulture

See "Regional Sources."

George W. Park Seed Co.

Highway 254 North
PO Box 31
Greenwood, SC 29647

- *Seeds, bulbs, and plants for flowers, vegetables, and berries; supplies.*
- *124-page catalogue, more than 950 color illustrations, free.*

The big firms like Burpee, Gurney, and Field are scattered all over the map in what they offer, while the comparably sized Park concentrates on vegetables and flowers. Though Park has no breeding program of its own, it is doing its best to catch up to Burpee in vegetable exclusives and novelties. Its Butterfruit sweet corns have a high reputation, as do its tomatoes and its early broccoli. There are a number of interesting summer squashes—including the cream-colored Park's Creamy and the Central American Gourmet Globe—and there is at least one distinctive variety to catch the eye in every vegetable type. Park has reduced its berry selections, ceding the field to its competitors, but Park cannot be touched by any of them in herbs and flowers. The herb selection is as fine as that of specialty herb houses, and the cactus group is also nice, the latter including even the "living stones" called lithops. Perennial flowers, pot plants, and houseplants are also Park specialties. The bulb selection has much less depth and is surprisingly weak in lilies, but the list makes up for it in the unusual lilylike offerings, including ginger lily, Amazon lily, and fairy lily. Lists of caladiums, cannas, and clematis are among the best I have around.

Park's Success With Seeds

by Ann Reilly

- *364 pages, many color illustrations, $12.95.*

Park's Success with Bulbs

by Alfred F. Scheider

- *173 pages, many color illustrations, $9.95.*

*Both from: George W. Park Seed Co.
Highway 254 North
PO Box 31
Greenwood, SC 29647*

All the usual information appears in these 2 books: for every plant in the encyclopedic lists, there is material on how to plant and propagate, where it does best, and what its habit and color are like. Thus far, the volumes are just souped-up catalogues, but what makes them remarkable are the wonderful photos of just-emerged plants and of not-yet-emerged bulbs. These appear for every listing, so from now on you should have no excuse for pulling a plant as a weed or for planting grape hyacinth where the snowdrops go. (For a review of *Park's Success with Herbs*, see page 141).

Pinetree Garden Seeds

New Gloucester, ME 04260

- *Seeds and bulbs for vegetables and flowers; tools, supplies, and books.*
- *96-page catalogue, 110 illustrations, free.*

Pinetree is set up to serve the intensive vegetable gardener and the small-space flower gardener. The seed packets are small and very reasonably priced. Cultural instructions for vegetables are geared specifically to intensive methods, and are more than adequate. There are many unusual selections among the vegetables, including a Dutch wax bean, a nonhybrid red cabbage, the sweet Jenny Lind melon, and a number of varieties chosen for earliness. The book list is long and interesting.

In Christian times, gardeners found their patron saints—St. Phocas and St. Fiacre. Phocas lived in the third century near Sinope on the Black Sea, where he cultivated a small garden. Welcoming strangers, he once entertained two visitors who were in fact searching for him to execute him as a Christian. So he dug his own grave in his garden, and led the visitors out to the graveside, inviting them to behead him. Which they did.

St. Fiacre, in the seventh century, has a happier story. He was a prince from Scotland or from Ireland who went to convert the Franks to Christianity. Living in a small garden-enclosure in a forest near Meaux, his sanctity was such that no wild animals would enter his garden, and so the legend grew up that his garden was miraculously enclosed.

Neither of these saints ever had the importance of Priapus, nor are they commemorated in gardens. In the Middle Ages, the cloister garden, the *hortus conclusus* or 'enclosed garden' of the Virgin Mary, and the garden of Eden all have immense religious significance, but they are not properly connected with the sacred grove.

—CHRISTOPHER THACKER, FROM *THE HISTORY OF GARDENS* (1979)

Plant Health Handbook

*by Louis Pyenson
AVI Publishing Co.*

- *241 pages, many illustrations, $19.50.*

This looks like a textbook, and it isn't pretty. There are no color pictures of your favorite bugs. Nevertheless, it is very thorough in its recommendations for the control of all the bugs, bacteria, viruses, mammals, and weeds that may attack any part of your garden. The text usefully considers the life cycles of the pests involved, but the best thing about the book is its numerous charts, broken down by many different types of planting, with specific information on symptom, cause, and cure. Most of the cures involve chemical pesticides and herbicides. Among the nicest charts are those that describe the action and effectiveness of most of the chemicals currently used in home gardens, together with notes on their relative toxicity.

Plant Propagation

*by Philip McMillan Browse
Simon & Schuster*

- *96 pages, spiral-bound, many illustrations, $9.95.*

Like its brother volume *Pruning* (see page 100), this is a remarkably well-illustrated guide to its subject. It is spiral-bound too, so you can lay it flat beside you on the work table. There are separate sections for all kinds of different propagation tasks and for special plant classes like ferns, alpines, and tropical trees and shrubs. Almost all procedures for taking and rooting cuttings, for division, and for layering are thoroughly covered. There is a whole chapter devoted to budding and grafting, going step by step through every procedure.

Plants, Man and Life

by Edgar Anderson
University of California Press

- *251 pages, some illustrations, $3.95.*

This must be the best botanical-book bargain in America. For some reason, the publishers seem to have filed it among books for "young adults," and the price is correspondingly reduced. It is the best book about "economic botany"—the study of useful plants —that exists for the general reader. It also features the musings, explorations, and experiments of an important botanist who just happened to be a fine writer and a great storyteller as well. If the book has a thesis, it is contained in the last sentence of the first chapter: ". . . the history of weeds is the history of man." Anderson traces and/or suggests possible scenarios for the transformation of weeds into crop plants like corn, as well as tracing the parallel travels of weeds and human beings. Along the way, he introduces us to the careers and ideas of N. I. Vavilov, the great Russian student of crop diversity, and Oakes Ames, the great man of American economic botany. There are also a-sides—skillfully woven into the argument—concerning his own work on tradescantias, the diversity of artichokes, the sunflower, the mixed gardens of Honduras (where he briefly worked), and the importance of dump heaps. The brief dictionary of all important crop plants, suggesting their origin and pattern of dispersal, is lovely, and it comes with an annotated bibliography that tells you where to seek further information. The annotated bibliography is a pleasure in itself, containing such things as *One Man's Life with Barley* and *Useful Plants of Guam* (1905). About this book Anderson writes, "Under this modest title is hidden one of the world's most fascinating volumes."

Plants of the Bible

by Harold N. and Alma L. Moldenke
Dover Publications

- *328 pages, some illustrations, $8.95 pbk.*

The Moldenkes' book is the standard work on the subject. It lists every plant the Bible mentions, with the relevant Scriptural passages and a brief history of the controversy about what the plant actually was. (The Tree of Knowledge was probably an apricot, for example.) As fascinating as such information may be on its own, you may also choose to use the identifications as the basis for a theme garden based on Biblical plants. If you do, it helps to live in a warmer climate or have a place to put the tenderer plants in winter.

DANDELION

Plants of the Southwest

See "Wildflowers and Native Plants."

Popular Encyclopedia of Plants

Edited by Vernon H. Heywood and Stewart R. Chant
Cambridge University Press

- *368 pages, many color illustrations, $37.50.*

This is an armchair encyclopedia for amateur economic botanists. It covers all the major families of the plant kingdom, selecting the genera and species that human beings use. It has more than 2,200 entries in all, and the 700 color photos cover more than 800 species. Like any book that tries to cover so much in such a brief compass, it can seem sketchy at times, but the entries are almost uniformly revealing.

Porter & Son, Seedsmen

PO Box 104
Stephenville, TX 76401

- *Seed and plants for vegetables and mainly annual flowers; books, supplies.*

Porter's is a regional catalogue that has gone out of its way to provide a very broad selection of vegetables, each chosen for its adaptability to not-always-ideal Texas conditions. The large tomato list includes Porter's Tomato and Porter's Pride, 2 varieties well known in the region. The list of peppers, sweet and hot, is also very long, as is the list of melons. The Israeli Ananas cantaloupe appears among the latter, along with an interesting melon I've seen nowhere else called the "cob melon." Then there's the selection of okra, which gives you 9 choices. It goes on and on. The firm also has an unusually large group of vegetable plants for sale by mail. The flowers list is shorter, but there is a comprehensive selection of supplies, chosen with the small gardener in mind. The books are selected for Texas gardeners.

Rawlinson Garden Seed

269 College Road
Truro, Nova Scotia
CANADA B2N 2P6

- *Seed for vegetables and mainly annual flowers.*
- *32-page catalogue, approx. 70 illustrations, a few color, free to Canada, $1.00 to U.S.*

The list is medium-sized for vegetables, smallish for flowers. For short-season growers, the vegetables are particularly worth a look, since they have been selected for earliness. The choices among the baking beans and the tomatoes are very distinctive: some varieties are heirlooms; others were developed locally for the climate of the Maritime provinces.

Reader's Digest Illustrated Guide to Gardening

Reader's Digest

■ *672 pages, many color and black-and-white illustrations, $22.98.*

You might not expect much out of it, but this turns out to be a terrific book, perhaps the best general garden book we have. There is virtually no topic that it doesn't cover—down to cacti and succulents, rock gardening, fruit trees, aquatics, greenhouse plants, ferns, irises, and orchids—with very useful and well-illustrated guides to planting, propagation, care, and sometimes even to hybridizing. Perhaps the only major ornamentals category without a section to itself is ornamental grasses. The step-by-step illustrations are most remarkable, particularly those in color, showing how to prune almost anything. (I don't agree, however, with the treatment of trees, in which the authors suggest pruning flush to the trunk, a practice that inhibits callousing.) The long lists of suggested species and cultivars for every kind of plant you might grow—except vegetables, which receive comparatively brief coverage—are generally useful and fairly comprehensive. Unfortunately, the editors have adopted a simplified, 3-division zone chart, which makes the hardiness ratings of the listed plants a little more difficult to gauge, but information on habit, color, propagation, and the like are very valuable. The section on pests and diseases is similarly comprehensive. The only thing not first-rate about the book is the small section of color photographs, which are lousy. People who already have their favorite references assembled may not buy the book, but everyone else should take a look. Incidentally, the book was produced in the U.K., but it is perfectly appropriate for the U.S. and Canada.

Rodale's Color Handbook of Garden Insects

by Anna Carr
Rodale Press

■ *241 pages, many color illustrations, $12.95 pbk.*

Know your enemy—and your friends. Both bad and good bugs—more than 300 in all—scamper across the pages of this book, generally in both larval and adult forms. Text describes range, feeding habits, natural predators, and *organic* means of control. It's an excellent reference for the gardener who eschews chemicals, and it is much more comprehensive than most of the cooperative extension publications (which usually do recommend chemicals). Even with a gallery of 300, however, the author has by no means exhausted the list of friends and foes, so if something unidentifiable appears, call your extension agent.

Rodale's Organic Gardening

33 E. Minor Street
Emmaus, PA 18049

■ *Variable-length, monthly magazine, many illustrations, some in color; annual subscription $12.97, 2-year subscription $23.97.*

It seems hardly necessary to mention this magazine, but here goes anyway. Robert Rodale has been a pioneer in organic gardening in America. His organization—through its endless books, through programs like the Cornucopia Project, and through its magazine—has probably been the most important force for the introduction of organic and regenerative gardening techniques into the mainstream. The magazine is not noted for its pretty graphics, and the articles on the floral side of the plant spectrum are usually fair to middling, but for the edibles gardener, the publication is well-nigh indispensable. The news items at the front of the magazine are usually up-to-the-minute, and they have cute titles like "Honk If You Hate Diazinon." The reader's questions section is unusually good, because it goes to real experts for the answers. A recent query about zucchinis, for example, was answered by Cornell's Henry Munger, one of the world's great squash men. Feature articles range from profiles of uncommon crops like Southern peas and gooseberries, to reports on pest management, comparison of vegetable varieties, surveys of historical gardens, and a whole section of recipes and kitchen ideas for dealing with the harvest. A zone-by-zone calendar at the back of the magazine tells you what you should be doing in the garden, whether you live in Saskatchewan or southern Florida. Robert Rodale contributes a more or less philosophical article to each issue, and in some he asks for readers' help on new projects.

Royal Horticultural Society

c/o J. R. Cowell
80 Vincent Square
London
ENGLAND SW1P 2PE

■ *Nonprofit organization dedicated chiefly to ornamental gardening.*
■ *Variable-length monthly The Garden, some color illustrations, annual subscription £19.00.*

The RHS is to horticulture much what the Vatican is to the Catholic Church. Its journal is British-oriented, but it has all sorts of articles of general interest. Most issues feature a visit to some great or noteworthy garden or nursery, and there are pieces on everything from clematis to winter gardens to earthworms.

Seaweed in Agriculture and Horticulture

by W. A. Stephenson
The Rateavers
9049 Covina Street
San Diego, CA 92126

- *241 pages illustrated, $7.00.*

They've brought this book in from the U.K. but it is perfectly relevant for gardening here. Here is good, detailed information on the benefits of fertilizing with seaweed, together with much on the available preparations and their use.

The Secret Life of Plants

by Peter Tompkins and Christopher Bird
Harper & Row

- *402 pages, $7.95.*

The book is half-delightful and half-maddening—which at least makes it a stimulating read. Anyone who wonders if patting his or her plants and singing to them will do any good will take heart at the positive evidence and supposed evidence here presented in a style that jumps from scholarly to mystical in a single paragraph. The accounts of emotional response in plants take us into the labs of researchers of the sort who can never repeat their experiments if a "doubter" is present, but also into the work of scientists of genuine achievement. In between come experiments and experiences influenced by everyone from Rudolf Steiner to Edgar Cayce, with every shade of looniness in between. There is also a good deal of perceptive reflection on the philosophy and usefulness of Steiner's biodynamic farming methods. The last little chapter on the Findhorn garden in Scotland is emblematic of the whole book: it is a sympathetic and moving portrait of some astonish-

ingly good gardeners who not only talk to their plants but meditate on their qualities while they turn them into food; at the same time, it is a tale of crazy Rosicrucians who learn what to do next via a medium! I only wish that the authors didn't constantly harp on the hostility of Establishment scientists to the wilder ideas. It makes the writers sound like cranks.

Semences Laval

3505 Boulevard St-Martin Ouest
Laval, Quebec
CANADA H7T 1A2

- *Seed and bulbs for vegetables, berries, annual and a few perennial flowers, and lawn grass; plants for roses and some ornamental and fruit trees and shrubs; tools and supplies; books.*
- *178-page catalogue, more than 525 illustrations, most in color, free.*

As the Cajun R&B accordionist Clifton Chenier would put it, *"Ça fait chaud!"* ("It's hot!") It's also in French, and the firm does most of its business in Canada, though it says it is looking into expanding the export market. Those who can order easily from the catalogue have a very good thing going indeed. The list of flower seed is very comprehensive for annuals, with an unusually good selection of houseplants as well. The vegetable list is mouth-watering. The choice is about as broad as I've seen for a major seed house, including such things as Oriental garlic, black bell peppers, fully 30 corns, 5 chicories, 29 cucumbers, pickles, and gherkins, an orange-red squash, numerous long string beans, white onions, and a black salsify. The plant lists are smaller, but pretty good, for trees and shrubs and for roses. The books, tools, and supplies section has almost everything you might call for, from grafting knives to whirligigs, with endless fertilizers and pest killers.

The Sex Life of Flowers

by Bastiaan Meeuse and Sean Morris
Facts on File

- *148 pages, some color illustrations, $19.95.*

It isn't all that steamy, but it is pretty fascinating. The brief history of the angiosperms is a bit ho-hum, though neat and accurate, but the chapters on the role of flower color, pattern, and scent in attracting and guiding pollinators to their favorite flowers are terrific. Watch out for the pictures of the carrion plant, which, as we see it, has succeeded all too well in attracting a lot of squirmy beetles into its pink maw.

ASPARAGUS

The Smallholder

Argenta, British Columbia
CANADA V0G 1B0

- *Variable-length, variable-frequency (2–4 times/year) magazine for homesteaders; 6 issues $11.00, 12 issues $20.00.*

This is a very wide-ranging, entirely reader-contributed information exchange for smallholders with holistic and leftist leanings. You will find anything and everything here, from listings for a society that promotes "polyfidelity" (otherwise known as bigamy) to information on experiences with using parsley to attract beneficial insects. It is an engaging and ecologically minded publication that is not above printing humor. For instance, a recent reprint from a Virginia state consumers' bulletin read in part, "You know you're a homesteader when you have chicken tracks, or worse, goat tracks on your car."

Soil and Civilization

by Edward Hyams
State Mutual Books

- *312 pages, illustrated $14.95.*

Agriculture made civilization possible, but it isn't often that historians dwell on the all-importance of the soil. Hyams elegantly chronicles the influence of deforestation, soil erosion, and the like, on the course of civilization, from Mesopotamia to the American Midwest. This is a fine volume for historians and ecologists.

Stokes Seeds

39 James Street, Box 10
St. Catharines, Ontario
CANADA L2R 6R6

Box 548
Buffalo, NY 14240

- *Seed for vegetables and flowers; tools and supplies.*
- *160-page catalogue, more than 525 illustrations, some in color, free.*

For my money, Stokes has the best seed catalogue in the business. It isn't too pretty, but the selection in most major categories is huge, and the cultural instructions are really outstanding. People may tell you that Stokes caters to commercial growers and is therefore no good for the home gardener, but Stokes's dual focus on home and market gardeners means a broader choice in many categories and a consistent focus on high-performance varieties, whether open-pollinated or hybrid. The Viking KB3 asparagus, for example, is more disease-resistant than any F1 hybrid. Stokes's selection is unparalleled in most of the major vegetables, especially for early types. In carrots, the firm not only offers the new, vitamin-rich A+ hybrid and a broad selection of ordinary carrot types, but 6 different baby carrots as

well. The choice of greenhouse cucumbers, bunching onions, parsley, and paste tomatoes is wide, where many companies offer 1 or 2 choices or none at all. Stokes breeders have been instrumental in the development of hybrid supersweet corns, 2 varieties of which are featured in the catalogue, along with many others. The firm is currently working on a broccoli with a better shoot-to-stem ratio, specifically for the home gardener, and on an interspecies hybrid between a cos and a Grand Rapids lettuce, producing a cos-flavored leaf in sandwich-garnish size. Stokes does not offer so many flower species as, say, Park or Burpee, but the choice of variety for the flowers it does list—particularly for old-fashioned favorites—is immense. The selection in pansies, petunias, salvia, snapdragons, stock, and sweet peas—as well as a number of lesser genera—is the best I have seen. There are 7 pages devoted to petunias alone! Originally an American company—and the company that introduced broccoli to the U.S.—Stokes is now based in Canada, with an American office in Buffalo. Gardeners should write to the address in their own country.

Sunset

Lane Publishing Co.

- *180- to 300-page monthly magazine, many illustrations, some in color; annual subscription $14.00.*

Sunset was founded back in 1898 as a promotional tool for the Southern Pacific Railroad; later it became a literary magazine; by 1928 it had turned into what is called a "shelter book"—a magazine devoted to home improvement—which it remains today. In the East it would be just one of a number of such periodicals, in the West it is an institution. As a Californian living in the East, I cannot find an issue of *Sunset,* brought out here by some fellow exile, without feeling irresistibly drawn to it. I just can't help myself. *Sunset* has not only been a booster for "Western living," but in some measure the creator of it. To open the magazine is to feel at home. Then, too, it is a more considerable publication than it may seem at first glance. Important Western landscape architects like Lawrence Halprin were first published in its pages, and when *Sunset* runs a major feature—on growing lantana, say—the garden centers of the whole region suddenly fill with lantana. And the magazine has an uncanny knack for producing how-to articles that are really usable. About a quarter of each issue is devoted to the garden, including the monthly "Garden Guides," keyed to specific Western regions and offering very complete suggestions for what to do in the garden, with one of the best new-and-noteworthy columns I've seen. Social scientists who try to get at the essence of California culture by considering Disneyland, Los Angeles architecture, or Marin life styles would probably do better to try analyzing *Sunset.* The Sunset Garden Books are reviewed on page 28.

Sunset New Western Garden Book

Lane Publishing Co.

- *512 pages, many illustrations, some in color, $14.95 pbk.*

Anyone gardening in the West without this book is not playing with a full deck. Sunset made up its own zone chart to take into account all the West's many microclimates, and every plant in the immense encyclopedia is keyed to this chart, so you get a very good idea of what will grow in your area. Descriptive text is excellent for both basic plantspersonship and specific plant listings. There are even good suggestions on such important matters as fire and erosion control.

Surry Gardens

PO Box 145
Surry, ME 04684

- *Plants for trees and shrubs, fruit trees and vines, perennials, rock-garden plants, roses, and ferns; landscape contracting.*
- *86-page catalogue, 45 illustrations, $2.00; 4-page mail-order list, free.*

The pity is that Surry offers so comparatively little by mail order. For all trees and shrubs, plus some of the perennials, you will simply have to visit the nursery. There, the choice is excellent among dwarf evergreens for the rock garden, landscape trees (some in large sizes), clematis, azaleas and rhododendrons, old and new roses (including a large number of rugosa hybrids), ferns, and flowering shrubs. The perennials list is very complete; fortunately, some of this list is available by mail, especially things for the rock garden. There are numerous uncommon species of common genera like *Campanula* and *Dianthus*, together with sometimes difficult rockery and alpine perennials like acaena, several gentians, and soldanella. For the serious ornamentals gardener, the catalogue and list are worthwhile. Although you can't order everything, you can read the good descriptive copy to give you an idea of how well many plants will do in the Northeast.

Sutton Seeds

Hele Road
Torquay
Devon
ENGLAND TQ2 7QJ

- *Seed, tubers, and bulbs for annuals and perennials, vegetables, some shrubs and houseplants, and lawn grass.*
- *128-page catalogue, more than 500 color illustrations, free.*

Sutton holds a quarter of the British mail-order market all by itself, so it is something like the U.K. equivalent of Burpee. Of course, it was founded about a century earlier than its American counterpart, was a leader in the development of lawn grasses, and has been purveyor to royalty for about as long as Burpee has been around. Most of what Sutton sells is actually grown in France, Italy, Holland, and California, so you might not expect too much here that can't be found in a large American catalogue. Not so. Look to Sutton's particularly for the old-fashioned flowers that the British love best—things like sweet peas, nemesias, geraniums, primulas, and snapdragons—and for species for the rock garden. Sutton holds a number of exclusives and a number of things it has bred itself for the flower trade, so the catalogue is indeed worth having. The illustrations are good enough to let you know what you are considering. Among the vegetables are quite a number of European varieties, including a tremendous number of peas and beans (especially runner beans) and distinctive selections even for such things as asparagus and onions.

T&T Seeds

PO Box 1710
Winnipeg, Manitoba
CANADA R3C 3P6

- *Seed, bulbs, and plants for annual and perennial flowers, vegetables, fruit trees, berries, ornamental trees and shrubs, roses, begonias, dahlias, and gladiolus; supplies.*
- *64-page catalogue, approx. 275 color illustrations, $1.00.*

A good, if not astonishingly wide-ranging, catalogue for the plains of Canada. The 40th-anniversary edition was dedicated to breeder Charles Walker of the Morden Research Station, who was responsible for some of the specially developed local varieties that the firm offers, including Mustang tomatoes and Morden Early cucumbers. In Walker's memory, T&T was giving away packets of Walker's last new release—the Charlie's Red Staker tomato—with every order. The list contains all the usual suspects, limited to those that thrive or at least survive on the northern plains. Among these are 3 apple trees released by the Prairie Fruit Breeding program. The annuals are sold as seed, the perennials as plants; shrub, tree, and rose lists are brief, but choice for the region.

COMMON WEED

Thompson and Morgan

PO Box 1308
Jackson, NJ 08527

- *Seeds, bulbs, and a few plants of flowers, shrubs, trees, cacti, and vegetables.*
- *194-page catalogue, more than 950 color illustrations, free.*

There are really no comparisons for Thompson and Morgan's flower-seed list. This British company, with American offices in New Jersey, has one of the broadest flower lists in the world, very strong in perennials and greenhouse plants. Many companies claim to have rarities, but T&M really has them, with what can be steep prices to match. The vegetable list is much briefer, but it is well worth looking at for its large number of European varieties not usually seen here. The tomato selections are unusually good, featuring a striped stuffing tomato, a good group of open-pollinated types, and a large choice of yellow-fruited varieties. They also stock tasty Israeli melons and such weirdos as flocculi, a broccoli-cauliflower cross. Also, if you happen to like Brussels sprouts, they have an inordinately large selection.

Twilley Seed Co.

PO Box 65
Trevose, PA 19047

- *Seed and bulbs for vegetables, berries, and annual and perennial flowers; tools and supplies.*
- *104-page catalogue, more than 425 illustrations, most in color, free.*

Little notes signed "Otis" still appear in the catalogue, though Mr. Otis Twilley passed away several years ago. Otis really loved hybrids, and so long as you do, too, you will get a lot of use out of the Twilley catalogue. The firm's featured vegetable varieties, called "Professional Seed Series," are all hybrids, some of them only available from Twilley. Though home gardeners may feel intimidated by the series name and the fact that they usually get second mention behind market gardeners in the catalogue text, some of the varieties are worth trying, particularly in the "Summer Sweet" corn series, which the firm claims is extremely widely adapted. The selection throughout in corn is really quite good, as it is for most major vegetables. A very useful feature of the list—and one I have seen nowhere else—is the charts that suggest recommended varieties of corn, tomatoes, and other vegetables for every state in the Union. The flowers list contains the usual, mainly annuals.

Vermont Bean Seed Co.

Garden Lane
Fair Haven, VT 05743

- *Seeds and a few plants for vegetables and flowers; supplies.*
- *94-page catalogue, more than 100 illustrations, some in color, free.*

As the name suggests, this company started from a bean collection, and its selection of open-pollinated beans remains a very fine one. Elsewhere, the catalogue is hybrid-heavy, with a good selection of vegetables for every cate-

gory, especially for salad greens, peas, and soybeans. The herb list is very strong. A few of the VBS exclusive offerings sound tantalizing. The flower list is brief and predictable but it includes a few nice wildflower mixes along with the garden varieties.

The Victory Garden Series

Crockett's Victory Garden

by James U. Crockett
Little, Brown & Co.

Crockett's Indoor Garden

by James U. Crockett
Little, Brown & Co.

Crockett's Flower Garden

by James U. Crockett
Little Brown & Co.

The Victory Garden Landscape Guide

by Thomas Wirth
Little, Brown & Co.

- *311–360 pages each, many color illustrations, $19.95 each pbk.*

There are two tricks to the Victory Garden series: personality and the month-by-month approach. It is very pleasant, not just surprising, to see how well the publishers have translated these advantages from TV to the printed page. While there are books that contain more information—the NGA's vegetable book, for example (see page 140)—there are none, I think, that so well combine reliable information with a personal and encouraging tone that makes you feel you will both succeed and have fun. With respect to the azalea as a houseplant, for example, Crockett says, "If I had to write a one-sentence summary of

azalea care, it would be this: keep them cool, keep them moist, and keep them after they flower." He always seems to strike just the right tone among folksy, entertaining, and instructive. The month-by-month approach is a bit jarring at first. (I suspected the authors were just taking the line of least resistance from TV show to book.) It is a little annoying to have to keep referring to the index for plants you are interested in or for year-round topics like bug control, but I found after awhile that the organization serves as a memory aid for actual hands-on gardening. By having to go to the month in which the calceolarias bloom, or the kale is planted, or the water garden is best installed, you have to keep in mind the regular rhythms of the gardening year. So the organizing principle isn't bad.

Crockett's Victory Garden does a fair job with annuals and perennials, as well as with all important vegetables. *Crockett's Indoor Garden* is just as useful, because Crockett made his living over the years publishing premium books on houseplants, so he knew what he was talking about.

The *Flower Garden* amounts to a very well-made anthology of the most popular garden flowers, with excellent notes on their culture. Like the other volumes, it is organized according to the gardener's calendar, introducing flowers during the season when they put on their finest show. Each month's chapter also features a sort of bonus: a design or maintenance chore, each with clear instructions for performing it.

Wirth's *Landscape Guide* is quite thorough, though it does not fit the month-by-month schema as well as the other titles. His instructions for measuring up the site are admirably clear, as are his comments on specific topics like planting for winter interest. Of the three, this volume might have done the best with a more conventional format.

The Virginia Master Gardener Handbook

Virginia Cooperative Extension Service
Publication 426-600
Virginia Polytechnic Institute and State
University
Blacksburg, VA 24061

- *492 pages in looseleaf binder, some illustrations, $15.00.*

Developed for the Virginia branch of the nationwide Master Gardener program, this is a very fine American garden book. It is neither beautiful nor particularly well written, but it is clear, noncondescending, and full of useful information. In fact, at the price, it is among the best basic gardening books that I know. According to people at the Virginia Cooperative Extension, it has been sold to several other state programs, as well as their own, and an updated version is now

DAHLIA

in process. Because it was put together by practical scientists, it offers more detail than we are used to seeing about such topics as soil and insect life cycles. The instructions for training fruit trees are, for a change, as detailed as the subject demands. Chapters on selection and care of vegetables and woody ornamentals are particularly impressive, but the sections on other garden plants are also more than adequate. Though the well-done diagnostics chapter stops short of recommending specific brands of pest control, its recommendations for the control of insects and disease are balanced and useful. Specific variety and species recommendations

among the plants are, of course, keyed to Virginia, but as this state has a varied climate resembling that of regions both north and south of it, the list is pretty useful for much of the temperate U.S.

Weeds of the North Central States

University of Illinois at Champaign-Urbana
College of Agriculture
North Central Regional Publication 281
47 Mumford Hall
1301 W. Gregory Drive
Urbana, IL 61801

- *303 pages, many black-and white illustrations, $3.00.*

Here is an enormously detailed and very well-illustrated weed-identification book for everyone living in the central band of states running from North Dakota to Oklahoma in the West and from Michigan and Ohio to Kentucky in the East. It also takes in most of the cosmopolitan weeds that plague the whole U.S. and Canada. Its advantage over the comparable California publication (see page 32) is its better regional adaptation for the central states and its much lower price. However, as it consists almost entirely of botanical descriptions, its role is pretty well limited to that of an identification tool.

Westcott's Plant Disease Handbook, Fourth Edition

Revised by R. Kenneth Horst
Van Nostrand Reinhold

- *803 pages, some illustrations, a few in color, $41.95.*

Maybe you won't rush out to buy it, but it is nevertheless both a fascinating and useful thing. The idea of a

book with chapter titles like "Blights," "Cankers," "Rots," "Rusts," and "Smuts" is intriguing in itself, but, more important, this is a very thorough and well-organized compendium of most diseases that might strike any plant in your garden. Descriptions of the disease's effect are clear, and controls are recommended, including both cultural and chemical methods. There is a long and helpful index in the back, organized by common name and genus, so that you can start with the plant and work back to identify the sickness. The text is mainly matter-of-fact, but, some intelligent asides on the history of disease control, especially for major crop plants, are interspersed. True enough, many more general garden books will tell you most of what you need to know about plant diseases—as will your county extension agent—but if you want more, here it is. This edition was publishd in 1979, so it's pretty up to date.

The Whole Earth Review

27 Gate Five Road
Sausalito, CA 94965

- *Variable-length quarterly, many illustrations, annual subscription $18.00.*

For my money, this is the best ecosensitive rag out there. Its politics are, I suppose, neoliberal, but with a California twist that makes them unpredictable and stimulating. Furthermore, they have an attitude toward writing that resembles few magazines other than *The New Yorker,* so there is a very good mix of firsthand travel reports, satire, cartoons, well-considered issues articles, and pieces by and about leading New Age thinkers. Besides that, there is a unique section each quarter devoted to reviews of books, catalogues, services, software, and so on. It frequently includes new—and sometimes obscure—sources for the gardener, homesteader, or small farmer.

The Wisley Book of Gardening

W. W. Norton & Co.

■ *350 pages, many illustrations, some in color, $25.95.*

It's subtitled "A Guide for Enthusiasts." In Britain, the word "enthusiast" must not have the slightly pejorative connotation it does here, because this is a very thorough and not at all condescending book. It includes everything from vegetables and fruit trees to alpines and ground covers, counting on the contributions of a variety of fine British garden writers, including Graham Stuart Thomas and Roy Lancaster. The Royal Horticultural Society agreed to sponsor it. The how-to's are clear and well-illustrated, and I like the often-long lists of recommended cultivars. The main problem with recommending this as a general gardening standby is that it is resolutely British, and it has not been adapted for the U.S. market. Therefore, the section on lawns, for example, while its general methods apply, will not be useful to gardeners who cannot successfully grow the fescues and bent grasses of England. Likewise, it may be a little jarring to read about the lack of native conifers, a lack we don't suffer, though the author of this section goes on to provide a thorough discussion of imported ones. For the somewhat experienced gardener with an Anglophile bent, however, this is a very nice reference book. There are good sections, for example, on raised-bed growing of alpines and on the alpine house. Sections on specialty plants like dahlias, fuchsias, mums, and rhododendrons are brief but very useful.

Wonder Crops

Natural Food Institute
Box 185 WMB
Dudley, MA 01570

■ *48 pages, a few illustrations, $5.00.*

The NFI has searched nursery catalogues, seed savers, and every other source to come up with a list—annually updated—of the hardiest, most productive, and all-around best fruit and nut trees, vegetables, flowers, herbs, cover crops, and prairie grasses. Each entry lists the variety, together with an assessment of its virtues and at least one source for obtaining it. According to the editors, they have selected the source with a more reasonable price when significant variation exists. Most of what is in here responds to the ecological gardener's love of heirloom varieties and unusual economic plants. Many of the listed sources are wonderfully arcane and much too small to list in a book like this. For example, it suggests something called the Dharma Farm in Maine as a source of about a dozen beans from Native Americans. There are some individuals listed as sources, too. The listings are not just hippy-dippy stuff: many are from agricultural experiment stations. There's also a group of "worst crops," things that have difficulty in the Northeast.

Worms Eat My Garbage

by Mary Appelhof
Flower Press
10332 Shaver Road
Kalamazoo, MI 49002

■ *100 pages, some illustrations, $7.95.*

Mary Appelhof keeps worms at work chomping on her kitchen garbage and incidentally producing some excellent compost. Here is a book about what she has done and how. The title alone is worth the price.

Wyatt-Quarles Seed Co.

PO Box 739
Garner, NC 27529

■ *Seeds, bulbs, and a few plants for vegetables, flowers, lawn grass, and pasture grass; supplies.*
■ *30-page catalogue, approx. 95 illustrations, some in color, free.*

Here's a very good, basic Southeast regional list of vegetables and flowers. The flowers are pretty much what you'd expect, but the vegetable list has some interesting nonhybrids and some less-common hybrids suitable for Southeastern growing. The field pea list is terrific, but unfortunately offered only in ½-lb. lots and up.

Goldenrod has many unusual uses. It can be made into a crown of gold for a Harvest Queen or a necklace for a child. Sewn onto a white bedsheet, it makes excellent cloth of gold. I lay under just such a sumptuous covering one summer day in my early teens when there was a regatta on Lake Chocorua. This was in that almost forgotten era before children were sent off to camp, when summer pastimes for the young were innocently contrived at home. On that bright New Hampshire mountain day so long ago, a parade of decorated canoes and rowboats was the first event in an afternoon of water sports, and, like every other family on the lake, we wanted to be in the parade. My sisters and I began the day by gathering bucketfuls of goldenrod, which my aunt spent the morning stitching onto a sheet in an intricate pattern—no stems or leaves showing, only the plumy golden blooms.

—KATHARINE S. WHITE, FROM *ONWARD AND UPWARD IN THE GARDEN* (1979)

2 Annuals and Perennials

Allwood Bros.

Mill Nursery
Hassocks
West Sussex
ENGLAND BN6 9NB

- *Seed and plants for carnations and pinks.*
- *23-page catalogue, free.*

Allwood is perhaps *the* dianthus nursery of the world. The firm admits only to having the largest collection in Europe, a good number of which are their important Allwoodii hybrids. You'll find old-fashioned garden pinks, laced pinks, rockery pinks, show pinks, Tyrolean trailing carnations, greenhouse carnations, and border carnations.

> This is one of Nature's mysteries—how from the best grass seed most luxuriant and hairy weeds come up; perhaps weed seed ought to be sown and then a nice lawn would result.
>
> —KAREL CAPEK, FROM *THE GARDENER'S YEAR* (1929)

Alpine Garden Society

Lye End Link
St. John's
Woking, Surrey
ENGLAND GU21 18W

- *Nonprofit society dedicated to alpine gardening.*
- *96 + / − page quarterly bulletin, many illustrations, some in color; annual seed distribution; wide publications list; annual membership £10.50 (approx. $16.40).*

Alpine and rock gardeners will join this society. The annual seed list alone is spectacular, numbering more than 4,000 species and varieties. It must be the largest such selection in existence. Then there is the very fine specialists' book list, including a number of hands-on and specific-genus books from the society itself. Most other in-print books on alpines appear, including a number of floras from other countries. The writing in the bulletins is first-rate, and verrry British, with quite thorough and mannerly explorations of every style and means of growing alpines, together with reflections on a great variety of flora.

American Begonia Society

See "Houseplants and Exotics."

TIGER LILY

American Daffodil Society

Route 3
2302 Byhalia Road
Hernando, MS 38632

- *Nonprofit organization dedicated to daffodils.*
- *Quarterly Daffodil Journal; annual membership $10.00, three years $27.50; book* Daffodils to Show and Grow, *$4.00.*

If you want to join this society, you should be crazy about daffodils. The book put out by the society lists 9,000 different cultivars!

American Dahlia Society

c/o Michael L. Martinolich
159 Pine Street
New Hyde Park, NY 11040

- *Nonprofit organization dedicated to dahlia culture.*
- *Variable-length quarterly bulletin, a few color illustrations, annual membership $8.00.*

The society is very much dedicated to breeding and shows, though it by no means despises beginners. The bulletin contains many show reports, notes on classification, and other arcana.

American Fern Society

Newsletter: Dr. Dennis W. Stevenson
Department of Biological Sciences
Barnard College
Columbia University
New York, NY 10027

Spore Exchange: Neill D. Hall
1230 N.E. 88th Street
Seattle, WA 98115

- *Nonprofit organization dedicated to culture and study of ferns and fern allies.*
- *Variable-length, bimonthly newsletter, Fiddlehead Forum; Spore Exchange; annual membership $8.00.*

This society also publishes the scholarly *American Fern Journal,* but unless you are interested in subjects like megaspore-surface morphology, stick to the $8.00 membership, which includes only the newsletter. The *Forum* publishes articles on the culture and protection of common and uncommon ferns; special issues deal with broad groups of ferns of a given region. At least one issue per year gives the very large list of species offered through the Spore Exchange, in return for $.25 postage. You can use the exchange without joining the society, but if you are that interested in ferns, you might as well join.

A smiling young man confronted me, saying he did not know if I would be interested, but he had brought these . . . and opened the van as he spoke.

'These' were giant pansies, thousands and thousands of them. The van's dark interior was a cavern of colour. Some royal hand had flung rugs of velvet over the stacks of wooden trays. Purples were there; and subtler colours than purple: bronze and greenish-yellow and claret and rose-red, all in their queer cat-faces of crumpled velvet. I stood amazed.

—V. SACKVILLE-WEST, FROM *GARDEN BOOK* (1983)

American Horticultural Society

7931 E. Boulevard Drive
Alexandria, VA 22308

- *Nonprofit organization dedicated chiefly to ornamental gardening.*
- *44-page bimonthly* American Horticulturist, *many illustrations, most in color; newsletter in alternate months; seed exchange; gardener's information service; plant finding service; discounts on books; annual membership $20.00, two years $35.00.*

Ornamental gardeners should look into the AHS; vegetable lovers will do better with the National Gardening Association (see page 140). The magazine articles are devoted mainly to design questions, including reviews of historic gardens, fairly sophisticated discussions of fine private gardens, and suggestions for plants to use in, say, a border or a water garden. Pamela Harper, a very knowledgeable plantswoman with one of North America's fine garden-photo collec-

tions (and an endless appetite for specificity and accuracy), contributes to the magazine with some regularity. Book reviews also appear in the magazine, preparing you to use the discount book club that the society runs. Each year, the AHS also offers a large selection of seed for distribution, drawn from the contributions of members, arboreta, and seed companies.

American Iris Society

c/o Carol Ramsey
6518 Beachy Avenue
Wichita, KS 67206

- *Nonprofit organization dedicated to the culture and improvement of every sort of iris.*
- *Annual seed exchange; book list; technical assistance; variable-length quarterly Bulletin, many illustrations, annual membership $9.50, three years $23.75.*

A large and serious group, with 24 regional branches, the AIS does everything imaginable with every sort of iris. There is a whole list of subsocieties specializing in medians, Siberians, spurias, Japanese, reblooming, Louisianas, species, Pacific Coast natives, and dwarf irises. The round robins of members with special interests has even gone so far as to set up a numerical fragrance rating for irises, partially to wit: "Unpleasant ratings: 1—slightly unpleasant odor, 2— fairly unpleasant, 3—definitely unpleasant, 33— very unpleasant and 333—so strong it turns your stomach." (There are also spicy and sweet ratings.) The *Bulletin* is packed with information. Some issues are devoted wholly to the culture and breeding of a single class of iris; others report on tours of well-known iris gardens, present show winners, and the like. The seed exchange is very extensive. One only wishes that the members would give tall bearded irises a rest, and spill off into the less overworked classes of the genus.

American Peony Society

250 Interlachen Road
Hopkins, MN 55343

- *Nonprofit organization dedicated to peony culture.*
- *44-page quarterly bulletin; seed bank; books on peony culture and identification; annual membership $7.50.*

"One wonders if the peony is all that one could desire," writes the society's president, Chris Laning, in a recent issue of the bulletin. Further on, he adds, "The seventies saw the striving for peonies with yellow flowers; now we are thinking about the greens, blues and purples as desirable. Maybe the nineties will be dedicated to dwarfs and reblooming miniatures." Clearly, the society has its work cut out, and it is steaming ahead, if the publication's generally good articles on culture and landscape use of the plants are any indication. There seems to be some controversy between the gardeners who grow for landscape use and those who grow for show, which to my mind is a healthy thing for all such flower-obsessed societies. The bulletin also contains advertisements from specialty nurseries, and the society offers a small list of books devoted to the peony. The seed bank the society maintains is of real value to peony enthusiasts; seeds are sent in exchange for $1.50 to cover postage and handling.

> I shall never forget my discovery of what is now Jackson Park when its lowlands were purple with phlox. Where are these flowers today? Did the designers of Jackson Park forget them, or were they ignorant of them?
>
> —JENS JENSEN, FROM *SIFTINGS* (1939)

American Rock Garden Society

c/o Buffy Parker
15 Fairmead Road
Darien, CT 06820

- *Nonprofit organization devoted to rock gardening.*
- *Seed exchange, library loan service, book list, variable-length quarterly bulletin, some illustrations, annual membership $15.00.*

As seems to be usual with rock-garden groups, the seed exchange is fabulously large, numbering about 4,000 entries each year. The selling and lending of books are also valuable services. The bulletin is very lively, perhaps the liveliest of all the rock- and alpine-club publications I have seen. There are travel stories, plant-hunting stories, reports on specific genera, and reviews of various cultural techniques. The society seems anxious to get people growing some of the neglected, if common, genera, as well as the rarities.

Anglewood Nurseries

12839 McKee School Road
Woodburn, OR 97071

- *Plants for ivy.*
- *8-page list, free.*

If you want something other than generic *Hedera helix*, here is a choice of more than 100 named cultivars. There are a couple of dozen different variegated ivies, plus heart-shaped, fan-shaped, bird's-foot-shaped, curlies, miniatures, and "oddities." There are even a few that the proprietor refers to as "ivy ivies," commenting, "These actually look like ivies." Cultivar names only appear in the list, so you will have to either take pot luck within a given type or get to know the cultivars before you buy. You can find out about joining the American Ivy Society here, too.

Appalachian Wildflower Nursery

See "Wildflowers and Native Plants."

Bay View Gardens

1201 Bay Street
Santa Cruz, CA 95060

- *Plant material for bearded and beardless irises.*
- *16-page catalogue, 2 color illustrations, $1.00.*

Proprietor Joseph Ghio has been hybridizing irises for more than 3 decades and is one of the leading growers of the Pacifica strains. The list is also strong in Mary Dunn's Louisiana hybrids, in spurias, and in bearded iris. Some are quite costly plants, suitable for collectors or breeders. At $30.00, for instance, you can have "Fortunata," with "melon-pink standards with creamy blue-white falls, banded pinkish melon. All petal edges have a picoteed laced edging." Good choices among older and more common introductions are available at much less daunting prices.

Blackmore & Langdon

Pentsford
Bristol
ENGLAND BS18 4JL

- *Seeds for begonias, delphiniums, and polyanthus primroses.*
- *14-page catalogue, more than 40 color illustrations, $2.00.*

In Britain, this firm sells plants, but it will ship seed to the U.S. for $2.00 per packet. Use a money order, not a check. The firm is very well known for its fine introductions, particularly in tuberous begonias and delphiniums. You ought to know what you are doing, however, before you try their begonias.

Kurt Bluemel, Inc.

2740 Greene Lane
Baldwin, MD 21013

- *Plants for ornamental grasses, bamboo, and perennials.*
- *22-page catalogue, $1.00; separate bamboos list, $1.00.*

This is the best grass list and one of the best bamboo lists in North America. There are almost two dozen choices among the *Carex* (sedges) here, a like number among the fescues, and almost that many *Miscanthus*. Almost every genus of ornamental grass is well represented, and handy charts at the back of the book describe the best traits and best uses of many of them. The separate bamboo list contains 102 varieties. The perennials list is much more selective, except among the astilbes, which number more than 30. Everywhere, Bluemel seems to have focused on the cultivars with the most desirable garden traits. The plant descriptions, though brief, tell most of what you need to know before you buy, and Bluemel is promising an expanded catalogue in the future.

Bluestone Perennials

7211 Middle Ridge Road
Madison, OH 44057

- *Plants for ornamental perennials and a few herbs.*
- *46-page catalogue, approx. 22 color illustrations, free.*

Bluestone offers an excellent selection of well-described perennials for the border. Unlike many perennials nurseries, it sells small plants—the size that commercial nurseries use for lining out in groups of 3 or 6—making its selections very reasonable in price. You can buy three plants from Bluestone for what one might cost from another supplier, so with a small amount of money, you can get enough plants to make a good, massed effect in the border. Of course, you will have to have a little more patience to allow them to reach full size. The list is quite comprehensive, with particular strengths in campanulas, pinks, and sedums. Unfortunately, though, the catalogue is not in strict alphabetical order.

Borbeleta Gardens

15974 Canby Avenue
Route 5
Faribault, MN 55021

- *Plants for lilies, day lilies, and Siberian irises.*
- *20-page catalogue, approx. 125 color illustrations, $3.00.*

Borbeleta's unusually well-illustrated catalogue features varieties drawn from the work of amateur hybridizers, and its listings are meant to serve the interests of these people. The most recent introductions are costly, but others are affordable. Included are such fine plants as the everblooming "Stella d'Oro" day lily. The lists are longish but not overwhelming, and the descriptions are brief but clear.

Busse Gardens

635 E. 7th Street
Route 2
Box 13
Cokato, MN 55321

- *Perennial plants.*
- *58-page catalogue, 60 illustrations, some in color, free.*

Next to the offerings from Carroll Gardens, Wayside Gardens, or White Flower Farm, the Busse catalogue looks pretty puny. This is an illusion. Though overall it does not have as much depth of coverage in each of the important perennial genera as do its competitors, it is very strong in several genera. The lists of hostas and day lilies are among the larger I have seen, and the catalogue is very deep in astilbe, bergenia, heuchera, monarda, phlox, tradescantia, Siberian irises, and species irises. The peony list is first-rate, including the tree peonies. Unlike its major competitors, Busse offers a very good group of wildflowers, including four trilliums.

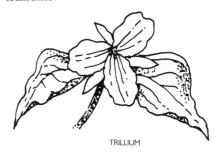

TRILLIUM

Caprice Farm Nursery

15425 S.W. Pleasant Hill Road
Sherwood, OR 97140

- *Plants for peonies, tree peonies, hostas, day lilies, and Japanese irises.*
- *24-page catalogue, approx. 14 color illustrations, $1.00.*

Proprietors Al and Dot Rogers more or less inherited this business from Walter Marx, a noted hybridizer of all the types of plants the Rogerses offer. Marx was particularly well known for his Japanese irises—he developed the Marhigo strains—and his varieties of these make up the bulk of Caprice's iris list. This said, the Rogerses have also made a very good effort to include plants from many leading hybridizers for everything they offer. The varieties are well described, including provenance and parentage. As one might expect from such a list, the brand-new named hybrids are quite costly, whereas the rest are more in line with what the ordinary gardener wants and can afford. Don't miss the lists of tree peonies and miniature hemerocallis, not to mention the very large group of herbaceous peonies.

Carroll Gardens

444 E. Main Street
PO Box 310
Westminster, MD 21157

- *Plants for perennials, grasses, herbs, vines, shrubs, trees, roses; bulbs.*
- *98-page catalogue, 59 illustrations, a few in color, $2.00.*

It's hard to know where to start to describe Carroll Gardens. The perennial list is of matchless depth, making it terrific for the specialist bed, border, or rock gardener. (Rockery plants are particularly well represented.) On the other hand, it offers a good deal of design advice for the perennials beginner, not to mention complete collections that the gardener can order as a group and plant according to the layout supplied! (I can't help thinking that this would take half the fun out of it, but the layouts make excellent guides for the imagination.) There is also a nice breakdown of recommended ground covers for sun and for shade. The grass list is unusually fine, as are the lists of summer bulbs and herbs, the

MUM

selection of all three resembling Park's. The rose selection is very complete for modern roses, and not bad for shrub roses. The shrubs and trees lists are selective, each including some rare varieties. The shrubs lists are deepest for those that do well in the mixed border, including Scotch broom, heaths and heathers, potentilla, and lilacs.

CHRYSANTHEMUMS

Mum nuts have many places to turn to find like-minded people. Contact the National Chrysanthemum Society, c/o Galen Goss, 5012 Kingston Drive, Annandale, VA 22009. In Canada, there's the Canadian Chrysanthemum and Dahlia Society, c/o G. H. Lawrence, 83 Aramaman Drive, Agincourt, Ontario, CANADA M1T 2PM. Real enthusiasts can go as far as Britain's National Chrysanthemum Society, c/o H. B. Locke, 2 Lucas House, Craven Road, Rugby, Warwickshire, ENGLAND CV21 3JQ.

Dooley Gardens, Route 1, Hutchinson, MN 55350.

Fleming's Flower Fields, PO Box 4617, Lincoln, NE 68504.
- Broad list.

King's Mums, PO Box 368, Clements, CA 95227.
- Broad list. Color catalogue $1.00.

The Lehman Gardens, 420 S.W. 10th Street, Faribault, MN 55021.

Mums by Paschke, 11286 Main Road, North East, PA 16428.

New England Mum Co., PO Box 51, Sorrento, FL 32776.

Reno Nurseries, 2718 Washington Street, Dubuque, IA 52001.

Sunnyslope Gardens, 8638 Huntington Drive, San Gabriel, CA 91775.
- Broad list.

Chadwell Himalayan Plant Seed

81 Parlaunt Road
Slough, Berkshire
ENGLAND SL3 8BE

- *Seed from the Western Himalayas for alpines, rock-garden plants, and perennials.*
- *6-page list, more than 50 illustrations; send 4 International Reply Coupons.*

Chadwell has connections with a big Indian seed firm, P. Kohli & Co. He himself is a long-time specialist in Himalayan flora and consults with Indian botanists on the topic. His selection is not huge, but it is chosen for the North Temperate Zone, and his illustrations give you a fair idea of what you are buying. Some of what he has in his list is quite rare, and a few are even new to cultivation. He promises an expanded list in the future.

Chehalis Rare Plant Nursery

2568 Jackson Highway
Chehalis, WA 98532

- *Seeds for primulas.*
- *1-page list, free.*

Most of what Herbert Dickson sells is only available at the nursery. Among his few seed listings is a group of garden auriculas that he has bred himself over the last 30 years.

Clifford's Perennial & Vine

Route 2
Box 328
East Troy, WI 53120

- *Plants for perennials, flowering vines, and a few woody ornamentals.*
- *18-page catalogue, 13 illustrations, free.*

This young nursery calls itself "suppliers of the cottage garden." The list is comfortable and the plants well described. It was refreshing not to be bombarded with choices in this list, but to see a good, selective list that tends toward the old-fashioned. The woody ornamentals consist of a few rhododendrons, azaleas, and magnolias, plus a tree peony and a kalmia. The vines are mainly clematis, with a few honeysuckles, trumpet vines, and the like, included as well. It looks as though Clifford's is taking its "cottage-garden" motto seriously.

Color Farm

2710 Thornhill Road
Auburndale, FL 33823

- *Plants for coleus.*
- *8-page catalogue, $.50.*

Vern Ogren has spent the last 20 years collecting heirloom varieties of coleus and breeding new ones. He provides well over 75 varieties, in different colors and patterns.

Color in Your Garden

See "Landscape Architecture and Design."

Companion Plants

See "Vegetables and Herbs."

The Complete Shade Gardener

by George Schenk
Houghton Mifflin

- *278 pages, many illustrations, some in color, $14.95 pbk.*

Here is easily the best book on the subject. Schenk ran an important native-plants garden in the Northwest for many years, before retiring to New Zealand or some such place. He writes with great authority and wit. Even his headings are entertaining—for example, "Bad Soil Dug Out, Ideal Soil Filled In: A Case History." He takes us along as he learns how to garden in the shade by trial and error, never hesitating to tell a funny story about himself. Meanwhile, you will find out all you need to know about planting, pruning, seasonal changes, soils, and whatever else it takes to make a lovely shade garden. His plant lists are long, adaptable, and very fine, and he even devotes a short section to vegetables.

The children next door came over this afternoon to ask for space for a garden. This happens every spring and fall, or whenever they see me planting something. I always allot a piece of ground, which they lay off neatly with a border of stones. Then they go about the business of digging and planting with great energy. They like little plants with little flowers—especially bulbs, because bulbs are easier to handle than seeds, or things with roots. Best of all are little bulbs with long names. Painfully and illegibly they print the names on plastic labels (which always get stepped on before the flower blooms). . . .

—ELIZABETH LAWRENCE, FROM *THE LITTLE BULBS: A TALE OF TWO GARDENS* (1986)

The Country Garden

Route 2
Box 455A
Crivitz, WI 54114

- *Seeds, bulbs, and plants for annual and perennial cutting flowers and drying flowers.*
- *74-page catalogue, $2.00; variable-length price lists, free.*

The choices are particularly good among the annuals (all from seed), since the proprietors have gone out of their way to stock as many colors of each species as they can. The special list for drying flowers is not so extensive, but it is choice, and it includes a few ornamental grasses. Perennial seed and plant lists are less varied, the same goes for the bulbs; still, they are pretty complete. Varieties are well described in the catalogue; there is less information in the price lists, but enough for the experienced gardener to make choices. What's awfully annoying about the catalogue is the cutesy and condescending text with which the writers begin the various lists. For example, the promotional suggestion that you might want to buy perennials seed "to get your hands on plants so new that we haven't mastered their propagation yet" does anything but inspire confidence in the firm, particularly as their perennials seed list is not all that adventurous.

Crockett's Indoor Garden

See "General Sources."

The Crownsville Nursery

PO Box 797
Crownsville, MD 21032

- *Container-grown plants for perennials, wildflowers, ornamental grasses, and herbs; a drip-irrigation system.*

Like Carroll Gardens (see page 56), Crownsville is a Maryland nursery with a very extensive list of temperate-climate perennials, grasses, and herbs. The Crownsville catalogue is unillustrated and not very pretty, but the serious perennials gardener will find it quite informative and worth perusing. In terms of species listed, it runs neck and neck with Carroll Gardens, with perhaps a few more of the rarer species and varieties than its competitor includes. Both the wildflower and grass lists contain some interesting surprises—like skunk cabbage (*Symplocarpus foetidus,*) snowy wood rush (*Luzula nivea,*) and prairie dropseed (*Sporobolus heterolepsis*). The grass list particularly is various and fine. The herbs group is similarly inclusive, featuring a number of scented geraniums.

C. A. Cruickshank, Inc.

1015 Mount Pleasant Road
Toronto, Ontario
CANADA M4P 2M1

- *Bulbs, plants, and seeds for perennials and annuals, miniature vegetables, woodland plants and houseplants; tools and supplies.*
- *72-page spring and fall catalogues, approx. 100 illustrations each, some in color; 12-page summer catalogue, approx. 15 color illustrations; all three, $2.00.*

Bulbs are the thing to look for at Cruickshank. Theirs is one of the largest lists in North America, much of it drawn from the great Dutch grower Van Tubergen. The spring catalogue is a grab bag of summer-flowering bulbs, houseplants, annual and perennial seed for the latest new varieties, herbs, woodland plants, and even seed for miniature vegetables. The summer catalogue features mainly splashy irises, with a few other things thrown in, including Oriental poppies, colchicum ("wonder bulbs"), and autumn crocus. The fall catalogue is mainly Van Tubergen material. It's strongest in the popular hyacinths, tulips, and daffodils, but the firm has made a good effort to include less common varieties of the favorite spring bulbs and a number of less well-known species. The species tulip selection is particularly good, as is the scilla. The fall catalogue is well worth looking at for gardeners in both Canada and the U.S., though if the Daffodil Mart in Virginia (see next entry) has its way, a large retail list from Van Tubergen may soon be available in the U.S., too.

DAHLIA

The Daffodil Mart

The Heaths
Route 3
Box 794
Gloucester, VA 23061

- *Daffodils and other flowering bulbs; tools and supplies.*
- *28-page catalogue, with 36 page color-illustrated Van Tubergen insert $1.00; 110-page Van Tubergen wholesale catalogue, 6 color illustrations, $5.00.*

As to daffodils, the Heaths have hundreds—more than I have seen from any other single source. In fact, they

DAFFODIL

offer more in any one subtribe than do most catalogues for the whole genus. The list is not pretty, but it is informative and comprehensive, including some very expensive show-quality bulbs, if you have got that particular bug. The information and products the Daffodil Mart provides for fertilizing daffodils and other bulbs are useful. The company is in a period of transition these days. According to its catalogue, it is offering other sorts of bulbs through a British Van Tubergen catalogue that comes as an insert in its own. I'm not quite sure how this works, but it's worth checking out. Also, and more important, it is offering the complete Van Tubergen wholesale list, a remarkably wide and various list of the finest of all sorts of Dutch-grown bulbs. It's worth $5.00 just to look at, since it includes many genera that seldom appear in our bulb catalogues. Minimum order from this catalogue is presently 100 bulbs, so you will either have to get together with friends or wait patiently until they have worked out a retail arrangement with Van Tubergen, which the proprietors say they are working on.

DAHLIAS

Here is a gaggle of dahlia-collectors' lists for the true enthusiast. If you are not already in the know about the things, it would be a good idea to get acquainted with The American Dahlia Society, c/o Mark Alger, 2044 Great Falls Street, Falls Church, VA 22043. You can also contact The Canadian Chrysanthemum and Dahlia Society, c/o G. H. Lawrence, 83 Aramaman Drive, Agincourt, Ontario, CANADA M1T 2PM.

Alger Gardens, 2044 Great Falls Street, Falls Church, VA 22043.

Alpen Gardens, 173 Lawrence Lane, Kalispell, MT 59901.

Bateman's Dahlias, 6911 S.E. Drew Street, Portland, OR 97222.

Blue Dahlia Gardens, Box 316, San Jose, IL 62682.
- Broad list of own introductions and others.

Campobello Dahlia Gardens, Route 1, Box 243, Campobello, SC 29322.

Carson Dahlia Farm, 245 Blauser Road, Castle Rock, WA 98611.

Connell's Dahlias, 10216 40th Avenue E., Tacoma, WA 98446.

Dahlias by Phil Traff, 1316 32nd Avenue E., Sumner, WA 98390.

Garden Valley Dahlias, 406 Lower Garden Valley Road, Roseburg, OR 97470.

Golden Rule Dahlia Farm, 3460 N. State Route 48, Lebanon, OH 45036.

Hooklands Dahlias, 1096 Horn Lane, Eugene, OR 97404.

Kordonowy's Dahlias, PO Box 1049, Castle Rock, WA 98611.
- Broad list of 800+ varieties.

Lamson & Sons Dahlias, Route 4, Box 4279B, Selah, WA 98942.

Land-a-Goshen Gardens, PO Box 178, Nooksack, WA 98376.

Sea-Tac Gardens, 20020 Des Moines Way S., Seattle, WA 98148.
- Broad list, some own hybrids.

Shackleton's Dahlias, 30535 Division Drive, Troutdale, OR 97060.

DAY LILIES

Out of a mere 15 species of *Hemerocallis* have come hundreds of cultivars. Below, you will find a number of collectors' lists. You can get a more complete list of sources, plus all sorts of useful information, from The American Hemerocallis Society, c/o Sandy Goembel, Route 5, Box 6874, Palatka, FL 32077.

Alpine Valley Gardens, 2627 Calistoga Road, Santa Rosa, CA 95404.
- Broad selection. Catalogue; send 1 first-class stamp.

Barnee's Garden, Route 10, Box 2010, Nacogdoches, TX 75961.

Lee Bristol Nursery, RR 1, Box 148, Gaylordsville, CT 06755.
- Broad selection.

Burkey Gardens, Loretto, PA 15940.

Cordon Bleu Farms, PO Box 2033, San Marcos, CA 92069.
- Catalogue $1.00; also iris.

Daylily World, PO Box 1612, Sanford, FL 32771.

Greenwood Nursery, 2 El Camino Real, Goleta, CA 93117.
- Catalogue $1.00.

Houston Daylily Gardens, PO Box 7008, The Woodlands, TX 77380.
- Catalogue $2.00.

Hughes Gardens, 2450 N. Main Street, Mansfield, TX 76063.

Joiner Gardens, 33 Romney Place, Savannah, GA 31406.

Lenington-Long Gardens, 7007 Manchester Avenue, Kansas City, MO 64133.
- Broad list, including many of my own well known hybrids. Catalogue; send 1 first-class stamp.

Maple Tree Gardens, PO Box 278, Ponca, NE 68770.

Meadowlake Gardens, Route 4, Box 709, Waterboro, SC 29488.
- Catalogue $2.00.

Oakes Daylilies, Monday Road, Route 3, Corryton, TN 37721.
- Very broad list, own and many other hybrids.

Pilley's Gardens, 2829 Favill Lane, Grants Pass, OR 97526.

Thundering Springs Garden, PO Box 2013, Dublin, GA 31021.

Dutch Gardens

PO Box 588
Farmingdale, NJ 07727

- *Spring-flowering bulbs.*
- *146-page catalogue, more than 200 color illustrations, free.*

Here is a bulb catalogue with voluptuous, full-page, larger-than-life pictures of many of its offerings. There are a few species tulips here, but the bulk of the plants are the latest and greatest spring-bulb hybrids in all the major classes (including horrid things like peony-flowering tulips). There are also nice groups of alliums and amaryllis.

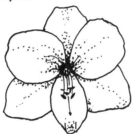
AMARYLLIS

Englerth Gardens

2461 22nd Street
Hopkins, MI 49328

- *Plants for day lilies, hostas, and irises.*
- *44-page catalogue, free.*

This is a long-established nursery with 3 obsessions. The day lily and hosta lists are very long, with brief descriptions. There is also a page or two of Siberian irises.

Fairway Enterprises

114 The Fairway
Albert Lea, MN 56007

- *Plants for hostas.*
- *1-page list, free.*

You must be nuts about hosta to order here. The selection of new named hybrids is very tempting, but while there are a few selections offered at $5.00 per plant, the majority cost $25 and up!

Fancy Fronds

1911 4th Avenue W.
Seattle, WA 98119

- *Plants for hardy ferns.*
- *Variable-length list, free*

Owner Judith Jones got started under the tutelage of an important British fern gardener, and her list is especially strong in English species and their varieties. She says it is also full of new fern introductions from around the Temperate Zone.

Ferncliff Gardens

SS 1
Mission, British Columbia
CANADA V2V 5V6

- *Plants for gladiolus, dahlias, peonies, and irises.*
- *16-page catalogue, free.*

Here are 4 very fine collections, all part of one nursery.

Fern Grower's Manual

by Barbara Jo Hoshizaki
Knopf

- *256 pages, many illustrations, a few in color, $11.95 pbk.*

The title tells the tale. The book does exactly what it ought to. Beginners will appreciate the introductory section on the morphology of ferns, which gives an illustrated primer on fronds, veins, spores, and other identifying marks. It's easy to understand, unlike many such "introductions." The cultural and propagation information is similarly usable, with useful touches, like a list of ferns that are easy to grow from spores. Ms. Hoshizaki has tried to include a broad list of species for all parts of North America and for a variety of garden conditions. Hundreds of species appear in the plant dictionary, with their preference for soil, light, propagation method, and the like.

Ferns to Know & Grow

by F. Gordon Foster
Timber Press

- *228 pages, many illustrations, $29.95.*

The new edition includes ferns from the South and the West, as well as from the Northeast. The suggestions for designing a fern garden are nice, as are those for interplanting ferns with wildflowers and for growing them indoors. There are good introductory sections on studying and collecting ferns in the field, and on their biology and morphology. The dictionary of more than 125 species is mainly devoted to American wild ferns, but includes some exotics for indoor culture, too. Text and illustrations for the dictionary are very botanical and somewhat technical, though they do provide useful cultural information.

A Field Manual of the Ferns & Fern-Allies of the United States & Canada

by David B. Lellinger
Smithsonian Institution Press

- *389 pages, some color illustrations, $45.00 hc., $29.95 pbk.*

Though I have generally left readers to the good offices of plant societies when it comes to books on individual specialties, I couldn't resist including this one, since ferns are so important to shade gardening and since the book comes from a not-so-usual source. It *is* written in botanese, but the clear descriptions of native habitat and garden use make it very useful for the gardener. The color photos—all grouped into a section in the middle of the book—are small but absolutely mouth-watering. If you are becoming interested in ferns, this resource should prove satisfying.

Fiske's Clematis Nursery

Westleton
Saxmundham
Suffolk
ENGLAND IP17 3AJ

- *Plants for clematis.*
- *40-page catalogue, 30 color illustrations, $1.00.*

The catalogue begins simply, "Three new clematis again this year!" They comprise one new and one old, little-seen variety found in New Zealand, plus one new variety from Poland. Fiske's has an amazing list of clematis, both hybrid and species. Most of the hybrids, at least, are available from American suppliers, but it is still worth having the Fiske catalogue for its completeness, its fine cultural suggestions, and the excellent variety descriptions. Reading the descriptions, you can tell at a glance how big the plant is, how big and what color the flowers, when the plant flowers, how and if to prune it, and even what exposure to plant it with. A nice Q&A section answers most common questions about clematis.

FERN

Fjellgarden

See "Wildflowers and Native Plants."

Flower Dictionaries

The Color Dictionary of Plants and Flowers

by Roy Hay and Patrick M. Synge
Crown

- *584 pages, many color illustrations, $12.95 pbk.*

The Complete Handbook of Garden Plants

by Michael Wright
Facts on File

- *544 pages, many color illustrations, $18.95.*

Simon & Schuster's Complete Guide to Plants & Flowers

Edited by Frances Perry
Simon & Schuster

- *522 pages, many color illustrations, $10.95 pbk.*

Taylor's Guide to Annuals

Taylor's Guide to Bulbs

Taylor's Guide to Perennials

Taylor's Guide to Groundcovers

Taylor's Guide to Houseplants

Taylor's Guide to Shrubs

Taylor's Guide to Vegetables

Houghton Mifflin Co.

- *Each more than 460 pages, many color illustrations, each $14.95 pbk.*

The Hay and Synge and Wright books are meant to be comprehensive dictionaries of ornamentals, embracing alpine and rock plants, annuals and biennials, greenhouse plants and houseplants, hardy bulbs, perennials, and trees and shrubs, all in one volume. With 2,500 color illustrations, Wright's book boasts 500 more pictures than its competitor; on the other hand, Hay and Synge list more recommended cultivars within each species. This means that Hay and Synge will generally give you a broader range of garden plants within any species, while Wright will give you a better sense of the varying looks within a genus or tribe. Wright's 2 pages of irises, for example, are about the best introduction to that complicated genus that I've seen. Both give comparatively short shrift to trees and shrubs, especially Hay and Synge.

Nevertheless, both are very serviceable and well-made books, though one feels that they may have bitten off slightly more than they can chew. The chief difference between them is that Hay and Synge is illustrated with color photos, while Wright is illustrated with color paintings. There's been debate for a long time as to which is the better way to illustrate a field guide: the photo fanatics say their method better shows true color and habit, while the painting advocates say that no photo can show enough detail to be really useful. When it comes to field guides, I think the painters are right, especially since the usual 4-color process used in book production can't duplicate the range of color the observer sees any better than a good painting can. Furthermore, a painting can consistently single out the important characteristics of the plants, whereas a photograph may be constrained to show the flower at the expense of the foliage and habit. Still, you can't help feeling a little extra sense of the real in a photograph, and in a book meant for garden planning more than for field identification, it is hard to choose between the 2 methods. The Hay and Synge photos do sometimes give too much of the flower and too little of the plant; the Wright paintings, though they are fine and

> With regard to seeds—some look like snuff, others like very light blond nits, or like shiny and blackish blood-red fleas without legs; some are flat like seals, others inflated like balls, others thin like needles; they are winged, prickly, downy, naked and hairy; big like cockroaches and tiny like specks of dust. I tell you that every kind is different, and each is strange, life is complex. Out of this big plumed monster a low and dry little thistle is supposed to grow, whereas, out of these yellow nits a fat gigantic cotyledon is supposed to come. What am I to do? I simply don't believe it.
>
> —KAREL CAPEK, FROM *THE GARDENER'S YEAR* (1929)

accurate, sometimes suffer from a washed-out look in the lighter tones (especially the pinks) and occasionally lose the illusion of depth.

The Simon & Schuster guide features pretty pictures and the accurate information for a fairly large number of the more common ornamentals, including houseplants. It's nice to have such a lot of variety in one volume, but I miss the more thorough coverage to be found in the Taylor multivolume series.

The Taylor guides were a very bright idea. It's simple: you take one fine garden encyclopedia—namely Taylor's—and combine it with one great library of garden photographs —Pamela Harper's. You fill in with other people's photos where Harper's leave a gap, divide the total into books on broad sorts of garden plants, format each to be like a field guide, and, *voilà*, you have a very handy series of photographic guides to a very wide range of plants. If you are designing a border by color, the

volumes may be particularly useful, since the photographs are organized according to color, not species. The text for each variety combines basic botanical descriptions with brief but clear cultural instructions. The introductory sections are full of hands-on information for general culture and propagation, together with a nice, illustrated key to the botanical terms used. There's even information on pests and diseases, plus a list of mail-order sources.

New volumes in the series are *Shrubs, Groundcovers, Vegetables,* and *Houseplants.* The virtues of the older volumes are repeated in the new. Even the vegetables books is useful, since it pictures and describes many lesser-known edible varieties and species. The groundcovers volume also contains a very nice section on ornamental grasses.

Foliage Gardens

2003 128th Avenue S.E.
Bellevue, WA 98005

- *Plants for hardy ferns, native and exotic.*
- *6-page list, $1.00.*

Proprietor Sue Olsen writes: "I began growing ferns from spore in 1968 as there were practically no sources for the plants. Several thousand plants later, I decided to open a nursery. I still run it on my own in the backyard, and normally have at least 100 species and 2,500 plants for sale per year." She propagates everything she sells; no plants are collected. As her description of herself might suggest, she writes lively, accurate, and straightforward descriptions of her ferns as well. It is definitely a specialist's list, but reading it makes the specialty look tempting. Rock, woodland, and indoor gardeners will all find something to intrigue them here.

The Fragrant Garden

by Louise Beebe Wilder
Dover Publications

- *405 pages, $6.50.*

"Fragrance speaks to many to whom colour and form say little . . ." begins Wilder. Her book was first published in 1932, and it is unlikely that anyone will top it. She has countless, charming reasons for growing fragrant plants, including the following: "Ancient books teach that the smell of many plants, rosemary among them, strengthens the memory." Several chapters are devoted to scents through the year, and there are sections on odorous shrubs, scented climbers, fragrant plants for the rock garden, bees and honey flowers, orchard and berry patches, night-scented flowers—and plants that smell rotten. Nothing scented is alien to her. Since Dover has been kind enough to keep this book available for us, I wish they'd do the same for her *Adventures with Hardy Bulbs.*

The Fragrant Path

PO Box 328
Fort Calhoun, NE 68023

- *Seed mainly for shapely and odorous annuals, perennials, vines, herbs, shrubs, and trees.*
- *32-page catalogue, a few illustrations, $1.00.*

The catalogue is literate, argumentative, and altogether delightful. Its author is not at all happy about the modern emphasis on flower size and color in the trade, instead preferring plants of fine shape and with fragrant flowers. It is worth having this list—even if most of the selections are common elsewhere—just for the elegant design ideas and the well-chosen historical facts that each entry contains. There are also quite a number of rarely seen and valuable garden plants, like the mock cucumber vine, the Hawaiian prickly poppy, two unusual nicotianas, a native lotus, two nice mulleins, the once-common vesper campion, and a lovely group of exotics, including many acacias and eucalyptus, for the greenhouse, house or warm-climate garden.

Gardening in the Shade

by Harriet K. Morse
Timber Press

- *242 pages, some illustrations, $12.95 pbk.*

This is a revised edition of a fine, hands-on shade gardening book that first appeared in 1962. Morse is a respected horticulturist who gardens on the Eastern seaboard, so people in that part of the country may prefer to start with her book rather than with George Schenk's more Western-oriented volume (see page 57). The plant palette is various, and all plants are very well described for cultural requirements and garden merit.

FROSTWEED

Gardening with Perennials

by Joseph Hudak
Timber Press

- *398 pages, some illustrations, $24.95.*

Here is an extremely useful book for planning perennial beds and borders. Its descriptive plant list is quite long, but the interesting thing about it is that it is organized according to sequence of bloom. You get a very good idea of what flowers, in what colors, will be blooming in any month. Then you can make your choices, and propagate and grow the plants according to Hudak's suggestions. All this is based on his experience in the Boston area, of course, so you may have to adjust timing for other parts of the country; he provides a rough guide for doing this.

> In reply to this charge I say that in one of the numerous phases of my life I also ruled over some beds of carrots and savoys, of lettuce and kohlrabi; I did it certainly out of a feeling of romanticism, wanting to indulge in the illusion of being a farmer. In due time it was obvious that I must crunch every day one hundred and twenty radishes, because nobody else in the house would eat them; the next day I was drowning in savoys, and then the orgies in kohlrabi followed, which were terribly stringy. There were weeks when I was forced to chew lettuce three times a day, to avoid throwing it away.
>
> —KAREL CAPEK, FROM *THE GARDENER'S YEAR* (1929)

The D. S. George Nurseries

2491 Penfield Road
Fairport, NY 14450

- *Clematis vines.*
- *2-page flyer, 1-page color flyer, free.*

This is a fine list of clematis, somewhat larger than that in general catalogues like Park's. It is weighted toward the very hardy Jackmanii hybrids, though it offers a few nice selections in the Patens and Florida groups as well, together with a few unusual species cultivars, including the golden-yellow *C. tangutica obtusiuscula.*

Gilson Gardens

3059 U.S. Route 20
PO Box 277
Perry, OH 44081

- *Plants for perennials, chiefly ground covers.*
- *24-page catalogue, 4 illustrations, free.*

This is a perennials nursery with a decent list, heavily weighted toward ground covers. The euonymus, ivy, and sedum groups are large and interesting. Minimum quantity is 5 plants for any one variety, which is not such a bad idea when you are buying ground covers. Gilson is a source for the red, white, and green *Houttuynia cordata,* a variegated ground cover from Japan often called Chameleon.

Gladside Gardens

61 Main Street
Northfield, MA 01360

- *Bulbs for gladiolus, dahlias, cannas, and unusual flowering bulbs.*
- *10-page list, $1.00.*

All parts of this list are interesting, but the proprietor's favorites are clearly the glads, of which a few named hybrids are her own introductions. The gladiolus list includes this and last year's premier new hybrids and good but not overwhelming numbers of upright, dragon, lacinated, double, and fragrant varieties, plus 2 odd species.

Groundcovers in the Landscape

by Emile L. Labadie
Sierra City Press
PO Box 2
Sierra City, CA 96125

- *314 pages, many illustrations.*

There are 125 groundcover plants listed in this volume, each with a fairly good black-and-white illustration and a description of its horticultural characteristics. Lists at the back of the book tell which plants are best in which situations. People in the warmer parts of the West will get the most use out of the book, since a number of the species listed are not hardy at colder temperatures. Nonetheless, it's a very good primer.

Hauser's Superior View Farm

Route 1
Box 199
Bayfield, WI 54814

- *Plants for perennials in quantity.*
- *6-page list, free.*

Most things here are the usual suspects, and I imagine that Hauser's is a large supplier to the nursery trade. Plants are sold in dozens or hundreds. While you are unlikely to want 100 hosta, you might well want a dozen, and the price is right.

Heirloom Gardens

See "Vegetables and Herbs."

Hermitage Gardens

PO Box 361
Canastota, NY 13032

- *Pools, waterfalls, water wheels, bridges, and other decorative items for the water garden.*
- *8-page catalogue, more than 50 illustrations, some in color, free.*

The pools come in quite a variety of shapes, and the rustic water wheels in at least 3 sizes. There is also lots of choice among the fiberglass rocks and waterfalls. Three simple, Japanesey bridges look somewhat more calm and elegant than the rest of the items.

Hildenbrandt's Iris Gardens

HCR 84
Box 4
Lexington, NE 68850

- *Plants for irises, peonies, Oriental poppies, hostas, and a few lilies.*
- *20-page catalogue, free.*

As its name suggests, hybrid irises, tall-bearded, and dwarf, are Hildenbrandt's specialty. The proprietor speaks modestly of "bringing you our little catalogue listing over 900 varieties." The very latest and costliest hybrids are not to be found here, but there are endless recent hybrids at medium prices, plus a good little selection of dwarfs and a long list of "proven favorites" offered at very reasonable prices, with discounts for quantity purchase. The poppy, peony, and hosta lists are small only in comparison with the huge iris inventory. To order from this nursery, you should have a good idea what you're looking for, since descriptions are brief.

Holbrook Farm & Nursery

Route 2
Box 223B
Fletcher, NC 28732

- *Plants for perennial flowers and shrubs; bulbs.*
- *54-page catalogue, 60 illustrations, $2.00.*

Holbrook is the kind of place that might get overlooked. Its list is large, but not as large as, say, Carroll Gardens'. But the variety descriptions here are very complete and interesting—better than those of most other catalogues of any kind. The plant-size information, for example, tells not only how tall the plant grows but how wide, a very useful bit of information for someone planning a garden. Proprietor Allen Bush also seems to take a fancy to both the white and compact forms of any given variety, and if you share his taste, you will find a number of less usual forms of common plants here. His selections among old-fashioned and native plants are sometimes quite distinctive, especially in the hypericums, Maltese cross, and potentillas, and in individuals like the native pachysandra called Allegheny spurge. The firm also has a good bulb list, strongest in narcissus but well represented throughout.

Homestead Division of Sunnybrook Farms

9448 Mayfield Road
Chesterfield, OH 44026

- *Plants for hostas, epimediums, day lilies, ivies, and a couple of ferns.*
- *26-page catalogue, $1.00.*

Most of the enthusiasm for ever-newer hybrids in the plant world has been generated by flowering plants and vegetables, but it appears that the foliage plants are now catching up. There are probably enough varieties of hosta, epimediums, and ivy in this catalogue to cover every county in the nation with a different one. The choice among hostas is particularly large, and if you don't see what you want, you can write to Homestead, since this list is drawn from a collection of more than 800.

Rock gardening in a place like Walnut Creek, California, does not really require wearing a hair shirt. Actually, it is not such a bad place. Located midway between the cold, damp fogs of San Francisco and the hot, dry furnace of the Central Valley, one might suppose that my garden would enjoy a pleasant combination of these two extremes. On the average, that is true. Unfortunately, our position is very much like the statistician's definition of an ideal situation: On the average, a person is very comfortable if his head is in an oven and his feet are in a refrigerator.

—FROM *BULLETIN OF THE AMERICAN ROCK GARDEN SOCIETY* (1986)

Hortico

723 Robson Road
RR1
Waterdown, Ontario
CANADA L0R 2H0

- *Plants for perennials, including bog species, grasses, and wildflowers.*
- *22-page perennials catalogue, free.*

Since Hortico is primarily a wholesaler, the catalogue is not pretty, but the firm sells quite happily at retail, too, and the list is well worth a look. The general perennials selection is wide and fairly deep, especially for aster, astilbe, true geraniums, day lilies, irises of all sorts, and phlox. Ornamental grasses are also well represented. Natives growers should look at the native bog, bulb, and wildflower lists. The bog list in particular is as large as that of most aquatics houses, and the selection is better for naturalizing. Some orchids, lilies, and trilliums appear too, among a good group of northern wildflowers.

Horticultural Systems

PO Box 70
Parrish, FL 33564

- *Native plants for freshwater and saltwater habitats; design service.*
- *3-page saltwater list plus 1-page freshwater list, free.*

For coastal gardeners from New Jersey to Florida and west to Texas, Horticultural Systems provides a basic, backbone palette of native plants. The firm appears to do a lot of reclamation work for commercial and government clients, but they sell by the plant as well as in bulk, so they may prove a reliable and experienced source to the gardener working beside or in salt, brackish, or fresh water. For salt habitats, there is a choice of about half a dozen species for dune and shore, including several grasses, a sunflower, and a morning glory; a slightly greater number of wetland species is heavy in grasses. Gulf residents may make good use of Southern natives like coontie (*Zamia floridiana*) and three different mangroves. The freshwater list is about two dozen plants long, and it is a kind of anthology of species offered by wildlife-food nurseries like Kester's, together with species offered for the bog by ornamentals nurseries like Lilypons. There is a very good choice among the rushes, grasses, and canes, with a few showy species like southern blue flag and pickerelweed.

IRISES

You could fill a whole book with descriptions of iris catalogues. You will find a number singled out for their own entries in this volume. Some of the rest appear here, though the list certainly isn't complete. The American Iris Society, with its many specialty subsocieties, is reviewed separately (see page 53). Canadians have their own Iris Society; contact V. Laurin, 189 Florence Avenue, Willowdale, Ontario, CANADA M2N 1G5. If you have seen one too many bearded iris, you might also be interested in the Aril Society International, c/o Donna Downey, 5500 Constitution N.E., Albuquerque, NM 87110.

Avonbank Iris Gardens, Radford University, PO Box 5961, Radford, VA 24142.
▪ Own and other hybrids of reblooming iris, especially tall bearded and especially for East and North; "a few near-everblooming."

Baldwin's Iris Gardens, PO Box 615, College Place, WA 99324.
▪ Bearded iris.

Cal Dixie Iris Gardens, 14115 Pear Street, Riverside CA 92504.
▪ Bearded iris.

Charjoy Gardens, 117 Acacia Drive, Lafayette, LA 70508.
▪ Louisiana iris.

Chehalem Gardens, PO Box 693, Newberg, OR 97132.
▪ Siberian and spuria iris.

Cherry Lane Gardens, 2988 Cherry Lane, Walnut Creek, CA 94596.
▪ Spuria iris, including own hybrids.

Circle N. Ranch, 18650 Birch Street, Perris, CA 92370.
▪ Long list of bearded iris and others.

Comanche Acres Iris Gardens, Route 1, Box 258, Gower, MO 64454.
▪ Tall bearded and other bearded iris. Catalogue $1.00.

Contemporary Gardens, PO Box 534, Blanchard, OK 73010.
▪ Louisiana, tall bearded, and median iris.

Cooley's Gardens, PO Box 126, Silverton, OR 97381.
▪ Tall bearded iris. Color catalogue $2.00.

Cooper's Garden, 212 W. County Road C, Roseville, MN 55113.
▪ Very good species list, with many tall bearded, Siberians, spurias, and Louisianas. Catalogue for first-class stamp.

Cordon Bleu Farms, PO Box 2033, San Marcos, CA 92069.
▪ Louisiana and spuria iris; also day lilies. Catalogue $1.00.

Deming Iris Gardens, 4122 Deming Road, Everson, WA 98247.
▪ Tall bearded iris. Catalogue $.50.

Gardens of the Enchanted Rainbow, Route 4, Box 439B, Killeen, AL 35645.
▪ Tall bearded, median, and reblooming iris.

Grandview Iris Gardens, HC86—Box 91, Bayard, NE 69334.
▪ Tall bearded iris.

Imperial Flower Garden, Box 255, Cornell, IL 61319.
▪ All kinds of iris, including Siberian, Japanese, and species; also Oriental poppies and day lilies.

Iris Acres, PO Box 189, Winamac, IN 46996.
▪ Bearded iris.

Iris Country, 118 S. Lincoln Street, Wayne, NE 68787.
▪ Tall bearded iris. Catalogue, $.50.

The Iris Pond, 7311 Churchill Road, McLean, VA 22101.
▪ All sorts of iris, including species. Catalogue $1.00.

Iris Ranch, PO Box 227, Cerrillos, NM 87010.
▪ Broad selection of all sorts. Catalogue $1.00.

J-Lot Gardens, Route 3, Box 496, Joshua, TX 76058.
▪ Reblooming iris.

Keith Keppel, PO Box 8173, Stockton, CA 95208.
▪ Good list of bearded iris. Catalogue $.50.

Kirkland Iris Garden, 725-20 Avenue W., Kirkland, WA 98033.
▪ Bearded iris, especially dwarf and median.

Laurie's Garden, 41886 McKenzie Highway, Springfield, OR 97478.
▪ Beardless iris; Pacific Coast natives; Siberian, water, crested, Japanese, and species iris.

Maple Tree Gardens, PO Box 278, Ponca, NE 68770.
▪ Bearded, aril-bred, and Siberian iris; also day lilies.

Maryott's Gardens, 1678 Andover Lane, San Jose, CA 95124.
▪ Tall bearded iris. Color catalogue $1.00.

Miller's Manor Gardens, 3167 E. US 224, Ossian, IN 46777.
▪ Bearded and Siberian iris.

Moonshine Gardens, PO Box 1019, Clearlake Oaks, CA 95423.
▪ Bearded iris, including rebloomers.

North Pine Iris Gardens, PO Box 595, Norfolk, NE 68701.
▪ Many bearded irises. Catalogue $1.00.

Mrs. Milton Ogburn, Route 1, Box 31, Smithfield, NC 27577.
▪ Many tall bearded irises.

Pacific Coast Hybridizers, PO Box 972, Campbell, CA 95009.
▪ Tall bearded iris, including rebloomers and own hybrids. Color catalogue $1.00.

Pleasure Iris Gardens, 425 E. Luna, Chaparral, NM 88021.
▪ Big list specializing in arils and their species, with others from virtually every category as well. Catalogue $1.00.

Rialto Gardens, 1146 W. Rialto, Fresno, CA 93705.
▪ Bearded iris, including rebloomers.

Riverdale Iris Gardens, 7124 Riverdale Road, Minneapolis, MN 55430.
▪ Good list of dwarf and median bearded iris. Catalogue $1.00.

Shannon Gardens of Oak Brook Farm, 30545 Tern Avenue, Shafer, MN 55074.
▪ Tall bearded iris.

Shepard Iris Garden, 3342 W. Orangewood, Phoenix, AZ 85051.
▪ Bearded, aril, aril-bred, spuria, and Louisiana iris.

Skyline Farms, Route 1, Box 162, Whitewright, TX 75491.
▪ Louisiana and bearded iris.

21st Century Gardens, 3237 Eisenhower Street, Eau Claire, WI 54701.
▪ Many bearded irises. Catalogue $1.00.

Huff's Gardens

617 Juniatta Street
Box 187
Burlington, KS 66839

- *Rooted cuttings of chrysanthemums.*
- *17-page catalogue, free.*

The Huffs have been growing mums for more than 40 years. These days, they list a mere 700 varieties or so, including about every type you can think of, plus some you can't. Among the choices are Japanese Ise types and a good group of the very late-blooming Cascade series. Descriptions are quite brief, but the "cultural tips" are authoritative, providing good general guidelines for pinching and disbudding, as well as for ordinary care. If you don't want to take a flying leap into the list itself, you can choose from a list of about a dozen collections. Here, the choices are made for you, though after you have grown the things, you may feel emboldened to tackle the varieties one by one.

LILY

International Geranium Society

4610 Druid Street
Los Angeles, CA 90032

- *Nonprofit organization dedicated to culture of true geraniums and pelargoniums.*
- *24-page quarterly* Geraniums Around the World; *Seed Center distributing unusual seed to members, annual membership $12.50.*

Members contribute the articles on culture, hybridization, travel, reminiscence, and the like. Each issue contains the Seed Center's current listings, as well as advertisements from specialty growers. Membership appears to be concentrated in California.

Klaus R. Jelitto

Postfach 56-01-27
D-2000 Hamburg 56
WEST GERMANY

- *Seed for perennials.*
- *68-page catalogue, 24 color illustrations; send 2 International Reply Coupons.*

The list of perennials is huge. It's also in German, but you will be able to figure out more or less what's going on, especially if you are a wild enough perennial or rock gardener to consider ordering from it. The selection of alpines is particularly nice. Be aware that only professionals are supposed to order from Jelitto, so you may have to have a nurseryman do it for you.

Jernigan Gardens

Route 6
Box 593
Dunn, NC 28334

- *Plants for day lilies, irises, and hostas.*
- *9-page list, SASE.*

There are more than 5 legal-sized pages worth of single-spaced day-lily listings here. At one variety per line, you get an idea of how many plants with names like Black Caesar, Buddha, and Little Dandy appear. Too many for my taste, but collectors will disagree. The hosta list runs a mere two pages and the irises but one, more than enough selection for most of us.

Kester Wild Game Food Nurseries

See "General Sources."

Klehm Nursery

Route 5
197 Penny Road
South Barrington, IL 60010

- *Plants for herbaceous and tree peonies, hostas, tetraploid day lilies, bearded iris, lilies-of-the-valley, and astilbes.*
- *68-page catalogue, more than 300 color illustrations, $2.00.*

This is perhaps the prettiest catalogue in the country, which is not really so odd when you consider that Klehm has been at work for well over a century. Klehm's peonies, called Estate peonies, are famous and lovely, and the firm lists hybrids from many other breeders as well. Klehm has recently shared in the development of a whole class of rock-garden peonies, which the catalogue has since introduced. There's also a nice list of Saunders tree peonies. This would be enough for most catalogues, but there are long lists of day lilies and hostas as well, plus a choice selection of irises. Instructions for the planting and care of all these different classes are excellent. Virtually everything is well illustrated and appropriately described.

Lakeshore Tree Farms

See "Trees and Shrubs."

Laurie's Garden

41886 McKenzie Highway
Springfield, OR 97478

- *Plants and seeds for all sorts of irises.*
- *5-page list, SASE.*

Laurie's offers a very good list of beardless irises. There are tons of named hybrids of Siberian and Japanese iris—a real collector's list. A smaller group of crested iris is also to be found here, but the most exciting things from the gardener's point of view may be the many iris species, especially the native Californicae, and the good number of water irises for the marsh or water garden.

Legg Dahlia Gardens

1069 Hastings Road
Geneva, NY 14456

- Tubers for dahlias.
- 16-page catalogue, free.

After 30 years in the business, Legg offers about 500 varieties of dahlias, from "tiny Pompons less than two inches in diameter" to "giant dinner plate size dahlias." Not all the 500 are listed in the catalogue, but for most of us that is just as well. If you are hunting a particular variety, write to Legg and ask about it. Descriptions of the cultivars in the catalogue are all very brief, so you do best not to use it unless you know what you are looking for.

LILIES

Here is a group of lily specialists. More information will come from the North American Lily Society, c/o Dorothy Schaefer, PO Box 476, Waukee, IA 50263.

Bluebell Lilies, 1432 Manor Lane, Blue Bell, PA 19422.

Fairyland Begonia & Lily Garden, 1100 Griffith Road, McKinleyville, CA 95521.
- Catalogue $.50.

Gaybird Nurseries, PO Box 42, Wawanesa, Manitoba, CANADA R0K 2G0.

Kent Lilies, 2009 Edgewood N.E., Grand Rapids, MI 49505.

Strahms Lilies, PO Box 2216, Harbor, OR 97415.
- Big list of Orientals. Catalogue $.50.

Trinidad Bay Bulb Company, PO Box 974, Trinidad, CA 95570.

Lilypons Water Gardens

6800 Lilypons Road
PO Box 10
Lilypons, MD 21717

PO Box 188
Brookshire, TX 77423

- *Plants for hardy and tropical water lilies and lotus; bog plants; all associated supplies, oxygenators, fish, other animals, pools and pool liners; ornaments and fountain heads; books.*
- *68-page catalogue, over 220 illustrations, most color, $4.00.*

Lilypons is certainly in line for most-beautiful-catalogue-of-all award. The pictures of the many lilies, lotus, and bog plants offered are remarkable. They have done a good job photographing the night-blooming tropicals, a type that has really come into its own since the development of outdoor lighting. Even the color pix of the filters and pumps are lovely! Only Van Ness can rival Lilypons for the variety of species offered: there are almost fifty "hardy" water lilies; over 30 day-blooming tropicals including many blue ones; 10 night-bloomers including the huge, almost frightening Victoria; another 10 lotus; two dozen hardy bog plants, plus a dozen irises; and another dozen tropical bog plants. Among the supporting cast are 4 oxygenating plants, 8 kinds of fancy fish, 2 sorts of prefabricated fiberglass pools, PVC liner, statuary (mostly ugly), fountains, appropriate books, and every sort of water cleaning or water moving chemical, pump, or filter. A nice feature is the step-by-step instruction for construction of a pool using PVC liner. The basic planting instructions are also good. If you find this too much to choose from, you can buy whole set-ups—rather like outdoor versions of a complete aquarium set—in six different forms, including everything from the prefabricated pool, to the plants, to the fish, to the snails. As the price of

the catalogue should indicate, this isn't an inexpensive hobby, but as the catalogue's beauty shows, it can be a rewarding one.

The cultivation of a rock garden appears in this way as an exciting and elevating sport; besides, it affords you innumerable thrilling surprises when, for instance, at the dizzy height of one yard you discover in the rocks a flowering tuft of the white edelweiss, or of Dianthus glacialis, or of some other so-called child of the highland flora. But what is the use of telling you who have not nursed all those miniature campanulas, saxifrages, campions, speedwells, sandworts, drabas, and iberises, and alyssums, and phloxes (and dryas, and erysimum, and house-leeks, and stonecrops), and lavender, and potentilla, and anemone, and chamomile, and wall cress (and gypsophila, and edraianthus and various thymes), (and Iris pumila, and the Olympic hypericum, and the orange hawkweed, and the rock rose, and gentian, and cerastium, and thrift, and toad-flax), (don't forget, of course, Aster alpinus, the creeping wormwood, erinus, spurge, soapwort, and erodium, and hutchinsia, and paronychia, and thlaspi, and aethionema or snapdragon, antennaria, and other innumerable and most beautiful little flowers, as, for instance, petrocallis, lithospermum, astragalus, and others no less important, like primulas, Alpine violets, and others) . . .

—KAREL CAPEK, FROM *THE GARDENER'S YEAR* (1929)

The Little Bulbs

by Elizabeth Lawrence
Duke University Press

- *248 pages, $10.95 pbk.*

Happily, there are companies that keep reprinting literate garden classics such as *The Little Bulbs*. Although the latest editors have had to do little to improve on a book that covered so many little bulbs, from the most to the least common, they have thoughtfully updated the source list, so we can find the things that Lawrence makes us so passionately desire. She is a rare garden writer—rarer even than those who can turn a phrase neatly or describe a plant well—because she writes more or less in dialogue with her friends and correspondents, chiefly with the redoubtable Mr. Krippendorf. Her first chapter, "The First Flower," starts thus: "As soon as spring is in the air Mr. Krippendorf and I begin an antiphonal chorus, like two frogs in neighboring ponds: What have you in bloom, I ask, and he answers from Ohio that there are hellebores in the woods, and crocuses and snowdrops and winter aconite. Then I tell him that in North Carolina the early daffodils are out but that aconites are gone and the crocuses past their best." Mr. Krippendorf gardens on a large scale; she gardens on a smaller one; other correspondents are from other parts of the nation and garden on plots as small as a window box. You can see that most of this information might have been conveyed in efficient little lists and chapters, with zone charts, suggestions for succession of bloom, and design hints for different scales and situations. Lawrence casts all this information into a narrative that never flags, but by the time you are done, you will find yourself better acquainted with the bulbs than if you had industriously pored over 100 lists.

Logee's Greenhouses

See "Houseplants and Exotics."

Lost Prairie Herb Farm

See "Vegetables and Herbs."

Louisiana Nursery

Route 7
Box 43
Opelousas, LA 70570

- *Plants for tropical and hardy water lilies, lotus, and bog species.*
- *64-page "Magnolias and Other Garden Aristocrats," catalogue $3.50.*

The company supports any number of expensive habits. Elsewhere, we have discussed their irises, magnolias, exotics, and what-have-you. Believe it or not, they also have two pages of aquatics. The lilies list is nice and very expensive, though it has little that is not offered elsewhere. Among the bog plants are a few not-always-seen species, including a crinum and a bronze-leafed floating heart.

Louisiana Nursery

See "General Sources."

John D. Lyon, Inc.

143 Alewife Brook Parkway
Cambridge, MA 02140

- *Spring- and autumn-flowering bulbs, mostly species and selections, plus some garden hybrids.*
- *4-page list, free.*

If you are looking for unusual species bulbs—particularly from the minor genera—Lyon ought to be about the first place you look. A good number of the species here are not offered in most general bulb catalogues. The lists of *Corydalis* and *Fritillaria* are remarkable, though the firm notes that supply is very limited, so you had better order early. The narcissus selection is also noteworthy. It contains a full half-dozen varieties of *N. bulbocodium*, not to mention species like *N. henriquesii* and some unusual cultivars. The company has changed its narcissus list recently, in an effort to avoid selling imported bulbs that have been collected in the wild. Not only is this change ecologically sound, but it doesn't seem to have hurt the list any.

McClure & Zimmerman

1422 W. Thorndale
Chicago, IL 60660

- *Flowering bulbs.*
- *28-page catalogue, more than 100 illustrations, free.*

McClure & Zimmerman offers most of what you'd expect from a fine bulb catalogue, but it goes farther, particularly in species bulbs (as opposed to the usual hybrids) of the more common types and of unusual, tender species. The species daffodils, crocuses, and tulips made my mouth water. Take, for instance, *Tulipa turkestanica,* an orange-based white, multiflowering tulip, the outside of whose petals are grayish, causing them to blend in with the foliage when the flowers close on a cloudy day. The lily selection is among the best around, as is the group of 17 different alliums. The catalogue touts new, California-bred hybrids of anemones, freesia, and ranunculus. Among the rare small bulbs and exotics, the firm has too many fine selections to name, but consider that they offer three ixias, while some catalogues list none. The iris selection is smaller than you might expect, but is unusual and worth looking at. It takes a few minutes to get used to this catalogue because it uses many abbreviations and a somewhat complicated zone chart. Entries are very well written, offering good ideas for the interplanting of different bulbs and odd bits of lore and description, like the following for *Bulbocodium vernum:* "appearing as if it had almost certainly slept in its clothes."

The Macdonald Encyclopedia of Alpine Flowers

Macdonald & Co.
Maxwell House
74 Worship Street
London
ENGLAND EC2A 2EN

■ *384 pages, many color illustrations, $18.00.*

This is another of those pretty color reference books originally produced by Mondadori in Italy. Simon & Schuster has published a number of them in the U.S., and I wish they had done this one, too. Generally, the great fault with the Mondadori volumes is that they are made for Europe, not the U.S. I was furious when I bought Simon & Schuster's mushroom field guide, only to discover that many American species were described but not pictured. (It struck me as particularly dangerous when the U.S. editor was compelled to describe a certain poison mushroom as looking much like the one in the picture, but not exactly!) The problem is decidedly less noticeable for alpine flowers, since collectors of alpines are generally quite happy to find out about all those wonderful European species. There are some American species included, but the emphasis is on Old World plants. Still, the book is gorgeous, copious, and better organized than any of the other Mondadori volumes I have seen.

Maroushek Gardens

120 E. 11th Street
Hastings, MN 55033

■ *Plants for hostas, clematis, and selected perennials.*
■ *12-page catalogue, free.*

The specialty is hosta. It's a respectable, not overwhelming, collection. Coverage elsewhere is spotty but interesting, especially in campanulas, primroses, and clematis.

> There are fanatical Phlox-men or Philophloxers, loudly sneering at Chrysanthemum-men, which courtesy these return in October, when Chrysanthemum indicum is in flower; there are melancholy Aster-men, who to all other gratifications of life prefer the autumnal aster; but of all the maniacs the wildest (besides, of course, the Cactus-men) are the Dahlia-men, or Georgians, who for some new American dahlia will pay a dizzy sum, perhaps even ten shillings.
>
> —KAREL CAPEK, FROM *THE GARDENER'S YEAR* (1929)

Maver Nurseries

Route 2, Box 265B
Asheville, NC 28805

■ *Seed and some plants for garden perennials, ornamental grasses, wildflowers, and alpines.*
■ *104-page general seed list, $5.00; write for specialty lists and to check availability of plants.*

A few years ago, this nursery relocated from Canada, and it has yet to put its mail-order plant business back into operation, but its ornamental seed list offers as much variety as you will find almost anywhere. The choice is not among cultivated hybrids so much as it is among all the gardenworthy species of a given genus. Collectors use this list, and, according to the proprietors, companies like Thompson and Morgan buy from it. For example, it offers 127 species and naturally occurring varieties of campanula, not to mention a number of named hybrids. As the list contains nothing but Latin names and brief descriptions, it requires careful study. The company is now working on a book that will list more than 5,000 different garden plants, each with a description and a list of commercial sources; ask for more information if you're intrigued.

Merry Gardens

Camden, ME 04843

■ *Plants for herbs, ivies, fuchsias, geraniums, and unusual houseplants.*
■ *One catalogue for houseplants, including cacti and succulents; one catalogue for other plants; $2.00 each.*

Merry Gardens is an older nursery whose proprietors have simply followed their bents in collecting. All the lists are sizable. The firm also sells little booklets on the culture of almost every type of plant it grows.

Messelaar Bulb Co.

150 County Road
Ipswich, MA 01938

■ *Flowering bulbs.*
■ *18-page catalogue, approx, 80 color illustrations, free.*

Messelaar has more than 40 years' experience in the trade. The list is large for the more common sorts of spring-flowering bulbs, but it is not by any means the most comprehensive list available. Selected varieties of the less common genera are also included. The illustrations are good. Minimum order is five of any one variety.

Milaeger's Gardens

4838 Douglas Avenue
Racine, WI 53402

- *Plants for perennials, roses, and prairie and woodland natives; garden-design service.*
- *32-page catalogue, 94 color illustrations, $1.00.*

Milaeger's wins the prize for helpfulness. Here is a sample of the catalogue copy: "Asclepias is pest free and butterflies and hummingbirds are attracted to it. You should be, too." The catalogue is very attractive and well illustrated, and it even offers hints on easy plants to grow and color combinations that do well together. You will not find as many varieties to choose from here as you will in the most hardcore perennials nurseries, but you will find most of what anyone actually grows. The rose list is comprehensive for modern types, including some of the older and less flamboyant hybrid teas. The woodland plants group contains the usual suspects, but the prairie flower and grass selection is really outstanding. Using it, you could form the backbone of a terrific Midwestern prairie garden. Perhaps unique to Milaeger's is the form of its garden design service: send $40.00, and you will receive a questionnaire about your garden and your wants for it. *Voilà!* The firm designs the garden and will send you the plants to fill it.

Mission Bell Gardens

2778 W. 5600 South
Roy, UT 84067

- *Rhizomes for tall bearded irises.*
- *20-page catalogue, free.*

The Hamblens of Mission Bell have been hybridizing tall bearded iris for the last 30 years. Their catalogue includes their own introductions, plus a lot of others, all at collector's prices. The descriptions are generally to the point, though occasionally they get carried away, as in this paean to "Rosecraft": "A vision in raspberry-violet . . . with lighter area accentuating violet tipped, rusty-henna beards." A vision of what?

Grant Mitsch Novelty Daffodils

PO Box 218
Hubbard, OR 97032

- *Bulbs for daffodils.*
- *28-page catalogue, approx. 70 color illustrations, $3.00.*

If you thought it took a good, full-color iris catalogue to drive you crazy, you haven't seen this daffodil catalogue. There are all kinds of collector's hybrids here—many of them pictured and many of them originated by Mitsch or his descendants. You don't have to be a collector to find these beautiful, but be aware that they are more costly than your average daffodil.

WATER LILY

Mohn's, Inc.

PO Box 2301
Atascadero, CA 93423

- *Plants for hybrid Oriental poppies.*
- *11-page catalogue, 23 color illustrations, free.*

Mohn's is the sole source for a new strain of poppy hybrids that it calls "Minicaps." According to the firm, these plants have very small seed pods and a 2–4 month blooming period. Each of the hybrids is well illustrated in the catalogue. Most of them look quite similar.

Montrose Nursery

PO Box 957
Hillsborough, NC 27278

- *Plants for cyclamen, garden perennials, and natives.*
- *11-page list, $1.00.*

Proprietor Nancy Goodwin propagates her own cyclamen—a very good thing, considering the depredations of collectors in the Mediterranean, whose work has succeeded in making many of the wild species rare. Goodwin has an astonishingly good selection, and her loving descriptions of what she offers are worth the price of the list all by themselves. She has also gathered a small group of unusual and very interesting perennials for sale, among them a number of woodland natives. Here, too, the descriptions are excellent, and one has the feeling that she has simply chosen her favorites out of what must be a delightful North Carolina garden.

Moore Water Gardens

PO Box 340
Port Stanley, Ontario
CANADA N0L 2A0

- *Plants for hardy and tropical water lilies, lotus, bog species, and oxygenators; fish; all supplies, fiberglass pools, fountain heads, PVC liner, prefabricated waterfalls; books.*
- *32-page catalogue, approx. 70 illustrations, a few color, free.*

Moore has been selling aquatics in Canada for over half a century. Its list isn't too pretty, but is fairly complete; the firm sells only in Canada. The water lilies and lotus lists are not so long as those of Lilypons or Van Ness, but they offer a good deal of choice. The bog list is quite interesting, with a few species not found in the other big waterplant catalogues, including 4 different taros and water hawthorne. The supplies list is as complete as could be wished, and there are several complete starter sets available for those who want convenience. Details on planting and winter care are useful, as is the diagram for lotus planting.

The Mother Earth News A-to-Z Flower Garden Favorites

Mother Earth News
PO Box 70
Hendersonville, NC 28791

- *176-page magazine-format book, many color and black-and-white illustrations, $3.95.*

At the price, this isn't a bad introduction to garden flowers. The book contains not only a fairly comprehensive A-to-Z listing, with descriptions, line drawings, and basic suggestions for use, but a number of articles on popular flowers like mums and roses, and on topics like water gardening and greenhouses. Still, I can't help feeling they have tried to do too much and keep the price too low. The color photographs are pretty awful, and much of the information in the listings could be gleaned from a good commercial catalogue. The articles mix some very good suggestions with others that are not so useful. For example, in their effort to make everything seem easy, the authors suggest that it is simple to buy flowering mums in the fall, plop them in the garden, and overwinter them. Only in the last paragraph of text do you discover that if you live in regions with "severe winters," you will have to dig them up again and put them in a cold frame or a basement for the winter.

Nature's Garden

Route 1
Box 488
Beaverton, OR 97007

- *Plants and seeds for rock-garden varieties, perennials, a few native trees and shrubs, woodland wildflowers, and hardy ferns.*
- *7-page list, $1.00.*

The whole list is pretty miscellaneous, but Western wildflower and rock gardeners may get good use out of it. The rock list is strongest in primulas and gentians; There are a couple of Oregon-native oxalis among the wildflowers, along with other interesting plants.

Nerine Nurseries

Bookend House
Welland nr. Malvern
Worcestershire
ENGLAND WR13 6LN

- *Bulbs for nerines.*

C. A. Norris is a remarkable fellow. He inherited half of his grandfather's bulb collection in 1959, studying it and gradually building it. In the 1970s, he went to South Africa, where he collected all of the described species but one, together with soil and climate data. Since then, he has continued to trade, breed, propagate, and study the things, until today his collection numbers about 50 species and subspecies, plus about 900 named cultivars. He has built a stock that he says is considerably in advance of the Exbury hybrids, with hardier plants and new colors and color combinations. How you can get them, he doesn't say. He is now looking into the possibility of forming a corporation to market his nerines better, but in the meanwhile, you'd better write to him.

North American Lily Society

c/o Mrs. Dorothy B. Schaefer
PO Box 476
Waukee, IA 50263

- *Nonprofit organization dedicated to the culture of the genus Lilium.*
- *64-page quarterly bulletin; 96-page yearbook; annual seed exchange and auction; books on culture, showing and history; annual membership $12.50, three years $31.25.*

The seed exchange sent more than 15,000 packets last year, so it is very active; particularly rare seed is auctioned. The selection is extremely wide, and the society helpfully provides a pamphlet on growing lilies from seed. The catalogue and yearbook are generally very businesslike, mainly containing scientific and technical information, lists of shows, and club reports and minutes. Nevertheless, a recent issue of the quarterly featured a delightful article by two Japanese members about the eating of lily bulbs in Japan. Like most plant societies, this is a place to discover all the arcane lily sources that are too small for me to list here.

Owl Ridge Alpines

5421 Whipple Lake Road
Clarkston, MI 48016

- *Plants for rock, alpine, and wildflower gardens.*
- *12-page catalogue, free.*

Judy Pearson is frank about what she knows and what she doesn't. If she's lost the species name of a given plant, but still likes it, she includes it in the catalogue with an enticing brief description. Overall, her nomenclature is variably accurate, but her enthusiasm is plain. There are not a lot of sedums or saxifrages here, nor any alyssum or aubrieta. There are a pretty large number of alpines and rockery plants selected apparently according to the preferences of an experienced rock gardener. Campanula, draba, geranium, iris, penstemon, phlox, and primula receive the most attention, and the lists of these are really worth a look. Natives gardeners should peruse the whole list, as there are interesting plants scattered all over it, including one Northeastern and one Northwestern iris, a very good group of penstemons, the lovely mound-forming *Phlox bifida*, and a valerian from Arizona.

Paradise Water Gardens

14 May Street
Whitman, MA 02382

- *Plants, pools, fish, all sorts of supplies, and books.*
- *50-page catalogue, many color and black-and-white illustrations, $2.00.*

"Everything for the water garden" is this firm's motto. The lists are indeed broad for everything from fish and oxygenators and water lilies and Higo irises, to submersible pumps and fountains. Paradise offers the biggest selection of prefabricated pools and waterfalls that I have seen. The lists of water lilies themselves seem to be slightly smaller than those of their major competitors, though the firm focuses on getting out new introductions quickly.

Peekskill Nurseries

Box 428
Shrub Oak, NY 10588

- *Plants for ground covers.*
- *9-page illustrated flyer, free.*

If you have a lot of ground to cover, this flyer will come in handy. Only the usual suspects appear: pachysandra (including a silver-edged variety), vinca, euonymus, ivy, and Bar Harbor juniper.

Yes, for the cultivator of a rock garden is not only a gardener, but a collector as well, and that puts him among the serious maniacs. You need only show him that your Campanula morettiana has taken root and he will come in the night to steal it, murdering and shooting because he can't live any longer without it; if he is too much of a coward, or too fat to steal it, he will cry and whine to you to give him a tiny cutting. That comes from having bragged and boasted of your treasures before him.

—KAREL CAPEK, FROM *THE GARDENER'S YEAR* (1929)

The Perennial Garden

by Jeff and Marilyn Cox
Rodale Press

- *304 pages, some color illustrations, $21.95.*

You might wonder why Rodale is doing a perennials book, but the Coxes have brought Rodale's holistic approach into the flower garden with good effect. The introductory chapters discuss the evolution of seed plants and the broad principles of garden design, then suggest where to place beds and borders. At the end of the volume is a long list of suggested species and cultivars with all the pertinent information for selecting and growing them. The best things about the book, however, are the chapters devoted to color harmony and to color-illustrated suggestions for lively appositions. Many books get shy when it comes to color. Not this one. They have charts relating color to the musical scales, to the planets, and to the "auras" of vice and virtue conveyed by each hue and tone. The aura chart is fun, suggesting among other things, that the lighter tones connote virtues while the darker shades suggest the Seven Deadly Sins. Using these charts, you could make music of the spheres in your garden, or pit saints against sinners. There is also a good deal of modern color theory, and some ideas for reflecting the color sensibilities of painters in the garden.

Perennials for Your Garden

by Alan Bloom
Capability's Books
Box 114
Highway 46
Deer Park, WI 54007

- *144 pages, many color illustrations, $19.95.*

Alan Bloom is a leading British nurseryman and breeder and winner of the RHS's prestigious Victoria Medal of Honor. This book amounts to a well-illustrated catalogue of his favorite species and cultivars, complete with his incisive comments on culture and placement. His introductory section about planning or rejuvenating beds and borders is suggestive but not overbearing. Derek Fell, quite a good writer and photographer himself, has adapted the text for American readers. Because he has left Bloom's cultivar recommendations intact, however, the book gives you a look at what the finest English perennial border contains. Since the English are kings of the perennial border, this is by no means a bad thing. Almost all the suggested plants will be available in the U.S. as well.

Pleasant Valley Glads

PO Box 494
Agawam, MA 01001

- *Bulbs for tall and miniature gladiolus.*
- *26-page catalogue, free.*

There are more glads here than anyone could grow, some with positively scurrilous-sounding names like "Vicki Cream," "Pert," and "Sweet Lips." Gladiolus hybridizers are no less prolific than their peers in the lily and iris worlds, it seems, and their prose is no less purple. The writer of this catalogue takes the county-fair approach, emphasizing the show qualities of the many offerings. "Spectrum Red," for example, "has one Grand Champion to its credit and numerous 3-spike champs." Most of us may not be as excited to hear this as the author is, but for all who are courting glad mania, here is an excellent list.

Prentiss Court Ground Covers

PO Box 8662
Greenville, SC 29604

- *Plants for ground covers.*
- *8-page flyer, 12 illustrations, free.*

Here is an unusually good selection of 12 ground covers, including such things as liriope and jasmine. You can order bulk quantities at good prices.

PRIMULAS

Primroses are getting a lot of attention these days, especially in the Pacific Northwest, which should clue you in that they don't like hot, dry summers. Your best starting information will come from the American Primrose Society, c/o Herbert Dickson, 2568 Jackson Highway, Chehalis, WA 98532.

Aberchalder Alpine Gardens, Gorthleck, Inverness-shire, SCOTLAND.
- Seed for primulas and alpines.

Bailey's, PO Box 654, Edmonds, WA 98020.
- Plants for show-quality auriculas and Julian hybrids.

Gordon Douglas, 87 Church Road, Great Bookham, ENGLAND KT2 3 EG.
- Seed for show-quality auriculas.

L. S. A. Goodwin & Sons, Goodwins Road, Bagdad, Tasmania, AUSTRALIA 7030.
- Seed for own polyanthus primroses.

Grand Ridge Nursery, 27801 S. E. High Point Way, Issaquah, WA 98027.
- Plants for primulas.

Brenda Hyatt, 1 Toddington Crescent, Bluebell Hill, nr. Chatham, Kent, ENGLAND ME5 9QT.
- Seed for fine, show-quality, and garden auriculas.

David Reath Nursery

PO Box 521
100 Central Boulevard
Vulcan, MI 49892

- *Plant material for herbaceous and tree peonies.*
- *26-page catalogue, 7 color illustrations, plus price list, $1.00.*

Peonies are gaining in popularity again, and Reath's nursery is a good place to get them. Too many collectors' catalogues read like a foreign language, comprehensible only to the initiated. Reath has gone out of his way to produce a very intelligent and

---

readable catalogue, not only listing and describing each of the many hybrids and few species he offers, but also providing a good deal of background on the whole subject of peony breeding. Reath propagates and sells the great hybrid herbaceous peonies introduced by Orville Fay, Lyman Glasscock, and A. P. Saunders, together with Saunders and Daphnis tree-peony hybrids. He has also crossed the two lines of tree peonies, creating a strain of his own sold under the name "New Era." Japanese tree peonies and a few other miscellaneous hybrids appear as well, along with two very hardy species peonies, one herbaceous and one "tree." In short, the catalogue is an excellent source of peonies for the gardener.

Rex Bulb Farms

PO Box 774
2568 Washington Street
Port Townsend, WA 98368

- *Bulbs for hybrid and species lilies.*
- *72-page catalogue, approx. 110 illustrations, most in color, $1.00.*

Among the more than 200 varieties offered in the huge and pretty Rex catalogue are all of your favorites plus many you have never heard of, especially among the Asiatic and Oriental hybrids. Like many specialists, the Rex people are wild about hybrids, and they keep up with the latest of everything, especially the Columbia-Platte and Strahm hybrids. The current year's introductions are always expensive because they are in short supply, but, to my eye, a lot of them look no lovelier than their predecessors. A notable exception is Bull's Eye, a yellow Columbia-Platte hybrid with what appear to be rough maroon brushstrokes instead of spots on the petals. The list of species lilies is also very good in this catalogue, though it is not nearly so well illustrated as the hybrid list.

Rice Creek Gardens

1315 66th Avenue N.E.
Minneapolis, MN 55432

- *Plants and bulbs for the rock garden and ground covers, including perennials, grasses, ferns, waterside plants, wildflowers, dwarf shrubs, conifers, and even a few cacti.*
- *16-page catalogue, 13 color illustrations, $1.00.*

In their introduction, the proprietors write enthusiastically, "Now you can find the plants you have read about!" Lucky you. If you are not already an experienced rock gardener—probably even if you are—you will have to keep plenty of references at hand in order to have any chance of making a selection from the enormous range of rock-garden plants offered here. The catalogue is helpfully broken into sublists for larger and smaller perennials for sun and shade, and for specialties like grasses and dwarf bulbs. Descriptions are very brief. Almost anything you could want can be found somewhere in the catalogue, including a good group of woodland and alpine natives that embraces rarer genera like *Shortia* and *Vancouveria*. A helpful how-to section at the back of the catalogue will help you get started in rock gardening, and if you simply can't make choices from the giant list, the proprietors operate a garden-design service, and will doubtless be willing to help you.

Right Plant, Right Place

by Nicola Ferguson
Simon & Schuster

- *292 pages, many color illustrations, $14.95 pbk.*

This is a very handy book if you are looking for something particular. It consists of 27 very nicely illustrated lists of plants, each placed according to a given attribute or to a particular place where it is best used. Within each list, plants range from sun lovers to shade tolerators, with information on height and color. It comes from the U.K., but Frederick McGourty, once head of the Brooklyn Botanic Garden's fine book series, has done a good job of keeping it relevant to the U.S. and Canada.

IRIS

Rock Gardening

by H. Lincoln Foster
Timber Press

- *466 pages, some illustrations, $22.95 pbk.*

Foster says at the outset that he is only going to deal with plants he has grown personally. Considering the immense range of the species he discusses, it's a wonder he ever had time to eat dinner. This is the classic rock-garden volume, not only for its information, but for its sensible attitude. Foster begins thus: "It is time to think in different terms [i.e., less elaborate] and consider possible and pleasant ways of bringing into our modest landscape some of the magic of alpine and saxatile plants. There are among them some of the easiest and most abundantly flowering garden plants, and also those challenging haunters of remote places, which by the difficulty of their taming lure us year after year to discover the secret of their adoption." He tackles soils, exposures, propagation, planting, both in general and for a great variety of alpine and rock plants. The illustrated suggestions for making such things as a planted retaining wall are unusually thorough, with plenty of variations for ledges and outcroppings.

Rock Gardens

by Jerry S. Stites and Robert G. Mower
Cornell Cooperative Extension
Bulletin 159
New York State College of Human Ecology
7 Research Park
Cornell University
Ithaca, NY 14850

- *30-page booklet, 70 illustrations, many in color, $3.00.*

Like many of the Cornell publications, this is an excellent value for the money. It also might be a good way for the would-be rock gardener to decide whether he or she really wants to get involved with this sort of thing. The instructions are good, basic, and no-nonsense. The list of several dozen recommended plants suffers from overly technical descriptions, but the comments on their uses in the rock garden are good, and the color illustrations are attractive and usually revealing of the plant's habit as well as color.

Royal Gardens

Dept. A11
Box 588
Farmingdale, NJ 07727

- *Flowering bulbs and plants for perennials.*
- *Spring and fall catalogues, 52–67 pages, more than 180 color illustrations each, free.*

I flipped open the fall catalogue to find a black iris as big as my hand staring blankly at me. The photographs here are very good. Because many are printed larger than life, they can also be scary. I thought the full-page fritillaria might devour me. A wide range of the more common bulb types appears in the catalogues, along with some less ordinary species tulips and interesting stuff like the plume-flowering *Muscari plumosum*. For the majority of gardeners, there is plenty of choice here, and, for all of us, the catalogues are a fine mnemonic aid, because of the pictures. The lovely violet-edged white Shirley tulips, for instance, stood out forcefully on a spread of varieties that pleased me less. Just be careful when you open the catalogue.

Savory's Greenhouses and Gardens

5300 Whiting Avenue
Edina, MN 55435

- *Plants for hostas.*
- *16-page catalogue, $1.00.*

Savory's propagates well over 100 varieties of hosta, and it hybridizes new ones of its own. Its list embraces most cultivated species plus numbers of named hybrids. Prices vary from reasonable to absurd.

Schreiner's Garden

3625 Quinaby Road N.E.
Salem, OR 97303

- *Plants for irises of all kinds, especially tall-bearded and dwarf.*
- *72-page catalogue, more than 350 color illustrations, $2.00.*

There are hundreds of hybrid irises here, many of them Schreiner's own introductions. Some of them are lovely indeed, and some are so ugly their own mothers couldn't love them. A few have such odd color combinations that they seem to have been dead for a week. Iris collectors and enthusiasts will love the catalogue, though. Schreiner is a leading breeder, and he himself calls the catalogue the "bible" of iris lovers. Descriptions are disgustingly sanguine, but they contain all pertinent information. There is a very good section on iris culture, in case you are just

catching the iris bug. I suppose I am prejudiced against the hybrid iris only because I have never seen irises so beautiful as the pale and delicate wild species that grow on the headlands above northern California beaches.

Scottish Rock Garden Club

c/o Dr. Evelyn Stevens
"The Linns"
Sheriffmuir
DunBlane, Perthshire
SCOTLAND FK15 0LP

- *Nonprofit organization devoted to the growing of rock- and peat-garden plants.*
- *Annual seed distribution; variable length, twice-annual journal,* The Rock Garden, *many illustrations, some in color; annual membership $12.00.*

Rock gardeners are collectors, and the seed exchanges of their societies tend to be copious. The SRGC's is only slightly smaller than the Alpine Garden Society's (see page 52), listing well over 3,500 species and varieties. The Scottish group, as one might expect, has a special interest in ericaceous plants, so it's a fine place to look for these. A recent seed list also seemed very strong in bulb-forming alpines. The society's journal maintains a pleasantly informal tone and a broad mix of articles. A recent issue contained at least half a dozen reports from collectors and visitors to alpine regions around the globe, together with reports on the culture of several genera and a light-hearted, informative article on the virtues of "shuffling," the frequent moving of one's plants to try different combinations and environments. The editor has a developed sense of irony, particularly about the weather and the shortcomings of plant societies, and his column also features a regular review of the results of growing recent acquisitions at the society's gardens.

Seawright Gardens

134 Indian Hill
Carlisle, MA 01741

- *Plants for day lilies.*
- *14-page list, $1.00.*

Robert Seawright described his business so well that I'll leave it to him: "One of the foremost sources of fine day lilies in the world. We deal in collector's items and fine breeding stock. Around July 25 you have to see it to believe it. Mark your calendar. . . . Begun as a hobby when R. Seawright was 12 years old, now a crossroads for day lily enthusiasts, collectors and hybridizers. Developers of the famous 'Jerusalem' tetraploid day lily." If the description appeals to you, so will the list. I like the way Seawright described his plants too. "Florence Bird," for instance, is "very refined light green-yellow self except for deeper green in the shallow throat. The flower opens out flat; wide petals are smooth, waxy and diamond-dusted. Beautifully branched." He cares for the whole plant, not just the flower, and he doesn't make his writing gooey with superlatives.

Seedalp

Case Postale 282
Ch–1217 Meyrin 1
Geneva
SWITZERLAND

- *Seed for alpine and other perennial plants.*
- *37 pages, free.*

This Swiss firm has a very broad selection of alpine plants, particularly in major genera like the saxifrages and campanulas. It's well worth a look, though it's written in French. The one tiny section in English is labeled "Sawing Instructions," so it's probably a good thing they stuck to French elsewhere.

Sequence of Bloom of Perennials, Biennials, and Bulbs

by R. G. Mower and R. E. Lee
Cornell Cooperative Extension
Bulletin 196
New York State College of Agriculture
and Life Sciences
7 Research Park
Cornell University
Ithaca, NY 14850

- *14-page booklet, 4 illustrations, $1.60.*

This little list is an excellent idea. In tabular form, it gives the bloom times of 295 perennial, biennial, and bulb-based flowers. The selection lists plants that are hardy in New York, and the time information is based on experience in central New York, but the booklet is a very handy primer on *sequence* of bloom, useful to gardeners in most of the temperate U.S. and Canada. The coverage is pretty good for the flower varieties that even experienced gardeners will try, though I wish they had included a table for shrubs as well.

Shady Oaks Nursery

700 19th Avenue N.E.
Waseca, MN 56093

- *Plants for shady places, including perennials, ferns, grasses, trees and shrubs, and wildflowers.*
- *36-page catalogue, $1.00.*

The Oslunds started their nursery when they were looking for shade plants to go beneath their stand of oaks; hence, the nursery's name. They would have to have a lot of oaks to plant all the numerous varieties they now offer in the catalogue. There are not too many things here that can't be found elsewhere, but it's a good idea to group together all the plants that like or will tolerate shade. The lists of epimediums, day lilies, and hosta are particularly extensive, and there are good color choices among such items as spiderwort, for which only one or two colors are commonly found. Grasses don't normally like shade, but a few that do appear here, along with a good selection of native wildflowers, 5 trilliums and the bottle gentian among them.

🌱 *TULIP*
🌀 The Fire by its own power meeting in the Birth of the Tulip the watery Substance, boils, consumes, and as it were burns it up, and thus brings the Tulip to a red Colour; and when it has evaporated the Substance of the Air by its heat, it remains moister, and causes the flower to be quite Red.

—HENRY VAN OOST, FROM *THE DUTCH GARDENER* (1700)

Siskiyou Rare Plant Nursery

See "Wildflowers and Native Plants."

Spring Hill Nurseries

6523 North Galena Road
Peoria, IL 61632

- *Plants and bulbs for perennials, shrubs and trees, roses, and a few berries.*
- *76-page spring catalogue, more than 250 color illustrations, $2.00; 60-page fall catalogue, under the Breck's firm name, more than 200 color illustrations, $2.00.*

Spring Hill does not list as many choices within a given species as do specialist perennials nurseries, but its spring catalogue is a good place for a gardener experimenting with perennials to begin. Above all, the illus-trations are unusually fine, and many of the offerings are grouped by type—dwarf, shade, color blend, daisies, cutting, and the like—so gardeners get an idea of the choices available for a particular use. Not that the catalogue should be restricted to beginners. There are appealing selections throughout, including a lovely pastel day lily called "Hall's Pink" and the Eveline dahlia, a pretty, full-flowered white variety with pink and yellow at the center. Spring Hill has what might be called a "county fair" selection of roses. There are crazy bicolors—the nicest of which is the new "Voodoo"—and the lavender "Blue Girl," the latter with a relative available in climbing form. The firm includes a free planting handbook with each order, which is a good thing, since cultural instructions are sparse in catalogue text and, where they exist, they are often a bit sanguine.

The fall bulb catalogue, offered under Breck's firm name, has the same virtues as its spring brother. It does suffer from the big-photo syndrome that makes you feel as though you've been hit over the head with a giant black tulip, but the selection is quite wide for the commonly grown genera. Two crocuses with lovely orange stamens—*C. etruscus* and *C. tomasinianus*—caught my eye. A thing called the "Buttercup iris"—yellow with green spotting in the throat—was also very attractive.

Swan Island Dahlias

PO Box 800
Canby, OR 97013

- *Tubers for dahlias; associated supplies.*
- *44-page catalogue, more than 100 color illustrations, $2.00.*

The family that runs Swan Island seems to live and breathe dahlias. They not only breed a good many of their own varieties, offering these plus many others in the catalogue, but they also sell knives for dividing tubers, indelible markers for identifying stored tubers—and a coffee substitute made from dahlia tubers! "Let your family experiment with the delicious and delightfully rich taste of DACOPA," says the ad. The range of choice here is very good, and the firm has provided a useful service by offering collections of 5 or 6 different dahlias, the members of each collection illustrated on a single page. On the whole, this is a very fine source for those who are seriously interested in dahlias, or for those who want to learn more about them.

Thaxter, Celia

An Island Garden

by Celia Thaxter
Bullbrier Press
10 Snyder Heights
Ithaca, NY 14850

- *130 pages, approx. 35 illustrations, some in color, $13.50 ppd.*

Among the Isles of Shoals

by Celia Thaxter
Wake-Brook House
Box 153
Hyannis, MA 02601

- *187 pages, $5.95.*

Thaxter's books—both written in the last quarter of the 19th century—deserve reprinting, and these 2 little presses should be praised for doing it. As good as Sackville-West and Jekyll are, I think Celia is a better writer for those of us with less than an estate to work with. I imagine Gertrude Jekyll in her combat boots, disciplining her plants to look natural; Thaxter is more modest. In *An Island Garden,* she describes her own work in her tiny garden—a mere 50 by 15 feet—

on Appledore Island off the coast of Maine. Her preferences for certain flowers and for certain combinations on the trellis, and her plan for the layout of her small, fenced plot, are still useful guides for the gardener—particularly the seaside gardener—but that is the least of it. The poetry for which she was well known in her day is almost forgotten now, but her prose should not be. Her descriptions are fine and lively, and she emphasizes what she actually does in the garden, not simply what it looks like. The tales of her battles with the slugs are stirring and funny, especially when she calls in the toads to her aid. She rises to plant at 4 A.M. while the sun is rising over the waves; she uses eggshells as pots for her seedlings; she plants lilies and water hyacinths in tubs. You may know the watercolors done of Celia in her garden by Childe Hassam. (They are in the Smithsonian.) All are reproduced in color in the book.

Among the Isles of Shoals does not have too much to say about gardening, but if you get hooked on Thaxter, this is perhaps her best book. It is a kind of human geography of the tiny islands on which she was raised. Since she had her garden on one of them, you may think of this book as a companion to the other. It includes geology, botany, history, memories of childhood, and tales of storm and shipwreck, all written in her limpid prose style. About one storm of her youth, when her father was a lighthouse keeper, she writes, "It raved and tore at lighthouse and cottage; the sea broke into the windows of that eastern chamber where the walnuts lay, and washed them out till they came dancing down the stairs in briny foam!"

Thomasville Nurseries

See "Roses."

Thompson and Morgan

See "General Sources."

Thon's Garden Mums

4811 Oak Street
Crystal Lake, IL 60014

- *Rooted cuttings of chrysanthemums.*
- *16-page catalogue, 53 color illustrations, free.*

Here is a well-illustrated list of more than 100 varieties of mums. The emphasis is on good American bedding types, including the very hardy Cheyenne series, developed by the USDA and said to tolerate temperatures as low as −40° F. You can buy either preselected collections or individual varieties. The listings helpfully tell relative height and flowering date for each.

William Tricker, Inc.

7125 Tanglewood Drive
Independence, OH 44131

- *Aquatic plants, fish, and supplies.*
- *32-page catalogue, more than 50 illustrations, many color, $1.00.*

Tricker claims to have originated water gardening in the U.S. As its first catalogue appeared in 1895, this is probably no idle boast. There is very little in the way of pools, fountains, or statuary here, but the list of plants for the pool and bog is superb. Some of the lilies are their own introductions. The catalogue is very well organized, and it is thoughtfully provided with all sorts of information on culture and care of plants and fish. There are several starter collections to choose from, not to mention a separate selection of lilies for the natural pond. Strictly from the point of view of aquatic flowers and plants, there is no better catalogue to be had.

Tyty Plantation

Box 159
Tyty, GA 31795

■ *Bulbs and plants for cannas, crinums, hymenocallis, zephyranthes, and other flowering bulbs for the South.*
■ *32-page catalogue, 79 color illustrations, free.*

A beautifully illustrated selection of cannas and crinums is to be found here, along with a miscellaneous group of subtropical bulbous plants and flowering shrubs for the South. Single and double forms of the Confederate rose (*Hibiscus mutabilis*) are among them.

Van Ness Water Gardens

2460 N. Euclid Avenue
Upland, CA 91786

■ *Plants for hardy and tropical water lilies, grasses, bog plants, and oxygenators; snails, all sorts of supplies, PVC liner, fountains, modular precast fiberglass ponds; books.*
■ *56-page catalogue, over 110 illustrations, many color, $3.00.*

Van Ness has lots of experience. The firm has done water gardens at Disneyland and the Los Angeles Zoo, among many other public and private places. Overall, the list is very large and comparable to the selection you will find at Lilypons, though each of them has distinctive items and new introductions. The Van Ness catalogue is not quite as pretty as its competitor's, but it is slightly more full of ideas and information. The 1986 catalogue had a lead article on the experience of a man who created his own small pond, a text on propagating lilies from the viviparous leaves, lots of details in the descriptions of each variety and in the introductions to sections, a whole essay on water management, very useful tips for installing and curing a cement pool, and an informative Q&A section. The firm also sells detailed information sheets

on a number of aquatics topics at $1.00 per sheet. I liked the modular pond sections, which can be combined to create a wide variety of shapes. Van Ness is also promoting water gardens on the very small barrel, tub, or pot scale, with information and supplies for creating them.

Veldheer Tulip Gardens

12755 Quincy Street
Holland, MI 49424

■ *Tulips and other spring-flowering bulbs.*
■ *4-page brochure, 91 color illustrations, free.*

This is a huge garden, containing several million tulips alone. There are windmills and Dutch-clad folks on the premises, and a wooden-shoe factory is next door. The mail-order list, though it contains most common genera of spring-flowering bulbs, is about average for its breadth and depth of coverage.

André Viette Farm & Nursery

Route 1
Box 16
Fisherville, VA 22939

■ *Plants for perennials, with many day lilies, irises, hostas, peonies, ornamental grasses, and Oriental poppies.*
■ *45-page catalogue with 2-page color-illustrated day lily insert, $1.50.*

A few years ago, the Viettes relocated from Long Island to Virginia, trying to escape the hubbub of the suburbs. Their bucolic surroundings do not seem to have slowed them down. The day lily list by itself is a complete collector's catalogue, featuring, among many others, the numerous and costly new hybrids devised by André and his two sons. There is also a large separate list of tall bearded iris, not to mention smaller ones for dwarf bearded, Siberian, and Japanese iris,

and for hosta, grasses, ferns, Oriental poppies, and herbaceous peonies. The perennials list is usefully divided into two: one for sun lovers and one for shade tolerators. The selection in both rivals that of Wayside Gardens (see page 79) and Carroll Gardens (see page 56), and the Viettes seem to make a special point of searching out lesser-known species and varieties of common genera, like a variegated bishopweed and purple-leaved bugbane. This is by no means the easiest catalogue to use, since it is virtually unillustrated and descriptions are very brief. Still, it ought to be one of the indispensables for the serious perennials gardener.

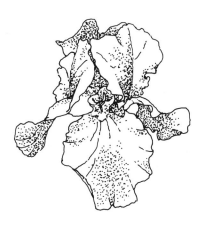

BEARDED IRIS

The Water Lily Society

PO Box 104
Buckeystown, MD 21717

■ *Nonprofit organization dedicated to culture of water lilies.*
■ *24-page quarterly newsletter* The Water Lily Journal, *a few illustrations, annual membership $12.50.*

The journal of this fledgling society, founded in 1985, is already a considerable publication. It doesn't look like much, particularly in contrast to the fancy color catalogues the big lily companies put out, but it is full of useful information, including accounts of a novice's difficulties in starting a pond, essays on hybridizing and on new introductions, reports of the discovery of new species and varieties, explanations of the nomenclature, details on the location of wild lily stands in North America, book reviews, and articles on the cultivation of selected plants. The president's message in the inaugural issue, lamenting the loss of native habitats containing water lilies, may herald some interest in the group for wildlands preservation. It is all intelligently written.

Water Lily World

2331 Goodloe
Houston, TX 77093

- *Pools, plants, fish, and supplies.*
- *Various lists, free.*

The selection of pools, of fish, and of supplies is decent. The choice of plants for pool and bog is good, though smaller than some. The oddest and most interesting things the firm supplies are pitcher plants—about 2 dozen varieties of the carnivores. The firm also sells what is billed as "a timely book" on carnivorous plants. What do you suppose "timely" means? The pool and bog plants are propagated in old rice fields in Texas, so they should be well adapted.

Wayside Gardens

Box 1
Hodges, SC 29695

- *Plants and bulbs for perennials, shrubs, trees, vines, ground covers, ornamental grasses, herbs, and a few fruits and berries; tools.*
- *132-page catalogue, approx. 900 color illustrations, $1.00 each, spring and fall.*

In an ideal world, one might order everything from ajuga to zelkova at Wayside, but that might be more

---

DELPHINIUM
The Delphiniums, or tall Perennial Larkspurs, are amongst the most beautiful of all flowers. They embrace almost every shade of blue, and, being usually of a tall and strong type, will make way among vigorous weeds, unlike many things for which we have to recommend an open space, or a wood with nothing but a carpet of moss under the trees.

One of the prettiest effects which I have seen was a colony of tall Larkspurs. Portions of old roots had been chopped off by the men when a bed of these plants was dug in the autumn, and the refuse thrown into a near plantation, far in among the shrubs and trees. Here they grew in half-open spaces, so far removed from the margin that they were not dug and were not seen. When I saw the Larkspurs in flower they were more beautiful than they are in borders or beds, not growing in such close stiff tufts, but mingling with and relieved by the trees above and the shrubs around.

—WILLIAM ROBINSON, FROM *THE WILD GARDEN* (1870)

---

excitement than any one garden could bear. The astonishing catalogue—among the few still printed on coated stock—has such good illustrations that I have more than once thought of cutting it up to make a paper garden on my corkboard, but that would destroy the appetizing and very informative text. There is no category of ornamental perennials, bulbs, shrubs, or trees, in which the list is not strong to very strong. A number of the more unusual selections come

---

from English plantsmen. Some of the rarities, British or not, are too odd for my taste. The Snow Queen hydrangea, for example, seems to have flowers too large for a self-respecting hydrangea, and the columnar Callery pear may find a use somewhere, but not, as the catalogue suggests, as a street tree. Many of the unusual finds, though, are delightful, like the American smoke tree or the lovely red-throated mock orange called Belle Etoile. Among the shrubs are a number of dwarf varieties that lend themselves to borders or small spaces; there is even a dwarf 3-foot tall pendulous white birch. Strengths among perennials include astilbe, phlox, and species clematis. The grass list is very fine, as is the choice of ground covers. Among the shrubs and trees, azaleas and rhododendrons, viburnum, lilacs, crab apples, cherries, and dogwoods are particularly well represented. (West Coast gardeners should note that some potted varieties cannot be shipped there, due to agricultural laws.) The rose list is very broad. Wayside's taste in hybrid teas runs to the conservative, so you will find many old favorites plus lovely new Meilland hybrids from France. Miniatures and floribundas are also present in abundance, but what really distinguishes Wayside's roses is the large number of older varieties they offer: gallicas, damasks, hybrid perpetuals, bourbons, and the like. The great, fat, fragrant Madame Hardy and La Reine Victoria are among the choices. This catalogue even offers a good, brief selection of woodland wildflowers. Founded in 1920, Wayside was bought out by the Park Seed Company in 1975, but the change doesn't seem to have done any harm.

Weston Nurseries

See "Trees and Shrubs."

White Flower Farm

Route 63
Litchfield, CT 06759

- *Plants and bulbs for perennials and shrubs; tools, furniture, books, and supplies.*
- *90–98 page catalogues, spring and fall; 150–200 illustrations each, mostly in color; $5.00 annual subscription, includes brief Christmas Note.*

The worst thing about the White Flower Farm catalogues is that you can't stop reading them. It's not just the very wide range of perennials, bulbs, and selected shrubs and dwarf evergreens that they offer; it's the suggestions, the reminders, the descriptions, and even the jokes. The advice on pruning, planting, planning the perennial border, and the like, is better than what you will find in many books, justifying the pretentious title, "The Garden Book," that the firm gives its alphabetical catalogues. The thorough planting charts for perennials and bulbs alone are a remarkable service to people planning a garden. (Do note that hardiness zones are based on the Arnold Arboretum's chart, not the USDA's.) Though the lists contain many plants for the rockery, for pot culture, or for naturalizing, the real love of these Anglophile plantsmen is the perennial border. This isn't a catalogue for those in search of rarities, though it contains unusual varieties. As the writers have said about chrysanthemums: "We choose varieties from the hybridizers on the basis of plant quality, habit of growth, and real differences in color—not on the basis of what is newly new in this overpopulated field." Hence, the lists are very selective, but they offer among the best choices anywhere for the 7 backbones of the perennial garden: daffodils, tulips, iris, peonies, delphinium, phlox, and chrysanthemums. Also very strong are anemones, aquilegia, asters, astilbe, azaleas, clematis, bedding dahlias, day lilies, daphne,

ferns, lilies, and hosta. The place has apparently made a specialty of heaths and heathers and of dwarf evergreens, making its basic lists hard to beat. Among pot and house plants, it has not only a fine selection of tender and forcing bulbs (especially amaryllis), but good groups of basket begonias, fuchsia, and lantana. According to the catalogue, the firm is planning to introduce more flowering shrubs and a selection of old roses

> One makes a mental note, or even a written note, and then the season changes and one forgets what one meant at the time. One has written 'Plant something yellow near the yellow tulips,' or 'Plant something tall behind the lupins,' and then autumn comes and plants have died down, and one scratches one's head trying to remember what on earth one meant by that.
>
> —V. SACKVILLE-WEST, FROM *GARDEN BOOK* (1983)

soon. It is a little misleading, perhaps, to single out species as strengths of the lists, since one of the things you trust at White Flower Farm is the quality of the selections the growers make. You feel that you could make an entire garden—from the amaryllis on the side table, to the fuchsias hanging in the patio, to the border, to naturalized bulbs or ferns in wilder areas—with nothing but this company's catalogues. You could even buy your tools, garden stakes, and furniture there. Of course, what you would end up with is a fine, Anglophilic flower garden. The list is not without class prejudices. Only mixed

gladiolus are offered, for example, because the named varieties are said to be gaudy; this reasoning has not prevented them from offering endless named varieties of lilies, which to my mind, are rather gaudy themselves. True enough, glads don't look right in the perennial border, but here, as elsewhere, the catalogue exhibits the taste of a crusty, firm-jawed meritocrat from Connecticut, Connecticut. This is a very good thing, because it means the writers are skillful, forthright, and have done their homework, but I think I like Granny with her glads as much as I like that crusty man in khakis. It's not surprising to learn that White Flower Farm's Eliot Wadsworth II joined with *The New Yorker* to purchase *Horticulture* magazine (see page 35) in 1981. *The New Yorker* has since sold its interest, but Wadsworth remains.

Gilbert H. Wild & Sons

1112 Joplin Street
Sarcoxie, MO 64862

- *Plants for peonies, iris, and day lilies.*
- *96-page catalogue, more than 225 color illustrations, $2.00.*

Wild's has among the finest collector's lists of peonies, irises, and day lilies in the country. Though it began by breeding peonies, the firm has diversified into hemerocallis hybridizing, at which it is unbelievably prolific. The catalogue lists well over a dozen new introductions annually, together with endless older day lilies by Wild and others. When it comes to day lilies, Wild is like the publisher who refuses to let older titles go out of print. Though the company does not breed irises, it keeps a good-sized list of those from the major breeders. After plowing through these, it is a relief to come to the comprehensive, but comparatively brief, group of peonies. It appears that peonies just don't lend themselves to massive hybridization, but, for whatever reason, the list is peppered with introductions dating all the way back to the 19th century, with very few from the 1980s. Saunders, Glasscock, Auten, Nicholls, and Wild hybrids make up the bulk of the list.

Wildwood Farm

10300 Highway 12
Kenwood, CA 95452

- *Plants and bulbs for perennials, California natives and Mediterranean natives, ornamental grasses, bamboo, and unusual trees and shrubs.*
- *6-page list, $1.00.*

California is an anthology of horticultural, as well as cultural, possibilities. So is this list. Owner Richard Monte is a landscape designer, and one gets the feeling that the list of plants is as much related to the vari-

The first job is to clean the worms inside and out. Wash adhering materials from them and place them in moist cornmeal or flour for 24 hours. This will enable them to be purged of all remaining parts of their past food.

Remove the mash and spread them on waxed paper. Remove any dead ones . . . . Place the live worms in a colander and rinse vigorously in cold water. If they are handled too hesitantly they will crawl through the holes. Tip them out onto paper toweling or a tea-towel and pat dry. They are now ready for use or they can be frozen for use later.

—FROM *EARTHWORMS FOR GARDENERS AND FISHERMEN* (1986)

eties he uses in his practice as it is to any overall principle. Though he provides nothing but Latin and variety names—with no descriptions—I could make out enough of the list to half-see a lovely California coastal garden taking shape in my mind's eye. There are some natives in here, chiefly among the trees and shrubs, like toyon, manzanita, and Matillija poppy. Then there is the stuff that Californians can put in their gardens and others must keep in the house, like the many varieties of abutilon offered. Lots of perennials, ground covers, and dwarf and nondwarf conifers are also listed. Check out the bamboos and the ferns and the grasses. Only beware that the list takes study.

Woodland Nurseries

See "Trees and Shrubs."

3   Trees and Shrubs

Adams County Nursery

PO Box 108
Aspers, PA 17304

- *Plant material for fruit trees.*
- *32-page catalogue, free.*

Adams County Nursery is a source for the chiefly modern varieties of apple, peach, pear, plum, apricot, nectarine, and sour and sweet cherry

 Plants which are moved every few years do not put down long tap roots and are unharmed by shifting, provided a few precautions are taken. Non-gardeners enjoy sunny weather, but we shuffling addicts can glory in gorgeous rain. When there is a long wet spell, colleagues at work notice my smug expression and guess that the blighter has been at it again. Actually, we put on plastic coats and shift plants while it is raining.

—FROM *THE ROCK GARDEN* (1986)

trees. One good old winter keeper called Smokehouse appears among the apples, along with Winter Banana, which most nurseries now use as a pollinator for Red Delicious strains. The descriptions of the virtues and vices of dwarf and semi-dwarf rootstocks are valuable, as are the texts describing the parentage of each strain. It's interesting, and a little scary, how many named varieties of apples come from so few older strains. The firm has been around since 1905, and it sells nationwide.

American Bonsai Society

Box 358
Keene, NH 03431

- *Nonprofit organization dedicated to bonsai.*
- *20-page quarterly* Bonsai; *4-page monthly newsletter* ABStracts; *annual membership $18.00.*

Both publications are a bit thin. *AB-Stracts* is meant to give news of upcoming events, which it does ade-

quately. Each issue of the quarterly features an interview with an expert, plus articles on everything from basic pruning to creating miniature rockscapes. The tone is generally dry but informative. Members also get discounts on bonsai books, plus the use of a lending library.

American Camellia Society

PO Box 1217
Fort Valley, GA 31030

- *Nonprofit organization dedicated to camellia culture.*
- *38-page quarterly* The Camellia Journal, *200-page* American Camellia Yearbook, *annual membership $12.50.*

Don't join unless you are crazy about camellias. The articles tend to be gossipy, and a good part of each issue of the journal is devoted to lists of shows, awards, and new cultivars. These folks were ecstatic about the discovery of yellow camellias in China, possibly because it gave them something new to talk about.

American Rhododendron Society

Mrs. Paula L. Cash
14885 S.W. Sunrise Lane
Tigard, OR 97224

- *Nonprofit organization dedicated to rhododendron culture.*
- *61-page quarterly, 11 pages of color illustrations; seed exchange; pollen exchange for hybridizers; conferences and discount books; annual membership $20.00.*

This society is quite serious. It even trades pollen, not to mention the seed of more than 1,300 varieties each year.

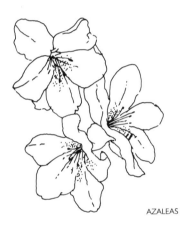

AZALEAS

Ames' Orchard and Nursery

6 E. Elm Street
Fayetteville, AR 72701

- *Plants for fruits and berries.*
- *12-page catalogue, free.*

Ames offers a nice, brief selection of fruits and berries on the basis of good disease resistance. Since Arkansas has a transition-zone climate, the choices will probably do well both north and south of there. There are apple and peach trees, strawberries, highbush blueberries (not for the South), blackberries, raspberries, and grapes. Most are recent releases, but I was interested in an heirloom apple called Hawaii Arkansaw, with what the firm describes as a "strong pineapple flavor." If you want an idea of the owner's temperament, consider their "package deals." One offers you two apples of his choice and is called "Dwarves! (sorry, no hobbits available)."

Every gardening book will tell you that "it is best to get seedlings from the seed." But they don't say that with seeds Nature has its own special habits. It is a law of Nature that either not one of the seeds will grow, or the whole lot. One says: "Here an ornamental thistle would look very well, say cirsium or onopordon." One buys a packet of each, one sows them, and rejoices how well the seeds come up. Some time later the gardener has to transplant them, and he is happy because he has one hundred and sixty pots with luxuriant seedlings; he says, this raising from seed is still the best thing. And then the time comes when the seedlings ought to be put in the ground; but what can he do with one hundred and sixty thistles?

—KAREL CAPEK, FROM *THE GARDENER'S YEAR* (1929)

Appalachian Gardens

Box 82
Waynesboro, PA 17268

- *Plant material for shrubs and trees; three odd English ivies.*
- *24-page catalogue, free.*

Appalachian Nurseries has been a well-known wholesale nursery for many years, specializing in unusual shrubs and trees. In 1986 the firm put out its first retail catalogue, under the name Appalachian Gardens. It must be finding it difficult to break the wholesale habit, since the minimum order is 4 items, but given that the list is strongest in shrubs, dwarf shrubs, and small trees, ordering 4 may make sense anyway. The list is enticing enough to make you want to buy 4, especially among the dwarfs. There is an unusual dwarf boxwood for bonsai, for example, a spreading *cephalotaxus* for ground covers, any number of nice false-cypress, and a small, mound-forming red-twig dogwood. This is also a source for less common midsize trees, such as cryptomeria and Japanese umbrella pine. In general, the variety descriptions are very good, right down to specific cultural suggestions, hardiness zones, and ultimate size, but occasionally the writers have forgotten to include one or more of these items, a fault they will probably correct in future catalogues.

Appalachian Wildflower Nursery

See "Wildflowers and Native Plants."

Applesource

Tom Vorbeck
Route 1
Chaplin, IL 62628

- *Service offering antique and specialty apples for examination and tasting.*

Tom Vorbeck has got a number of specialty apple growers together to offer more than 50 varieties of heirloom apples. If you want to taste some of these old cultivars before you grow them, here is your chance.

AZALEAS AND RHODODENDRONS

Every region where azaleas and rhododendrons can be grown has a good number of nurseries catering to the collector. Often, the nurseries also stock other ericaceous plants—kalmias, heath, and heathers—and some of them have branched out into flowering shrubs like pieris and camellias as well.

J. Blaauw & Co., PO Box 33, Red Bank, NJ 07601.

Bull Valley Rhododendron Nursery, Route 1, Box 134, Aspers, PA 17304.
- Good selection of hybrid rhodos. Catalogue $1.60.

Cardinal Nursery, Route 1, Box 97, State Road, NC 28676.
- Many hybrid rhodos. Catalogue $1.00.

Chambers Nursery, 26874 Ferguson Road, Junction City, OR 97448.
- Azaleas and rhodos.

Clay's Nurseries, PO Box 3040, Langley, British Columbia, CANADA V3A 4R3.
- Azaleas, rhodos, and kalmias.

The Cummins Garden, 22 Robertsville Road, Marlboro, NJ 07746.
- Azaleas, rhodos, and kalmias, including dwarf and small-leaved rhodos; dwarf conifers and other companion plants, too. Catalogue $1.00.

Bill Dodd's Rare Plants, Drawer 377, Semmes, AL 36575.
- Azaleas and rhodos, focusing on natives; a few other ericaceous and miscellaneous plants.

Dogwood Hills Nursery, Route 3, Box 181, Franklinton, LA 70438.
- Many azaleas, plus other flowering shrubs. Catalogue $2.00.

Eastern Plant Specialties, PO Box 40, Colonia, NJ 07067.
- Rhodos, kalmias, and other ericaceous plants. Catalogue $2.00.

Flora Lan Nursery, Route 1, Box 57, Forest Grove, OR 97116.
- Azaleas and rhodos, plus other flowering shrubs and conifers.

The Greenery, 14450 N.E. 16th Place, Bellevue, WA 98007.
- Especially azalea and rhodo species.

Hager Nurseries, RFD 5, Box 2000, Spotsylvania, VA 22553.
- 1,500 azalea varieties from more than 50 hybridizers.

Hall Rhododendrons, 1380 Quincy Drive, Junction City, OR 97448.
- More than 2,000 varieties of species and hybrid rhodos.

Harstine Island Nursery, E. 3021 Harstine Island, North Road, Shelton, WA 98584.
- Azaleas, rhodos, and more.

Hass Nursery, 256 Ervin Road, Philomath, OR 97379.
- Azaleas and rhodos, plus pieris. Catalogue $2.00.

Marc Henry Nursery, 10415 72nd Avenue N.E., Brooks, OR 97305.
- Azaleas; daphne.

Hillhouse Nursery, RD 1, Marlton, NJ 08053.
- Linwood azaleas.

Island Gardens, 701 Goodpasture Road, Eugene, OR 97401.
- Azaleas and rhodos.

Mowbray Gardens, 3318 Mowbray Lane, Cincinnati, OH 45226.
- Many hybrid and species rhodos; also seed.

Rhododendron Farm, PO Box 242, Mountain Home, NC 28758.
- Many rhodos.

Roslyn Nursery, 211 Burrs Lane, Dix Hills, NY 11746.
- Fine list of azaleas and rhodo species and hybrids; kalmia, pieris, and other flowering shrubs; dwarf conifers. Catalogue $2.00.

Sonoma Horticultural Nursery, 3970 Azalea Avenue, Sebastopol, CA 95472.
- Many species and hybrid rhodos, vireyas, azaleas, and companion plants. Catalogue $1.50.

Stubbs Shrubs, 23225 S.W. Bosky Dell Lane, West Linn, OR 97068.
- Many azaleas. Catalogue $2.00.

Transplant Nurseries, Parkertown Road, Lavonia, GA 30553.
- Azaleas and rhodos.

Trillium Lane Nursery, 18855 Trillium Lane, Fort Bragg, CA 95437.
- Many rhodos.

Vireya Specialties Nursery, 2701 Malcolm Avenue, Los Angeles, CA 90064.
- Vireya rhodos.

Westgate Gardens Nursery, 751 Westgate Drive, Eureka, CA 95501.
- Many rhodo species and hybrids.

Whitney Gardens, PO Box F, Brinnon, WA 98320.
- Azaleas and rhodos. Catalogue $1.00.

Azalea Society of America

PO Box 6244
Silver Spring, MD 20906

- *Nonprofit organization dedicated to azalea culture, with many local chapters.*
- *29-page quarterly* The Azalean, *annual membership $15.00.*

Local chapters take care of education, plant sales, and the like. The national group puts out the magazine, which is far less clubby than one might expect. A recent issue, for example, had a sensible article on flower arranging with azaleas, starting from the principle that most of us really use, regardless of what the books tell us: remember what patterns you like in the garden, and abstract them for the arrangement. The quarterly also culls articles from professional journals, like Henry T. Skinner's account of his travels in search of native azaleas. "Much as one would have liked to linger in this intriguing collecting area," writes Skinner, "the azaleas of the north were now calling much too loudly." He goes to quiet them, and we go along. The magazine accepts advertising, so it is a good place to discover the more and less common sources of these plants.

Bear Creek Nursery

PO Box 411
Northport, WA 99157

- *Seedlings and plants for antique apple varieties and other fruit and nut trees and shrubs.*
- *30-page catalogue, free.*

In spite of the fact that the proprietors refer to their customers as "tree friends," Bear Creek produces an outstanding catalogue, especially of apples. As dedicated as the firm is to old-fashioned varieties, its choices by no means cling to this tendency. Variety introductions as recent as 1983 appear among a group of more than 70 different apples drawn from American, European, Japanese, and even Russian sources. Most of the varieties loved by antique apple enthusiasts

BOYSENBERRIES

are here—including Red Astrachan, Maiden's Blush, Spitzenburg, and Wolf River—along with real rarities like New York's Primate and Red Hook and a blushing porcelain-skinned Russian called Lubsk Queen. The plum and pear lists are more predictable, but the latter is very representative, including even the Japanese pear-apple Nijiseiki. Selections for nut trees of all sorts, as well as for fruiting and nutting ornamental shrubs, are worth a look, particularly

if you want landscape trees that will also feed you or your friends. Bear Creek is a source for the hybrid chestnut—a cross between American and Manchurian strains—that is supposed to preserve the habit of the American elm while resisting blight.

The Book of Edible Nuts

by Frederic Rosengarten, Jr.
Walker & Co.

- *384 pages, many illustrations, $35.00.*

Here is a natural history and archeology of nuts. Rosengarten will not tell you how to grow them, but he does describe almost everything else about them, including recipes for their use. The 12 major nuts grown in this country each get a chapter; 30 more nuts follow, including things that are not strictly nuts—like kolas, lichees, and chufas—chosen for their interest as economic plants. It's a very readable set of capsule histories. The pictures alone are fascinating: on one page, you may find an Attic almond-shaped vase, on another a machine that shakes pecans from the trees!

Bovees Nursery

1737 S.W. Coronado Street
Portland, OR 97219

- *Plants for azaleas and rhododendrons, plus a few trees and shrubs, dwarf shrubs, dwarf conifers, and alpines.*
- *48-page catalogue, plus periodic price lists, $2.00.*

The Bovees have been turning out one of the best azalea and rhododendron lists in the business since 1952. For species rhododendrons, the catalogue reads like a manual, offering a thorough overview of the type. Unlike a manual, however, it offers

the species for sale. There are also good groups of both small- and large-leaved hybrid rhododendrons, plus vireya species and hybrids and a few tender Maddennii species. The deciduous azaleas list has not only a brief selection of Knapp Hill, Ghent, and Exbury hybrids, but a nice group of native species and the Smith-Mossman selections of *R. occidentale*. There's also a decent list of evergreen azaleas, both species and North Tisbury and Robinhill hybrids. If you're not tired after all that, you can play with the little lists of unusual trees, shrubs, vines, and alpines. Have fun.

Brussel's Bonsai Nursery

8365 Center Hill Road
Olive Branch, MS 38654

- *Starter plants, specimen bonsai, and tools and supplies.*
- *12-page catalogue, more than 50 illustrations, free.*

The selection of species for starter plants is serviceable, as is the list of pots and tools. Most of the illustrations are fairly good black-and-white shots of the imported specimen bonsai, ranging in price from around $60 to more than $1,000.

Burnt Ridge Nursery

432 Burnt Ridge Road
Onalaska, WA 98570

- *Plants for unusual fruit and nut trees, shrubs, and vines.*
- *2-page list, free.*

A good group of fig trees figures among the more ordinary offerings. There are also things like chinquapin, piñon pine, monkey-puzzle tree, akebia vines, silver vines, pineapple guavas, kiwis, and loquats.

California Nursery Company

Niles District
Box 2278
Fremont, CA 94536

- *Plant material for fruit and nut trees, two sequoias, bamboo, and grapevines.*
- *8-page list, free.*

Here is a good selection of the usual suspects among fruit trees, including a nice group of figs. Less common are the avocados, kiwis, an olive, and a number of dwarf citrus trees. The grape selection includes the major wine varieties. Balled and burlapped 1-gallon sizes of giant sequoia and coast redwood are also available. No descriptions appear in the catalogue, as it is meant chiefly for commercial growers.

California Rare Fruit Growers

Fullerton Arboretum
California State University
Fullerton, CA 92634

- *Nonprofit organization dedicated to the culture of fruits many people have never even heard of.*
- *32-page quarterly newsletter, 92-page yearbook, annual membership $10.00.*

Cherimoyas, pawpaws, and kiwis are among the more common things these people like to grow. They do very good research as well in search of such stuff as antique apples, and late, low-chill peaches. Still, they venture far afield, to the Hottentot fig, the Yellow Mombin, biriba, the toad tree, and the Pili nut. There is no end to the kinds of fruits and nuts they are interested in, as a perusal of the yearbook will demonstrate. As the group is meant for amateurs, the articles tend to be lively and informative. Ten dollars is not a lot to pay for a year's information—plus the seed and plant exchanges the group sponsors—so I think any moderately serious fruit enthusiast ought to look into CRFG, though much of what they like can be grown outdoors only in California or the Deep South.

Camellia Forest Nursery

125 Carolina Forest
Chapel Hill, NC 27514

- *Plants for camellias, azaleas, and unusual varieties of other trees and shrubs.*
- *12-page list, free.*

This nursery was founded to sell the owners' camellia selections. Their plans to expand further were thwarted by the winter freezes of 1984 and 1985, but they have been doing in-habitat collecting of some unusual ornamentals in China and Japan. The propagated plants are starting to become available, so if you live in a milder climate, you might do well to send for the unusual list.

Carlson's Gardens

Box 305
South Salem, NY 10590

- *Plants for azaleas, rhododendrons, mountain laurel, and lilac.*
- *38-page catalogue, $2.00; selected color pictures available at $.50 each.*

Carlson's claims to have the largest selection of hardy azaleas and rhododendrons available by mail. The list is big in almost every category. Among the azaleas, there are natives, many Knapp Hill–Exbury hybrids, Ghents and Molles, New Zealandish Elams, Royals, Kurumes, Schepens, Linwoods, Robin Hills, Gables and Kaempferis, Glenn Dales and Great Lakes; there are even a number of dwarf and late-blooming varieties with possibilities for the rock garden, together with a large selection of the North Tisbury evergreen azaleas that are useful as ground covers. As for the rhododendrons, there are Shammarellos, Leaches, Gables, a number of small-leaved varieties, plus the hard-to-find Dexters. The plants are well described, and the catalogue includes a good section of cultural instructions; color photos of some varieties can be had by sending 50 cents for each. If you live in the North or East and are nuts—or are considering becoming nuts—about the rhodos tribe, this catalogue is a must. The firm is well set up to handle first-time orders; it encourages phone calls and will help you choose varieties from the huge list. A handy calendar showing the sequence of azalea bloom comes with the catalogue. The list of mountain laurels is 10 varieties long and growing; only 2 varieties of lilacs appear in the catalogue, but these are container-grown and should be simple to get started.

Carroll Gardens

See "Annuals and Perennials."

Cascade Forestry Service

RR 1
Cascade, IA 52033

- *Plant material for lumber, shade and nut trees, and shrubs; tools.*
- *12-page flyer, 5 illustrations, free.*

If you live nearby and want to choose from a good selection of large-size shade trees and ornamental shrubs, you should check out Cascade. Otherwise, the gardener will have less use for this company than the farmer does. Its main business is the sale of trees for timber, nuts, and windbreaks, and it has a fine selection for these purposes. Brief as it is, the list is a little anthology of the economic uses of trees, featuring the best hard-woods for veneers, the best firewood trees for difficult sites, the best nut producers, and the best Christmas trees. The firm also is among those that sell a dandy tool called the Ost Planting Bar, complete with instructions that almost make it look like fun to plant a whole windbreak.

Converse Nursery

Amherst, NH 03031

- *Plant material for 200 varieties of apples.*
- *1-page list, free.*

Converse has a remarkable list of apples old and new, all of them offered on a semidwarf rootstock. This is perhaps the largest selection of apples offered anywhere, but you should be aware that not all of the list is available every year. In 1986, a good half of it was not. Know what you are looking for when you come to Converse, since the list is unadorned with description.

Cumberland Valley Nurseries

Route 1
Shaffee Lane
PO Box 471
McMinnville, TN 37110

- *Plants for peach, plum, nectarine, cherry, apricot, apple, and pecan trees.*
- *6-page flyer, free.*

Here's a list of 96 peach varieties—including one with red flesh—plus smaller groups for the other trees. You must know what you are buying to shop here. The varieties are well described for sequence of ripening, freeness of stone, and abundance of bud; there is no information on hardiness or chill requirements. You must also want to plant a lot, since the minimum purchase of $25 amounts to a dozen small trees or 7 or more large ones.

Designing and Maintaining Your Edible Landscape Naturally

See "Landscape Architecture and Design."

Dilatush Nursery

780 Route 130
Robbinsville, NJ 08691

- *Plants for dwarf conifers.*
- *6-page catalogue, free.*

This is a specialist nursery that does no mail order, but it is so good at what it does that it ought to be included here. The list of the more often-used dwarf conifers—Hinoki cypress, juniper, and spruce—is quite good, though you could also go to White Flower Farm (see page 80) for most of it. The selection of dwarf pines is really remarkable, embracing dwarf varieties of at least 15 species. The nursery is currently working on the development of high-grafted forms for landscape use; its principals also offer garden-design services using dwarf conifers. If you have caught this bug, these are people you should be in touch with.

Earl Douglass

RD 1
Box 38
Red Creek, NY 13143

- *Nuts and seedlings for hybrid chestnut trees.*
- *3-page flyer, 1-page price list, $.25.*

Douglass missed the American chestnut he knew from his childhood. Having secured his own grove of blight-resistant Manchurian chestnuts, he added a dozen American chestnuts, children of a tree that had

survived the blight. The result was a natural cross of the two, providing tasty nuts, an American chestnutlike habit, and some disease resistance. As Douglass freely admits in his charming brochure, the trees are variable in character and some will develop blight canker. However, he has a neat method he claims to use to treat the cankers successfully, and he seems very willing to discuss with correspondents any and all ways for bringing back the American chestnut.

> Theirs is a long and complicated story, a story just now beginning to be unraveled but about which we already know enough to state, without fear of successful contradiction, that the history of weeds is the history of man.
>
> —EDGAR ANDERSON, FROM *PLANTS, MAN & LIFE* (1967)

Dutch Mountain Nursery

7984 N. 48th Street
Augusta, MI 49012

- *Plants for trees and shrubs attractive to birds and wildlife.*
- *4-page flyer, free.*

The nursery's professed interest is in plants that attract wildlife, but there are a number of fine, uncommon ornamentals in its simple list. The dogwoods and viburnums are very well represented. Among the nicer unusual species included are striped maple (*Acer pennsylvanicum*), flowering ash (*Fraxinus ornus*), Osage orange (*Maclura pomifera*), trifoliate orange (*Poncirus trifoliata*), and wafer ash (*Ptelea trifoliata*). If you are looking for something in particular, this is a good place to look, even if you are not an ornithologist.

Eccles Nurseries

PO Drawer Y
Rimersburg, PA 16248

- *Seedlings for conifers.*
- *20-page price list, 14 illustrations, free.*

A fine source if you are starting a Christmas-tree farm, Eccles also offers a few small lots for the home gardener. A feature called the "Backyard Special" offers 75 seedlings—which calls for quite a backyard—but Colorado blue spruce, Austrian pine, and Japanese black pine are offered in smaller quantities. There is also a selection of 3 pines for the woodlot.

Ecological Fruit Production in the North

by Bart Hall-Beyer and Jean Richard
Bart Hall-Beyer
RR 3
Scottstown, Quebec
CANADA J0B 3B0

- *270 pages, some illustrations, $11.50.*

A very fine introduction to fruit growing for those who live in northerly climates or at high altitudes, written by two very experienced fruit growers who are by no means sanguine about the hardiness of trees. If you are tired of losing trees that were suggested as "fairly" hardy for your area, this is a good place to learn what really works.

Edible Landscaping

Route 2, Box 343A
Afton, VA 22920

- *Plants of fruiting vines and trees.*
- *12-page catalogue, a few illustrations, free.*

A most unusual list of fruit plants, offering a dozen varieties of cold-hardy kiwis, half a dozen of gooseberries, 15 of figs, and even a pawpaw. Other berries appear, including blackberries, mulberries, and currants. I suppose the fact that some of these are trees and shrubs—two rugosa roses are offered, along with an edible dogwood, not to mention the pawpaws and mulberries—while others are vines, qualifies this as a catalogue for edible landscaping, but the good cultural instructions are directed at producing fruit, not at garden design.

PAW PAW

Eisler Nurseries

PO Box 465
Prospect, PA 16052

- *Plant material for ornamental trees and shrubs, vines, and ground covers.*
- *57-page catalogue, free.*

I ought to leave Eisler out, since it does not ship and since, if you don't live near Pittsburgh, you will not find it easy to visit it yourself. On the other hand, these guys have provided landscape material to the United Nations, the White House, and the Missouri Botanical Garden, among many other public projects and estates, and they have one of the best selections of landscape-sized trees and shrubs in North America. The choice of sizes for each type is really astonishing. You can get a maple up to 12-inch caliper here! Many of the varieties are not uncommon, but flipping through the catalogue, you come on the rare Pink Spires clethra and the Yeddo euonymus, both striking and unusual. If you are doing a large landscape project in the East or Midwest, it may be worth seeing if your landscape architect can get Eisler's plants trucked to you.

Endangered Species

PO Box 1830
Tustin, CA 92680

- *Plants for bamboo, palms, cycads, succulents, grasses, and trees and shrubs; books; fine pots.*
- *55-page catalogue, approx. 35 illustrations, $5.00.*

This is a strange, often funny, and very comprehensive catalogue of generally costly plants, especially bamboos and palms, both of which are divided according to size and to relative hardiness (though "hardy" palms and bamboo may be so only to, say, 0° or 10° F). For those with the climate or the greenhouse, however, the list is astonishingly varied, with dozens of choices in each size range, ranging from low-growing things that, in the case of bamboo, could be used for ground covers, to huge plants topping 80 feet in height. Each section is prefaced with a Q&A-format introduction that should help the beginner tell what will do best where. The descriptive text for each species is usually good, and it is exceptionally frank. When the proprietor knows nothing about a plant, he says so, and on occasion he will even instruct you not to buy the plant! (Honest or not, it's an entertaining rhetorical trick.)

Fedco Trees

Box 340
Palermo, ME 04354

- *Plants for fruit and nut trees and shrubs.*
- *6-page price list, free; catalogue, $.50.*

The minimum order is $50, which is at least 5 apple trees, or rather more of the other fruit and nut trees and shrubs offered. The apple list is good, including a few old Maine apples, plus popular heirlooms like Red Astrachan and Roxbury Russet. The selection of nuts and small fruits is geared for Far Northern gardens.

Fowler Nurseries

525 Fowler Road
Newcastle, CA 95658

- Bare-root plants for fruit and nut trees, berries, grapes, and perennial vegetables.
- Price list, free; 60-page catalogue, $2.00.

This 75-year-old California company serves mainly the commercial orchard trade, but it offers an attractive retail catalogue, with excellent, modern fruit selections for the home orchard. The firm began with pears, and its list is still very strong in them. Particularly interesting are the 8 strains of Asian pear-apples and the 6 varieties of red pears. Late in her life, a daughter of the California-Mexican grandee Mariano Vallejo wrote with longing of the pear orchards of her childhood, where different varieties ripened all season long. Fowler will not give you the same varieties, but its list of pears could well give you the same long season of pear crops. The catalogue also has very good selections of almonds and prunes.

Foxborough Nursery

3611 Miller Road
Street, MD 21154

- Plant material for trees, shrubs, and dwarf and unusual conifers.
- 12-page catalogue, $1.00.

Foxborough will probably not be your first-choice nursery, simply because it sells mainly wholesale. Also, the list consists of nothing but names, so you must know what you are looking for. For a number of genera, however, their stock is quite various and worth the trouble if you want a very special plant. The conifer list is strong everywhere, but especially in named cultivars of false-cypress, spruce, pine, and hemlock. There are also good choices among the named hybrids for flowering shrubs like witch hazel, pieris, and kalmia.

Tilling the soil consists, on the one hand, in various diggings, hoeings, turnings, buryings, loosenings, pattings, and smoothings, and on the other in ingredients. No pudding could be more complicated than the preparation of a garden soil; as far as I have been able to find out, dung, manure, guano, leafmould, sods, humus, sand, straw, lime, kainit, Thomas's powder, baby's powder, saltpetre, horn, phosphates, droppings, cow dung, ashes, peat, compost, water, beer, knocked-out pipes, burnt matches, dead cats, and many other substances are added. All this is continually mixed, stirred in, and flavoured. . .

—KAREL CAPEK, FROM *THE GARDENER'S YEAR* (1929)

Friends of the Trees Society

PO Box 1466
Chelan, WA 98816

- Organization running a perennial seed exchange, publishing a newsletter and yearbook, and promoting tree planting.
- 80-page yearbook, $4.00; variable-length Actinidia Enthusiasts Newsletter, $3.00 per issue.

The yearbook is the thing, unless you want to know all about the Actinidia, or hardy kiwis. The yearbook is what happens when one man, Michael Pilarski, tries to put together an agroecological, permacultural, reforestational, Gaiaistic, and voluntary-povertistic sourcebook with a seed exchange to boot. It is both charming and valuable, with only an occasional embarrassing moment. Information and resources for obtaining and propagating tree seed is fine, as are the endless lists of books, pamphlets, magazines, and organizations having to do with all kinds of sustainable agriculture, horticulture, and forestry. There are a number of gaps in the coverage, but Pilarski's enthusiastic essays plus the resources he provides will lead you in the right direction. His essay on hoedading—working as a high-speed tree planter—is a real gem, though it has little to do with the rest of the book. He has also thrown in a little speculative fiction about a young man who goes to sleep and wakes up in Washington state in the 21st century. What is most poignant about the story is that the utopia our hero finds resembles nothing so much as the old visions of the Garden City movement. Come to think of it, however, if the Garden City ever does work, it will work in the Pacific Northwest.

The Fruition Project

PO Box 872
Santa Cruz, CA 95061

- Nonprofit organization dedicated to disseminating fruit and nut trees to people who will plant them in public.
- Biannual 8-page newsletter, $10.00.

The newsletter may not be worth $10.00, but it goes to fund a worthwhile idea. The project gives away fruit and nut trees in the Santa Cruz area, and it has stimulated the creation of Massachusetts's statewide fruition program. Newsletter articles keep you informed on the growth of the movement. The promotional letter begins, "You and I both want to see the Garden of Eden replanted." Even if you don't, this seems a good group to foster.

Garden of Delights

See "Houseplants and Exotics."

Girard Nurseries

Box 428
Geneva, OH 44041

- *Plant material for trees and shrubs, especially azaleas, rhododendrons, and conifers; bonsai plants; plus a few nut trees.*
- *20-page catalogue, more than 50 color illustrations, free.*

Girard's is well known for its azaleas and rhododendrons, and for its interesting cultivars and selections of other shrubs and trees. For all this, however, the catalogue doesn't try to daunt you with an immense list, so this is an excellent place to go if you are making your first venture beyond the garden-center realm of trees and shrubs. The text and photographs are for the most part clear, and the distinctive features of the selections are well described. There are very choice lists of both native and hybrid azaleas and rhododendrons, and of dwarf conifers, along with a section devoted to bonsai plants especially for the beginner. Other trees and shrubs are also well chosen, including Girard introductions such as a rainbow-foliaged leucothoe and deep gold juniper, and selected forms like weeping versions of ginkgo and mountain ash.

Golden Bough Tree Farm

Marlbank, Ontario
CANADA K0K 2LO

- *Plants for fruits, nut, and ornamental trees and shrubs.*
- *22-page catalogue, 23 illustrations, $1.00*

This is a good, basic tree and shrub list for the Canadian gardener; American orders are discouraged. All varieties have been carefully chosen for Northern hardiness, and very good zone charts for all regions of Canada are featured. There are particularly nice choices among the oaks and lin-

dens, including the very hardy burr oak, two English oaks, and the silver linden. Among the nut trees are the cold-adapted shagbark hickory and Manchurian walnut. Hardy peaches, apricots, pears, cherries, and many plums appear. New and old apples and crab apples are well represented, and there is a selective list of evergreens for landscape and foundation planting, and for bonsai. The writing in the catalogue is intelligent and opinionated.

Gossler Farms Nursery

1200 Weaver Road
Springfield, OR 97478

- *Plant material for magnolias and other ornamental trees, shrubs, and vines.*
- *20-page catalogue, 8 color illustrations, $1.00.*

Gossler Farms is in a class with Wayside Gardens, Greer Gardens, or Louisiana Nursery. Its list is smaller than the other firms', but it is comparably choice, possibly even more so. The proprietors reveal feeling for the magnolia that is nothing short of adoring, to wit: "But the forces of hybridization, nuclear radiation, meristematic propagation have unleased [sic] a cornucopia of improved plants unimagined by the Creator in the original genesis—Adam, Eve, apples, snakes, magnolias, etc." Their enthusiasm has led the Gosslers to seek the finest magnolia cultivars available, from England to San Jose. There are dozens of magnolias on the list. Even where the species is quite common—as are *M. soulangiana* or *M. stellata*—Gossler offers a number of rare named cultivars for it. Among the other shrubs and trees appear species that few people know of, together with unusual cultivars of more common genera. Gossler is among the best places in the country to find the following: decorative-barked maples; the beautyberries (*Callicarpa*);

the uncommon and graceful *Corylopsis*, spring-flowering alternatives to forsythia; a number of daphnes; fully 5 varieties of *Eucryphia*, a lovely genus grown mainly in the West; lots of witch hazel; lots and lots of stewartia and snowbells (*Styrax*); and a deep-red-flowering pieris. These aren't just rarities; they are highly ornamental plants that are not too often found in the trade. There is also quite a good list of the new showy kalmia cultivars. The catalogue requires considerable study—since the Gosslers refuse to include information on zone hardiness and ultimate size and since there are no pictures or common names to remind you just what this stuff is—but your work will be amply repaid. This is one of the finest tree and shrub lists in North America.

Greenmantle Nursery

3010 Ettersburg Road
Garberville, CA 95440

- *Plant material for antique and other selected varieties of apples, pears, plums, peaches, cherries, chestnut trees, and black locust trees; shrub, species, and old-fashioned roses.*
- *30-page catalogue, approx. 30 illustrations, $3.00.*

Greenmantle was founded to serve northern California homesteaders, and the cultural information is directed to helping them. There is much other information, however, useful to the rest of us, not least of which is the motto "Put your ego in your compost heap." You might not expect a company that lists its more than 50 antique apple varieties by the sign of the zodiac in which each ripens to have much of interest to say about the botanical and culinary qualities of the apple. Strangely enough, though, the catalogue has about the best fruit variety descriptions I have seen anywhere for the old-time varieties, and it has done an unusually thorough job of searching out less common antique fruits and nuts in the farms and homesteads of its local area. Fruit growers around the country should be interested in the list, not just for its information but as a source of varieties for their own areas. As the proprietors point out, Humboldt County has an unusual California climate, suitable for the cultivation of fruits that generally do well in both the Northeast and the South. The area is also fortunate to have been the home of Albert Etter and his brothers, a group of once-noted hybridizers who worked there early in the century. Albert Etter said of his home, "The climate of Ettersburg is just like heaven, only we have to work." Etter's strawberries, long lost to all but a few local people, are being resurrected by Greenmantle, which also offers a number of unusual chestnut hybrids that Etter was working with in the 1920s. The essay on Etter and the reflections on rootstocks are in themselves worth the price of the catalogue. Though Greenmantle offers newer, disease-resistant varieties of many fruits, it has gone out of its way to come up with some old-timers among pears, plums, peaches, and cherries—types of fruit for which old varieties are generally less available. For a review of the firm's rose list, see page 159.

Greer Gardens

1280 Goodpasture Island Road
Eugene, OR 97401

- *Plant material for rhododendrons, azaleas, trees and shrubs, ornamental maple cultivars, and bonsai; books.*
- *82-page catalogue, approx. 116 color illustrations, $2.00.*

Greer Gardens began as a hobbyist's collection, and the list shows the marks of an avid collector: it is very large, very enthusiastic, and tries to be very accurate. The result is a catalogue that is a good deal more useful than it is fun to read. There is little new or exciting material from the world of rhododendrons that does not appear here, though after reading through the list of hundreds of cultivars—each apparently more luscious and indispensable than the last—I had a case of mental indigestion. It was a relief to come to the large list of species rhododendrons, including the lovely, bell-flowered *R. williamsianum.* Rhododendrons really are spectacular plants; you will find here one of the best available lists of them. Still, they are also a good example of the tendency in the horticultural world to breed a plant to death in search of variations on a few characteristics. The species rhododendrons, on the other hand, really do look different, and I am glad that Greer is paying attention to them as well. The purple prose aside, the catalogue text is very well done for size, parentage of hybrids, and hardiness. Nice, shorter lists of vireyas and evergreen and deciduous azaleas also appear.

BONSAI PRUNING KNIFE

That would be enough for most catalogues, but the Greers go on. There are very extensive lists of maple cultivars and conifers, with a whole special selection devoted to trees and shrubs suitable for bonsai. The general list of ornamental trees and shrubs—with edible kiwi fruit and Japanese pear-apples thrown in for good measure—is quite choice, comparable to the fine group at Gossler Farms. Many unusual birches, heathers, and dogwoods can be found here, along with callicarpa, eucryphia, pieris, stewartia, styrax, and vibur-

num. Greer is another source for the new, floriferous kalmia cultivars. To top it off, the firm offers a very broad book list, particularly for rhododendrons, azaleas, and bonsai. Among them are two books by the proprietor, Harold Greer: *Greer's Guidebook to Available Rhododendrons*, an even more complete guide to the field than the catalogue, and Salley and Greer's *Rhododendron Hybrids: A Guide to Their Origins.*

Grimo Nut Nursery

RR 3
Lakeshore Road
Niagara-on-the-Lake, Ontario
CANADA L0S 1J0

- *Seedling and grafted plants for nut trees.*
- *8-page list, $1.00.*

Ernest Grimo manages to get more useful information into 8 pages than many people can get in a whole catalogue. His list includes walnuts, butternuts, heartnuts, hybrid filberts, hickory, pecan, chestnuts (including American chestnut), and a few others. All are quite well described, both in text and in a handy chart that comments on nut size and flavor and other matters of import. The page of cultural instructions is excellent.

Grootendorst Nurseries

15310 Red Arrow Highway
Lakeside, MI 49116

- *Rootstocks, dwarfing rootstocks, and custom grafting service for a variety of fruit trees.*
- *8-page flyer, free.*

This is the same Grootendorst who runs the remarkable Southmeadow Fruit Gardens (see page 102). When not busy looking for fine fruit varieties, he sells rootstocks and does custom grafting.

Hall Creek Nursery

HCR 60
Box 195
Bonners Ferry, ID 83805

- *Plant material for nut trees.*
- *1-page list, free.*

The list is 5 items long—all cold-hardy nut trees: Chinese chestnut, European filbert, black walnut, Carpathian walnut, and heartnut. Hall Creek sells chiefly to major mail-order nurseries, but will sell to individuals too. It's a bit cheaper to order direct from this nursery, though you should note that, like a number of other wholesale suppliers, it does not offer any guarantee on its trees.

FUCSHIA

Harmony Farm Supply

PO Box 451
Graton, CA 95444

- *Dwarf and standard plants for fruit and nut trees; plants for berries; all kinds of supplies and tools (see page 188).*
- *38-page catalogue, approx. 20 relevant illustrations, $2.00*

California orchardists will get the most use out of Harmony's plant list and accompanying information. Included is a complete map of chill hours for northern California, plus illustrations showing very clearly how to plant and protect fruit and nut trees. The descriptive text is very good about evaluating varieties for reliability in the region, including helpful suggestions for marginal types. The proprietors seem to be Luther Burbank freaks, and they stock a couple of his plums, plus a Burbank peach and elephant garlic. Otherwise, the list is an amalgam of modern and heritage types. The apples

tend to be the old-fashioned kinds; among them appears an old California variety that Harmony calls Sierra Beauty, and there are the usual favorites of antique apple lovers. The citrus list includes kumquats, lime quats, mandarins, and blood oranges, though unfortunately none of these can be shipped. Minor fruits like pineapple guava, figs, kiwis, mulberries, and persimmons are also well covered. The pear list is very strong in Japanese pear apples. It's worth looking at the berries too, since, especially for strawberries, the firm lists a good choice of the varieties specifically created for the Far West.

Heard Gardens

5355 Merle Hay Road
Johnston, IA 50131

- *Plants for lilacs, and unusual trees and shrubs.*
- *4-page list, free.*

The list doesn't look like much (though it should look nicer in coming years). Don't let it fool you, though. Proprietor Bill Heard has a collection of more than 200 varieties of lilacs, including French, Carpathian, Yugoslavian, Russian, Canadian, and Dutch hybrids. The collection was started by his father more than 50 years ago. If you are looking for a particular lilac, Heard is the man to ask. Nevertheless, lilacs are really a sideline for him. As a landscape architect, he has worked on public projects in 20 states, including the National Arboretum and the White House. As a designer, he has imported and even developed some interesting landscape plants. He is a source of the European beech, and he developed a columnar sugar maple called "Greencolumn," for which he is the lone mail-order source. (George Ware at the Morton Arboretum thinks this cultivar will make a great street tree in the Midwest.)

Heaths & Heathers

PO Box 850
Elma, WA 98541

- *Plants for heaths and heathers.*
- *4-page list plus 1-page cultural sheet, free.*

Heather Acres has been in business as a wholesale nursery for more than a quarter-century; Heaths & Heathers is its retail list. It includes more than 100 choices of heath and heather varieties. If you are just starting to garden with these plants, you can order a 12-plant starter collection or a 10-plant selection for the rock garden. If you are already wild about the things, you can write the company about non-listed varieties you may be seeking, since it grows about 180 more than the retail list includes. The wholesale catalogue, offered for $1.00, contains most of these supplemental listings.

Hidden Springs Nursery

Route 14
Box 159
Cookeville, TN 38501

- *Rooted cuttings and plants for fuchsias.*
- *6-page flyer, free; booklet,* Fuchsias in the South, *$2.95.*
- *Seedlings and plants for edible, nitrogen-fixing, and timber-bearing trees and shrubs. (For herbs list, see page 134.)*
- *28-page catalogue, $.60; 5-page price list, free.*

It is hard enough to find a good fuchsia nursery, much less one that specializes in varieties for the South and East. The cuttings and plants are propagated from plants grown at the Tennessee nursery and acclimatized there. There are 54 varieties offered, including standards, bushes, and trailing plants. Descriptions and instructions are good, but, for those who want to get serious about growing fuchsias in these climates, the firm also offers a detailed and helpful cultural booklet.

Hidden Springs also offers an idiosyncratic list of well-described trees and shrubs. The theme is edible landscaping, and it manages to embrace everything from apples to Russian olive. The apples include antique and up-to-the-minute varieties, even the ancient Roxbury Russet. There is also a good selection of figs, kiwis, pears, and flowering quinces, together with a choice of pinyon or Korean stone pine for pine nuts. All kinds of berrying shrubs that today are seldom eaten by people are included, among which are two nitrogen-fixing pea shrubs. A red-foliaged *Rosa rugosa* and a fast-growing paulownia for timber are thrown in for good measure. It's worth a look.

Hillier Nurseries

Ampfield House
Ampfield, Romsey
Hants
ENGLAND S051 9PA

- *Plants for trees, shrubs, vines, roses, and a few hardy perennials; books.*
- *100-page catalogue, 68 color illustrations, $1.00.*

Hillier is a very important source of ornamental trees and shrubs. The breadth of its catalogue—numbering more than 5,000 varieties—is astonishing, as are the introductions they have made over the years. The rose list alone will be delightful to shrub-rose enthusiasts, but everywhere the firm's offerings are deep and strong. If you are serious *and* picky, you will certainly want to consult the catalogue. Hillier has considerable experience shipping its plants overseas, for a price. You might also use the color section as a source of inspiration for things you may be able to find in the U.S. The firm also produces 2 well-respected manuals of trees and shrubs. One is a pocket book listing and describing about 3,500 varieties, with 600 color illustrations and tables for helping you choose the ones you want. The other is a full-fledged manual of 8,000 varieties with lots of cultural information. The first runs about $9.00 paperback, the second about $10.25, but you should write Hillier's for exact details.

Hortica Gardens

PO Box 308
Placerville, CA 95667

- *Plants and seeds for bonsai specimens; bonsai tools; books, some imported from Japan.*
- *14-page catalogue, $1.00; 1-page seed list, free; 1-page tool list, free.*

This small company has a good reputation among bonsai specialists and beginners. Though many of the varieties listed are useful for the garden or as indoor plants, most are adapted to bonsai and miniature landscaping. The list is a nicely selected one—not too intimidating to the beginner nor too limited for the specialist—and several collections designed strictly for beginners are offered. The tools list is very comprehensive, but the proprietors have helpfully singled out those tools indispensable for the beginner. This is a very simply but thoughtfully put-together catalogue.

Hortico

723 Robson Road
RR 1
Waterdown, Ontario
CANADA L0R 2H0

- *Plants for shrubs, trees, vines, and fruiting vines.*
- *33-page catalogue, free.*

Shop here if you know what you're looking for. It's mainly a wholesale business—liners and cuttings are available in minimum quantities of 10—but plants are available at retail. The selection is good and strong, particularly for shrubs. Many are named varieties.

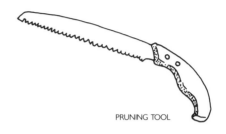

PRUNING TOOL

Howlett's Coastal Zone Nursery

31427 W. Pacific Coast Highway
Malibu, CA 90265

- *Plants for chiefly exotic trees and shrubs, suitable for cultivation in zones 9 and 10.*
- *23-page catalogue, free.*

Howlett's does not do mail order and, for that matter, sells strictly wholesale, so why include it? The reason is its extremely wide selection of landscape-size trees and shrubs that will thrive along the southern coast of California. The exotic greenhouse plants of most of the U.S. will prosper outdoors in parts of California, and this firm has a very good list of plants from all around the Pacific Rim, with particular strength in Australian natives. There are palms, tree ferns, bottlebrushes, banyans, exotic evergreens, and so on. Just to keep things from looking too otherworldly, Howlett's also stocks a good group of the natives and naturalized exotics that form the backbone of many California landscapes: pepper trees, coast redwoods, Monterey cypress, California sycamore, toyon, Catalina ironwood, and olive trees. The wholesale prices listed are fairly high, but if you are looking for very particular specimen trees and shrubs, the catalogue is worth checking. Your garden center can order for you.

How to Identify Rhododendron & Azalea Problems

Washington Cooperative Extension
Publication EB-1229
Washington State University
Pullman, WA 99164

- *25 pages, many color illustrations, $3.50.*

Three cheers for the cooperative extension services, once again. Here is a nicely illustrated guide to just about anything that might happen to your rhododendrons or azaleas, whether resulting from nasty beasties or from cultural deficiencies. A lot of the solutions involve pesticides, but who's complaining? It's seldom you find such a compact and useful little volume.

> I have often been astonished at our indifference to the memory of those preceding us who have introduced useful [plants] into our country, the fruits and [beauty] of which we enjoy today. The names of these benefactors are chiefly unknown, yet their benefits continue from generation to generation. . . .
>
> —JACQUES HENRI BERNARDIN DE SAINT-PIERRE FROM *ÉTUDES DE LA NATURE XIII* (1789)

Hughes Nursery

1305 Wynooche W.
Montesano, WA 98563

- *Plants for Japanese maples.*
- *10-page list, $1.00.*

Here is a good, broad list of Japanese maples for landscape and bonsai. Trees are high- or low-grafted, according to intended use. The proprietors have very usefully organized the list by habit of plant and color of leaves, making the usually overwhelming list of *A. palmatum* and *A. japonicum* cultivars seem much less forbidding. Descriptions of individual plants are brief but revealing. Best of all, they have tried to find translations for Japanese cultivar names, so you will know that those hard-to- pronounce names mean things like "village on a mountain," "flock of skylarks," and "seven red apparitions."

The Hundred Finest Trees and Shrubs for Temperate Climates

Plants & Gardens, volume 13,
number 3
Brooklyn Botanic Garden
1000 Washington Avenue
Brooklyn, NY 11225

- *80-page handbook, many black-and-white illustrations, $2.25.*

This is the handiest introduction to garden trees and shrubs that I know. Experts may carp that certain species have been unfairly excluded. Well, let them use Michael Dirr's book (see page 97) instead. For the rest of us, the BBG booklet is unintimidating and very valuable. Information is geared to gardeners'—not botanists'—needs, and the illustrations generally show the plant's strongest points, its habit, flowers, or foliage. The choice of flowering trees and shrubs is particularly good. Leaving pretty much aside the well-known and much-hybridized genera like roses and rhododendrons, it focuses on the specimen and accent plants that most of us need to know better. Gardeners in California and Florida should note that subtropicals and tropicals have been excluded, but most of the plants included are valuable for their gardens as well.

International Bonsai Arboretum

412 Pinnacle Road
Rochester, NY 14623

- *Nonprofit organization dedicated to bonsai.*
- *40-page quarterly* International Bonsai, *many illustrations, some in color; mail-order books, many from Japan; tools and pots; instruction; annual subscription $20.00.*

You can't visit the arboretum except by appointment, but the magazine is wonderful, the kind of thing a bonsai fetishist will slaver over. Each issue contains a chapter in the continuing series of illustrated pruning guides for a variety of different plants. The illustrations are captioned with both challenging and encouraging instructions like "Pinch every branch" (pointing to a pine loaded with branches) and "Beautiful texture develops from warty bark." There are also copious examples—some schematic and some in color—of the work of masters, and many brief articles on display, design, and design aids. The arboretum's book list, featuring many untranslated volumes from Japan, is the place to look when you have finished with all the English-language bonsai books. You can even buy bonsai containers here. The pages devoted to advertising seem to list just about every major supplier of bonsai, plants, tools, and equipment.

International Forest Seed Co.

PO Box 290
Odenville, AL 35120

- *Seedlings of pines and hardwoods.*
- *No catalogue.*

Come all you hoedaders and other forest planters. This American branch of a Swedish company sells containerized—not bare-root—seedling for reforestation. If you want a few acres or more, these people are worth contacting.

International Oleander Society

PO Box 3431
Galveston, TX 77552

- *Nonprofit organization dedicated to oleander culture.*
- *2-page quarterly* The Nerium News; *free seed exchange; sale of cuttings; annual membership $5.00.*

One wouldn't think that oleanders, as lovely as they are, would inspire a whole society, but they have. Galveston is the "Oleander City," and interest appears to be centered there, but the society has members as far afield as the island of Diego Garcia in the Indian Ocean, whence one member wrote in a recent newsletter to say that he had succeeded in reestablishing the oleander there. Good for him.

Ison's Nursery

See "Vegetables and Herbs."

Johnson Nursery

Route 5
Box 29JR
Ellijay, GA 30540

- *Plant material for fruit and nut trees, roses, grapes, and berries; tools and supplies.*
- *19-page catalogue, approx. 80 color illustrations, $1.00.*

Johnson has quite a good choice of fruits—many selected for Southern climes, but some superhardy and hard-to-find varieties as well. There are some crazy peaches here, including Peento, a very sweet doughnut-shaped variety, and a number of pickling peaches. The list is very good for old and new, big and small, and early and late types. Hagen Sweet is a pickler that comes from a seedling found growing wild near the Johnsons' farm. Selections are also very well made for other stone fruits and apples. You can get Arkansas Black here, as well as a red-blushed green apple called Big Green. The pears include a couple of Asians, as well as the usual suspects and a local variety, and the berry list includes the Dorman-red raspberry, supposedly the best adapted to zones 7–10. While you're ordering, you might want to get your Corona long-handled or Felco hand-grip shears here. There are 5 choices among the Felco shears, one for left-handers.

V. Kraus Nurseries

Carlisle, Ontario
CANADA L0R 1H0

- *Plants for fruit and ornamental trees and shrubs; some berries and grapes; roses.*
- *13-page catalogue, free.*

The firm is bigger in wholesale than in retail. Even the retail catalogue is in the style of a wholesale one, listing nothing but names, sizes, and prices. Still, the selection is fairly wide in all classes. Hidden among the alphabetical lists are nice groups of lilacs, clematis, apples, plums, and a large number of roses. These last include the usual modern types, plus minis and a few old shrub roses.

Michael & Janet L. Kristick

155 Mockingbird Road
Wellsville, PA 17365

- *Plants for dwarf conifers and Japanese maples.*
- *12-page catalogue, free.*

This list reads like a poem: column after column of the variety names of conifers and the Japanese variety names of maples. That is all there is to the catalogue, so the buyer must know what to look for and then correspond with the Kristicks for further information. The selection is large. If you have caught the dwarf conifer or the bonsai bug, get to know the Kristicks.

VIBURNUM

Lake County Nursery

Route 84
Box 122
Perry, OH 44081

- *Wholesale nursery offering plant material for ornamental trees and shrubs, ornamental grasses, and perennials.*
- *96-page catalogue, free.*

An important wholesaler, especially for flowering crab apples, Lake County offers hundreds of choices in a variety of sizes, the smaller ones bare-root and the larger ones balled-and-burlapped. The firm has patented a number of new crab-apple varieties, along with smaller numbers of other trees and shrubs. The plant-patent laws seem to have given their breeders a push: 25 proprietary varieties are out, and hundreds more are being developed. You can't buy retail from Lake County, but you can get your garden center to order from it. Look especially at its lists of tall maples, barberries, quinces, dogwoods, ornamental grasses, junipers, crab apples, hybrid poplars, lilacs, and viburnums, if you're in the market for any of these. The catalogue is worth having regardless, since in addition to its list, it has unusually good charts on hedges, shrubs, trees, and ground covers.

Lakeshore Tree Farms

RR 3
Saskatoon, Saskatchewan
CANADA S7K 3J6

- *Plants for hardy ornamental and fruit trees, shrubs, and perennials; landscaping and tree-moving service.*
- *24-page catalogue, approx. 75 color illustrations, $1.00.*

The catalogue is not stuffed with unusual plants, but it contains among the best general lists imaginable for the Northern plains. A number of varieties come from local breeding and research stations, and all are selected not only for hardiness and attractiveness, but for the kind of things a plainsperson needs. The list of columnar willows for screening is very good; there are two currants, one quite unusual, for cold-climate hedges; and the selection of red- and yellow-twig dogwood is nice, providing winter interest. Good choices also appear among the peashrubs, spirea, shrub roses, and junipers. The fruit list does its best, and there are 4 uncommon flowering cherries. The perennials selections are basic. Heeling and planting instructions for trees and hedges are very clear, and the catalogue features grouped lists of the varieties valuable for a particular habit, foliage color, drought resistance, or shade tolerance.

Landscape Plants in Design

by E. C. Martin, Jr.
AVI Publishing Co.

- *496 pages, many illustrations, $55.95.*

The book styles itself "A Photographic Guide," and with more than 1,900 photographs of at least 650 varieties of trees, shrubs, vines, and ground covers, it lives up to its self-image. The author has visited many gardens in order to get pictures of the specimens doing what they do best in the landscape. When I first heard of this book, I thought I had at last come upon the perfect reference for selecting trees and shrubs for the garden. However, as good as the volume is for learning about the habit and texture of landscape plantings, the photographs are not of the best quality and too many of them show public landscape settings. Also, as the author and most of his pictures come from the South, the selection is weighted toward warmer-climate species. Nonetheless, gardeners around the country can make good use of the book, though probably at the library.

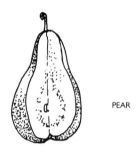

PEAR

Lawson's Nursery

Route 1
Box 294
Ball Ground, GA 30107

- *Plant material for fruit and nut trees.*
- *36-page catalogue, free.*

Bernice Lawson writes; "We have looked over the old mountain home and come up with some apples that were thought to be extinct. We now have over 230 different old-fashioned trees." In his introduction to the catalogue, her husband, James, says: "We are still a small mail-order nursery and don't have any plans to become big. . . . I personally graft or bud each tree we grow. . . . I dig each tree, usually the same day the tree is shipped out. . . . This is just a hobby that has gotten a little out of hand." The Lawsons have collected not only all the more popular antique apples, but a number of rare local varieties, like the Hog Sweet and the Limbertwig, as well. There are even a couple of old English cider apples. Variety descriptions are generally very good. The list of other fruits and nuts is smaller, but worth a look.

Living off the Land

See "Vegetables and Herbs."

Living Tree Centre

PO Box 797
Bolinas, CA 94924

- *Plants and scionwood for antique apples; seed for a few heirloom vegetables; books on biodynamics.*
- *50-page catalogue/handbook, $5.00.*

Take a deep breath before you start reading this one, and promise to keep an open mind. I nearly threw it away when in the introduction by Jesse Schwartz ("Ph.D., C.E., M.S., B.C.E., chief propagator") I read the following: "Heirloom apples are to a large extent humans' creations, being the result of the efforts of generations of horticulturalists labouring, for the most part, autonomously [*sic*]. So much are they the products of particular historical epochs that they have, in our opinion, become anthropomorphized. . . ." He goes on to describe one variety as "reminiscent of fine handmade 18th-century furniture," another as neighborly, a third as intellectual, and a fourth as aesthetically thrilling. It pays to put up with Jesse, however, since the list of antique apples he offers is a good one, rich in varieties that he has recovered from old California orchards. Surprisingly, the text describing the selected apple varieties is coherent and useful, and the section on planting and training apple trees is very good indeed. It isn't long, however, before Jesse lets loose again, in his essay on John Chapman, aka Johnny Appleseed. I agree Chapman is a much more odd and interesting figure than the usual legend tells, but the claim that "John Appleseed was a true American spiritual master" is a little more difficult to swallow. Schwartz also offers us an essay entitled "The Orgone Energy Accumulator Used to Enhance Plant Growth."

Louisiana Nursery

See "General Sources."

Manual of Woody Landscape Plants

by Michael A. Dirr
Third Edition
Stipes Publishing Company
1012 Chester Street
Champaign, IL 61820

■ *826-page book, numerous illustrations, $29.00.*

It is too bad that this book looks like a botanical tome, because it is about the most useful encyclopedia of garden trees and shrubs that you could wish. The pictures here are only of leaf and bud patterns, but, unlike almost all better-illustrated guides, the varieties included are specifically for the garden maker, not for the walker in the wilds. Descriptions of color, texture, bark, rate of growth, and general gardenworthiness are included with each entry, together with very useful notes on pests and diseases and on propagation. Coverage is better for the eastern half of the country, but by no means limited to it. Dirr can be opinionated and charming at the same time. He does not, for example, like camellias; he goes all out on their pests and diseases: "spot disease on the leaves, black mold on leaves and stems, leaf gall, leaf spot, flower blight, stem cankers, root rot, leaf

blight . . . Florida red scale, numerous other scales, mealy bugs, weevils, Fuller rose beetle, thrips, spotted cut worm, numerous other insects, rootnema . . . bud drop, chlorosis, oedema, sunburn, salt injury." If anyone would dare grow them after that, he remarks, ". . . a few plants are fine but a grove represents boredom." It should be said, however, that his bug lists are often extensive; don't let them scare you away, and if you are moderately serious about your woody ornamentals, don't let the heft and the price scare you away from the book.

Maplewood Seed Company

6219 S.W. Dawn Street
Lake Oswego, OR 97034

■ *Seeds of Japanese maple cultivars and maple species.*
■ *3-page flyer, free.*

More than 70 cultivars of *Acer palmatum* and about half that many other small maple species make up the whole list. That's plenty. If you don't already know your Japanese maples and you want to figure out what's going on here, it would be best to look at a copy of J. D. Vertrees's *Japanese Maples*. Maplewood thoughtfully provides Vertrees's address, should you wish to order an autographed copy.

Matsu–Momiji Nursery

PO Box 11414
Philadelphia, PA 19111

■ *First- and second-year grafts of Japanese maples, black pines, and spruce; bonsai plants; bonsai tools; accent plants.*
■ *13-page list, free.*

This is another good source for Japanese maples and pines. The *Acer palmatum* cultivars are helpfully divided

into subgroups, and each receives a line of comment about its special features. A very diverse selection of bonsai plants, some trained by the nursery and some in Japan, is available by mail. The Japanese bonsai are quite costly. This firm has bonsaied everything from azaleas to zelkova; the imported ones are elms, maples, and pines. There is a short list of unusual, mainly dwarf or low-growing perennials and shrubs as well.

PEACH TREE
If the kernels be bruised and boiled in vinegar, until they become thick, and applied to the head, it marvellously makes the hair to grow upon bald places or where it is too thin.
—FROM *CULPEPER'S COLOR HERBAL*

Maver Nursery

Route 2
Box 265B
Asheville, NC 28805

■ *Seed for trees and shrubs.*
■ *14-page list, $1.00.*

Maver deals mainly with professionals, but it sells in packet and ounce sizes for the little guy, too. There are well over 1,000 species listed here, but they appear by Latin name only, with no information about them. (A separate book with more descriptive information is available for $5.00.) All in all, this is a fine and wide-ranging list, but it is best left to people who know just what they are looking for, and who are confident about their ability to propagate what they get. Along with most species normally cultivated in the U.S., Maver lists 5 albizias, 7 yuccas, and the polynesian tapa-cloth tree! The firm also buys seed, so if you are cultivating anything unusual, you might give it a try.

May Nursery Company

PO Box 1312
Yakima, WA 98907

- *Nursery stock for a wide variety of fruit and nut trees.*
- *32-page catalogue, free.*

Since May serves mainly as a purveyor to the commercial orchardist, the varieties offered are the latest and the best for mass production. This doesn't mean they aren't tasty, but it does mean that emphasis is on uniform ripening and crack-resistant fruits, and, in general, on efficient varieties. There are piles of Red and Golden Delicious apple varieties, for example, but the tasty snow apple and the old Summer Rambo appear as well. The selections are all nicely described, especially with information on who will pollinate whom, perhaps the most useful bit of information a beginning orchardist can have. Minimum purchase is 10 trees.

J. E. Miller Nurseries

Canandaigua, NY 14424

- *Plant material for fruit and nut trees, ornamental trees and shrubs, berries, grapes, and a few perennial vegetables and flowering shrubs; tools and supplies.*
- *64-page catalogue, more than 230 illustrations, most in color, free.*

Through most of its range, this catalogue offers the usual suspects. All are grown along the Canadian border and are guaranteed hardy. The outstanding lists here are of apples, peaches, and grapes. Miller has been in the forefront of nurseries bringing back the older varieties of apples; its list is now as wide and varied as that of many specialty suppliers. Not that it ignores the moderns, all of which are offered in high-yielding dwarf forms called "comspur." They even have a nearly black apple, should you want one. The peach list is shorter,

but with some excellent hyperhardy choices. There are more grapes— early, middle, and late season, wine grapes, and seedless—than you can shake a stick at, including a black seedless. The ornamental trees and shrubs are disappointingly brief. A 32-page planting guide comes free with each order.

CONIFER

The Morton Arboretum

Lisle, IL 60532

- *Nonprofit arboretum for study and education regarding woody and herbaceous plants.*
- *48-page quarterly magazine, some black-and-white illustrations, annual subscription $6.00; 4-page Plant Information Bulletins, published irregularly and inserted in quarterly, or available separately at $.25 each. Annual membership $25.00, including free admission, discount on and preferential admission to garden courses, free subscription to publications.*

The Morton Arboretum offers courses on everything from wildflower identification and prairie gardening to landscaping and outdoor photography. As such, it is a valuable resource to people in the Chicago area. Many Midwesterners are also familiar with its important work in prairie restoration. Readers all over the country should be interested in its quarterly and Plant Information Bulletins. The magazine contains 3 or 4 articles per issue, most of an ecological bent and most about woody plants. They are written for popular audiences, often by senior members of Morton's scientific staff, such as dendrologist George Ware. A recent issue

excerpted Jean Giono's lovely profile of a tree planter, *The Man Who Planted Hope and Grew Happiness*, following it with an article by Ware about an oak-planting project in Illinois. Another issue had a general article on the energy economy of leaves and an appreciation of the possum and the persimmon, which is called possumwood in the South. The plant bulletins provide widely applicable aid in diagnosing and dealing with the diseases and pests that attack trees. You can get a complete list of available bulletins by writing the arboretum.

Musser Forests

PO Box 340
Route 119N.
Indiana, PA 15701

- *Seedlings and transplants for trees, shrubs, and ground covers; tools and supplies.*
- *40-page catalogue, approx. 182 color illustrations, free.*

If you are looking for landscape trees and hedges, Musser's catalogue will be most helpful. There are few uncommon varieties here, but the range of species and varieties is good. The best things are the pictures, which clearly show the habit of the plants and often demonstrate the way they are best used in the garden. Musser began as an evergreen nursery. Many years ago, it introduced Scotch pine as a Christmas tree, and today it operates a 10,000-acre Christmas-tree farm that ships nationwide. As you might expect, Musser has a very good selection of evergreen trees, some for Christmas trees but many for landscape, hedge, and ground cover as well.

Native Trees of the Intermountain Region

See "Wildflowers and Native Plants."

New York State Fruit Testing Cooperative Association

Geneva, NY 14456

- *Plant material for fruit trees and berries.*
- *Annual membership fee $5.00; 31-page catalogue, 2 color illustrations, free.*

The cooperative offers members the chance to grow and report on their success with a wide variety of fruit and berry plants, some well established in cultivation and some recent, experimental strains. The catalogue offers plant material for sale, operating much as a retail list does, but the selection is well worth looking at and the text is extremely informative. In fact, you can find out more about the commonly and uncommonly grown strains of fruit and berries here than you can in any retail catalogue. You may not need to be aware that the M9 dwarf rootstock is "unusually attractive to mice," but you may be edified to hear that the common Jonagold is a sterile triploid and is also cross—incompatible with Golden Delicious. This is a very good thing to know, since a miniorchard of the two varieties will not bear fruit, and since a planting that includes Jonagold may benefit from some extra pollinators in the mix. The association helpfully offers a selection of ornamental and crab apples that not only are fine choices for the edible landscape, but will help pollinate your orchard. All the major fruits are well represented, with especially good lists of apples both new and antique. This is not surprising, since the cooperative is associated with The New York State Agricultural Experiment Station at Geneva, among the nation's leading apple breeders since 1885. The excellent list of European plums is a little harder to explain, but it turns out that the station has been very active in plums as well. Mulberries and crab apples are more often grown as orna-

mentals than as edibles today, but the association has a fine old Russian fruiting crab and a tasty mulberry.

Nolin River Nut Tree Nursery

979 Port Wooden Road
Upton, KY 42784

- *Plant material for more than 100 varieties of nut trees.*
- *2-page list, free.*

Nolin River offers black and Persian walnuts, pecans and Northern pecans, butternuts, chestnuts, heartnuts, hickory, and hicans. They don't just have 1 or 2 varieties of each, but between 6 and 35! The list provides no descriptions, but the proprietors, Lisa and John Brittain, are willing to correspond with potential customers about the virtues of any varieties in their list. In the future, they plan to stock persimmons and pawpaws too.

North American Fruit Explorers

10 S. 055 Madison Street
Hinsdale, IL 60521

- *Nonprofit organizaton devoted to sharing information on the culture of fruit trees.*
- *Quarterly journal* Pomona; *annual membership $8, two years $15.*

Dedicated enthusiasts, amateurs, and nurserymen run NAFEX and its journal *Pomona*. Articles and advice are contributed by members. There is hardly an issue of *Pomona* that will fail to contain some item of interest for virtually any fruit or berry gardener. There are serious articles on grafting, pollination, culture, pests, and diseases, along with reports from the standing committees on every sort of fruit, discussing both efforts to find old cultivars and results with varieties members are cultivating. Sometimes, there is an official plant-

exchange column; in other issues, wants and needs are scattered through the articles. Particularly useful are the reports from individuals about their experiences in the orchard or berry patch. A recent issue had very good advice on fruit-thinning the Canadice grape and a fine list of hardy versus susceptible apples and pears drawn from a grower's experience with a fireblight outbreak. Some comments are aphoristic, such as the following: "Rock phosphate in latex paint is said to keep off rabbits." The members are very acute, not to say acid, in their comments on the difference between what a nursery says a variety will do and what it actually does, so readers of *Pomona* can get a better idea about some plants before they buy.

Northern Nut Growers Association

Richard Jaynes, Vice-President
13 Broken Arrow Road
Hamden, CT 06518

- *Nonprofit organization offering publications and information on nut culture.*
- *172-page annual report, 18-page quarterly bulletin; annual membership $13.00; Handbook of North American Nut Trees, $17.50 postpaid.*

If you want to network with nut enthusiasts, here's your chance. The annual report and the bulletins are full of the latest information on the culture of most nuts you can think of, including jojoba and macadamia. Good lists of sources—many of which are too small to be included in this book—appear, together with information on seed sales and exchanges from local chapters. The recently updated *Handbook* is an authoritative source on every aspect of nut growing. Both can be enjoyable reading (see the quotation, page 248).

Nuccio's Nurseries

PO Box 6160
Altadena, CA 91001

- *Plants for camellias, azaleas, and a few gardenias.*
- *54-page catalogue, free.*

The Nuccios have been breeding camellias and azaleas since 1950, and they are among the people responsible for the particularly awful variety names of some of the former—things like "Bob Hope," "Dreamcloud," and "Tickled Pink." Still, they have a fine reputation as breeders. Some of their introductions are offered in the garden-center trade or in other catalogues, but here you can find them all, together with a very broad selection of other people's cultivars. The camellia list includes not only endless Japonicas, but a good list of the earlier-blooming Sasanquas, not to mention species, hybrids, and Reticulatas. Two classes of Japanese specialties—the single-flowered Higo strains and the varieties selected for foliage—look very appealing. The azalea list is strongest in the more tender strains, especially kurumes and indicas (Indians), and it features a goodly group of the Japanese Satsuki azaleas, a very variable, often-sporting strain. The Japanese favor Satsukis for bonsai, but Nuccio's suggests them as landscape and pot plants.

Nursery Source Manual

Brooklyn Botanic Garden Record, vol. 38, no. 3.
Brooklyn Botanic Garden
1000 Washington Avenue
Brooklyn, NY 11225

- *88-page booklet, 18 illustations, $2.50.*

The manual is a terrific resource for anyone seeking a particular ornamental tree or shrub, especially if he or she lives in the Northeastern quarter of the United States. The book is very well organized and clearly written, with suggestions on the garden-worthiness and hardiness of many varieties. In terms of scope, it does for the East much of what *Sunset's New Western Garden Book* (see page 47) does for the West, plus one thing more: each of what must be at least 1,500 entries includes not only a description of the plant in question, but a key that tells you where to get it.

Old Fashion Apple Trees

Route 1
Box 203
Gatlinburg, TN 37738

- *Plants for antique apple varieties, plus a few other fruits and nuts.*
- *16-page catalogue, free.*

Henry Morton specializes in the old apple varieties of the Appalachian Mountains. Limbertwigs are his specialty-within-a-specialty. He has about 15 varieties of this interesting type, along with another 60 or so other heirlooms. Many varieties have been collected in the region.

Ornamental and Shade Trees for Utah

by E. Gregory McPherson and Gregory H. Graves
Utah Cooperative Extension Bulletin EC-406
Utah State University
Logan, UT 84322

- *144-page book, many black-and-white illustrations, $7.00*

This remarkable introductory tree manual is meant for the Intermountain region, but the majority of the trees it lists do well in other regions too. Each of the 100 selections, divided roughly into 4 groups according to ultimate size, comes with a good landscape-oriented description; a nice chart evaluating the plant for park, lawn, screen, and utility purposes; and terrific illustrations. A black-and-white photo shows the habit of each, and reproductions of botanical illustrations attractively present the bud, twig, leaf, and flower. Western gardeners will find a number of varieties they may have felt were lacking in the BBG's *Hundred Finest Trees and Shrubs* (see page 94), including Western species and cultivars of poplar, willow, pine, oak, catalpa, and locust.

BONSAI PLANT

Pruning

by Christopher Brickell
Simon & Schuster

- *96 pages, spiral-bound, many illustrations, some 2-color, $7.95 pbk.*

This is about the best general pruning book I've seen, with just the right mix of breadth and depth in its coverage. Furthermore, it opens up flat, so you can lay it beside you while you work. The step-by-step instructions are extremely well illustrated, and they are detailed enough to be truly useful. You can find out how to do ordinary shaping and pruning chores, and how to renovate old and neglected trees and shrubs, how to prune and train fruit trees and berry vines, and how to prune roses of all the major classes. The detail in the section on training fruit trees and vines is particularly admirable, and not seen that often.

Pruning Simplified

by Lewis Hill
Garden Way Publishing

- *208 pages, many illustrations, $12.95 pbk.*

The descriptions are wordier than they might be, but the book is eminently usable for all the basic pruning chores, from ornamentals to fruit trees to vines and ground covers. When it comes to more formal pruning and training—for espaliers or topiary—the information is too sketchy to be helpful.

Raintree Nursery

391 Butts Road
Morton, WA 98356

- *Plants for edible landscaping, including fruits, berries, nuts, mushrooms, kiwis, citrus, woodlot and wildlife trees, roses, and ornamentals.*
- *70-page catalogue, a few illustrations, free.*

What a wonderful catalogue! The list of varieties is not particularly large, but it is serviceable, including a few heirlooms among the apples. The owners seem to have taken the notion of "edible landscaping" seriously, so each fruit or other tribe's section comes with a boxed description of the best landscape and culinary uses, together with information on culture, pests, pollination, and anything else you might need to know. Apples are available on a variety of rootstocks, and the catalogue features a very useful pollination chart for all of them. I shouldn't give you the idea that the lists are *small* here; they are as large as those of many bigger nurseries, but the emphasis is on usefulness, not rarity, in the edible landscape. The lists may not be murkily deep, but their range is really grand, including such things as cherimoyas, hardy bamboo, huckleberries, salal, and sand cherries. All of this is really directed at people in the Pacific

Northwest, though I think that the rest of us may find this catalogue quite useful, too.

Santa Barbara Seeds

See "Houseplants and Exotics."

Shanti Bithi Bonsai

3047 High Ridge Road
Stamford, CT 06903

- *Bonsai plants, books, tools, and supplies.*
- *6-page catalogue, more than 70 color illustrations, plus 8-page price list, $3.00.*

Proprietor Jerome Rocherolle thinks he has the largest collection of imported bonsai in the U.S. Sources for the plants include Japan, Korea, China, and Taiwan. The catalogue features absolutely stunning photos of a couple of dozen specimens. It's no wonder the nursery recently won a gold medal from the Chicago Horticultural Society. Prices are quite high for finished plants, ranging from $50 to around $1,500. Starters are cheaper. My favorite, a three-trunked zelkova pictured without its leaves, looks priceless, and I suppose it is, since it isn't for sale. Pots and tools are high-quality. The tools are helpfully offered in sets.

The Shrub Identification Book

The Tree Identification Book

both by George W. Symonds
William Morrow

- *Shrubs: 379 pages, many illustrations, $12.95 pbk.*
- *Trees: 272 pages, many illustrations, $10.95 pbk.*

These 2 excellent volumes were originally published in the early 1960s.

Each offers cross-listed photographic keys for identifying shrubs and trees by means of their bark, buds, leaves, fruits, flowers, and sometimes even habits. Unfortunately, the pictures are in black and white, and the coverage for the named cultivars of major species is skimpy or lacking. Nevertheless, the photos are clear, and they cover most of the species you will be interested in. The books are particularly useful to winter botanizers and to people who have bought a property but don't know what's growing there.

JAPANESE YEW

Shrubs and Vines for American Gardens

Trees for American Gardens

both by Donald Wyman
Macmillan

- *Shrubs: 613 pages, some illustrations, $29.95.*
- *Trees: 502 pages, many illustrations, $24.95.*

Wyman is copious, Wyman is careful, and Wyman is bright. Both volumes are full of excellent lists, containing plants grouped by such useful categories as order of bloom and color of twigs. The very long dictionaries of recommended trees and recommended shrubs and vines—including some favorite cultivars for many of them—assess the foliage, flowers, and habit of each, recommending specific landscape uses. The illustrations do not consistently show either leaf shape or habit, however, and I was disappointed to find no consistent information on the rate of growth for the trees. The books make an effort to cover all regions of the country, so you will find good selections for zones 9 and 10 here, too.

Shrubs in the Landscape

by Joseph Hudak
McGraw-Hill

- *291 pages, many illustrations, a few in color, $38.50.*

The illustrations are average-to-rotten, but Hudak more than makes up for this weakness by offering us descriptions of more than 1,000 different shrubs for the landscape. Though I miss Michael Dirr's fine and opinionated writing (see page 97), Hudak's shrub book does pay more consistent attention to the specific cultivars of a given species than does his competitor. Then too, Hudak is better for the shrubs you might use in the South or the Far West. The early chapters contain useful information on planting and caring for shrubs and for setting them effectively in the garden.

Southmeadow Fruit Gardens

Box SM
Lakeside, MI 49116

- *Plants for antique and rare varieties of fruits, grapes, gooseberries, and currants.*
- *112-page catalogue, approx. 200 illustrations, $8.00; variable-length price lists, free.*

Horticultural societies are fond of distributing medals. I hope that they have settled a good hundredweight of them on Mr. Theo C. J. Grootendorst, the proprietor of Southmeadow. Among all the fine companies offering heirloom and unusual varieties of fruit trees, his is the finest. His catalogue is costly, but it lists more than 500 varieties of apples, grapes, pears, gooseberries, medlars, peaches, currants, plums, and cherries. Furthermore, its text is more stimulating and informative than that of most books. Many firms have big apple lists, but Grootendorst's other lists are each as

large as others' apple lists, and his own apple list is astonishing. He is fond of old-time varieties, but the selections also include many fine, less commercially viable strains from the various experiment stations. He has spent more than a quarter-century looking for some things, like the Lola peach. Lola hasn't appeared yet, but he did come up with an old cross of it, called Lola Queen.

Spring Hill Nurseries

See "Annuals and Perennials."

Steve Ray's Bamboo Gardens

909 79th Place S.
Birmingham, AL 35206

- *Plants for cold-hardy bamboo.*
- *24-page catalogue, 25 illustrations, free.*

Ray offers 30 varieties of bamboo—from dwarfs to giants—in a well-made catalogue. The photos are not so good, but they do show the plants' habit. The descriptions are first-rate, with specific information as to the hardiness of each (generally around 0° F). The cultural information is very good, reflecting the proprietor's more than 25 years' experience with bamboo.

Stonehurst Rare Plants

1 Stonehurst Court
Pomona, NY 10970

- *Plants for dwarf and unusual conifers and Japanese maples.*
- *16-page catalogue, $1.00.*

Here's a very large list—by name only—of dwarf conifers. There are more than 1,200 conifer varieties and 300 Japanese maples. Either know exactly what you are looking for or visit the nursery to see what you are buy-

ing (or both). A few varieties are Stonehurst's own introductions. The proprietors are now adding more high-grafted varieties for Japanese and rock gardens.

> The love of dirt is among the earliest of passions, as it is the latest. Mud-pies gratify one of our first and best instincts. So long as we are dirty, we are pure. Fondness for the ground comes back to a man after he has run the round of pleasure and business, eaten dirt, and sown wildoats, drifted about the world, and taken the wind in all its moods. The love of digging in the ground (or of looking on while he pays another to dig) is as sure to come back to him as he is sure, at last, to go under the ground, and stay there. To own a bit of ground, to scratch it with a hoe, to plant seeds, and watch their renewal of life—this is the commonest delight of the race, the most satisfactory thing a man can do.
>
> —CHARLES DUDLEY WARNER, FROM *MY SUMMER IN A GARDEN* (1871)

Sunset Nursery

4007 Elrod Avenue
Tampa, FL 33616

- *Bamboo.*
- *2-page list, plus 3-page descriptions and recipes, free.*

A small bamboo list where the description of types and qualities is lively. It includes a few recipes for the shoots. The list itself is relatively unadorned, so ask before you buy. I get the feeling that Sunset won't ship these things far, which is probably just as well, since many won't thrive much farther north.

Sunsweet Fruit & Bulb Nursery

Box Z
Sumner, GA 31789

- *Plants for fruit and nut trees and grapes; plants for flowering bulbs.*
- *32-page catalogue, more than 100 color illustrations, free.*

Here is an attractive catalogue for gardeners in the Deep South. Fruit, nut, and grape varieties are selected for those that do best in that region. There is an unusually large and appetizing-looking group of figs, along with mainly modern varieties of most other types. The flower list specializes in things like cannas, hymenocallis and crinum lilies, and it duplicates what is found at Tyty Plantations (see page 78), a firm with which Sunsweet is apparently associated. Note that Sunsweet sells bulbs for a banana tree hardy in the South.

> Medicinal virtues: Nothing is better than the leaves or flowers of this peach tree to purge choler and the jaundice from children and young people. They are given as a syrup or as a conserve. The fruit provokes lust. The leaves bruised and laid on the belly kill worms; and boiled in ale and drank, they open the belly.
> —FROM *CULPEPER'S COLOR HERBAL*

Dean Swift Seed Company

PO Box B
Jaroso, CO 81138

- *Seed for conifers, shrubs, and a few wildflowers.*
- *2-page list, free.*

Do you need to plant the whole ranch and want to do it with Rocky Mountain or Southwestern native trees and shrubs? Dean Swift is your source. He collects the seed of conifers from Arizona to South Dakota, offering them in minimum quantities of 1 pound. His shrubs and wildflowers list is brief but attractive, including a couple of succulents.

Thomasville Nurseries

See "Roses."

Tollgate Garden Nursery

20865 Junction Road
Bellevue, MI 49021

- *Seeds, seedlings, and grafted varieties of pawpaws.*
- *Brief list, SASE; "Paw Paw Bulletin," $3.25.*

Hortus Third may dismiss the whole genus with "one species is sometimes cultivated," but the pawpaw has its champion in Corwin Davis of Tollgate. He has spent the last quarter-century growing and studying the pawpaw. You can buy his wisdom in the bulletin, or in seeds and plants to try yourself.

Trees for Every Purpose

by Joseph Hudak
McGraw-Hill

- *229 pages, many illustrations, a few in color, $39.95.*

The bulk of this book is a catalogue of 257 landscape trees, well chosen to reflect what is common in all different regions of the nation. The information is a good deal less extensive than Dirr provides in his *Manual of Woody Landscape Plants* (see page 97), but there is still plenty here for the gardener who is just deciding what to plant. Best of all are the boxed drawings that show leaf, flower, and fruit details, together with a scaled drawing of habit and height of each tree both at typical nursery transplant size and at maturity. For some reason, however, there is no information on rate of growth. People in the coastal West and the South will find good reason to prefer this book to Dirr's, since it makes a more thorough effort to cover the landscape trees that grow best in those warmer climates.

> FIR TREE
> From this tree is gotten the Strasbourg turpentine, . . . a good diuretic, and of great use in gonorrhea and the fluor albus.
> —FROM *CULPEPER'S COLOR HERBAL*

Trees of North America and Europe

by Roger Phillips
Random House

- *224-page book, numerous color illustrations, $14.95.*

The "and Europe" of the title appears in small print, which is the tip-off that this is a British book adapted for the American market. Still, its fine illustrations make it quite a useful volume. It includes only about 500 entries, but this is enough to make it a pleasant reference guide or a tool for choosing landscape trees. Color photographs show leaf, flower, and fruit very clearly for all entries, and bark for some. Fine silhouette drawings show the habit of each tree. The text is informative, but a bit dry, and I wish it said more about garden values and less about economic and historical matters. In fact, if someone could cross the pictures in this book with the text and coverage of Dirr's *Manual of Woody Landscape Plants* (see page 97), the resulting hybrid would be a classic.

Tripple Brook Farm

37 Middle Road
Southampton, MA 01073

- *Plants for annuals and perennials and for fruiting and ornamental shrubs and trees.*
- *20-page catalogue, some illustrations, free.*

It's hard to know what to make of this catalogue. The owners tell us they are trying to bring all sorts of underused plants into our gardens. Their catalogue is indeed charming, well-written, and diverse. There is a little of everything in here, from kiwis and pineapple guava, to native and naturalized wildflowers, to more or less ordinary shade trees. The only considerable group in the catalogue consists of about 20 bamboos.

Tyty Plantation

See "Annuals and Perennials."

Q—Somebody told me bamboo will tear up my sidewalks, driveways, and even lift the foundation of my house.

A—Baloney, nonsense, balderdash! (Excuse me). I have never seen it happen. This same person probably has also heard about the mythical torture wherein people are killed by rapidly growing Bamboo shoots piercing their bodies. It just doesn't happen—the new bamboo tip is very soft, and follows the easiest path of growth. I do assume that you are talking about *concrete* sidewalks and driveways. If you are referring to asphalt or brick or stone pavers set on sand—that's a different matter.

—FROM *ENDANGERED SPECIES* (1986)

Valley Nursery

Box 4845
Helena, MT 59604

- *Trees and shrubs for cold climates.*
- *2-page list, free.*

Here's an agreeable selection of very hardy varieties of landscape plants. There are a few perennials—including the native bitterroot—plus vines and ground covers, but the bulk of the list is trees and shrubs. There is little information in the list, but it contains an intriguing group of choices. There's a hardy boxwood from Saskatchewan, a native yucca, a good selection of roses (including Morden hybrids), and quite a number of mountain ash, together with at least 100 other choices.

Vineland Nurseries

PO Box 98
Vineland Station, Ontario
CANADA L0R 2E0

- *Plants for dwarf and unusual conifers, ericaceous plants, Japanese maples, and bamboos.*
- *8-page catalogue, free.*

This is a collector's list strongest in conifers, with a good group of heathers too.

Maude Walker

PO Box 256
Omega, GA 31775

- *Plant material for blueberries, muscadines, and fruit and nut trees and vines.*
- *16-page catalogue, 42 color illustrations, free.*

Walker puts out a very attractive catalogue of fruit and nut varieties for the South. The emphasis is on productivity, not rarity or the antiquity of the varieties. There are 8 or 9 choices each among the blueberries; many of the selections are attractively illus-

trated. The catalogue has smaller choices among strawberries, blackberries, raspberries, figs, pomegranates, apples, pears, plums, peaches, persimmons, pecans, walnuts, filberts, and chestnuts.

Waynesboro Nurseries

Route 664
PO Box 987
Waynesboro, VA 22980

- *Plant material for fruit and ornamental trees and shrubs, as well as berries.*
- *48-page catalogue, approx. 200 illustrations, most in color, free.*

No other state of Virginia's size straddles as many climatic zones. (It runs from zone 5 in the northwest to zone 8 in the southeast.) The list contains not only the fruit, foliage, and flowering trees and shrubs that do well throughout the temperate zone, but a number of selections for both northern and southern ranges. The apple group is good and varied; the peaches include both a number of old favorites and 4 Virginia Agricultural Experiment station varieties, the latter known for their hardiness. There are pecans for both North and South, and figs and persimmons strictly for the south. Most of the ornamental list is serviceable but not adventurous. Exceptions are the fine selections of ilex, crab apples, and conifers, particularly yews. A number of less common varieties of abelia, elaeagnus, and spirea (one is the spike-flowering *S. billiardi rosea*) liven up the shrubs group. At 4 each, there are too many forsythias and honey locusts. One of the best features of the catalogue is its charts: for fruits they show the first bearing age of the varieties offered and for shade trees and yews they show the ultimate size and habit of the plants.

Wayside Gardens

See "Annuals and Perennials."

Weston Nurseries

PO Box 186
E. Main Street
Hopkinton, MA 01748

- *Plant material for ornamental trees and shrubs, perennials, fruit and nut trees, and berries.*
- *216-page catalogue, 18 color illustrations, free.*

This is a lot of catalogue for free. Weston is known to many gardeners as the introducer of the PJM rhododendron hybrids; its breeding program has also produced some other rhododendrons, a number of fine azaleas and red-budded kalmia. To people in the Boston area, the nursery is known for its garden center, one of the best in the East. The catalogue is various and complete, selected from the more than 2,000 varieties of evergreens and broad-leaves, 250 deciduous trees, 500 shrubs and 1,000 perennials grown at the nursery. All varieties are selected for their usefulness and hardiness in New England climates. The nursery says that it will ship some perennials UPS, and that individuals can place orders to be delivered by truck as far south as New Jersey, but for those who can't visit the garden center, it is probably the best idea to ask your local nursery to order for you.

Whitman Farms

1420 Beaumont N.W.
Salem, OR 97304

- *Plant material for ornamental trees and shrubs, plus some cuttings for small fruits.*
- *1-page list, free.*

Among the ornamentals, only Latin names appear, and the selection is so odd that only the terrific gardener can decipher the list at a glance. True, there are quite a number of maples, but most are unusual or rare species. Then there are things like *Arbutus*

unedo (strawberry tree), a *Clerodendrum* (harlequin glory-bush), and *Exochorda giraldi* (pearlbush), all quite lovely-looking and all seldom seen in the trade. There are more than 75 choices in all, and, though I didn't try to decode all of them, it appears that quite a number are interesting landscape plants while some (like the bladdernuts) are not. This list would be fun to play with on a winter's evening, puzzling over the choices and perhaps coming up with something really special. The fruits list is easier to figure out, and it offers a very good choice of varieties among the currants and the gooseberries.

Wildwood Farm

See "Annuals and Perennials."

Winter Guides

Winter Botany

by William Trelease
Dover Publications

- *396 pages, many illustrations, $6.95 pbk.*

Winter Tree Finder

by May Theilgaard Watts and Tom Watts
Nature Study Guild
Box 972
Berkeley, CA 94701

- *58 pages, many illustrations, $1.50 pbk.*

It's a lot of fun to identify deciduous plants in winter, and learning to know them by their "skeletons" makes it all the easier to recognize them in the leafy season. Then, too, if you're looking at property in winter, you may well want to figure out what's growing there. Trelease's classic volume first appeared in 1918, and it is still among the best winter guides you

will find. It covers a considerably larger field than does the Wattses' book, embracing shrubs and vines as well as trees. The language, however, is pure botanese, and the illustrations, though very clear, show only buds, leaf scars, and twig patterns. The Wattses' book covers only trees for the Eastern half of the nation, but it gives lots of well-illustrated hints—nuts and seed pods, as well as twigs and buds—and its key is easy to use. Also, the lovely little pamphlet fits comfortably in any pocket, so it's handy to take along.

Womack's Nursery Company

Route 1
Box 80
De Leon, TX 76444

- *Plant material for nut and fruit trees, ornamental trees, grapes, and berries.*
- *30-page catalogue, 14 illustrations, free.*

Here's a decent catalogue for the South. Being a Texas catalogue, its illustrations contain rulers, hands, or dimes to demonstrate the great size of its pecans and pears, but at least there is one ruler to show how small the pit of the Sam Houston peach is. The widest choice is among the pecans, which are divided according to whether they do better in the East or the West. "For a rough boundary line for eastern and western varieties," the text advises, "draw a line from San Antonio through Fort Worth to Tulsa." Through all of the fruits and right down to the enormous Brazos blackberry, a fair proportion of the selections come from the Texas A&M breeding station. Emphasis everywhere is on efficient varieties, the sort that do well in commercial or home plantings. The ornamentals section, though brief, has choice natives, including the Mexican plum.

Woodland Nurseries

2151 Camilla Road
Mississauga, Ontario
CANADA L5A 2K1

- *Plant material for rhododendrons and azaleas, unusual shrubs and trees, and perennials.*
- *30-page catalogue, $1.50.*

Woodland is very experienced with the rhodo tribe and offers a very fine, numerous, but not overwhelming selection for Northern gardens. Other shrubs are very well represented, including some less common genera and good choices among the euonymus, mahonia, potentilla, lilacs, and viburnum. The perennials list is good for the rock garden.

One cussedness of gardening is the problem of the plant you desire larger actually dwindles, whereas the one that has attained perfect size insists on growing.

—FROM *THE ROCK GARDEN* (1986)

Worcester County Horticultural Society

30 Tower Hill Road
Boylston, MA 01505

- *Scionwood from an antique apple orchard.*
- *List free with self-addressed envelope.*

There are 110 antique apple varieties to choose from in this simple list, but be aware that it offers scionwood, so if you order from it, have your rootstock and your grafting tools handy.

Zilke Brothers Nursery

8924 Cleveland Avenue
Baroda, MI 49101

- *Plant material for fruit trees, berries, ornamental trees and shrubs, and roses.*
- *22-page catalogue, free.*

This is a good, serviceable basic list that shouldn't be overlooked by people living in the region. It contains nothing startling, except for a terrific list of flowering crab apples.

4 *Wildflowers and Native Plants*

Arthur Eames Allgrove

PO Box 459
Wilmington, MA 01887

- *Plants for native woodland species and wildflowers; terrarium plants and gift planters.*
- *6-page wildflower planting guide plus 3-page price list, $3.00; 4-page terrarium and woodland plant list, $.50.*

I don't know what to make of this stuff. It seems pretty casually put together—with amateur illustrations, rough-looking charts, and a mish-mash of offerings—but there is a good deal of information in the wild-flower guide, and the list of woodland plants Eames offers is helpful. The guide lists soil and light preferences, plus size and flower color, for well over 100 wildflowers and ferns, mainly Eastern natives or naturalized species, not quite half of which are offered for sale in the current list. The sale items are strongest in native ferns, bulbs, trilliums, and ground covers. Among the miscellaneous wildflowers appear pitcher plant and rattlesnake plantain. A little folder that comes with the guide gives some basic guidelines on soil preparation and planting depths for various species and types. The separate terrarium list mainly duplicates the plants offered in the guide.

> Many primitive peoples plant brilliant flowers around their homes. Inquiries by understanding anthropologists demonstrate that these gaudy plants are not just for ornament, they are for magic: they are scaring away devils. Coxcomb and amaranth are planted in primitive grainfields for the same purpose; who is to know from our present evidence which is the older use, the plant grown for food, or the plant deliberately grown for protection against evil spirits?
>
> —EDGAR ANDERSON, FROM *PLANTS, MAN & LIFE* (1967)

Appalachian Wildflower Nursery

Route 1
Box 275A
Reedsville, PA 17084

- *Seeds for an idiosyncratic list collected around the world.*
- *1-page flyer.*

Don Hackenberry must be mad, but we are glad that he is. He has collected wildflower seed from Appalachia to Oregon to Kazakhstan to Hokkaido, testing and developing them at home until he can offer them in his unprepossessing but remarkable list of seeds and plants. He is currently working on a daphne from Beijing and an endangered gentian from Oregon. The list is 100 plants long, especially strong in kalmia and rhododendrons, gentians, phlox, and primulas. This is not a selection for beginners, but Hackenberry claims he will offer his customers advice by phone in the evenings. It's a service worth using.

Applewood Seed Co.

PO Box 10761
Edgemont Station
Golden, CO 80401

- Seeds for a wide selection of species and mixes.
- 24-page seed catalogue, color and black-and-white illustrations, free.

A handsome, informative catalogue that will appeal to gardeners who may never have grown wildflowers before. There are no surprises in it. Indeed, several of the listed species are cosmopolitan weeds like cornflower, not American natives. For those interested in fast results for the garden or meadow, however, the company offers an unusually wide variety of seed mixes, each selected for success in a specific geographic region. Also valuable are the unusual number of dwarf varieties and the mixes tailored for ground-cover or "knee-high" results. Healthy wildflowers can overwhelm a small garden, so size control is important. And do check out their "Sof-Pot," a sort of sturdy and attractive sack that does duty as a pot for annuals, vegetables, and indoor plants.

The Audubon Society Nature Guides

Knopf

Atlantic and Gulf Coasts

Deserts

Eastern Forests

Grasslands

Pacific Coast

Western Forests

Wetlands

- Each 600+ pages, many color illustrations, each $14.95 pbk.

Every time there's a good idea for a field guide, the Chanticleer Press has it. Chanticleer prepared the *Taylor's Guides* to garden flowers for Houghton Mifflin (see page 60), and they are also responsible for this habitat-oriented series from Knopf. Unfortunately, the effort to tackle the whole flora and fauna of an ecological province is such an immense task that the editors have had to be selective in what species they include. For some volumes, this means that plants get comparatively short shrift. Nonetheless, if you are a natives or wildflower gardener, the guides will give you a colorful sense of the natural palette you are working with, both as to overall habitat and as to indigenous, naturalized, or migratory species.

BUTTON BUSH

Bernardo Beach Native Plant Farm

Star Route 7
Box 145
Veguita, NM 87062

- Plants for native and arid-land shrubs, trees, vines, and herbaceous ground covers and perennials.
- 12-page catalogue, free.

Judith Philips' catalogue of natives is cheerfully and thoughtfully presented. She isn't a stickler for the "native" label; she includes a number of frankly confessed exotics like the jujube and Russian olive. Given the difficulty of the climate, it is probably just as well that she hasn't been too strict about what gets in. Still, the natives list is just broad enough to be intriguing and useful, without becoming overwhelming. Philips has been working on a book, *Southwestern Landscaping with Native Plants*, which will be out by the time you read this. From her catalogue writing and selection, the book will probably warrant a look.

Boehlke's Woodland Gardens

W. 140 N. 10829 Country Aire Road
Germantown, WI 53022

- Plants for natives, wildflowers, ferns, and naturalizing perennials for woodland, prairie, and meadow.
- 8-page catalogue, 26 illustrations, send 2 first-class stamps.

Boehlke's is a well-written and prettily illustrated catalogue, embracing most of the species that Northern growers like. Plants for different situations are grouped separately, and the perennials for naturalizing are segregated. Much of the stuff here is available at other wildflower nurseries as well, but the lakeside daisy caught my eye. It is a diminutive yellow daisy, native to a small area along the Great Lakes.

Busse Gardens

See "Annuals and Perennials."

Richard, James, and Katherine Clinebell

RR II
Box 176
Wyoming, IL 61491

- *Seed for prairie-native forbs and woodland natives.*
- *3-page list, free.*

There's nothing to the list but Latin and common names, so don't wade in here unless you know what you're doing. Prairie and woodland selections are both very nice, though it appears that the Clinebells prefer to sell all seeds in fairly large quantities. Like most conscientious prairie nurseries, they never take plants from the wild, and they are anxious to trade seed with other collectors who can document county of origin.

The Crownsville Nursery

See "Annuals and Perennials."

Desert Plants

University of Arizona
Boyce Thompson Arboretum
PO Box AB
Superior, AZ 85273

- *Variable-length quarterly, many illustrations, some in color, annual subscription $12.00.*

Desert Plants is a scholarly journal whose editor has been known to complain about "intellectual scurvy," the debility that results when scientists guard their specialties from all contact with the outside world. As a result, perhaps, his quarterly contains botanical research that is also useful for nonspecialists. A recent issue contained a thorough and well-illustrated monograph on *Salvia*, a genus full of fine ornamentals. There was also an article on the economic and horticultural uses of rabbitbrush, and a fascinating piece on the many decades of travail that resulted in Arizona's first flora, a book that is still used by both botanists and native-plant gardeners. Geographer Conrad Bahre consulted rafts of 19th-century Arizona newspapers (including the *Tombstone Epitaph*) to produce an article on the influence of wildfire on the grassland ecosystem of the region. This is by no means a scurvy journal, and it is well worth the attention of Southwestern natives gardeners.

Directory to Resources on Wildflower Propagation

National Council of State Garden Clubs
4401 Magnolia Avenue
St. Louis, MO 63110

- *331 pages, 7 illustrations, $3.00.*

Seldom has so homely a book contained so much worthwhile data. Prepared with state highway departments in mind, it looks like tables of actuarial figures. Actually, it provides column after column listing the native wildflowers and grasses of the seven different macroregions of the nation. Each entry tells how to prepare and cultivate seed, describing the full height of the plant and when it blooms. A bibliography for every region shows where to go for further information on propagating plants. Some of these are hard to find—Agronomy Report No. 87, for example—but others are little known but available gems that may be just what you need for your own situation. The relevant publications of native plant societies and botanical gardens are particularly well indexed.

The Earth Manual

by Malcolm Margolin
Heyday Books

- *237 pages, many illustrations, $8.95 pbk.*

This isn't really a gardening book at all. In fact, it's more of an antigardening book, but it is very useful for people who want to preserve the native landscape as is, adding only such things as will protect or restore it. Particularly adapted for homesteaders or country-home people with a comparatively large amount of land, it will help you preserve existing vegetation, add plants that harmonize with the natural landscape, and control erosion damage.

Earthside Nature Center

3160 E. Del Mar Boulevard
Pasadena, CA 91107

- *2½-acre garden of California natives.*
- *Annual seed list of California natives.*

Improbably enough, this place is run by the Girls Club of Pasadena, but its guiding spirit is Kevin Connelly. Since starting in 1971, he has created a garden that contains over 500 species of California natives, including shrubs, annuals, and perennials. Nineteen different environments are represented. Connelly is a serious collector, known to keep a notebook of all local brushfires so that he can return the next spring to search the sites for rare "fire followers," natives that seed only in burned-over areas. He prides himself on careful identification of plants, so what you order from his seed list is indeed likely to be what you will get. The list goes from common to rare, and seeds are available on a first-come-first-served basis. Good luck.

Field Guides

The Audubon Society Field Guide to North American Wildflowers, Eastern Region

by William Albert Niering
Knopf

- *863 pages, many color illustrations, $13.50 pbk.*

The Audubon Society Field Guide to North American Wildflowers, Western Region

by Richard Spellenberg
Knopf

- *863 pages, many color illustrations, $13.50 pbk.*

A Field Guide to the Wildflowers of Northeastern and North Central North America

by Roger T. Peterson and
Margaret McKenny
Houghton Mifflin

- *420 pages, many illustrations, some in color, $15.45 hc., $10.70 pbk.*

A Field Guide to Rocky Mountain Wildflowers

by John J. Craighead et al.
Houghton Mifflin

- *277 pages, many illustrations, some color, $17.45 hc., $12.70 pbk.*

A Field Guide to Southwestern and Texas Wildflowers

by Theodore F. Niehaus and
Charles L. Ripper
Houghton Mifflin

- *449 pages, many illustrations, some color, $18.45 hc., $12.70 pbk.*

A Field Guide to Pacific States Wildflowers

by Theodore F. Niehaus and
Charles L. Ripper
Houghton Mifflin

- *432 pages, many illustrations, some color, $16.45 hc., $11.70 pbk.*

Newcomb's Wildflower Guide

by Lawrence Newcomb and
Gordon Morrison
Little, Brown & Co.

- *490 pages, many illustrations, some color, $6.95 pbk.*

The differences between the 2 main nationwide series—the Audubon (published by Knopf) and the Peterson (published by Houghton Mifflin)—can be told at a glance. The Peterson series is divided into more volumes, and it includes more species total than does Audubon's. The Audubon series is illustrated with color photographs, whereas the Peterson guides are illustrated with black-and-white line drawings, supplemented by a good number of color paintings. Which to choose? If you are actually going into the field and want to make sure identifications, I think the Peterson is the better bet: not only are there more species in each volume, but the drawings and paintings show detail for both flower and foliage. The key is fairly easy to learn to use. For the gardener who cares only about the more conspicuous species, however, and who may not worry about precise identification or who may actually be ordering the plant from a wildflower nursery, the Audubon series' pictures give an undeniable *frisson* of the real, and the written descriptions are quite as fine and precise as those in the Petersons.

The Audubon books use a similar, easy-to-learn key for finding the flower in question, combining color and shape. One annoying thing about the Audubons is that the color plates and the text are in separate sections of the book, so you find yourself flipping back and forth all the time.

The *Newcomb's* guide covers an area west to Wisconsin, south to Virginia and Tennessee, and north to Quebec. The illustrations are drawings and paintings, both accurate and visually appealing. Newcomb has kept the very nice 3-digit key system that he first used in his unillustrated guide for the New England Wildflower Society (see page 118). You assign the first digit for flower type, the second for plant type, and the third for leaf type. It's a sure and simple method, and here you can check it against the illustrations to see if you have it right. But you do have to go through one step more here than you did in his earlier book. From the 3-digit key, you must proceed to a "locator key" that takes color and other factors into consideration, and only then arrive at the correct entry. Still, it is certainly in the running for the finest guide to its area.

Fjellgarden

PO Box 1111
Lakeside, AZ 85929

- *Rock-garden and alpine plants, particularly Arizona natives.*
- *14-page catalogue, 11 illustrations, $1.00.*

Proprietor Sonia Lowzow lives at an altitude of 7,200 feet in the White Mountains of Arizona; she is also an accomplished rock gardener. Put the two together and you have a collector's list of remarkable interest. She has developed a lovely shorthand for describing her plants' preferences, including a soil nomenclature that comes complete with simple recipes for making the right sort of soil. Her choice list of alpines, subalpines, and bog plants includes material from around the world, but the matchless thing about the list is the large number of collected and propagated Arizona flowers she offers. Some are new to cultivation and available nowhere else. Her introductory essay on their habitat and cultural requirements is first-rate.

Flowering Plants in the Landscape

Edited by Mildred E. Mathias
University of California Press

■ *254 pages, many color illustrations, $16.95.*

The book is meant to be a pictorial guide to flowering plants that do well in tropical/subtropical climates, particularly in California. It has been very influential there, partly for the exotic plants it lists. Chapter 5 is devoted exclusively to California natives, each well illustrated in color. There is no end of good native plant suppliers in California, but not enough catalogues or books that show what you are buying. Here is a good place to look.

Forestfarm

990 Tetherow Road
Williams, OR 97544

■ *Plants for woody and herbaceous natives, fruits, other useful species, and non-native ornamentals.*
■ *56-page catalogue, 24-page insert, $2.00.*

Forestfarm started out propagating Western natives, where it is still strongest, but it has since branched far afield, especially into unusual woody plants from Australia and the Far East and into edible fruiting varieties now usually grown as ornamentals. Consider that the catalogue

matches good groups of ceanothus, manzanita, and even mountain mahogany, with Eastern natives like leatherwood and a huge group of Australian eucalyptus. Among the herbaceous perennials, you will find two Dutchman's pipes, one native to the East and one to the West, and an iris selection that includes several Pacific natives, the Pacific Coast hybrids, a couple of Eastern natives, and a couple from the Far East. Fruiting plants run the gamut from actinidias and pawpaws, through pineapple, guava, salal, Japanese raisin tree, wild plum, and coast huckleberry.

Gardenimport

See "General Sources."

A Garden of Wildflowers

by Henry W. Art
Garden Way Publishing

■ *290 pages, many illustrations, $12.95 pbk.*

Though it lacks the color illustrations that would bring its pages to life, this is a first-rate introduction to growing native wildflowers. Art is a declared enemy of the "wildflower" mixes that include naturalized cosmopolitans like Queen Anne's lace and purple loosestrife, so his well-annotated list of 101 wildflowers contains only natives. The list is designed to cover the whole country, so if you are really serious about growing only what is in your region, you will just find the commoner species in this book. Still, it is a very good middle ground for someone who wants to start growing natives. The plant-by-plant catalogue describes culture and propagation requirements for each, and it offers a suggested list of natives

to plant as its companions. The black-and-white illustrations are finely detailed. Appended to them is a map showing the native range of each plant. There are also useful charts showing the hardiness, flowering sequence, and light and moisture preferences of each. Among the source lists at the back of the book is a nice one that tells you which botanical gardens around the country offer native plants for sale.

Bait mousetraps with pumpkin seeds. It is better bait than cheese.
—FROM BAER'S AGRICULTURAL ALMANAC (1897)

Gardens of the Blue Ridge

PO Box 10
Pineola, NC 28662

■ *Native and naturalized plants, chiefly from Eastern woodlands.*
■ *34-page catalogue, 21 color illustrations, $1.00.*

Founded in 1878, this nursery has been run by the Robbins family for 95 years, making it one of the oldest wildflower operations around. It offers a lovely list of Eastern perennials, shrubs, and trees, including 22 ferns, 8 trilliums, and special sections for rock-garden and aquatic plants, for orchids, and for native kalmia and rhodos. The color photos are superb, and it's a shame there are so few for the 250 plants listed. Except for the rhodos, the catalogue is unfortunately weak on cultural instructions, so the beginner must take a chance or study up. The *Cypripedium acaule*, for example, looks very attractive, but it is *very* hard to grow.

Grasses: An Identification Guide

by Lauren Brown
Houghton Mifflin

- *240 pages, many illustrations, $9.95.*

My only complaint about this book is that there is no companion volume for the West. It covers the native and introduced grasses of the Northeast, extending to the West into Minnesota and to the South as far as southern Illinois. The keyed field guide to wild grasses, embraces most of the major species. The illustrations look practically like brush paintings, though they seem to show sufficient detail for identification. The entries describe the origin and character of each species, and its uses as well.

AZALEA

Green Dragons and Doll's Eyes

by Donna Levy
Cornell Plantations
1 Plantations Road
Ithaca, NY 14850

- *106-page book, many illustrations, $7.95.*

The book is meant as a trail guide to the Mundy Wildflower Garden at Cornell Plantations, but it is a very fine resource for any wildflower gardener in the East. The Mundy garden includes habitats from meadow to marsh to woodland, and the text describes the native and naturalized wildflowers growing in each. A series of terrific wildflower gardens for different habitats might be planned using the selection found here. Following the habitat-by-habitat guide are complete alphabetical charts of the native and naturalized wildflowers, ferns, shrubs, and trees of the region.

Griffey's Nursery

1670 Highway 25-70
Marshall, NC 28753

- *Plants native to Eastern woodlands.*
- *8-page list, free.*

Griffey's has a good, selective list of native trees, shrubs, and forbs, though the $20 minimum purchase is steep. The entries give little description or cultural information, but the Griffeys will answer queries from customers. The list covers much the same ground as Gardens of the Blue Ridge (see page 111). It is stronger, however, in native trees, and it contains a selection of native berry plants. Elsewhere, the Griffeys generally give less choice than their competitor, but in each field, they offer at least 1 or 2 varieties that Blue Ridge does not.

Growing and Propagating Wildflowers

by Harry R. Phillips
University of North Carolina Press

- *331 pages, many illustrations, a few in color, $24.95.*

Is this the best of the wildflower books? At least for collecting and propagating, I think it is. Phillips covers mainly the more common species from about 100 different genera, but his plant dictionary gives you a palette that is quite copious enough to start with. Among a lot of the more usual cultural information for each species, he gives you unusually deep information on when the seed is ripe, how to tell whether it is, and exactly what the seed looks like. Coverage is good for carnivorous plants and ferns, as well as forbs.

Grow Native Shrubs in Your Garden

by F. M. Mooberry and Jane H. Scott

- *68 pages, many illustrations, $4.95.*

Landscaping with Native Plants

by Elizabeth N. duPont

- *72 pages, many illustrations, $9.95.*

Both from: Brandywine Conservancy
PO Box 141
Chadds Ford, PA 19317

Here are two very fine resources for natives gardeners in the Middle Atlantic region. The shrubs volume contains dozens of native species, each well-described and with excellent cultural instructions. It is organized by season, a thoughtful touch that will help the garden planner. The landscaping volume contains a great deal of information in just a few pages. It describes everything from the plants themselves, to the physiography of the region, to its natural plant communities, to the means of constructing retaining walls. The plant lists are good and thorough.

Growing California Native Plants

by Marjorie Schmidt
University of California Press

- *366 pages, many illustrations, some in color, $15.95 hc., $7.95 pbk.*

You can't do much better than this for a book on California natives. It's quite thorough for both woody and herbaceous species, and the chapters are divided into annuals, perennials, bulbs, shrubs, and trees. Each of the hundreds of entries for individual species not only describes the plant but goes into considerable detail regarding garden usefulness.

Growing Wildflowers: A Gardener's Guide

by Marie Sperka
Scribner's

■ *288 pages, many illustrations, $10.95 pbk.*

Sperka owned and operated Woodland Acres Nursery in Wisconsin for more than 25 years, so it would be hard to match the extent of her experience with wildflowers. (She was also a talented hybridizer and came up with the bleeding-heart cultivar "Luxuriant.") The bulk of this book is the detailed plant list, but she opens with uncommonly good suggestions for propagation, care, and so on. I particularly like her method for clearing a weedy woodland—using sheets of newspaper spread over the ground, topped with 10-10-10 fertilizer, and left to decompose for a year, at the end of which you should have both a clear and a fertile soil. Plant descriptions include bloom period, plant height, and color, shape, and habit, plus good cultural notes. The list is broad but particularly nice for bulbs, trilliums, irises, violets, and orchids. Her orchid culture method is practically a propitiatory rite, including the placing of rocks around the plant (to provide a cool root run), the insertion of a twig near the root (to mark the spot), and the application of a mulch of grass clippings. People in the West and Southwest will get less use out of this book than people living in more temperate regions.

Growing Woodland Plants

by Clarence and Eleanor Birdseye
Dover Publications

■ *223 pages, many illustrations, $4.50.*

This has been the standard reference on the topic since 1951, provided you live north of Virginia and east of Montana. The Birdseyes write straightforwardly but with enough flair to keep you going through the very complete chapters of suggestions and plant lists. Consideration of woodland habitat and soil gets down to very useful instructions, including the proper use of pH papers, and there are some detailed recipes for woodland soil. The information on collecting plants—prefaced with a warning about not disturbing endangered species—is unusually thorough, down to ideas for digging out long-rooted plants inch by inch. The propagation methods are sensible and doable, generally involving no more than a flower pot and cellophane, though there is a lack of information on breaking seed dormancy. The plant dictionary contains about 200 species, including ferns and club mosses, with descriptions of flower, habit, economic and garden uses, and preferences for soil, temperature, and sun. There are an unusual number of orchids in the list, and because the Birdseyes warn about the difficulty of growing some, they don't inspire confidence in the others.

A Guide to Mountain Flowers

Utah Cooperative Extension
Bulletin EC-355
Utah State University
Logan, UT 84322

■ *60-page booklet, many black-and-white illustrations, $1.00.*

The Utah Cooperative Extension keeps coming up with good little books. This one is an introduction to Rocky Mountain flora. It is too sketchy to serve as a field guide, but for gardeners who want to grow native plants and know what habitats they come from, it is quite a handy reference. Each of the herbaceous species considered is given a line drawing and a brief description. Charts at the back indicate what mountain zone each plant grows in and what color its flowers are.

Hardesty Associates

See "Landscape Architecture and Design."

High Altitude Gardens

See "General Sources."

Home Grown Prairies

Bob and Mickey Burleson
Box 844
Temple, TX 76501

■ *20-page, photocopied, no illustrations, $1.50.*

Talk about hands-on experience. The Burlesons own a large ranch near Temple, Texas. One day, they thought that they would like to plant part of it—say, a hundred acres—to native prairie. The people at the local Soil Conservation Service told them to find established Czech and German farmers in the area, since such folks have always maintained native prairie on their spreads, in the belief that prairie hay makes their stock sweat less! The Burlesons were off. Eight years later, they had established their hundred acres with over 350 species of prairie natives, all of them collected and planted by hand. The 20-page photocopied paper is clearly written and distills years of hard-earned experience into a few thousand words of detailed how-to. A grass-and-forbs list for Texas is included.

Hubbs Bros. Seed

1522 N. 35th Street
Phoenix, AZ 85008

- *Seeds chiefly for Arizona natives.*
- *1-page list, free.*

This is as simple a seed list as you will find. The 135 entries contain common name and Latin name, nothing more. There are some good, unusual plants here—coyote melon, alligator juniper, and tree tobacco among them. The last of these is a pretty shrub that poisoned more than one settler who mistook its leaves for those of a similar-looking salad herb found in the East. The strength of the list is its grasses, native and otherwise. There are more than 30 choices, including Southwestern favorites like buffalo grass and galleta.

Jewels of the Plains

by Claude A. Barr
University of Minnesota Press

- *256 pages, some color illustrations, $19.95.*

Barr was a Montana rancher for many years. During one bad period, he started supplementing his income by taking wildflower photos. Eventually, he became one of the most knowledgeable natives gardeners on the Great Plains. The book includes a brief, engaging physiography of the Plains region, but the bulk consists of Barr's A-to-Z dictionary of plants. It shows unusual depth and penetration, and Barr is a good storyteller. Most of the entry about a certain dwarf achillea is made up of his tale about the day he found it, while taking some kids out for a hike. (He brought his treasure home in a pocket handkerchief.) There are more than 100 photographs, all very attractive and all taken by Barr.

David Kropp

The Kropp Company
11662 S. Book Road
Plainfield, IL 60544

- *Prairie landscape architect*

When I spoke with David Kropp, he was sitting at his window looking out over a winter prairie covered with snow. Farther off, there were acres of newly plowed fields with great flocks of migratory birds wheeling over them. "This is prairie country," he said. Few people know that landscape better than he does. He has created native gardens throughout the upper Midwest, from open informal prairie, to woodland edges, to elaborate front yards in suburban homes. Avoiding commercial seed mixtures, he buys strictly from local nurseries, putting sixty to eighty species in a single planting. One of his clients had a home sandwiched between one belonging to a Victorian flower gardener and another belonging to a lawn fanatic. Kropp massed colorful forbs to the Victorian side of the property and made a neat phalanx of grasses to the lawn side, allowing the two to mix in the middle of the yard. Kropp is a rare hybrid: a superb native plantsman with a designer's eye.

La Fayette Home Nursery

Route 1
Box 1A
La Fayette, IL 61449

- *Plants and seed for natives forbs, shrubs, and trees.*
- *Catalogue, $1.00.*

From what I learned of La Fayette in doing an article on wildflower gardening, it is one of the best of the Midwestern natives nurseries. It is certainly the oldest, having passed its 100th anniversary in 1986.

Landscape Plants from Utah's Mountains

by Richard Sutton and Craig W. Johnson
Utah Cooperative Extension
Bulletin EC-368
Utah State University
Logan, Utah 84322

- *135 pages, $2.00.*

Any serious native-plant enthusiast in the Intermountain region will have a field day with this book. It is limited to the trees, shrubs, and ground covers—evergreen and not—that grow wild in that area, and the authors' aim is to bring many lesser-used, gardenworthy plants to the attention of gardeners. Each of the more than 100 species listed is described for every characteristic you can think of: leaf color, fall color, flower color, flower period, fruit or berry, habit, drought tolerance, wind resistance, insects, diseases, transplantability, palatability to animals, etc. Some of the plants, like blue spruce and creeping Oregon grape, are frequently found in gardens. Many others are not. Where possible, the authors have provided a commercial source for the plant in question.

Larner Seeds

PO Box 407
Bolinas, CA 94924

- *Seed for wild forbs, shrubs, and trees; relevant books.*
- *12-page catalogue, 5 illustrations. $.50.*

Though this list of more than 200 species contains natives from many Western states and even some naturalized exotics, it is strongest in California natives. This isn't a wild-and-woolly stuffed-full list like Las Pilitas's (see next entry), but it is a pleasant and gentle introduction to California natives, including some lovely and less common plants like miner's lettuce, soap lily, and a number of eriogonums and native grasses. The book list is a short compendium of the important volumes you will find useful in growing California natives. Larner also publishes a little pamphlet, *Seed Propagation Techniques,* which sells for $1.00. It's a brief, decent, and usable guide to getting native seed to grow, with specific instructions for such techniques as stratifying seed.

CALYPSO BULBOSA

Las Pilitas Nursery

Star Route
Box 23X
Santa Margarita, CA 93453

- *California native trees, shrubs, forbs, and grasses.*
- *34-page catalogue, some illustrations, $4.00.*

Who would pay $4.00 for a catalogue in blurry 4-point type, with lousy illustrations and countless misprints? If you have the slightest interest in California natives, you would. This is one of the finest catalogues I have ever strained my eyes over. It is astonishing, funny, and informative on every topic from the edibility of some its entries to the numerous microclimates in the California landscape. Every listing gives both *Sunset* and USDA recommended climate zones for planting. There are many recommendations for companion plantings and appropriate garden settings. Among

the hundreds of plants listed are 13 varieties of penstemon and 27 of ceanothus. This catalogue deserves a better printer, but don't miss it.

Laurie's Garden

See "Annuals and Perennials."

Little Valley Farm

RR 1
Box 287
Richland Center, WI 53581

- *Plants and seeds for native wildflowers and a few shrubs; relevant books.*
- *12-page catalogue, more than 50 illustrations, $.25.*

The upper Midwest is chock full of good little wildflower companies, it seems. Here is another one. There's nothing really startling about the selections here, but the species are well described and their preferred habitat is indicated. Like many such catalogues, Little Valley's is worth checking not only for the more common stuff, but for the few rarer things that creep in. The book list is really fine, including several resources designed in and for the region.

Maver Nursery

See "Annuals and Perennials."

Midwest Wildflowers

PO Box 64
Rockton, IL 61072

- *Seeds for wildflowers.*
- *16-page catalogue, 12 illustrations, and 1-page list, free.*

The catalogue is handsome and very informative, but it lists only 12 of the 171 species offered by the company.

For culture and other information about the rest, the gardener must rely on his or her own knowledge or on one of the mail-order books that Midwest offers for sale. The list is a good mix of native and introduced wildflowers for prairie and woodland, strong on prairie species for summer bloom, but weaker for spring and autumn.

Milaeger's Gardens

See "Annuals and Perennials."

Montrose Nursery

See "Annuals and Perennials."

Moon Mountain Wildflowers

PO Box 34
Morro Bay, CA 93442

- *Wildflower seed, by individual species and in mixes.*
- *34-page catalogue, illustrated, $1.00.*

There are no surprises among the more than 50 species of wildflowers offered here. What is more surprising is the variety of mixes Moon Mountain has put together and the care they have taken with the catalogue. There are 6 different mixtures for California, including an "urban" one, not to mention specialized mixes for other parts of the country. All the species are cross-listed for their viability in shade, sun, existing grassland, and clay soils, and for their usefulness as cut flowers. Every species is keyed to the regions in which it grows best and for its time of bloom.

SHOOTING STAR

The Morton Arboretum

Lisle, IL 60532

- *Leaflets on prairie restoration, free.*

The arboretum has an active prairie restoration project in which individuals can participate as seed collectors. It publishes a very good 1-page flyer on collecting prairie seed, for their purposes or your own. The 4-page leaflet on "Restoring Illinois Tall Grass Prairie" is a fine, basic how-to guide, with references for further information and a useful list of local nurseries in Illinois and Wisconsin. The arboretum also offers a species list for prairie restoration, the sort of thing you might use as a checklist in creating a prairie garden.

The National Wildflower Research Center

2600 FM 973 North
Austin, TX 78725

- *Nonprofit organization dedicated to wildflower research.*
- *Quarterly newsletter, annual membership $20.00.*
- *State-by-state listing of wildflower sources, free.*

Their very first newsletter (Spring, 1984) features Ladybird Johnson standing in a field of wildflowers. This is only right, since the center is the latest of her brainchildren for beautifying Texas and the nation at large. The land for the test gardens and the original operating funds were her gift. Directed by David Northington, a capable botanist from Texas Tech, the center is already experimenting with a range of natives and commercial wildflower mixes. It is also trying every planting technique known to man and the highway department, plus a few the staff has thought up on its own. The newsletter reports on results of all these tests and keeps readers abreast of wildfloweriana around the country. But one of the best things about this organization is that it can tell you, on request, where to find as many wildflower and natives sources as they have been able to turn up for any of the fifty states. Some of these lists are still pretty spare, but they are to be updated. Updating will be important, since some of the listings go out of date when a hobbyist chucks a parttime seed business for an MBA program, but almost every list contains a valuable source or two, of the kind you might not hear of otherwise. If you are a strict nativist, you will of course frown at the reprints from the Applewood Seed Company catalogue that come appended to each list. Sure enough, the plants included may not be natives, and some—heaven forbid—are really garden perennials. But all this should scare no one away from the center's serious and growing effort.

Not yet have we reached Tipton. Behold a white flower, worthy of a better name, that the farmers call "sheep's tea." Behold purple larkspur joining the lavender larkspur. Behold that disreputable camp-follower the button-weed, wearing its shabby finery. Now a red delicate grass joins in, and a big purple and pink sort of an aster. Behold a pink and white sheep's tea. And look, there is a dwarf morning glory, the sweetest in the world. Here is a group of black-eyed susans, marching like suffragettes to get the vote at Tipton. Here is a war-dance of Indian Paint. And here are bluebells.

—VACHEL LINDSAY, FROM *ADVENTURES WHILE PREACHING THE GOSPEL OF BEAUTY* (1914)

Native Seeds, Inc.

14590 Triadelphia Mill Road
Dayton, MD 21036

- *Seeds for wildflowers.*
- *4-page leaflet, 10 color illustrations, free.*

The botanists who run this company have made a short list of wildflowers—only 27 species in all—selecting them for their beauty and adaptability to most U.S. climates. Seed packs contain complete planting instructions. The leaflet illustrations are excellent. This is a good choice for the wildflower beginner who nonetheless wants to create his or her own garden with a small, manageable palette.

COMMON EVENING PRIMROSE

Native Sons

379 W. El Campo Road
Arroyo Grande, CA 93420

- *Plants for California-native wildflowers, trees, and shrubs.*
- *16-page catalogue, no illustrations, free.*

Native Sons has a good list to keep on hand for comparison with Las Pilitas Nursery (see page 115). The former is strictly wholesale, so you will have to convince your local garden center to order what you want. The catalogue is not at all descriptive. If you want to plop large trees right into your landscape, the firm offers 8 natives—California buckeye, incense cedar, tanbark oak, California sycamore, coast live oak, island oak, coast redwood, and bay laurel—all in a 24-inch-box size.

Native Trees of the Intermountain Region

by Carl M. Johnson
Utah Cooperative Extension
Bulletin EC-407
Utah State University
Logan, UT 84322

- *82 pages, many black-and-white illustrations, $6.00.*

Another good woody plants guide from the Utah Extension (see also page 247), which contains about 86 trees in all, most natives and all growing wild in the area. The author has done a fine job of photogaphing all of them to show habit, scale, foliage, and bark texture. The text gives a nice idea of what happens to the tree's look as it ages, and it describes the leaves, flowers, twigs, and bark separately. The volume digests the author's own wide experience and the scholarly literature into a brief and useful guide.

The Natural Garden

38W443 Highway 64
St. Charles, IL 60174

- *Plants and seeds for prairie forbs and grasses.*
- *22-page catalogue, $2.00.*

You can order the price list for free, but the full catalogue is worth the $2.00. It contains all sorts of useful planting and design advice, and the species are listed in an ingenious shorthand that tells you briefly most everything you'll need to know. The list is extremely broad, including quite rare species like the Kankakee mallow. Some must be ordered well in advance, since the owners will only collect the seed at your bidding. (The catalogue tells you which species this restriction applies to.) Not to scare the beginner away, there are also good collections for different prairie conditions.

Natural Gardens

113 Jasper Lane
Oak Ridge, TN 37830

- *Plants and seed for native and naturalized flowers and shrubs; some garden perennials.*
- *18-page catalogue, $.50.*

No wildflower mixes are to be found here. The list contains well-described native and naturalized species, some of which are widely available and others of which are less-common Southeastern natives. Even where the type is common, Natural Gardens offers more choice of species: there are five goldenrods, three lobelias, four monardas, and four sunflowers.

Natural Landscaping

by John Diekelmann and Robert Schuster
McGraw-Hill

- *276 pages, many illustrations, some color, $24.95.*

If you live in the Northeast or Midwest, you are lucky: you can make use of this fine book. The authors have described in great detail—but readably—the chief plant communities of the Eastern temperate zones, explaining what grows where and why. Having literally laid out the groundwork for you, they then consider the design of gardens that will harmonize with the existing plant communities. The chapter on design around the home uses only a single example, but the authors have taken particular care to make it one that anthologizes the characteristics of many small-home sites. A separate chapter tells how to work in open fields and in the larger landscape, and there are also chapters about shade and wetlands design. Every plant community they discuss has a list of its constituent species at the back of the book, and there is even a guide to the parks and gardens you may visit to see both the commu-

nities and their species. The book will not tell you how to lay a path or propagate plants, but if you are already a competent gardener, it will give you countless ideas.

Nature's Design

by Carol A. Smyser et al.
Rodale Press

- *390 pages, many illustrations, a few in color, $22.95.*

Of all the books I know that describe landscaping with native plants, this one has the broadest application and the most complete how-to information. Of course, I miss here the brilliant and loving descriptions of native plant communities that appear in Diekelmann and Schuster's book (see previous entry), and I was more than once annoyed by phrases like the following: "Unless it stems directly from the ecological characteristics of the site, and unless it uses native plants, a landscape just isn't natural." Let's not be so picky! On the other hand, the authors are not among those who try to tell you that gardening with natives is a snap. If you are ready for the effort, they will give you a very complete idea of how to proceed, from drawing a site plan, to putting in paving and walls, to propagating plants, to deciding which species to use. Very helpfully, they have developed native-species lists for every region of the country, with information on native habitat, growth habit, and propagation for each species. Throughout the chapters, when it comes to describing, say, the placement of shade trees or windbreaks, they also suggest the most appropriate species to use for the region. There are even instructions for making birdhouses!

Nature's Garden

See "Annuals and Perennials."

New England Wild Flower Society

Garden in the Woods
Hemenway Road
Framingham, MA 01701

Garden in the Woods Cultivation Guide

■ *61 pages, a few illustrations, $5.50 ppd.*

Nursery Sources: Native Plants and Wild Flowers

■ *53 pages, $4.50 ppd.*

Pocket Key to Common Wild Flowers

by Lawrence Newcomb

■ *104 pages, $5.95 ppd.*

Wild Flower Notes

■ *Variable-length, twice-annually newsletter, some illustrations, subscription $5.50 ppd.*

The New England Wild Flower Society has been around since 1922, long before the present vogue for wildflowers. Its gardens are justly famous, as is its expertise. Though Northeastern gardeners will benefit most from the society, the *Cultivation Guide* and *Nursery Sources* are extremely valuable for natives and wildflower gardeners throughout the country. If you should be a lucky New Englander, it is well worth joining the society, the price of membership being $15.00 per year. (Members get the *Notes* and a newsletter free.)

The *Cultivation Guide* won't help you with specific germination techniques, though its bibliography tells you where to learn about that topic. On the other hand, it catalogues more than 270 species of natives and naturalized flowers, describing preferred soil, sun, pH, and the color, size, and

bloom time of each. More helpful still, it contains a whole section of lists telling which of the species grow well together.

Nursery Sources, like the SCSA's source book (see page 121), lists as many sources of native and naturalized plants as the compilers could find. If you are a serious enthusiast, you'd do well to look at both, since they don't duplicate each other. The New England Society's volume performs the additional service of telling you whether a firm collects, propagates, or buys in its seed and plants.

Newcomb's Wildflower Guide is well known as a terrific field guide, but before he published the full-blown book, he had already done the *Pocket Key to Common Wild Flowers* for the society. Uncharacteristically, in these days of full-color field guides, the *Pocket Key* is completely unillustrated, but it is so ingeniously organized that it is perhaps easier to use than most of the glossy picture books. Each species is assigned a three-digit number—the first referring to flower color, the second to flower parts, and

OPUNTIA MICRODASYS

the third to leaves. When you look under the relevant number, you find only those plants that fit the general description. I can't think of a better way to identify flowers in the field. Be aware, however, that the book is meant for people in the Northeast.

Wild Flower Notes is full of articles about the society's wildflowers and natives and about their important students, but it is directed mainly at New England enthusiasts.

The New Wildflowers & How to Grow Them

by Edwin F. Steffek
Timber Press

■ *200 pages, some illustrations, a few color, $17.95.*

Steffek's book is well regarded by wildflower gardeners—partly, I imagine, because he succeeds in covering so much territory. He lists and describes more than 560 species of herbaceous and woody ornamentals, even azaleas and rhododendrons, illustrating about a tenth of them with nice color pictures. The list is weighted toward the Eastern part of the country, but Steffek has made an effort to include Western species as well, making his book more wideranging than Sperka's (page 113). You will find clarkias, mariposa lilies, manzanitas, and darlingtonias here, for example. There are herbaceous plants, bulbs, shrubs, and nice group of carnivorous plants. Descriptions include decent cultural information. I have one complaint and one question: his A-to-Z list takes some getting used to, since he shifts with abandon from Latin to common names in his headings; also in the title, what does he mean by "New"?

North Carolina Native Plant Propagation Handbook

North Carolina Wild Flower
Preservation Society
Totten Garden Center, 457-A, UNC
North Carolina Botanical Garden
Chapel Hill, NC 27514

■ *79 pages, $5.00.*

Here's a nice A-to-Z list of native plants, both herbaceous and woody, for North Carolina gardens. The cultural and propagation information is serviceable, and there is a decent introduction to seed collection and storage. The separate section on propagating ferns is particularly good, as is the list of seeds that need stratifying and the information on when to sow seed for any of the plants included in the book. The authors have thoughtfully singled out 24 natives for their ease of cultivation. The bibliography is worth looking at.

Orchid Gardens

6700 Splithand Road
Grand Rapids, MI 55744

- *Plants for native and naturalized wildflowers, mosses, ferns and a few woody plants; a few garden perennials and lilies; books.*
- *17-page catalogue, $.50.*

According to proprietor Norma Phillips, the post office has changed her address eleven times, but she has been propagating and selling wildflowers at the same place since 1945. Her cultural instructions are very good and, unlike a number of the national wildflower companies, they are not too sanguine. If anything, she is positively intimidating about the cultural requirements of the plants she sells, but this will not scare experienced natives growers away. The list is quite long and varied, with everything from woodland to streamside and meadow species. Native violets and ferns are a specialty, along with the difficult club mosses. Mrs. Phillips offers three or four species of native orchids, depending on the state of her propagating beds. She will not let you buy her orchids except when an equal or greater dollar value in other plants is ordered, and she is positively forbidding about their chance of blooming.

Owl Ridge Alpines

See "Annuals and Perennials."

Painted Meadows Seed Company

PO Box 1865
Kingston, PA 18704

- *Wildflower seed.*
- *4-page leaflet, 5 color illustrations, free.*

If you want a wildflower meadow with a minimum of trouble, Painted Meadows is a good company to go to. Its list is only 12 species long, selected for color, adaptability and a full season of bloom, and it is offered in a single, standard mix sold by the pound.

Passiflora

PO Box 99
Germanton, NC 27019

- *Seeds and plants for wildflowers; books.*
- *8-page catalogue, 34 color illustrations, $1.00.*

There is nothing startling about this list. Indeed, it comprises the 34 wildflowers most commonly grown around the country. Some are not native even to the U.S., much less to the Southeast, and I wish the authors had excluded chicory, or at least warned people that it can be invasive. On the other hand, all of the plants are very well illustrated in color, and, unlike many companies listing these species, Passiflora sells plants, not just seed.

The Theodore Payne Foundation

10459 Tuxford Street
Sun Valley, CA 91352

- *Nonprofit, membership organization offering seed of natives by mail order.*
- *4-page list, free.*

Theodore Payne was one of California's pioneer native plantsmen. Among other things, he provided

most of the native plant material for the Santa Barbara Botanic Garden's excellent collection. The Foundation carries on his work, with the help of member volunteers from the Los Angeles area. The 21-acre nursery is open to visitors and sells plants onsite. The mail-order list contains a good selection of native California wildflowers and their cultivars; it is especially strong in lupines.

CALIFORNIA POPPIES

Plants of the Southwest

1812 Second Street
Santa Fe, NM 87501

- *Native and naturalized wildflower, shrub, tree, and grass seed; indigenous and drought-tolerant vegetable seed.*
- *48-page catalogue, 30 color illustrations, $1.00.*

This is one of the finest seed catalogues available for gardeners working in the difficult Southwest. The listings are extensive, and each entry is well described, including important cultural hints. The company also offers a number of unusual wildflower mixes, a terrific selection of grasses, and special cutting-garden, hummingbird-garden, and kitchen-garden assortments, the last of these complete with the *Pueblo Indian Cookbook*. The catalogue makes good reading as a reference, and the illustrations (all of wildflowers) are excellent.

Prairie Moon Nursery

Route 3
Box 163
Winona, MN 55987

- *Plants and seeds for prairie-native forbs, grasses, and shrubs; books.*
- *28-page catalogue, $.50.*

Son of Douglas and Dorothy Wade of Windrift (see page 124), Alan Wade has, if anything, outdone his parents. Like theirs, his list is simple and unadorned—not for the rank novice—but it is even richer in prairie species than the terrific list from Windrift. His seed sources cover the upper Midwest, and the list contains, among many others, 3 anemones, 7 milkweeds, 8 asters, 5 gentians, 5 blazing stars, and about 17 grasses and sedges. He also offers a variety of mixes for dry, mesic, and wet conditions in tall- and short-grass prairie. The book list is outstanding, including how-to prairie handbooks and historical works like Steven Foster's *Echinacea Exalted*, an account of the many medicinal uses of the purple coneflower.

Prairie Nursery

PO Box 365
Westfield, WI 53964

- *Plants for prairie natives: forbs, grasses, and shrubs; books.*
- *38-page catalogue, 39 illustrations, $1.00.*

It is what its name suggests: a topflight nursery for prairie forbs and grasses. There are more than 200 entries in the list, weighted heavily toward forbs but with a good representation of the important grasses and the few native shrubs. Many of the entries are illustrated, all contain a fine description of the plant, noting its appearance, size, bloom period, and ethnobotanical information. If a plant will take a long time to mature in your garden, the entry will tell you

how long. Separate lists suggest which plants to grow in dry, mesic or wet soils, and there are collections for attracting butterflies and birds, and for the tall- and short-grass prairies. The book list contains several important regional publications that will be of great help to the prairie gardener.

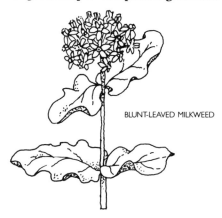

BLUNT-LEAVED MILKWEED

Prairie Propagation Handbook

by Harold W. Rock
Wehr Nature Center
Whitnall Park
5879 S. 92nd Street
Hales Corners, WI 53130

- *74 pages, $3.79.*

Rock has written a handy pamphlet for prairie gardeners in Wisconsin and Northern Illinois, though residents of other areas can certainly use it as well. He outlines at least 5 different propagation methods, keying each of the more than 250 forbs and grasses he lists to 1 or more of the methods. There are handy lists of the backbone species for all prairies—wet to dry—and every one of the plants in the dictionary comes with a suggested time for seed harvest, if you are collecting your own. The bibliography at the back is very, very good. It will take you years to exhaust it. The Wehr Center can also send you sheets about nursery sources, prairie planting techniques, and native ferns for the landscape.

Clyde Robin Seed Company

PO Box 2855
Castro Valley, CA 94546

- *Wildflower seed and mixes, with selected herb, tree, and shrub seed.*
- *54-page catalogue, 40 color illustrations of wildflowers, $2.00.*

Robin's firm has little interest in natives, but it does provide a list that rivals Applewood's for adaptable wildflowers. These are the people who gave us "Meadow in a Can," but they also offer a number of mixes for different regions, plant sizes, and periods of bloom. The species list is predictable, including a fair number of cosmopolitans like chicory and cornflower, but the fine illustrations make the catalog worth the price. Descriptions are a bit sanguine. Indian paintbrush, for instance, is characterized as "will grow anywhere." That may be so, but some people have a hard time getting Indian paintbrush seed to germinate. Still, Robin is a big, dependable company and a good place for the wildflower gardener to begin.

The Root Book

by Norma Phillips
6700 Splithand Road
Grand Rapids, MN 55744

- *103-page book, many illustrations, a few in color, $9.50, $1.25 handling.*

The author runs Orchid Gardens (see page 119), and the book is a planting guide for much of the material she sells. It digests a lot of the wisdom she has acquired over almost half a century of propagating wildflowers. Some of her general tips—like making leaf mulch by running a lawnmower over the leaves or burying a rotting oak log beneath a bed where you want acid soil—are really useful. The plant-by-plant section—though the information it contains is generally available elsewhere—is distinguished by the very nice photographs showing actual roots at their correct soil depth and attitude for planting. There are 73 different species included, embracing orchids and club mosses. If you are a serious natives or wild gardener, this book is worth a look.

Seed Identification Manual

by Alexander C. Martin and William D. Barkley
University of California Press

■ *221 pages, many illustrations, $35.00.*

The book covers more than 600 native and introduced plants of the West, grouped by habitat: farmlands, wetlands, and woodlands. There are 824 black-and-white photographs showing the seeds both enlarged and at actual size, together with descriptions of each seed, its resulting plant, and the habitats it prefers. It is wonderful just to see the variety of seeds, some like hedgehogs, cowries, or limpets, others like jades, feathers, or coins. Quite a number of the plants are classified as weeds, but among them are many of the plants prized by natives and wildflower gardeners.

Selected California Native Plants with Commercial Sources

Saratoga Horticultural Foundation
15185 Murphy Avenue
San Martin, CA 95046

■ *67 pages, $4.75 ppd.*

This very plain and useful book consists largely of a big chart of California natives, divided into herbaceous plants, ferns, and trees and shrubs. Each species listed is described for habitat, special comments, recommended planting size, planting sea-

son, and propagating season. The accompanying list of 54 nurseries and seed companies is keyed to the species list, so you know who has what. Look, too, at the fine bibliography of local literature on the subject.

Shady Oaks Nursery

See "Annuals and Perennials."

Siskiyou Rare Plant Nursery

2825 Cummings Road
Medford, OR 97501

■ *Plants for alpine and dwarf rock-garden species, including Northwestern natives and dwarf conifers.*
■ *68-page catalogue, plus supplementary lists, 25 illustrations, $1.50.*

In the West particularly, rock-garden nurseries tend to specialize in natives as part of their business. Siskiyou's immense 1,000 + -plant list includes a mere 200 natives, but they form a choice list of herbaceous perennials, ferns, and woody ground covers and shrubs. There are, for example, 15 different lewisias, an equal number of penstemons, the lovely and rare kalmiopsis, a nice dwarf kalmia, several orchids, the dwarf arctic birch, and 4 native gentians. Otherwise, the catalogue is very strong in most alpine genera from around the world, including the rare acantholimon from Greece, South American calceolarias, heather, campanulas, chrysanthemums, daphnes, shooting stars, dwarf brooms, gentians, saxifrages, club mosses, violets, and phlox. Among the last of these are the large-flowering hybrids from Chihuahua, Mexico. There are also strong groups of dwarf conifers and rhododendrons, together with other selected woody dwarfs. This is a very large and first-rate list; its plants are well described.

Sources of Native Seeds and Plants

Soil Conservation Society of America
7515 N.E. Ankeny Road
Ankeny, IA 50021

■ *32 pages, $3.00.*

Here's a handy list of many of the native-plants providers around the country. Each entry tells whether the given company stocks forbs, grasses, and/or shrubs and trees. Since some of the firms don't do mail order, and since I haven't the space to list every one of them, you will find some listings in this pamphlet that you don't find in this volume. The SCSA promises to update the list, though my copy is from 1982.

Southwestern Native Seeds

Box 50503
Tucson, AZ 85703

■ *Seed of native wildflowers, shrubs, trees, and succulents.*
■ *5-page list, 5 illustrations, $1.00.*

For the serious grower of Southwestern natives, this is the very best list imaginable. All species are selected for their flowers or foliage, and there are 330 of them in all. There are any number of rarities here, some to be found nowhere else in the trade. Tabular descriptions of each tell not only its outstanding garden qualities and the colors of its flowers, but also the county it comes from and the elevations where it grows best. Any gardener west of the Rockies can find something irresistible in this remarkable list.

Dean Swift Seed Company

See "Trees and Shrubs."

Texas Natives

How to Grow Native Plants of Texas and the Southwest

by Jill Nokes
Texas Monthly Press (address below)

- *404 pages, some color illustrations, $26.95.*

Landscaping with Native Texas Plants

by Sally Wasowski and Julie Ryan
Texas Monthly Press
PO Box 1569
Austin, TX 78767

- *288 pages, many color illustrations, $23.95.*

Native Plants for Landscaping in Northern New Mexico

Native Plants for Landscaping in Southern New Mexico

Native Plant Society of New Mexico
PO Box 5917
Santa Fe, NM 87502

Despite its title, the Wasowski and Ryan book does not contain a lot of suggestions for landscape design, though a few sample plans are scattered through the volume. It does cover about 100 species of Texas natives—herbaceous and woody—with beautiful color photographs and excellent descriptive entries detailing all pertinent information plus suggestions for landscape uses. A special dividend is the section on prairie planting at the back, supplied by Bob and Mickey Burleson, who also sends out a fine, mimeographed planting guide themselves. Jill Nokes's book focuses on the collection and propagation of more than 350 species, some of which are illustrated with lovely color paintings. The notes for seed collecting and propagating are unusually detailed and clear. She gives you a far larger palette than do Wasowski and Ryan, but she doesn't tell you as much about how to use the plants in the landscape. The Texas gardener is lucky to have 2 such fine books on natives; elsewhere in the nation, perhaps only California is so lucky.

Both the Texas books will be of service to many Southwestern gardeners, too, but non-Texans should look into the 2 volumes from the Native Plant Society of New Mexico. I was not able to see them myself, but the society has a good reputation.

ERYNGO

Vermont Wildflower Farm

Route 7
Charlotte, VT 05445

- *Seed for wildflower species and mixes.*
- *16-page catalogue, 36 color illustrations, free.*

I had heard that the wildflower gardens the Allens maintain near Charlotte are varied and particularly rich in woodland flowers. The catalogue, attractive as it is, was a disappointment, since the farm apparently sells only the common meadow species—individually and as mixes—by mail. Nevertheless, the mixes are well selected for a variety of regions and situations. Visit the farm, if you can.

Wayside Gardens

See "Annnuals and Perennials."

Weber Native Plant Nursery

237 Seeman Drive
Encinitas, CA 92024

- *Native plants of southern California.*
- *Annual 1-page availability list, plus fact sheets on selected varieties, free.*

Most of California's native plant companies are in Northern California. One exception is Weber, located in San Diego County. Weber focuses on California natives from and for southern California. The list is strong everywhere from ground covers to perennials to trees and shrubs, and the learned fact sheets provide more than enough information for growing them. If you don't know the plant already, it's a good idea to ask for advice or to consult the relevant fact sheet first.

White Flower Farm

See "Annuals and Perennials."

Wildflower

c/o James Hodgins
90 Wolfrey Avenue
Toronto, Ontario
CANADA M4K 1K8

- *"Canada's National Magazine of Wild Flora."*
- *Quarterly, $15.00 annual membership fee for The Canadian Wildflower Society.*

This fine, simply produced periodical should interest wildflower gardeners in the northern tier of the United States, as well as in Canada. There is a feature on a single species in each issue, describing in great detail where to find it and what to do with it. Other articles cover everything from wildland travel to regional flora to plant explorers, and there is a section of book reviews. One of the best things about *Wildflower* is the seed exchange it operates and updates quarterly.

The Wildflower Source

Box 312
Fox Lake, IL 60020

- *Woodland wildflower plants.*
- *7-page list, some inserted photographs, $1.00.*

The list is strongest in orchids and trillium; there are seven of the former and six of the latter. Among the asarums is an interesting native mottled ginger, *Asarum shuttleworthii*, and you can get large, container-grown plants of European ginger here, as well. The list is otherwise interesting and unusual for its selection of woodland plants.

GAILLARDIA

The Wild Garden

by Violet Stevenson
Viking Penguin

- *168 pages, many color illustrations, $27.50.*

The book is part of a series that the company brings in from the U.K. Like its companions, it too will probably soon be available in paperback at a more reasonable price than listed above. *The Wild Garden* is well worth having for people who want a wild look to their gardens. It is *not* for lovers of American natives, but it does a very fine job of tracing the evolution from the "wild" garden of William Robinson—a matter of rough style, not of ecological plantings—to the more recent wild garden, which puts more emphasis on native and naturalized species of the local countryside. The result is a mixed approach, which admires natives without disallowing cultivars. The author and editors have gone out of their way

to make the volume useful for American gardeners, adapting it to some of the wildflower species more commonly grown here and using a sprinkling of American photos. There are many suggestions—together with sample plans and plant lists—for wildflower lawns and meadows, woodland gardens, heaths and heathers, ferns, herbs, plants to attract butterflies, and water and rock gardens, all in natural styles. Advice on soils, propagation, care, and the like are generally adequate. Plants for different situations are gathered in alphabetical charts at the back, with all sorts of relevant information about them. My only complaint about the charts is that, while the author has clearly chosen species that we can use in the U.S., she has left out even some of our more common wildflowers, like purple coneflower and California poppy. Personally, I find her advice admirable but intimidating, and I run to my Thomas Church to be reassured that pictorial beauty is not the only end of gardening.

Wildginger Woodlands

PO Box 1091
Webster, NY 14580

- *Plants, seeds, and spores for native and naturalized wildflowers, ferns, and shrubs; books.*
- *13-page catalogue, 30 illustrations, $1.00.*

Phyllis Farkas grows all of this very large list at her home just south of Lake Ontario and in a 20-acre woodland nearby. It's a one-woman show, so you may have to wait a while for some of the material you order. The catalogue starts with the best possible warning against simply strewing seed and expecting it to grow: it's Matthew 13:3–8, in which seeds fell by the wayside and upon stony places, and the fowl devoured them and the sun scorched them. Thereafter, she launches into a list of more than 185

species. (Cultural instructions for some of these appear at the back of the catalogue.) I won't try to summarize it, but do take a look. There are 8 trilliums and 15 violets.

Wildland & Native Seeds Foundation

2402 Hoffman Drive, N.E.
Albuquerque, NM 87110

- *Nonprofit organization promoting conservation and propagation of natives; annual membership $25.00 (associate), $10 (subscribing affiliate).*
- *Custom collecting of hard-to-find New Mexico and Arizona natives.*

For the serious Southwestern natives gardener, this foundation is a valuable resource. Its custom collecting is done mainly for researchers, but it provides a free referral service to individuals seeking particular species. If you collect seed yourself in Arizona or New Mexico, it is worth becoming at least a subscribing affiliate, in order to receive the periodical flyer "Seed Collector's Notes." Issues are devoted to topics from collecting methods, to species and genera, to hazards of collecting.

> Maybe you can understand how I feel. The middle of winter is just that—the middle. It's not the end of one thing and the beginning of something new, but rather an arbitrary date selected by, I'll bet, a committee. The choice of January 1 as the beginning of a new year must have been a compromise. Sort of like the platypus or camel.
> —FROM *GLEANINGS IN BEE CULTURE*, (1987)

Wildwood Farm

See "Annuals and Perennials."

Windrift Prairie Shop & Nursery

RD 2

Oregon, IL 61061

- *Seeds and plants for prairie-native forbs and grasses.*
- *6-page flyer, $.40.*

Douglas and Dorothy Wade started growing prairie natives in 1965 and quickly found themselves running a nursery. It's a remarkable mom-and-pop operation, not only for its fine list of uncompromisingly pure prairie forbs and grasses, but because the Wades' son Alan has gone on to start his own prairie nursery up in Minnesota (see page 120). Doug Wade is a bitter enemy of exotics, so don't expect to find any California poppy or purple loosestrife on his list. It is also a very simple catalogue, giving only common and Latin names plus character of native habitat. You will find that almost all seeds and plants are propagated from material collected in remnant prairie (mostly around railroad tracks) in the Wades' area of Illinois.

Woodlanders

1128 Colleton Avenue

Aiken, SC 29801

- *Plants of native and uncommon exotic trees, shrubs, ferns, and flowers.*
- *12-page list, free; 24-page descriptive catalogue, 11 illustrations, $1.50.*

Woodlanders offers one of the best lists of Southeastern natives available, particularly in trees and shrubs. Of the several hundred selections, most are best adapted to zones 5–8. There are 19 rhododendrons listed, mainly natives, plus 5 native phloxes, and many lesser-known species of outstanding genera, such as the American wisteria. Recently, Woodlanders has been searching overseas for garden plants, coming back with a number of interesting Oriental and Australian varieties, as well as the true Mediterranean laurel and myrtle—plants the Southerner is lucky enough to be able to grow.

Wyrttun Ward

See "Vegetables and Herbs."

GARDEN PHLOX

Yerba Buena Nursery

19500 Skyline Boulevard

Woodside, CA 94062

- *California native plants, and native and exotic ferns.*
- *12-page catalogue, no illustrations, $1.00.*

The selection of more than 250 native forbs, trees, and shrubs is similar to Las Pilitas's (see page 115). Unlike the Las Pilitas catalogue, this contains no descriptions or instructions. The nursery is located in the San Francisco Bay area, though, and it has a very nice demonstration garden where the visitor can see what all these strange plants actually look like in cultivation. Yerba Buena's fern list, on the other hand, is 71 varieties long and among the best available. The company stocks everything from the California goldback to the silver-pink Japanese painted fern.

5 Vegetables and Herbs

Ahrens Strawberry Nurseries

RR 1
Huntingburg, IN 47542

- *Strawberry plants, plus a few other berries, grapes and asparagus, fruit trees, and growing supplies.*
- *34-page catalogue, full color, free.*

Among the big Eastern strawberry firms—like Ahrens, Allen, and Brittingham—Ahrens has the largest selection and the cheapest prices. Its beautiful catalogue is unusually informative. Like its competitors, Ahrens has picked up a useful chart from the USDA comparing the ripening characteristics, fruit quality, and disease resistance of every one of the varieties it carries. The strawberry is the most widely distributed of all temperate-zone fruits, but Ahrens offers cultivars chiefly for the areas east of the Rockies and north of the Gulf states. A number of other berries also appear in the catalogue, including a not-too-thorny gooseberry for those who are longing for a good gooseberry fool.

STRAWBERRIES

Allen Company

PO Box 1577
Salisbury, MD 21801

- *Strawberry plants, plus some other berries and asparagus.*
- *48-page catalogue, 27 color illustrations, free.*

Allen is the oldest strawberry firm in the country, dating to 1885, and was a pioneer in the propagation of the certified virus-free plants that now dominate the market. The Allens were instrumental in the creation of the USDA-Maryland cooperative breeding program that has developed many outstanding varieties. The company maintains stock of all existing varieties, presenting a selection of 25 or so in its catalogue each year.

I should issue a Raspberry Edict. It would enact that no gardener, under the penalty of having his right hand cut off, must plant raspberries near the hedge. Tell me, what has a gardener done to have everlasting raspberry suckers from his neighbour's garden sprouting in the middle of his rhododendrons? These raspberries sprawl underneath the ground for miles; no hedge, wall, or trench, not even barbed wire or a warning notice, will stop them; a raspberry sucker will shoot up in the middle of a bed of carnations or evening primroses, and there it is! Every single one of your raspberries ought to become black with lice! Raspberry suckers ought to sprout in the middle of your bed. Warts as big as ripe raspberries ought to grow on your face.

—KAREL CAPEK, FROM *THE GARDENER'S YEAR* (1929)

American Gourd Society

PO Box 274
Mount Gilead, OH 43338

■ *Nonprofit organization for the culture of ornamental and useful gourds; numerous brief publications, newsletter, and seed exchange; annual membership $3.00.*

Dedicated gourd people are generally craftspeople too. When you join this society, you get a membership card, a sheet on how to keep and dry gourds, and a list of publications. Then you can start carving, everything from dippers and figurines to bird houses and banjos. There are also those who simply collect colorful, ornamental gourds or raise such useful ones as luffa. The newsletter contains reports from local chapters, request letters like "Since Mr. Odom died, I need a new source for bushel-basket gourds," illustrated reports like, "Here is a photo of my gourd musical instruments. The dulcimer on the left is tuned by a skate key." The book-and-pamphlet list is quite nice, including a reprint of L. H. Bailey's *The Garden of Gourds*. A separate periodical lists seed and other items for sale. One recent correspondent offered a selection that gives you an idea of the variety of gourds: "dumbbell, lump-in-neck bottle, penguin, pow-derhorn, dipper, Chinese bottle, Indonesian bottle, Hercules club, retort, kettle, sugar trough, calabash, Costa Rica bottle, caveman's club, syphon, club, Japanese bottle, Indian club, maranka, dolphin, giant club, water calabash, calabash pipe," and more.

American Medicinal Plants

by Charles F. Millspaugh
Dover Publications

■ *806 pages, many illustrations, $12.00 pbk.*

Here's the classic manual on medicinal herbs, originally published in 1892. Unfortunately, Dover had to convert Millspaugh's brilliant color plates to black-and-white in order to reprint the book at a reasonable price. The volume was originally meant for students of the pharmacopoeia, so it is not a rattling good read. Still, it's stuffed with information on 1,000 native or introduced plants, including pictures, descriptions, habitats, and preparations for pharmacological use.

Ancient Herbs in the J. Paul Getty Museum Garden

by Jeanne D'Andrea
The J. Paul Getty Museum
17985 Pacific Coast Highway
Malibu, CA 90265

■ *91 pages, many illustrations, $10.00.*

For those with the antiquarian interest in herbs, here is a very fine introduction to the herbs used in ancient Greece and Rome (all of which are grown in the Getty garden). D'Andrea's scholarship is first-rate, and her essays provide a fascinating account of the religious, magical and medicinal uses of 21 herbs. It is also a fine reference for those looking into the earliest roots of modern botany.

Arkansas Valley Seed Company

PO Box 270
Rocky Ford, CO 81067

■ *Seed for grains, cover crops, reclamation grasses, and turfgrass.*
■ *4-page list, free.*

Though it is used to dealing with big customers, this firm does sell by the pound. It offers a fine selection of grain, cover, and pasture grasses.

Barney's Ginseng Patch

Route 2
Box 43RTP
Montgomery City, MO 63361

■ *Ginseng and goldenseal seeds, roots, guides, and manuals.*
■ *34-page catalogue, illustrated, free.*

The catalogue is a mess, but Barney knows about ginseng. He buys and sells the roots and seeds, offers information on markets for ginseng root, and sells cultivation manuals by mail. Ginseng is an important cash crop in the Southeast, and the catalogue is aimed at growing for profit.

Becker's Seed Potatoes

RR 1
Trout Creek, Ontario
CANADA P0H 2L0

■ *Potato eyes.*
■ *2-page list, 1-page planting instructions, free.*

A nice list of about 25 varieties of potato—some old, some recent introductions, and some experimental strains. Canadians can order in lots of 25 or 50 eyes; U.S. customers must order a minimum of 50.

Beginning Hydroponics

by Richard E. Nicholls
Running Press

- *126 pages, some instructions, $7.95.*

Nicholls makes it seem possible, and even desirable, to try hydroponics on a small scale, and I mean small. Using this book, you can start as small as a single pot. He provides good hands-on instructions, a simple comparison of the different methods, and a comprehensive list of sources of supply.

> Someone asked him the price of [a huge melon]. "All I wants is de price ob de chicken, sah!" Seeing no chicken about, an explanation was asked. "Why you see, sah, early in de spring, before plantin' time comes, I take a young chicken with seven dry watermelons seeds—just seven—and just as soon as he got dem seven seeds down his troat, I kills him and sah, I plant dat der chicken in de middle ob de patch."
>
> —FROM *BAER'S AGRICULTURAL ALMANAC* (1897)

Better Vegetable Gardens the Chinese Way

by Peter Chan
Garden Way Publishing

- *103 pages, many illustrations, a few in color, $9.95 pbk.*

Chan was trained in mainland China and has since brought his knowledge of raised-bed gardening to the Pacific Northwest. The book is charmingly written, if poorly designed, and it is peppered with pithy sayings in Chinese and English like, "If the people work hard, then the earth won't be lazy." Photos of Chan's own raised-bed garden are beautiful and inspir-ing. The information is serviceable, though planting dates for vegetables are geared to the Pacific Northwest. It's a relaxed introduction to an attractive and workable system.

Biodynamic Farming & Gardening Association

PO Box 550
Kimberton, PA 19442

- *Nonprofit organization dedicated to a sort of organic agriculture with philosophical roots in the work of Rudolf Steiner.*
- *80-page quarterly* Biodynamics, *many illustrations; discounts on some books and on biodynamic compost and growth promoters; annual membership $20.00.*

Though Rudolf Steiner's ideas about life force may be too much for most of us, biodynamics has been an important and pioneering branch of organic gardening for many years. The magazine features many articles on the future of market gardening and the small farm, with practical suggestions for organic gardeners. Even where an article ends up talking about the mystical laws of form and the role of the Holy Spirit—as did a recent one about "Mound Gardening"—the story of what the family actually did is valuable. And even the crazier parts of it are provocative. The organization is also the source for most of the important literature of the biodynamic movement.

Boston Mountain Nurseries

Route 2
Box 405-A
Mountainburg, AR 72946

- *Berry and grape plants.*
- *10-page catalogue, no illustrations, free.*

Blackberries, raspberries, dewberries, wineberries, strawberries, blueberries, and grapes: anything resem-bling a berry will be found in Boston Mountain's catalogue. It lists 2 berries I've never heard of: the youngberry, a sort of firmer-fruited boysenberry, and the tayberry, a big-fruited Scottish cross between the raspberry and the blackberry. The firm was founded when the present proprietor's father, migrating in search of work during World War II, learned the vineyard trade and returned to Arkansas with his knowledge. Boston Mountain is now an important wholesale outlet, but it does substantial retail trade as well. The blackberry list is particularly strong, and all plants are hardy to zone 5. The catalogue recommends the best kitchen uses for each variety offered by Boston Mountain Nurseries.

Bountiful Gardens

Ecology Action
5798 Ridgewood Road
Willits, CA 95490

- *Nonprofit organization offering to the general public seed of nonhybrid vegetables, herbs, cover crops, and flowers; fertilizers, tools, supplies, books.*
- *78-page catalogue, approx. 30 illustrations, $1.00. Annual membership, including catalogue and newsletter $30 (supporting), $50 (sustaining).*

This is a one-stop mail-order shopping center for organic gardeners, particularly those influenced by John Jeavons's fine *How to Grow More Vegetables . . .* (see page 135). The seed list is a good selection of heirloom and European varieties. Since the organization's main focus is the creation of a healthy, living soil, the fertilizer and cover-crop selections are extensive and good. The kelp fertilizer from Chase Organics of England is also available here. The book list is quite good, including a number of books and research papers written by John Jeavons or by other members of Ecology Action.

Brittingham Plant Farms

PO Box 2538
Salisbury, MD 21801

- *Strawberry plants, plus a few other berries, grapes, and asparagus.*
- *28-page catalogue, 27 illustrations, mostly black-and-white, free.*

Another entry among the big Eastern strawberry nurseries, Brittingham has been in business for more than 40 years. Like the Allen Company, it has the good fortune to be part of the stringent USDA-MD cooperative that assures vigorous, virus-free plants. The catalogue is by no means as pretty as those of its competitors Ahrens and Allen, but the planting instructions are excellent.

CARROTS

Bunting's Nurseries

Box 306C
Selbyville, DE 19975

- *Strawberry plants, plus asparagus, rhubarb, and horseradish.*
- *18-page catalogue, 11 illustrations, free.*

An old Eastern strawberry nursery like Ahrens, Allen and Brittingham, Bunting's carries most of the usual suspects for the Northeast, Mid-Atlantic and Midwest. The catalogue is not particularly attractive, but the information is solid, including a nice section on planting methods. The firm also offers 10 different mixed selections, chosen for flavor, long season, large berries, or the like. The USDA chart comparing earliness,

fruit quality, and disease resistance of the offered varieties is also included.

Butterbrooke Farm

78 Barry Road
Oxford, CT 06483

- *Open-pollinated vegetable seed.*
- *4-page leaflet, free; quarterly newsletter and special seed list to members of seed cooperative; annual membership $6.00.*

Proprietor Thomas Butterworth is a biology professor who went back to the land. When he bought a farm in the mid-1970s and began growing vegetables by the French Intensive Method, he was soon in possession of surplus produce and surplus seed, which he sold through a local co-op and later began to trade with friends. The network of friends has expanded into an organized nationwide seed cooperative with several hundred members. All are dedicated to the preservation and propagation of nonhybrid vegetable seed. Butterworth now offers to the general public a good list of about 75 varieties, selected for short season, but it is well worth the $6 fee to join the co-op, both for the newsletter and for the special seed list offered only to members. The newsletter combines practical growing tips with scholarly articles on agroecological topics; the latter come with excellent bibliographies drawn from scientific journals. The members' seed list is rich in discoveries. Butterworth is now working on a tiny pumpkin that fits in the palm of your hand and a tomato shaped like a banana pepper. The IPB tomato is almost as early as Siberia (see Siberia Seeds, page 144), but unlike Siberia, it produces all season long. Butterworth was the first to release the Super Italian Paste Tomato—4 times larger than most paste tomatoes—a variety he found on a local Connecticut farm and has since supplied to other mail-order houses.

Caprilands Herb Farm

534 Silver Street
Coventry, CT 06238

- *Plants and seeds for herbs; herb products.*
- *8-page flyer, free.*

The list is a potpourri, mixing herbs plants and seeds; cards; herbal oils, potpourris, and pomander balls; herb-scented hangers and pillows and sachets and hotpads and even umbrellas; dolls; wreaths; and endless books about herbs and about Caprilands written by the proprietors. The herb list is large for both plants and seeds, and there are numbers of scented geraniums.

The Community Garden Book

by Larry Sommers
National Gardening Association
180 Flynn Avenue
Burlington, VT 05401

- *121-page book, many illustrations, $8.95.*

A very good resource book for anyone starting a community garden. It says very little about growing plants, but it tells most of what you need to know about finding land, raising money, improving the soil, and managing the garden. The resource lists will lead you to most of the important local publications on the subject.

Companion Plants

Route 6
Box 88
Athens, OH 45701

- *Plants and seed for herbs, broadly defined.*
- *36-page catalogue, 12 illustrations, $1.50.*

Four hundred varieties of herb plants and one hundred of herb seeds make this one of the bigger lists of such things around. To Peter and Susan Borchard, the proprietors, an herb is any plant useful for medicine, seasoning, tea, dyes, dried arrangements, or scents. This makes for a very broad field, including many plants now grown chiefly as ornamentals. Lists of basils, scented geraniums, mints, sages, thymes, and wormwoods are very long. Ornamental gardeners should look at this list, as should veggie and herb people. A number of natives appear scattered throughout. Why is the firm called Companion Plants? Well, for $3.00 the proprietors offer a big chart of the companionate relations among 54 herbs and vegetables, suggesting what combinations grow well together.

POTATO BEETLE

The Cook's Garden

Box 65
Londonderry, VT 05148

- *Gourmet vegetable seed.*
- *16-page catalogue, a few illustrations, free.*

Like the other gourmet vegetable firms that have sprouted in the last decade, The Cook's Garden gets most of its list from European seed suppliers. The selection of seed for the likes of tomatoes, beans, and squash is small and interesting, but the glory of the catalogue is its long list of lettuces and salad herbs: 35 lettuces, 13 chicories, and 28 miscellaneous items including mâche, arugula, and cress. Among the lettuces are 5 intended specifically for greenhouse growing. All of the varieties are grown in Vermont, so the Northeastern gardener can count on getting the seed of hardy plants. Good descriptions and instructions accompany each variety.

Corns

Carl D. Barnes
RR 1
Box 32
Turpin, OK 73950

- *Seed exchange specializing in all types of maize.*
- *Variable-length lists of dent, sweet, flint, pop, flour and pod corns.*

Carl and Karen Barnes don't buy and sell seed; they trade it, with the intention of keeping alive as many varieties of nonhybrid corn as possible. All told, their lists comprise well over 500 varieties. The network of traders for which Corns is the node numbers more than 1,000 growers. The organization will send seed free to those who propagate it and return it; it also accepts contributions of seed. If you have never grown corn, keep in mind that this plant cross-pollinates readily, so you will either have to grow each variety well separated from any other variety or learn the special technique of hand-pollination.

The Crownsville Nursery

See "Annuals and Perennials."

Culpeper's Color Herbal

Edited by David Potterton
Sterling Publishing Co.

- *224 pages, many color illustrations, $14.95 pbk.*

It was a nice idea to take Culpeper's 1649 herbal, reprint his comments, add notes on modern usage, and illustrate each entry with new color paintings. It's a very pretty book, and Culpeper is never dull reading. You can't learn how to cultivate herbs here, but you learn quite a lot about astrology, humours, Renaissance medicine, and Culpeper's own colicky disposition.

Designing and Maintaining Your Edible Landscape Naturally

See "Landscape Architecture and Design."

Edible Landscaping

See "Trees and Shrubs."

Elysian Hills

RFD 1
Box 452
Brattleboro, VT 05301

- *Seed for Gilfeather turnip.*

By all accounts, this is a very sweet and tasty turnip, a Vermont heirloom grown quietly in the Brattleboro area for many years. The Schmidts of Elysian Hills have registered it with the USDA and say they are exclusive suppliers of it. It's an interesting question to me whether or not an heirloom variety ought to be protected under the Plant Variety Protection Act— usually used to patent new hybrids— but given that these people are in part responsible for preserving it, they probably deserve our business. For a Thanksgiving dinner, I once tried to make *Himmel und Erde* (Heaven and Earth), a tasty-sounding potato-and-turnip dish with a poetic name. It was awful! I think that what was missing was a turnip like this one.

The Encyclopedia of Organic Gardening

See "General Sources."

Far West Fungi

PO Box 428
South San Francisco, CA 94080

- *Spawn, supplies, and book for growing mushrooms.*
- *4-page flyer, free.*

The species offered are button, shi-itake (several strains), the old-fashioned almond (*Agaricus subrufescens*), tree-oyster (*Pleurotus ostreatus*), and hon shimeji (*Llophyllum sp.*). The firm says it is the first to introduce the last of these in the U.S. Perhaps the best thing is the mini-farms, with shi-itake, tree-oyster or button mushrooms all pre-inoculated, activated, and ready to produce.

Fred's Plant Farm

Route 1
BOX 707
Dresden, TN 38225

- *Sweet potato plants.*
- *1-page list, free.*

A good list of 16 varieties of sweet potato plants, weighted toward the softer varieties sometimes called yams. The list is slightly larger than that offered by the Margrave Plant Company (see page 137), though Fred's does not offer the reduced-price "Beginner's Specials".

G. Seed Co.

PO Box 702
Tonasket, WA 98855

- *Open-pollinated vegetable, herb, and flower seed.*
- *56-page catalogue, 15 black-and-white illustrations, $1.00.*

Will Ross produces an unusually fine catalogue of heirloom seeds, chiefly for the vegetable and herb gardener. He grows all the offered varieties at both high and low elevations in northern Washington state, so his selections are well adapted to most of the interior Northwest. The descriptions of each offering are really first-rate—including lore and nutritional, cultural, and harvest information—and he has a number of unusual varieties, including virus-free tepary beans, some early Indian corns, and the Egyptian walking onion.

The Gardener's Handbook of Edible Plants

Sierra Club Books

- *420 pages, many illustrations, $25.00 hc., $12.95 pbk.*

The Complete Book of Edible Landscaping

both by Rosalind Creasy
Sierra Club Books

- *379 pages, many illustrations, some in color, $25.00 hc., $14.95 pbk.*

The introductory section of *The Complete Book*, where Creasy goes on about design with edibles, seems to belabor her very fine idea somewhat. I found her capsule history of landscape design unenlightening, and I was surprised that she did not make more of medieval gardens or of vernacular dooryard gardens. It begins to get exciting when she starts listing edible plants for the herbaceous and shrub borders and for hedges and boundaries and foundations. The illustrations offer any number of interesting design ideas for different parts of the garden and different situations, but I wish they had not settled for quite such impressionistic watercolors. I particularly like her schemes for an entryway dominated by bays, dwarf peaches, almonds, plums, and pecans, not to mention the fall-foliage garden of edible plants. The bulk of the book is a very helpful listing of edibles, with notes on their landscape value and how to work with them, including a neat "effort scale" to help you judge whether you want to take the trouble or not. In most cases, she selects preferred varieties or cultivars for the edible landscape. Be aware that you will not learn how to train fruit trees or vines here; Creasy suggests that you buy them ready-made. The *Handbook* is essentially a revised and expanded version of the plant dictionary from *The Complete Book*, confessing, I suppose, that the latter was not "complete."

Gardening for All Seasons

by Members of The New Alchemy Institute
Brick House Publishing Co.
34 Essex Street
Andover, MA 01810

- *309 pages, some illustrations, $12.95 pbk.*

The New Alchemy Institute is nothing if not ambitious—one of its other books is called *Tomorrow Is Our Permanent Address*—and its projects have generally borne fruit. *Gardening for All Seasons* is meant to help home and community gardeners benefit from the Institute's experiments. Holism is second nature to the Institute, so the book not only covers outdoor and greenhouse culture of edibles, but the raising of fish, chickens, and bees as well. Waste from the fish and chickens goes into the garden as fertilizer; the fish ponds serve as a heat reservoir for the solar greenhouse. You get the idea: this is New Age homesteading, aimed at getting your food-production habits to resemble the workings of a natural ecosystem. The Institute's greatest original work has been on the solar greenhouse, but the book is also a compilation of organic experiments originated by others and used at New Alchemy. Each chapter has a long and useful list of other sources of information, some of which can give you direct step-by-step information, as this book usually does not. Reviews of other people's ideas often contain valuable suggestions for making them really work in a climate like New England's. I found their comments on the drawbacks of no-till permaculture particularly interesting.

Gardening: The Complete Guide to Growing America's Favorite Fruits and Vegetables

by The National Gardening Association
Addison-Wesley

- *432-page book, many color and black-and-white illustrations, $19.95.*

There are more books about fruit and vegetable gardening than I care to think of, but, for the average gardener, this one is the very best that I have seen. It will not tell you about the latest organic methods or extol the virtues of double-digging—two things you may very well want to learn about elsewhere—but it clearly explains and demonstrates with convincing charts and illustrations most everything you will need to know to grow any of the ordinary sorts of vegetables and fruits. The little extra effort is what makes the difference in this book: many books tell you not to plant near trees, but this one shows how far beyond the drip line a tree's roots extend. Some say a window sill is a fine place to raise seedlings; this book explains why window-sill-grown seedlings can be leggy. Everyone says nitrogen is important as fertilizer; this book explains the virtues and uses of 3 different forms of nitrogen. The sample garden layouts provided here respond to people's actual needs, so not all of them are rectangular, and one provides a nice design for a mixed, edible landscape. The A-to-Z vegetable listing and separate fruit listing

are remarkable for their excellent organization and completeness. For many types, a box evaluates the generally available varieties. Where a crop has different requirements in different parts of the country—lettuce, for example—there is separate regional information. When varieties are listed or evaluated, at least one source for each is included. As if all this were not enough, the color illustrations are also fine, and among them appears a very useful rogue's gallery of pests and diseases, with recommendations for dealing with each. Even where the book fails—as in its first- and last-frost-date maps—it fails because it is trying to be more valuable than most. The maps are very hard to read, but if you succeed in figuring them out and in doing the associated math to determine your precise planting times, you will probably have an accurate tool. The National Gardening Association also puts out a series of inexpensive "Garden Guides" to the basic crops, but I would rather shell out the money for the book and get it all in one nice-looking volume.

Gardening with Herbs

by Harriet B. Flannery and
Robert G. Mower
Cornell Cooperative Extension
Bulletin 123
New York State College of
Human Ecology
7 Research Park
Cornell University
Ithaca, NY 14850

- *40-page booklet, 70 black-and-white illustrations, $1.25.*

This booklet is a very good value for the beginning herb gardener. Though it offers few specific ideas for designing herb gardens, it is clear and helpful on the propagation and culture of annual and perennial herbs. A well-

illustrated list of 50 herbs contains descriptions, instructions, and brief, cogent suggestions for culinary, medicinal, and ornamental uses. If your aim is simply to add herbs to an existing garden, this source may be all you need.

The Garden Seed Inventory

Edited by Kent Whealy
Seed Saver Publications
PO Box 70
Decorah, IA 52101

- *450 pages, $12.50 pbk.*

This 450-page masterpiece is not easy to read or use, since it was produced on a computer and is full of abbreviations and odd spaces. Nevertheless, it is far and away the best key available to the companies offering open-pollinated vegetable and heirloom fruit seed for sale or trade. There are 239 companies and more than 3,000 varieties listed, each variety cross-listed for the companies that carry it.

Garden Way's Joy of Gardening

by Dick Raymond
Garden Way Publishing

- *365 pages, many color illustrations, $17.95 pbk.*

This is an extremely comprehensive book about edibles gardening, and, unlike most such books, it was written by one, apparently very experienced, gardener. Aside from beautiful charts and illustrations, plus all the usual information, you get the benefit of Raymond's little tricks and shortcuts, like using a kitty litter made of alfalfa meal as a compost starter! I don't know whether this one is quite as good as the NGA's *Gardening* (see page 131), but you should definitely compare the two before deciding for yourself.

Giant Watermelons

PO Box 141
Hope, AR 71801

- *Watermelon and cantaloupe seed.*
- *3-page flyer, free.*

This firm grows BIG melons, the kind it takes several people to lift. The watermelon seed is from the red-fleshed Carolina Cross strain, and you can order it randomly or selected from particularly large melons (165 pounds and up). Also available is seed from the Blue Rind variety, whose melons average a mere 120–140 pounds, and seed from a cantaloupe that tips the scales around 30 pounds.

Good & Wild

Apartado Postal #40
Camalu, B.C.N. 22910
MEXICO

- *Irregular, variable-length publication, some illustrations, plus periodic letters and seed distributions, annual membership $7.50.*

A guy named Paul W. Jackson puts this together, apparently on a mimeograph machine. His aim is to broaden our knowledge of neglected food plants and help get them more widely planted in the Third World. I cannot think when I have seen a better-hearted newsletter. It is simply astonishing and, to anyone interested in lesser-known food plants, it is also edifying.

Growing and Using Herbs and Spices

by Milo Miloradovich
Dover

- *231 pages, a few illustrations, $4.95.*

Though it was first published in 1952, Miloradovich's book is still refreshing today because it starts with useful chapters on how and where to grow herbs before plunging into the lore of herbs and spices. Indeed, the best thing about the book today—when there is anything but a shortage of herb treatises—are its lists suggesting herbs for different regions of the country and for different types of gardens and levels of skill.

Hartmann's Plantations

310 60th Street
PO Box E
Grand Junction, MI 49056

Box 254
Earleton, FL 32631

- *Plants for highbush, rabbiteye and hybrid blueberries.*
- *16-page catalogue, free; 8-page Florida blueberry variety handbook, $.30; "Hints on Blueberry Growing for the Home Gardeners," free; pruning guide, free.*

Through their 2 catalogues, the Hartmanns offer over 20 Northern highbush and 15 Southern highbush and rabbiteye blueberries. Some new, dwarfer varieties—with both lowbush and wild blood in their veins—are also available. The nursery seems to serve mainly commercial growers, but the catalogue has very nice descriptions for the home gardener, including descriptions of the ornamental characteristics of the different plants. The hints and pruning sheets are useful and complete.

The Heirloom Gardener

by Carolyn Jabs
Sierra Club Books

- *310 pages, some illustrations, $9.95 pbk.*

Would-be seed savers will start with Jabs. Her timely book argues for the preservation of genetic diversity, profiles pioneer seed savers like John Withee and Carl Barnes, suggests sources for old open-pollinated seed of crop plants, and gives good, detailed accounts of how to save your own seed. There is a chapter of profiles of the major vegetable crops, talking mainly about the formerly wide and now reduced availability of a number of choice varieties. There is also lots of information on resources to help you hunt for old varieties and to create an authentic "period" vegetable garden. Jabs tells you how to proceed for crops that must be isolated to ensure cross-pollination.

Heirloom Vegetable Garden

Heirloom Garden Project
Department of Vegetable Crops
Cornell University
157 Plant Science Building
Ithaca, NY 14853

- *Heirloom vegetable seed and descriptive materials.*
- *36 varieties plus 14-page descriptive mimeo, $10.00; 36 varieties plus 28-page Cornell Cooperative Extension Bulletin 177, $12.00; 22 varieties plus mimeo, $6.00; 22 varieties plus bulletin, $8.00; bulletin only, $3.00.*

Any of the above packages will take you from nothing to a complete garden of 19th-century vegetables in a single season. Cornell's outstanding vegetable-crops people, Roger Kline and Robert Becker, have gathered 36 open-pollinated varieties that major seed firms still offer. Descriptive information includes everything from complete layouts for the garden to historical sketches of the available crops. Much of the mimeo information is duplicated in the bulletin, but the latter also contains fine vintage illustrations and recipes culled by the Genesee County Museum's Lynne Belluscio, together with a good bibliography. If you buy the bulletin alone, ask for the 2-page "Heirloom Vegetable Seed Source List," which tells where to get the varieties.

Hemlock Hill Herb Farm

Hemlock Hill Road
Litchfield, CT 06759

- Perennial herb plants.
- 24-page catalogue, 6 black-and-white illustrations, $.50.

The descriptions are very brief; cultural instructions are absent, except in the case of the 6 illustrated herbs. Nonetheless, the list is comprehensive, including some unusual species like skirret.

Herb and Ailment Cross Reference Chart

United Communications
PO Box 320
Woodmere, NY 11598

- 30 x 40-inch wall chart, $10.00.

If you are interested in a simple way to treat anything from aches to worms —including gangrene, lockjaw, and excess sexual desire—you will be fascinated by this chart. It looks positively Byzantine—just the kind of thing that appeals to herb fanatics—but it is actually rather easy to use and covers a great variety of herbs. The information has been gathered from herbals and pharmacopoeia. It contains the usual cautions against really using it, but you white magicians will have to make your own decisions about that.

The Herb Basket

Practical Press
Box 1773
Brattleboro, VT 05301

- 24-page, 6-times-yearly newsletter, annual subscription $15.00.

The editors contribute an article or two on growing, storing, and using herbs, but the majority of the newsletter is made up of reprints from newspapers around the country. It's a useful clipping service, especially when it comes to herb recipes and sources for plants and seed.

The Herb Garden

by Sarah Garland
Viking Penguin

- 168 pages, many color illustrations, $27.50.

Look for this book to come out in paperback, as it is one of a series that Viking has brought in from England; most of its brother volumes are already in softcover. I think it is the best of the lot. The bulk of the book focuses on the design of herb gardens and on the cultivation and use of a wide variety of species; it offers many different ideas for planting herbs, some laid out as full garden plans and others representing attractive and doable details, like a miniature knot garden or an herb collection planted in the checkerboard formed by square pavers.

An Herb Garden Companion

Cornell Plantations
1 Plantations Road
Ithaca, NY 14850

- 124-page spiral-bound book, many illustrations, $13.95.

The book is a companion for those touring Cornell Plantations' remarkable herb gardens, but it's a fine volume all by itself. The best thing is the checklist that comprises the greater part of the book. Hundreds of herbs, grouped according to use or kind, are treated, with information on size, botanical family, flower color, and a paragraph of lore.

Herb Garden Design

by Faith H. Swanson and
Virginia B. Rady
University Press of New England

- 165 pages, many illustrations, $30.00 hc., $15.95 pbk.

This reminds me of the old pattern books that furniture makers put out in England during the 18th century. It is simply full of ideas for designing herb gardens, illustrating more than 50 different gardens, complete with layout and planting plan. There are historical themes, fragrance themes, herb gardens for every size, exposure, and location around the home, and so on. It's really a remarkable book and might well give ideas to gardeners who don't design strictly with herbs. The book ends with a chapter about the authors' experience designing their own herb garden, including some good detailed discussions of the joinery you can use in making raised beds with wood. On the whole, this is a good source for herb gardeners.

The Herb Gardener's Resource Guide

by Paula Oliver
Northwind Farm
Route 2
Box 246
Shevlin, MN 56676

- 82 pages, $7.95 pbk.

What Beverly Dobson does for roses (see page 158), Paula Oliver has done for herbs. There are well over 500 listings in the book, each about a seller of herb seeds or plants, herb preparations, or herb publications. She tackles a number of sources that I could not fit in this book, and, even where we happen to list the same ones, she will tell you more about their particular virtues than I can.

Herb Gathering, Inc.

5742 Kenwood Avenue
Kansas City, MO 64110

- *Gourmet vegetable and herb seed; seed for flowers to be dried.*
- *16-page flyer, no illustrations, free.*

The company started out selling fresh herbs, a practice they have continued by mail on an as-available basis. In 1984, it bought the J. A. Demonchaux seed catalogue business and now offers several hundred varieties of mainly European vegetables. The selection is well worth looking at, not only for its breadth but for varieties specially selected for home hydroponics.

The Herb Quarterly

PO Box 275
Newfane, VT 05345

- *48-page magazine issued five times per year, many illustrations, annual subscription $20.00.*

Almost every article in this literate and well-put-together magazine contains recipes and/or uses for the herbs it discusses. The monthly herbal astrology feature tells what herbs go with what signs and suggests some propitious prandials like Libra bean dip. In a recent issue, there was a literary piece about Andrew Marvell and gardening, an article about bath herbs with practical suggestions, a gatherer's reflections, a recipe for wild fruit concoctions, and more.

Hidden Springs Nursery

Route 14
Box 159
Cookeville, TN 38501

- *Herb and tree plants.*
- *30-page catalogue, no illustrations, $.60; 4-page order form, $.35.*

Hidden Springs started with fuchsias (now offered in a separate catalogue)

and has recently added herb plants and trees for edible landscaping. The herb list is really first-rate, offering several varieties of most common herbs—there are 8 thymes, for instance—and a long list of scented geraniums.

A History of the Strawberry

by Stephen Wilhelm and James E. Sagan
California Cooperative Extension Service
University of California
6701 San Pablo Avenue
Oakland, CA 94608

- *298 pages, some illustrations, $10.00.*

The endpapers alone are enticing, showing the routes of dispersal around the Western world of *Fragaria virginiana* and *Fragaria chiloensis*, two types most important to the breeding of the modern commercial varieties. Not that the authors neglect the woods strawberry, *F. vesca,* the most widespread and anciently cultivated species, of which they remark, "By its delicate tendrils the woods strawberry has enlaced the world." The book is an altogether attractive work of scholarship, leading from the earliest mention of the fruit in herbals to the latest varieties and commercial techniques. The authors being Californians, there is perhaps a little more about the California industry than the non-specialist might wish, but they have not skimped in their research elsewhere.

M. Holmes Quisenberry

4626 Glebe Farm Road
Sarasota, FL 33580

- *Seed for tomatoes.*
- *1-page flyer.*

According to his son, the tomato that William Holmes bred for his truck

farm was so big and tasty that people drove from miles around to buy it. Eventually, his dad started selling by mail, and Mr. Quisenberry has continued the tradition.

The Home Vegetable Garden

by Leonard D. Topoleski
Cornell Cooperative Extension
Bulletin 101
New York State College of Agriculture and Life Sciences
7 Research Park
Cornell University
Ithaca, NY 14850

- *31 pages, some illustrations, $1.00.*

Professor Topoleski's booklet is a conservative beginner's manual for gardeners in New York state, though the information is useful for most of the Northeast. The writing is dry and occasionally intimidating, but it is clear and practical. Basic information on mulches and chemical weed and bug killers is particularly good. There is also a centerfold, depicting 12 common weeds, as well as a handy list of vegetable varieties recommended for New York State.

Horticultural Enterprises

PO Box 810082
Dallas, TX 75381

- *Chile-pepper and Mexican herb seed.*
- *4-page flyer, 2 illustrations, free.*

This international selection of 31 chiles is supplemented with a few other staples of the Mexican kitchen: tomatillos, jicama, chia, cilantro, epazote, and tatume. Though it includes a number of Far Eastern and European peppers, it is strongest on those items you would want if you were cooking recipes from the fine Mexican cookbooks of Elisabeth Lambert Ortiz or Diana Kennedy. Red chiles contain almost twice the vitamin C of their generally cooler counterparts, so if you wonder why people would eat firebombs, here may be a reason.

How to Grow More Vegetables (Than You Ever Thought Possible on Less Land Than You Can Imagine)

by John Jeavons
Ten Speed Press

- *144 pages, some illustrations, $10.95.*

This is the primer for the biodynamic/French Intensive Method (b/FIM), a high-yield vegetable-gardening method first popularized in this country by Alan Chadwick at the University of California at Santa Cruz. The writer runs Palo Alto's influential Ecology Action, a group that has been practicing this method for more than a decade. More organic even than Rodale, the b/FIM people begin a garden with organic fertilizers and switch over to homegrown compost. Instructions for creating raised beds and for composting are very useful and complete, though the book's layout can make them seem confusing. Useful to all gardeners are the very thorough charts listing the nutritional and cultural characteristics of a large group of vegetable, grain, and tree crops; the suggested garden layouts; and the cross-referenced list of companion plants.

Hydroponic Society of America

See "Tools and Supplies."

Insect Diseases in the Home Vegetable Garden

by Arden F. Sherf and Arthur A. Muka
Cornell Cooperative Extension
Bulletin 141
New York State College of Agriculture and Life Sciences
7 Research Park
Cornell University
Ithaca, NY 14850

- *17 pages, some illustrations, $1.00.*

An excellent, well-illustrated primer about pests and diseases, this 18-page booklet is a good value for a buck. Though it pays lip service to organic and integrated pest-management techniques, it is generally conservative, offering standard chemical solutions to insect and disease problems. If you use chemicals, this booklet is probably all you will need; if you do not, it is still valuable for the comprehensive lists and descriptions of pests and their infected prey.

Ison's Nursery

Box 191
Brooks, GA 30205

- *Plant material for muscadine grapes, all sorts of berries, and fruit and nut trees; tools and supplies.*
- *16-page catalogue, 26 illustrations, some in color; free.*

Ison's regards an order of 150 muscadine vines as a small one, but the firm does sell to the home gardener. William Ison has been involved in muscadine breeding, and the list is very complete, numbering 23 varieties. Otherwise, the list of berries and fruit and nut trees is well chosen for the South. Cultural information is good throughout, including suggestions for trellising grapes. If you do a lot of trellising, you may be interested in a gadget called the "Max Tapner HT-B," which quickly and gently fixes vines to wires.

Johnny's Selected Seeds

Foss Hill Road
Albion, ME 04910

- *Vegetable, herb, and flower seed; tools and supplies.*
- *96-page catalogue, 200 illustrations, free.*

Though Johnny's offers seed for annual flowers and for a good selection of herbs, its glory is vegetable seed. The catalogue is perhaps the best in the business. Several hundred varieties—keyed for everything from beginner's gardening to far northern hardiness and accompanied by temperature guides for best germination—offer as much selection as anyone could want. A number of the varieties were introduced by Johnny's, like the Tongue of Fire bean, a lima relative that does well in the North, where most limas do not. Cultural instructions are superb, variety descriptions excellent, and though the illustrations are mostly black-and-white, they show good detail. There are even recipes. Legume seed for cover crops is also offered, and the selection of organic pesticides, tools, and growing covers is good. As if this were not enough, Johnny's is also one of the few remaining retail companies that runs its own breeding program for the introduction of new varieties.

Johnson Seed Co.

227 Ludwig Avenue
Dousman, WI 53118

- *Heirloom and modern vegetable seed.*
- *12-page catalogue, no illustrations, free.*

This is a historian's seed list. Jim Johnson was the gardener at a prominent living-history farm, Old World Wisconsin, before he started his own business. Though there are a number of modern hybrids among the almost 200 varieties listed, the old, open-pollinated varieties are listed with year and source of introduction.

Kalmia Farm

PO Box 3881
Charlottesville, VA 22903

- *Sets for topset, potato and multiplier onions, and for shallots and garlic; bulbs for flowering allium and a few other ornamentals; hardy kiwis.*
- *12-page catalogue, 17 illustrations, free.*

This is a good spot to get the old-fashioned and versatile onions of the aggregatum and proliferum groups. Some of these can be used both green and as mature bulbs, and all produce their own sets. Three varieties each of shallots and garlic also appear. Among the flowering allium are both giant and low-growing varieties. It seems odd that despite its name, the place offers no kalmia, nor anything like it.

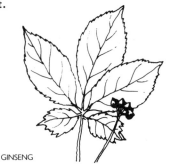

GINSENG

The Kimberton Hills Agricultural Calendar

PO Box 155
Kimberton, PA 19442

- *41-page agricultural calendar/almanac, with associated essays, some illustrations, $8.00.*

This is perhaps the most serious and thorough moon-signs planting calendar that I know of. Not that it is only moon signs; it takes into account all the relative motions of sun, plants, stars, and moon. The moon, it seems, acts mainly to focus cosmic energy. If you are susceptible to such methods, you will adore the calendar—with its many attached articles and speculations on matters micro- and macrocosmic, all influenced by the thought of Rudolf Steiner.

Kitazawa Seed Co.

1748 Lane Avenue
Santa Clara, CA 95051

- *Oriental vegetable seed.*
- *4-page list, no illustrations, free.*

Kitazawa has been around since 1917. The list is brief and contains no cultural instructions, but it has most of the important Oriental vegetables and herbs. There are 6 different Chinese cabbages and 7 daikons, which makes it a worthwhile source.

Wm. Krohne Plant Farms

Route 6
Box 586
Dowagiac, MI 49047

- *Strawberry plants; asparagus roots.*
- *8-page color flyer, free.*

Here are 19 varieties of strawberries—mainly the usual selection—with a handy chart for distinguishing the virtues of each.

Lagomarsino Seeds

5675-A Power Inn Road
Sacramento, CA 95824

- *Seed for vegetables, turfgrass, reclamation grass, and flowers.*
- *12-page catalogue of vegetables, free.*

For many of the common vegetables, there is not much to choose between the Lagomarsino list and, say, Burpee's. Lagomarsino's is distinctive when it comes to shell beans, cucumbers, melons, onions, peppers, pumpkins, squash, and tomatoes. There, the catalogue often betrays an Italian influence, whether via direct imports of chicories or drawn from California farming with its Italian-American heritage.

D. Landreth Seed Company

180-188 W. Ostend Street
Baltimore, MD 21230

- *Seed for vegetables, herbs, grass and flowers.*
- *50-page catalogue, 70 illustrations, $2.00.*

Landreth has been in business since 1784, making it arguably the oldest seed house in the U.S. The catalogue contains both hybrid and heirloom varieties, many of the latter offered in Landreth lists for more than a century. Descriptions and cultural instructions are fine, though the catalogue is hard to find your way around in. There are nice surprises, old and new—like Reid's yellow dent corn, Stowell's evergreen sweet corn, and a self-blanching cauliflower.

Le Jardin du Gourmet

Box 85
West Danville, VT 05873

- *Seed and bulbs for gourmet vegetables and herbs; dried and canned gourmet items.*
- *16-page catalogue, a few illustrations, $.50.*

While Raymond Sauffroy was a restauranteur in New York, he was well known for his shallot and herb sauces. Now transplanted to Vermont, he offers the bases of his sauces to the home gardener, together with a good selection of European vegetable seed. He sells sets for ordinary shallots, the fall-planted gray shallots, the sought-after Frogs' Legs shallots, and Rocambole, which are called Spanish shallots, though they look more like garlic. The list of vegetables and culinary herbs is the equal of other gourmet seed companies, and Sauffroy also offers a selection of herb plants, for people who hate to propagate. Among the vegetables are a few oddities like Portuguese cabbage and a white, flat pumpkin from Africa, but perhaps the greatest service he offers are the little 22-cent packages of seed he will provide for the small-scale gardener.

Le Marché Seeds International

PO Box 566
Dixon, CA 95620

- *Seed for gourmet vegetables and herbs.*
- *44-page catalogue, approx. 85 illustrations, $2.00.*

Le Marché offers what is very probably the largest selection of gourmet vegetable seed available in North America. It is unusually broad-based, listing a good group of Asian vegetables and American corns, along with extensive lists of the presently popular European salad and cooking veggies. It even has ground cherries and a purple Sicilian artichoke! International recipes are included in the catalogue, together with excellent descriptions and cultural instructions. The firm has recently started sending out short lists of items specially selected for autumn planting, among which are a number of varieties that are to be picked as babies.

Living Off the Land

PO Box 2131
Melbourne, FL 32902

- *4–6 page bimonthly newsletter about subtropical food growing, annual subscription $10.00; book* Living Off the Land: A Subtropic Handbook, *$3.50.*

Brief as it is, the newsletter offers a feature in each issue on a different potential food crop that you can grow in subtropical climes. Things as common as sweet potatoes and bananas and as odd as quail grass and jaboticaba are discussed. Subscribers participate in a seed exchange, and wants and haves are published in each

issue. Some issues have a group of recipes to help you make better use of what you grow.

Lockhart Seeds

PO Box 1361
Stockton, CA 95205

- *Seed for vegetables, fruits, and green-manure crops; tools and supplies.*
- *61-page catalogue, over 80 illustrations, most color, $1.00.*

Lockhart's list is put together with the market grower in mind, so it is strongest in the uniform and disease-resistant varieties that do well in California's market and other commercial gardens. Nevertheless, there is a wide selection, and the whole catalogue is organized in a no-nonsense chart form that helps you see quickly the size, color, days-to-maturity, and disease resistance of each. The bean and onion lists are particularly nice, including a speckled Italian bean called Bacciccia that I have not seen elsewhere.

Lost Prairie Herb Farm

805 Kienas Road
Kalispell, MT 59901

- *Plants for herbs, ground covers, and rock-garden species.*
- *20-page catalogue, free.*

The herb list is very large, though slightly less so than the one from Companion Plants (see page 128). Otherwise, the catalogues take much the same attitude, explaining how things like coneflower, which we now use as ornamentals, were once used for medicines and other purposes. A number of the selections in both catalogues are nice choices for beds and borders. Lost Prairie has actually added a separate list of ground-cover and rock-garden plants to its catalogue, all of which are hardy in Montana. A pleasant essay on low-cost rock gardening accompanies the list.

Makielski Berry Nursery

7130 Platt Road
Ypsilanti, MI 48197

- *Plants for raspberries, strawberries, other berries, grapes; plants for fruit trees.*
- *20-page catalogue, a few illustrations, free; 10-page growing guide, free.*

Red, black, and purple raspberries are the specialty at Makielski. There are selections that should do well in both the Northeast and Northwest, and a few will grow as far south as Maryland. The lists of other berries, grapes, asparagus crowns, and fruit trees are up to snuff, though they contain nothing unusual. Be sure to request the growing guide, a very good miniprimer for the culture, pruning, and training of climbing berries and grapes. In short, here is yet another good berry nursery.

Margrave Plant Company

117 Church Street
Gleason, TN 38229

- *Sweet potato plants.*
- *1-page list, free; grower's guide, free.*

Since sweet potatoes don't do well north of southern New Jersey or central California, they are often underrepresented in the catalogues of the big Northern seed and plant companies. Margrave offers 12 sweet potatoes, mainly the popular softer-fleshed varieties that are often called yams. The selection of different flesh colors is wide, and several varieties are of the compact, "bunch" type, which takes less room in a small garden. Sweet potatoes are very nutritious; if you have a long growing season, you can create additional bounty by planting vine cuttings from already-developed plants as the season goes along.

Medicines from the Earth

Edited by William A. R. Thomson
Harper & Row

- *176 pages, illustrated, $12.95.*

There are many reasons to grow herbs, but if you are interested in the pharmacological properties of herbs and all kinds of plants, here is the place to find out more. More than 250 different plants are analyzed for their active chemical agent, their range of uses, and the like. Instructions for harvesting and preserving the things also appear. The authors note that they have only scratched the surface with the huge number of plants that may have pharmacological value.

Medieval English Gardens

See "Landscape Architecture and Design."

The Medieval Health Handbook

George Braziller

- *153 pages, many illustrations, many color, $25.00 hc., $15.00 pbk.*

Herb books almost always make a fuss over the medieval use of herbs, but we seldom get a chance to take an unmediated look at what medieval medicine was like. This very pretty volume is art-historical in approach, discussing and picturing pages from 5 illuminated manuscripts that were composed in the Po Valley of Italy during the 13th and 14th centuries. The illuminations are not only lovely to look at, they are annotated with comments (translated into English) about the appropriate use of herbs and of other remedies, referring to the doctrine of the Humours.

A Modern Herbal

by Mrs. Maude Grieve
Dover Publications

- *2 volumes, 912 pages, some illustrations, $16.45 for both.*

Dover has kept Mrs. Grieve's classic in print. It isn't meant to be read straight through. The people who have done that can probably be counted on the fingers of one hand. Instead, the book is an extremely comprehensive reference for all kinds of useful herbs, blending cultural suggestions, details of use, recipes for dishes and decoctions, and citations from ancient and modern authorities. Mrs. Grieve writes pretty drily, and she always has her native Britain in mind, but hers is a key dictionary for the serious herb lover.

Monticello

See "Regional Sources."

Moose Tubers

Box 1010
Dixmont, ME 04932

- *Seed potatoes, onion sets, Jerusalem artichoke seed, and cover-crop seed.*
- *4-page list, free.*

Moose has an unusually good group of seed potatoes, about 15–20 varieties in all, depending on the year. The minimum order is $25, which amounts to at least 450 feet of potato rows, if you buy only potatoes. Two fine old-time varieties—Green Mountain and Irish Cobbler—appear on the list, as does the popular yellow-fleshed Carole from Germany. Descriptions of all varieties are excellent, though cultural instructions are lacking. Some people wonder whether a given potato is better for baking, boiling, or frying. To find out, float the tuber in a brine of 1 gallon of water and 1 gallon of salt. If it sinks, bake it.

The Mother Earth News

PO Box 70
Hendersonville, NC 28793

- *Variable-length bimonthly magazine, many color and black-and-white illustrations, annual subscription, $18.00.*
- *A-to-Z Home Gardener's Handbook, 176 pages, many color and black-and-white illustrations, $3.95.*
- *Green Thumbs and Blue Ribbons, 176 pages, many color and black-and-white illustrations, $3.95.*
- *Guide to Almost Foolproof Gardening, 176 pages, many color and black-and-white illustrations, $3.95.*
- *The Abundant Vegetable Garden, 224 pages, some color and black-and-white illustrations, $14.95.*

The magazine is devoted to all sorts of how-to and self-sufficiency advice, with emphasis on right-livelihood and ecological means. Text tends to be enthusiastic, and it is usually best when it reports the experience of individuals. The 3 publications offered for $3.95 each (*see above*) share the magazine's strengths. Each is a magazine-format book, mixing theme articles and how-to guides. You will have to read sentences like, "Let's plow into the how-tos of cultivating green beans," but what follows can be genuinely useful. The *A-to-Z Handbook* has the best text of any of them when it comes to planting and growing specific crops; individual varieties are recommended based on garden experience, and some of the tips are really tips. *Foolproof Gardening* contains several interesting articles—including one about composting using plastic sacks and an interview with John Jeavons—but it is too miscellaneous for my taste. The best of the 3 is *Green Thumbs and Blue Ribbons*, which consists of illustrated profiles of 34 vegetable gardeners around the country. Each comes with a garden plan, and reports on each gardener's success with different exposures, different vegetable varieties, and different pest controls. It's the kind of book that gives you nothing for 20 pages and then, eureka, a sudden inspiration. I would love to see this idea carried out in more durable, trade-book form.

The Abundant Vegetable Garden puts some of what appeared in the above publications into trade-book form. Though the writers have done away with the rah-rah style of the magazine text, they have instead substituted writing that is often too dry. The information on specific vegetables could, for the most part, be gathered from seed packets. A section on cold frames shows a number of interesting types but gives no idea how to make them. Likewise, there is just enough information on succession planting to confuse the beginner or put the experienced gardener to sleep. Nevertheless, there are 3 very helpful sections to the book: the 10 lovely illustrations of sample garden layouts are inspiring and understandable; the section on companion planting is comprehensive and first-rate; and the evaluation of various pest controls, including a critical look at organics like rotenone, is valuable for both beginners and master gardeners.

Mountain Seed & Nursery

PO Box 9107
Moscow, ID 83843

- *Vegetable and herb seed; flower seed.*
- *14-page catalogue, $1.00.*

The company was founded in 1975 by Dr. Arthur Boe, who developed a number of very early tomatoes as horticulturist at the University of Idaho. Mountain specializes in early varieties of all sorts of vegetables, selected for the inland Pacific Northwest and for high elevations. When you stop to consider that most seed for all mail-order vegetables is actually grown in

the West, however, you will not be surprised to find that a company like Burpee duplicates most of the listings in the Mountain catalogue. Mountain's real advantage is in tomatoes and corn, where it offers a number of uncommon varieties specially selected for the region. Its second advantage is price: most packets sell for less than 75 cents.

The Mushroom Cultivator

by Paul Stamets and J. S. Chilton
Homestead Book Co.
6101 22nd Avenue N.W.
Seattle, WA 98107

- *415 pages, many illustrations, $25.00.*

Many of us may be content with periodically buying our little ready-to-go mushroom farm, but for those who really want to grow a whole range of species, this is the best how-to resource that I know of. It will tell you all you need to know about inoculating, growing, fighting pests, and the like. You can even find out how to harvest and store your own spawn.

MUSHROOMS

Mushroompeople

PO Box 158
Inverness, CA 94937

- *Shiitake mushroom spawn and associated tools and books.*
- *24-page catalogue, 12 illustrations, $2.00.*

Not a company run by mycoform mutants, Mushroompeople offers any, all, and only shiitake mushroom

spawn, tools for growing it, and books about shiitake and mushrooms in general. Eleven different strains are listed, available in plugs or sawdust. Minimum quantities and costs are fairly high, directed chiefly at commercial growers or shiitake nuts. For less specialized fanatics, the firm has a fine list of mail-order mushroom books, including its own reissue of Rolf Singer's classic *Mushrooms and Truffles*.

MUSHROOMS

Here are 3 more excellent fungus catalogues. Others are listed separately.

Fungi Perfecti, PO Box 7634, Olympia, WA 98507.
- Fine, broad list of spawn and supplies. Catalogue $2.50.

Kurtzman Mushroom Specialites, 815 S. Harbor Way, Richmond, CA 94804.
- Good list includes some rare species; supplies. Catalogue $1.00.

Western Biologicals, PO Box 46466, Station G, Vancouver, BC, CANADA V6R 4G7.
- Broad list of spawn and supplies, including tissue-culture supplies. Catalogue $2.00.

National Colonial Farm

3400 Bryant Point Road
Accokeek, MD 20607

- *Nonprofit organization maintaining farm of colonial-era vegetable and fruit varieties.*
- *Many educational services; 2-page list of publications, free.*

One of the most serious of the living-history farms, the National Colonial Farm has an active program in agri-historical research and a very carefully made set of colonial gardens. The farm has a fine collection of heirloom vegetables, fruits, and flowers. For those interested in building a history garden, the pamphlets on colonial crops, husbandry, and tools are indispensable. Each costs $3.00, plus $1.00 for postage.

National Gardening Association

180 Flynn Avenue
Burlington, VT 05401

- *Nonprofit organization dedicated to vegetable and fruit gardening.*
- *54-page monthly magazine* Gardening, *many color illustrations, annual membership $18.00, 2 years $32.00; discount on NGA books and garden guides, garden answering service, seed swap.*

This group didn't become a membership organization until 1978, but it already has a quarter of a million members. The fine magazine must have something to do with it. Like so many local garden clubs, it features many contributions from members, but the quality of text and pictures is unusually high. Hands-on solutions are the emphasis, along with frequent reviews of everything from vegetable varieties to watering systems, evaluating different choices. A few pages of "seed swap" offers appear in each issue, a lot of them for common stuff, but some of them for odd heirlooms like the Little Greasy string bean. The NGA's fine garden book is reviewed on page 131.

Native Seeds/SEARCH

3950 W. New York Drive
Tucson, AZ 85745

- *Nonprofit organization offering to general public a list of Southwestern native food- and-dye plants, and to members a grower's network, newsletter, workshops, bibliographies, recipes, and 10 percent discount on all purchases.*
- *12-page periodical newsletter* Seedhead News; *28-page catalogue, $1; $10 annual membership, $25 annual contributing, $100 lifetime.*

The catalogue is free to members, $1 to the rest of us; the newsletter comes free with membership. There is no more interesting catalogue for the serious Southwestern vegetable gar-

dener. Since the authors have provided a rough key for translating their desert planting code into a code for temperate climates, other gardeners may also be tempted by the many unique offerings among the more than 200 varieties listed. Ethnobotanist Gary Paul Nabhan—author of *The Desert Smells Like Rain*—is this organization's guiding light, so the selected varieties are well described, particularly as to origin. Most of the seed has been collected

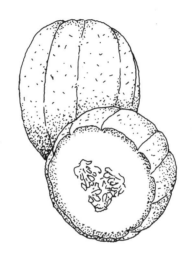

HYBRID CANTALOUPE

from the tribes of the arid Southwest and Mexico, or from the wild. There are countless beans, endless corns, and a good group of squashes. The organization discovered a panic grass that was thought to be extinct; was instrumental in bringing the dwindling chiltepine—a pea-sized firebomb of a chile—into cultivation; and has acquired seed of the recently discovered perennial teosinte. All of the above are offered to the general public, and the grower's network for members promises still rarer seed. The book list is worth looking at, too, since it lists publications from Native Seeds/SEARCH, from its sister organization Meals for Millions, and from hard-to-find academic sources. A wholly admirable group.

Natural Gardening Research Center

See "Tools and Supplies."

New England Farm Bulletin

See "Regional Sources."

New Roots for Agriculture

by Wes Jackson
University of Nebraska Press

- *151 pages, illustrated. $6.95.*

Jackson is opinionated, perhaps even crotchety, but his ideas are original and well worth hearing about. He is an avid permaculturist who has gone Masanobu Fukuoka (see page 141) one better: instead of simply leaving the land unplowed and sowing his crop-plant annuals each year, Jackson envisions an agriculture based on *perennial* crops. That few of these exist does not daunt him. At the Land Institute of Salina, Kansas, he is busy trying to create perennial crop plants of economic importance. The title of his book is therefore a pun of sorts, and the book will give you a good idea of what he is doing. For those who get hooked, you can subscribe to the institute's triquarterly *The Land Report*. It's also possible to work there as an intern. Contact the institute (Route 3, Salina, KS 67401), for information.

No-Dig, No-Weed Gardening

by Raymond P. Poincelot
Rodale Press

- *272 pages, 96 photos, $17.95 hc., $10.95 pbk.*

Rodale seems to be getting into new methods for gardening. In 1985 it brought out Mel Bartholomew's *Square Foot Gardening* (see page 144), and in the following year it released Poincelot's book. Like Bartholomew's, Poincelot's idea is meant to keep gardening organic while making it easier. Poincelot says he happened on his basic method via a gardening friend named Bill Loefstedt, who one day appeared in the author's garden to show him how you could install a pepper plant by growing the transplant in a Styrofoam cup, then using a bulb planter to make a hole for it in the garden. Together with a number of ideas for reducing or eliminating weeding—by using mulches or an oscillating hoe—and improvements to the basic Styrofoam cup, this is the substance of the method. It makes pretty good sense, especially with Poincelot's recommendations for improving root aeration in the cup. The title of the book is slightly misleading, since you must make a good garden soil before you can use the method and since even using a bulb planter or a dibble is a sort of digging. What you don't have to do is keep tilling the garden year after year. (Poincelot's reasons for not doing so are persuasive.) Unless you buy transplants from commercial sources, however, your effort will instead go into producing quality transplants, which he very thoroughly shows you how to accomplish.

Old-Time Herbs for Northern Gardens

by Minnie Watson Kamm
Dover

- *256 pages, some illustrations, $2.75.*

I like a book that organizes its contents by families (not genera or species) of plants, because it helps to suggest a relationship between species that we usually don't consider as similar. Quite a few of our culinary herbs are members of the carrot family (*Umbelliferae*), and those that aren't are mainly members of the mint family (*Labiatae*). Kamm uses this basic chapter organization to list over 100 herbs, most of which can be grown in colder-climate gardens. The book is almost entirely lore, with little cultural instruction. Information on the earliest uses and origins of the plants is generally sketchy, but she has done a wonderful job of culling quotes and fact from the writers and gardeners of more recent times. From an 18th-century poetic salad recipe, she quotes, "Let onion atoms lurk within the bowl/ And, half-suspected, animate the whole."

The One-Straw Revolution

by Masanobu Fukuoka
Rodale Press

- *181 pages, illustrated, $9.95.*

Fukuoka is the leading guru of permaculture, a man who just stopped plowing his fields and, by letting nature takes its course, managed to create a farm of mixed crops and field plants that is very productive and relatively immune to disastrous pest invasions. His is the ultimate in natural farming or gardening. The book is an inspiring account of his methods.

Park's Success with Herbs

by Gertrude B. Foster and Rosemary F. Louden
George W. Park Seed Co.
Highway 254 North
PO Box 31
Greenwood, SC 29647

- *192 pages, many color illustrations, $9.95.*

To my mind, this is the best handbook of herb culture that is available.

It looks quite a bit like an expanded Park catalogue—no wonder, since it uses many of the same illustrations—but the lively writing strikes the best possible balance between simple organization and detailed information. There is first-rate material on habit, culture, and use for every herb covered, together with recipes when appropriate. Some tropical, as well as temperate, species are included. Foster and Louden toss off a terrific amount of useful knowledge with ease and grace. It's comprehensive and a very good buy.

Peaceful Valley Farm Supply

See "Tools and Supplies."

Peace Seeds

1130 Tetherow Road
Williams, OR 97544

- *Seed for vegetables, herbs, grains, and flowers.*
- *8-page flyer, free.*

More than a decade ago, Alan Kapuler started gathering seed with the goal of collecting all the species used by humans among the 360 botanical plant families on earth. So far, he is up to 150 families and 3,250 species. A mere 200 of these appear in the Peace Seeds list, but it is one of the oddest and most intriguing selections I have ever seen. Organized by family, the list reminds its readers of the sometimes strange relations in the plant kingdom. (Carrots, for example, are a sort of annual ginseng.) It includes everything from wild blackberries to ornamental celosia to two species of edible cactus selected by Kapuler's hero Luther Burbank. Five unique publications explaining just what Kapuler is about, are offered at reasonable prices. Write for information about these publications when you send for the flyer.

Permaculture Institute of North America

6488 Maxwelton Road
Clinton, WA 98260

- *Nonprofit organization dedicated to sustainable and regenerative agriculture and garden design.*
- *16-page quarterly newsletter* The Permaculture Activist; *variable-length quarterly* International Permaculture Journal; *discount on mail-order books relating to sustainable agriculture and permaculture design; annual membership $25.00.*

Self-sustaining or even self-renewing usable landscapes are the goal of this group. To some members, even a compost heap is too unnatural, and in general they are one step beyond the common run of organic gardeners. The term "permaculture" comes from Australia, and until recently the *International Permaculture Journal* has been edited there, making it more inspirational than useful to the rest of us. Future issues are to be edited by the group's chapters around the world, so the focus should broaden. The North American institute puts out its own newsletter, including lots of information on meetings and design courses in the U.S. and Canada, reviews of books, and features about such things as tree crops, aquaculture, and successful examples of permaculture. Just what is permaculture? On this continent, it seems to have attracted a number of different ideas, all aimed at reducing the use of chemical pesticides and fertilizers, reducing farm labor and soil erosion, and producing closed-system gardens and farms that put back into the soil most of or more than what they take out. Members and sympathizers are into things like aquaculture tanks for passive-solar heating, fish production, and fertilizer production. One new project of PINA is exploring the use of geese to weed commercial crop fields. This is a serious group, and it will be interesting to see just how many of its ideas prove practicable.

Plants of the Southwest

See "Wildflowers and Native Plants."

Reader's Digest Magic and Medicine Plants

Reader's Digest

- *464 pages, many color illustrations, $21.99.*

The title is a bit of a come-on, since the book is much stronger on medicinal than on magical uses of herbs. Nevertheless, it is a gorgeous handbook that, despite the crowded herb library, deserves a place on your shelf. The historical introduction is sort of goofy in parts, as it tries to cover many centuries in a few pages, but the plant-by-plant list is just astounding, with color photos *and* paintings for each herb. Details on cultivation and lore are strong for each plant, and there is a separate section for tropical and subtropical herbs, an area too often neglected. Later chapters review the uses of herbs for cooking, dyeing, and other purposes, with good hands-on suggestions.

Redwood City Seed Company

PO Box 361
Redwood City, CA 94064

- *Seed of open-pollinated vegetable, herb, dye, and other useful plants; mail-order pamphlets and books.*
- *32-page catalogue, 40 illustrations, $1.00.*

Leave it to northern California to produce a hippie with the virtues of a Yankee proprietor. Craig Dremann started Redwood City Seeds in 1971, while he was still in high school; he typesets his catalogue himself on a 1930s linotype machine. Hard as it is to read the small type, the catalogue is well worth the effort for any gardener with an interest in what Dremann calls "useful plants." His is among the most comprehensive lists of open-pollinated vegetable, herb, and medicinal seed available in North America, embracing varieties from Europe, Asia, Africa, and the Americas. Dremann is an enthusiast who trades, collects, and tries seed from around the world. He didn't like the Oxheart carrot he could find in the U.S., so he searched until he found a variety in England that pleased him. Along with good selections of the predictable vegetables, he offers rarities like miner's lettuce, the very hot, wild Pequin and Tepin chiles, an American white pumpkin, a pink bean grown only around Santa Maria, California, 3 unusual species of the Physalis genus, and deadly nightshade. His list of books and pamphlets—some of which he wrote himself—is the best I know of for gardeners interested in heirloom and open-pollinated varieties. Among the selections are a number of old, hard-to-find USDA pamphlets, including the charming *Usefulness of the American Toad* (1904). Catalogue descriptions are excellent for use of varieties, but can be sketchy on culture.

Otto Richter and Sons Ltd.

Box 26
Goodwood, Ontario
CANADA L0C 1A0

- *Plants for herbs; tools, supplies, books, and herbal products.*
- *80-page catalogue, some illustrations, $2.50 CAN, $4.00 U.S.*

This is a fine and wide-ranging herb catalogue. Indeed, since it even includes a few gourmet vegetables plus some odd South African herbal shrubs, one might call it a catalogue of economic plants, not strictly herbs. It is among the most complete that I have seen, and that goes for its book list as well as its plants list. Only Canadians can order from the selection of organic pest controls and beneficial insects.

The Rosemary House

120 S. Market Street
Mechanicsburg, PA 17055

- *Plants and seeds for herbs; herbal stuff of every kind.*
- *26-page catalogue, $2.00.*

These people will have you serving herb tea with herb cookies and herb butters at tea parties. They will have you killing your cat's fleas with pennyroyal. They will have you ordering from their astonishing list of botanicals to make your magic potions. The first thing they ever sold, lo these many years ago, was wedding rice with rosemary and rosebuds. Baby soap, sachets, herb books of all descriptions, and essential oils, and the like, are stuffed into the catalogue as well. The list of herb plants is medium-sized, the list of seed is larger. The firm also lists lesser-known herb periodicals, should you want to subscribe. If this sounds intriguing, you'll just have to see for yourself.

The Seed Finder

by John Jeavons and Robin Leler
Ten Speed Press

- *150 pages, many illustrations, $4.95 pbk.*

Jeavons and Leler highlight a selection of 22 seed and nursery companies that stock a good selection of old-fashioned and home-garden varieties of vegetables, fruiting plants, and ornamentals. Jeavons and his group of organic gardeners have had plenty of experience with growing every vegetable you can think of for best flavor, yield, and nutrition. For each seed company, the authors have singled out a list of the varieties they feel are best for the home gardener.

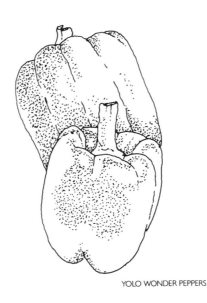

YOLO WONDER PEPPERS

Seed Savers Exchange

PO Box 70
Decorah, IA 52101

- *Nonprofit organization dedicated to the trade and preservation of open-pollinated vegetable and fruit varieties.*
- *256-page* Winter Yearbook, *256-page* Harvest Edition; *$10 annual membership, $7 fixed-income, $14 Canadian or Mexican; $20 sustaining; $100 lifetime.*

It is far too tedious to count the hundreds of varieties of open-pollinated vegetables and heirloom fruits offered for trade by members of the Seed Savers Exchange through their *Winter Yearbook.* This remarkable organization, founded and run by Kent Whealy, is the best single source there is for the *serious* gardener interested in nonhybrid seed. The *Harvest Edition* reports on the talks and workshops given at the group's annual Camp Out, and offers tons of information on the proper ways to propagate, store, and ship seed. If you are a buyer, not a trader, consult Whealy's *Garden Seed Inventory* (see page 131).

Seed Saving Techniques of the National Colonial Farm

by Mary Ann Klein
Research Report No. 25
National Colonial Farm
3400 Bryant Point Road
Accokeek, MD 20607

- *56 pages, $4.00.*

This is a very good beginner's guide to the nuts and bolts of saving seed from nonhybrid vegetable and herb plants. Mary Ann Klein runs the National Colonial Farm's heirloom garden of 70 vegetables and 50 herbs, so the advice she offers has the virtue of hands-on experience, as well as research. For more advanced techniques, see *The Heirloom Gardener* (page 132).

Seeds Blum

Idaho City Stage
Boise, ID 83706

- *Seed for heirloom vegetables, herbs, ornamentals, and flowers for drying.*
- *52-page catalogue, approx. 65 illustrations, $2.00.*

Run by two young women who built everything, including their office itself, from scratch, Seeds Blum has one of the fine collections of nonhybrid and heirloom varieties in the country. The cultural instructions are concise and clear, and there are a number of seed collections offered for different needs and situations, including one for a child's garden, another for the apartment dweller, and another for the winter gardener. Two pages are devoted to a useful chart of companion plants with ornamental qualities, perfect for edible landscaping. Complete garden layouts are offered with some of the collections. The firm has a unique arrangement whereby experienced gardeners can propagate selected plants for seed, selling the seed to the company.

Selected Essays 1963–1975

by Carl O. Sauer
Turtle Island Foundation
2845 Buena Vista Way
Berkeley, CA 94708

- 391 pages, $9.95 pbk.

Sauer was an extremely influential photographer; many of his suggestions—about man's ultimate ancestors being woman-led coastal gatherers rather than hunters, about the importance of fire in the ecology of the prairies, and about the dispersal routes of crops and cultures—are still hotly debated today. Read these essays, and when you are done, you might want to try his *The Early Spanish Main*, a history of the Spanish conquest of the Caribbean and Central America, which is a remarkable consideration of the mound-garden practices of the indigenous peoples.

Shaker Seed Industry

by Margaret Firsbee Somer
The Shaker Museum Foundation
Old Chatham, NY 12136

- 61 pages, a few illustrations, $2.00.

This little book was written as a doctoral dissertation, so the text is meant to inform, not excite, you. Still, it is very interesting material, since the Shakers were among the first seed sellers in America. Details on the Shakers' cultivation, harvest, and business practices are enlightening, including quotations like the following: "We, the undersigned, having for some time past felt a concern, lest there should come loss upon the joint interest, and dishonor upon the gospel, by purchasing seeds of the world, and mixing them with ours for sale; and having duly considered the matter, we are confident that it is best to leave off the practice, and we do hereby covenant and agree that we will not, hereafter, put up, or sell, any seeds to the world which are not raised among believers (excepting melon seeds)." Watch out for the melons!

Shepherd's Garden Seeds

7389 W. Zayante Road
Felton, CA 95018

- Seed for gourmet vegetables, herbs, and flowers for drying.
- 60-page catalogue, approx. 40 illustrations, $1.00.

This is the most appetizing vegetable seed catalogue there is. The variety of descriptions, recipes, and even the illustrations are terrific. There are collections of French, Italian, and Continental varieties, one of each of drying flowers, vegetables, and chili peppers. Proprietor Renee Shepherd believes that European vegetable varieties—which have less distance to travel from field to market—are superior in flavor to American varieties. Her list is therefore heavy on European imports and, as such, compares favorably with her competitors at Le Marché and Le Jardin du Gourmet.

Siberia Seeds

Box 3000
Olds, Alberta
Canada T0M 1P0

- Seed for early tomatoes.
- 8-page flyer, $.50.

Siberia Seeds began when Cynthia Driskill won a little money on a lottery ticket and took her family for a picnic in the country. At a little greenhouse, they found a tomato that had been brought from Russia a generation before. It sets fruit at 38°F! Beginning with this variety, the Driskills are building a company that offers both heirloom and outstanding hybrid tomato seed, all selected for cold Northern climes.

Southern Exposure Seed Exchange

PO Box 158
North Garden, VA 22959

- Seed for heirloom vegetables, herbs, flowers; a few hybrids.
- 60-page catalogue, 14 illustrations, $2.00.

Southern Exposure has perhaps the best list of nonhybrid vegetables in the East. Its catalogue is a must-have for all vegetable gardeners in the Mid-Atlantic states, though other heirloom growers will certainly want to look at it. Particularly strong in tomatoes, onions, beans, corns, and sunflowers—some of the varieties of which are offered nowhere else—the list includes what are among the best cultural instructions I have seen. A 2-page planting calendar for the Mid-Atlantic region appears at the back.

Square Foot Gardening

by Mel Bartholomew
Rodale Press

- 352 pages, some illustrations, $14.95 hc., $11.95 pbk.

Bartholomew was an engineer before he retired, and he has done here what engineers do best: taken an amorphous set of practices and codified them into a workable system. He got his baptism by fire in a community garden where the lots were too large and too labor-intensive to keep the gardeners enthusiastic. After a year's experience, he decided to devise a method for keeping the size manageable and the work load light. Gardening in 4x4-foot blocks, 16 one-square-foot patches to the block, was his answer. The general tenor of his recommendations reflects the informal practice of many skilled vegetable gardeners, especially in cramped urban areas, but his system makes an excellent framework for avoiding overambitious projects and for calculating what you actually need. All the information required to grow by Bartholomew's method—including planting plans and suggestions for trellising, crops—appears in this very thorough book. Even intensive gardeners may be interested in the method, because instead of focusing on the hallowed recommendations of gurus, it simply looks for what works with the least effort, embracing many of the virtues of intensive gardening without its obsessions.

Square Root Nursery

4764 Deuel Road
Canandaigua, NY 14424

- Plants for grapes; books; supplies.
- 14-page catalogue, 7 color illustrations, free.

This is the most helpful grape seller for home gardeners I've seen. The list contains about 40 varieties, including table, seedless, cold hardy, and European wine grapes. There's also a good group of French hybrid wine grapes, somewhat easier to grow than the true Europeans. What sets Square Root apart, however, is its extremely clear and thorough planting and pruning guide. It comes with each order, and, should you be ambitious enough to order European wine varieties, you will get a special supplement to help you deal with them. The firm will also send you free plans for a nice-looking grape arbor, plus a recipe for "Best in the Universe" blackberry wine.

The Sunflower

by Charles B. Heiser, Jr.
University of Oklahoma Press

- 198 pages, some illustrations, a few color, $10.95.

This is a lovely and various portrait of the sunflower—its uses, origins,

travels, and improvement—by a pupil of the great botanist Edgar Anderson. Heiser is passionate about the genus, and he is unusually able to convey both love and knowledge. Consider his dilemma on the train west from St. Louis to Berkeley in 1945: "I saw thousands of sunflowers on the way, and it was frustrating not to be able to examine them." At one stop, he indeed leapt from the train and ran a quarter-mile back along the tracks to collect some, much to the wonder of his fellow travelers. This enthusiasm is contagious.

Sunnybrook Farms

9448 Mayfield Road
PO Box 6
Chesterland, OH 44026

- Plants and seeds for herbs; dried herbs and herbal products; plants for ivies and houseplants.
- 26-page catalogue, $1.00.

The herb plant list is quite long, with a lot of variety within the major genera. The separate group of scented geraniums is also extensive. There is a smaller list of seeds. All in all, it's one of the more comprehensive herb catalogues. Of course, it also lists several dozen ivies and a selection of houseplants including hoyas. For $25, you can get a culinary herb-garden kit, complete with design and all cultural information.

Taylor's Herb Garden

1535 Lone Oak Road
Vista, CA 92084

- Plants for herbs.
- 22-page catalogue, 26 color illustrations, $1.00.

The illustrations alone in this catalogue are worth a dollar, since they

show some of the lesser-known plants —like lion's ear and Mexican bush sage—in settings that will give you ideas for landscaping. This is not the sort of list that offers you dozens of basils and scented geraniums. It is selective within single genus, but the breadth of genera covered is very great.

Territorial Seed Company

PO Box 27
Lorane, OR 97451

- Seed for vegetables, herbs, and a few flowers; supplies.
- 56-page catalogue, approx. 25 illustrations, free.

The catalogue is like a course about growing vegetables west of the Cascades in the Pacific Northwest. Territorial scrupulously tries all the varieties it offers on a difficult test ground, using organic methods. Selections are specifically oriented to grow in the difficult, cool conditions of the region. The choices are particularly valuable for vegetables like corn, cucumbers, tomatoes, peppers, eggplant, and melons. Varieties include both open-pollinated and hybrid types, each with good descriptions and really outstanding cultural instructions.

Tomato Grower's Supply Co.

PO Box 2237
Fort Myers, FL 33902

- Seed for tomatoes; equipment and supplies.
- 34-page catalogue, approx. 30 illustrations, free.

The firm offers more than 100 varieties of mainly hybrid tomatoes for every conceivable purpose. In each category, there are a few good selections for Florida and the humid South.

The Tomato Seed Co.

PO Box 323
Metuchen, NJ 08840

- Seed for all sorts of tomatoes.
- 24-page catalogue, free.

Is there room in the world for two tomato specialty companies? These folks and Tomato Growers Supply Co. (see previous entry) are going to find out. TSC certainly has a larger list than its competitor. It numbers about 300 varieties, including big and little; red, yellow, and white; common commercial varieties and some lesser-known ones from agricultural research stations and even from Japan; and oddities like the pepper-shaped Jersey Devil. Descriptions are basic, but detailed enough to let you know what you are dealing with. If a variety is especially good for a given region, the copy will tell you so. Here, you can also buy huckleberries, 5 different husk tomatoes, a green and a purple tomatillo, and the tamarillo, or tree tomato. None of these last are really tomatoes, of course, though the huckleberry is in the same genus.

Tsang and Ma

PO Box 294
Belmont, CA 94002

- Seed for Oriental vegetables and herbs; oils, sauces, and cooking supplies.
- 8-page flyer, free.

Probably the most various selection of Oriental vegetables available, the Tsang and Ma list includes such oddities as Chinese fuzzy gourd and dry-water spinach. Kitazawa Seed generally offers more choices of variety for the popular species, but Tsang and Ma's variety descriptions are better, and the firm also offers everything from oil to sauces to woks. Some of the sauces were developed according to Tsang and Ma's own recipes.

The Vegetable Garden

by M. Vilmorin-Andrieux
Ten Speed Press

- 620 pages, many illustrations, $11.95.

This must be one of the most comprehensive books on vegetables ever written. It was the work of leading French nurserymen and first appeared in English translation in 1885. Recently, Ten Speed Press reprinted it, an act for which it deserves all praise. The gardener who is looking for the latest and the greatest in vegetable varieties will of course find little of interest here, but everyone else will have a ball. The cultural information is fascinating—providing a very good glimpse of the advanced propagation and cultivation ideas of the time, many of them still relevant—and the descriptive lists of the varieties then available are staggeringly long and really mouth-watering. There are, for example, 14 different artichokes and well over 125 types of beans! The volume also qualifies as an herbal, since it lists a great number of common and uncommon herbs. The authors even dabble in natural history, with some bright observations on the constancy of vegetable species in spite of every effort to breed something new into them. Seed savers and heirloom gardeners dote on this book, because it both shows them what they have and suggests new old varieties to look for.

Vegetable Growing Handbook

by Walter E. Splittstoesser
AVI Publishing Co.

- 325 pages, some illustrations, $24.50.

The book is like a sheaf of cooperative extension pamphlets, conveniently gathered under one cover. Like many extension publications, it goes into the whys, the wherefores, and

other details regarding planting, culture, and care that most garden books overlook. Especially helpful are the charts, which cover everything from transplantability of different vegetables, to the relative nutrient content of different manures, to additions needed to correct soil pH. The pest-control section gives good weight to organic and cultural methods and is realistic about the uses and toxicity of pesticides.

Well-Sweep Herb Farm

317 Mt. Bethel Road
Port Murray, NJ 07865

- Plants and seed for herbs and perennial flowers; dried flowers.
- 34-page catalogue, $.75.

Companion Plants (see page 128) has a huge list of herbs, but this one may be larger. At least it offers a distinctive selection of the more common herbs, and it is stronger than Companion Plants in bulb-based and shrubby herbs. For example, Well-Sweep has 8 myrtles, where Companion has only 2. It has 2 barberries and 15 alliums, where Companion has none of either. Well-Sweep has an even larger selection of scented geraniums than does Companion. Companion, on the other hand, has a lot more hyssop. Unfortunately, the Well-Sweep list is strictly a list, without descriptions of any kind. The serious herb gardener would do well to pore over both catalogues.

Willhite Seed Co.

PO Box 23
Poolville, TX 76076

- Seed for vegetables and melons.
- 52-page catalogue, 109 color illustrations, free.

Willhite is particularly known for its watermelons and other melons, of which it offers substantial lists. Several of the watermelons were developed in-house. Also strong are the selections of cucurbits, corn, tomatoes, and Southern specialties like okra and cowpeas. The catalogue is beautifully illustrated, with excellent variety descriptions, but cultural information is limited to a basic planting guide. Willhite sells its more than 350 varieties nationwide, but for every vegetable, there are a few good selections well-suited to Southern growing conditions. For people who ordinarily order from Burpee or Park, Willhite might offer an intriguing alternative.

PAK CHOY

Wilton's Organic Potatoes

Box 28
Aspen, CO 81611

- *Organic seed potatoes.*
- *No catalogue.*

Wilton's offers only Norgold russets and Norland reds, but they are certified and organically grown. They are also raised at an altitude of 8,000 feet, an elevation like that at which potatoes were originally raised in the Andes. The word from people like James Beard has been that this gives Wilton's potatoes an unusually fine flavor.

Wonder Crops

See "General Sources."

Wyrttun Ward

18 Beach Street
Middleboro, MA 02346

- *Plants for herbs and wildflowers.*
- *33-page catalogue, $1.00.*

The plants are sold in groups of 3. The herb list is not quite so extensive as some, but it is quite respectable. Zone-hardiness information is lacking; descriptions of the lore relating to the herbs is very good. Here you will find out, for example, that the Pied Piper is supposed to have used valerian to lure the rats out of Hamelin and that southernwood has been used to repel moths. Special collections are offered for dyers, cooks, Shakespeare enthusiasts, sorcerers, and those who garden by signs of the zodiac. The wildflower list is selective, but contains many of the species Eastern gardeners look for. Incidentally, "wyrttun" is Anglo-Saxon for herbs, and a "wyrttun ward" is an herbskeeper.

Dr. Yoo Farm

PO Box 290
College Park, MD 20740

- *Seed for Oriental vegetables; spawn for shiitake, reishi, and other Japanese mushrooms.*
- *24-page catalogue, 86 illustrations, free; 20-page shiitake growing guide, 44 illustrations, free.*

Among the catalogues listing strictly Oriental vegetables, Dr. Yoo's is the most useful. The variety selection is good, and there are usually clear cultural instructions. He offers an unparalleled variety of Oriental mushrooms, some of which are less difficult to grow than shiitake. If you really want to grow shiitake, the guide gives an idea of how to proceed, but keep in mind that you must begin by felling an oak tree and wait 5 months to 2 years for the first crop.

> If it were of any use, every day the gardener would fall on his knees and pray somehow like this: "O Lord, grant that in some way it may rain every day, say from about midnight until three o'clock in the morning, but, you see, it must be gentle and warm so that it can soak in; . . . that there may be plenty of dew and little wind, enough worms, no plant-lice and snails, no mildew, and that once a week thin liquid manure and guano may fall from heaven. Amen."
>
> —KAREL CAPEK, FROM *THE GARDENER'S YEAR* (1929)

Your Nutritious Garden

National Gardening Association
180 Flynn Avenue
Burlington, VT 05401

- *44-page book, some black-and-white illustrations, $3.95.*

A basic veggie-growing guide for beginners, that is also a little too scattered. The vitamin chart is, I suppose, a useful thing to have, but why waste space on promoting vegetable gardens as cancer fighters? The whole thing is written in a cutesy style that sometimes makes it hard for the writer to get the real points across. How many gardeners will respond to a section headed "Invite a Worm to Lunch" anyway? When it comes to step-by-step guides for planting and growing individual types of vegetables, the booklet is much more useful, but if you are really a beginner, you will be distressed to find that there is no index. When step #1 is "Harden off plants," it may take a good deal of flipping before you can find the spot where you learn just what that means.

6 Cacti and Succulents

Abbey Gardens

4620 Carpenteria Avenue
Carpenteria, CA 03013

- *Plants and seedlings for succulents and cacti.*
- *47-page catalogue, over 100 color illustrations, $2.00.*

The lovely illustrations in this catalogue make it a visual primer of the world of chiefly exotic succulents and cacti. At the same time, Abbey provides an extensive list for collectors— so extensive that a few of the offerings have not been identified as to species. A good proportion of the list is propagated from material that was originally collected, but the firm says that it offers no plants from the endangered species list without first obtaining government permits. Not much appears in the way of cultural instructions, but lists for the major genera are prefaced with a note about ease or difficulty of culture. There are things as beautiful as bombax and notocactus here; things as horrid as *Calibanus hookeri*, which resembles cowpies covered with fescue; and things as strange as *Crassula pyra-*

midilis, which your child may mistake for a green robot. All lithops fanatics will be pleased to find more than a dozen species of "living stones" offered at Abbey Gardens. The firm is strong in all of the following areas: among the succulents, agaves, aloe, crassula, echeveria, euphorbia (amazing), haworthia (also amazing), sanseviera, and mesembryanthemums; and among the cacti, copiapoa, coryphantha, echinocereus, gymnocalycium, mammillaria (amazing), and notocactus. To top it off, there are a good few tillandsias and other bromeliads. Succulent nuts can pay $3.00 per year to receive a special list of rare plants, complete with photos and details about their collection.

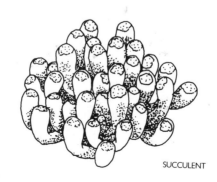

SUCCULENT

Altman Specialty Plants

553 Buena Creek Road
San Marcos, CA 93069

- *Plants for many succulents and a few cacti; books.*
- *36-page catalogue, more than 200 illustrations, some in color, $1.00.*

If you want to see very good photographs of the range of absolutely crazy habits of succulents and cacti, this is the place to look. The owners started this nursery to help them work their way through school in psychology and social work. By the time they'd earned their degrees, they were more interested in the succulents than in counseling. Now, they are large wholesale suppliers, with a good-sized retail mail-order trade. The lists here are not the longest you will see, but they are extremely choice. The owners' training has stood them in good stead, since they seem to have made selections guaranteed to startle and arouse the human psyche. There's an aloe (*A. plicatilis*) that reaches out to you with fingers like a sea anemone's; an echeveria that looks like a lettuce; an alluaudia that resembles a Hawaiian war club; and a mesembryanthemum that looks like pulled teeth. The range of the catalogue is wide, and the book list includes both beginner and expert material.

BOOJUM

Aztekakti

PO Box 26126
El Paso, TX 79926

- *Plants and seed for cacti, succulents, and arid-land trees.*
- *9-page catalogue, free.*

The medium-long list is as much for the arid Southwestern landscape gardener as for the collector. A number of South American species appear among the cacti. The succulents are strong in agave and yucca.

Boojum Unlimited

PO Box 64293
Tucson, AZ 85740

- *Seed and plants for boojum (Fouguieria columnaris) and a few other cacti and succulents.*

Proprietor Bob Perrill is promoting boojum as a houseplant. The Baja California native looks, says Perrill, "like an upside down carrot with short side branches." *Hortus Third* describes it simply as "a bizarre tree." Regardless, you will soon be able to get it from Perrill, along with species of *Ferocactus*, *Bursera*, and *Agave*, all native to roughly the same area. He is well-qualified to offer this stuff, since he spent 15 years collecting it for the Arizona-Sonora Desert Museum in Tucson.

British Cactus & Succulents Society

c/o W. C. Keen
8 Stonehouse Close
Cubbington
Leamington Spa
UNITED KINGDOM CV32 7 LP

- *Nonprofit organization devoted to culture of cacti and succulents.*
- *Annual seed-distribution list; variable-length quarterly journal, many illustrations, a few in color; annual Bradleya, 96 pages, many illustrations; annual membership $15.00 w/o Bradleya, $30.00 w/Bradleya.*

Unless you are deeply involved and scientifically inclined, you can do without *Bradleya*. The journal itself can get very technical, with article titles like "Some Succulents of Malawi (Part Two)," but it also contains much of use to collectors and natural historians, including things like "How Do Succulents Cope with Fire?" and "A Repotting Challenge." The monographs of genera in the journal tend to be focused for the collector, not the botanist. There are also reports on collecting trips and garden visits. The illustrations in a recent issue showed some lovely trained caudiciforms.

Cacti and Succulents for the Amateur

by Charles Glass and Robert Foster
Van Nostrand Reinhold

- *72 pages, many illustrations, $4.95.*

If you want to become a cactus nut or fancier, here is the best place to begin. The authors were the original editors of the CSSA's journal. They are knowledgeable, witty, and wise. On the attraction of growing cacti and succulents, they rhapsodize on the admirable adaptation of these plants to difficult conditions, their beautiful geometry, and the following: "When you get right down to it, though, the

original attraction, more often than not, is that here's a weird-looking piece of plant, which a friend yanked off his or her plant, which you can just plunk down in a corner somewhere and it'll grow. That's a great beginning." Not that they are sanguine about the ease of cultivating cacti. Their instructions are detailed and first-rate. There's also very good material on propagation, including an unusually sensible and simple section on growing from seed. They even make nomenclature seem interesting. The plants themselves are discussed on a family-by-family basis, singling out the genera that are most actively collected. A separate section deals with difficult but rewarding genera.

The Cactus & Succulent Society of America

c/o Miss Virginia F. Martin
2631 Fairgreen Avenue
Arcadia, CA 91006

- *Nonprofit organization dedicated to culture of cacti and succulents.*
- *45-page bimonthly Cactus & Succulent Journal, many illustrations some color, annual subscription $20.00, annual membership $26.00.*

The CSSA's journal is among the best-assembled plant society publications that I've seen. It mixes articles by avid growers with fairly lively scientific monographs, travel guides to the species of protected wild areas, collectors' reports, and advice for beginners. The annual sale offering of the International Succulent Institute is published here as well, listing dozens of cacti and succulents with fair illustrations and excellent descriptive text. The debate now going on in the society centers on the problems of whether or not to allow endangered species in shows and how to control illicit collecting of wild rarities.

Cactus by Dodie

934 E. Mettler Road
Lodi, CA 95240

- *Plants for cacti and succulents; books, supplies.*
- *18-page catalogue, free.*

Here is a very large cactus list, with not a bad selection of succulents as well. All the major genera of cacti are represented, and there are several dense pages of mammillarias alone. Crassulas and haworthias are the best represented among the succulents. Know what you seek, since the list contains only names. The book offerings are a short but good list of the references a cactus maniac needs.

The Cactus Primer

by Arthur C. Gibson and Pask S. Nobel
Harvard University Press

- *296 pages, many illustrations, $39.50.*

From the title, you'd think this is a simple little book. It isn't. It's a complete biology of cacti, and a very good one. If you are already a cactus maniac, look for it. If not, wait until the mania has fully possessed you before you venture in.

California Epi Center

PO Box 1431
Vista, CA 92083

- *Rooted and unrooted cuttings for epiphyllums and other flowering cacti and succulents; supplies.*
- *48-page catalogue, over 100 color illustrations, $2.00.*

Aside from being a noxious pun, the firm's name refers to the fact that it specializes in hybrid "epis," or epiphyllums, commonly known as orchid cactus. The selection of these is quite broad, including both day- and night-bloomers, and is full of the usual horrid names, like Bambi and

Satin Doll. There are also nice groups of the Easter and Christmas cacti (*Rhipsalidopsis* and *Schlumbergera*), together with lots of rhipsalis and a longish list of the lovely and inappropriately named rattail cacti (*Aporocactus, Aporophyllum*, and others). Some hoya, aloe, euphorbia, haworthia, and miscellaneous epiphytic cacti appear as well. The cultural instructions are adequate, and the list of supplies includes everything from pots and baskets to fertilizer and rooting powder.

Christa's Cactus

529 W. Pima
Collidge, AZ 85228

- *Seed for cacti, plus some succulents, native and exotic trees and shrubs, and wildflowers.*
- *12-page list, free.*

Christa Roberts puts out the kind of catalogue a specialist will love. It contains a very wide choice of species, each species little described, but the devotee will know what to look for. Most of the cacti are Southwestern natives, from ranges that extend north into Utah and south deep into Mexico and Baja. A number of Argentine species also appear. There is lots to choose from among most major cactus genera, but the list is very strong in coryphanthas, echinocereus, gymnocalyciums, mammillarias, and sclerocactus. Among the hedgehog cacti, for example, is one found on only a few islands in Baja California. The succulents list is shorter but strong in native areas, including groups of agave, yucca, ocotillo and its relatives, and lewisias from California and Oregon. Exotic families like the Euphorbiaceaea and the mesembryanthemums (including lithops) are also well-represented. The brief list of trees and shrubs is very good for Southwestern native species, and it offers a good selection of eucalyptus and acacia as well. The

wildflowers list has only a few well-chosen species of true natives, but I was intrigued by the 3 collections it mentions, each containing seed collected in a very specific locale.

Country Cottage

Route 2
Box 130
Sedgwick, KS 67135

- *Plants for sempervivums.*
- *9-page periodic lists, free.*

As Micki Crozier says, "About 12 years ago, a friend in Oregon sent me a half-dozen semps." Predictably, her garden was soon full of them. She now offers about 400 varieties.

Encyclopedias

Cacti and Succulents

by Gunter Andersohn
EP Publishing Ltd.
Bradford Road
East Ardsley
Wakefield
ENGLAND WF3 2JN

The Illustrated Encyclopedia of Succulents

by Gordon Rowley
Crown

- *256 pages, many color illustrations, $17.95, out of print.*
- *312 pages, many color illustrations, $19.95.*

The Encyclopedia of Cacti

by Dr. Willy Cullmann et al.
Alphabooks
Sherbourne
Dorset
ENGLAND DT9 3LN

- *340 pages, many color illustrations.*

Rowley uses the word "succulents" in the larger sense, embracing cacti as well, so what we have here are the finest popular natural histories of cacti and succulents that I have seen. Neither Rowley nor Andersohn is intimidating to the beginner, though each thoroughly covers every conceivable topic from native habitats, to cultivation and propagation, to morphology and nomenclature. Both are very well illustrated, the Andersohn volume perhaps a little more so, since he has traveled the world taking many of the photographs himself. Especially well-done in Andersohn are the consideration (and photos and charts) of native habitats and ethnobotanical uses of the plants. Andersohn covers about 150 genera of cacti and 75 of other succulents, with maybe a little more detail on specific species for cultivation than Rowley.

Rowley's is the classic volume in the field, and it is extraordinarily well written. Its dictionary of the families and genera of cacti and succulents is perhaps less usable as a grower's guide, but it succeeds in giving a fine overall picture of the whole field. Also, Rowley provides a separate section for the popular caudiciforms. Here again is a case in which the cactus and succulents nut will buy both volumes.

Cullmann's classic cactus volume, embracing about 750 species, has been recently revised. It's an excellent book for the collector, though the beginner may first want to consult Rowley or Andersohn for an overview of the field. The material on morphology, growth, cultivation, propagation, and nomenclature is accurate and not too technical. Collectors will like the chart comparing the different nomenclatures that have been devised for the family. The dictionary is prefaced by a key, making it usable as a field guide (though a bulky one), but it is organized alphabetically by genus, so it is easy for the fancier to use. Cultural instructions appear for each genus, with a realistic assess-

ment of the ease or difficulty of growing the things. The species listings are full of botanese.

BROMELIAD

Phyllis Flechsig Cacti & Succulents

619 Orpheus Avenue
Encinitas, Ca 92024

- *Plants and cuttings for cacti and succulents.*
- *18-page catalogue, $1.00.*

Phyllis has a broad, medium-sized catalogue for collectors. The list is strongest in natives of Baja California and Mexico, and it features her own epiphyllum hybrids, together with good choices among the other epiphytic flowering cacti. The succulents list is briefer, but with a comparatively wide selection for agaves and aloes. Though the catalogue is not illustrated, her descriptions are unusually good, so you will have a fair idea what you are buying.

Grigsby Cactus Gardens

2326 Bella Vista Drive
Vista, CA 92084

- *Plants for cacti and succulents; supplies.*
- *43-page catalogue, approx. 120 illustrations, $2.00.*

Another fine, wide-ranging cactus/succulents catalogue, this one has the added advantage of singling out those species and hybrids best suited to the beginner's talents, while still offering a broad choice for the specialist. This is no accident, since David Grigsby writes the beginner's column for the

Cactus & Succulent Journal. Emphasis here is on the showier genera, including crassulas, euphorbias, haworthias, sansevierias (remarkable), gymnocalyciums, lobivias, mammillarias, notocactus, rebutias, and sulcrorebutias. The good black-and-white photos help to show the loveliest plants, including *Notocactus scopa* var. Muriellii, which resembles the lights of the Tivoli Gardens, and the odd *Pelecyphora aselliformis*, which looks like the decorated knob for a stickshift. The text is often lively, if brief: "It's hard to believe this plant," or "A rare species with very hairy stems." Grigsby says he has brought a number of species into cultivation for the first time, though he seems to be scrupulous about avoiding the use of collected endangered species. Supplies include pumice, fertilizers, pots, and tongs and tweezers. Established customers may ask for the supplementary "wish letter," including some plants not found in the catalogue.

Honingklip Nurseries

See "Sources of Sources."

Intermountain Cactus

2344 S. Redwood Road
Salt Lake City, UT 84119

- *Plants for winter-hardy cactus.*
- *7-page list, free.*

Intermountain has sought out all those cacti that will thrive outdoors in climates where the temperature may drop to -20° F. This means that there are quite a number of opuntia (prickly pears and cholla), a good list of echinocereus (barrel cacti), and a few coryphanthas and neobesseyas. The text often tells the limit of the plant's native habitat, making a useful hardiness guide for those who want to grow them.

K&L Cactus & Succulent Nursery

12712 Stockton Boulevard
Galt, CA 95632

- *Plants and a few seeds for succulents and cacti, including epiphytic cacti; books and supplies.*
- *38-page catalogue, over 100 illustrations, some color, $2.00.*

All plants in this very comprehensive catalogue are listed by genus and species, but the descriptions often supply the common names, names that go a long way to explaining people's fascination with cacti and succulents. There are plover eggs, climbing sea onion, Mexican boulder, necklace vine, giant cowhorn, pregnant plant, purple scallops, chocolate soldier, elks horns, split rock, blue pickles, inchworm, peppermint stick, string of peas, penis plant, and the spotted toad—an anthology of metaphors all in the service of the effort to explain just what plants with species names like *horrida*, *spinosa*, and *paradoxa* actually look like. K&L's catalogue does not go as deeply into each genus as do some of the specialty catalogues (except in euphorbias), but the list is unusually broad, embracing everything from agave and lithops to kalanchoe and haworthia, to mammillaria and opuntia, to epiphytic cacti. Regardless, all the major genera are represented here, most in as much detail as even the moderately passionate collector could wish. Some plants are available in more than one size. The supplies list is comprehensive, including not only the usual fertilizers, insecticides, and plant labels, but a nice line of terra cotta pots as well. A four-page book on cultural requirements comes with each catalogue, and for those who want more, there is a very complete listing of mail-order books available for the asking. All in all, a very decent source.

Kirkpatrick's

27785 De Anza Street
Barstow, CA 92311

- *Seed for cacti and succulents.*
- *6-page list, free.*

This is a completely unadorned list of species, best for collectors, featuring strong lists of the major cactus genera and unusual examples of lesser-grown genera.

Gerhard Kohres

Wingertstrasse 33
D-6106 Erzhausen
Darmstadt
WEST GERMANY

- *Seeds for cacti, succulents, and tillandsias.*
- *30-page seedlist, free.*

Collectors take note. Kohres lists more than 3,000 different varieties. The list is strongest in cacti and mesembryanthemums, though there is no shortage of anything. The list is in German, but that doesn't matter much, since the bulk of it is nothing but Latin names.

Lauray of Salisbury

See "Houseplants and Exotics."

Lexicon of Succulent Plants

by Herman Jacobsen
Blandford Press
Link House, West Street
Poole, Dorset
ENGLAND BH15 1LL

- *1,069 pages, $37.50*

This is the updated, standard botanical reference to the noncactus succulents. Use it in the library.

Merry Gardens

See "Annuals and Perennials."

Mesa Garden

PO Box 72
Belen, NM 87002

- *Plants and seeds for cacti, mesembryanthemums, and a smaller number of succulents.*
- *35-page plant catalogue, 51-page seed catalogue, each free.*

There are many, many cacti and many, many, many mesembryanthemums, especially lithops, offered here. The succulents lists seems tiny in comparison, but it is as large as that of many nurseries. These are unadorned, extremely comprehensive lists for the collector.

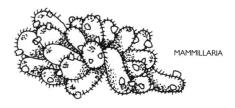

MAMMILLARIA

New Mexico Cactus Research

PO Box 787
Belen, NM 87002

- *Seed and a few plants for cacti and succulents.*
- *Variable-length lists offering roughly 1500 species each, $1.00.*

Here is a very important source for the collector. Proprietor Horst Kuenzler buys, sells, and trades seed worldwide, and his list is among the most comprehensive there is for cacti. For those with species in which he is interested, he does offer to exchange seed. About 90% of the list is cacti, according to Kuenzler, and they are drawn from sources throughout North and South America and from collectors abroad. Descriptions are brief, with a note about origin.

Popular Exotic Cacti in Colour

by Edgar and Brian Lamb
Blandford Press
Lind House, West Street
Poole, Dorset
ENGLAND BH15 1LL

- *176 pages, many color illustrations, $6.95.*

The Lambs have done any number of color cactus and succulents guides for Blandford Press, of which this is the latest. They are also the authors of a 5-volume illustrated reference guide, which you may obtain through some of the specialty cactus nurseries. They can be so prolific because they run a huge nursery of the things, numbering around 9,000 species; moreover, they periodically send to their subscribers both their catalogues and a selection of color plates that they have taken of items in the collection. If you want to get involved with the Lambs directly, write to The Exotics Collection, Brian M. Lamb, 16 Franklin Road, Worthing, Sussex, ENGLAND BN13 2PQ.

As to this volume, it lists about 100 of the more popular genera of cacti, each with a picture of a prominent member of the genus, plus notes on the habits, looks, and cultivation of the important species. It is a useful introduction to the field.

Rainbow Gardens Nursery and Bookshop

PO Box 721
La Habra, CA 90633

- *Plants for flowering cacti, plus hoyas and some other cacti and succulents; extensive book list specializing in cacti, succulents, and bromeliads; relevant supplies.*
- *24-page catalogue, approx. 100 color illustrations, plus 14-page book list, $1.00.*

Here's an attractively illustrated catalogue, chiefly of flowering epiphytic cacti. Many are epiphyllums, but there are also Christmas and Easter cacti, plus rhipsalis and rattail cacti. Each section begins with brief cultural directions, including suggestions for soil mix. About a dozen hoyas appear, too.

The book list is wonderful for *all* cacti and succulents, numbering more than 170 different titles gathered from around the world. A lot of these are specialists's books, but beginner's guides are well covered, too. The bromeliads book list includes only a bit more than 2 dozen titles.

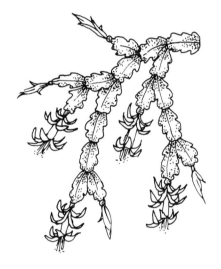

CHRISTMAS CACTUS

Red's Rhodies & Alpine Gardens

15920 S.W. Oberst Lane
Sherwood, OR 97140

- *Sempervivums and sedums; books.*
- *8-page list, plus 2 color-illustrated sheets, $.50.*

Red's seems to have started with rhododendrons and been taken over by sempervivums and sedums, about 400 of the former and 100 of the latter. It's definitely a list for collectors, though each variety is briefly described. Also, a daphne, some shallots, and pleione orchids bulbs are to be found here. You figure it out.

Jim & Irene Russ, Quality Plants

HCR 1
Box 6450
Igo, CA 96047

- *Plants for sedums, sempervivums, and relatives.*
- *7-page list, $.50.*

Even if the humble houseleek is the only one of these succulents you know, take a look at this list of a few hundred species and cultivars. It is a collector's list, but the plants are well described, especially those that have been added to the catalogue since the Russes inherited the mail-order business from Helen Payne of Oakhill Gardens. Good information on hardiness and native habitat should give the gardener some ideas about where to use the plants. Rock gardeners especially should take note of this list.

Shein's Cactus

3360 Drew Street
Marina, CA 93933

- *Plants for cacti and succulents.*
- *8-page list, $1.00.*

Anne Shein's résumé gives you a good idea what the world of plant shows is like: at the national CSSA show, she has won Best Succulent in Show, Best Cacti in Show, Overall High Point in Show, and the Scott Hazelton Award, an award for general excellence in successive years. She is also a CSSA judge for some shows. The mania for rating has always struck me as an annoying thing about plant societies, but in a specialty as overwhelmingly large as cacti and succulents, it seems a necessity, assuring a high standard of accuracy and knowledge. From her awards, you should expect Shein's list to be pure and true-to-name. It is also very long for cacti, including larger specimens in some less common genera, plus numbers of mammillaria.

Singer's Growing Things

17806 Plummer Street
Northridge, CA 91325

- *Plants for succulents; supplies and books.*
- *22-page catalogue, 34 illustrations, $1.50.*

Singer's is a broad list of succulents, with emphasis on caudiciform plants, that is, plants with swollen stem bases. The list is wider than it is deep, except for the large group of euphorbias and related plants (including monadeniums) and of sansevierias. The usual supplies appear, along with a fine selection of books.

Southwest Seeds

Vivi Rowland
200 Spring Road
Kempston, Bedford
ENGLAND MK42 8ND

- *Seed for cacti, succulents, and other desert plants; books.*
- *12-page catalogue; send 2 International Reply Coupons.*

There's nothing but the names of plants here—almost 3,000 of them. The catalogue is well organized by type and region of origin. The lists of lithops, mesembryanthemums, and South American cacti are particularly interesting, though all the lists are very long. There are choice groups of bulbs from the South African veldt and of carnivorous plants mixed in as well.

Ed Storms, Inc.

PO Box 775
Azle, TX 76020

- *Plants for succulents, especially lithops and other mesembryanthemums; books and supplies.*
- *40-page catalogue, over 135 illustrations, $1.50.*

Mr. Storms loves the bizarre. He glories in the stone-like lithops, the other bulbous and fleshy mesembryanthemums, and the often-hairy star-flowering asclepiads. He also has a very good, if not very deep, list of other succulents for collectors and enthusiasts. For mesembs and lithops, he is the best source in North America—he must have over a hundred lithops and an equal number of other mesembs. All are briefly or not at all described, but each section is prefaced with good cultural instructions, and the pictures give you a good idea of what crazy thing you are buying. Storms even sells the fine color prints of lithops taken by the world expert Desmond Cole, to whom he refers you for seed, if by chance you don't find what you are looking for in his own catalogue. The book list includes his own volume on mesembryanthemum culture, plus *Excelsa*, the journal of Zimbabwe's Aloe, Cactus & Succulent Society, a good place to find out more about the genera he loves best. As if this were not enough, he has bothered to group some of his plants into preselected collections, for both beginners and collectors. One offers every one of the Cole-derived lithops in the catalogue at a mere $275!

Sunnyvale Cactus

679 Pearl Street
Reading, MA 01867

- *Cuttings. for winter-hardy cacti*
- *4-page list, free.*

If you want to grow cacti outdoors in the North, Art Scarpa will do his best to help you. He offers more than 50 different varieties—all hardy to at least 0 °F, and many hardy at even lower temperatures.

Swakaroo Nursery

Mrs. D. T. Cole
PO Box 85046
Emmarentia, Transvaal
SOUTH AFRICA 2029

- *Seed for lithops.*
- *Variable-length list, $1.00.*

Mrs. Cole's husband is the world authority on lithops and possesses the world's best collection. Ed Storms is proud to say that his own vast collection is derived from Cole's seeds. To a lot of us, they all look the same, but not to Storms or to Cole. If you are of their opinion, you may want to get that rare, rare little lump of flesh directly from Cole.

Guy Wrinkle/Exotic Plants

See "Houseplants and Exotics."

Roy Young Seeds

79 Pearcroft Road
Leytonstone
London
ENGLAND E11 4DP

- *Seeds for cacti, succulents, and other exotics.*
- *16-page catalogue, plus periodic supplements; send 2 International Reply Coupons.*

Young lists more than 2,000 different varieties in his main catalogue alone; the supplements add about 1,000 more. There's little to the list but names, but it is so copious that serious cactus and succulent lovers will give it a look.

There are at least 60 ways to say that a plant is not smooth, that it has fuzz, hair, prickles, or roughness of some sort: aculeate, aculeolate, asperous, bristly, bullate, canescent, chaffy, ciliate, ciliolate, coriaceous, corrugated, downy, echinate, floccose, flocculent, glandular, glanduliferous, glumaceous, glutinous, hairy, hispid, hispidulous, hirsute, hirsutulous, hirtellous, hoary, lanate, lepidote, nodose, paleaceous, pannose, papillose, penicillate, pilose, pilosulous, prickly, puberulent, puberulous, pubescent, rugose, scabridulous, scabrous, sericeous, setiferous, setose, setulose, spinous, spinulose, strigose, strigulose, tomentose, tomentulose, velutinous, velvety, verrucose, verruculose, villose, villosulous, villous, vicid, and woolly.

—ROGER TORY PETERSON AND MARGARET MCKENNY, FROM *A FIELD GUIDE TO WILD-FLOWERS OF NORTHEASTERN AND NORTH CENTRAL NORTH AMERICA* (1968)

7 Roses

All–America Rose Selections

PO Box 218
Shenandoah, IA 51601

- *Nonprofit organization dedicated to testing and evaluating new rose cultivars; annual awards to a selected few new roses.*
- *12-page flyer, free.*

The AARS was founded in 1938 by rose breeders who hoped to improve the quality of the new cultivars coming on the market. Each year, roses entered in AARS trials are test-grown in 23 public gardens around the country, where they are evaluated by local experts. The highest-scoring ones receive the AARS award, an indication that they are widely hardy and gardenworthy. The society deals only with new classes: hybrid teas, floribundas, grandifloras, miniatures, modern climbers, and tree roses. Their brief pamphlet includes basic instructions for selecting a site for a rose garden and for planting and pruning, but it is most useful for its lists of all the AARS winners still in commerce and of AARS test gardens.

The American Rose Society

Box 30,000
Shreveport, LA 71130

- *Nonprofit organization dedicated to rose culture.*
- *32-page monthly.* The American Rose, *some illustrations, some in color, annual subscription $15.00; 50-page* Handbook for Selecting Roses, *$.50; 224-page* American Rose Annual, *some illustrations, available to members; annual membership $20.00, includes free all publications listed above, plus help with sources for scarce roses and advice from rosarians on your specific problem.*

There are really 3 levels of involvement with this society. The first is just to buy the handbook for 50 cents. If it were not such a little thing, the hundreds of old and new cultivars and species listed would probably seem overwhelming. As it is, it is fun to play with, because most of the roses come with a numerical rating for quality, developed from comments sent in by members. If you are about to buy a rose, you can flip through the handbook to see how real rose fanatics have evaluated your choice. The handbook also lists top-rated cultivars for all the modern classes, plus the new AARS winners for the current year. The next level of involvement is to subscribe to the magazine, which contains generally useful information on culture and surveys of old and new roses, plus articles on such things as companion planting for roses and antique rose postcards. And if you are passionate enough about the flowers to buy the magazine, you might just as well join the society and receive the handbook, and the annual as well, all as part of the membership fee. The annual is pretty clubby, has a generally rah-rah tone, and is, in my opinion, only for those who have caught genuine and persistent rose mania. Member-contributed articles broach the latest topics in hybridizing, disease prevention, rose showing, variety research, and the like. There are also lists of all the new roses registered since the preceding annual, of AARS winners, of top exhibition roses, and of the latest members' ratings of existing cultivars. Decide for yourself just how involved you are with roses.

Antique Rose Emporium

Route 5
Box 143
Brenham, TX 77833

- *Plants for old roses and companion perennials.*
- *50-page catalogue, more than 135 illustrations, many in color, $2.00.*

Begun in 1984, this company has gotten off to a tremendous start. More than 120 varieties of old roses are listed here, both named cultivars and collected varieties that the proprietors have yet to identify. Some of the plants are drawn from sources like the National Arboretum and the Huntington Botanical Gardens. There are a dozen or more choices among species roses, noisettes, teas, hybrid perpetuals, polyanthas, and hybrid musks. Selections are smaller for the other old-rose groups, but there are a good half-dozen bourbons, including Souvenir de la Malmaison and La Reine Victoria. You can also find progenitors of modern groups, including La France, first of the hybrid teas, and Gruss an Aachen, arguably the first floribunda. Wilhelm Kordes's seminal Crimson Glory, a great red hybrid tea from 1935, is about the most modern rose in the catalogue. Some selections favor the Southern gardener's climate, especially those from the tender tea and china groups. The perennials list is selected for plants that go well with roses, but it includes some interesting choices of its own, especially among Texas natives like the yellow Hinckley's columbine. The illustrations are the only disappointing thing about the catalogue: the color shots are too small and often a bit muddy. Cultural and variety descriptions, on the other hand, are excellent. The entry for Souvenir de la Malmaison, for example, quotes a 19th-century Texas nurseryman to

this effect: "How I envy the grower who first saw that plant bloom, the seed of which he had sown, feeling that such a gem was *his*!"

The Book of Old Roses

by Trevor Griffiths
Michael Joseph Ltd.
44 Bedford Square
London
ENGLAND WC1

- *168 pages, many color illustrations, $14.95 pbk.*

Griffiths lives in New Zealand, where he grows an amazing collection of old roses. The 400 photographs in this book are all taken by him, mainly of his own collection! The volume is slightly less wide-ranging than Beales's *Classic Roses* (see page 157), but it is friendlier in both tone and organization. The long rose dictionary—embracing 600 different roses—is organized by garden types, not botanically, making it more convenient for a gardener to use. Furthermore, though the entries contain somewhat less detailed information than in the competitor, there appear to be a few more cultivars listed in many of the old-rose categories than are listed in Beales. Also, since Griffiths has included fewer roses in his book, he is able to illustrate a larger number of those he does list. The comparison is probably academic, since old-rose lovers will doubtless end up buying both books.

A Book of Roses

by William Bryant Logan
William Morrow

- *124 pages, many color illustrations, $10.00.*

This is the little rose book I wrote. It's a lot of money for a small book,

but people seem to find it a good gift book. The best thing about it, I think, is the selection of roses made by Peter Malins, then rosarian of the Brooklyn Botanic Garden. We could only include 55 or so, and Malins was terrific at choosing just the right combination of old and modern roses. He was kind enough to provide our illustrator, Drew McGhie, with the flowers to draw from life, and his enthusiasm and knowledge, I hope, inspired me to write pretty decent entries for each flower.

Carroll Gardens

See "Annuals and Perennials."

RUGOSA ROSE

Classic Roses

by Peter Beales
Henry Holt & Co.

- *432 pages, many color illustrations, $50.00.*

The more than 1,000 species and cultivars that appear in this nicely illustrated compendium are mainly old roses, but some of the more respected modern climbers and shrub roses, and even a few hybrid teas, are included as well. There is a brief historical introduction, focusing on the evolution of different garden types, and considerable, well-illustrated information on budding and grafting. The chapter on landscape uses of roses is the weakest. For some reason, the otherwise lovely dictionary is organized by botanical, not garden, classes of the genus, which makes it a bit difficult to use, but the information for each entry is first-rate and the 550 color photos are fine. Where appropriate, separate pictures will show both the flower and the hips.

Climbing Roses Old and New

- *203 pages, some illustrations.*

The Old Shrub Roses

both by Graham Stuart Thomas
J. M. Dent & Sons
Aldine House
33 Welbeck Street
London
ENGLAND W1M 8LX

- *232 pages, some illustrations.*

Almost every one of Thomas's guides to the different classes of garden plants is a classic of its sort, since the author has the rare advantages of wide experience with the plants, a good designer's imagination, and an uncommon ability to convey what he knows clearly and attractively. Both these volumes, though not extensively illustrated, are standard references for rose fanatics because Thomas not only covers a great number of species and cultivars, but gives you very good ideas about what to do with the plants in the garden. Both books are available through Capability's (see page 250).

Combined Rose List

Beverly R. Dobson
215 Harriman Road
Irvington, NY 10533

- *102 pages, $10.00.*

This should be subtitled *Beverly Dobson's Miracle.* If you are a rose fanatic and haven't got it, get it. Dobson has collected a list of every old and modern rose variety available around the world, totaling more than 7,000 entries, with a code explaining who is offering it and referring you to the several pages of nursery addresses in-cluded. That's all, though in her brief preface she tells you how to get an import permit if you are bringing in a rose from abroad. She lists many more sources of roses than I can possibly fit in this book, so don't fail to consult her. While you are at it, you may as well subscribe to her *Rose Letter* (see below).

The Dictionary of Roses in Color

by S. Millar Gault and Patrick M. Synge
Grosset & Dunlap

- *191 pages, many color illustrations, $14.95 pbk.*

Here's a serviceable general rose dictionary, including a brief history, basic instructions about culture, propagation, and the like, and a list of well over 500 species and cultivars. Completely illustrated with color photographs, about half of the dictionary section is devoted to hybrid teas, floribundas, and other modern classes. This book puts old and modern roses together, and could have devoted more pages to both. Also, this is one of those books that put its illustrations in a separate section from the text, and it's a chore to keep jumping back and forth.

Bev Dobson's Rose Letter

215 Harriman Road
Irvington, NY 10533

- *8-page bimonthly newsletter, a few illustrations, annual subscription $7.50.*

Dobson's is quite a fine newsletter and a fit companion for her *Combined Rose List* (see above). In part, it serves as a supplement to the list, reviewing new nurseries that have come to her attention and amending and amplify-ing the previous year's list. It also includes book reviews, lists of booksellers, accounts of travels in search of roses, overviews of certain rose types, tales of nursery visits, abstracts from her lively correspondence, and rose-identification queries. In short, it is about as full as 8 pages can be.

One of my children once remarked that there was nothing that I wouldn't do for my roses. The remark was made after I spent a wet spring day carrying plastic bags of manure from an otherwise inaccessible part of a field—and doing my back no favours in the process.

Of course I denied the comment vehemently. But I wasn't being let off. The conversation went something like this:

"You wouldn't lie for your roses?"

Of course I wouldn't."

"Then why do you grow some freesias at the back of the greenhouse just to make people think the scent comes from the roses?"

"Well maybe I would tell a little white lie . . ."

"And what about stealing?"

"Me, steal! That's one thing I wouldn't do."

"Don't you remember once coming home with a couple of cuttings of roses that you shouldn't have had?"

"Well, that was different . . ."

"Yes, we know—the cuttings got caught in your coat."

"But . . . but . . ."

—FROM *THE ROSE* (1986)

Greenmantle Nursery

3010 Ettersburg Road
Garberville, CA 95440

■ *Plants for old roses, plus some older hybrid teas and floribundas.*
■ *28-page catalogue, $3.00; 1-page rose list, free.*

Greenmantle is found elsewhere in this book for its list of older fruit-tree cultivars, and, to tell the truth, only a few pages of the catalogue are devoted to rose descriptions. The 1-page sheet contains a larger selection of roses—more than 160 in all—though plants are not described there. It might seem strange that a fruit nursery also offers old roses, but both specialties provide the chance to indulge a passion for collecting. Furthermore, the Greenmantle rose selection is particularly strong in fruiting rugosa and species roses. It also lists "useful" roses like Kazanlik, a damask from Bulgaria that has been an important source of attar of rose. This is not to say that there aren't quite a number of purely ornamental roses: fair-sized groups of gallicas, damasks, albas, centifolias, mosses (including white moss), bourbons, hybrid perpetuals, chinas, hybrid musks, and teas appear. Three miscellaneous categories—"Rambling Roses," "Bedding Roses" and "Special Shrubs"—list climbers, ramblers, a few noisettes, mainly older hybrid teas and floribundas, and some of the more unusual species hybrids. Among the shrubs appear several of the great Kordes hybrids, including both Fruhlingsgold and Fruhlingsmorgen. A lot of the plants for this collection have been imported from England, where the love of old roses is not such a recent revival as it is in North America. About 50 of the choices appear in the catalogue, with good descriptions, but for the rest, the gardener will have to go hunting in sourcebooks. It's a good idea to check carefully before selecting roses. Although many of the old roses are tougher plants than the modern ones, some are susceptible to various plagues, and some are very tender.

Did you read that a number of people in the United States would like to take the rose as their national flower? It's a battle that has been going on since 1959—and would you believe that there is vociferous opposition in favour of the marigold?
—FROM *THE ROSE* (1986)

Handbook on Roses

Plants & Gardens, vol. 36, no. 1
Brooklyn Botanic Garden
1000 Washington Avenue
Brooklyn, NY 11225

■ *84-page book, many illustrations, $3.05 ppd.*

There are two great virtues to the BBG handbooks: first, they are brief; second, they are written by a variety of true experts. The rose volume was edited by David Stump, president of Jackson & Perkins. Contributors include great breeders like Reimer Kordes and Sam McGredy. You can quickly find out how to do anything you want with a rose—from growing it in a container to breeding a new one—using the more than a dozen theme articles that appear. Advice on planting, pruning, and winter care is clear and concise. An article and a photo essay provide suggestive ideas for using roses in the landscape. The pieces seem particularly topical in light of the later comments by breeders about the probable future of roses as bedding plants. I was especially charmed by the piece written by J. Benjamin Williams, a prominent private breeder, who confesses: "For twenty years, I ate, drank and slept roses. . . . A half million crosses later, after producing and sowing some two hundred thousand seeds, I narrowed my forty-eight thousand seedlings down to two hundred fifty promising plants. Of these, fifteen have been named and registered, and ten are available for sale in this country." So that's how they do it.

High Country Rosarium

1717 Downing Street
Denver, CO 80218

■ *Plants for roses.*
■ *9-page catalogue, 10 illustrations, free.*

I'd heard a lot about High Country and was disappointed to find its 1986–87 catalogue so brief, but it turns out that the firm is switching over to tissue-culture propagation, so only a fraction of its 200 varieties of old, species, and shrub roses are listed in the catalogue. Look for the return of a bigger list soon. Even as it is, it is quite good. All roses are on their own roots, making them smaller than hybrids and a bit harder to establish, but improving their hardiness. All the roses High Country grows are tempered for the conditions of the West's high plains and mountains. The list this year was small but choice, still quite strong in species, including the native *R. woodsii*. For those who want to try growing from seed, the firm sells a few species as seed. Also, look at the hedge, bird lovers, and drought-tolerant collections.

Hillier Nurseries

See "Trees and Shrubs."

Historical Roses

1657 W. Jackson Street
Painesville, OH 44077

- Plants for old and modern roses.
- 7-page flyer, free.

Ernest Vash is a long-time rose collector who turned pro, and his list is remarkably long for old roses, containing a good number of hybrid perpetuals, floribundas, hybrid teas, and climbers. The descriptions are very brief, so buyers must know what they seek or do their own research. Some of his old roses are comparatively scarce in the trade; he seems to be the only source for at least 2.

Jackson & Perkins Co.

PO Box 1028
Medford, OR 97501

- Plants for roses, plus a few fruits and berries, bulbs, and trees.
- 40-page catalogue, more than 90 color illustrations, free.

J&P is a leading breeder and introducer of modern roses. William Warriner, its chief of research, seems to win an average of at least one AARS award per year. In 1980 he took 3: one for the hybrid tea Honor, one for the floribunda Cherish, and the third for a grandiflora called Love. The firm stocks all the latest and greatest in those 3 classes and has recently come up with a new set of hybrids—called "Flora-Teas"—from crosses between hybrid teas and floribundas. To my mind, it is a sign of the excessive inbreeding among rose developers that the company not only came up with the new crosses, but slapped a trademark restriction on the name Flora-Tea. J&P is *not* the only creator of such crosses. Most breeders are now putting effort into hybrids among the hybrid tea, floribunda, and miniature classes in an effort to produce good bedding plants that also yield superb

cut flowers. J&P just owns the name. A number of the varieties are also available as "tree" standards.

Keener Classics

205 E. Edgewood
Friendswood, TX 77546

- Plants mainly for old roses.
- 5-page list, free.

This is a miscellaneous list of old roses for the South. The list has little to say about each rose, but Keener is also selling a book called *Old Garden Roses for the Gulf South* for $6.95, which may be worth a peek.

V. Kraus Nurseries

See "Trees and Shrubs."

Krider Nurseries

See "General Sources."

Lowe's Own-Root Roses

6 Sheffield Road
Nashua, NH 03062

- Plants for around 500 varieties of old roses, some custom-propagated; plant identification service.
- 24-page catalogue, $2.00.

Malcolm Lowe's old-rose collection was more than 20 years old before he started selling roses in 1984. The selection is quite large for everything except teas and noisettes, which territory Lowe is ceding to the numerous old-rose nurseries now springing up. The damask perpetuals, or Portlands, are a specialty here. It would be hard to find a wider choice of them than Lowe offers, and his catalogue descriptions, though brief, are very good. Be aware that custom-propagation orders take at least 18

months to fill, and that orders are dependent on supply—a particularly important limitation, since many of the roses are difficult to establish on their own roots. In some cases, grafted plants may be offered as an alternative. Lowe will identify old roses for you at a rate of $3 per plant.

> 🌱 I find that a real gardener is not a man who cultivates flowers; he is a man who cultivates the soil. He is a creature who digs himself into the earth, and leaves the sight of what is on it to us gaping good-for-nothings. He lives buried in the ground. He builds his monument in a heap of compost. If he came into the Garden of Eden he would sniff excitedly and say: "Good Lord, what humus!"
>
> —KAREL CAPEK, FROM *THE GARDENER'S YEAR* (1929)

The Makers of Heavenly Roses

by Jack Harkness
ISBS, Inc.
5602 N.E. Hassalo Street
Portland, OR 97213

- 175 pages, many illustrations, some color, $29.95.

Harkness himself is a prominent rosarian who has known some of the more than a dozen rose raisers and breeders whom he profiles. In effect, the book is a set of linked biographies that make up a history of modern breeding, beginning with Guillot (the originator of 'La France') and ending, at his publisher's insistence, with the author. Harkness knows how to tell a story well, so aside from getting a good idea as to where many prominent cultivars came from, we also get a feel for the pleasure of the chase. In the case of Joseph Pernet-Ducher, for instance, Harkness tantalizes us with reports of the slow progress of a not very promising yellowish seedling that Pernet-Ducher had managed to obtain, finally revealing it as the first true yellow hybrid tea.

Milaeger's Gardens

See "Annuals and Perennials."

MINIATURE ROSES

In the ordinary rose world, there is a lot of interest in old roses now, so the collectors are researchers. Miniature roses, on the other hand, have given rise to enthusiastic breeders and collectors of new varieties. Some collectors' lists of minis appear below.

BDK Nursery, PO Box 628, Apopka, FL 32704.

Gloria Dei Nursery, 36 East Road, High Falls Park, NY 12440.

McDaniel's Miniature Roses, 7523 Zemco Street, Lemon Grove, CA 92045.

MB Farm Miniature Roses, Jamison Hill Road, Clinton Corners, NY 12514.
- Own, Lyndon Lyon, and other hybrids.

The Mini Farm, PO Box 501, Bon Aqua, TN 37025.

Miniature Plant Kingdom, 4125 Harrison Grade Road, Sebastopol, CA 95472.
- Roses and other minis. Catalogue $1.00.

The Rose Garden & Mini Rose Nursery, PO Box 203, Cross Hill, SC 29332.

Rosehill Farm, PO Box 188, Galena, MD 21635.
- Lovely color catalogue, free.

Springwood Miniature Roses, Port Credit, Box 255, Mississauga, Ontario, CANADA L5G 4L8.

Tiny Jewels Nursery, 9509 N. Bartlett Road, Oklahoma City, OK 73131.

Tiny Petals Nursery, 489 Minot Avenue, Chula Vista, CA 92010.

Mini-Roses

PO Box 4255
Station A
Dallas, TX 75208

- *Plants for miniature roses.*
- *16-page catalogue, 10 illustrations, free.*

This company breeds little roses with awful names like "Beautyglo" and "Touch o' Midas." It also propagates and sells a very wide selection of other peoples' minis, plus a few microminis and climbing minis. The plants can be very useful for containers, patios, hanging baskets, and the like, though this list emphasizes the show quality of many of its offerings. Should you bog down in the listings, turn to the back, where you will find a large number of collections for different purposes.

Nor'East Miniature Roses

58 Hammond Street
Rowley, MA 01969

- *Plants for miniature roses.*
- *16-page catalogue with 6-page folded supplement, more than 65 color illustrations, free.*

People who already know miniature roses know that the Savilles, the proprietors of this firm, are active and well-respected breeders. The list is full of their introductions, along with those of others. Some micros and climbers appear, together with miniature "tree" roses. The catalogue is interesting to collectors but also very good for people who've never grown roses before. The color illustrations are very good, and the Savilles' descriptive copy is readable. I have never liked miniature roses, but some of the bicolors here look really lovely and somehow appropriate to their size. Those sensitive to saccharine

flower names will also appreciate the Savilles' comparative restraint.

Pixie Treasures Miniature Roses

4121 Prospect Avenue
Yorba Linda, CA 92686

- *Plants for miniature roses.*
- *14-page catalogue, 19 color illustrations, $1.00.*

Pixie puts out a very manageable and attractive list of minis, plus a few microminis. The firm lists both its own introductions and those of other hybridizers. There are climbers, standards, mosses, striped, and green minis, along with the usual little bushes in the expected colors. One particularly interesting variety is a russeted thing called "Indian Princess," bright orange on one side and umber on the other. The illustrations are few but unusually nice, and, in general, this is a welcoming, not too jam-packed, minis catalogue.

MINIATURE ROSE

Rose Acres

6641 Crystal Boulevard
Diamond Springs, CA 95619

- *Plants for modern and old roses.*
- *2-page list, SASE.*

Here's another nursery born of a hobby. The list is various and intriguing, with special strengths in single-flowered and musk roses. Only the name and classification appear in the list. They are all own-root plants.

Roses

by Gertrude Jekyll and Edward Mawley
N. W. Ayer Co.
Box 958
Salem, NH 03079

- *301 pages, some illustrations, a few in color, $23.50 hc., $10.95 pbk.*

Generally, I've given you the Antique Collector's Club reprints of Jekyll, since they are generally better illustrated and since I see them more frequently in bookstores. But Ayer has reprinted the same volumes, often with introductions by Graham Stuart Thomas. His introduction to her *Roses* is particularly good, so the Ayer reprint deserves recommendation here. Jekyll was among the first people in modern times to consider the landscape and garden uses of the rose. The notions of roses as hedges, as tree climbers, as ground covers, and the like are due in part to her writing. The illustrations alone, showing several design ideas, are remarkable. As she particularly loved the species roses and the old shrub and rambler varieties, her work is relevant today, as we are rediscovering just those types.

Roses by Fred Edmunds

6235 S.W. Kahle Road
Wilsonville, OR 97070

- *Plants for roses; gloves and Felco shears.*
- *32-page catalogue, 59 color illustrations, free.*

The Fred Edmunds list has been around for a long time, and it continues to make a very nice selection of hybrid teas, grandifloras, floribundas, and a few climbers, chiefly for serious growers and people interested in shows. The choices are weighted to the old and new introductions of great modern rose names like Kordes, McGredy, Warriner, Meilland, and Tantau. The Kordes selections are particularly strong. The illustrations are attractive, and the text is sprightly. If you live in the Pacific Northwest, the proprietor's reports on the trickiness or ease of culture for the varieties he grows will be especially informative.

Roses of Yesterday and Today

802 Brown's Valley Road
Watsonville, CA 95076

- *Plants for old and unusual roses; pegging stakes.*
- *80-page catalogue, over 50 illustrations, $2.00.*

One of the oldest and finest companies in the field of heritage and unusual roses, Roses of Yesterday and Today also produces just about the best flower catalogue I know of. Though it contains many rarities, it is not so much a collector's catalogue as a rose lover's catalogue. There are well over 250 varieties offered, many of them true old-rose types, but proprietor Patricia Wiley is not above listing newer but lesser-known hybrids of outstanding beauty, like the 1976 grandiflora "Earth Song." You can find the true "American Beauty" rose here, in both a bush and a climbing form, as well as many other hybrid perpetuals; the lovely paper-barked chestnut rose; a delightful, nearly single old hybrid tea called "Kathleen Mills;" the climbing "Raubritter," which the English love; and polyanthas and bourbons and musks and gallicas and centifolias and damasks and a few each of noisettes, chinas, teas, and Portlands. The text is very informative for all important garden qualities, and the firm has even quoted letters from customers about the plants they have ordered and grown. The catalogue begins with a very valuable description of the relative hardiness of the different types, and black-and-white photos are very clear. The color cover shows a large arrangement of roses in a vase, with a tissue-paper overlay identifying each rose in the arrangement; so instead of just a pretty cover, you get color renderings of the flowers of 2 dozen offered varieties.

Roseway Nurseries

205 N. Main
PO Box 269
Ridgefield, WA 98642

- *Plants for modern roses.*
- *8-page catalogue, 24 color illustrations, plus 3-page list, free.*

Roseway does a lot of wholesale business. Its retail mail-order list offers a wide choice of hybrid teas and grandifloras, plus floribundas and climbers.

Royal National Rose Society

Chiswell Green, St. Albans
Herts
ENGLAND AL2 3NR

- *Nonprofit organization dedicated to rose culture.*
- *Variable-length quarterly* The Rose, *some color illustrations, annual subscription £8.00.*

The Rose is a welcoming and friendly journal, perhaps more comfortable than its U.S. counterpart (see page 156). It does have its share of highbrow discoveries and serious-minded discussions: Graham Stuart Thomas proudly pictured the newly rediscovered *Rosa chinensis* var. *spontanea* on a recent cover. Nonetheless, it is also very funny—and interesting to beginners. Sean McCann contributes a wonderfully opinionated column every quarter, featuring comments like the following: "Yes, they have produced plants that are said to be roses and are as easily obtainable all the year round as cabbages and lettuces. The only problem is that, like the cabbage and the lettuce, the rose as it is being produced in the laboratory has lost its heart." The British society is not at all hostile to the newer classes of roses, but it is very hospitable to the old roses and to uses of the rose in the landscape. There are novice columns in every issue, along with suggestions for budding and grafting, brief histories, guides to choosing roses, and even anagrams and puzzles.

Sequoia Nursery— Moore Miniature Roses

2519 E. Noble Avenue
Visalia, CA 93277

- *Plants for miniature roses.*
- *Several 2-4-page leaflets annually, color-illustrated, free; 44-page book,* The Breeding and Development of Modern Moss Roses, *many illustrations, $3.00.*

The list is not as long as some, but it consists of the selections made by noted breeder Ralph Moore; some of these are offered as miniature "tree" roses in one of the yearly leaflets. The most interesting varieties here are the striped roses and the moss roses; Moore has been a pioneer in breeding both. Moore's little book is a very good firsthand account of how a breeder gets from a bright idea—in this case, the idea of creating ever-blooming miniature moss roses—to

finished introductions, while inventing some mossy floribundas on the way.

Spring Hill Nurseries

110 W. Elm Street
Tipp City, OH 45371

- *Plants for modern roses.*
- *32-page catalogue, approx. 75 color illustrations, free.*

Spring Hill's rose catalogue is called "American Beauty Roses, " but it has nothing to do with the real "American Beauty" rose. In fact, the company seems to have created its own prize —"American Beauty Rose of the Year"—to award to itself. This promotional tool is irritating, but the roses—mostly hybrid teas and grandifloras, with a few floribundas and a number of climbers and "tree" roses thrown in—are outstanding. This is a good place to find most of the conservative hybrid teas, including "Mister Lincoln," "Chrysler Imperial," "Fragrant Cloud," and "Peace." The firm also keeps up with the latest AARS winners. For some reason, there is an abnormally wide selection of mauve and purplish roses in this catalogue, so if you love such things, this is an excellent place to find them.

Stocking Rose Nursery

785 N. Capitol Avenue
San Jose, CA 95133

- *Plants for modern roses.*
- *24-page catalogue, 19 color illustrations, free.*

The nursery has been around for more than half a century, selling hybrid teas, floribundas, grandifloras, and other modern classes. The present list is respectably wide-ranging, with a few older selections, plus all the latest and most startling. Descriptions are good, including name of hybridizer and date of introduction.

Thomasville Nurseries

PO Box 7
Thomasville, GA 31799

- *Plants for roses, evergreen and native azaleas, day lilies, and liriope.*
- *28-page catalogue, 25 illustrations, a few in color; free.*

Thomasville can be counted on to list the latest AARS award winners, but what is best about the catalogue is that it offers many of the older winners—plus other fine roses for the South. Here, you can find hybrid teas like "Garden Party," "King's Ransom," "Tiffany," and the still matchless "Charlotte Armstrong." Among the floribundas, too, recent selections appear, together with fine older ones like "Cecile Brunner" and "Europeana." The same mix appears for climbers, and some of the older modern types are available as "tree" roses. Thomasville's list is not limited to roses. The group of evergreen azaleas, chiefly indicas and kurumes, is medium-sized and quite good, but the real strength among the azaleas comes in the natives, including a couple of rare species from Georgia and Alabama. The day lily list is long, and there are 7 different liriopes.

Valley Nursery

See "Trees and Shrubs."

Wayside Gardens

See "Annuals and Perennials."

8 Houseplants and Exotics

African Violet Society of America

PO Box 3609
Beaumont, TX 77704

- *Nonprofit organization dedicated to the culture of African violets.*
- *74-page bimonthly magazine; annual membership $13.50.*

Few can be as serious about African violets as these people are. They write poems to African violets, breed them, show them, travel in search of them, make up acrostics that hide the names of favorite varieties, register them, list them, select them, and give prizes for them. In a recent issue of the magazine, Sylvia Mather was able to write: "It is common knowledge that the first *Saintpaulia* species was discovered by Baron Walter von Saint Paul Illiare, growing at about 300 feet above sea level somewhere near the coastal town of Tanga, Tanganyika, East Africa, in the year 1892." What, then, is *uncommon* knowledge? As with most such societies, it is also a good place for enthusiasts to find out about sources and books too specialized for me to list.

Alberts & Merkel Bros.

2210 S. Federal Highway
Boynton Beach, FL 33435

- *Plants for bromeliads, orchids, and tropical foliage plants.*
- *Variable-length separate lists for bromeliads, orchids, and foliage plants, $1.00 each.*

Here are 3 collector's lists from a firm that has been growing tropicals for almost a century. Except for the illustrated bromeliad lists, the lists are unadorned, but the selection is very good. The general tropicals include

AFRICAN VIOLET

aglaonemas, alocasias, anthuriums, citrus, gesneriads, cycads, dieffenbachias, dracaenas, episcias, ferns, hoyas, marantas, platyceriums, and so on. The orchids list has offerings in all the commonly grown genera.

All About Houseplants

by Montague Free
Doubleday

- *365 pages, many illustrations, a few in color, $5.95 pbk.*

This classic houseplant reference was first published in 1948. In the new edition, revised and expanded by Marjorie Dietz, it may still be the best houseplant book on the market, even if it's not the prettiest. Free is a charming writer and a knowledgeable gardener. He gives you all that you might expect from such a book, including general care and propagation instructions, plus suggestions for indoor settings from dish gardens to aquatics tubs. His plant list is very large and comprehensive, including goodly numbers of cacti and suc-

AFRICAN VIOLETS

Judging from the following list, there is probably no one in North America who doesn't live near an African violet supplier, and the list is not by any means exhaustive. The more prominent growers and nurseries have been featured separately with their own entries.

The African Violet Co., 100 Floral Avenue, Greenwood, SC 29647.
- Plants and cuttings for African violets.

Alice's Violet Room, Route 6, Box 233, Waynesville, MO 65583.
- Catalogue $.25.

Aquatica, 8360 Solano Drive, Thornton, CO 80229.
- Seed for African violets. Catalogue $2.00.

Jeanne P. Bohn, PO Box 174, Hygiene, CO 80533.
- Catalogue, $.25.

Cape Cod Violetry, 28 Minot Street, Falmouth, MA 02540.
- Large selection of plants and cuttings. Catalogue $1.00.

Carousel of Violets, 1903 Margaret Street, Winston-Salem, NC 27103.
- Cuttings and supplies. Catalogue $1.00.

Country Girl Greenhouse, PO Box 83, Sterling, CT 06377.
- Catalogue, $1.00.

Dvorsky's African Violets, 31 Park Street, Binghamton, NY 13905.

Fischer Greenhouses, Oak Avenue, Linwood, NJ 08221.
- Nice color catalogue.

Lorine Friedrich, 9130 Glenbury, Houston, TX 77037.
- Plants for African violets and other gesneriads; catalogue $.50.

Growin' House, 37 Shaw Crescent, Barrie, Ontario, CANADA L4N 2Z3.
- Catalogue $1.00.

Hortense's Honeys, 12406 Alexandria, San Antonio, TX 78233.
- Own show-quality hybrids from prominent breeder.

Joan's Windowsill Gardens, PO Box 943, Center Moriches, NY 11934.
- Cuttings for African violets and other gesneriads. Catalogue $.35.

JoS Violets, 402 Dundee, Victoria, TX 77904.
- Cuttings, plants, and supplies for African Violets.

Knull African Violets, 26614 Timberline Drive S.E., Kent, WA 98042.
- Calatogue $.50.

Kolb's Greenhouses, 725 Belvedere Road, Phillipsburg, NJ 08865.

Lakeside Violets, 62 Brady Road, Lake Hopatcong, NJ 07849.
- Catalogue $2.00.

Lloyd's African Violets, 2568 E. Main Street, Cato, NY 13033.
- Wide list, some own hybrids, catalogue $.50.

Mary's Plant and Gift Shop, PO Box 244, Culloden, WV 25510.
- Plants and cuttings from a fine, select list.

Meek's African Violets, 214 Goodrich Avenue, Syracuse, NY 13210.
- Catalogue $1.00.

Mighty Minis, 7318 Sahara Court, Sacramento, CA 95828.
- Plants and cuttings for minis. Catalogue $1.00.

Nadeau Seed Co., 48 Queensbrook Place, St. Louis, MO 63132.
- Seeds, plants, cuttings, and supplies.

Patty's Plant Place, Route 2, Box 41, Cheney, KS 67025.
- African violets and other gesneriads. Catalogue $.50.

Plant Villa, 16 Fullerton, Belleville, IL 62221.
- Plants and cuttings for African violets and other gesneriads. Catalogue $.35.

Plants 'n' Things, Pollock Road, RR 2, Keswick, Ontario, CANADA L4P 3E9

- African violets and other gesneriads. Catalogue $1.00.

Ray's African Violets, Rte 1., Box 244, College Station, TX 77840.
- Plants, cuttings, and supplies. Minis and trailers especially.

Skagit African Violets, 3632 N. Woodland Place, Mount Vernon, WA 98273.
- Does its own hybridizing.

Suni's Violets, PO Box 32, South Kent, CT 06785.
- Plants, cuttings, and supplies.

Susan's Bloomers, PO Box 187, 3094, Champaign, IL 61821.
- Minis. Catalogue $.50.

Tiki Nursery, PO Box 187, Fairview, NC 28730.
- African violets and other gesneriads.

Tomara African Violets, Route 3, Box 116, Fayette, MO 65248.
- Catalogue $.30.

Travis Violets, PO Box 42, Ochlocknee, GA 31773.
- Own and other hybrids.

Violet Cousins by Karen, 6072 N. Dower, Fresno, CA 93711.
- Plants and cuttings for African violets and other gesneriads. Catalogue $1.00.

The Violet Nook, 1814 N. Nevada Avenue, Colorado Springs, CO 80907.
- Plants, cuttings, and supplies.

The Violet Showcase, 3147 S. Broadway, Englewood, CO 80110.
- Good list of African violets and supplies. Catalogue $1.00.

Violets by Court, 87 Mahan Street, West Babylon, NY 11704.

Violets c/o Cookie, 2400 Knightway Drive, Gretna, LA 70053.

Violets Collectible, 1571 Wise Road, Lincoln, CA 95648.
- Catalogue $.50.

Wilson's Violet Haven, 3900 Carter Creek Parkway, Bryan, TX 77802.
- Plants and cuttings for African violets. Catalogue, $1.00.

---

culents, bulbs, fruit trees, and trailers and climbers. What I like best are his pronouncements. "The chief defect of the shrimp plant," he declares, "is its tendency to gawkiness and bare legs." (He also offers a remedy.) Then there is devil's-tongue: "I submit that it should never be brought into the house during the time its flowers are discharging their offensive odor, which at its height is sufficiently strong to gag a maggot."

All About Orchids

by Charles Marsden Fitch
Doubleday

■ *276 pages, many illustrations, a few in color, $15.95.*

Fitch has spent more than a quarter-century with orchids, and however dry his writing seems, it tells you what you need to know for indoor or outdoor culture. There are separate chapters on the top 6 genera, plus a dictionary of about 60 more.

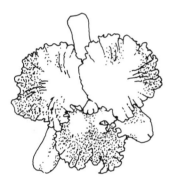

AQUI-FINN "KALEIDESCOPE" ORCHID

Amaryllis, Inc.

PO Box 318
Baton Rouge, LA 70821

■ *Amaryllis—named cultivars, species, and double hybrids—and a few other bulbs.*
■ *6-page catalogue, free; large poster of Hadeco bulbs, 25 color illustrations, $2.00.*

Ed Beckman sells a few day lilies and miscellaneous bulbs, but his real love is amaryllis. He imports numbers of amaryllis from Dutch growers like Van Meeuwen and Ludwig and from the African firm Hadeco. A few more come from India, and the double amaryllis he offers is hybridized in the United States. The Hadeco and Van Meeuwen amaryllis are well, if briefly, described, but the others are listed mainly by name or species. It's a very wide selection from a man who knows his stuff. Beckman points out that the Hadecos, unlike the Dutch varieties, are field grown, so they are generally hardier.

> 🌱 I usually drew in the evening in some tourist cabin or motel. In the case of rare orchids, gentians, or other species, where prudence forbade my picking them, I often drew them while lying flat on the ground. But most of the flowers were drawn in motels. In my suitcase I carried a 200-watt daylight bulb that I often substituted for the weak 40- or 60-watt bulb in my quarters. To this day I am able to look at each drawing and bring back by association the place where I found the flower, the circumstances in which I drew it, and incidents— some pleasant, others trying. This odyssey was very educational.
>
> —ROGER TORY PETERSON AND MARGARET McKENNY, FROM *A FIELD GUIDE TO WILDFLOWERS OF NORTHEASTERN AND NORTHCENTRAL NORTH AMERICA* (1968)

American Begonia Society

PO Box 1129
Encinitas, CA 92024

■ *Nonprofit organization dedicated to begonia culture.*
■ *24-page bimonthly* The Begonian, *seed exchange, mail-order books; annual membership $15.00.*

Plant societies are wonderful ways for people to become amateur explorers, scientists, breeders, and historians. Consider this report of a trip down the Tapajos river in Brazil from a recent issue of *The Begonian*. After describing the jungle, the heat, the mosquitoes, and the prevalence of bromeliads, the author gets to the point: "From the small boat Tom could see a patch of color among the leaves. . . . Along the bank was a somewhat open area, perhaps 200 feet across, where there was a huge stand of wild *Begonia* with flower clusters of the most marvelous and intense shade of red." The magazine also includes items on culture, flower arranging, and the history of varieties. Seed offered for sale through the seed fund is listed in the magazine. The members are interested in every begonia there is, including tuberous- and fibrous-rooted, shrub and cane and Rex. The group sells the key reference books by mail, and will provide you with a useful list of specialty growers.

American Gloxinia and Gesneriad Society

5320 Labadie
St. Louis, MO 63120

■ *Nonprofit society dedicated to the culture of as many of the roughly 120 genera of the family Gesneriaceae as members can lay hands on except for* Saintpaulia ionantha, *the African violet.*
■ *46-page bimonthly* The Gloxinian, *some color illustrations; seed exchange; annual membership $10.00, three years $25.00.*

Gloxinias are the flagship of the gesneriad fleet, but members' interest is by no means limited to them. A good two dozen genera are included in the seed-fund listing published in a recent issue of the *The Gloxinian*. It may be that the variety of plants in their favorite family makes these people unusually literate and charming. Whatever the reason, the magazine is not only informative but fun to read. There is a lively debate afoot on the value of hybrids and the primacy of flowers, including some hilarious advice from the pseudonymous columnist "Blabby." Those who associate gloxinias with their grandmother's living room will be interested to hear that gesneriads can be grown on window sills, in rock gardens, in basements and greenhouses, and even as garden annuals.

American Orchid Society

600 S. Olive Boulevard
West Palm Beach, FL 33405

- *Variable-length monthly* Bulletin, *many color illustrations, annual subscription $28.00.*

As a society publication, the *Bulletin* gives first place to hands-on information about culture, propagation, new hybrids, and the like. It is perhaps less interested in general scientific articles than are the independent orchid journals, though it includes a fair mix of general articles on common and uncommon genera, plus travel and plant-hunting articles. Attention is also given to native orchids. As usual with such magazines, the pictures are lovely. There was even a recent pictorial of vintage orchid postcards. Look, too, for the fine large section of advertisements for all orchids and orchid-related items.

Annalee Violetry

29-50 214 Place
Bayside, NY 11360

- *Plants for African violets.*
- *4-page list, $1.00.*

This is a well-described, collector's list of African violets. The unusual, striped "pinwheel" hybrids—which can only be propagated from suckers —are scarce and comparatively costly, but not exorbitant. There are more than a dozen choices among these, together with more than 100 other named cultivars, some developed at Annalee and many from other prominent breeders. If you have been frightened by your grandma's array of lavender African violets, this list gives you a good idea of the much fuller color range available. Trailers, miniatures, and variegated-foliage types appear along with plants of the ordinary form.

AUSTRALIAN NATIVES

Gardeners in the Far West and Southwest are liable to find quite a number of Australian species mixed in with the lists of local or regional nurseries; eucalypti, acacias, callistemons, banksias, and the like, are all of Australian origin. For those who are wild about Australian flora, here is a selective list of specialists, mainly located in Australia. If your madness persists, you might find it worth your while to join The Society for Growing Australian Plants, which publishes a magazine on the subject. For information, write c/o Glen Harvey, 5 Ellesmere Road, Crymea Bay, N.S.W., AUSTRALIA 2227.

Austraflora of Utah, PO Box 579, Santa Clara, UT 84765.
- Hardy eucalyptus.

Bushland Flora, PO Box 189, Hillarys, W.A., AUSTRALIA 6025.
- Broad selection of seed for native wildflowers, shrubs, and trees.

H. Grant—Australian Seeds, 90 Wingewarra Street, Dubbo, N.S.W., AUSTRALIA 2830.
- Seed for natives adapted to dry-land conditions.

International Seed Supplies, PO Box 538, Nowra, N.S.W., AUSTRALIA 2541.
- Seed for everything including natives. Color catalogue $3.00.

Nindethana Seed Service, Washpool Road, RMB 939, Woogenilup, AUSTRALIA 6324.
- Seed for many natives.

D. Orriell—Seed Exporters, Villa 11, Madeira Gardens, Mt. Yokine, W.A., AUSTRALIA 6060.
- Seed for a great variety of natives and exotics. Extensive list $3.00.

Southern Seeds, The Vicarage, Sheffield, Canterbury, NEW ZEALAND.
- Seed for New Zealand natives suitable for the rock garden. A charming list from collection made by a pastor and his wife.

Vaughan's Wildflower Seeds, PO Box 66, Greenwood, W.A., AUSTRALIA 6024.
- Seed for Australian wildflowers.

The Banana Tree

715 Northampton Street
Easton, PA 18042

- *Corms, seeds, bulbs, and a few plants for bananas and other exotics, mainly but not exclusively tropical.*
- *19-page catalogue, $.75.*

The Banana Tree is a wonderful toy store for the serious grower of exotics, but since it sells mainly seeds and bulbs, the gardener must be a proficient propagator to enjoy it. Some of the species offered can be grown outdoors in semitropical parts of the United States, but most are indoor plants and many require carefully controlled greenhouse conditions. There are several dozen species of banana to choose from, a dozen protea, seldom seen species of bird-of-paradise and yucca, numerous palms and palm-like plants, trees like the baobab and the monkey-puzzle, a thorny shrub called "titty fruit" (*Solanum mammosum*), a half dozen heliconia, and no end of other stuff. Some of Fred Saleet's customers are botanical gardens, which accounts for listings like *Acrocomia vinifera*, "A 30' feather type palm known for its unique sharp spines on the trunk."

BANANA

On the other hand, he lists quite a number of plants that could do well in an ordinary house (or outdoors in California), like abutilon, acacia, the aforementioned monkey-puzzle tree, and lots more. There are also quite a few true trees, best for outdoor planting where possible. One question I would like to ask Saleet is whether he has ever sold any ailanthus. He is, I think, the only nurseryman I've come on who actually lists this weedy and almost unkillable tree.

BEGONIAS

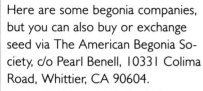

Here are some begonia companies, but you can also buy or exchange seed via The American Begonia Society, c/o Pearl Benell, 10331 Colima Road, Whittier, CA 90604.

Antonelli Bros., 2545 Capitola Drive, Santa Cruz, CA 95062.
- Catalogue $1.00.

Fairyland Begonia & Lily Garden, 1100 Griffith Road, McKinleyville, CA 95521.
- Catalogue $.50.

Paul P. Lowe, 5741 Dewberry Way, West Palm Beach, FL 33415.
- Broad list, some own hybrids. Catalogue $1.00.

Blackmore & Langdon

See "Annuals and Perennials."

The Bromeliad Society

2488 E. 49th
Tulsa, OK 74105

- *Nonprofit organization dedicated to the culture of bromeliads.*
- *46-page bimonthly journal, some color illustrations; seed exchange; specialty books; annual membership $15.00.*

The pineapple is a bromeliad; so is Spanish moss; so are members of about 45 other genera. Society members are most interested in about a dozen of these, including the lovely *Tillandsia.* The magazine contains everything from reports of new species to notes on using "Liquid Nails" adhesive to glue plants to their supports. Illustrations are unusually good. Like most specialty societies, this one is a good place to get books on the culture of its favorites and to learn about unusual sources for the plants. Seed-fund offerings appear periodically in the journal, covering at least 18 of the more popular genera, plus a list of hybrids.

BROMELIADS

As many bromeliads specialists as there are, there could still be many more, since the family embraces 45 genera and more than 2,000 species in total.

Beach Garden Nursery, PO Box 697, Delhi, CA 95315.

Bromeliad Brokers, PO Box 435, Washingtonville, NY 10992.

Claire's Bromeliads, 720 Balour Drive, Encinitas, CA 92024.
- Broad list. Catalogue $1.00.

Cornelison Bromeliads, 225 San Bernardino Street, N. Fort Myers, FL 33903.

Dana Co., 4626 Lamont, Corpus Christi, TX 78411.

BROMELIAD AECHMEA

De Leon's Bromeliad World, 8880 S.W. 80th Street, Miami, FL 33173.

His 'n' Hers Bromeliad Nursery, 2112 W. Carol Drive, Fullerton, CA 92633.
- Catalogue $1.00.

Jerry Hoernig, 3228 Gerle Avenue, Placerville, CA 95667.
- Catalogue $.50.

Kent's Bromeliad Nursery, 703 Pomelo Drive, Vista, CA 92083.

Marilynn's Garden, 13421 Sussex Place, Santa Ana, CA 92705.

Marz Bromeliads, 10782 Citrus Drive, Moorpark, CA 93021.

M. Oppenheimer Bromeliads, PO Box 960, San Antonio, TX 78284.
- Catalogue $1.00.

Plant Ranch, 2020 Tweed Street, Placentia, CA 92670.
- Catalogue $1.00.

W. K. Quality Bromeliads, PO Box 49621, Los Angeles, CA 90049.

John Brudy Exotics

3411 Westfield Drive
Brandon, FL 33511

- *Seed for exotic trees, shrubs, and some herbaceous plants.*
- *12-page catalogue, $1.00.*

Huysman's Des Esseintes—the hero of his novel *Against Nature*—loved every sort of hideous exotic flower; what he was to ugliness, John Brudy seems to be to size. Brudy's list is strong in all sorts of chiefly tropical exotic trees and shrubs, but big leaves and flowers really turn him on. Consider the amorphophallus, which "grows from large subterranean bulb-like formations (called 'corms') which attain a size of 12 to 20 inches in the wild. After a size of about 8 to 10 inches is reached. . . . the corm puts up a big blossom. . . . The flower is shaped like a huge, hooded Calla lily, is generally from 12 to 20 inches in diameter, and is colored a deep, velvety purple with cream markings." Try that in the living room. Then there is the aptly named bat-wing coral tree (*Erythrina vespertilio*), of which Brudy remarks, "No other tree has leaves remotely like this." Overall, the list is not quite as extensive as say, The Banana Tree's, but for the subtropical or greenhouse gardener, it has many items of interest, including quite a number of eucalypti and many shrubs/trees with edible fruits. Scattered through the catalogue are a few exotics less tropical in nature, including some Italian cypresses, the Irish shamrock, and a Chinese elm. It may be hard for neophytes to start any of this material from seed, but Brudy has included a really first-rate set of instructions for germinating all the plants he lists, together with some general dos-and-don'ts and a troubleshooting guide. For enthusiasts of tropical exotic trees and shrubs, particularly of those plantings with large leaves, this source can't be beat.

STRELITZIA

Buell's Greenhouses

PO Box 218 RTP
Eastford, CT 06242

- *Plants for African violets, gloxinias, and other gesneriads.*
- *32-page list, $.25 plus stamped, self-addressed envelope.*

Stand back for this one. The list is immense, numbering several hundred African violets alone, not to mention a number of the gloxinia hybrids for which Albert Buell is known and the species and/or cultivars of about 23 other genera. There are more than 800 listings in all, and Buell claims to be raising about 140,000 plants at his nursery. Don't send for the list unless you love the things or feel ready to fall in love with them.

Clargreen Gardens

814 Southdown Road
Mississauga, Ontario
CANADA L5J 2Y4

- *Plants for orchids and other tropicals.*
- *16-page orchid catalogue, $1.00.*

The minimum order is $45.00, but as individual prices are by no means low, this isn't a very formidable amount. The species list is wide-ranging and excellent, with good brief notes on form, color, bloom time, preferred temperature, and cultural requirements. The species selections embrace more than 40 genera, including a very large group of paphiopedilums. There are also lists of hybrids, most notably cattleyas.

CARNIVOROUS PLANTS

Here are a few places of interest for devotees of the flesh-eaters. You might also visit the Carnivorous Plant Bog at the Fullerton Arboretum, or join the International Carnivorous Plant Society. Write to the Fullerton Arboretum, Fullerton, CA 92634.

Black Copper Kits, 266 Kipps Street, Hackensack, NJ 07601.
- Carnivorous plants for terrarium culture.

Carnivorous and Unusual Seeds, 3 Normandy Avenue, Para Hills, Adelaide, S.A., AUSTRALIA 5096.
- Seed for Australian tuberous droseras and others.

Carolina Exotic Gardens, PO Box 1492, Greenville, NC 27834.
- Carnivorous plants. Catalogue $1.00.

Hungry Plants, 1216 Cooper Drive, Raleigh, NC 27607.
- Tissue-cultured plant material. Catalogue $1.00.

Lee's Botanical Gardens, PO Box 7026, Ocala, FL 32672.
- Plants for carnivores and exotics.

Marston Exotics—Carnivorous Plants, Turners Field, Behind Town, Compton-Dundon, Somerton, Somerset, ENGLAND TA11 6PT.
- Fine selection of seed and books for carnivores. One of the best. Illustrated catalogue $1.00.

Peter Pauls Nursery, Canandaigua, NY 14424.
- Nice color list, with wide selection, including darlingtonias, and terrarium supplies; owner-authored book *The Carnivorous Plants of the World*, available by mail.

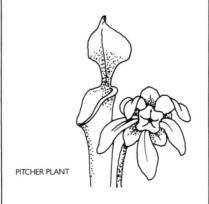

PITCHER PLANT

The Cymbidium Society of America

c/o Mrs. Jo Johnston
6881 Wheeler Avenue
Westminster, CA 92683

- *Nonprofit organization dedicated chiefly to the culture of cymbidium and paphiopedilum orchids.*
- *Variable-length bimonthly* The Orchid Advocate, *many color illustrations, annual membership $15.00.*

Chiefly a West Coast society, the Cymbidium Society also has a branch in New Zealand. The magazine contains no-nonsense reports on breeding and culture of cymbidiums and paphiopedilums around the world, but the texts are directed at serious amateurs, not scientists. Arcane sources appear among the advertisements, but the best thing about the publication is its mouth-watering illustrations.

Dow Seeds Hawaii

PO Box 30144
Honolulu, HI 96820

- *Seeds for tropical and subtropical palms, flowering and foliage plants.*
- *86-page catalogue, approx. 150 illustrations, some in color, $5.00.*

The parent company hails from New Zealand, but the list is very strong in tropicals and subtropicals from around the world. Unfortunately for the eager buyer, it sells *only* wholesale. Still, if you are a lover of palms, tree ferns, or other exotic specialties that Dow lists, you may be able to get together with a group of fellow-enthusiasts to purchase the minimum quantity, or you might get a specialty retail nursery to send for that ravenala you just *must* have. Serious growers of exotics will probably want the catalogue just to pore over or to keep up with what the trade is introducing.

Endangered Species

PO Box 1830
Tustin, CA 92681

- *Plants for bamboo, palms, cycads, phormiums, and other tropical foliage plants.*
- *56-page catalogue, approx. 35 illustrations, $5.00.*

This catalogue is also reviewed in the Trees and Shrubs chapter (see page 88), but I couldn't resist including it here for its tropical bamboos and palms and its fair selections of cycads and phormiums. The miscellaneous list of exotic foliage plants is short, but well worth a look for unusual species and rarer varieties of common ones.

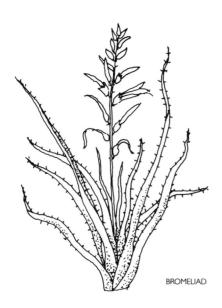

BROMELIAD

Exotica

by Alfred B. Graf
Roehrs Company
136 Park Avenue
East Rutherford, NJ 07073

- *2,580 pages in 2 volumes, many color illustrations, $187.00.*

If you are crazy enough about exotics to buy this double tome, you probably already have. It weighs in at 18 pounds and contains a good 16,000 illustrations. Not only a fine doorstop,

it is also the best reference work in existence about tropical and hardy exotics. Plants grown for flowers and foliage are included, with pictures and all kinds of information. If you don't buy it yourself, you might talk your public library into buying it. People interested strictly in tropical exotics can refer instead to Graf's *Tropica*, and those who want a briefer and handier guide to all exotics can see his *Exotic Plant Manual*.

Exotic Plant Manual

by Alfred B. Graf
Roehrs Company
136 Park Avenue
East Rutherford, NJ 07073

- *840 pages, many illustrations, some color, $37.50.*

This is a very well put together reference book that contains all that most exotics growers need to identify, propagate, and care for their plants. It is not as comprehensive as *Exotica*, but let's not be picky. There are well over 4,000 photos here, plus introductions to the culture, ecology and who-knows-what of all major families, together with an extensive alphabetical listing by genus and species at the back. There are even photographs showing suggested indoor and outdoor settings for exotic plants. For the record, the following tropical genera and types are discussed at length: aroids, begonias, bromeliads, cacti, dracaenas, bananas, gingers, figs, palms, ferns, and vines. Among subtropicals appear broad-leaved evergreens, bamboos, conifers, cycads, herbs, oxalis (and shamrocks), and succulents. A separate section on flowering plants embraces gesneriads, geraniums, orchids, and many more. It is too bad that all the photos aren't in color, but for that you wil have to go to (and pay the price for) *Tropica*.

> *FILIPENDULA (Meadowsweet)*
> It groweth in the brinkes of waterine ditches and rivers sides, and also in meadowes: it liketh watery and moist places, and groweth almost every where. It floweth and flourisheth in June, July, and August.
>
> . . .
>
> The leaves and floures farre excell all other strowing herbes, for to decke up houses, to straw in chambers, halls, and banqueting houses in the summer times for the smell thereof makes the heart merrie, delighteth the senses: neither doth it cause headache, or lothsomenesse to meat, as some other sweet smelling herbes do.
>
> —FROM *GERARDE'S HERBALL* (1596)

Fairchild Tropical Garden

10901 Old Cutler Road
Miami, FL 33156

- *Nonprofit botanic garden, specializing in tropical and subtropical plants.*
- *Classes, annual plant distribution and sale; variable-length quarterly Garden Bulletin, many illustrations; annual subscription $6.00, annual membership $25.00, family membership $40.00.*

Miami residents know what a remarkable place the Fairchild Garden is, not only for the over 5,000 tropicals and subtropicals it displays, but for the form of the garden itself. It was designed by William Lyman Phillips, an associate of Frederick Law Olmstead. Newer areas contain gardens of Florida and Bahamas natives. Even if you are nowhere near Miami, however, you will find the *Garden Bulletin* both stimulating and useful. Because Fairchild is so heavily involved in research, it can draw on the talents of plant explorers to contribute fascinating accounts of their travels in search of Cycad X. The tales are often as interesting for ethnography as they are for botany. A recent issue, for example, contained an account of the search for the supposed *Zamia chiqua*, which turned out to be something else altogether. A clue in the search for the plant was the huge seed cones that the botanists found piled by doorways in certain villages—the seeds were used for tortillas! Most issues also contain profiles of plants you might grow at home or in the greenhouse; species from the garden's large collection of cycads and palms are prominent among these.

Fennell Orchid Company

26715 S.W. 157 Avenue
Homestead, FL 33031

- Plants for orchids; large display garden.
- 8-page beginner's catalogue Your First Orchids, approx. 25 illustrations, free.

Fennell is a downhome company that follows the time-honored American tradition of real service and relentless self-promotion. The firm runs the 10-acre Orchid Jungle near Miami, "where every lady gets an orchid." According to the beginner's catalogue, the Fennells were instrumental in making orchids popular indoor plants for North American gardeners, back in the 1950s. That catalogue offers a short list of the major genera—cattleyas, dendrobiums, phalaenopsis, oncidium, miltonia, and vanda, including some miniatures—typed by color, not species. The cultural instructions offered for each are very good, though of course, the company uses the text to sell its own potting medium and orchid food. There are several collections available, including the "One of Each," which offers 17 plants at $365, "only one dollar a day!"

Fischer Greenhouses

Oak Avenue
Linwood, NJ 08221

- Plants for African violets and a few other gesneriads; supplies.
- 12-page catalogue, 145 color illustrations, $.50.

If you are starting to like gesneriads, and African violets in particular, Fischer is a good place to find out what they look like. Almost every variety offered is clearly illustrated in color, so the catalogue is a little anthology of the color forms and types commonly available. Not to say that the section on African violets isn't long. It is, but compared to some of the crazier specialty houses, it is refreshingly brief.

Fox Orchids

6615 W. Markham
Little Rock, AR 72205

- Plants for hybrid orchids and some other tropicals; supplies, corsage supplies, books.
- 35-page catalogue, free.

The wide-ranging list from this very experienced company includes more than 250 cattleya hybrids, grouped according to color pattern. The phalaenopsis list is also quite long, and there are smaller numbers of most of the usually cultivated genera. Among the other tropicals appear small groups of staghorn ferns and bromeliads. The supplies list is comprehensive. Because the catalogue is so broad, it doesn't pause long over any given hybrid, but introductory paragraphs for each genus tell the beginner whether the plants are easy or hard to grow. The books list contains a very good selection of volumes for beginners, including the Oregon Orchid Society's *Your First Orchids and How to Grow Them*.

G&B Orchid Laboratory

2426 Cherimoya Drive
Vista, CA 92084

- Plants for orchids; laboratory propagation supplies.
- Variable-length list, free.

If you are a budding breeder and into meristem tissue culture, here is a good place to get all sorts of growing media, chemicals, and glassware. The firm also offers a list of named cultivarsfor sale—chiefly phalaenopsis, cattleyas, cymbidiums, dendrobiums, and the other commonly grown genera.

Garden of Delights

2018 Mayo Street
Hollywood, FL 33020

- Plants and seeds for exotic fruit trees and palms.
- 7-page fruits list, 3-page palms list, free.

The selection of exotic fruits is particularly interesting. Both lists contain Latin and common names only, so you must know what you are doing.

Garden World

2503 Garfield Street
Laredo, TX 78043

- Plants for bananas, pineapples, bromeliads, Latin American herbs, and other tropical useful and ornamental plants.
- Catalogue, $1.00.

Even the old catalogue lists around 30 banana varieties, both ornamental and edible, plus a handy article about growing them. The proprietors collect a lot of what they sell. Look for the new catalogue, which promises to list a far wider range of offerings.

Gesneriad International and Saintpaulia International

Box 102
Greenwood, IN 46142

- *Nonprofit organizations dedicated to the culture of all gesneriads, including African violets, and of other exotics as well.*
- *60-page bimonthly Gesneriad Saintpaulia News, many illustrations, some in color; seed exchanges; annual membership to either society, including magazine subscription, $8.75; annual membership to both societies $9.25.*

Those who love gesneriads are lucky; there are at least four different societies for them to join. Here are two of them, and they share a single magazine. For others, see pages 164 and 166. The magazine is full of useful, member-contributed articles, though it is a bit less literate than the publication of the American Gloxinia and Gesneriad Society. On the other hand, the question-and-answer format of several of the articles is very convenient for people who need to know quickly what to do.

Glasshouse Works

Church Street
Box 97
Stewart, OH 45778

- *Subtropical and tropical greenhouse plants and houseplants; succulents; unusual perennials.*
- *Two 48-page catalogues, some illustrations, plus specialty lists, $1.50.*

This firm keeps an astounding number of species and varieties on hand: about 10,000 by its count. Not quite half of these get into one of the catalogues or lists each year. (Plans are afoot for an exotics manual to list and describe many more of them under one cover.) "Plants traditional and unusual" is how the Works describes itself. From what I can tell, it is heavy on the unusual, including such things

as the Australian "beefoak tree," an African "fat grape," something that has "tinkertoy stolons supporting colonies of brilliant red leaves," and so on. There *are* some common things like leopard plant and Jerusalem cherry, but even among the commoner stuff you will find odd species and forms, like a succulent morning glory from Central America. The tropicals are worth looking at in themselves, but mixed in with them is a very fine selection of succulents—with many mesembryanthemums, euphorbias, haworthias, and caudiciform plants—and quite a number of dwarf conifers, ericaceous plants, and perennials for the rock garden. In short, if you are a mad gardener, you will probably enjoy these lists.

The Good Housekeeping Encyclopedia of House Plants

by Rob Herwig
Hearst Books/Morrow

- *288 pages, many color illustrations, $19.95.*

I liked best the illustrated discussion of different growing situations, from window-sill pots, to hydroponic and self-watering gardens, to a variety of greenhouse ideas. The how-to sections here are unusually good, too, describing common problems and their solutions, as well as general instructions. The usual information on propagation, care, and bug control appears. The plant dictionary is very large, embracing 1,500 species and cultivars, with 700 color photographs. Unlike some of the smaller houseplant books, this does not attempt to dispose of huge families like the cacti, the orchids, or the gesneriads in a single mass entry. It breaks the genera down into their own listings instead.

Goodman Greenhouses

4780 Falstaff Road
Greenwood, CA 95635

- *Plants for African violets and begonias.*
- *4-page list, free.*

There are about 600 African violets in this list, a good selection of other gesneriads, and a couple of dozen begonias.

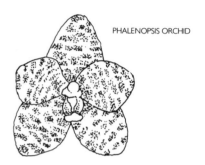

PHALENOPSIS ORCHID

Great Lakes Orchids

28805 Pennsylvania Road
Romulus, MI 48174

- *Plants, hobby flasks, and community pots for orchids.*
- *27-page catalogue, 17 color illustrations, free.*

Here's a first-rate catalogue of orchids, whose weakness is its virtually complete lack of cultural instructions. Still, as the fact that the firm sells both plants and seedlings would suggest, it is probable that most customers are not rank beginners. The list of species orchids is particularly fine, with good groups of aerides, dendrobiums, epidendrums, laelias, odontoglossums, oncidiums, paphiopedilums, and phalaenopsis; many miniature species are also available. A specialty seems to be masdevallias, gorgeous little things that look like squadrons of swept-wing fighters from some tropical air force. For the deeply interested, Great Lakes will send separate lists of more flask, community pot, and masdevallia listings.

Himalayan Plants

See "Annuals and Perennials."

Honingklip Nurseries

See "Sources of Sources."

Jerry Horne

10195 SW 70 Street
Miami, FL 33173

- Plants for exotics.
- 6-page list, SASE.

Jerry Horne begins his list by greeting "Fellow Plant Nuts." What you will find among the selections are good groups of aroids, palms and cycads, bromeliads, and epiphytic ferns, plus a lot of miscellany. Among other things, Horne promises to list every known species of *Platycerium*, well qualifying him for the epithet he uses in his greeting. There are numbers of alocassia and anthuriums here too.

C. W. Hosking— Exotic Seed Importer/Exporter

PO Box 500
Hayle, Cornwall
ENGLAND TR27 4BE

- Seed for tropical and subtropical plants.
- 21-page list, $2.50.

Well over 700 species and varieties appear here, with brief notes on origin, appearance, and other information. Sometimes the entries are mysterious, as the Chinese Jellow vine (a ficus), about which Hosking comments, "The famous Ae Yu Jello and lemonade drink is made from the ripe fruits." The list is impossible to summarize; it includes plants from virtually every tropical region of the globe. Expert exotics growers should have a lot of fun with it.

HOYAS

There are a few hoya specialists. A good source of information for the beginner and collector can be found in the 32-page quarterly bulletin published by the Hoya Society International, PO Box 54271, Atlanta, GA 30308. Here are two specialists:
Hill-N-Dale, 6427 N. Fruit, Fresno, CA 93711.
Green: Plant Research, PO Box 735, Kaaawa, HI 96730.

The Hyponex Book of Houseplants

The Hyponex Co.
Copley, OH 44321

- 256 pages, many color illustrations, $3.95.

The first of the many color photos occupies a full page and shows an array of Hyponex products for indoor gardening. Crass commercialism, you may think, but consider how rare it is to find a color-illustrated reference work for under $10, much less for under $5. This one has some faults—for instance, it continually tells you that a given plant will thrive in the "average house" without telling you whether or not your house is average—but it is generally very informative, not only for most species of the commonly grown indoor plants, but for general propagation, pest control, and light and humidity requirements as well. The A-to-Z list of plants will by no means put you on to every possible African violet, begonia, or cactus, but where a family or genus is full of choice, it at least tries to offer a range of selections. The photos are generally good, as are the cultural instructions. There is even a section on making gift plants like poinsettias and cyclamen survive and bloom again.

The Indoor Garden

by John Brookes
Crown

- 288 pages, many color illustrations, $24.95.

It's good to see an indoor-garden book that focuses on design—few volumes provide such an attractive overview regarding the use of plants in interior design. The color photos are spectacular throughout, and it's particularly inspiring to see the variety of containers Brookes has selected. Illustrations of leaf texture are also very useful.

For similar sexual reasons, Aphrodite-Venus is also associated with gardens. Pliny says that Plautus speaks of gardens as being under the guardianship of Venus, though the Roman cult of Venus as goddess of gardens seems to have lapsed by the end of the republic. Goddess of the rose, the flower of purity, desire and passion, her role is like Flora's, though never undergoing so violent a transformation in post-Renaissance times.

Last, the god Terminus should be mentioned, for his statues—*Terms*—served as landmarks, protecting boundaries, whether of a state, or of a rural property. As garden ornaments, to line a walk or to close a vista, they survive until modern times, often becoming confused with statues representing other persons—Faunus, for example, or Priapus.

—CHRISTOPHER THACKER, FROM *THE HISTORY OF GARDENS* (1979)

International Aroid Society

PO Box 43-1853
South Miami, FL 33143

- *Nonprofit organization dedicated to study and culture of aroids.*
- *40-page quarterly Aroideana, some illustrations, annual membership $15.00.*

If you are into aroids, you will find the mainly scientific and technical material discussed here very interesting, even sexy. The pictures themselves are enough to cause a sensation of pleasure or revulsion, depending on your bent (remember that *Monstera* is a genus of the aroids, as are *Anthurium* and *Philodendron*, plants that in the wild can have leaves up to 8 feet long). Since some of the articles are reports of expeditions in search of these plants, the texts are livelier than most scientific writing. An article in a recent issue told of the author's search in Gabon for *Pseudohydrosme gabunensis*. The flowers are huge inverted clown hats that look big and mean enough to swallow monkeys. They are so rare that the author only found a couple. The society does no formal plant exchange, but members can list their wants in the magazine.

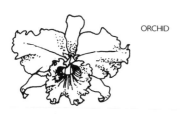

ORCHID

International Tropical Fern Society

8720 S.W. 34th Street
Miami, FL 33165

- *Nonprofit organization dedicated to culture of exotic ferns.*

The society no longer publishes a magazine, but will send you a list of local chapters, on request. The chapters publish their own newsletters.

J&L Orchids

20 Sherwood Road
Easton, CT 06612

- *Plants for orchids.*
- *45-page catalogue, 25 illustrations, $1.00.*

J&L's is an extremely fine list of chiefly species orchids. Unlike many, it is prefaced with adequate cultural instructions, and a little dot marks each species that is recommended for easy culture. Still, it is perhaps the widest ranging mail-order source there is of blooming-size species orchids. Even among common genera like *Cattleya* there appears an unusual choice like *Cattleya dormaniana*, producing mahogany flowers with bright violet lips. You will have much to choose from even in less common genera, including *Encyclia*, *Pleurothallis*, *Bulbophyllum*, and *Gastrochilus*. Many sophronitis, oncidiums, and dendrobiums are also present, along with a good few miltonias, but Janet and Lee Kahn are really nuts about masdevallias and the aptly named draculas. (The latter appear to have both fangs and a stinger.) They not only list several pages of masdevallias, but offer collections of them and the standard monograph on the genus as well. Many miniatures are scattered through the catalogue.

Jones & Scully

18955 S.W. 168th Street
Miami, FL 33187

- *Plants and seedlings for orchids; supplies and books.*
- *74-page catalogue, more than 240 color illustrations, $5.00.*

Jones & Scully is probably the largest orchid supplier in the world. The catalogue is massive. The species selection alone is very wide, including a number of Brazilian species, and there are endless hybrids for the more popularly grown genera. Get it.

Kartuz Greenhouses

1408 Sunset Drive
Vista, CA 92083

- *Flowering houseplants and greenhouse plants, especially begonias and gesneriads, with many flowering vines and shrubs, and passion flowers.*
- *52-page catalogue, with yearly supplements, more than 40 illustrations, $2.00.*

Michael Kartuz has built a very fine list of tropical and subtropical plants over the last quarter-century. There are well over 500 varieties to choose from among the begonias and gesneriads alone; about 2 dozen genera of gesneriads are represented. There is a small but choice selection of miniature plants, some for the terrarium. Among these are the miniature Hawaiian series impatiens, introduced to the trade by Kartuz some years back. The very choice selections of flowering shrubs and vines may be planted outdoors in our mildest climates. This is one of those rare catalogues that should interest everyone from the conservatory fanatic to the occasional houseplant grower to the outdoor gardener along the Southern coast.

Kensington Orchids

3301 Plyers Mill Road
Kensington, MD 20895

- *Seedlings and plants for orchids; books and supplies.*
- *10-page list, free.*

When it comes to getting orchid supplies, you can get almost everything you need by mail from these people, except pots. The orchids list itself is fairly strong in cultivars of the usually grown genera, especially phalaenopsis, cymbidiums, cattleyas (including Art Shade cattleyas), and paphiopedilums, with some miltonias and brassias thrown in. The group of miniature cymbidiums is nice.

As of this date, 9/86, I do not have a greenhouse, but grow 85% of our collection under lights, leaving the hardier *Columnea*, *Aeschynanthus*, *Codonanthe*, and *Nemathanthus* to natural light on our enclosed porch. Although I get many calls asking "Is this the greenhouse?", I am just a small operation, a 1¼ person business growing all of these plants in our home. I do about 90% of the work myself, as Jim is a full time chemist employed outside the home. In addition to filling orders, there is other equally important work to do. Watering, bug control, propagation, repotting and bookkeeping to mention a few. Somehow all of these things must be squeezed into a 24 hour day, a 7 day week. I now have about 1,000 varieties of gesneriads, although not all of them are listed in my catalog. Many are grown in multiples to be sold as plants, so I have between 3,000–4,000 hungry little plant mouths to feed on a regular basis. In addition, I have 2 little human mouths to feed, Emily and Hanna, and that in itself is a full time job.

—FROM *ROBERTS' GESNERIADS 1987 CATALOGUE*

Lauray of Salisbury

Undermountain Road
Route 41
Salisbury, CT 06068

- *Plants for gesneriads, begonias, cacti and succulents, orchids, and a few other houseplants.*
- *50-page catalogue, $1.50.*

All gesneriad, begonia, and cactus and succulent fetishists must already know about Lauray. For each, the firm offers quite a wide selection of genera, species, and hybrids. Know what you seek, because the descriptions are quite short. The orchids list is less broad, though still extensive, and it uses a shorthand that only the cognoscenti understand. Among the "other houseplants" appear a goodly number of hoyas and peperomia.

Wm. O. Lessard

19201 S.W. 248th Street
Homestead, FL 33031

- *Bulbs for bananas.*
- *7-page catalogue, free.*

Lessard will sell you bulbs for 31 different bananas. You will have to figure out how to grow them yourself.

GESNERIAD

Logee's Greenhouses

55 North Street
Danielson, CT 06239

- *Begonias; indoor and greenhouse plants; herbs.*
- *122-page catalogue, 110 color illustrations, $3.00.*

This is a beautiful and gigantic catalogue from a firm almost a century old. In the main, you'll need another source to tell you how to grow the things it offers, but there is hardly a kind of indoor plant that you will not find listed—and gorgeously illustrated—here. Begonias of all sorts are a specialty, taking up a full third of the catalogue, but there are also lots of pelargoniums and an astonishing miscellaneous list. Collectors of cacti and succulents, gesneriads, citrus, ferns, fuchsias, camellias, and such specialties may find the 1-to-2 dozen choices here skimpy for their needs, but general houseplant enthusiasts will be thrilled. There's even a very fine list of herbs for outdoors, and some of the other offerings, like abutilon and calliandra, can be grown outdoors as well, climate permitting.

Louisiana Nursery

Route 7
Box 43
Opelousas, LA 70570

- *Plants for alocasias, tropical vines, palms, bamboo, bananas, and others.*
- *64-page "Magnolias and Other Garden Aristocrats" catalogue, $3.50.*

Louisiana Nursery is many specialty nurseries all lumped together. Its magnolias and irises are famous (see pages 38 and 68), but it offers quite a selection of tropical and subtropical flora as well.

Lyndon Lyon Greenhouses

14 Mutchler Street
Dolgeville, NY 13329

- *Plants and rooted cuttings of African violets, plus a few other gesneriads.*
- *8-page catalogue, 64 color illustrations, $1.00.*

For the record, these folks were the first to create a "double pink" African violet. When such a thing was still rare, they were offered $1,000 for a single plant. They have also been important breeders in the development of miniature, trailing, and large-flowered hybrids. The catalogue is thankfully brief, though it contains many new and old African violets, including the Chimeras, plus a few other gesneriads. The nicest thing about it are the arrays of color photos, which admirably show the color and pattern of flower and leaf, for each of more than 60 varieties.

Rod McLellan Company

1450 El Camino Real
South San Francisco, CA 94080

- *Plants for orchids.*
- *24-page catalogue, over 125 color illustrations, $1.00.*

The Rod McLellan catalogue shows its orchids against a background of the Golden Gate Bridge and of the skyline of South San Francisco. In fact, the company's retail store is located off the El Camino in a light industrial section of South San Francisco. The bridge is nowhere in sight, but the very setting of the place made it all the more wonderful to me as a child. Accompanying my mother to McLellan's or to a florist's shop in San Francisco whose name I never could spell, I had the feeling of leaving the world for paradise. Now, when I read the catalogues of all those orchid companies full of rare species orchids, I am not as awed by the strangeness of McLellan's assortment of cattleyas, cymbs, sophronitis, miltonias, paphiopedilums, and phalaenopsis, but I still admire the sheer loveliness of the shop. The catalogue, likewise, is richly done in color with fair cultural instructions, making it a good place for the beginner as well as the explorer. There are a few specimens of the more exotic genera here, but you go to McLellan's for a good choice among the more common genera, offered by a firm that has been shipping orchids for almost a century. I particularly liked, for example, two of their green cattleya hybrids, Irish Helen and Jade Parade 'Pixie Puff.' The awful names aside, the contrast of lubricious green petals and startling lips is delightful. The list of sophronitis is also unusually large. McLellan's has a mini-greenhouse that you can pop over outdoor orchids to raise their humidity level, plus potting mixes, plant food, and books.

Ann Mann's Exotic Plants

9045 Ron-Den Lane
Windermere, FL 32786

- *Plants for orchids and other exotics; supplies and books.*
- *39-page catalogue, $1.00.*

These are the folks who market Husky-Fiber potting medium, but they also have an extensive plant list. There are several dozen choices each among the aroids (especially anthuriums), bromeliads, and hoyas. The orchids list is strong in the usually grown genera, especially in the cattleyas, with both species and hybrids represented. The list is by name only, with brief descriptions of color.

Merry Gardens

See "Annuals and Perennials"

The Miracle Houseplants

by Virginie F. and George A. Ebert
Crown

- *288 pages, many illustrations, a few in color, $3.98 pbk.*

It's all gesneriads, piles of them, and not just African violets. There is quite enough here for the collector, though the beginner will not find the book intimidating. A brief introductory botany of the family is followed by thorough instructions for cultivation and propagation. The very long plant dictionary includes more than 60 genera, with many cultivar recommendations for most of them. The book was recently updated to take into account changes in nomenclature and some second thoughts that the authors have had about cultural techniques. It's too bad that

some of the update material is simply appended at the back; it might have been nicer to work it into the existing text.

Rebecca Northen

Home Orchid Growing
Dover Publications

- *375 pages, many illustrations, some in color, $37.50.*

Orchids as House Plants
Dover Publications

- *148 pages, many illustrations, $2.95.*

Miniature Orchids
Van Nostrand Reinhold

- *189 pages, many illustrations, a few in color, $20.50 pbk.*

Northen's are perhaps the most respected orchid-culture books in the field. They've been around for quite some time, and they keep being updated. *Home Orchid Growing* was recently revised, and a number of color illustrations were added. It's a very complete hands-on book for the serious orchid grower, and it's clearly and attractively written. Among much other material, there are 2 whole chapters on cattleyas, a chapter on hybridizing, another on dealing with seedlings and growing from seed, and long considerations of many common and unusual genera.

Orchids as House Plants is perhaps the best book for the beginner. It doesn't tackle the whole field at once, but clearly sets out cultural instructions for growing orchids indoors under all kinds of different conditions. A specific chapter on cattleyas is followed by several more chapters that treat about 20 additional genera in logical groups. The material is well selected and illustrated for the beginner.

Miniature Orchids is Northen's newest book, and it amounts to a small encyclopedia of orchids that grow anywhere from about ½ inch to 6 inches high. Each entry is well described for bloom time, looks, native range, and so on, but I wished for a little more information on the culture of each.

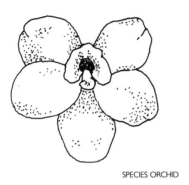

SPECIES ORCHID

Orchid Digest

c/o Mrs. Norman K. Atkinson
PO Box 916
Carmichael, CA 95609

■ *Variable-length bimonthly, many color illustrations, annual membership $18.00.*

Much like its sister publication, *The Orchid Review* (see below), the *Digest* pictures the latest and greatest in the orchid world, explorations of common and uncommon genera, and very good regular columns and features on propagation, greenhouse culture, and general culture. The beginner will feel welcome here. The *Digest*'s photos are, if anything, even sexier than the *Review*'s. You will find some lovely old orchid paintings reproduced here, as well as fine color photographs. The editors have even been known to give us a 2-page orchid centerfold, where the gorgeous thing appears larger than life. Being an American publication, it is especially copious in information and pictures

relating to the most popular genera here, especially cattleyas and paphiopedilums.

Orchid Genera Illustrated

by Tom and Marion Sheehan
Van Nostrand Reinhold

■ *207 pages, many color illustrations, $19.79 out of print.*

You will still find the Sheehans' delightful orchid paintings and descriptions appearing periodically in the American Orchid Society *Bulletin.* This book is a compilation of them, providing an introduction to 61 of the more commonly cultivated genera in the huge family of more than 800. The paintings are a striking combination of strict botanical illustration—showing exploded as well as complete views of the flowers—and graceful line and coloring. When you see the lips and the calyxes of an orchid broken out from the rest of the flower—looking so much like a snake or a weapon, a vulva, mask, or bird—you understand the fascination of the *Orchidaceae.* The Sheehans' written description of the genera do a good job of avoiding unnecessary botanese, while still giving you a decent idea how to identify and grow the things.

The Orchid Review

Katukelle House
Victoria Village
Trinity, Jersey
Channel Islands
UNITED KINGDOM

■ *Variable-length monthly, some color illustrations, annual subscription $31.00.*

For some reason, orchid journals share something of the tone of a men's magazine like *Playboy.* The articles are indeed various and genuinely appealing, but the photographs are

stunning and calculated to drive fanatics wild. The color shots in the *Review* are usually of the latest RHS award winners and of new intergeneric hybrids and the like. They combine the appeals of beauty, novelty, and rarity. Articles may be inhabitat profiles of a genus, discussion of culture or propagation, and so on. Especially attractive are the plant-hunting tales like the hunt for the "lost" pleione, *P. coronaria.* "A great hurrah rose from the group when pleiones were found," the author recounts. Just in the nick of time, of course, while everyone is preparing to depart, a porter appears bearing an orchid that he apologetically describes as not exactly like the common pleione species he had been shown. It is the Lost Pleione (and it is pictured in the article). Cultural tips in this journal are also imaginative, as is the suggestion for sterilizing agar in your microwave.

Orchids by Hausermann

2N 134 Addison Road
Villa Park, IL 60181

■ *Plants for orchid species and hybrids, supplies, books.*
■ *56-page catalogue, more than 225 color illustrations, $1.25.*

Here is a gorgeous catalogue and a list whose breadth is hard to beat. It starts out with a brief introduction to the cultural preferences of orchids, enough to lay out the groundwork but not to use for actual growing. (You can use the fine book list to supply this lack.) Not many cultivated genera are missing here, but the greatest strengths of the catalogue lie in the endless phalaenopsis hybrids and the equally endless mericloned cattleya hybrids. The fine illustrations make for a visual anthology of the orchid world.

ORCHIDS

There are a wide variety of sources specifically for orchids. Some of them are listed here.

Beall Orchid Co., 3400 Academy Drive S.E., Auburn, WA 98022.
- Plants and seedlings for orchids. 18-page catalogue, free.

Carter & Holmes, PO Box 668, Newberry, SC 29108.
- Plants and seedlings for orchids, ferns, anthuriums, and other tropicals; supplies.

Creole Orchids, PO Box 24458, New Orleans, LA 70184.
- Plants for hybrid and species orchids. 15-page catalogue, free.

Finck Floral Co., 16195 S.W. 184th Street, Miami, FL 33187.
- Plants, seedlings, and community flasks for orchids. Various lists, free.

Huronview Nurseries, 1811 Brigden Side Road, Brights Grove, Ontario, CANADA N0N 1C0.
- Plants for orchids; supplies. 14-page catalogue, free.

Limrick, Inc., 6900 S.W. 102nd Avenue, Miami, FL 33173.
- Plants for orchids, heliconias, and other tropicals.

Orchid Imports, 11802 Huston Street, North Hollywood, CA 91607.
- Plants, seedlings, and community pots for species orchids. 2-page catalogue, free.

Orchid Species Specialties, 42314 Road 415, Coarsegold, CA 93614.
- Plants for terrestrial and epiphytic orchid species; supplies.

Owens Orchids, PO Box 365, Pisgah Forest, NC 28768.
- Plants for mainly hybrid orchids. Three 2-page lists, free.

Penn Valley Orchids, 239 Old Gulph Road, Wynnewood, PA 19096
- Plants for mainly hybrid orchids. 28-page catalogue, $1.00.

Riverbend Orchids, Route 1, Box 590E, Biloxi, MS 39532.
- Plants for hybrid orchids, chiefly compact growers. 16-page catalogue, free.

George Shorter Orchids, PO Box 16952, Mobile, AL 36616.
- Plants and seedlings for species orchids.

Orchids for the Home and Greenhouse

Plants & Gardens, vol. 41, no. 2
Brooklyn Botanic Garden
1000 Washington Avenue
Brooklyn, NY 11225

- 88 pages, many illustrations, some color, $2.95 pbk.

The Brooklyn Botanic Garden's method of assembling a handbook from the contributions of a variety of experts usually results in a large volume of dependable information at a reasonable price. It does in this volume, too, but the orchid world is so various and its classification so confusing that the innocent reader may be left with the feeling that he has only scratched the surface. There is no general survey or introductory article to lay out the territory, and the essay on orchid classification is clear but forbidding in tone. Fortunately, the articles on actual cultural practice are extremely helpful, especially the one on mistakes that beginners often make. There are two good pieces on miniatures, one by noted hybridizer Frank Fordyce, and separate culture articles on paphiopedilums and cattleyas. There's even an article on how to raise orchids from seed more easily than you may have thought possible. The historical and popular scientific articles are informative. All in all, this is a volume to get once you have already begun growing, perhaps just as you are making your first mistakes.

Orchid Species Source Book II

by J. F. Spatzek
Twin Oaks Books
4343 Causeway Drive
Lowell, MI 49331

- 90 pages, $9.50.

This list covers about 3,000 species representing 326 genera. Each listing is coded for at least 1 commercial source from which you may obtain the plant. About 80 different sources are listed at the back, including a few in Southeast Asia, Brazil, Central America, and England. It's a simple but mouth-watering treasure for the orchidist.

Orgel's Orchids

18950 S.W. 136th Street
Miami, FL 33187

- *Plants for orchids and carnivorous plants.*
- *2-page carnivore list, free.*

For some reason, Orgel Bramblett didn't send me his orchids list, but I understand that it contains mainly species orchids. His carnivore list is large, including a good couple of dozen exotic nepenthes, as well as a good dozen each of sarracenia and drosera, the American pitcher plants and the sundews respectively. There are a few other flesh-eaters too, plus limited supplies of sarracenia hybrids. Somehow, the thought of hybridizing pitcher plants gives me the feeling I should keep the cat away from them.

Protea Gardens of Maui

RR 2
Box 389
Kula, Maui HI 96790

- *Plants, blossoms, and dried arrangements of protea and relatives.*
- *1-page color flyer, 30 color illustrations, free.*

The photos of protea and banksia are enough to make the enthusiast slaver and the rest of us blink. If you want to surprise someone, send them a bouquet of these. It isn't clear that the species shown on the flyer are always available as live plants, but if you want them, you can check with the firm and see.

Rainforest Flora

1927 W. Rosecrans Avenue
Gardena, CA 90249

- *22-page Genus Tillandsia, 10 color illustrations, write for price.*

The firm sells bromeliads and tillandsias wholesale, but it also offers this valuable introduction to the tillandsias for the general gardener.

Steve Ray's Bamboo Gardens

See "Trees and Shrubs."

Rhapis Gardens

PO Box 287
Gregory, TX 78359

- *Container-grown dwarf rhapis, or lady palms, plus one sago palm; pots and books.*
- *30-page mail-order catalogue, approx. 50 illustrations, $1.00; 52-page handbook Secret of the Orient, many illustrations, some in color, $5.00.*

All the hoopla that the catalogue raises about the "treasures of the Orient" and the favorites of cultured Victorians is tiresome, but the fact remains that dwarf lady palms are terrific houseplants. Rhapis Gardens claims to be the only company in the U.S. that grows its own, as opposed to importing them. It offers a good selection of lady palms, some with variegated foliage, plus books relating to their culture and ornamental pots to put them in.

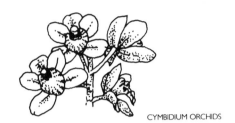

CYMBIDIUM ORCHIDS

Rhapis Palm Growers

31350 Alta Vista Drive
Redlands, CA 92373

- *Plants for* Rhapis excelsa *and R. humilis; ceramic and plastic pots.*
- *8-page brochure, 32 color illustrations, plus descriptive sheets, $2.00.*

There are about 50 choices, both variegated and all-green. All are imported from Japan, and the color brochure is in Japanese.

Roberts' Gesneriads

5656 Calyn Road
Baltimore, MD 21228

- *Plants and cuttings for gesneriads.*
- *32-page catalogue, $2.00.*

There are 900 species and varieties to choose from here—and not one of them is an African violet! The sinningias list is particularly impressive, but there are many choices among the almost 50 other genera listed. According to proprietor Barbara Roberts, hers is the largest and most varied commercial collection of gesneriads in the nation. She is constantly adding new varieties, both from private hydridizers and from institutional collectors. All of this seems to have made her both proud and harried. If you are a serious collector of gesneriads, you should have her catalogue.

Santa Barbara Orchid Estate

1250 Orchid Drive
Santa Barbara, CA 93111

- *Plants for species and hybrid orchids.*
- *32-page cymbidium catalogue, 27-page species catalogue, plus catalogues for cattleyas, paphiopedilums, lycastes, outdoor orchids for California, and others, each free.*

One of the largest selections you will find anywhere. The species list is huge enough, but the cymbidium catalogue is even bigger. There must be almost 1,000 cymbidiums, including species, hybrids, and miniatures! These are real collector's lists, but I was surprised at how good the cultural instructions are for the cymbidiums: you could buy and grow the things on the basis of the catalogue information alone. The firm did not send me its other catalogues, so I can't comment on them, but overall it claims to offer orchids in more than 200 genera. Californians may be particularly interested in the list of outdoor orchids, though most of the plants in the cymbidium list will do well outdoors as well.

Santa Barbara Seeds

PO Box 6520
Santa Barbara, CA 93160

- *Seed for exotic fruit trees.*
- *5-page list, SASE.*

Here is a list of about 21 different kinds of tropical fruit trees, including 5 different cherimoyas. Be aware that fruit will not necessarily come true from seed.

Seagull's Landing Orchids

PO Box 388
Glen Head, NY 11545

- *Plants, flasks, and community pots chiefly for miniature cattleyas.*
- *12-page catalogue, free; 4-page flyer, 21 color illustrations, free.*

Seagull's Landing is a leading breeder of miniature cattleyas, hybrids that reach only 6-10 inches in height. Cultural instructions are brief.

Shelldance, Inc.

2000 Highway 1
Pacifica, CA 94044

- *Plants for bromeliads.*
- *Inventory price list, $1.00.*

Shelldance is probably the most important bromeliad nursery in the country. The owners have propagated a lot of material from their own collecting trips throughout Latin America. They also had the good fortune to inherit the important David Barry collection of bromeliads. Then, too, they are a major importer of European hybrids. You will find several hundred species and hybrids in their simple list.

SLO Gardens

4816 Bridgecreek Road
San Luis Obispo, CA 93401

- *Cuttings and rooted cuttings for hoyas.*
- *8-page list, free.*

There are almost 100 different hoyas listed here, enough to fill a conservatory or bury the living room. The business grew out of the owners' collection. Descriptions of the varieties are brief, but the cultural information at the front of the list is very good indeed.

SOUTH AFRICAN NATIVES

A surprising number of our garden plants are of South African origin. The exotic protea have been popular recently, but the list of others is long and full of important genera like *Gladiolus*, *Erica*, *Pelargonium*, *Clivia*, *Zantedeschia*, *Arctotis*, *Gazania*, and *Gerbera*.

Akkerdrai Seeds, PO Box 9, Lynedock, Cape, SOUTH AFRICA 7603.
- Proteas and others.

Avon Seeds, 29 More Road, Bristol, ENGLAND BS20 9HN.
- Proteas.

Bio-Quest International, PO Box 5752, Santa Barbara, CA 93150.
- Seeds, bulbs, and plants for a good selection of South African natives, chosen for their adaptability to California gardens. Catalogue $1.00.

C 'n' C Protea, 387 Carmen Plaza, Camarillo, CA 93010.
- Seeds for proteas.

Cape Seed & Bulb Co., PO Box 4063, Idasvalley, Stellenbosch, Cape, SOUTH AFRICA 7609.
- Seeds; extensive, illustrated catalogue of South African natives, $2.00.

Exoticana Seeds, PO Box 184, Greytown, SOUTH AFRICA 3500.
- South African natives.

Feathers Wild Flower Nursery, PO Box 13, Constantia, SOUTH-AFRICA 7848.
- Seed for South African natives.

Indigenous Gladiolus Nursery, 44 Nederburgh Street, Welgemoed, Bellville, SOUTH AFRICA 7530.
- Bulbs and seed.

Parsley's Cape Seeds, PO Box 1375, Somerset West, Cape, SOUTH AFRICA 7130.
- Seeds for proteas and others; catalogue $1.00.

Protea Seed & Nursery Suppliers, PO Box 98229, Sloanpark, SOUTH AFRICA 2152.
- Proteas and others.

Rust-En-Vrede Nursery, PO Box 231, Constantia, SOUTH AFRICA 7848.
- Seed for native bulbs, especially members of the lily family, plus some disa orchid species.

Stewart Orchids

1212 E. Las Tunas Drive
San Gabriel, CA 91778

- *Plants for orchids.*
- *18-page catalogue, 32 color illustrations, plus variable-length descriptive inserts, free; 4-page catalogue of supplies, free.*

In 1986, Stewart merged with Armacost & Royston, creating one of the largest orchid nurseries and most potent breeding programs in the world. Most of the new firm's work is in cattleyas, paphiopedilums, cymbidiums, and phalaenopsis, but the catalogue lists plants from other genera as well, among them a lovely spray-forming *Rhyncostylis gigantea*. This is an important catalogue for orchid growers to keep up with; once you get the first one, they will send supplements. For the most part, the breeding program seems to be yielding fine flowers, though I was depressed to see an example of the new "Colorama" hybrids, a laeliocattleya with red and yellow markings splashed across it, making it resemble some horribly mutated pansy. The separate supplies list is complete and useful.

Success With House Plants

Edited by Anthony Huxley
Reader's Digest

- *480 pages, many color illustrations, $21.99.*

The text is useful, the pictures adequate, but as with the *Reader's Digest Guide to Gardening* (see page 45), the very best things are the lists. The comprehensive houseplant list here includes more than 600 varieties. There are probably more than 600 varieties of African violets and begonias alone, so the book is by no means complete. Still, if you are a generalist when it comes to houseplants, this will be a valuable resource.

Sunset Nursery

See "Trees and Shrubs."

Tinari Greenhouses

2325 Valley Road
Box 190
Huntingdon Valley, PA 19006

- *Plants for African violets; tools, supplies, and books.*
- *15-page catalogue, 64 color illustrations, $.35.*

Tinari presents a good group of standard, variegated, miniature, and trailing African violets. The list is not quite so overwhelming as those of some other African violet specialists. Most of the tools and supplies you will need are offered here, including Safer's soap, trimming tools, and a variety of plant stands and lights. Among the books listed in the illustrated catalogue is *Our African Violet Heritage*, by Mrs. Tinari, for $4.95.

Tropica

by Alfred B. Graf.
Roehrs Company
136 Park Avenue
East Rutherford, NJ 07073

- *1,120 pages, approx. 7,000 color illustrations, $125.00.*

This is *the* reference work for tropical and subtropical plants. Unlike Graf's other two great works (see page 170), its illustrations are all in color, making it a terrific aid for plant identification. There are grasses, bamboos, herbaceous plants, flowering and foliage trees and shrubs, vines, ferns, palms, conifers, cacti and succulents, and even carnivorous plants. You may not be able to afford it, but you should find a place where you can use a copy. It's a worthwhile investment for anyone interested in tropical plants.

Patricia Trumble Orchids

3897 N. 57th Street
Boulder, CO 80301

- *Plants, seedlings, and flasks for more than 350 genera of orchids.*
- *Various lists, free; 5-page* How to Grow Orchids In Colorado, *free.*

Specialties are cattleyas, paphs, and phalaenopsis, with a good number of species from many other genera, to boot. The lists are quite wide-ranging. Best of all, perhaps, is the little booklet for Colorado growers, who are often blessed with too much light and too little humidity. The recommendations are specific and useful, and there is a chart suggesting the appropriate conditions for a wide variety of genera.

Twin Oaks Books

4343 Causeway Drive
Lowell, MI 49331

- *Bookseller selling only volumes about orchids.*
- *Variable-length catalogues, free.*

George Woolfson lists over 375 orchid titles here. You can find just about anything here, if it is in print, recently out-of-print, or reprinted. There is an Indian reprint of Veitch's *Manual of Orchidaceous Plants*; the orchid papers of the great Harvard botanist Oakes Ames plus his daughter's compilations of his miscellaneous orchid jottings; Stewart's orchid wheel, which lets you dial up cultural instruction and pest control information for most of the major genera; every orchid flora imaginable from every country imaginable; and proceedings of the World Orchid Conference. It's a long list, but Woolfson's sprightly copy makes it fun to read. And you're sure to find the book you were searching for.

Wildwood Farm

See "Annuals and Perennials."

Wilson Plant Sales

PO Box 400
Roachdale, IN 46172

- *Plants for geraniums, African violets, and other exotic houseplants.*
- *16-page catalogue, 69 color illustrations, free.*

This is a good general list for the houseplant grower, not for the collector. The geraniums include rosebud, ivy-leafed, scented-leaf, Lady Washington, zonal, and miniature types. The choice of types is similarly wide for African violets, and there is also a page full of begonias. Otherwise, the list is strong in unusual flowering and fruiting houseplants like bleeding-heart vine (*Clerodendrum*), chenille plant, lipstick vine, shrimp plant, and golden candle.

> It is true that the tropical conditions favour and breed a very large number of orchids, many of which are, indeed, air-plants; but, on the other hand, there are orchids adapted to every clime and condition, latitude and altitude, making them the most widely distributed family in the floral kingdom. . . .
>
> It is their creed, their banner under which they have conquered their "place in the sun"—"In Hoc Signo Vinces," might be their motto. And throughout our vast country, from Greenland to Mexico, from flat Cape Cod to lofty Mount Shasta, we find their tiny banners fluttering, to announce their victory in the struggle for existence.
>
> —HERBERT WALDRON FAULKNER, FROM *THE MYSTERIES OF THE FLOWERS* (1917)

World Insectivorous Plants

PO Box 70513
Marietta, GA 30007

- *Carnivorous plants; relevant books.*
- *12-page catalogue, more than 50 illustrations, plus periodic updates, $1.00.*

A lot of preparation has gone into this tasty catalogue. Sections are divided not only according to genus but according to habitat origin, and every species is described, illustrated, and rated for ease of culture. The choice is delicious, including not only common droseras, and sarracenias, but rarer members of those genera, as well as unusual and difficult marsh pitcher plants, a choice of nepenthes, and even some butterworts and bladderworts. A separate section gives followable directions for creating a carnivorous-plant terrarium. Here is a place to find out how to join the International Carnivorous Plant Society, too. Beginners and fanciers will both get use out of this catalogue; in fact, they'll eat it up.

BUTTERWORT

Guy Wrinkle/Exotic Plants

11610 Addison Street
North Hollywood, CA 91601

- *Plants for exotics, chiefly of African origin.*
- *4-page list, free.*

Wrinkle propagated most of what he offers from material he has collected on field expeditions in Africa. Some of the species are quite rare in cultivation. His list of succulents, bulbs, and cycads is long, though unadorned, so you had best be a collector before you venture into it.

Your First Orchids and How to Grow Them

Oregon Orchid Society
PO Box 14182
Portland, OR 97214

- *72 pages, some illustrations, a few in color, $4.75.*

Like a Brooklyn Botanic Garden booklet, this admirable little guide consists of a number of articles, each written by an expert in the area. It seems to have been in print practically since the beginning of time, so it must satisfy its readers. Articles cover everything from home and greenhouse culture to native orchids and all the commonly grown genera. The writing can be quite lively, as in an article by Mrs. Scott Hyde on the first orchid she ever grew. "Growing orchids is a wonderful hobby for husbands," she remarks. "You always know where he is, and he knows where you are when he's at the office." Hints like these make the guide most enjoyable reading.

9 Tools and Supplies

Applied Hydroponics of Canada

2215 Walkley
Montreal, Quebec
CANADA H4B 2J9

- *Containers, books, kits, growing media, and supplies for hydroponics.*
- *6-page catalogue, black-and-white illustrations, free.*

Here is a basic list of supplies for home hydroponics of both house-plants and vegetables. There is a good choice of kits and books to get you started. Lighting is also available, though the firm helpfully informs its American customers that they will do better buying their lights in the U.S.

BCS Mosa, Inc.

PO Box 1739
Matthews, NC 28106

- *Combination tiller, mower, snow-blower, and so on.*
- *14-page catalogue, color illustrations, free.*

If you have a big enough job to do, you might want to consider investing in a versatile tiller/mower. These Italian machines come in several different sizes, most convertible for various garden uses. One even has an attachment that turns it into a small tractor with wagon. The cutter bars have power reverse, a useful feature if you have difficult terrain to mow.

> Now then Clementine!
> Please consider this: If a garden tool is still on the market after 50, 75, or maybe even 100 years, it must have the proper qualities for the job. If these tools had not worked well for your gardening grandparents, they would be "long gone." So Clemy! Perhaps you should wake up to these facts and consider these historic tools as we honor them here on our catalog cover. New Ideas, we admit, are great, But don't lose sight of these tried-and-true garden-tool varieties. Grandma wouldn't like that.
>
> —FROM *WALT NICKE'S GARDEN TALK* 1986 *CATALOGUE*

Beneficial Insectary

245 Oak Run Road
Oak Run, CA 96069

- *Beneficial insects.*
- *8-page fly flyer, free; 1-page grasshopper flyer, free.*

BI specializes in getting rid of flies and grasshoppers. It is therefore of most use to homesteaders. The brochure suggests release procedure and schedules, as well as describing the virtues of its 3 different fly parasites. Describing his fly parasites the author enthuses: "Their need for flies, in order to reproduce, provides a strong and natural incentive to do all the work: search and destroy." The grasshopper killer is a pathogen.

Better Yield Insects

PO Box 3451 Tecumseh Station
Windsor, Ontario
CANADA N8N 3C4

- *Beneficial insects and yellow-strip traps.*
- *8-page flyer, color illustrations, free.*

This firm specializes in good bugs for the greenhouse that attack whiteflies, mites, aphids, and thrips.

Dorothy Biddle Service

U.S. Route 6
Greeley, PA 18425

- *Tools and supplies for flower arrangers and indoor gardeners.*
- *16-page catalogue, more than 75 illustrations, $.25.*

Dorothy Biddle was a well-known professional flower arranger who had had difficulty finding the supplies she needed in her upstate New York town. She therefore started this business out of her own need, and in the hands of her daughter, it remains a fine source of clippers, snippers, pinholders, other holders, tapes, pebbles, and all the paraphernalia a flower arranger needs.

Bonsai Creations

See "Furniture and Ornament."

The Bonsai Farm

13827 Highway 87 S.
Adkins, TX 78101

- *Bonsai tools, supplies, books, and starter plants.*
- *36-page catalogue, black-and-white illustrations, $1.00.*

The range of pots, supplies, and tools here is huge and impressive. I can't imagine any tool you might need that isn't included here. The list of pre-bonsai starter plants, though it is tucked away at the end of the catalogue, is intriguing. It includes not only the usual bonsai species, but a number of others, too, particularly subtropical plants and some Texas natives. Here, for example, you can get the Bahama black olive, Texas baby bonnets, buttonwood, and Texas ebony. These plants and the tools offered make Bonsai a good source.

Bramen Co.

PO Box 70
Salem, MA 01970

- *Solar vent openers; English tools.*
- *8-page catalogue, black-and-white illustrations, free.*

The vent openers are automatic, and the company will send you plans for a cold frame to build around them. The things also work in your greenhouse. The trowels are by Strongbeam; the pruners by Rolcut.

Brighton By-Products Co.

PO Box 23
New Brighton, PA 15066

- *Tools, fertilizers, pest controls, greenhouses and greenhouse equipment, irrigation supplies, carts, sprayers, pots, and just about everything else.*
- *126-page catalogue, black-and-white illustrations, $5.00.*

Here's another of those great, huge catalogues of every kind of supply you might imagine. It's meant for the pros, but if you need larger quantities or know what you're looking for, you may find some comparative bargains here. Felco #7 pruners, for example, were listed at almost $15.00 cheaper here than in a prominent catalogue.

Cart Warehouse

PO Box 3
Point Arena, CA 95468

- *Garden carts.*
- *16-page catalogue, free.*

If you want to get a quick idea of what's available in garden carts, here is the place to do it. The Garden Way cart is here, as are several other brands and styles; and there are plans for making your own cart using the warehouse's supplies. The Muller

barn cart—a big, removable polyethylene tub set on an aluminum frame—looks interesting.

Charley's Greenhouse Supplies

PO Box 2110
LaConner, WA 98257

- *Kits for greenhouses and sunrooms, associated supplies, accessories, and tools.*
- *32-page catalogue, more than 150 illustrations, free.*

Charley's not only offers kits, but it can provide you with all the accessories you would need if you were building your own greenhouse from scratch. There are all sorts of fans, watering aids, heaters and insulators, pots and propagation tools, and building supplies. Since the catalogue is aimed specifically at the hobby greenhouse grower, you can bet that what you see here will be of a scale that you can use.

Clapper's

1121 Washington Street
West Newton, MA 02165

- *Tools and supplies.*
- *32-page catalogue, more than 75 color illustrations of tools, free.*

Clapper's is an upmarket mail-order firm specializing in furniture and tools. In this, it resembles Smith & Hawken (see page 212). The tools selection is perhaps a little less wide-ranging than S&H's, but the quality and choice of basic garden tools is first-rate. There are 2 whole pages of pruning shears, including Felcos in 5 different sizes. A lot of Wilkinson products appear here, too; as well as Solo backpack sprayers and the Gardena watering system. The line of spades and forks is from Spear & Jackson. The choice of pole pruners is about the best I've seen.

Common Sense Pest Control Quarterly

Bio-Integral Resource Center
PO Box 7414
Berkeley, CA 94707

- *Variable-length quarterly, some illustrations, annual subscription $30.00; reprints available separately.*

Perhaps you aren't interested enough in pests to subscribe to a journal devoted to them, but you can certainly use at least the reprints. The Resource Center is dedicated to integrated pest management (IPM), and one of its back issues will probably have an extended discussion of the beastie you want to control. Not that the quarterly isn't fascinating; it includes a good deal of historical information as well as means of control. House as well as garden pests are discussed.

Dare Products

860 Betterly Road
Battle Creek, MI 49016

- *Electric-fencing equipment.*
- *16-page color catalogue, free.*

Farmers are Dare's main customers, but if you have the skill and confidence—not to mention the need—to design and build your own electric fencing, here is a good selection of insulators, posts, and wire.

DoDe's Gardens

1490 Saturn Street
Merritt Island, FL 32953

- *Supplies for houseplants, especially for African violets.*
- *15-page catalogue, more than 50 illustrations, free.*

As the catalogue's purple ink might indicate, this company loves African violets, but when it comes to soil

amendments, growing trays, and pesticides, DoDe's has a good selection for all sorts of houseplants. There is even a "plant tonic" and a sort of plant food that is supposed to mitigate the effects of overwatering.

The Dramm Co.

PO Box 528
Manitowoc, WI 54420

- *Manufacturers of a variety of watering and spraying devices.*
- *14-page catalogue, color illustrations, free.*

Dramm sells its own waterbreaker nozzles, quick-release connectors, water shutoffs, watering wands, and watering cans. It also makes two portable power sprayers, one gasoline-powered and one electric. Both look genuinely portable. There's also a nice selection of dribble rings and tubes for watering potted plants, plus greenhouse misters. Dramm is also into hand-forged iron standing and bracket hooks, very spare and elegant-looking.

GARDEN CART

Drip Irrigation Garden

16216 Raymer Street
Van Nuys, CA 91406

- *Drip-irrigation systems.*
- *8-page catalogue and design manual, $.25.*

The manual is not that easy to read, largely because of confusing layout

and small print, but the writing style is clear. The firm has experience with such systems on large and small scales, installed outdoors and in greenhouses.

EarthWay Products

PO Box 547
Bristol, IN 46507

- *Garden carts, seeders, spreaders, and high-wheel cultivators.*
- *Various sheets, free.*

Well-balanced, wide-wheeled garden carts are an EarthWay specialty. There are 4 models. Most of the seeders and spreaders are for pros, but some may be useful to the larger-scale home vegetable gardener. One of them, called the "Plant-Rite" row seeder, is an ingenious device for the smaller gardener. You roll it along the ground, using a long handle. Attached to the roller is a dispenser calibrated for all sizes of seed. The high-wheel cultivators have plow attachments as well. They look sturdy and old-fashioned, but they will fold up for storage.

Equipment Consultants and Sales

2241 Dunwin Drive
Mississauga, Ontario
CANADA L5L 1A3

- *Accessories and supplies for greenhouses.*
- *4-page catalogue, 13 illustrations, free; inserted color catalogue of propagators and trays, 16 pages, many color illustrations, free.*

Here's a leading Canadian supplier of shades, vents, misters, heaters, watering systems, and other necessaries for the home greenhouse. ECS also is the Canadian distributor of the plastic pots, propagators, and trays made by Stewart in England.

Fanno Saw Works

PO Box 628
Chico, CA 95927

- *Saws.*
- *10-page illustrated catalogue, free.*

Fanno has been making great saws since 1921, when A. A. Fanno revolutionized the orchard industry with a wholly new pole saw. The list of things the firm makes reads like a poem: pole saws, pole pruners, folding saws, utility saws, special-purpose saws, custom saws, orchard saws, camping saws, gardening saws, tree-surgery saws, construction saws, and, of course, saw scabbards. The Fanno folding saws, for tree and shrub pruning, are famous, but you should get the catalogue so that you can admire the full line. The lovely #9 pole saw looks like it belongs in The Metropolitan Museum's arms and armor collection. There are some real beauties here.

Foothill Agricultural Research

510 W. Chase Drive
Corona, CA 91720

- *Beneficial insects for pest control.*
- *7-page list, free.*

The list is charmingly titled "Better Bugs by F.A.R." The firm says that it constantly collects or buys insects that come from wild settings so that the gene pool of these beneficial bugs is kept vigorous and the bugs effective. The text describes what each critter likes to eat, to wit: "The ladybug is possibly the most widely known beneficial insect in the world. They feed on a wide range of soft-bodied insects in many different crops and are legendary for their ability to consume aphids." The firm offers 6 other species that attack specific enemies, from various forms

of scale to snails. In fact, the snail killer is another snail, the decollate snail, and catalogue text is very good about the virtues and drawbacks to this form of snail control. Foothill seems to go to extra effort all around. Often, ladybugs are collected and shipped during hibernation. When they wake, they tend to fly away. Foothill keeps them until what it calls "the spring flight portion of their life cycle" has passed.

Gardener's Eden

PO Box 7307
San Francisco, CA 94120

- *Tools, supplies, and gadgets.*
- *48-page catalogue, approx. 45 color illustrations of tools and supplies, free.*

There is not much here that you can't find elsewhere as well, but the selection is of very high quality, and looking at it may remind you of things you need. On the other hand, you may be able to do without goatskin garden gloves or a copper watering can. This is one place to get the small, lightweight Lescha garden shredder, not to mention an electric leafblower. There are a variety of better-quality rakes, shears, pruning saws and loppers, an English dibble, and hand tools—also good, cheap pull-on garden booties, garden clogs, kneepads, and the like.

Gardener's Supply Co.

128 Intervale Road
Burlington, VT 05401

- *All kinds of tools and supplies.*
- *32-page catalogue, color illustrations, free.*

GSC is pretty well known for its fine and apt selection of garden tools and supplies. Much of what you find in other upscale catalogues—the Lescha shredder, Gardena watering system,

and the like—appears here too, but you have the feeling that the selection has been made more for continual usefulness than for cachet or mere beauty. There's an unusually simple, functional wire compost bin, as well as a drum composter. The poly row cover and frames are attractive and functional. Tools are chosen for tasks, including a double digger, a raised-bed builder, and the Warren hoe. The greenhouse kit uses double glazing and features an unusual long roof slope for the south side. The garden carts are famous.

Garden Way Manufacturing Co.

102nd Street & 9th Avenue
Troy, NY 12180

- *Garden tillers, lawn mowers, garden carts, and shredders.*
- *Various color brochures, 32-page color tiller catalogue, 4-page color raised-bed gardening brochure, all free.*

Garden Way has been making power tillers for more than 50 years. The 3 models of Troy-Built tillers it now offers are substantial, dependable tools. Even the smallest is not particularly lightweight; on the other hand, all come with a lifetime warranty. There are quite a number of attachments you can add to the tillers; perhaps the neatest is a hiller/furrower that makes drainage ditches, crop furrows, and raised-bed gardens quite simply. The firm has a separate brochure showing how to use this device to make raised beds. Garden Way's garden cart also has a very fine reputation. I'm not sure it was the prototype for the various wide-wheeled, balanced, plywood carts that are now on the market, but it seems to me it's been the one to beat for a long time. The other power tools, like the tillers, are sizable and powerful.

E. C. Geiger

Box 285
Route 63
Harleysville, PA 19438

- *Greenhouses, accessories, and supplies; "everything for the grower."*
- *184-page catalogue, several hundred illustrations, free.*

This catalogue is aimed at professional growers, and a lot of the items offered are geared to a professional scale. Still, it is an enormous book full of interesting products and gadgets, the sort a grower can really use. Minimum quantities for some items tend to be high, but Geiger is still a good place to check for everything from grow bags to insulation materials. Some fine shears, knives, and other tools appear here, too, often at prices slightly cheaper than those of the upmarket retail-trade firms. There are also neat things like the "Little Wonder Seeder," a device that automatically spreads seed in nursery flats. You can even get a machine that will call you on the phone if your greenhouse freaks out.

Goldblatt Tools

511 Osage
Kansas City, KS 66110

- *Shears, clippers, loppers, and saws.*
- *100-page catalogue, 4 pages and 23 color illustrations relevant to garden tools, free.*

Most of Goldblatt's blades are Teflon-coated, making them less liable to foul with sap. The pruning shears—3 bypass and 1 anvil types—look particularly good, all with red PVC handles so they are hard to lose. There are quite a number of grass, hedge, and lopping shears to choose from. One very long tree pruner has an 11½ foot fiberglass pole with both a saw blade and rope-pull shear at the end. Prices are comparatively reasonable.

Goserud Products

Highways 84 & 87
Pine River, MN 56474

- *Lawn edgers; innovative hoes and weeders.*
- *1-page flyers, free.*

This company makes a small line of fine-quality hand tools. The lawn edger uses sharp carbon-steel blades. It also offers a push/pull hoe and a couple of nicely designed cultivators.

One hundred fifty patents have been issued to flying machine inventors, and hundreds of patents to inventors of horseless carriages for the roads, to be propelled by electricity, by steam, by gas or gasoline, hot air, springs, and perpetual motion, but none of these patent claptraps are practicable. The only use thus far is for the papers to frighten farmers into selling their horses before the horseless age comes.

—FROM *BAER'S AGRICULTURAL ALMANAC* (1897)

Great Lakes IPM

10220 Church Road, N.E.
Vestaburg, MI 48891

- *Pheromone lures and traps; other traps; insect nets.*
- *16-page catalogue, free.*

This company offers traps and lures for just about every bug that might plague you. Often, such traps are used only to monitor the presence of a particular critter, but some are designed to help cut down the population. There isn't much how-to here, since the firm is geared to commercial growers. I liked the insect nets included at the back: if all else fails, chase the bugs down!

Green Earth Organics

9422 144th Street E.
Puyallup, WA 98373

- *Tools, organic supplies, and pest controls; books.*
- *32-page catalogue, many illustrations, $1.00.*

Here's a fine regional organics company, with some distinctive selections. All the usual organic soil amendments and pest controls can be found here, along with an effective-sounding predatory nematode named Scanmask. There's also a rotary cultivator that looks like a lawn mower, and a pair of versatile clippers for snipping everything from flowers to metal.

Green River Tools

5 Cotton Mill Road
PO Box 1919
Brattleboro, VT 05301

- *Garden tools, some soil amendments and ornaments, and a bit of furniture.*
- *32-page catalogue, more than 110 color illustrations, free.*

If you want to buy garden tools by mail—or if you are just a tool nut—Green River's catalogue is the first place to look. The selection is outstanding, generally expensive, and extraordinarily wide. I spent 10 minutes trying to think of something that wasn't in it, and all I could come up with is the dibble, but maybe I just missed it. Well, there doesn't seem to be a drip-irrigation system either. Otherwise, you will find everything from 2 sizes of double-diggers, to scythes and hay rakes, to stirrup hoes, multiattachment wheel hoes, and Korean hand hoes, to children's tools, to any number of shears, including Felcos, to shredders and compost bins, to complete watering systems. The German birdhouses are very nice-looking, too, as is the line of handmade willow furniture.

Gro-Tek

RFD 1
Box 518A
South Berwick, ME 03908

- *Tools, gadgets, and supplies for greenhouse and garden.*
- *39-page catalogue, more than 85 illustrations, $1.00.*

This young company has gone out of its way to come up with neat gadgets and the latest eco-tech greenhouse supplies. It offers an attractive zip-up field notebook in 2 sizes, something I haven't seen elsewhere. The solar card—a simple tool to help you determine what parts of the garden will be shaded between 9 A.M. and 3 P.M. at different times of the year—looks very good, if it works. Then there are indoor hoses, a device to tell you when basket plants need water, a number of hose nozzles, custom-made sunshades in a variety of densities, a paintable shading material for the greenhouse, Monsanto 703 greenhouse film, greenhouse glazing, and storage tubes for passive-solar heating. Almost everything else required for the small greenhouse, plus lots of organic fertilizers and pesticides, are to be found here, too. The book list is very complete for greenhouse gardeners. Check it out.

Growing Crazy

PO Box 8
Tawas City, MI 48764

- *Organic fertilizers, soil amendments, pest controls; books.*
- *10-page catalogue, $1.25.*

Here's a good choice of botanical and biological insecticides, traps and lures, and fertilizers. Included in this catalogue the firm also offers an interesting-looking and reasonably priced duster/fogger. It's driven with a hand crank.

Grow-N-Energy

PO Box 508
Baldwin Place, NY 10505

- *Pots, baskets, propagators, and other supplies for greenhouse or indoor growing.*
- *12-page catalogue, approx. 50 illustrations, free.*

Here is a good and pretty basic selection of supplies for the small home greenhouse. It is not overwhelmingly large, nor is it at all intimidating.

Harmony Farm Supply

PO Box 451
Graton, CA 95444

- *Biodynamic and organic fertilizers; organic pest controls; tools; fruit and nut trees and vines; cover crop and lawn seed; books.*
- *39-page catalogue, approx. 63 illustrations, $2.00; brief quarterly newsletter lists featured and new products, plus classes at the store, for established customers.*

Harmony offers a very thorough and thoughtful catalogue directed mainly at the organic orchardist; in coming years it will publish a separate catalogue listing its tools and supplies, but for now, these appear in the same catalogue with a very nice northern California fruit and nut list (see page 92 for review). Most organic gardeners will want to look at the catalogue, whether they grow fruit trees or not. The usual run of organic pest controls and beneficial insects appears, along with 2 powders specifically directed against fruit-attacking moths and a variety of pheromone traps for different specific pests. The catalogue is also strong in watering systems: it lists both the well-respected Gardena system and a pretty wide choice of drip-irrigation systems and parts. The shears, pruners, and saws are all very high quality, including the Felco shears most used in orchards, the Fanno folding saw, and 2 beautiful Japanese saws (one folding and one sheathed). For fruit growers,

the long pruner Harmony offers is very useful, because it can either lop and prune branches or cut and hold fruit located high in the tree. The Japanese hand sickles are good for clearing grass and brush. Both electric and hand-operated shredders are listed here, the latter able to handle twigs up to little-finger size. The fertilizer list is comprehensive for organic matter, including small and large lots of biodynamic compost, all kinds of meal and manure, and even bat guano. Harmony is also a source for biodynamic compost starter and organic soil inoculants, not to mention seed for cover crops. Even the book list is thorough.

Once when I was lecturing in Iowa on a below-zero winter day, I remarked that I had never met a box-elder bug face to face. Whereupon the amused garden club members told me to look down at the rug I was standing on! . . . The one comforting thing in pest control is that injurious insects are pretty well divided up around the country. No one section has more than its fair share.

—CYNTHIA WESCOTT, FROM *THE GARDENER'S BUG BOOK* (1973)

Homestead Carts

6098 Topaz Street N.E.
Salem, OR 97305

- *Garden carts.*
- *4-page brochure, black-and-white illustrations, free.*

Here's a good, sturdy garden cart with wide-tread wheels and an adjustable handle. There are 2 different sizes.

Hortica Gardens

See "Trees and Shrubs."

Hubbard Folding Box Co.

15980 Rush Creek Road
Osseo, MN 55369

- *Wooden folding boxes.*
- *6-page brochure, complete with folding-box business card, free.*

"In this world of 'new and improved' . . . products that rise in the competitive solar system only to set soon thereafter . . . it is comforting to reflect that some items withstand the test of time. Among this list of unfailing traditions are found, of course, baseball, hot dogs, apple pie, and the Hubbard wire sewn, *folding* wooden box." So Hubbard says, and given the fact that it's been around since 1898, it's probably not exaggerating too much. The boxes are pretty and convenient, and Hubbard will print whatever you like on them. They have side handles and come in a variety of sizes. Use them for holding the harvest, storing your tools, or whatever.

Hydro-Gardens, Inc.

PO Box 9707
Colorado Springs, CO 80932

- *All supplies, including greenhouses, for hydroponic gardening.*
- *19-page home greenhouse catalogue, free; 77-page commercial greenhouse catalogue, $4.00.*

An experienced hydroponics supplier with a very large list for the commercial grower, Hydro-gardens has also developed a home hydroponics catalogue, listing everything from a little window-sill greenhouse kit to real, substantial greenhouses, with all the supplies necessary to get them producing. If you have never looked into hydroponics, you might do a little reading first, since except for the window-sill toy, it requires a considerable investment of energy and money.

Hydroponic Society of America

PO Box 6067
Concord, CA 94524

- *Nonprofit organization dedicated to hydroponic growing.*
- *Bimonthly newsletter; 36-page list of suppliers and books; annual membership $25.00.*

One of the nicest things the society puts out is its source list. Every sort of company making supplies for the hydroponic grower appears here, many with full-page descriptive advertisements, and there is a good list of books.

International Irrigation Systems

LPO 160
1555 Third Avenue
Niagara Falls, NY 14304

- *Drip-irrigation systems.*
- *Brochures, price lists, and layout sheet, free; 12-page* Derek Fell's Automatic Garden, *color illustrations, $1.00.*

This company makes Irrigro drip-irrigation systems. If you already know what you want, you can simply choose from the various brochures, but if you want a ready-made, vegetable-garden system, you can order the Derek Fell brochure, telling you just what you need and how to install it.

Introduction to Integrated Pest Management

by Mary Louise Flint and Robert van den Bosch
Plenum Press

- *240 pages, many illustrations, $19.95.*

Integrated pest management (IPM) is basically a careful formulation of the principles on which old-time farming had to depend. Flint and van den Bosch do a workmanlike and not too technical job of telling how it works, focusing on life cycles of bad and beneficial bugs, and on acceptable pest populations as opposed to total eradication. This is a text with more information than you will probably need, but if you are an organic gardener, I don't think you will mind.

The Japan Woodworker

1731 Clement Avenue
Alameda, CA 94501

- *Saws and flower clippers from Japan.*
- *Variable-length catalogues, many illustrations, $1.50.*

Most of what appears here is for the serious woodworker, but the clippers and the saws are wonderful for gardeners. I once took a walk with a furniture maker who makes chairs out of natural wood cut from second-growth maples. He carried a wonderful Japanese saw that cut through the trunks like butter. Watch out for the blades of these things because they're deadly; it is best to buy them with a sheath.

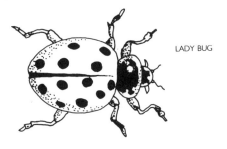

LADY BUG

Johnson's Industrial Supply Co.

1941 Karlin Drive
St. Louis, MO 63131

- *Earth augers.*
- *Various sheets, free.*

JISCO makes those nice augers that attach to a power drill. They are very handy when you have to deep-fertilize a number of trees.

Kemp Co.

160 Koser Road
Lititz, PA 17543

- *Drum composter, electric shredder/chipper.*
- *4-page brochure, color illustrations, free.*

The composter isn't little or particularly pretty, but it will prepare compost in around 14 days. Some assembly is required. If you have the space and need for such a thing, consider this one. Kemp also makes a nice-looking, heavy-duty electric shredder called Samson. It's a bit bulkier than some of the others in its price range, but it is versatile. You can set it on its side and sweep leaves right into it.

The Keth Co.

Box 645
Corona del Mar, CA 92625

- *Tools, supplies, and books for cutting flowers and for flower arranging.*
- *20-page catalogue, more than 70 illustrations, free.*

This firm has a wide selection of items for cutting, preserving, and arranging flowers. There are a number of conventional pin holders, plus 5 choices among the Japanese well-kenzan. The choice among clippers and stem strippers is good, including a Swiss flower gatherer that holds as it cuts and a group of Japanese arranging tools. The few vases and other containers offered are disappointing.

King's Natural Pest Control

224 Yost Avenue
Spring City, PA 19475

- *Beneficial insects.*
- *2-page list, free.*

The proprietor must be fond of insects; he/she also sells insect model kits for decorating the home. A good list of beneficials is available here, and the firm also sells Safer's insecticidal soap, which is safe to use around many of the friendly bugs and may help you control the enemies while the good guys are getting established.

The Kinsman Co.

River Road
Point Pleasant, PA 18950

- *Shredders, tools, compost bins, cold frames, metal arbors, and gadgets.*
- *Various brochures, free.*

This company imports the following: Sheffield Pride garden tools, lovely English things; the small, electric Steinmax shredder; Juwel cold frames, with an automatic open/close option; prefab compost bins; a versatile system of easy-to-assemble arches and arbors; and things like watering cans and kneelers. Since the firm has not invested in the fancy catalogues or the very wide inventory that others who stock these brands generally have, it may be worth checking them for slightly better prices on the same items.

LaMotte Chemical Products Co.

PO Box 329
Chestertown, MD 21620

- *Soil-test kits.*
- *3-page color flyer, free.*

LaMotte released the first commercially available soil-test kits back in 1928, and its kits are still the standard against which others are measured. Piles of them appear in the big wholesale catalogue, but most of us can make do with one of three models designed for the home gardener and shown on the color flyer. Model EL is the one you find in all the upmarket garden-supply catalogues. Not only is the kit accurate and well made, but it comes with the *LaMotte Soil Handbook,* a somewhat dry but very useful booklet about soil nutrients. Among other things, it contains terrific charts on the relative nutrient intakes of vegetables and on the preferred pH of several hundred species of ornamentals.

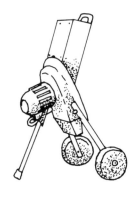

SHREDDER

A. M. Leonard, Inc.

6665 Spiker Road
PO Box 816
Piqua, OH 45356

- *Garden, orchard and nursery tools.*
- *78-page catalogue, over 500 illustrations, free.*

Because it supplies nurseries, Leonard has a wider choice of high-quality tools than you are likely to find in any catalogue directed strictly at home gardeners. On the other hand, the descriptions tend to assume that you already know what you are looking for, and that names like Fanno, Felco, Fiskar, Sandvik-Pradine, True Friends, Corona, and Wilkinson will speak volumes to you. As you might expect, the company also has a fine selection of greenhouse supplies and of serious tools like soil augers and a positively mouthwatering group of pruning and budding knives. There is also a wide choice of garden carts and wheelbarrows.

Little Wonder

11028 Street Road
Southampton, PA 18966

- *Electric and gas hedge trimmers, cultivators, edgers, and blowers.*
- *8-page color catalogue, free.*

A lot of Little Wonder's well-respected power tools are sized for the professional, but the cultivator—at about 20 pounds—is a handy thing to have at home. The company also has a small electric edger and an electric hedge trimmer.

Luster Leaf Products

PO Box 1067
Crystal Lake, IL 60014

- *Soil-test kits and pH meters.*
- *4-page color brochure, free.*

Here's a range of testing devices, including a few that do rapid, separate tests of N, P, and K levels. There are so many sorts of meters you'd begin to feel like a utility company if you used them all. You can even test for acid rain.

Mainline North America

PO Box 348
London, OH 43140

- *Rotary tillers, with attachments.*
- *Brochure, free.*

Most of us will probably rent tillers as needed, rather than buy them. These are top-of-the-line Italian models: expensive, powerful, and versatile. The cheapest goes for $1,200, but even the cheapest is higher-powered than most you will see. They have the added advantage of attachments that include mowers and log splitters. Still, they are probably only for the large-scale gardener.

Mantis Manufacturing Co.

1458 County Line Road
Huntingdon Valley, PA 19006

- *Convertible tiller/weeder/trimmer; portable power sprayer.*
- *8-page tiller brochure, color illustrations, free; 4-page sprayer brochure, color illustrations, free; 4-page shredder brochure, free.*

One of the things American manufacturers may eventually be remembered for is bringing the concept of "all-purpose" items to its highest stage of development. This is what the Mantis tiller tries to do. It is designed for home gardens, weighing in at only about 20 pounds, but you can hook little attachments to it that trim hedges and borders, dethatch the lawn, and cultivate the soil. It's a nifty idea. The newest downscaling idea from the firm is a power sprayer, mounted on wheels, that you can use for spraying whole vegetable or flower gardens quickly and easily. The company also imports a Swiss chipper.

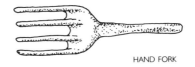

HAND FORK

Memory Metals

84 W. Park Place
Stamford, CT 06901

- *Devices to open and close vents and cold frames automatically.*
- *Various brochures, free.*

This is a firm that hopes to prosper using the shape-memory effect (SME) of certain alloys. There are endless applications for metals that can be cued to change shape under different environmental conditions, but most useful to gardeners are hinges that open and close automatically with changes in temperature.

Meridian Equipment Corporation

4-40 Banta Place
Fair Lawn, NJ 07410

- *Importers of English tools.*
- *8-page catalogue, color illustrations, free.*

The tools are so pretty you may hesitate to use them. Aside from that, the most noticeable thing about the catalogue is the number of fine hand tools with long handles. Weed forks, lawn and border shears, even a trowel and hand fork, are all long-handled. They have two lines, one quite expensive and one moderately priced. Both look serviceable.

Micro Essential Laboratory

4224 Avenue H
Brooklyn, NY 11210

- *Hydrion soil-test papers.*
- *No catalogue.*

The firm makes extremely handy tools for rough measurement of soil pH, using a litmus paper that turns different colors according to the pH reading. You compare the colored paper to a color-coded pH chart to get the reading.

Molded Fiber Glass Tray Co.

E. Erie Street
Linesville, PA 16424

- *Plastic flower boxes, planters, tubs, seed flats, and trays.*
- *2-page color flyer, free.*

This firm makes the simple Bo-Kay brand pots, flats, and trays in unobtrusive styles and a nice group of colors.

Natural Gardening Research Center

Highway 46
PO Box 149
Sunman, IN 47041

- *Organic pest and disease controls; beneficial insects; seed for cover crops and lawns; organic soil amendments.*
- *32-page catalogue, approx. 80 illustrations, many in color, free.*

This unusually informative catalogue combines the virtues of a cooperative extension bulletin and a sales brochure. A color-illustrated list describes the common pests and diseases—chiefly, but not exclusively, of vegetable and fruit crops—telling which plants they attack and how to control them by organic methods. Of course, most of the methods involve using the products the company sells, but some are simply sanitary measures. The products themselves are very well described, including information on such important topics as how to keep beneficial insects around and how many parasitic nematodes of what age will really do the job. There's also a good chart of recommended cover crops, and the soil amendments the firm sells are backed with a good deal of text explaining their virtues. The selection of control products—insects, dusts, sprays, traps, envelopes, and row covers—is as wide as any I have seen.

Natural Pest Controls

8864 Little Creek Drive
Orangevale, CA 95662

- *Beneficial insects.*
- *1-page list, free.*

Here is another company you can try for the usual run of beneficial bugs. Since the firm is located in the Sacramento Valley, it also goes in for mos-quito control. You can buy powdered or liquid BT *(Bacillus thuringensis)* here, not to mention mosquito fish.

I had a giant tiller once
Of which I grew quite fond.
It only threw me in the mud
And never in the pond.
—FROM MANTIS MANUFACTURING CO. 1986 CATALOGUE

Necessary Trading Company

648 Main Street
New Castle, VA 24127

- *Biological soil management and natural pest controls; sprayers and dusters; books.*
- *16-page periodical "Newsalogue" tabloid, more than 75 illustrations, $2.00.*

There really is some news in the "Newsalogue": it is a good place to find out about nonprofits doing work in alternative and organic agriculture and gardening. Mainly, it is devoted to selling the company's ultraorganic pesticides, fertilizers, compost supplies, and the like. From the look of the book list—heavy as it is in biodynamics publications—the proprietors are at least sympathetic to the organic mysticism emanating from Rudolf Steiner and his pupils. Altogether, it makes for a fine and somewhat unusual list. The pest controls favor traps, plus all kinds of oils and dusts: BT, ryania, rotenone, liquid copper, dormant oil, lime sulfur, Safer's soap, Bordeaux mix, and pennyroyal, citronella, eucalyptus, garlic, cedarwood, sweet orange, and bay oils. Some beneficial insects are to be found here, too. The list of organic fertilizers is among the longest I've seen. There is far too much stuff to mention, but the text is an invaluable

help in solving real problems and building a healthy garden step-by-step. The mix of books, tools, and products on theme-oriented pages has something of the feel of the old *Whole Earth Catalogue.*

Walter F. Nicke

19 Columbia Turnpike
Hudson, NY 12534

- *Garden tools, birdfeeders, gadgets, and books.*
- *47-page catalogue, over 225 illustrations, $.50.*

Walter Nicke is one of the older firms in the mail-order tool business for home gardeners. The proprietor describes his company pretty well: "Who else would have snail bait holders?" he writes. The selection of everything from traditional "tit bells"—suet-filled feeders from which the tits and other such birds hang belly-up—to odd-looking Danish hand tools is very wide and quirky. A lot of the gadgets look more useful than such things usually are. He lists, among many other things, a potato barrel (to grow a barrelful of potatoes), an adjustable seed sower, a window-shelf extender, a soil sifter, and some very fine English propagators. When it comes to tools, he has most of the good imported stuff you will find in the trade—things like Felco pruners, Solo sprayers, and Sheffield Pride spades—together with some items selected particularly for the elderly and handicapped. He also likes American tools, of which he writes as follows: "Now then Clementine! Please consider this: if a garden tool is still on the market after 50, 75, or maybe even 100 years, it must have the proper qualities for the job." The text throughout the catalogue is written in a similarly crotchety and entertaining style. By the way, the snail bait holders are his best sellers.

North American Kelp

Cross Street
Waldoboro, ME 04572

- *Soil amendments made from the kelp Ascophyllum nodosum.*
- *14-page catalogue, black-and-white illustrations, free.*

NAK harvests and processes its kelp on the coast of Maine, making meals, liquids, and powders for conditioning the soil of outdoor gardens and houseplants. The catalogue tells you recommended rates and times for application.

Northern Wire Products

PO Box 70
St. Cloud, MN 56302

- *Plant supports.*
- *Various brochures, free.*

The most interesting support here is a collapsible rectangular tomato cage called the "Tomato Ladder."

OFE International

PO Box 161302
Miami, FL 33116

- *Pots, moss, growing media, and other supplies for orchids.*
- *20-page catalogue, more than 45 color illustrations, free.*

The illustrations make growing media look lovely, and there are a good 2 dozen choices. The selection is similarly wide in basketry, including wire baskets that come prelined with sphagnum moss. You will also find all kinds of tree ferns, in the form of plaques, poles, balls, and pots. Tools, food, and pesticides appear, to boot. A first-rate catalogue for orchid growers. (Bromeliad and epiphytic fern people will probably get a lot of use out of it, too.)

Ohio Earth Food

13737 Duquette Avenue N.E.
Hartville, OH 44632

- *Organic soil amendments and pest controls.*
- *10-page catalogue, free.*

Here's another good regional organics company, with the sort of fertilizer list that will make organic gardeners yearn to sift the products through their fingers. OEF sells Earth-rite, a complex composted fertilizer, plus other goodies like ground seashells from Bermuda and granular Norwegian seaweed extract.

Peaceful Valley Farm Supply

11173 Peaceful Valley Road
Nevada City, CA 95959

- *Organic pest and disease control; beneficial insects; organic soil amendments; tools and supplies; plants for fruit trees and vines, ornamental trees, and shrubs; seed for lawns, cover and forage crops, and wildflowers; flowering bulbs.*
- *102-page catalogue, approx. 250 illustrations, $2.00; 55-page fall supplement, many illustrations, $2.00.*

An astonishingly general supply company for the organic farmer and gardener, Peaceful Valley must list every good bug, every organic pesticide or other-i-cide, every trap, and every organic fertilizer, soil amendment, and inoculant known. Descriptions and instructions for use are good, as is the list of sprayers and spreaders and insect foods. The same greenhouse offered by Smith & Hawken is available from Peaceful Valley, and the quality of the seeders, spreaders, wheel hoes, pruners, shearers, hand tools, saws, and you-name-its is high. The saw selection includes several Fannos in different sizes and a nice group of Japanese models. If you have the slightest in-

terest in organic methods, this is a good catalogue to have on hand. It is practically a primer of the materials available through the trade. The fall supplement is more of the same, plus an expanded list of bulbs for the spring.

Plantjoy

3562 E. 80th Street
Cleveland, OH 44105

- *Genuine Peruvian sea-bird guano.*
- *6-page brochure, free.*

If you want the real thing, here it is. The proprietors are perhaps needlessly defensive about the stuff, being sure to tell us that it doesn't smell and that the cormorant (the sea bird in question) is not a scavenger but a lover of "nutrition-rich anchovies." The brochure tells you how to apply it most economically to most kinds of plantings. The NPK rating is 13–8–2. Be careful how you use it. It's powerful.

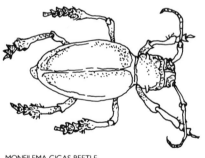

MONEILEMA GIGAS BEETLE

Proen Products Co.

2777 9th Street
Berkeley, CA 94710

- *Sprinklers, hose couplers, hose-end root feeders, and edgers.*
- *Color brochure, free.*

Proen is the source of the original "squarespray" sprinklers, whose charming motto is "It gets the corners."

Radio Steel & Manufacturing Co.

6515 W. Grand Avenue
Chicago, IL 60635

- *Wheelbarrows, garden carts, spreaders, and outdoor furniture, all unassembled in boxes.*
- *12-page color barrow, cart, and spreader catalogue; 8-page color furniture catalogue; both free.*

Yes, they still make the Radio Flyer children's wagon, not to mention about 15 models of wheelbarrows, garden carts, and lawn and rotary spreaders. The furniture is simple and serviceable: metal-framed with wooden slats. You put it together yourself. Along with seats, benches, and tables, there are even a couple of porch gliders.

BEE

Rain Bird National Sales

145 N. Grand Avenue
Glendora, CA 91740

- *Watering devices.*
- *No catalogue for consumers.*

These are the people who invented the "impulse" sprinkler. Here is the address, in case you have any questions to ask the firm. You must buy from retail outlets, however. One item of note: most stores today seem to be carrying the newer Rain Bird sprinkler model, with its blocky plastic base. A good deal of the pleasure of the original came from its beautifully curved wire base, which somehow always made me think of the elegance of the Whirlybird helicopter. If you share my obsession, you will be pleased to learn that Rain Bird

still makes one that looks like the original, though it seems the curved base is now plastic. Ask for model RG-25.

Raindrip, Inc.

14675 Titus Stret
PO Box 44913
Panorama City, CA 91412

- *Drip-irrigation systems.*
- *15-page color catalogue, 46-page planning guide, both free.*

Raindrip's catalogue may look intimidating. How do all these neat little pipe joints fit together? The planning guide is unusually thorough at telling you where and how. It's a little rougher going than some of the how-to's offered by other drip companies, but it really does give you all the information you need to design, maintain, and install a system yourself.

Reuter Laboratories

8450 Natural Way
Manassas Park, VA 22111

- *Natural pest controls, mainly based on milky spore, BT (Bacillus thuringensis), or pheromone traps.*
- *8-page catalogue/wholesale brochure, more than 25 color illustrations, free.*

Reuter seems to be bucking to become the Ortho of the organic pest-control trade. The firm also sends out little brochures, noting their advertising and chumminess with magazines like *Organic Gardening* and *Horticulture*. You can always tell Reuter products because they are named ATTACK, prefixed with the name of the critter each is supposed to control. The slickness of its marketing is a little disturbing, but who can fault a company with such decent aims? One hopes, however, that it will not drive out of business all the smaller companies that offer a higher proportion of information to hype.

Rincon-Vitova Insectaries

PO Box 95
Oak View, CA 93022

- *Beneficial insects.*
- *4-page brochure, free.*

The firm's attractive brochure opens with the motto "Invite a friend to dinner . . .", flanked by a large and friendly-looking ladybug. Aside from ladybugs, the other "friends" it sells are lacewings, trichogramma wasps, cryptolaemus beetles, *Encarsia formosa*, predatory mites, and fly parasites. Rincon-Vitova is one of the oldest companies in the business. Heretofore, they've supplied mainly commercial growers, but the new brochure represents an effort to sell to ordinary gardeners.

Ringer Research

6860 Flying Cloud Drive
Eden Prairie, MN 55344

- *Organic fertilizers and soil amendments; tools, shading, fencing, and books.*
- *20-page catalogue, color illustrations, free.*

Ringer sells organic feeds, amendments, and pest controls for everything from lawns to houseplants. Among the many neat aerating and watering tools is a tree-feeding auger that attaches to an ordinary power drill. Also, take a look at the netting for protecting fruit trees and the braided-nylon vegetable trellises.

RL Corporation

1000 Foreman Road
Lowell, MI 49331

- *Sprayers, hose reels, and hose couplers.*
- *12-page color brochure, free.*

Here are a lot of American-made ways to go-with-the-flow. There are 4 models of pump sprayers at different price levels, plus a few hose-end models. Lots of quick-couplers and sprinklers, too.

A. I. Root Co.

Box 706
Medina, OH 44258

- *Everything for beekeeping and honeymaking.*
- *45-page catalogue, many illustrations, free; variable-length monthly,* Gleanings in Bee Culture, *many illustrations, annual subscription $11.20, two years $21.70; 96-page book,* Honey Plants, *many illustrations, $2.50.*

Root has the corner on bee supplies and information. The only thing it doesn't supply are the bees themselves, though you can get its free pamphlet *Beginning with Package Bees,* which tells you how and where to order the hymenopterans, and what to do when you get them. For the rest, Root has it: hives, escapes, fume boards, frames, queen excluders, pollen traps, food supplements, smokers, veils, helmets, gloves, sting lotion, melters, processors, extractors, jars, buckets, every necessary book, posters, sweat bands, and "Honey for Sale" signs. They even have a selection of colored labels to affix to your honey jars.

Root has been around for more than a century, as has its well-respected magazine *Gleanings in Bee Culture.* Beyond its singularly mellifluous title, the magazine is as copious as the catalogue. There are reports on every strain of bee, every method of caring for them, plants bees like, means of making honey, and interviews with beekeepers. There are also lively features such as "The Adventures of Lance Ashemore, Apiary Inspector." The problem of vicious Africanized bees seems to be the topic of the hour, and there is

plenty of reflection on it. A recent issue reported on a group's visit to Nicaragua, where the visitors were able to observe two ends of the sting spectrum: the Africanized bees, who they said might follow the keepers for half a mile from the hive, and the Central American stingless bees. If you are beginning with bees, here's a good magazine to start with, and you should never outgrow it.

Honey Plants is a field guide with a difference. It describes several hundred different plants, many of them natives, together with information on where they grow plus an assessment

> But if I mentioned the words "plant-lice" I should also have added that in June green-fly should be destroyed. For this there are various powders, preparations, tinctures, extracts, infusions, and fumigations, arsenic, tobacco, soft soap, and other poisons, which the gardener tries one after the other, as soon as he notices that on the roses the green and succulent lice have seriously increased. If you use these expedients with a certain care, and in due quantity, you will find that the roses sometimes survive this destruction uninjured, except for the leaves and buds, which look somewhat blasted, while the plant-lice thrive under this treatment so that they cover the twigs like dense embroidery. Afterwards it is possible—with loud expressions of disgust—to squash them on one twig after the other. In this way they are destroyed, but for long afterwards the gardener smells of tobacco extract and grease.
>
> —KAREL CAPEK, FROM *THE GARDENER'S YEAR* (1929)

of the quality of the honey that bees can make with them. The photos vary in quality, but most are useful for identification. At the price, it's a terrific and unique reference.

Scovil Hoe Co.

PO Box 479
Higganum, CT 06441

- *Hoes.*
- *2-page sheet, free.*

Here are carbon-steel hoes in 4 traditional shapes. They are very well made, using a unique "eye" to join blade to handle.

H. B. Sherman Manufacturing Co.

1450 Rowe Parkway
Poplar Bluff, MO 63901

- *Sprinklers and other hose supplies.*
- *20-page color catalogue, free.*

This is a wide and attractive line of sprinklers, quick-couplers, nozzles, and the like, some of plastic and some of brass. If you're shopping around, check this catalogue out.

Allen Simpson Marketing & Design Ltd.

1 Albert Street
Eden Mills, Ontario
CANADA N0B 1P0

- *Supergrip hand tools and telescoping rake.*
- *Various sheets, free.*

Simpson makes the very sturdy, one-piece alloyed Supergrip tools. The telescoping rake handle comes with a locking system that lets you detach the rake and turn any of the other tools into long-handled models.

Smith & Hawken

25 Corte Madera
Mill Valley, CA 94941

- *Garden tools and greenhouse kit.*
- *40-page catalogue, more than 85 color illustrations of tools, free.*

Paul Hawken is forever writing about the need for mail-order firms to provide the finest products and the best and most courteous service, so you should never have to worry about what you'll get when you order from his company. The catalogue is very beautiful, and the descriptions are appetizing. Often, Smith & Hawken makes the little extra effort that matters to people. The greenhouse kit, for example, comes with its own tools for building, and the catalogue tells you about how much it will cost to

RUBBER BOOTS

buy glass for the walls, if you don't choose their plastic ones. Then there is the lovely illustration that shows how a Bulldog spading fork is made from a single piece of metal. When customers write with suggestions, the firm sometimes does take action: people wrote asking for a hopper to make it easier to use the Lescha electric shredder, and Smith & Hawken now provides one. The list includes most tools you will need, each of the highest quality. The Japanese hatchet and pruning saws are particularly attractive. Drip irrigation, the Gardena watering system, and good backpack sprayers also appear. You can get

every kind of watering can from plastic to copper. Selections of clothes, boots, kneelers, and assorted gadgets are also available.

Snow & Nealley

739 Odlin Road
Box 876
Bangor, ME 04401

- *Dibbles, bulb planters, axes, and mauls.*
- *2-page illustrated flyer, free.*

S&N got going just as the Civil War was winding down, and it hasn't stopped since. Its axes are beautiful, durable, workable, and famous, but you should know that they also make extremely fine long- and short-handled dibbles and bulb planters. The Cape Cod weeders that you often see advertised come from here, too.

Specialty Manufacturing Co.

2356 University Avenue
St. Paul, MN 55114

- *Carts, hose reels, and hose couplers, wands, and nozzles.*
- *10-page color catalogue, free.*

Most of this stuff appears at garden centers. I like the look and weight of the firm's orange plastic wheelbarrow. There's also a handsome folding cart that works as a hand truck or a trash-bag holder.

Survival Equipment Co.

PO Box 80
Oley, PA 19547

- *The "Woodman's Pal" billhook.*
- *1-page sheet, free.*

The Woodman's Pal is an evil-looking combination tool that might have

been carried by a medieval warrior. It's meant for clearing brush. If I were the brush, I'd run.

Tools & Techniques for Easier Gardening

Edited by Lynn Ocone and George Thabault
National Gardening Association
180 Flynn Avenue
Burlington, VT 05401

- *48-page book, many illustrations, $6.00 ppd.*

The NGA puts out several books for special gardening situations. This one is the most generally useful. For any handicapped gardener, or for those who can't bend over much or get a firm grip on a tool, it is very helpful. It selects and reviews the best tools available for people with such limitatons. It also lists aids that make it easier to handle ordinary tools, and it even has a few do-it-yourself ideas for homemade kneelers and the like.

Trickle Soak Systems

PO Box 38
Santee, CA 92071

- *Distributors of a wide variety of drip-irrigation systems.*
- *70-page product catalogue, black-and-white illustrations, $3.95; 37-page "Drip Irrigation for Landscape and Garden," black-and-white illustrations, $3.95.*

The novice could drown in the immense product catalogue, a mail-order supermarket of drip-irrigation equipment. Fortunately, the company has created a terrific little book for home gardeners who may want to use drip irrigation. It offers a clear and well-illustrated introduction to the whole idea, together with enough specific information to let you decide on what means and quantities are right for your needs. Read it first, then tackle the product catalogue.

Tropical Plant Products

PO Box 547754
Orlando, FL 32854

- *Baskets, pots, tree-fern fiber objects, growing media, and other supplies for orchids and other exotics.*
- *16-page catalogue, 22 color illustrations, free.*

This firm has anything an orchid likes, plus a few things orchids couldn't care less about. Its tree-fern repertoire includes not only pots, plaques, balls, and poles, but a number of totems and other sculpted shapes. There is also a good choice of Peters fertilizers for general houseplant use and for particular exotic plants.

TSI Co.

1322 North Avenue
Bridgeport, CT 06604

- *Tools and supplies for arborists, landscapers, and other professionals.*
- *106-page master catalogue, more than 500 illustrations, free.*

The catalogue is really meant for pros. Among every sort of tool for trees and shrubs, for example, it lists a whole line of pneumatic saws, shears, and loppers—all lovely things if you have the compressor to run them. But it is also a very fine and well-priced source of all kinds of good tools that are appropriate for home users. It is my favorite kind of catalogue: not too pretty, but you never know what terrific device the next page will show you. There are boots for loggers; Havahart animal traps; deer and rabbit repellent and tanglefoot; chainsaws; Solo sprayers; True Friends shears; all the Felco shears; a large selection of True Temper rakes, spades and forks; fencing and netting and row covers; a rake that works as its own shovel; terrific gloves made for people who use chainsaws; mattocks and axes; utility carts by Rubbermaid; a wide range of saws, loppers, and hedge shears; soil augers; seed spreaders; and, of course, tree-planting bars. Also, if you really are going to make your own landscape plan or you want to sketch the property you are buying, TSI offers fine tape measures, a variety of templates, and easy-to-use clinometers. You can even get from TSI a raised-relief topographic map of the area you live in. Prices for many tools are less than you would pay when ordering from one of the color-catalogue, upmarket mail-order firms.

Unique Insect Control

PO Box 15376
Sacramento, CA 95851

- *Beneficial insects.*
- *4-page catalogue, 6 illustrations, free.*

Here is another source for good bugs. The catalogue features little essays on each of the species offered, containing a lot of interesting tidbits. Did you know, for example, that there are 72,000 ladybugs per gallon?

Urban Farmer Store

2121 Taraval Street
San Francisco, CA 94116

- *16-page catalogue, 12 illustrations, $1.00.*

The Urban Farm people are specialists in drip irrigation. Their catalogue not only gives you a broad choice of the best in such systems, but it tells you a good deal about their advantages and offers basic installation advice. It's a good way to find out if you want to use drip irrigation and here's your chance to get the goods quickly, if you do.

Wells & Wade

PO Box 1161
Wenatchee, WA 98801

- *Fruit-picking buckets and bags; pruning shears and pole pruners.*
- *Various sheets, free.*

Wells & Wade is an important supplier to the Northwest's orchard industry. The buckets and bags are great for the home orchard, too. They hang from your shoulders, making picking quicker and easier. The shears are of professional quality.

Wilson Safety Products

PO Box 622
Reading, PA 19603

- *Safety masks, goggles, other devices.*

It can be annoyingly hard to find a good mask when you need to work with toxic materials. Wilson has a whole line of them, including some specifically designed for pesticide applications.

Yonah Manufacturing Co.

PO Box 280
Cornelia, GA 30531

- *Polypropylene cloth for greenhouse shading.*
- *Fact sheets and cloth samples, free.*

You can get shade cloth in densities from 30 to 92 percent. A helpful page among the fact sheets recommends different shading percentages for different sorts of greenhouse plants. The company makes up the shading to your specifications, complete with grommets. The cloth can also be used to shade landscape plants. You will appreciate the samples, which give you a real feel for what you are buying.

10   Furniture and Ornament

Ascot Designs

286 Congress Street
Boston, MA 02110

- *Importer of treillage, garden seats, antique ornaments, and cast stone ornaments and paving.*
- *28-page cast stone catalogue from Minsterstone, many color illustrations, free; assorted brochures and price list, free.*

Ascot is a fine source of top-quality cast stone from Britain. They make everything with it: seats, fountains, paving, balustrades, urns and vases, finials, sundials, and birdbaths. The generally simple and classically designed selections in the Minsterstone catalogue are lovely and functional. The iron and mild-steel treillage and benches are equally appealing, particularly a set of Gothic chair and seat, with backs in the shape of simple Gothic arches. The antiques are beautiful and costly.

BENCH

Axelsson Metal Design

PO Box 222598
Carmel, CA 93922

- *Ornamental metalwork in iron, bronze, copper, and stainless steel.*

Chris Axelsson is an award-winning designer of elaborate gates and other metalwork. The leaf and branch patterns in his ornamental gates are enormously detailed, down to the suggestion of veining on the leaves and little birds on the branches. The style is rhythmic and symmetrical. These are substantial and beautiful objects at substantial prices. He likes to work on commission.

Backhouse, Inc.

4121 Hillsboro Road
Suite 301
Nashville, TN 37215

- *Adirondack lawn chairs, and other garden furniture in the same style.*
- *12-page folder of color inserts, $3.00.*

Backhouse is a very young firm that makes well-finished Adirondack chairs, ottomans, chaises, love seats, and side tables for the garden. The materials are Honduran mahogany, joined with wooden pegs and epoxy. All items are available in white or green.

Bench Manufacturing Co.

56 Winthrop Street
PO Box 158
Concord, MA 01742

- *Makers of benches, picnic tables and light fixtures.*
- *Four 4-page color brochures, free.*

The firm makes furniture chiefly for public parks. The benches are wooden-slatted with decorative Victorian iron arms and legs. Because they are available in a variety of widths, it is possible for a gardener to order sizes that will fit a smaller space. Two other items look interesting for the larger garden. One is a simple backless bench with a slightly bowed seat, good for a pathside seat or placement deep in a large garden.

The other is a durable hexagonal seat, for use as a landscape-tree surround.

Mr. Birdhouse

2307 Highway 2 W.
Grand Rapids, MN 55744

- *Aluminum purple-martin house.*
- *4-page brochure, free.*

"Martins show a strong preference for aluminum houses," says the pushy advertising copy with which the brochure is stuffed. For all the hype, the birdhouses do seem to be well made, with removable sides for cleaning out old nesting material and a roof system that keeps the insides dry. Not only that, Mr. Birdhouse will sell you a pole and pulley, so you can hoist the thing up without a ladder.

> Gardeners have certainly arisen by culture and not by natural selection. If they had developed naturally they would look differently; they would have legs like beetles, so that they need not sit on their heels, and they would have wings, in the first place for their beauty, and, secondly, so that they might float over the beds.
>
> —KAREL CAPEK, FROM THE GARDENER'S YEAR (1929)

Bird 'n Hand

40 Pearl Street
Framingham, MA 01701

- *All sorts of bird feed.*
- *15-page catalogue, color illustrations, free.*

Sunflower seed—whole, shelled, or broken up for small-billed birdies— thistle seed, hearts of peanut, white millet, cracked corn, safflower seed, and grit are what's sold here: gourmet food to attract gourmet birds like finches, chickadees, grosbeaks, cardinals, juncos—and the occasional grackle.

Bomanite Corporation

81 Encina Avenue
Palo Alto, CA 94301

- *Colored, imprinted, and textured concrete paving.*
- *4-page flyer Concrete Paving Systems, 30 color illustrations, free; 4-page list of licensed contractors and sales representatives, free.*

Bomanite is one of the world's great makers of textured concrete paving. It offers more than 50 styles, suitable for patio paving, entryways, or driveways. The styles that imitate tile and setts are practically as elegant and attractive as the real thing, and much cheaper. Even the imitation random-stone pattern would work for a driveway. (It is used as such at the J. Paul Getty Museum in Malibu.) The only failures, I think, are the styles that simulate brick and river rock. These just look fake. Bomanite also makes an interesting material called Grass-crete, which consists of filigreed slabs whose holes can be filled with soil and planted in grass, making a green-patterned surface that is strong enough to park a car on. I have seen one instance where the stuff was used to create a whole field of X-shaped grass patches.

Joseph A. Bonifas

Black Oak Forge
9090 Spencerville Road
Spencerville, OH 45887

- *Ornamental gates in steel, stainless, or bronze.*

The Bonifas garden gates are minimal by the standards of today's often-ornate craftwork. A half-dozen lightly worked vertical elements may be topped with a few graceful curves that end in single leaves. A gate like this is a fine introduction to the garden because it prepares you for the forms within, lets you see through to them, and does not call too much attention to its own undoubted craftsmanship. Bonifas creates one-of-a-kind pieces on commission.

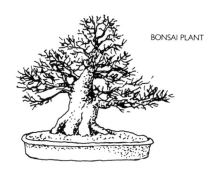

BONSAI PLANT

Bonsai Creations

2700 N. 29th Avenue
#204
Hollywood, FL 33020

- *Bonsai pots, tools, stands, and supplies; books; Japanese tools; finished bonsai and prebonsai plants.*
- *43-page illustrated catalogue, free.*

This is among the widest selection of bonsai pots that I've seen. The pots are from 3 different Japanese makers, and there are some hand-painted porcelain pots, too. There's also a selection of plastic pots and trays and a collection of plastic and wooden stands in many styles. The bonsai tools section is smaller, but it's supplemented with a number of fine Japanese tools for flower arranging and general gardening, including a nice group of the Silky pruning saws. The book list is comprehensive for bonsai. When it comes to plants, you'll find almost 50 different choices of prebonsai material, embracing most of what you'd expect. The finished bonsai and miniature landscapes are hard to judge from the small photos. I think most of us would enjoy them, though a fancier might find fault. Let him do his own.

Bow House

Bolton, MA 01740

- *Pool and garden structures.*
- *Poster showing a variety of structures, plus price list, free.*

Bow House got its start during the last recession, when the proprietor was looking for a way to stimulate the depressed building trade. He started with a reproduction of the Temple of the Winds at Kew Gardens, and Bow House has gone on from there. A version of the temple is still available, along with the following: a solar shower, a belvedere, an orangerie, a doghouse, a utility building, a Japanese bridge, a "shandy" (open gazebo), a cabanabar (a gazebo-bar hybrid), a pavilion, a Japanese tea house, a well, an arched arbor, and a pergola. If this sounds eclectic, you should send for the poster to see what it all looks like sketched on a single page, with kids and bikini-clad women strolling around.

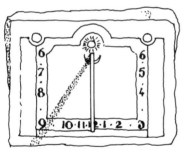

SUNDIAL

Peter Bramhall

Box 163
Bridgewater Center Road
Bridgewater, VT 05034

- *Bronze and other metal sculpture.*
- *4-page brochure, free.*

Bramhall's sculpture shows a strong African and modernist influence, skating the line between figurative and abstract. The pieces have a strong, solid, knobby but smooth look, like a cross between heavy machinery and primitive cult figures. They are remarkable things to stumble on in the garden or landscape.

Cal-Ga-Crete Industries

803 Miraflores Avenue
San Pedro, CA 90731

- *Concrete tiles for paving and wall veneers.*
- *10-page brochure, nearly 50 color illustrations, free.*

The very nicely illustrated brochure shows just how ambitious the textured concrete makers can get. One style imitates wood, and another looks like "used brick." Most of the choices in quarry-tile patterns look fine, including a number that are cast into hexagonal, octagonal, or a sort of Mexican-looking hourglass shape. The octagonal style, inset with real Mexican glazed tile, looks lovely. Some of the wall veneers are intriguing, including a number patterned on historical styles like Aztec and Romanesque.

Carruth Studio

7035 N. River Road
Waterville, OH 43566

- *Birdbaths, bird feeders, statues, and plaques cast in white concrete or terra cotta.*
- *1-page flyer, 6 color illustrations, free.*

George Carruth designs garden sculpture that his wife says has "a slightly medieval flavor." It also has a slight greeting-card flavor—all picture animals, mainly smiling cats with some sheep and bunnies, too. The one human figure is a squat St. Francis, with animals of course. The plaques indeed look medieval, since the relief figures are framed in Romanesque arches. They are mainly light-hearted, however, and would make good garden surprises, set into a wall. The really charming rabbit and cat birdbaths—each cast in the

form of the animal, with a hollowed-out back for the bath—have a similarly whimsical tone.

Cassidy Bros. Forge

U.S. Route 1
Rowley, MA 01969

- *Ornamental wrought iron gates, fences, balconies, sundials, and gazebos.*
- *4-page color brochure, free; 8-page brochure.*

The forge produces a variety of traditional-looking iron gates and fences. The work ranges from the simplest vertical-bar fences to curlicued and monogrammed gates. Commission work is a specialty here, so you can probably get them to do work to your design specifications. I very much like a simple arched trellis that appears in the brochure. The style is clean and architectural, but not overbearingly modern.

Kathleen Cerveny

Cervenova Studios
7714 St. Clair Avenue
Cleveland, OH 44103

- *Ceramic tiles and wall reliefs.*

Among the most interesting things Cerveny makes are working wall-mounted sundials, made out of many handmade ceramic tiles. She works on commission and can produce relief work in tile for garden-wall installations.

Charleston Battery Bench

191 King Street
Charleston, SC 29401

- *Victorian bench.*
- *4-page flyer, free.*

The firm makes only a very nice oak-slatted bench with decorative iron framing. It is modeled very closely on the park benches of Charleston.

Charley's Greenhouse Supplies

See "Tools and Supplies."

Child Life Play Specialties

55 Whitney Street
Holliston, MA 01746

- *Wooden play equipment for children.*
- *28-page catalogue, more than 50 illustrations, most in color; free.*

Most of the products are based on a simple, 3-ladder form—2 vertical and 1 across the top—that makes even the support structure into a thing to mess around on. Based on it, you can add swings, ropes, rope ladders, canvas-covered "treehouses," trapezes, punching bags, and slides. You can also make a jungle gym by combining the appropriate vertical ladders. A playhouse, a seesaw, and a wooden sandbox are also available. They even make a trolley slide that you can hang between 2 trees. Most of the items are available finished or in kit form.

Clapper's

1121 Washington Street
West Newton, MA 02165

- *Garden furniture, tools, and books. For review of tools, see page 184.*
- *32-page catalogue, 36 color furniture illustrations, free.*

The furniture is in 2 basic styles: English and Italian. To get a more American, and specifically Southern, look for some of the English designs, they have painted the furniture white and emphasized those big square planting boxes that, to my mind, never stop looking like crates. You can get some Chippendale designs and the Lutyens Runnymede bench in white. The Lutyens design also comes in unpainted teak, as do simple slatted-back and backless benches. At 56 inches, the Clapper's Lutyens bench is shorter than that available from other sources. The Italian styles are quite attractive, both the teak lounger and the big garden parasols done in canvas-covered beech or oak.

🌿 ON GARDEN STATUARY
We arrived with that Victorian penchant for Gothick, and are of equal date with Christmas trees and cuckoo clocks. Our pedigree can be seen to mount at least

to the Kobolds, those legendary delvers
    who with water and choke-damp wrought such Grimm mischief; nor should you overlook
    all the achondroplastics

of the Spanish and Salzburg courts; remember
    Velasquez, and that mankind defines itself by the monsters at its edge,
    if Bacon's notion holds good.

—ROBERT DRUCE, FROM *JOURNAL OF GARDEN HISTORY* (1985)

Columbine

RD 3
Box 212
Blairstown, NJ 07825

- *Terra-cotta architectural columns and pedestals.*

The fine, simple terra-cotta columns are available in more than a dozen colors, and they come in modular sections, making them relatively easy to construct. Columbine also offers small pedestals in the same color range. The flat-topped capitals are easy to build a pergola on top of, and the structure can bear the weight. Here is a way to build a garden temple for the landscape or introduce a powerful architectural element into a smaller garden.

Robert Compton, Ltd.

Star Route
Box 6
Bristol, VT 05443

- *Stoneware fountains and planters.*
- *8-page catalogue, 8 color illustrations, $2.00.*

Compton makes "stacked" fountains, using natural forms that resemble assemblages of udders, funnels, or mushroom heads. The shapes are generally graceful, and the sound of the water falling from level to level is reported to be lovely. You can buy the fountains glazed or unglazed, in several sizes, suitable for indoor or outdoor use. If you use them outdoors, remember to bring them inside before the cold weather sets in. They aren't hardy.

Concrete Paving Stones

13090 S.E. Orient Drive
Boring, OR 97009

- *Stepping stones and interlocking pavers.*
- *4-page color brochure, free.*

Here's a range of textured and shaped concrete paving stones. They are tough enough for paving the driveway, and some are attractive enough for the poolside or the porch. The company is one of those that has created a hollow grid system, so you can let plantings grow to cloak the surface.

Country Casual

17317 Germantown Road
Germantown, MD 20874

- *Garden furniture.*
- *16-page catalogue, 46 color illustrations, $1.00.*

Along with the usual run of English Chippendale designs and Lutyens benches, the firm offers several less prevalent styles. The dining table and side-chairs of the "Aurora suite," another English import, are really striking. The chairs are simple, 3-piece fanbacks, and the fan pattern is repeated in the tabletop. The effect is at once refined and rustic, though the

CHAIR

gaps between pieces of the tabletop look as though they would eat the cutlery. The other unusual English collection, called "The Wickham Collection," is certainly distinctive, but I'm not sure I like it. It consists of square-patterned stools and seats, and octagonal-patterned drinks tables, dining tables, and tête-à-tête love seats. The seats and tabletops are joined in 2 different tones of teak, the complete surface formed by means of concentric bands. The craftsmanship is beautiful, but you must judge the effect for yourself. Look at the "Mayan Collection," purportedly based on ancient Mayan designs. To me, it looks Scandinavian, but whatever it is, it is really something. The S-curved coffee table is distinctive, but the folding chairs are the thing. Both seat and back are made of straight slats gathered at the outer edges. The result is a chair that almost looks like some kind of forest cradle, and it slopes so far back that you may indeed feel unsure whether you are sitting or lying in it. A number of the styles are also available as porch or garden swings, and there are a few planting boxes (some displaying little finials) and other accessories.

Country Floors

300 E. 61st Street
New York, NY 10021

- *Wall tiles, floor tiles, and terra-cotta planters.*
- *96-page full-color tile catalogue, $10.00; 16-page ceramic accessories catalogue, 27 color pictures of planters, $2.00.*

The tiles come from all over the Mediterranean, from Portugal, from France, and from Mexico. A few are made in the U.S. Most are new, but there is a section of antique tile, too. The choice of wall tiles is extraordinary. If you can imagine all the styles from Mozarabic to floral to modern, you will have an idea of what the catalogue offers. Unfortunately, most of this material is not guaranteed for outdoor use, though a salesperson I spoke to said that a number of her clients had successfully used it outdoors, even in New York's climate. A lot of the terra-cotta floor tile from Mexico, Spain, and France, on the other hand, is suggested for patio or terrace use. The choice of shapes, sizes, and tones is awfully large. The accessories catalogue has 2 pages full of terra-cotta planters, pedestals, and garden ornaments, most highly decorated. Several planters in the shape of sarcophagi are attractive, but, though the figures on them are generally grouped in antique or medieval styles, the figures themselves have sometimes metamorphosed into rather cutesy cherubs. I like best a really gigantic square planter decorated with simple swags on each face.

The catalogues are beautifully done, but if you want to see the stuff in person, there are stores in Los Angeles, Miami, and Philadelphia, as well as New York.

Crowther of Syon Lodge

Syon Lodge
Busch Corner
London Road
Isleworth
Middlesex
ENGLAND TW7 5BH

- *Antique garden ornaments and gates.*
- *28-page catalogue, 52 illustrations, free.*

Crowther has gathered architectural ornaments from all over the world for more than a century. Its stock depends on what it finds, but it is weighted toward the classical styles (mainly in 19th-century versions), plus some rustic and grotesque material. The catalogue I saw had the following for the garden—or should I say for the estate garden: statuary, including 2 wonderful arch-necked mythological beasts; marble seats; a number of estate-size stone vases and finials; several wellheads, one from 17th-century Italy; 2 garden temples; and a 53-foot-wide gate. If you have the means to buy from Crowther, you will probably visit in person.

Cypress Street Center

330 Cypress Street
Fort Bragg, CA 95437

- *Redwood Adirondack-style furniture.*
- *8-page catalogue, color illustrations, free.*

Here are some basic and reasonably priced models of the Adirondack chair and loveseat, along with compatible tables and the like. They are made of redwood and come partly assembled.

Dalton Pavilions

7260 Oakley Street
Philadelphia, PA 19111

- *Gazebos.*
- *12-page catalogue, 24 color illustrations, free.*

This firm sells elaborate, red-cedar gazebos in 4 different period styles: the Victorian Gazebo, the Classic Gazebo (actually the least period-looking), the Williamsburg Gazebo, and the Victorian Pagoda. Three of them use a fair amount of latticework in the walls. My favorite is the Williamsburg, with its low surround of S-curved slats. All come with benches and table, and they are available as kits or finished structures. Dalton has a national dealer network and can send you information on the dealer nearest you.

Duncraft

Penacock, NH 03303

- *Bird feeders, birdseed, and related items.*
- *32-page catalogue, 93 color illustrations, free.*

Among its many bird feeders, seed mixes, and accessories, Duncraft offers another neat new tool for foiling squirrels called the "Squirrel Spooker Pole," which features a sliding sleeve that can eject the varmint when it tries to climb the pole. One wonders about the diabolical fellow who invented it, but it looks harmless and effective. Most of the feeder styles—together with a few simple bird-baths—are done in Plexiglas, and there are a good number of choices for affixing directly to your window. The catalogue also has suet and hummingbird feeders, and some wooden feeders as well. Particularly attractive are a stocking for dispensing thistle seed and a couple of feeders meant for suspending fruit. The catalogue is attractive, and the offerings various.

Erkins Studios

604 Thames Street
Newport, RI 02840

- *Importers of just about everything, including Italian and English ornaments and planters, and English wooden and iron furniture.*
- *36-page catalogue of ornaments, finials, statues, fountains, seats, and so on, $4.00. Various brochures of English garden furniture and Italian terra-cotta pots.*

A lot of the Italian stuff—be it in cast stone, bronze, or terra cotta—will downright horrify you. If you are of a baroque turn of mind, sweet horror is just what you are looking for, so you will be glad. The selection is wide, particularly in statuary and fountains. A few of the English sculptures in bronze are attractive for the rest of us, especially a lovely baby holding two turtles in her hands. There's also a very crazy and slightly *moderne* Orpheus, not to mention gaggles of cherubs and menageries of animals. Some of the English lead planters are really lovely, with simple medieval-looking decoration. Separate brochures show the usual tasteful English garden furniture, in teak, plus a selection of Italian terra-cotta pots.

> In Columella's poem on gardening, the modest Roman garden is to be protected by the simple statue of the god:
>
> . . . chuse the trunk of some huge ancient tree; Rough-hue it, use no art; *Priapus* make with frightful member, of enormous size; Him, in the middle of thy garden, place, And to him, as its guardian, homage pay, That with his monstrous parts he may deter The plund'ring boy; and with his thret'ning scythe, The robber from intended rapine keep.
>
> —CHRISTOPHER THACKER, FROM *THE HISTORY OF GARDENS.* (1979)

Everlite Greenhouses

PO Box 11087
Cleveland, OH 44111

- *Greenhouses and solariums; associated supplies.*
- *18-page catalogue, color illustrations, $5.00; 28-page price list and design specs, free.*

Everlite was the first firm in the country to make aluminum greenhouses, and its designs have become the common model for the industry. Its line is somewhat broader than that of many other firms, and it provides design advice and custom installation. Glazing is inch-thick. As with most such greenhouses, the look is clean and functional.

Exotic Blossoms

PO Box 2436
Philadelphia, PA 19147

- *Plain and planted topiary frames; distributors of English Haddonstone cast stone ornaments.*
- *4-page topiary list, free; 48-page color Haddonstone catalogue, write for price.*

The firm says it is the largest shipper of topiary frames in the world. There are about 75 cute choices, mostly animal shapes. The Haddonstone catalogue is something else altogether. A lot of these very fine English reproductions of Neoclassical garden ornaments are fit for an estate. There are seats and benches, urns, finials, balustrades, and even whole temples and pavilions. You may not have room for such follies, but you may be interested in the planters and troughs—which Exotic offers a wide variety of—with nicely done finishes, including scales, leaves, figures, swags, basketweaves, and scallops. There is even a nice alpine trough, rough and plain. A few of the statues are less demanding of an estate setting, particularly a lovely reddish peregrine falcon.

Five Artists at NOAA

Essay by Patricia Fuller
The Real Comet Press
932 18th Avenue E.
Seattle, WA 98112

■ *50 pages, some illustrations, a few color, $11.95.*

It's a lot to pay for a little book. Also, it's a book about artists' landscape projects installed at the Seattle station of the National Oceanic and Atmospheric Administration. Still, unusual among such books, it includes a number of interesting projects at a scale small enough to give you ideas. Some lovely stonecutting and austere bridgework has gone into one path and rock terrace, designed by Scott Burton. George Trakas contributed a thing called "Berth Haven," a lakeside dock which makes remarkable use of a blonde wood decking and very industrial-looking steel. Walking from one surface to another is an experience in itself. The large sound garden by Douglas Hollis is out-of-scale for our purposes, but the idea is very intriguing. (It is flanked by starling, gull-wing benches made of perforated metal.) Addresses for the artists are included at the back.

Florentine Craftsmen

46-24 28th Street
Long Island City, NY 11101

■ *Importers of fountains, statuary, gazebos, sundials, seats, and other ornaments.*
■ *56-page catalogue, many illustrations, $3.00.*

The open, wrought iron gazebo, with its filigreed roof, would do very well in a classic garden setting. The various statues of children and animals and cherubs will appeal to some of us. Pots and urns range from the elegant to the ostentatious. There are several nice-looking aluminum seats and benches, with slatted seats and a vari-

ety of lovely patterns in the backs. One of them, called the Corinthian design, is plain nuts, with backs in the shape of Corinthian capitals! The selection of classically styled sundials and birdbaths is worth a look. The fountains are hideous.

Foster-Kevill

15102 Weststate Street
Westminster, CA 92683

■ *Wood and fiberglass planter boxes.*
■ *4-page flyer, 7 illustrations, free.*

If you like planter boxes, here is a good selection of them, each available in different sizes. There are some with plinth bases, and a few of the patterns are distinctive.

Garden Concepts Collection

PO Box 241233
Memphis, TN 38124

■ *All kinds of garden ornaments and furniture.*
■ *44-page illustrated catalogue, $3.00.*

There are gates and arches and benches and seats, urns and gazebos, mailboxes and Venuses, birdbaths and bird tables, bird condos, weather vanes and columns, wind chimes and lights, fountains and statues and jars. There's also a fabric garden pavilion by Laura Ashley. If you are in the market for high-quality, unusual, and fairly costly fixtures for the garden, you would do well to examine this catalogue. The gate, arch, and arbor (gazebos, too!) section gives you a look at more or less elaborate Anglophile styles, ranging from very open to very closed. Generally, I found the urns and fountains more ordinary, except for some wild Corinthian and Egyptian columns and pedestals. I loved the dragonfly weather vane.

Gardener's Eden

PO Box 7307
San Francisco, CA 94120

■ *Garden furniture, ornaments, plants, seed, gadgets, and tools.*
■ *50-page catalogue, approx. 160 color illustrations, free.*

I often get annoyed with this chic catalogue, with its terra-cotta watering cans, its French gardener's soap, and its bird-shaped baskets, but it always has a few very good ideas in it. One is the simple, modular set of red-cedar benches and planting boxes, just the other side of homemade in look, but functional, attractive, and versatile. Similar in effect is the Dutch pine planting box that doesn't try to look like anything more than a nice crate. The 2 more elaborate garden benches—one a self-supporting swing—are nice-looking kits at a reasonable price. I also love the plastic-bag patio lights, modeled on Southwestern *luminaria*, but giving the effect of something between lighted shopping bags and a Japanese *bon* festival. There are endless other gadgets, from quail faucets to rabbit planters, so you will just have to get the catalogue and look.

Garden Appointments

PO Box 1745
Shepherdstown, WV 25443

■ *Furniture and ornament.*
■ *Illustrated flyer, free.*

It is about time that someone got to work on American garden furniture, and Garden Appointments takes the challenge. The firm's first entry into the market is a lovely, dark green bench, based on the Chippendale-influenced design of Thomas Jefferson. The locally-inspired Shepherdstown garden obelisk is also among the current offerings; look for more from this firm, including pieces by 20th-century American designers.

Genie House

PO Box 2478
Vincentown, NJ 08088

- *Garden lighting.*
- *24-page catalogue, more than 65 illustrations, free.*

The fixtures are handcrafted with unusually fine detail to reproduce historical styles. The company has supplied such places as the White House and Monticello.

Anne Goldman

1972 Meadow Road
Walnut Creek, CA 94595

- *Ceramic planters and vases.*

Anne Goldman carves clay. She makes planters and vases in what are often classical shapes and plain earth tones, then works them until their surfaces resemble rough tree bark or membranes seen under a microscope. It is really astonishing stuff, and if you can afford the prices that individual craftspeople must charge, you should look into it.

Gothic Arch Greenhouses

PO Box 1564
Mobile, AL 36633

- *Kits for acrylic greenhouses; related supplies.*
- *4-page brochure, color illustrations, free.*

The frames are redwood or cedar; the glazing is a corrugated acrylic that admits more light than flat planes would. The shape is indeed arched. To my mind, this makes the greenhouses most attractive when freestanding, though lean-to models are also available.

Greenlee Landscape Lighting

1220 Champion Circle
Suite 116
Carrollton, TX 75006

- *Lighting fixtures and design.*
- *8-page color-illustrated brochure, free; single-sheet specifications for different models.*

Greenlee lights are not meant to be seen; they are meant to create effects. Many are uplights which fit into the ground plane; some are to be mounted on trees and planters. They are generally sleek and unobtrusive. Customers in the South and California can use the firm's custom-design service; others must simply purchase the fixtures.

Barbara Grygutis

273 N. Main Avenue
Tucson, AZ 85701

- *High-fired ceramic sculpture, sometimes combined in settings with other materials like brick and natural stone.*

Her blue and black ceramic work can resemble tall, jagged outcroppings of impossible stone or rhythmic groups of shiny teeth. The effect of these things in an architectural garden or landscape setting is really lovely. In 1985 Grygutis installed a garden in Tucson mixing native brick, weathered stone, pebbles, an arc and pedestal of ceramic tiles, and a pair of her tall monoliths. I have seen many attempts to imitate Japanese rock-garden styles, but this pun on the style is one of the most successful. It is both appropriate to its place in the desert Southwest and a witty attempt to hold desert monochromes at bay. Just what her work will be for a specific garden depends on her collaboration with owners and landscape designers in creating a garden setting.

Heath Manufacturing Co.

PO Box 105
Coopersville, MI 49404

- *Redwood planters; birdhouses.*
- *12-page catalogue, approx. 60 color illustrations, free.*

Heath supplies a lot of retail garden centers. If you want to get an idea of the full range of options commonly available in the trade, the catalogue is a small anthology. Among the birdhouses are a number of purple-martin houses in different sizes and styles.

Heritage Arts

16651 S.E. 235th Street
Kent, WA 98042

- *Tools and pots for bonsai.*
- *14-page illustrated catalogue, $2.00.*

A very wide selection of unglazed and glazed pots and containers for bonsai, together with a list of every tool you could possibly need. The brand name of the tools is Kaneshin, which may mean something to you.

Heritage Lanterns

70A Main Street
Yarmouth, ME 04096

- *Handmade bracket, post, and hanging lanterns in generally Colonial styles.*
- *48-page catalogue, more than 80 illustrations, many in color, $2.00.*

Heritage is one of the good Eastern handiwork companies that must be doing a booming trade, now that authentic restorations of colonial and period homes are in vogue. The choice of styles embraces most everything you can think of along Colonial and European lines, and the fixtures are available in copper, brass, or pewter.

Hilltop Slate Co.

Route 22A
Middle Granville, NY 12849

- *Quarries and special-finish slate.*
- *2-page brochure, free.*

Hilltop quarries its slate in New York and Vermont, offering natural slate for flagstones, paving, and wall applications. You can also get the stone finished in red, green, black, or even purple.

The House of Boughs

Edited by Elizabeth Wilkinson and
Marjorie Henderson
Viking Penguin

- *226 pages, many illustrations, $35.00.*

Often in the shuffle between plants and design, garden ornament gets left out. Perhaps this is why so much of the furniture and ornament offered looks so similar. This book is a wonderful antidote to that sameness. It is something of a pattern book, showing countless pictures and providing capsule histories for everything from apiaries to wells. The illustrations are first-rate, covering a wide range from the most formal and elaborate structures and ornaments to the most spare and rustic.

Huntington Pacific Ceramics

PO Box 1149
Corona, CA 91718

- *Bricks for paving.*
- *2-page color sheet on landscaping ideas; 2-page color sheet showing all pavers; 6-page color brochure* Architectural Bricks and Pavers; *all free.*

This is a terrific brick company that makes all kinds of bricks in a variety of widths and depths, and offers bull-nose pavers, with one contoured end. The landscaping-ideas sheet shows some very attractive pool settings created with Huntington's bricks. For most, several different shades of red and brown are available. The 6-page brochure contains complete specifications.

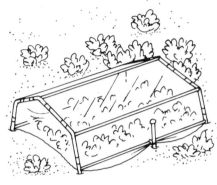

CLOCHE FRAME

Hyde Bird Feeder Co.

56 Felton Street
PO Box 168
Waltham, MA 02254

- *Bird feeders and birdseed.*
- *20-page catalogue, 37 color illustrations, free.*

Hyde makes nothing but bird feeders, including suet feeders and hummingbird feeders, plus various devices for fending off squirrels. Much of the line is based on Plexiglas housings, though many of the styles are more thoughtfully finished than those you commonly see on the market. A few are of the old-fashioned wooden-house type, one actually in the shape of a covered bridge.

Idaho Wood

PO Box 488
Sandpoint, ID 83864

- *Wood-framed lighting, mailbox, house numbers.*
- *12-page catalogue, more than 30 color illustrations, free.*

The company makes the sort of smooth, "all-natural"-looking wooden lights that go well with a deck, a Western wooden house, or a forest path. There are bollard lights, post lights, and wall lights. The mailbox is hexagonal, and you can have your address carved on it.

International American Ceramics

4942 E. 66th Street
PO Box 6600
Tulsa, OK 74156

- *Floor tile and pavers.*
- *28-page color catalogue, free.*

IAC makes tough ceramic floor tiles in a whole range of colors. They will do best in entryways or on patios.

International Bonsai Containers

412 Pinnacle Road
Rochester, NY 14623

- *Bonsai containers.*
- *6-page flyer, 37 color illustrations, free.*

Here is a very wide selection of bonsai containers, from trays to deep bowls. The pictures are quite clear.

Jackalope

2820 Cerrillos Road
Santa Fe, NM 87501

- *Pottery and statuary and paving, generally from Mexico and Central America.*
- *4-page flyer, free.*

Unfortunately, Jackalope has stopped sending out its big color catalogue, and its present flyer gives little idea of the immense variety of stuff that it has in the store. The firm sends trucks into Mexico all year long, looking for lovely pots, jugs, statues, and all sorts of ornaments. The store itself is large, but there's an even larger selection piled all over a gigantic yard. If you can visit, do; if you can't, you might try calling with a list of your wants.

Janco Greenhouses

9390 Davis Avenue
Laurel, MD 20707

- *Greenhouses and solariums.*
- *48-page catalogue, more than 100 color illustrations, $2.00.*

Janco makes attractive, modern greenhouses, as well as glass walls and skylights for solariums. There are many models, some lean-to and some with pitched roofs, all made with aluminum framing and insulated glass. The color pictures in the catalogue show the products in a variety of home-garden situations. Janco has a nationwide dealer network to build the things for you.

Kim Lighting

16555 E. Gale Avenue
PO Box 1275
Industry, CA 91749

- *Landscape lighting fixtures.*
- *6-page foldout brochure, 43 color illustrations, free.*

F. B. Nightingale, the founder, was making garden lighting back in the 1930s, and the company is still a leader in the field. Much of its work is for public spaces—including its custom lighted-fountain business—but it offers an excellent selection of up, down, and spread lighting for the garden. The brochure contains a very useful section on the principles of garden lighting, using color photos and black-and-white schematics to show what effect different kinds of lighting will have. The portfolio of fixtures includes some very well-finished spread lights in the shapes of mushrooms and campanulate flowers, available in copper and bronze or aluminum.

Sue Fisher King

3075 Sacramento Street
San Francisco, CA 94115

- *Italian terra-cotta planters and ornaments; white-wire Victorian furniture and gazebos.*
- *4-page brochure, 15 illustrations, free.*

The planters are available in all the usual styles, with a pleasing emphasis on simple shapes. Only 2 drawings of the white-wire furniture and gazebos appear in the brochure, but they look distinctive, offering a refreshing change from all that tasteful English

wooden stuff. King invites your inquiries about the other furniture she offers in the same style.

Kuma Enterprises

11 E. 57th Street
New York, NY 10022

- *Terra-cotta urns, obelisks, friezes, tables, and ornaments.*
- *22-page catalogue, 22 illustrations, free.*

Kuma imports really outstanding reproductions of traditional garden ornament from Italy. The urns and friezes are remarkably detailed, and they have none of the cuteness that often creeps into the human and animal figures in other pieces of the same style. A few of the pieces—including a very architectural doghouse that doubles as a table—were designed by noted French designer Loup de Viane.

URN

Live Oak Railroad Co.

111 E. Howard Street
Live Oak, FL 32060

- *Victorian-style benches, mailbox, and hitching post.*
- *6-page flyer, color illustrations, free.*

If you like the park-bench style—wooden slats with worked iron framing—Live Oak sells 2 unusually attractive styles, one modeled on the benches that grace Charleston's streets. (There's a small one of these, made for children, too.) The mailbox is so bulky and odd that the postman will never have trouble remembering where to find it.

The London Architectural Salvage and Supply Co.

St. Michael's Church
Mark Street (off Paul Street)
Shoreditch
London
ENGLAND EC2A 4ER

- *Antique and reproduced architectural ornaments, including fences and gates, seats and benches, flagstone, antique beams, statuary, urns, columns, gazebos, and summerhouses.*
- *1-page information sheet, free.*

The firm describes itself charmingly: "In 1974 the redundant Church of St. Michael and All Angels (James Brooks 1863) was taken over as LASSCo's permanent home and since then the company has pioneered the field of Architectural Salvage through times when that business has become both fashionable and necessary. . . . Over the years LASSCo has been involved in some of the most infamous demolition jobs in the UK, and nowadays draws on sources as far away as the USA, France, Spain, and Eastern Europe." If you have the means to undertake a search for the kind of stuff it offers, you will have to write LASSCo with your wants. Among the sample photos it sent to me were a crazy baroque rustic seat, done in iron with a flowers-and-foliage pattern, and a gorgeous iron bench that is worked in the patterns of fern leaves.

Rob MacConnell

White Crane
37 Ethel Avenue
Mill Valley, CA 94941

- *Raku-fired sculpture.*

MacConnell has crafted a number of temple stones and similar Oriental pieces, many with inscribed calligraphic texts. The stones range from 18 inches to 7 feet and will look well in the Oriental garden. They have a rough, well-used appearance. Be aware, however, that you can only use his sculpture outdoors in a mild climate that is not subject to freezes.

Machin Designs

652 Glenbrook Road
Stamford, CT 06906

- *English conservatories, garden pavilions, covered garden seats, summerhouses, and a few pots and planting baskets; modular trellis system in classical style; pagoda-roofed bird table.*
- *10-page brochure The English Garden, 24 illustrations, most in color, listing seats, pavilions and miscellaneous, $3.00; 32-page Machin Conservatories (more than 90 color illustrations) and 28-page Machin Designs: Architectural Details (complete elevations and dimensions), $5.00 for both.*

The buildings Machin offers are all remarkably lovely, and so are the catalogues, though the prices are remarkably steep. All the material is imported from England. The conservatories are quite elaborate, and the catalogue not only shows the selection, but provides fine photos of the different styles in a variety of sites, together with colored drawings suggesting how the buildings might be placed in town or country. The conservatories come in ogee, vaulted, and lean-to models, adaptable to many sizes and situations. The other garden houses are simpler, but all have an elegant English period look. Most of the roofs are bell-shaped or pagoda-shaped, though the covered seat has a pitched roof. All are finely detailed and finished. By the time this book is in your hands, the company will also be offering a modular system of traditional trellising for garden screens, as well as several different widths of rectangular panels, pitched-top and oval-top panels, and a trellised gateway. When you can't stand to look at another garden structure, try the bird table, the Versailles planter boxes, and the terra-cotta pots. The pots are especially nice, one with swags and one in a basketwork style.

Daniel Mack Rustic Furnishings

225 W. 106th Street
New York, NY 10025

- *Rustic furniture.*
- *12-page catalogue, 19 illustrations, $1.00.*

Mack makes some of the loveliest rustic furniture I have ever seen. His work for interiors is incomparably light and graceful; for outdoor furniture, he works with heavier woods, mainly cedar, but he is able to carry the whimsical and ideogrammatic quality of his work into these as well. It is best to work with him on commission, since he likes to respond to the client's wishes.

DECORATIVE TRELLIS

Thomas Meyers Studio

26 RR 1
Old Hancock Road
Antrim, NH 03440

- *Stained glass.*

The country is full of fine stained-glass makers who mainly work on residential and church interiors. Thomas Meyers does, too, but I was struck by a photo of an entry gate he built for a home in New Hampshire. The framing of the wide double doors looks like off-the-shelf, fabricated metal, but Meyers has filled it with a terrific latticework of antique and beveled glass, creating a play of refracted light and sight lines that makes the gate private but very inviting.

Robert Mihaly

Artifistudios Applied Arts
1611 Rosewood Avenue
Lakewood, OH 44107

- *Primarily wall surfaces and freestanding sculptural design in clay.*

The wonderful thing about Mihaly's wall tiles and his pottery is the texture he works into it. His unglazed red stoneware wall tiles, for example, are worked until they look like redwood bark. His pots are in unusual, asymmetrical shapes, with lines, folds, nodes, and cracks visible.

Nampara Gardens

2004 Golf Course Road
Bayside, CA 95524

- *Japanese-style bridges, lights, and bench.*
- *6-page brochure, 4-color illustrations, free.*

The company makes both a high and a low electric lantern, plus simple bridges and a bridge-back bench, all in a Japanese-looking style and all out of redwood. None of the work is finely detailed, but it has generally attractive, archetypal lines. The bridges are available in 3-, 4-, and 6-foot sizes. Nicest of all is the bench, which unfortunately is not pictured in the brochure. Its graceful, arched back imitates the shape of the bridge rails; the seat and supports are in a simple English style.

Norstad Pottery

253 S. 25th Street
Richmond, CA 94804

- *Clay and stoneware planters.*
- *1-page flyer, 3 illustrations, free; 1-page size and price list, free.*

The planters, designed by architect Eric Norstad, come in a variety of sizes and shapes. He will also custom-design large planters, fountains, and birdbaths. The glazed stoneware pots are pretty enough, but I can't help thinking they look a little like stoneware dishes and cooking pots. The plain clay pots, on the other hand, are lovely indeed (but unfortunately not pictured in the flyer). The hexagonal pots are elegant and unadorned; the round ones come with a circle of rough, apparently handmade incisions or raised beads.

PLANTER

Northern Greenhouse Sales

Box 42
Neche, ND 58265

Box 1450
Altona, Manitoba
CANADA R0G0B0

- *9.5-mil woven poly for greenhouse covers; connecting strips and cinch strapping.*
- *10-page brochure and other literature, free.*

Bob Davis has written the most charming greenhouse catalogue I have seen. He lives in southern Manitoba, where the first frost can come in August. Lacking the means to construct a double-glazed glass greenhouse, Bob experimented with a thicker-than-normal poly cloth, making the frame for the greenhouse out of rebar, the iron rods used in reinforced concrete. All he sells is the poly cloth, but his brochure is full of perfectly delightful information on things like building that rebar greenhouse for under $100, scavenging a fan for the greenhouse by dismantling people's abandoned oil heaters, and extending the season by planting strawberries and vegetables in truck and automobile tires. I suppose that none of these ideas are peculiar to him, but the engaging and thorough manner in which he presents them make them seem like *the* sensible solution for cheaply extending your growing in a difficult climate. His methods don't make for architectural loveliness, of course, but they do have the beauty of simplicity and efficiency.

Park Place

2252 Wisconsin Avenue N.W.
Washington, DC 20007

- *Distributors of teak furniture, Victorian iron furniture, and beveled glass for doorways.*
- *Various color brochures and price lists, free.*

Park Place has Weatherend, Sherwood, and Lister teak furniture in the usual English estate styles. The selection is pretty broad. The Victorian material is ornate but chunky-looking, and it includes tables and street lamps, as well as benches and seats. There is also some oak furniture and a variety of odds and ends, such as mailboxes and hitching posts.

Charles C. Parks

44 Bancroft Mills
Wilmington, DE 19806

- *Figurative sculpture, chiefly in bronze.*
- *36-page catalogue, many illustrations, some in color; write for price.*

Parks is a distinguished sculptor in bronze and welded steel. He has done everything from monumental and religious figures to seated children and a bronze octopus. He has a fine eye for detail and weight, and his figures look at once relaxed and archetypally posed. The drapery, when present, is also realistic, including even blue jeans and belts.

Ross L. Peacock Madison Avenue Gallery

985 Madison Avenue
New York, NY 10021

- *Original bronze garden sculpture by Else Martinus.*
- *Photos and prices sent on request.*

Peacock is the New York gallery for Dutch artist Else Martinus. I happened on her stuff while wandering by the gallery and was struck by it. Her bronze children look innocent but not cutesy, perhaps because of the material and the classical treatment of the subjects, whose features are those of ordinary modern children. It is very relaxed sculpture in a very refined style. If you like children and can afford an original bronze, her work is worth looking into.

GARDEN STATUARY

The Plow & Hearth

560 Main Street
Madison, VA 22727

- *Furniture, ornaments, tools, and gadgets.*
- *32-page catalogue, approx. 145 color illustrations, free.*

A general garden and kitchen mail-order company, many of whose wares resemble those of Gardener's Eden, The Plow & Hearth lists some sturdy-looking wooden seats, porch swings, and gliders, plus a folding Adirondack chair, a line of Adirondack rustic furniture, and loads of other stuff, including reconditioned Electrolux vacuum cleaners and army surplus ammo boxes. I found the rustic furniture a little too blocky, and, to my eye, it looks mass-produced. Still, the prices are quite reasonable, and it could look nice in the right setting.

Popovitch Associates

346 Ashland Avenue
Pittsburgh, PA 15228

- *Garden lamps.*
- *Send for photos.*

Don and Rose Popovitch make some sweet, informal floraform lamps, using copper and glazed ceramics. The firm is fairly new, but it promises to offer 6 different styles in its "Nature Series" by the end of 1987. The photo it sent me showed 2 low path lamps, both in the shape of campanulate flowers with a single straplike leaf. The leaves and standards were copper, the flowers ceramic and glazed, the one a dark blue and the other a dusty green. Detailing was not remarkable, but the overall form was attractive.

Lynn H. Poulter

Hawkes Design
Unit 112
Woodland Hills, UT 84653

- *Bronze door pulls.*

There are lots of decorative bronze faucet heads available these days; Lynn Poulter is doing the same thing for door pulls. She offers some very finely detailed pulls in the shapes of horses, mermaids, and blooming flowers and will also do custom work.

Radio Steel & Manufacturing Co.

See "Tools and Supplies."

Reed Bros.

6006 Gravenstein Highway
Cotati, CA 94928

- *Hand-carved redwood garden furniture and garden accessories.*
- *Variable-length catalogue with illustrated inserts, $7.00.*

Duncan Reed and his 8 apprentices make up the whole shop, but they turn out a considerable range of gray-stained redwood furniture, planters, and ornaments for the garden. The look of the pieces is distinctive, combining very blocky construction—necessary when working with redwood—with finely detailed leaf and animal patterns carved on the backs and elsewhere. My favorite of his garden benches is one with nothing but the smallest bit of scrollwork outlining the long back. It looks both very rustic and very elegant. There are a number of lounge chairs, deck chairs, and animal-shaped planters that are worth seeing, too. Reed must also have the distinction of having made the most elaborate picnic table ever.

Replogle Globes

1901 N. Narragansett Avenue
Chicago, IL 60639

- *Bronze, iron, or aluminum sundials.*
- *8-page catalogue, 24 color illustrations, $1.00.*

Replogle is one of the largest makers of globes in the world, but it also has a nice selection of cast-metal sundials. All are traditional in style, both flat and armillary (globe-shaped). Among the choices are 2 comparatively simple dials, one to be hung on a wall and one to be set into paving stone. The firm even offers a paper sundial that you can carry around with you. The version of the old alarm-clock dial—which used a magnifying glass to set off a little cannon at noon—is pretty but unfortunately doesn't work.

Robinson Iron Corporation

PO Drawer 1235
Alexander City, AL 35010

- *Wrought iron ornaments.*
- *8-page illustrated brochure, free.*

Robinson is very skilled at working and restoring decorative iron. Among other commissions, the firm has been involved in recasting the ironwork for the Bethesda Fountain in New York's Central Park. The brochure pictures mainly elaborate urns, fountains, statuary, and some beautiful custom gates. At first glance, not too much is surprising here, but the quality of the craftsmanship makes the catalogue worth a closer inspection. If you need fine custom work done and can afford it, this is a very good bet.

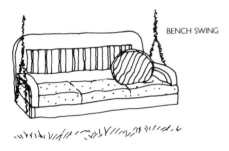

BENCH SWING

The Rocker Shop

1421 White Circle N.W.
PO Box 12
Marietta, GA 30061

- *Porch rockers and porch swing.*
- *4-page brochure, 13 illustrations, free.*

Ben Franklin is supposed to have designed the big, comfortable Brumby rocker. Be that as it may, it was a popular piece of furniture made by the Brumby Company in Marietta from shortly after the Civil War until World War II. Joel Chandler Harris wrote *Br'er Rabbit* while sitting in one. It is big and wide, with a lovely cane back and seat. The Rocker Shop has brought it back into production, as

the leader of a line that features 3 more rockers in similar styles, one for children. The company also offers a simple, slatted porch swing that is unaccountably lovely.

Mary Roehm

Clayworks
PO Box 960
Maples Road
Ellicottville, NY 14731

- *Porcelain and terra-cotta claywork, especially columns.*

If Columbine's columns (see page 201) are simple and spare, Mary Roehm's are wild. They may be topped by what looks like a cross between a beehive and a stack of plates. These would make a riveting focus in the garden.

Romaflex, Inc.

1815 Drew Road
Mississauga, Ontario
CANADA L5S 1J5

- *Rubber pavers.*
- *4-page color flyer, free.*

Elastocrete is the brand name of this company's rubber flooring material. It comes in a few shapes and colors and is considerably more attractive than the industrial-grade black pavers that line many city playgrounds.

Santa Barbara Greenhouses

1115-J Avenida Acaso
Camarillo, CA 93010

- *Partly prefabricated redwood-frame greenhouses; associated supplies.*
- *16-page catalogue, color and black-and-white illustrations, free.*

Glass or corrugated fiberglass is the glazing. Lean-to or freestanding, the redwood frames are simple and at-

tractive. All are glazed floor-to-ceiling, which makes them harder to keep warm in some climates, but also makes them prettier and gives you more planting room.

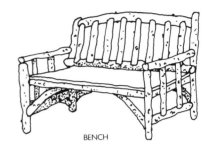

BENCH

San Francisco Victoriana

2245 Palou Avenue
San Francisco, CA 94124

- *Decorative wood and plaster moldings.*
- *60-page catalogue, many silhouettes of offered styles, $3.00.*

If you are restoring a Victorian house, this handsome catalogue will be of great use to you. SFV offers at least 200 off-the-shelf styles of Victorian moldings for both exterior and interior use. You can find everything from the simplest wooden wall molding to plaster brackets showing an alluring Lorelei in relief. For people without the house to work on, the ornaments could find a place on a garden wall.

Schwartz's Forge & Metalworks

PO Box 205
Forge Hollow Road
Deansboro, NY 13328

- *Ornamental metalwork.*

Joel Schwartz does a lot of fine ornamental door-and-grill work for architectural settings, but he has also done a few very interesting garden gates. One was constructed out of interlacing parabolas, topped with matching spirals and 2 birds beak-to-beak. The effect is unusual and delightful.

Sculpture Cast

PO Box 426
Roosevelt, NJ 08555

- *Limited editions of artist-designed statuary in bronze and cast stone.*
- *Variable-page brochure, with illustrated inserts, free.*

The selection varies according to what the associated artists produce and how quickly it sells—since the firm says it does not do second editions. The inserted cards consist of clear black-and-white pictures of the pieces, with descriptions of size, material, and quantity produced, and a brief biography of the artist. The artists are serious realists, usually well exhibited and with work in important collections. Emily Kaufman and Jeanna Pasley had some very fine sculptures of children in the catalogue I received, and Hilda Steckel had a funny and charming George Segal-like adult birdwatcher, his binoculars scanning the sky. All work is produced in cast stone or terra cotta, as well as bronze, making the pieces more affordable for those of us who have yet to become CEOs or financial barons.

Sculpture Design Imports

416 S. Robertson Boulevard
Los Angeles, CA 90048

- *Imported terra-cotta planters, urns, and 1 bench; carved stone statuary, benches, finials, and fountainpieces; Italian marble statuary and pedestals.*
- *32-page catalogue, 126 illustrations, some in color, $5.00.*

There is a very wide choice of terra-cotta pots here, and the simpler ones are quite lovely. The basket-weave styles and the other decorated urns and pots are generally less successful. Very simple amforas and Mediterranean-looking jugs are also attractive, and not often seen elsewhere. Unless your taste runs to Beverly Hills rococo, forget all the statuary and such, and yet, all of these faithfully copied old cherubs and lions and gods and wrestlers and Venuses are really so awful that they are practically charming.

Shakertown

1200 Kerron Street
Winlock, WA 98596

- *Fancy gingerbread Victorian shingles and siding.*
- *12-page brochure, free.*

For those with the house to accept it, Shakertown has a varied line of cedar shingles and siding. They are well illustrated and described in the catalogue, together with ideas for installing them.

Mark Sheehan

PO Box 1815
Ketchum, ID 83340

- *Sculpture and sculptured lighting, chiefly in mild steel.*

Sheehan works strictly on commission, so his work varies considerably with the wishes of his clients, but he seems to favor a sprung and asymmetrical style, full of tendrils and curving lines. He has made both free-standing sculpture and path lamps for the garden.

Smith & Hawken

25 Corte Madera
Mill Valley, CA 94941

- *Garden furniture and ornaments.*
- *24-page catalogue, approx. 45 color illustrations, $1.00.*

Paul Hawken has become a sort of New Age economic guru, thanks to his book *The Next Economy* and to his articles in the *Whole Earth Review*. His writing has a lot to say about the virtues and the means of mail-order selling—and his work is taken seriously in part because he has developed such a fine mail-order business himself. Smith & Hawken has been known for its catalogue of tools and garden supplies; recently, the firm has begun issuing a separate catalogue for furniture and ornaments. The choice among imported English benches, seats, and tables includes the usual Lutyens and Chippendale styles, along with a number of traditional but less commonly available styles. The airy backs of the "Suffolk Seating"—made with thin rectangles crossed by diagonals at the vertices—

 Apropos of garden statuary: a disquisition upon a minor genre

Must we be precluded because of our scale?
    A moment's thought will suggest that figures of a size to assert themselves
        among cedars, would appal the eye in a suburban plot. But we, sir,
        like you, will never admit the megalomaniac view. Discreetly
        the lupins overarch us

and silvery-fluted on our far skyline
        your palely-gleaming dustbin
is a lofty belvedere: that is romance
        enough for such pastoral

comedians as we are, whom you may trust
        not to make a lupanar
of your lawns.

—ROBERT DRUCE, FROM *JOURNAL OF GARDEN HISTORY* (1985)

are appealing. The undulating "wag-onbacks" of the "Cotswold" models—they look like webbing—deform the usual rectilinear quality of English seats in a lovely way. A very crazy but somehow elegant thing called the "Loveknot Garden Bench" has a back based on sections of circles. Look too at the hoopbacked iron benches; it is refreshing to see them, given the present prevalence of wood in the upper echelon of the trade. Among the offerings from American makers are single and double Adirondack lawn chairs and a number of different pieces in the blocky, carved redwood style now becoming popular. The redwood pieces are nice, but I don't like them as well as Duncan Reed's (see page 210). You can also get Victorian edging tiles, thatched dovecotes, and many more items besides.

Strassacker Bronze

PO Box 931
Spartanburg, SC 29304

- *Bronze sculpture, lamps, and fountains.*
- *75-page catalogue, many color illustrations, $10.00.*

Strassacker is a German company that casts original and limited-edition garden statuary, along with some figural and nonfigural fountains and garden lamps. The choice is enormous, both for full-round and relief figures, including the usual animal, bird, woman, and child themes, plus some less common motifs. I was particularly impressed with one tall figure of a sinuous woman in a simple dress and shawl, holding a staff in one hand and reaching toward the ground with another. A plain, ball-in-hand lamp in Art Nouveau style was also striking. But the majority of the figural sculpture seemed to me only partly successful. Some is cutesy,

and some puts too much detail into the drapery, hair, and face, giving the figures too much anecdotal reality for my taste.

Sturdi–Built Manufacturing Co.

11304 S.W. Boones Ferry Road
Portland, OR 97219

- *Partially prefabricated greenhouses and solariums; associated equipment.*
- *12-page catalogue, color illustrations, $2.00; 12-page accessories catalogue, black-and-white illustrations, $1.00.*

The 2 catalogues are well put together, offering many clearly explained options. The firm has been making redwood-frame greenhouses for about 30 years, and its selection of styles is very wide. It will also do custom modifications for you. The glazing is standard, but there is a thermal, shaded fiberglass option for a bit more money. The basic styles are more functional than they are attractive, but the firm's versatility has made for some very attractive installations, particularly in combination with the modern wooden homes of the West. On the other hand, Sturdi-Built has an apparently popular round greenhouse that looks like it was deposited by extraterrestrials. The products come partly preassembled with the doors already hung, so installation should be pretty simple.

Summit Furniture

PO Box S
Carmel, CA 93921

- *Garden furniture.*
- *7-page catalogue, approx. 24 color illustrations, free.*

The teak seats and benches are designed by an American, Kipp Stew-

art, and manufactured in Thailand. They are extraordinarily supple in look, with simple slatted backs and seats that bow and curve. I lust after the "First Cabin Bench," and if I ever make the collection of folding chairs I would like to, I would include the substantial, graceful "First Cabin Folding Chair." There is also an interesting chair that doubles as a dining chair and, matched with a folding table, reclines into a full-length lounge. The planters and light fixtures are meant to match the style of the furniture, but seem clunky.

Summitville Tiles

PO Box 73
Summitville, OH 43962

- *Quarry tile, ceramic tile, and floor brick.*
- *35-page general catalogue, some color illustrations relevant to garden uses, free.*

The brick—which is made of extruded shale—comes in a number of different textures, including a diamond tread and a grooved tread. It is frequently used in industrial plants, but the patterns make interesting choices for the garden. The quarry tile and brick come plain or in flashed colors. The firm will custom-glaze its ceramic tile to almost any color.

Suncraft

414 South Street
Elmhurst, IL 60126

- *Kits for greenhouses; associated supplies.*
- *Color brochure with inserts, free.*

Suncraft's "Superior" greenhouses are aluminum-framed with glass glazing. Lean-to and freestanding models are available. You have to do some work to build these—including some cutting and drilling in aluminum and glass—but the price is certainly right.

Sun Designs

PO Box 206
Delafield, WI 53018

- Books and plans for garden structures.
- 4 different volumes, 96–102 pages each, many illustrations, some in color; $7.95 each.

There are very few outdoor structures that Sun Designs has not thought of. It can send you complete plans for bridges, outhouses, lemonade stands, cupolas, birdhouses, cabanas, doghouses, barns, and more sorts of gazebos than you thought existed. The 4 volumes are as follows: *Gazebos and Other Garden Structure Designs; Bridges and Cupolas; Privy: The Classic Outhouse Book;* and *Backyard Structures* (cabanas, barns, studios, etc.). Each book contains at least 1 complete building plan, but the volumes serve mainly as illustrated portfolios of the plans that the company offers separately at prices from around $5 to about $40. The plans are very thorough and peppered with useful captions. They are not for a carpentry illiterate, but they are far easier to read and use than are ordinary blueprints.

Sunglo Solar Greenhouses

4441 26th Avenue W.
Seattle, WA 98199

- Acrylic solar greenhouse kits.
- 6-page brochure, color illustrations, free.

Sunglo makes both lean-to and freestanding greenhouses at competitive prices. Frames are aluminum, and windows are of a two-ply, insulated acrylic. Though the greenhouses are by no means works of beauty, they are simple enough in design to be versatile. The firm can install them, for an additional fee.

Topiary, Inc.

41 Bering Street
Tampa, FL 33606

- Topiary frames.
- 7-page catalogue, free.

Here's another good choice of cute, animal-shaped topiary frames, if you like that sort of thing.

GAZEBO

Tom Torrens: Sculpture Design

PO Box 1876
Gig Harbor, WA 98335

- Steel bells, gongs, and sculpture.
- 5-page illustrated description and price list, free.

The biggest part of Torrens's work consists of elegant, cylindrical bells, either set in sculptural standards or provided with chain for hanging. They are lovely and distinctive indeed. The sculptor has paid attention not only to the limpid form of the bells themselves, but to the hooks and eyes and chains that join the bell to its standard. The torii-style standards on some emphasize the Japanese influence on his design, though the bells have an Oriental flavor of their own. He has made everything from bells more than 4 feet tall to little ones that you can hang from the garden gate. The gongs are also lovely, though it's hard to guess how

you might use them. Torrens does other metal sculpture—including fountains, gates, and abstract pieces—so people with a particular object to commission might consult him as well.

David Tresize

2901 Pheasant Branch Road
Middleton, WI 53562

- Wall reliefs and garden statues in limestone and marble.

Tresize is a classically trained sculptor who can put an extra bit of care into the creation of traditional garden sculpture. A freestanding figure of Pan that he did for a private garden was a remarkable expression of the god's character: sitting with its hooves exposed, the figure, with a pensive and detailed face, was flanked by two large wings. Obviously, this was not your ordinary bit of garden statuary, but it uncannily caught the dilemma of a god more comfortable on earth than on Olympus.

Marian J. Vieux

1963 N. Summit Avenue
Milwaukee, WI 53211

- Tree-sculpture installations.

Vieux wraps trees. She takes a stand of second-growth forest and, when she is done, its trunks and branches are blue, red, black and zebra-striped. The wrapping is done with fiber, leather, and vinyl. It lasts only 1–6 months, but she produces Cibachrome prints of the installations, so you can keep a permanent record of them. The compositions are quite startling. They serve to reinforce, not detract from, the natural geometrical composition of the forest.

Vine Arts

PO Box 03014
Portland, OR 97203

- *Indoor and outdoor topiary frames.*
- *Color-illustrated catalogue, $2.50.*

Janet Schuster makes wire frames for topiary. Her catalogue is a menagerie of everything from bunnies and turtles to sizable deer. She will also undertake custom work.

Vixen Hill Manufacturing Co.

RD 2
Phoenixville, PA 19460

- *Modular cedar gazebos.*
- *4-page brochure, 14 color illustrations, free.*

You get your choice of Victorian and colonial styles here, though in truth they look much the same; only the details of railings and moldings are changed. Still, they are fairly attractive, and each is available in 4 different sizes: 9-, 12-, 15-, and 21-foot diameters. Just so you have an idea of who the company is aiming at, consider that the promotional copy recommends the gazebos not only for gardens, but for malls and for the "commercial campus."

Walpole Woodworkers

767 East Street
Walpole, MA 02081

- *Rustic cedar furniture and other garden furniture; wooden outbuildings; fencing.*
- *30-page furniture catalogue* Leisure Living, *more than 100 illustrations, some in color, $1.00; 16-page small-building catalogue, more than 25 illustrations, free; 28-page fencing catalogue* Beautiful Surroundings, *more than 90 illustrations, most in color, free.*

Walpole started making cedar fencing during the Depression, when wood was plentiful and hands were cheap. Finding itself with more wood than it needed, the company designed and began building a line of simple cedar-post furniture. From there, it went on to outbuildings—not elegant summerhouses or gazebos, but attractive, functional, pitch-roofed wooden structures with working doors and watertight windows. A year or two ago, Walpole took one further step—including a variety of furniture from other makers in its *Leisure Living* catalogue. The furniture comes partially assembled, but you must do the final construction yourself. It uses simple mortise-and-tenon joinery reinforced with screws and should be no trouble to put together. Because of its unfinished cedar-pole construction, the stuff has a generally rustic look, but the most attractive pieces are those that don't go out of their way to look countrified. The variety of outdoor pieces is as wide as you could wish, and because it's in kit form, it is less expensive than comparable finished furniture. I was particularly attracted by the canopied double swing. The furniture catalogue now features other stuff as well, including an American-made version of the ubiquitous European market umbrella; a nice set of wicker from St. John's; some of the often seen and widely useful outdoor dining and seating collections from Brown Jordan, and an extremely nice set of blue-cushioned white furniture from France.

The buildings are based on a modular system that lets you mix and match for any use, including tool shed, cabana, stable, storage room, playhouse, or screened-in summer dining area. If you live in New England, Walpole can install it for you; otherwise, you must do it yourself or hire someone locally.

When it comes to fences, Walpole makes everything from palisades to post-and-rail to picket to butted-board. The firm will also custom-design fencing, and, from the look of the fine catalogue, it appears that there are few things it cannot do. In fact, the catalogue itself would make a fine introduction to fence options for the garden. Walpole installs its own fencing in New England.

After having finished grafting roses the gardener finds that he ought again to loosen the baked and compact soil in the beds. This he does about six times a year, and invariably he throws out of the ground an incredible amount of stones and other rubbish. Apparently stones grow from some kind of seeds or eggs, or continually rise out of the mysterious interior of the earth; or perhaps the earth is sweating these stones somehow. The garden—or cultivated soil, also called humus, or mould—consists mainly of special ingredients, such as earth, manure, leafmould, peat, stones, pieces of glass, mugs, broken dishes, nails, wire, bones, Hussite arrows, silver paper from slabs of chocolate, bricks, old coins, old pipes, plate-glass, tiny mirrors, old labels, tins, bits of string, buttons, soles, dog droppings, coal, pot-handles, washbasins, dishcloths, bottles, sleepers, milkcans, buckles, horseshoes, jam tins, insulating material, scraps of newspapers, and innumerable other components which the astonished gardener digs up at every stirring of his beds. One day, perhaps, from underneath his tulips he will unearth an American stove, Attila's tomb, or the Sibylline Books; in a cultivated soil anything may be found.

—KAREL CAPEK, FROM *THE GARDENER'S YEAR* (1929)

Robert Walsh

Route 2
Box 101
Arkansaw, WI 54721

- *Ornamental iron, often with inset bronze pieces.*
- *Brochure with illustrated inserts, free.*

This is a small blacksmith shop that does fine iron work. Walsh's commissions have included gates for the Minnesota governor's mansion. Generally speaking, his style is medium-light, playing off the rectilinear form of a gate against the curved patterns of leafy and flowery branches. One small sculptural gate he has done—it's really a sculpture that is a pun on a gate—was a remarkable little polychromed piece, consisting of a simply worked blue rectangle inhabited by green fiddleheads and a nest of pink circles.

West Rindge Baskets

Rindge, NH 03461

- *Hand-woven ash baskets.*
- *4-page color brochure, free.*

There must be a couple of dozen of them, from picnic baskets to fruit-harvest baskets to trugs and planters. The firm has been making them, using much the same techniques, since 1925.

Wild Bird Supplies

4815 Oak Street
Crystal Lake, IL 60014

- *Bird feeders, birdhouses, feed, and supplies.*
- *32-page catalogue, approx. 85 illustrations, free.*

Here is every sort of wooden or plastic feeder, including feeders that attach to your window, hummingbird feeders, and simple suet feeders. Do you want a heated birdbath for the winter? You'll find it here. There is a wide variety of martin houses—some quite ambitious—plus some birdhouses in kit form.

Willsboro Wood Products

Box 336
Willsboro, NY 12996

- *Rustic cedar and oak furniture.*
- *12-page catalogue, black-and-white illustrations, free.*

The rustic cedar furniture has too much of a machine-made look for my taste. It is neither rough-hewn enough to look genuinely rustic, nor well enough finished to look elegant. Nevertheless, it looks extremely sturdy and serviceable. The picnic table here is well worth a look, as is a very nice folding version of the Adirondack chair, done in oak.

Dan Wilson & Co.

Highway 401 North
PO Box 566
Fuquay-Varina, NC 27526

- *Furniture and planters.*
- *5-page flyer, 12 illustrations, free.*

This is a 10-man craft shop, dedicated to reproducing traditional styles of wooden garden furniture and planters. The planters are the usual cratelike things, with finials and a variety of slatted patterns. The furniture is mainly in English styles, though the selection of patterns for bench backs is somewhat wider than in other catalogues. An extremely simple plank-backed bench was particularly lovely. Most furniture is of teak or mahogany.

BIRD BATH

Winterthur's Gift and Garden Sampler

Winterthur Museum and Gardens
Winterthur, DE 19735

- *Garden ornaments, plants and seeds, gifts.*
- *24-page catalogue, more than 80 color illustrations, free.*

There is more for the house than for the garden in this catalogue, but the few garden ornaments it offers are worth looking at. I particularly liked a pair of large cast iron storks and a couple of iron ducks. The lead-glazed basket-weave planter is very small and charming, but my favorite was a little heart-shaped plant hanger—a bracket-hung planter that frames a small plant in a light, simple heart of cast iron.

Wood Classics

RD 1
Box 455E
High Falls, NY 12440

- *Wooden garden furniture in kit or finished form.*
- *12-page catalogue, 14 color illustrations, $1.00.*

Wood Classics makes a number of different styles, all simple in look and all available in either teak or mahogany. The joinery is better than you might expect from a firm that offers kits, since most of the visible joints are finished with wooden pegs, not metal screws. I was a little skeptical about seeing the Adirondack lawn chair in mahogany, but I must admit it doesn't look bad. The seat, bench, and table set that makes up the "Versailles Line" looks elegant and versatile. The backs and seats are gracefully bowed. There is a lounge, some English-style seats and benches, a set of poolside rockers, a simple porch swing, and some planters and a birdfeeder, as well. The firm's picnic table is based on the Shaker trestle table and is one of the prettiest such things I have seen.

Woodplay

PO Box 27904
Raleigh, NC 27611

- *Children's play equipment.*
- *12-page catalogue, 42 illustrations, many in color, free.*

Here is a company that, like Child Life (see page 201), offers freestanding swing, slide, and jungle gym combinations that you can build yourself. The Child Life designs are based on 3-ladder construction, whereas Woodplay mixes ladders with a metal-pole crosspiece from which swings and the like are suspended. The choice of modular combinations and accessories is very wide. You can make up a unit that has everything from a lookout tower to a slide and a rope swing. Seesaws, balance beams, and sandboxes are also available.

Zanesville Stoneware Co.

309 Pershing Road
PO Box 605
Zanesville, OH 43702

- *Stoneware for indoor and outdoor use.*
- *20-page color catalogue, free.*

Zanesville offers an extremely broad choice of planters from 3 to 26 inches in diameter, available glazed or unglazed and in many colors. The styles are mainly traditional, some finished with vertical or horizontal striping and a few with swags or diamond-weave patterns. These are not outstanding pieces in themselves, but they are fine enough to serve as containers in almost any setting.

11 Landscape Architecture and Design

The Adventurous Gardener

by Christopher Lloyd
Random House

■ *248 pages, a few color illustrations, $17.95.*

The Well-Chosen Garden

by Christopher Lloyd
Harper & Row

■ *176 pages, many color illustrations, $18.45.*

Both of these books are composed of the pithy notes of a very experienced and imaginative gardener. Essentially, they are witty recountings of Lloyd's garden practice, under such headings as "Doubts and Torments" (about when to prune what), "Roses Need Company" (about roses in the landscape), and "Conifers Without Gnomery" (about a more relaxed use of ornamental conifers). The first volume listed above is particularly good on things like pruning and taking cuttings; the second one is unfailingly stimulating about landscape ideas.

The American Woman's Garden

Edited by Rosemary Verey and Ellen Samuels
Little, Brown & Co.

■ *192-pages, many color illustrations, $29.95.*

Rosemary Verey, who also co-edited the earlier *The Englishwoman's Garden*, points out in her introduction to this volume that the great thing about Gertrude Jekyll and Vita Sackville-West is that they gardened with their own hands, not via a team of experts. The present volume is a compendium of articles by American women who have done likewise. Each piece is accompanied by unusually fine photographs. The pictures are the thing. Even where the garden is of a scale that most of us will never manage, the photographers have focused on fine appositions of plants and of design elements, aspects of the garden that might inspire anyone. Then, too, many of the gardens—the best ones, to my mind—are on a small scale, so the whole plan may prove useful. The texts vary in style, but all reflect the enthusiasm and experience of women who would never hear of "low maintenance." My favorite, both for text and pictures, is the Connecticut garden of Ruth Levitan. Not only has she bit by bit created one of the nicest woodland gardens I've ever seen, she reveals in her writing the funny and pleasing story of a family at work on a landscape.

> The truth, of course, is that cacti deserve their special cult, if only because they are mysterious. The rose is beautiful, but not mysterious; among the mysterious plants are the lily, gentian, golden fern, the tree of knowledge, ancient trees as a whole, some mushrooms, mandrake, orchids, glacial flowers, poisonous and medicinal herbs, water-lilies, Mesembryanthemum, and cacti.
>
> —KAREL CAPEK, FROM *THE GARDENER'S YEAR* (1929)

The Art of Planting

by Graham Stuart Thomas
David R. Godine

■ *310 pages, many illustrations, some in color, $24.95.*

Thomas describes this book as "a catalogue of my own thoughts" about garden planning. His long chapter on color in the garden is a wide-ranging discussion of both theory and practice, full of apt suggestions and comments. Thomas has a very light touch, and he is not above dropping in mildly shocking remarks like the following: "A scheme which I have long had in mind but have never found the opportunity of using is coppery purple foliage with a foreground of orange flowers and lime-green leaves." The chapter on foliage textures is also very engaging, as is the long, wonderful list of plants according to both foliage texture and color. And you can find any number of bright ideas for the landscape uses of bulbs, roses, hedges, trees, and shrubs.

COREOPSIS

The Brickman Group

Long Grove Road
Long Grove, IL 60047

The largest landscape architecture firm in the country, Brickman has branch offices in Pennsylvania, New Jersey, Maryland, and Missouri. Along with a lot of large-scale work, it has also done many residences. The style is tasteful low-maintenance. The examples I have seen made best use of water features—both formal and informal—and of ground shaping. Lawns are set on gentle slopes, with well-placed trees.

> As for you, Campanula Alpina, I will make you a deeper bed. Work! even this messing with the soil you may call work, for I tell you it strains your back and knees; you are not doing this work because work is beautiful, or because it ennobles, or because it is healthy, but you do it so that a campanula will flower and a saxifrage will grow into a cushion. If you wish to celebrate anything, you should not celebrate this work of yours, but the campanula or saxifrage for which you are doing it. And if instead of writing articles and books you stand at a loom or a lathe, you would not do the job because it is work, but because you would get for it bacon and peas, or because you would have a crowd of children, and because you would like to live.
>
> —KAREL CAPEK, FROM *THE GARDENER'S YEAR* (1929)

Burton & Spitz

2324½ Michigan Avenue
Santa Monica, CA 90404

Pamela Burton and her younger partner Katherine Spitz are prominent members of the New Wave in California landscape design. Burton writes and lectures about the influence of postmodern art and ideas on gardens, particularly about the need to create rich symbolic tensions in a space. They have created many, many residential gardens in the Los Angeles area, the best of which elaborate the fertile contradictions between genius of place and aspirations of culture. One garden mixes areas of "oasis," using lots of color and water, with areas of "desert," featuring drought-tolerant native plants. Another contrasts design elements drawn from the European past with a plant palette of natives. To organize the contrasts, Burton and Spitz have had to develop facility in the handling of garden rooms and the links between them. A few of their gardens have used water for links, moving the visitor from swimming pool to *koi* pond to stream, to secret pool. Many of their spaces have also made use of the imagery of California agriculture, particularly citrus orchards. In such a naturally eclectic place as Los Angeles, their approach seems very valuable, since it focuses the contradictions that have been running all over the place for a century. You might expect their work to seem frenetic, but in fact, it is welcoming and embracing, having the quality of what they call "sanctuary."

A. E. Bye

523 E. Putnam Avenue
Greenwich, CT 06830

Some have argued that Bye's subtle gardens owe much to the English tradition of the landscape garden, but it is probable that the native-garden ideas of the Danish-American Jens Jensen are just as important to him. Bye generally works on a large, country scale. His creations are at first glance hard to tell from the general look of the countryside, because they intentionally draw their form and most of their plant material from the existing landscape. His work serves to bring the house into relation to its surroundings, layering native plant communities in a pattern that leads up to the dwelling or linking the habitation to the land form through the use of sinuous walls. His own book, *Art into Landscape, Landscape into Art*, is out of print, but it is worth looking for at the library.

Chinese Gardening

The Chinese Garden

by Maggie Keswick
Rizzoli International Publishers

- *216 pages, many illustrations, some color, $19.95 pbk.*

The Gardens of China

by Edwin T. Morris
Scribner's

- *288 pages, many illustrations, a few in color, $37.50.*

Creating a Chinese Garden

by David H. Engel
Timber Press

- *160 pages, many illustrations, a few in color, $38.95.*

The first 2 of these volumes are really cultural histories of the Chinese garden, and both are quite serviceable. I prefer the Keswick book because it takes a less pat view of the nature-culture question in China. There has recently been a sort of fad for the Chinese garden, based on the Chinese love of nature and understanding of ecological principles. Morris by no means falls headlong into this trap, but he does seem to promote something along these lines when he comments that "the modern taste for nature first appears in China," a crabbed concept if ever I heard one, for it is not *modern* to the Chinese at all. Perhaps the difference between Keswick and Morris's approach is clearest in the way they begin their books: Keswick starts with a chapter about the history of the idea of China in the West, where Morris starts with a consideration of Chinese philosophy. Keswick is always aware that there is a tension between Chinese practices and our understanding of them; Morris is not. She understands that nature was not for the ancient Chinese

anything comparable to the Romantic cult of Nature in the West; rather it was a symbol of universal order, rather as a Greco-Roman temple might be for us. There is no doubt that all this is very relevant to us today, particularly when it comes to thinking spiritually about ecology, but Keswick's approach is more gingerly and, to my mind, more entertaining as well. Her book also has the advantage of a fine concluding essay by Charles Jencks on the whole nature/culture question. This said, I should also say that I very much like Morris's concluding chapter on ways in which the Chinese garden might be adapted for the West.

Engel's book is specifically for the practical gardener, but it is also a brief and intelligent introduction to Chinese ideas. Because Engel is so experienced with Japanese garden-design concepts, he is remarkably good at contrasting the Chinese garden with the Japanese. His comments on garden making can either be applied literally—using the fine groups of photographs showing many choices for a given style or garden material—or taken on a more abstract level, concentrating on space division, garden circulation, directed views, contrast, depth, and sequence. Among the literal borrowings, the intricate Chinese paving patterns illustrated here (and in the other 2 books) seem ripe for imitation.

Color in Your Garden

by Penelope Hobhouse
Little, Brown & Co.

- *239 pages, many color illustrations, $34.00.*

Most garden design books fade off into generalities when it comes to using color. There simply isn't the space to consider the matter as it deserves. It's a very good thing, then,

that Hobhouse has devoted a whole, wonderfully illustrated book to the subject. Her chapters are broken down by color, with extensive plants lists and indications of the blooming sequence of each. There is also considerable material on successful color and textural juxtapositions.

Common Landscape of America, 1580-1845

by John R. Stilgoe
Yale University Press

- *429 pages, some illustrations, $12.95 pbk.*

Stilgoe, once a pupil of the fine landscape writer and teacher John Brinckerhoff Jackson, has written a remarkable volume about the American organization of space from the Colonial period until just before the Civil War. Though it won the Bancroft Prize for historiography, it is really as much a geography as it is a history, organized into chapters concerning different facets of the landscape: roads, farmsteads, the grid, sawmills, factories, furnaces, and the like. He has tried to drive a wedge between the American preoccupations with the city and the wilderness, arguing for the importance of the manmade rural landscape, a creation both of oral tradition and sophisticated planning. The book is incredibly detailed but seldom boring—including minutiae such as Daniel Boone's renunciation of American citizenship in favor of Spanish, in order to receive a land grant! Though it seldom talks about ornamental gardens, it is a fine antidote to all those design volumes which either assume we are debased Europeans or impose a set of rules on a supposed *tabula rasa*. Stilgoe tells us what we have had and explores our attitude toward it. There are perhaps few better summaries of the American attitude to the land than the one contained in the early 19th-century quotation with which he begins his last chapter: "The Americans love their country not, indeed, as it is, but as it will be. They do not love the land of their fathers; but they are sincerely attached to that which their children are destined to inherit. They live in the future, and make their country as they go on."

> 🌱 Our eyes do not divide us from the world, but unite us with it. Let this be known to be true. Let us then abandon the simplicity of separation and give unity its due. Let us abandon the self-mutilation which has been our way and give expression to the potential harmony of man-nature. The world is abundant, we require only a deference born of understanding to fulfill man's promise. Man is that uniquely conscious creature who can perceive and express. He must become the steward of the biosphere. To do this he must design with nature.
>
> —IAN L. McHARG, FROM *DESIGN WITH NATURE* (1971)

The Contained Garden

by Kenneth A. Beckett et al.
Viking Penguin

- *168 pages, many color illustrations, $12.95 pbk.*

This is a sort of complete garden book in miniature, with soil, climate, planting, propagation, design, pest control, and plant variety information all tailored for container growing. As such, it often repeats information you may well have from other books, but when it comes to making mixed container plantings and designing groups of pots to fit a given situation, the advice is quite detailed and useful. As with so many garden books, this is a British import, but it is well-adapted for American use. Only the color photographs remain exclusively British. It's too bad, because although the complex plantings give us many good ideas, the ambience in which they are set is too often unlike those we encounter here in the U.S. The detailed list of container plants, complete with variety recommendations, is handy, though perhaps it is skewed a bit too far to warmer climate species. The volume opens with a few nice pages of pictures representing every kind of readily available pot or planter, which makes for a solid vocabulary. I wish they'd included a few found-object pots as well. (One of my favorite container gardens was planted in old tennis shoes.)

Cottage Garden Designs

The Hampton Gardener
PO Box 620
Southampton, NY 11968

- *One of a series. 12-36 pages, many illustrations.*

The Hampton Gardener has published some very handy and well-researched booklets, useful to anyone planning a perennials garden. In addition to *Cottage Garden Designs*, Hampton publishes *Design for Shaded Gardens*, *English Garden Designs*, and *Perennial Border Designs*. The firm is a wholesale nursery specializing in perennials, so they know whereof they speak. The volumes are essentially pattern books, with paint-by-numbers illustrations telling you exactly what to plant where in the overall scheme. Each volume covers a number of different garden situations and styles. The Cottage and English garden books actually model the plans on historical gardens or garden types. Note that the plant selections for "English" gardens are adapted for American use.

Designing and Maintaining Your Edible Landscape Naturally

by Robert Kourik
The Edible Landscape Book Project
PO Box 1841
Santa Rosa, CA 95402

- *400 pages, many illustrations, $16.95 pbk.*

This fat book is of particular interest to gardeners in Northern California, but many of its recommendations can be applied elsewhere. Kourik goes into an enormous amount of detail about designing a garden to integrate edible plants, from ground-hugging herbs to fruit trees.

Design on the Land

by Norman T. Newton
Harvard University Press

- *714 pages, many illustrations, $35.00*

Dry as the writing can be, this book contains about the best one-volume synopsis of the history of landscape design that I know. Everyone will tell you that Queen Hatshepsut imported trees, but it takes Newton to assess the form of her mortuary temple at Deir-el-Bahari. His assessments of the great gardens of classical antiquity and of Europe are clear, detailed, accurate, and revealing. The plans and elevations that accompany many of these descriptions tell you as much about the actual look of the places as could pages of text. (Some of the drawings come from Harvard's collections and are not widely seen outside this book.) In modern times, Newton focuses more on public parks and expositions than on private gardens, but he is always lucid, providing a remarkable window into the designed world.

Design with Nature

by Ian McHarg
Doubleday

- *198 pages, many illustrations, $15.95 pbk.*

In his introduction, Lewis Mumford calls this "a book to live with." He wasn't kidding. It would take any number of readings to absorb it all, in spite of McHarg's uncannily accessible and even inspiring way with topics like physiography and ecology. The book is really directed toward land planners, not gardeners, but I strongly recommend it for 2 reasons. First, it is a founding text of modern ecological planning, important not only to large-scale planners but to all those landscape designers and gardeners who speak of designs appropriate to the land. Second, it is a short course in the ecology and physiography of almost any region you might be gardening in. When another book admonishes you to fit your garden into the landscape, McHarg will tell you in great and enthralling detail just what that means. By the way, McHarg likes cities, which to my mind already sets him head and shoulders above quite a number of "ecologists."

The Education of a Gardener

by Russell Page
Random House

- *382 pages, a few illustrations, $8.95.*

"I last had a garden of my own when I was eighteen," confesses Russell Page at the outset of this fine memoir. No matter. He has since created everything from a window box to a corporate-headquarters garden for clients all over the world. Page is the master of what we might call a reception-and-response aesthetic, shaping his gardens as a harmony of society and nature, house and landscape, plant and soil. He forthrightly declares, "I know that I cannot make anything new." The book is modest and proud at the same time, telling everything from Page's chance introduction to horticulture to his uniquely various experiences with gardens and gardeners. It ends with a charming portrait of the garden he might make, if he had the place and time.

Engel/GGP

204 W. 27th Street
New York, NY 10001

David Engel and his group are perhaps the leading landscape designers in America, when it comes to using Japanese garden principles in an American way. Engel gardens don't look Japanesey—they are not full of lanterns or rock galleries or bamboo—but they are everywhere informed by a Japanese sense of the importance of space, contrasting materials, and intriguing asymmetry. The gardens are never all of a piece; they are evolving compositions that must be explored to be experienced. His use of stone—contrasting formal and informal shapes—and his symbolic use of plant groupings to suggest elements of landform are among the group's hallmarks.

English Cottage Gardens

by Ethne Clarke and Clay Perry
Viking Penguin

- *160 pages, many color illustrations, $25.00.*

This is a gift for your favorite flower gardener. Text is brief, though lively, and the captions sometimes, but not always, tell you what flowers you are seeing. The photos are the thing. The cottage garden is a sort of idealization of the English middle-class gardening styles, and when the gardens are taken in full flower, they are striking. The book ranges through the seasons, taking each of a number of gardens at their peak. Some terrific ideas appear here—including a low wall inlaid with bits of crockery collected from the plate-smashing booth at church bazaars—but mainly it is a collection of flower gardens to wish for.

Falcon & Bueno

4061 Battersea Road
Coconut Grove, FL 33133

The team embarks on whole site projects, Falcon designing the house and Bueno the garden. It is a fertile collaboration, because Florida is one of the few places in the country where indoor/outdoor living is more than a summer-season thing. House and garden make full use of the subtropical climate, typically borrowing not only from vernacular architectural styles but from the colorful palette suited to the place. The structures themselves provide the main elements of color, plants filling in with foliage color, texture, and accent flowers. Doors open to walled patios, which themselves extend into further garden rooms delimited by trellises, hedges, or allees of palms.

Barbara Fealy

4805 S.W. Chestnut Place
Beaverton, OR 97005

If you garden in the coastal Northwest, you had better be used to shade and rain. Fealy's gardens make good use of both, counting heavily on ericaceous plants and on natives of the region's forests. Though her work makes prominent use of shrubs and trees, hers is by no means the usual low-maintenance, deck-and-woodland style. She pays plenty of attention to hard surfaces and paths through the garden, and she has a particularly sensitive eye for the placement of stones and boulders as focal points along the way.

Fundamentals of Landscape Planning

by James B. Root
AVI Publishing Company

- *158 pages, many illustrations, $29.95.*

The book would serve well as the text for an introductory course in landscape architecture. Its virtue, as compared to most design volumes made for gardeners, is that it briefly explains the physical and chemical properties accounting for such things as soil composition, acidity, and the effect of fertilizers. The section on the basic principles of design is not rich in examples, but it does do a nice job of laying out the basic options for the composition of space.

The Garden Book

by John Brookes
Crown

- *287 pages, many color and black-and-white illustrations. $22.50.*

John Brookes is a well-respected garden designer in Britain. In some ways, *The Garden Book* may be seen as a response to his countryman Hugh Johnson's well-known *The Principles of Gardening.* Perhaps, on the other hand, the 2 books are simply complementary. Where Johnson concentrates on plants and plantsmanship—the traditional English garden virtues—Brookes is the exponent of modern garden design and concentrates on space planning. I recall how

miffed I was to discover that Johnson didn't mention the great American garden designer Thomas Church until the brief section on modern design at the very end of his book. Brookes starts right out with a nice synopsis of modern design and its relevance for us, illustrating his points with American examples drawn from the work of Church and Christopher Tunnard.

RABBIT

He clearly believes that gardens are for living in, not simply for admiring. Of course, Brookes is not without Old World ideas. Whenever he refers to the swimming pool, he prefaces the words with the adjective "fashionable," reminding me of the English cabinet minister who at the turn of the century sent a spy to look at the new pool at Andrew Carnegie's English manor. The servant reported, "Well, it does savor of the parvenoo." Regardless, Brookes' approach to gardening by way of design is a good idea, and it is well carried out in this book. As with all such books, some of the advice about site, climate, and the like seems self-evident, but in almost every case, Brookes backs up his general observations with excellent photographs and drawings that really are illuminating. Too many of the photographs are of European origin, but the whole section of example gardens—chosen for their archetypal appropriateness to a given site problem—can still give New World gardeners ideas. Furthermore, each of the gardens is faced with one or more alternative plans for the same space, executed in fine color drawings on the facing page. As often happens in

books of this nature, when it comes to suggesting how to actually make the garden, there is a large gap between the good general advice and some very specific and difficult-looking instructions. This is particularly true when it comes to building a wall or surveying the whole garden area. To Brookes' credit, he's fit a lot of information into a small space, using illustrations to help us visualize the process. For the first time, I think, I actually understand how "boning"—the rough measurement of a slope's gradient—is done.

Garden Design

by Douglas, Frey, Johnson, Littlefield, and Van Valkenburgh
Simon & Schuster

- *224 pages, many color illustrations, $35.00.*

I edited this book. The pictures are generally very strong, and unlike many such all-color garden volumes, their subjects are predominantly American. The text tries to skirt the line between over general "advice" and over specific instructions: where it succeeds best is in laying out an unusual number of choices for the gardener to consider. I felt that we had too little on planting design, but what we do have, written by landscape architect Michael Van Valkenburgh, is very good. Look too at the "Designer's Choice" section, where Susan Littlefield profiled the work of 15 prominent designers. William Lake Douglas, Susan Frey and Norman Johnson—all at the time editors at the American Society of Landscape Architects—provide chapters on design principles, personal style, and history. If you want to see examples of the work of some of the people I consider in this chapter, you can find them in *Garden Design.*

Garden Design Magazine

American Society of Landscape Architects
1733 Connecticut Avenue N.W.
Washington, DC 20009

■ *116-page quarterly, many color illustrations, annual subscription $20.00.*

When *Garden Design* started a few years ago, it seemed to have trouble deciding whether to simply feature ASLA members' work or to tackle broader issues of the residential landscape. There was a notable break between the very fine (and nowadays almost impossible) estate gardens and the sometimes undistinguished recent works that appeared side by side. Though the break is still sometimes noticeable, the magazine as a whole has matured into a good balance of well-illustrated articles about specific gardens, notes on ornamental genera, and columns about landscape elements. The general quality of the members' gardens included seems also to have risen, as has the quality of the photographs and the layout. The groundplans of all featured gardens are included in a section at the back. All that I could wish of the magazine now is that it do for the home garden what Grady Clay managed to do with landscape architecture in general during the 1950s and 1960s, when he made the society's professional magazine *Landscape Architecture* into a forum for the exchange of ideas about what the common landscape should look like and how designers might go about changing it.

The Gardener's Garden

Photographs by Jerry Harpur
David R. Godine

■ *158 pages, many illustrations, most in color, $27.50.*

Harpur combed Britain for fine gardens by professional gardeners, combining his own sensitive photographs with texts contributed by the gardeners themselves. Some of the writing is a bit dull, but some is fine indeed, including Peter Borlase's story of how he was hired. The then-head gardener first put a watering can in his hand and told him to water only the pots that needed it; then, he made the young man shoot a wood pigeon using only one cartridge! The gardens are mainly on the estate scale, so the specific design lessons here are few. The pity is that Harpur's very good photos have been reproduced so poorly in the book. You get a good idea of mass and color, but they lack that detail that makes you say, "That's exactly what I want to try!"

The Gardener's Handbook of Edible Plants

See "Vegetables and Herbs."

Isabelle C. Greene & Associates

34 E. Sola Street
Santa Barbara, CA 93101

Isabelle Greene has created hundreds of gardens in and around Santa Barbara and on the coast of Southern California. Her work is remarkably sensitive to the requirements of climate, to the needs of the clients, and to her own vision of each space on which she works. She is particularly fond of drought-tolerant natives and succulents, but her settings for these and other plantings depend on very fertile imagination.

Hardesty Associates

855 Oak Grove Avenue
Suite 205
Menlo Park, CA 94025

Nancy Hardesty and her team regard themselves as stewards of the land, meaning that they like to keep and nurture what is there. The firm won an ASLA Award of Merit in 1984 for their work on the Portola Valley Ranch development in the oak-and-grass lands west of Palo Alto in northern California. They are specialists in the fitting of habitations to their ecosystem, particularly for the coastal region they know best; the ASLA jury praised them for focusing on the preservation of whole ecosystems, not just the endangered species. The spiral-bound *Oak Woodland Preservation and Land Planning* volume, prepared as part of the Portola Valley project, is a terrific resource for people who garden in California's coastal oak regions. It contains notes on the planting and care of many native herbaceous and woody plants—in-

---

BIRD OF PARADISE
It was proposed, that the Queen's health be drunk. An odd, ill-favoured little fellow in the company expressed his opinion, that Queen Caroline were better styled her Botanick, than her Britannic majesty, on account of her botanizing, and great regard for the Linnaeans. And he described the monstrous flower, that had lately come to his Majesty's gardens at Kew from the Cape Colony, named for her majesty's natal German Province of Strelitz.

—MICHAEL TEWES AND GEOFFREY SHARP, FROM *THE ALMANAC OF WIT* (1779)

cluding many different oaks—plus suggestions for inviting wildlife and dealing with the common weeds.

Heavenly Caves: Reflections on the Garden Grotto

by Naomi Miller
George Braziller

- *141-pages, many illustrations, $10.95 pbk.*

This sounds like a book to skim, but it isn't. Scholarly as Miller's book is, it is a fascinating exploration of the variety of grottoes made from classical Greek times until the end of the 19th century. To me, it was a revelation to learn that those twin icons of high culture—the Parthenon and Mount Parnassus—have foundations that are honeycombed with grottoes dedicated to Pan and other not-quite-respectable gods. Miller's suggestion that grottoes represent the whole gardening impulse in miniature is lovely, helping one to focus on the continual tension between nature and design that is found in all gardens. As usual, I was disappointed to find little information on recent grottoes and a scant chapter on the Christian grotto, the main avenue of these things into our own world. (People in immigrant Catholic neighborhoods will be familiar with dozens of more or less elaborate grotto-ized Virgins.) When I complained to a friend who is a fountain of information on almost any subject, he immediately put me onto a book edited by Steven Ohrn, from Iowa State University Press, called *Passing Time and Traditions,* which contains a long, illustrated profile of Iowa folk artist Paul Friedlein. Friedlein's amazing grottoesque stonework is much influenced by the grottoes of the German Franciscans.

Above all, Miller's book made me want to do elaborate and baroque things in the garden. Perhaps it will do the same for you, in which case you might consult the essay on Friedlein for a beautiful example of where you might end up.

Herb Garden Design

See "Vegetables and Herbs."

The History of Gardens

by Christopher Thacker
University of California Press

- *288 pages, many color and black-and-white illustrations, $16.95 pbk.*

I have put a lot of garden history and scholarly reflection into this book, because it seems to me that we are now in a time when we should consider and use the whole range of garden traditions, not just the lowest maintenance or most limpid modernist ideas. Thacker's book gives a somewhat compressed but altogether lively account of that history from Babylon to Russell Page, with a few side trips to the Middle and Far East. Unfortunately, it says nothing at all about New World gardening, and it suffers in regard to plain-people's gardens, concentrating entirely on the great works. The Far Eastern sections seemed weakest to me, but the chapters on the great French and English gardens of the 17th and 18th centuries were very good. Among other things, Thacker points out that gardens were then central to European high culture. His descriptions of the theatrical uses of French gardens, and his fine discrimination between the styles of English gardening that

are often lumped under "landscape school" are both valuable. Overall the text is a virtual bibliography in itself, with many well-chosen quotes and old and new illustrations, but the volume also includes a good bibliography at the back. Gardeners who want to know more may find that their first library stop will be to peruse Marie-Luise Gothein's classic *A History of Garden Art.*

LINDEN

Innocenti & Webel

The Studio
Box 250
Greenvale, NY 11548

This team began working on Long Island's estate gardens back in the 1930s, but then made an uncommonly successful transition to smaller spaces, preserving a moderately formal style that is nonetheless very relaxed in tone. The firm now works a whole "L" of the nation, stretching from New York through Florida to Texas. They use hard surfaces (always related to the material of the house) extensively, and they create both ornamental and swimming pools that contribute to the overall shape of the garden. They are also experts at creating interest in a flat yard by means of more or less formal parterres, filled with massed, appropriate plantings.

Italian Villas and Their Gardens

by Edith Wharton
Da Capo Press

- *270 pages, $8.95 pbk.*

What Norman Newton's terrific section on Renaissance Italian gardens (see page 221) lacks in colorful writing, novelist Edith Wharton more than makes up for. Of course, the gardens do not now look exactly as she described them, but her descriptions are remarkably evocative without being florid. In this book, you get 2 classics in one: a great travel book and a fine garden book.

Japanese Gardening

A Japanese Touch for Your Garden

by Kyoshi Seike, Masanobu Kudo, and David H. Engel
Kodansha

- *80 pages, many color illustrations, $18.75.*

Space and Illusion in the Japanese Garden

by Teiji Itoh
Weatherhill

- *229 pages, many illustrations, a few in color, $11.95 pbk.*

There are endless books about the Japanese garden, but most of them are just glossy picture books. These 2 are among the more interesting. The first is an introduction to Japanese garden materials, not to their philosophy. The authors suggest adapting a corner of your garden to the Japanese manner, or using some of the materials in a non-Japanese garden. The second approach seems more interesting to me, perhaps because I have less than fond memories of the perfect Japanese courtyard gar-

den outside my dentist's window when I was a child. The garden felt as separate from my ordinary experience as the whirring drill. Nevertheless, the pictures are the thing in the first book: the authors have made little pictorial anthologies of paving and gravel treatments, other pathway ideas, fences, lanterns, bridges, and the like. The specific planning section at the end gives very complete instructions for placing stones and for building bamboo fences.

Teiji Itoh's *Space and Illusion* doesn't pretend to cover the whole range of Japanese gardens, sticking to courtyard and borrowed-landscape gardening, but it is wonderful for its double focus and for its comparative lack of posturing. Itoh has in fact done very much what the Japanese garden itself does—making a virtue of the strong contrast of opposites. The garden may play light against shadow; Itoh plays the most inward-looking Japanese garden—the *tsubo-niwa*, or courtyard garden—against the most outward-looking—the borrowed landscape garden. In doing so, he has also provided us with a well-focused historical and philosophical look at the 2 forms of Japanese practice most adaptable to the West.

Thomas Jefferson's Garden Book

Edited by Edwin Morris Betts
American Philosophical Society
PO Box 40098
Philadelphia, PA 19106

- *704 pages, some illustrations, $25.00*

This book includes Jefferson's garden notebook, complete with his plans for Monticello and elsewhere, but Edwin Betts has created the majority of the book from Jefferson's voluminous correspondence about plants and the garden. The result is a

wonderful life in letters and notes of America's most ambitious early gardener. So detailed are the entries that the preservationists at Monticello are now using them to reconstruct Jefferson's original gardens. His curiosity and willingness to experiment were endless. At one period of his life, he was desperate to start olive plantations in Virginia; then it was breadfruit trees. His correspondence stretched around the world. I would like to have this book by my bedside for the rest of my life (along with the book of the correspondence between Jefferson and John Adams), and as soon I can afford to buy it, I will.

Gertrude Jekyll

The Gardener's Essential Gertrude Jekyll

David R. Godine

- *283 pages, $8.95 pbk.*

Children and Gardens

Antique Collector's Club
Woodbridge,
Suffolk,
ENGLAND

- *110 pages, many illustrations.*

Colour Schemes for the Flower Garden

Antique Collector's Club

- *326 pages, many illustrations, some in color.*

Lilies for English Gardens

Antique Collector's Club

- *152 pages, some illustrations, some in color.*

Wall and Water Gardens

Antique Collector's Club

- *177 pages, many illustrations, some in color.*

Wood and Garden

Antique Collector's Club

- *286 pages, some illustrations, a few in color.*

It is hard to believe that Gertrude Jekyll didn't publish her first book until the age of 56. She wrote 13 of them in all; the ones listed above (written between 1899 and 1908) are the major ones that have been re-printed, except for *Roses* (see page 162). Perhaps the uninitiated would do best to start with *The Essential Gertrude Jekyll,* an anthology of her work that groups quotations from her books according to theme. Then, if you have the money and the nerve, you can plow through the individual volumes.

ORCHID

Jekyll is deservedly revered for her insistence on softer and more natural landscapes, the use of hardy plants, and the composition of gardens into a series of nested "pictures." The more informal styles of planting beds, borders, and woodlands owe much to her inspiration and writing. Nonetheless, she was a tough lady who worked in army boots. In her first volume she wrote, "I have lived among outdoor flowers for many years, and have not spared myself in the way of actual labor, and have come to be on closely intimate and friendly terms with a great many growing things, and have acquired certain instincts which, though not clearly defined, are of the nature of useful knowledge." From such a painstaking statement of her qualifications, one might expect a woman who is just as stringent with plants and indeed, she seems always to be trying to decide whether a given flower is worthy of her interest or not.

Journal of Garden History

Taylor & Francis
Rankine Road, Basingstoke
Hants
ENGLAND RG24 0PR

- *Variable-length quarterly, many illustrations, annual subscription $48.00.*

As its price suggests, this fine, scholarly journal, edited by John Dixon Hunt, is not for the casually interested. It contains articles and reviews chiefly by professors on all aspects of garden and park design. Most articles cover British or continental gardens and designers—almost always with a very specific focus—but there is more than occasional material on such things as early American gardening, great (and lesser known) American gardens in European styles, and even a piece on Western Canada's first landscape architect. Now and again, there's even a poem. Book reviews also concentrate on British titles, but for many gardeners who have trouble keeping abreast of U.K. books not published here, this may be a real service. The magazine also does an annual bibliography.

David Kropp

See "Wildflowers and Native Plants."

Landscape Architecture

by John Ormsbee Simonds
Second Edition, 1983
McGraw-Hill

- *331-pages, many black-and-white illustrations.*

Few textbooks ever achieve the style, grace, and general usefulness of this one. For all that Simonds is a bit of a knee-jerk ecologist and for all that the quotations with which he peppers the text savor of the 60s (when the first edition came out), this book provides the professional or amateur gardener with an entire design vocabulary, attractively set forth and beautifully illustrated with Simond's clear sketches. It is not a how-to book, so you will not learn a lot about actual installations. What you will find out about are the many possible relations of man to the land, with countless persuasive suggestions for defining volumes, designing walls or fences, establishing the emotional quality of line, using water features, fitting the garden to the site, and you name it. He even provides checklists of matters to consider when designing in different geographic regions. Like many landscape architects, he claims perhaps too large a role for the professional planner, but his book has certainly given nonprofessionals a remarkable set of tools for making decisions on their own. His paeans to the earth can be tiresome, but they are basically right-minded, and whenever the writing threatens to get technical, they give it a little goose.

SENSITIVE FERN

The Landscape Book

by Jack E. Ingels
Van Nostrand Reinhold

- *273 pages, many illustrations, $23.50.*

Here is what you expect from a landscape textbook. It's dry and written to a fairly low level of comprehension. Nevertheless, it is serviceable for most major design topics, especially for the nuts-and-bolts of putting a landscape plan on paper. For some reason, it has an unusually good section on arid-land gardening for the Southwest, complete with a very good, annotated list of appropriate plants for that landscape.

The Landscape of Man

by Susan and Geoffrey Jellicoe
Prairie Avenue Bookshop
711 S. Dearborn
Chicago, IL 60605

- *400-pages, many black-and-white illustrations, $19.95 pbk.*

I have not read the revised edition of this recently out-of-print classic. It is probably the best one-volume introduction we have to the history of man in the landscape. Geoffrey Jellicoe is one of Britain's leading landscape designers. Look for it.

Landscape Plants in Design

See "Trees and Shrubs."

PALM

Landscape Techniques

Edited by A. E. Weddle
Van Nostrand Reinhold

- *265-pages, many illustrations, $19.50 pbk.*

Written for and by professionals, the book is very technical and very British. In fact, Van Nostrand has simply released the U.K. edition here, without any adjustment for the American market. Still, it is written by authorities like Sylvia Crowe and Brian Hackett, so its advice is worth seeing for those who want nitty-gritty information that must usually be translated for North American use. For the general reader, the illustrations and the charts are extremely helpful. Among the latter appears a very good list of the relative growth rates of landscape trees and a comparison of the relative cost and wear-resistance of different paving materials. Probably most of us will see this one in the library.

Lois Lister

145 Farnham Avenue
Toronto, Ontario
CANADA M4V 1H7

Lister was born in England, and her Toronto gardens show the British regard for a strong but informal plan, filled out with lovely foliage and flower borders. Her designs work by gradual transitions, level changes, and linking paths, not by "rooms." Aside from her wonderful eye for the composition of herbaceous borders, her gardens are notable for the very sensitive use of hard paving materials in combination. She may create a lawn-flanking path out of flagstone, for instance, marking points of interest and seating by means of granite sets that intrude a little way onto the path. She is very careful in the placement and design of pools, realizing that if they are not well-designed for ornamental value, they may simply be eyesores for most of the year. People who like to work with their own flower gardens will be happy to know that she encourages clients to participate in working out the contents of beds and borders.

The Low Maintenance Garden

by Graham Rose
Viking Penguin

- *168 pages, many color illustrations, $12.95.*

"There is a myriad of solutions to the problem of reducing gardening effort," writes Graham Rose, but he doesn't seem to have found many of them. According to his introduction, we are in the midst of a revolution which is offering us better and hardier plants, improved watering systems, lovely pesticides and herbicides, and all sorts of labor-saving devices. In fact, that revolution is the better part of a century old, though admittedly it did not really take off until after World War II. Though he goes out of his way to make even fairly elaborate garden features—like an artificial pond—seem easy, his how-to section at the back includes propagation techniques like air- and ground-layering, hardly the kinds of techniques I associate with "low maintenance." The only thing that really qualifies the book for its title, I suppose, is that it includes no gardens with large expanses of grass to mow. It isn't a bad book, really, but the effort to make everything seem easy results in some overly sanguine remarks. A cement pond, for example, is not necessarily either easier or more flexible than one made with PVC, and you can't simply fill it and add the plants. (Concrete releases lime into the water, so it must be treated.) Furthermore, a wildflower meadow is not just a matter of clearing the ground, raking in the seed, and sitting back for the rest of your life. Most "wildflower" mixes include a large percentage of annuals, so you will have to reseed your meadow more often than you may think.

Robert E. Marvin and Associates

Route 4
Box 10
Walterboro, SC 29488

Robert Marvin is a fine Southeastern landscape architect, who, among many other projects, has done the garden design for a number of houses at Hilton Head, South Carolina. Both his parents were raised on South Carolina plantations, so he comes from a cultural and physical milieu that suits him well for design in his region. Like a number of postwar landscape architects, he is in his glory when he can work as a team with the building architect, the two designing the total living environment. He has a real commitment to the home as "a place where the habits, hobbies, pleasures and friendships of the entire family can find expression." It is good to see a landscape architect who suggests, among other things, that the living room might be replaced with a hobby room, so the whole family can *do* things together. Outdoors, he works to combine hard-surfaced seating areas or decks with extensions into the garden that express the character of the place. For a home on the South Carolina coast, for example, he fit a broad patio into the southern angle of the house, extending a curvilinear sand space from it that extends toward the beach but is framed by a low, brick sea wall. From one corner of the patio, a long boardwalk extends along the beach, articulated with an informal beach deck about halfway down its axis. The design for his own home is extremely naturalistic, matching a lovely rustic deck with the surrounding native woodlands, relating the simple geometry of the wooden house to the garden with an outline of angled beds raised on a tier of brick.

Medieval English Gardens

by Teresa McLean
Viking Penguin

- *298 pages, a few illustrations, $25.00.*

McLean has an interesting biography. Among other things, she worked for a year with Mother Teresa in Calcutta.

Whether or not this fact betrays a long interest on the writer's part in matters Christian, it is true that the best parts of this book are its accounts of medieval monasteries and its reflections on the Marian cult of the rose. She puts the matter succinctly and beautifully: "Mary's motherhood enclosed the whole of heaven and earth within her womb, within the space of a single round rose." She probably drew the description from a phrase used by the 4th century St. Ephrem of Syria, which she later quotes: "The God whom the whole earth could not contain did Mary contain and carry." It's enough to make you a rose gardener. For the rest, the text on medieval secular gardening is too rich in lists and account books, too brief in its laying out of the social fabric of the time. The bulk of the book amounts to entries describing the primary plants used in medieval gardens, with more or less interesting notes on their provenance, culture, and lore.

Natural Landscaping

See "Wildflowers and Native Plants."

Nature's Design

See "Wildflowers and Native Plants."

The Necessity for Ruins

by John Brinckerhoff Jackson
University of Massachusetts Press

- *129 pages, $6.95.*

In "Nearer Than Eden," a perceptive essay in this remarkable book, the author writes, "Whenever we search the garden for mythical reminders, whenever we search for traces of the Garden of Eden or the experience of a

mystical state of being, we are searching in the wrong place. The garden satisfies the aspirations of everyday existence: work shared with a few companions, family or neighbors, work that has quality and measure, capable at best of humanizing a small fragment of nature." I have never seen a better definition of the pleasure of gardening. In this essay and in "Gardens To Decipher," Jackson gives us suggestive portraits of the common and the designed gardens, illuminating the whole history of the field in just a few pages. The other essays in the book—on the street, the garage, the sacred grove, the need for ruins (not restorations), and the landscape as theater—may strike you, as

> I am strongly for treating garden and wooded ground in a pictorial way, namely with large effects, and in the second place, with beautiful incidents, and for so arranging plants and trees and grassy spaces that they look happy and at home, and make no parade of conscious effort.
>
> —GERTRUDE JEKYLL, FROM *WOOD AND GARDEN* (1983)

they struck me, with the force of revelation. Jackson is no nativist and no ecologist—his knowledge ranges over the whole Western tradition—but he is certainly among the best and most lively observers of the American landscape scene we have. If you get hooked, read *Landscapes* next. (It's also from the U. of Mass. Press.) After that, you will perhaps want to tackle the magazine he founded in 1951 and ran until 1968. It is called *Landscape* and subtitled "Magazine of Human Geography." It may be hard to find it in the library, but if you can, you will be glad you did.

Oehme, Van Sweden & Associates

3813 N Street N.W.
Washington, DC 20007

Oehme and Van Sweden are experts at making the most dramatic uses of smaller spaces, though their practice is not limited to them. The larger ornamental grasses, and similar plants with striking forms and arresting textures and color, are the hallmarks of many of their works. Like most designers who work on the scale of modern American homes, Oehme and Van Sweden start formally near the house, gradually erasing straight lines and formal feel as they approach the perimeter of the property. Their style makes very heavy and designed use of the above-mentioned plants, and it should be noted that one of the best things about the grasses they favor is that they may persist through winter, adding excellent color and texture to what might otherwise seem a barren landscape.

The Oxford Companion To Gardens

Edited by Jellicoe, Jellicoe, Goode and Lancaster
Oxford University Press

■ *635 pages, some illustrations, a few color, $49.95.*

The price is high, but the book delivers. There are over 1500 entries covering gardens, designers, and landscape terms from around the world. Over 200 experts contributed to the tome, including such leading folks as John Brookes, Garrett Eckbo, Sylvia Crowe, John Dixon Hunt, Geoffrey and Susan Jellicoe, Graham Stuart Thomas, and Diane Kostial McGuire. All together, they leave few stones unturned, from ancient Greek *paradeisos* to the landscape work of Lawrence Halprin. Particularly nice is the large number of entries devoted to modern gardens and design. As usual, there is too little focus on the common gardens of ordinary people, but if they had tried to include such things, you wouldn't have been able to lift the book. Being an old fan of the Jellicoes' *Landscape of Man,* (see page 228), I was a little put off by the alphabetical format here, particularly in comparison with that remarkable historical survey of the field. I learned from the *Companion,* however, that the historical book is about to come back into print. Hurrah!

Paradise as a Garden in Persian and Mughal India

by Elizabeth B. Moynihan
George Braziller

■ *168 pages, many illustrations, $9.95 pbk.*

Moynihan's focus on the "paradise" garden makes not only an interesting and not too abstruse discussion of the type, but a very nice introduction to the civilization of the region. This is all to the good for gardeners, since the garden played such an important role in those cultures and since a great number of our garden plants made their way into Western gardens during the period she studies. She has, for example, fascinating pages on Islamic and Norman Sicily, showing how the shifting patterns of invasion resulted in the transfer of important useful and ornamental species. You can find out how we got the peony, the apricot, the crocus, and any number of other plants. The work is also a fine account of early irrigation and agricultural practice, including such tidbits as the Safavids' use of "pigeon towers" as a source of fertilizer.

For those who would like to read a fine garden designer's book on the same subject, you can go to the library to find Sylvia Crowe's out-of-print *The Gardens of Mughal India.* She gives a very good reason for our continued interest in the paradise: there, for the first time, the strictness of geometry was combined with luxuriance of organic growth.

Plants in the Landscape

by Philip L. Carpenter et al.
W. H. Freeman & Co.

■ *481 pages, many illustrations, $33.95.*

Here is a much-used textbook for the professional. Its brief history of landscape design is interesting to the gardener, as is the nice chapter on the origin of our common landscape plants. Most of the rest deals with such things as cost estimates and large-scale projects. If you want to get an idea of how your landscape architect figures out how much to charge you, here is a place to find out.

The Principles of Gardening

by Hugh Johnson
Simon & Schuster

■ *272 pages, many color illustrations, $17.95 pbk.*

Sections on the history of design are stuck at the back of the book, which is appropriate since this is a volume for the beginning plantsperson. As such, it is one of the finest available. Johnson's introductions to all sorts of plants for every situation are really first-rate, and his sections on soil, water, light, plant exploring, nursery practice, and other related topics are models of clarity for the general reader. It *is* a British book, transplanted to our continent, so you will find not-too-relevant sections on things like "The Peat Garden," but overall the coverage is very fine indeed. Where the genus is complex—as in roses or tulips or azaleas—Johnson provides at least a well-made and illustrated summary of the garden types and at most a whole genealogy of the modern types. The only thing that bothers me about the book is the virtual lack of coverage of American ideas and styles, natural perhaps in a British plantsman. Still, given the horrors that American low-maintenance landscaping has often created, Johnson can't be blamed for his position.

Pursuing Innocent Pleasures: The Gardening World of Alexander Pope

by Peter Martin
Archon Books
925 Sherman Avenue
PO Box 4327
Hamden, CT 06514

- *310 pages, some illustrations, $27.50.*

With its plain purple cover and its many footnotes, this volume looks like scholarship, and indeed it is, but it's scholarship of the finest humanistic sort. All the ground has been covered before, but Martin chooses to focus on Pope's life as a gardener, both at his own place, Twickenham, and among the gardens and estates of his friends. What we get then, is a Pope's-eye-view of the gardens of his time. Pope is just the person for this, because unlike many of his contemporaries, he gardened on a comparatively small scale and according to his own tastes. He regarded himself as a lover of nature, but he viewed classical culture in a way that made his gardens anything but endless woods and meadows. The challenge for us is to come to terms with Pope's

elaborate grotto, his mount, and his shell-festooned temple as examples of a "natural" style. The poet wrote, "Simplicity is the Mean between Ostentation and Rusticity." He gardened with and in the name of nature, but not simply by means of nature, making him a lively antidote to some of our more naive ecological notions. It would be fun to read this book against Jane Brown's *Vita's Other World* (see page 232), a similar effort to focus on a prominent British figure's life in the garden. Both books twine their subjects' poetry with their gardens, but Pope was a great poet at a time when gardening was central to his culture, while Vita Sackville-West was a minor poet who found refuge in her garden at a time when gardening had become marginal to the wider culture. His was an assertion of a vibrant culture; hers was a holding action against a terrifying one. Vita's Sissinghurst is perhaps the most famous private garden in the world today, and Pope's attracted similar attention during his lifetime.

Rhetoric and Roses: A History of Canadian Gardening, 1900-1930

by Edwinna Von Baeyer
Fitzhenry & Whiteside
195 Allstate Parkway
Markham, Ontario
CANADA L3R 4T8

- *197 pages, many illustrations, $29.95*

It is good to see a garden history that focuses on Canada as a whole, though it's too bad Von Baeyer chose to limit herself so strictly as to period. The strongest material is on the great estate gardens, including some very surprising gardens set in the wilds of the Yukon. She has tried to include reflections on the role of vernacular and civic gardening—chiefly on the

City Beautiful and the School Garden movements, and on the influence of the railroad. I wish that there were more on these.

Room Outside

by John Brookes
Thames and Hudson

- *192 pages, many illustrations, $10.95.*

This was Brookes' first design book for the general public. Published in 1969, it was first released in this country in 1985. Though some of the material seems dated—especially styles of paving, seating, and the like—it is still a very valuable source-book for principles of modern garden design. In fact, I prefer it in many ways to his more recent and extremely thorough *The Garden Book,* because it is clean, direct, and not overstuffed with information and suggestions. In everything from title to illustrations to text, *Room Outside* embodies the modern approach. Brookes wrote in his introduction, "We have allowed ourselves to be conned into believing that the garden is only a set-piece for showing off plants." In the 60s in England, those were fighting words, as were his frank espousal of American and Scandinavian garden ideas. Still, they were moderated by a continuing respect for actual work in the garden, perhaps the strongest thing about the British tradition. He writes, "There is a difference between hard manual labour, which should be kept to minimum, and pottering. Pottering is to be recommended for anybody suffering from any form of nervous tension." The black-and-white photographs and the drawings illustrate design ideas and methods which, for the most part, have lost none of their relevance today. The book is incisive, written with grace and humor.

The Victory Garden Landscape Guide

See "General Sources."

Vita Sackville-West

V. Sackville-West's Garden Book

Edited by Philippa Nicolson
Atheneum

■ *250 pages, a few color and black-and-white illustrations, $9.95 pbk.*

Vita's Other World

by Jane Brown
Viking Penguin

■ *240 pages, many illustrations, a few color, $20.00.*

There are not one but several industries dedicated to writings by and about Vita Sackville-West. Back in the early 70s, we college kids were fascinated with her son's *Portrait of a Marriage,* a lively book about the many love affairs and abiding love for each other of Vita and her husband, Harold Nicolson. This, we thought, was a model for open marriage. It was therefore doubly enjoyable to me to read Vita on gardens and Jane Brown's gardening biography of Vita, since they revealed that the epitome of radical love I had idolized was in many ways a very conservative woman of unflaggingly aristocratic taste.

Philippa Nicolson has edited the four volumes of Vita's garden writing—all of which first appeared in her newspaper columns—into one volume, organized by the months of the year. In one of her fine travel books about her time in Persia, Vita had written that one can say only one thing about Persian gardens . . . and say it again and again. Reading her garden

writing, one is tempted to say that people of taste say only one thing about gardening . . . again and again. She doesn't like garish flowers—the climbing rose "American Pillar" is her particular enemy—and she is none too fond of the horticultural experiments that produce, say, the double-flowering snowdrop. What makes this collection of occasional pieces very valuable, however, is not her strictures but her suggestions. Here you will find a charming and tentative exposition of her original idea for a one-color garden, a disquisition on arranging cut flowers as a means of planning color schemes for the border, an idea for growing clematis on a horizontal trellis, a number of suggestions of her favorite varieties or species of many, many plants and in short, more good ideas than usually appear between a single set of book covers.

Brown's biography, though its occasional chumminess with the reader becomes annoying, sets Vita's garden writing in the context of a full and emotionally difficult life. Brown believes that a person's garden reflects his or her deepest feelings—that the garden is a sort of biography in itself—and in Vita's case, she proves her point delightfully. There are not only considerations of her subject's own gardens—from the estate garden of her childhood, to her gardens in Persia and at Long Barn and Sissinghurst—but information on other gardeners and gardens she knew: people like Norah Lindsey, Jekyll, and Lutyens, and places like Hidcote. The period photographs wonderfully illustrate the evolution of Vita's gardens. Brown's effort to show the relations between Vita's poems—mainly *The Land* and *The Garden*—and the actual gardens is stimulating. It gives us nice chunks of a poetry little seen these days, and it convincingly shows that both garden and poem were responses to the changes that two wars brought to Vita's world.

Hal E. Stringer & Associates

4579 Lake Shore Drive
Waco, TX 76710

Stringer is another designer who has worked at Hilton Head, but the majority of his private gardens have been done in Texas. He designs everything from tiny courtyards to large estates. There seems to be little surprising in his work, but the modern outdoor-living style of Southern gardens is confidently expressed. He is particularly good at combining hard surfaces for dining and entertaining with the existing trees in the landscape, framing the trees with plantings that may be as simple or as various as the client wants. One of his Texas gardens uses a stepped amphitheater to separate patio from the deeper garden. Viewed from the house, the steps are invisible, making the transition immediate; seen deeper in the garden, the hard geometry of the steps smoothes the transition to the architecture of the house.

Three Gardens: The Personal Odyssey of a Great Plantsman and Gardener

by Graham Stuart Thomas
Capability's Books
Box 114
Highway 46
Deer Park, WI 54007

■ *189 pages, many illustrations, $29.95.*

Thomas is one of the great British plantsmen of this century. His reflections on the apprenticeship he served in his father's gardens and the formative influences on him are worth reading in themselves. The sections on his own gardens are rewarding both for their biographical interest and for the discussions of the planting plans that formed them. It's good to find a gardener so well able to tell what he has done and why.

TKA – Landscape Architects

8801 Lafayette Road
Indianapolis, IN 46278

Principal John Clayton Thomas works in a subtle, naturalistic style. Areas of lawn, streams, and other features may be articulated with low walls or banks of native stone. Simplicity and informality are important. An entryway, for example, may be emphasized only by a slight slope given to the lawn in front of it.

Michael Van Valkenburgh

23 Myrtle Avenue
Cambridge, MA 02138

Here is a young garden designer who teaches planting design at Harvard. He does lovely work on the scale of a small country place or suburban/urban yard, articulating spaces within the gardens by means of witty puns on classical architectural features. The gardens may contain column-based arbors in radically simplified styles, pathway arches made of painted metal tubing, or gabled archways that repeat the line of the accompanying house. He is also skilled at matching pathway materials and colors to ingenious combinations of groundcovers, foliage and flowering plants, and hedges. His control of textures and colors is delightful.

How much I long sometimes for a courtyard flagged with huge grey paving-stones. I dream of it at night, and I think of it in the daytime, and I make pictures in my mind, and I know with the reasonable part of myself that never in this life shall I achieve such a thing, but still I continue to envy the fortunate people who live in a stone country . . . . In this courtyard should grow all kinds of low plants between the flags, encouraged to seed themselves freely . . .
—*V. SACKVILLE-WEST'S GARDEN BOOK* (1983)

12 Regional Sources

Because state cooperative extension services, botanical gardens, arboretums, and horticultural societies so frequently provide advice and information tailored specifically to their regions, I have placed all of their listings here together with some of the more important historical gardening sites. In some cases, a publication produced by a local or regional group will be valuable to gardeners elsewhere; such publications are simply listed here, but marked with an asterisk (*) to indicate that they are discussed in the appropriate section of GBS. Please note that in the case of cooperative extensions, I have not listed every relevant publication published by a given group. Pamphlets on pruning, pests, general culture, and the like, are available from almost every cooperative extension, and many of the different extensions share a single publication. What I have tried to include are all those pamphlets and books specifically geared to the problems and opportunities of the group's own region. Titles with no price in the entry are offered free of charge. If you want a

complete list of the titles offered by any of the listed state organizations, just request it from the appropriate address I have supplied. The extension catalogues are good reading in themselves, since they cover everything from clothing and family life to swine and group dynamics. Where else could you find a pamphlet on "Wall Attachments," another on "Soil Injection of Sewage Sludge for Crop Production," a third on "Vital Signs in Animals," and a fourth on "How to Motivate People in Groups?" I suspect that the cooperative extension publications are among the most underused resources in the country. By writing to the listed address, you can also get a list of the county agents in your state. The agent for your county is the person to go to for direct advice. Many botanical gardens, arboretums, and horticultural societies also offer help with specific gardening problems. Please note that not every state's cooperative extension is listed here; when a state did not respond to my queries, I could not provide an entry. I hope this does not reflect upon their service in general.

Alabama Cooperative Extension Service

Auburn University
Auburn, AL 36849

A good run of sheets and pamphlets on ornamentals, turf grasses, fruits and vegetables, and insect and disease control are available from this service, free of charge.

Alabama Gardener's Calendar
Pecan Production
Rhododendrons in Alabama

Alaska Cooperative Extension Service

University of Alaska
Fairbanks, AK 99701

Alaska has advantages as well as disadvantages for the gardener, and the extension service can provide information on both. In "Carrots in Alaska," for instance, we learn that the disease called aster yellows does not occur in the state, so carrots there are never bitter. The publications catalogue is worth having, since you can order from it everything from a pamphlet on grantsmanship or marketing the uniqueness of a small town to sheets about reindeer health, sealskins, building log cabins, and air-raid shelters for animals. The home gardening list is not long, but all items on it are tailored to Alaska growing. Pamphlets are free unless otherwise marked.

The Compost Heap in Alaska

Gardening in Southeastern Alaska, $.65

A Key to Flower Growing in Alaska, $1.00

Landscape Plant Materials for Alaska, $5.00

Sixteen Easy Steps to Gardening in Alaska, $.75

Vegetables and Fruits for Alaska:
Recommended Varieties for Interior Alaska
Recommended Varieties for South Central Alaska
Recommended Varieties for Southeastern Alaska

Fennel, radish, wild oat, all of these plants are Mediterraneans. In those countries they mostly grow pretty much as they do in California, at the edges of towns, on modern dumps and ancient ruins, around Greek temples and in the barbed-wire enclosures of concentration camps. Where did they come from? They have been with man too long for any quick answer. They were old when Troy was new. Some of them are certainly Asiatic, some African, many of them are mongrels in the strictest technical sense.

—EDGAR ANDERSON, FROM PLANTS, MAN & LIFE (1967)

Arizona Cooperative Extension Service

University of Arizona
Room 301
Forbes Building
Tucson, AZ 85721

The Arizona extension offers an unusual run of pamphlets on fruits, nuts, vegetables, and ornamentals, largely because the flora and the physiography of the state are out of the ordinary. Through the Boyce Thompson Arboretum and the Office of Arid Land Studies, it also offers a fine magazine, *Desert Plants,* and a number of books, bibliographies, and reports on jojoba, Indian water rights, and appropriate technology. Larger pamphlets, books, and magazines are priced; Arizona residents may order their first 10 extension reports free, the remainder at $.05 per page. Out-of-state residents pay $.05 per page for any report.

Annual Flower Guide (Southern Arizona), 4pp.

Annual and Perennial Gardens Above 4,500 Feet, 8 pp.

Bulbs for Northern Arizona, 7 pp.

Bulbs for Southern Arizona, 4 pp.

Cactus, Agave, Yucca, and Ocotillo, 2 pp.

Care and Weeding of Desert Landscapes and Rock-Covered Areas, 4 pp.

Conquering Home Yard Caliche, 2 pp.

Deciduous Fruit Varieties (3,500–7,000 Feet), 2 pp.

Desert Plants, quarterly, annual subscription $12.00*

Flowering Periods for Common Desert Plants, poster, $1.00*

Ground Covers for Arizona Landscapes, 16 pp.

Hot Weather Effects on Landscape Plants, 3 pp.

Jojoba and Its Uses, $5.00

Landscape Vines for Southern Arizona, 8 pp.

Mesquites in the Landscape, 4 pp.

Overseeding the Desert (discusses wildflower seeding), 1 p.

Palo Verdes in the Landscape, 4 pp.

Perennial Flower Guide (Southern Arizona), 4 pp.

The Pocket Gopher in Arizona, 2 pp.

Production of Jojoba in Arizona, 2 pp.

Roses for Arizona, 7 pp.

Arkansas Cooperative Extension Service

PO Box 391
Little Rock, AR 72203

Send for the catalogue. It has a good list of leaflets about the care and protection of most major vegetables and fruit trees, all offered free. The "Family Life" section offers 16 sheets about "Cradle Criers," followed by publications called "Understanding Depression" and "Dealing with Anger."

Vegetable Gardening in Arkansas, $2.65

Vegetable Varieties for Arkansas Gardeners

Bernardo Beach Native Plant Farm

See "Wildflowers and Native Plants."

The Blue Ridge Farm Museum

The Blue Ridge Institute
Ferrum College
Ferrum, VA 24088

■ *Living-history farm, the educational arm of the Institute.*

The Institute runs an unusually good and serious program for the study of indigenous Blue Ridge culture. The farm now has an 1800 farmstead with kitchen garden, and a 1900 subsistence-farm project is under way. Visiting groups can participate in farm chores, and the Institute sponsors a folk-life festival on the 4th Sunday in October, complete with coon dogs and a draft-horse-and-mule show.

Brooklyn Botanic Garden

1000 Washington Avenue
Brooklyn, NY 11225

▪ *Annual membership $15.00, includes 4 issues of* Plants & Gardens *(quarterly newsletter), shop discounts, plant information service, and access to research library.*

The many booklets offered in *Plants & Gardens* are highly respected. Several are reviewed in appropriate places throughout this volume. Members of the Garden receive the 4 current numbers in the series free. The brand-new newsletter is very attractive and is most useful for its culling of ideas from professional horticultural journals and its "Where to Find It" column. Brooklyn, however, offers nowhere near the selection of courses that its sister institution, the New York Botanical Garden (see page 244), does.

California Cooperative Extension Service

University of California
6701 San Pablo Avenue
Oakland, CA 94608

Get the catalogue. Each of the sections on home orchards, home yards, and vegetables contains more how-to-grow and how-to-protect pamphlets than do the whole publications lists of many states. The brochures meant for commercial growers include interesting ones on integrated pest management for fruit and nut trees and for leaf crops. Aspiring vintners will want to look at the recommendations on grape varieties for different parts of the state. Here is my limited choice of the most intriguing titles:

An Annotated Checklist of Ornamental Plants of Coastal Southern California, $12.00

An Annotated Checklist of Woody Ornamental Plants of California, Oregon, and Washington, $4.00

Fruit, Nut and Grape Varieties for Home Orchards:
  Mother Lode Counties, $1.00
  San Mateo and San Francisco
  Counties, $4.00

Generalized Soil Map of California, $2.00

Growers Weed Indentification Handbook, $55.00 with binder, new sheets in groups of 16, $4.25 per group*

Growing Coast and Sierra Redwoods Outside Their Natural Ranges, $1.00

A Guide to Shrubs for Coastal California, $1.75

A History of the Strawberry, $10.00*

Insect Identification Handbook, $6.50*

Landscape Trees for the Great Central Valley of California, $1.25

Native California Plants for Ornamental Use, $1.00

Ornamentals for California's Middle Elevation Desert, $1.00

Planning for Your Mountain Property, $1.00

LILAC

California Garden

San Diego Floral Association and Garden Center
Casa del Prado
Balboa Park
San Diego, CA 92101

▪ *Bimonthly magazine, some black-and-white illustrations, annual subscription $5.00.*

Its title aside, this is a magazine for *Southern* California gardeners. Its local calendar and garden-clubs listings are great for networking in the San Diego area. A helpful section called

"Now Is the Time" reminds you of what to do with specialty plants and ordinary garden plants and vegetables during the season of the issue. Each issue features reader-contributed articles, especially on the exotics that can be grown outdoors or indoors in Southern California.

Connecticut Cooperative Extension Service

University of Connecticut
College of Agriculture and Natural Resources
U-35, 1376 Storrs Road
Storrs, CT 06286

You will do best to send for the catalogue. Very good lists of pamphlets are offered for such topics as plant diseases, fruits and berries, greenhouses, houseplants, plant pests, lawns and gardens, trees, and vegetables. The subject of each pamphlet is usually narrowly defined.

Connecticut Soils Primer, $.40

Growing Strawberries in Connecticut, $.50

Conner Prairie

13400 Allisonville Road
Noblesville, IN 46060

▪ *Living-history pioneer settlement, 1823 mansion, and 1836 village.*

Located very close to Indianapolis, this is one of the more elaborate living-history museums in the country, featuring mock weddings, court sessions, temperance society meetings, and so on. Well-made herb, dye, vegetable and flower gardens are planted in the three separate areas of the museum, and courses on period gardening are offered regularly.

Cornell Plantations

One Plantations Road
Ithaca, NY 14850

- *Arboretum and botanical garden.*
- *Classes in horticulture; extensive tree, herb, and wildflower plantings; 16-36-page quarterly* Cornell Plantations; *annual membership $6.00.*

A great place to learn about gardening, especially about wildflowers and herbs, the Plantations also publish two fine books, *An Herb Garden Companion* and *Green Dragons and Doll's-Eyes,* the latter about wildflowers. Both are meant as guides to the Plantations' gardens, but they are excellent general reference books as well. The quarterly has one newsy issue per year; the other three are devoted to quirky and interesting topics, such as the ancient spice trade and the shapes of snowflakes.

Desert Plants

See "Wildflowers and Native Plants."

Florida Cooperative Extension Service

University of Florida
Gainesville, FL 32611

No list of publications exists, and the state extension service refers callers to local county agents. One good publication, which is produced at Florida A&M in Tallahassee, is *Grow a Row of Vegetables in Florida,* a folder that includes recommended varieties and planting instructions for most home vegetable crops. It is free to Florida residents.

Flowering Plants in the Landscape

See "Wildflowers and Native Plants."

Georgia Cooperative Extension Service

Hoke Smith Building
University of Georgia
Athens, GA 30602

Georgia's publication list contains the usual information on pest and disease control, lawn care, propagating and pruning, and the use of ornamentals like azaleas and roses. The number of pamphlets about problems could frighten off would-be settlers, with titles like "Stray Voltage in Dairies," "Accident Extrication Procedures," "Controlling Head Lice," and "Snakes and Their Control."

Centipede Lawns
Bermudagrasses in Georgia
Ornamentals for the Georgia Mountains

Rose Culture for Georgia Gardeners
Small Garden Plan for Georgia

Greener Gardening, Easier

E. Dexter Davis
26 Norfolk Street
Holliston, MA 01746

- *4-page monthly newsletter, annual subscription $10.00.*

Davis's newsletter is a sometimes crotchety and very miscellaneous thing, but it is of interest to gardeners in the Northeast and especially Massachusetts. It contains garden tips, addresses of interesting smaller societies and groups, information on soil testing, and suggested varieties of plants drawn from local nurseries. One never knows what one will find here. One book review is of a popular paperback on general gardening; the next may discuss a 200-copies-only encyclopedia of American woods, complete with 16 volumes of actual wood sections! A recent piece of garden advice suggested that you practice your seed-sowing technique by doing it indoors on a piece of soft cloth, until you get the spacing right.

Hans Herr House

1849 Hans Herr Drive
Willow Street, PA 17584

- *Historic 1719 farmstead, oldest Mennonite meeting house in America.*

Located near Lancaster, this place maintains a kitchen garden and an orchard of antique apple varieties, as well as a museum of agricultural implements. Gardeners can get information here on the gardening and horticulture of the 18th century.

The Horticultural Society of New York

128 W. 58th Street
New York, NY 10019

■ *Nonprofit organization, newsletter, and education programs guide; copublishes* Garden, *bi-monthly; "Plant-Line" call-in service; library; annual membership $25.00; full annual membership $50.00.*

The New York "Hort" runs many classes and garden tours—some for members only, some for which members receive a discount. It also sponsors the prestigious New York Flower Show. Members can call the Plant-Line service for help with gardening questions. As one might expect from a horticultural society founded in 1900, the smell of Guerlain wafts through the place, in the wake of many bright, older plantswomen. Local chapters of garden-specialty clubs frequently meet here. There are a couple of more unusual services at the "Hort," too. The Community Services Program is endlessly helpful to the city's large number of community gardeners. The library has excellent periodical resources and a pretty good book collection, though you must pay the $50.00 membership fee if you want to check books out.

Idaho Cooperative Extension Service

University of Idaho
Moscow, ID 83843

You can learn a lot about the character of a state by looking at what its extension service publishes. The publications list for grains, sugar beets, and, of course, potatoes is a lesson in the Idaho economy. Potato advice is plentiful: one leaflet concerns "Thumbnail Cracks in Potatoes"; another, entitled "Influencing Seed Tuber Behavior," sounds like

seed psychology; and a third is a complete computer simulation of potato physiology. In all aspects of horticulture, except ornamentals, the Idaho extension is very strong. There are specific leaflets for each of the major vegetables, and the lists of sheets about soils, fertilizers, and pests seem endless.

Flowering Crabs for Idaho Gardens, $.25

Fruit Varieties for Idaho, $.50

Ornamental Hedges for Idaho, $.35

Plant Materials for Landscaping—A List of Plants for the Pacific Northwest, $.50

Potato Varieties for Idaho, $.35

Selecting Turfgrasses for Idaho Lawns, $.35

Tomatoes for Southeastern Idaho, $.25

University of Idaho Soils Handbooks, $17.00

Vegetable Varieties for Home Gardens in Idaho's Cooler Areas, $.35

Vegetable Varieties for Idaho Gardens, $.35

Illinois Cooperative Extension Service

University of Illinois at Champaign-Urbana
College of Agriculture
47 Mumford Hall
1301 W. Gregory Drive
Urbana, IL 61801

Illinois has a small but unusually good set of publications—many of them full-fledged books—for the home gardener. Some are of interest not only to Illinois residents but to people throughout the Midwest. County-by-county soil profiles are also available.

Beekeeping in the Midwest, 160 pp., 85 illustrations, $5.50

Dwarf Shrubs for the Midwest, 171 pp., 364 illustrations, $8.00

Flowering Trees for the Midwest, 100 pp., 170 illustrations, $8.00

Groundcovers for the Midwest, 188 pp., 200 illustrations, $8.00

Growing Illinois Trees from Seed, Circular 1219, $1.50

Illinois Fruit and Vegetable Garden Schedule, 40 pp. $2.00

Illinois Lawn Care and Establishment, $1.50

Landscaping Your Home, 246 pp., $5.00

Nut Growing in Illinois, Circular 1102, $.15

Tree Fruit and Nut Varieties for Illinois Home Orchards, Circular 998, $.10

Vegetable Gardening for Illinois, 140 pp. $6.00

Weeds of The North Central States, 303 pp., $3.00*

Indiana Cooperative Extension Service

Purdue University
Horticulture Department
West Lafayette, IN 47907

Indiana has a separate publications list devoted to home-yard and garden topics. It is strong in most areas, including flowers, houseplants, and landscape architecture. Leaflets are narrowly focused, so it's best to send for the list and choose what you need yourself. The Department of Horticulture runs a quite extensive vegetable-and-flower garden at Purdue, where gardeners can look at both commercially available and experimental varieties.

Iowa Cooperative Extension Service

Iowa State University
Horticulture Building
Ames, IA 50011

The publications offered for the home gardener represent a small fraction of the huge list of items on every aspect of rural life, from stress on the farm to drug withdrawal in chickens. Still, the home vegetables and fruits list is very good. Iowa is a state that offers county-by-county soil surveys. It also offers a home-garden telephone reference service, called Hortline. You can call 1-800-262-2224, toll free, Monday through Friday.

Characteristics and Sources of Apple Cultivars

Characteristics and Sources of Pear Cultivars

Landscape Plants for Iowa, $3.00

Suggested Vegetable Cultivars

Shuffling is good for you, Margaret & Henry Taylor Cousin John started it. He's a solid sort of chap, the kind who sits in the correct spot in his room to listen to Mahler on his hi-fi. Though not to my knowledge a Fred Astaire fan, he sure is a conifer freak, and artistic with it. "That *Picea albertiana conica* of yours is a ghastly green, quite out of place beside its neighbours". Proud of our plant we naturally scoffed, but after John's departure, thinking that there might just be something in his suggestion, we shuffled the plant to another site. It hurt to admit it, but the conifer collection did look better.

—FROM *THE ROCK GARDEN*. (1986)

Jourdan-Bachman Pioneer Farm

11418 Sprinkle Cut Off Road
Austin, TX 78754

■ *Nonprofit organization running an 1880s Texas farm; some heirloom seed distributed on-site; mimeographed book,* A Guide to Heirloom Seeds, *free.*

The farm re-creates a cotton planter's, a sharecropper's, and a

---

homesteader's lifestyle, all on one piece of property. You can get some heirloom seed here, but the nicest thing the farm has is *A Guide to Heirloom Seeds.* A lot of the information has been picked up from Carolyn Jabs's books (see page 132) or other sources, but Eve Williams's list of heritage seeds for Texas, complete with sources, is unique and useful. Many of the varieties she lists have no current source, so you might enjoy combing the region in search of them. Williams says she has also developed an heirlooms list for orchard trees of central Texas, also available free.

Oliver H. Kelley Farm

15788 Kelley Farm Road
Elk River, MN 55330

■ *Historical farm formerly owned by a founder of the Grange; extensive involvement in heirloom crops and vegetables; 3-page list of historical documentation and modern sources for varieties grown on the farm, free.*

Among the members of the Association of Living History Farms and Agricultural Museums (ALHFAM), Tom Woods at the Kelley Farm is one of the most active people in heirloom gardening. He has done careful research on the varieties once grown at the farm and has prepared a good list telling where he found out about them and where to get them.

Kentucky Cooperative Extension Service

University of Kentucky
College of Agriculture
Lexington, KY 40546

A good number of the Kentucky pamphlets and sheets are directed at the commercial grower, but, even among these, there is useful information for the gardener, free.

Cool Season Flowers for Spring and Fall Planting, 4 pp.

Cultivating Ginseng in Kentucky, 12 pp.

Fruit and Nut Varieties for Kentucky Home Plantings, 4 pp.

Guidelines for Choosing Hedges for Kentucky Yards, 16 pp.

Home Vegetable Gardening in Kentucky, 72 pp.

Kentucky Nursery Grower's Directory (lists the stock of all wholesale nurseries in the state; could be used to get your garden center to order something), 74 pp.

Trees, Shrubs, Groundcovers, and Vines Suitable for Kentucky Landscapes, 20 pp.

Vegetable Cultivars for Kentucky Gardens, 7 pp.

Living History Farms

2600 N.W. 111th Street
Des Moines, IA 50322

■ *Living-history farm.*

A huge and well-established project, this farm covers 600 acres, embracing an Ioway Indian village, an 1840 farm, an 1870 village, a 1900 farm, and an experimental modern farm. All contain documented collections of historical vegetable and field-crop varieties, but the Indian village and the experimental farm are the rarest and the most interesting of the group. The Ioway garden attempts to reproduce Native American techniques as well as crop varieties. The modern farm contains a number of new experimental field crops such as kenaf, amaranth, and multi-ear corn, together with a virtual anthology of maizes, from teosinte (a probable ancestor of corn) through pod corns, flint corns, flour corns, Indian corns, shoepeg corn, and important Corn Belt and experimental strains. You might also visit the Henry A. Wallace Crop Center, where you can play "AgriGamble," a game about the economic risks of modern agriculture!

The Living History Sourcebook

by Jay Anderson
American Association for State and
Local History Press
172 2nd Avenue N.
Suite 102
Nashville, TN 37201

■ *469 pages, many illustrations, $19.95.*

Many living history farms and museums contain heirloom or historical gardens, and some offer both advice and seeds. If you want to learn which are in your area, the *Sourcebook* is the place to look. It will also give you a fair idea of how people started doing this sort of thing. Instead of going native, you might call it "going historical." Regardless, it's had by-and-large pleasant results for gardeners who like old varieties of vegetables, fruit trees, and flowers.

Maine Cooperative Extension Service

100 Winslow Hall
University of Maine
Orono, ME 04469

One very nice thing that the Maine extension offers is a set of bulletins directed specifically at part-time farmers, who are becoming prevalent throughout the Northeast. Publications about fruit and potato production are also very extensive. You may be interested in the children's ag-series, featuring titles like "Meet Mollie Moo," or the insect leaflet on the "confused flour beetle." The latter is undoubtedly aimed at ending the bug's perplexity by eliminating it.

Flowering Crabapple in Maine
Plant Hardiness Zone Maps for the State of Maine
The Soils of Maine

Vegetable Varieties for Maine
Woody Ornamental Plant Hardiness Trials
Woody Plants for Landscape Planting in Maine

Maine Organic Farmers & Gardeners Association

PO Box 2176
Augusta, ME 04330

■ *Nonprofit organization dedicated to organic gardening techniques. 32-page bimonthly tabloid The Maine Organic Farmer & Gardener; bimonthly newsletter; crop certification; supplies and assistance; annual Common Ground Country Fair; annual membership $15.00; annual subscription for nonmembers $8.00.*

Every country resident and part-time farmer in Maine and the Northeast will get a lot of use out of this group and its fine paper; organic growers elsewhere will find enough in it to make the subscription worthwhile. It already seems to have a pretty far-flung circulation; a recent issue included a letter from Forest Shomer of Abundant Life Seed Foundation in Washington State. The same issue featured some very thorough and useful articles on general topics such as trellising grapes in the organic garden and choosing and planting different oak species. The transcript of a miniconference on the apple offered interesting and realistic proposals for the use of beneficial insects in the orchard. There is also a lot of news, some local and some not. The University of Vermont, *MOF&G* reports, has started an alternative agriculture major that, among other things, requires Hatha yoga as a form of physical education. The paper also reported on the opening of a USDA alternative agriculture information center in Maryland. Maine residents will not want to miss the Common Ground Country Fair held annually in Windsor, a sort of alternative county fair with ex-

hibits devoted not only to every phase of organic growing but to appropriate technology and lifestyles as well.

Michigan Cooperative Extension Service

Michigan State University
Department of Horticulture
Plant and Soil Sciences Building
East Lansing, MI 48824

Michigan's cooperative extension service puts out one of the most thorough publications lists in the nation. Just reading the titles gives you a pretty good idea of what life is like in the state. The insect, weed, and disease publications are very well put together and illustrated; there are vegetable- and fruit-garden tips for all major types. Especially nice are the numerous publications about every aspect of agricultural planning and economics, from beginning farmer's guides to pamphlets on no-till and regenerative agriculture. There are so many vegetable, ornamental, and lawn garden sheets and pamphlets that you had best send for the catalogue.

Familiar Trees of Michigan
Grasses for Lawns in Michigan, $.10
Guide to Identification of Common Weed Seedlings of Michigan, $.65
Guide to Identifying Plant Disease Symptoms, $.70
Heritage Gardening, $1.50
Insects and Diseases of Vegetables in the Home Garden, $.30
Winter Injuries to Trees and Shrubs in Michigan, $.35.

Minnesota Cooperative Extension Service

Room 3 Coffey Hall
1420 Eckles Avenue
St. Paul, MN 55108

Minnesota has a good mix of materials on ornamentals, fruits, and vegetables. Send for the list, so you can look at the separate "Vegetable Variety Reports" offered for most common vegetables and berries. The reports are geared to commercial growers, but they give yield and other data for most of the varieties the home gardener will grow. It's also worth having the complete list to browse through the pamphlets of growing advice for specific crops and ornamentals.

Apple-Crabapple-Pear Varieties for Minnesota, $.50

Azaleas and Rhododendrons for Minnesota, $.20

Fruits for Minnesota, $.20

Garden Lilies in Minnesota, $.20

Know Your Minnesota Apples, $.20 (out of stock at this writing, but may come in again).

Native Shrubs and Vines for Landscaping, $.20

Native Trees That Can Be Used for Landscaping, $.50

Plum, Cherry, Apricot Varieties for Minnesota, $.20

Suggested Vegetable Varieties for Home Gardeners in Minnesota, $.50

Trees, Shrubs and Vines for Minnesota Landscapes, $3.00

The Minnesota Horticulturist

Minnesota State Horticultural Society
161 Alderman Hall
1970 Folwell Avenue
St. Paul, MN 55108

■ *Magazine, 9 issues per year, many color and black-and-white illustrations, annual subscription $12.00.*

The Minnesota "Hort" has been around for more than a century. It founded the arboretum at the University of Minnesota and the Horticulture and Landscape Architecture departments there, not to mention the state's fruit-research stations. It isn't surprising, then, that its maga-

zine is uncommonly well written, well illustrated, and altogether appealing. Take, for example, this opening to a recent article on melons: "One marvels to see a dog playing a violin, not because the dog is playing well, but because it is playing at all. The same goes for growing melons here in Minnesota's heartland." The story goes on to a pithy review of cultivars, with some detailed suggestions for growing. Features also deal with ornamentals, houseplants, and fairly sophisticated aspects of garden design. There are good columns with garden tips, information on pests and diseases, and descriptions of exemplary private gardens.

Mississippi Cooperative Extension Service

Mississippi State University
PO Box 5446
Mississippi State, MS 39762

The extension publications are free to Mississippians; the state service suggests that you get them directly from your county extension agent. A good variety of sheets on the culture and care of popular ornamentals and edibles is available, but I can't resist mentioning two others specifically. First, the service offers blueprints for 6 different greenhouses, all suitable for the home gardener and some fairly easy to build. Second, it has a very nice booklet called "Planning the Home Landscape." Every state has a brochure on this subject, but few of them are this clear and full of suggestions. A neat little paper tool comes with this book, providing you with scaled measurements, templates for marking in different sizes of trees and shrubs on the plan, and a French curve for drawing in lines. This is an extremely handy device for someone

making his or her first landscape plan. Too many home-landscaping books tell you how easy it is to draw a landscape plan, then bury you in details. I wish they might all be so thoughtful as Mississippi's.

Greenhouse Designs, 1 p. description plus blueprints

Planning the Home Landscape, 16 pp. plus paper tool

Dear Blabby,
    I bought a cutting of your hybrid x *Kohleriantha* 'Oodles of Noodles,' which you featured in your catalogue. Having grown it under all sorts of conditions, I can certainly attest that it is one tough plant. However, it is also the ugliest I have ever seen. All I get are a few brown-tipped leaves and hundreds of stringy rhizomes that grow everywhere, including out of the drainage holes of the pots, from where they proceed to invade my other plants and choke them out. Why did you ever release that hybrid?

                    Baffled in Buffalo

Dear Bison,
    From your letter, it is obvious that you know nothing about the etiquette of hybridizing. Yes, I know that 'Oodles of Noodles' is incredibly ugly and will never flower, but it is a totally new intergeneric hybrid. No one else has succeeded in crossing *Kohleria* 'Brownleaf' and *Smithiantha* 'Nuttin' but Trouble' before, so this makes 'Oodles of Noodles' a first-rate scientific discovery, and puts me in line for a Hybridizer of the Year award.

—FROM *THE GLOXINIAN* (1986)

Missouri Botanical Garden

PO Box 299
St. Louis, MO 63166

■ *Nonprofit organization, annual membership $35.00; Missouri Botanical Garden Bulletin, annual subscription, $12.00.*

Missouri has one of the country's great botanical gardens, noted for its fine, unusual botanists. Edgar Anderson, the author of *Plants, Man, and Life* (see page 44), a distinctive contribution to popular botany, was there, as was Victor Muhlenbach, who spent a lifetime studying the flora of St. Louis's railroad rights-of-way. The present director, Peter Raven, is the world's leading authority on tropical flora and a popular spokesperson for rain forest conservation. On the staff is Julian Steyermark, a tropical botanist who has been cited in the *Guinness Book of World Records* as the most prolific plant collector in the world. The public sees some of the results of the tropical research in the Climatron, a remarkable geodesic greenhouse devoted to tropical plants. The membership fee includes free admission to the garden (otherwise, $1) and to the arboretum 40 miles away, and a free subscription to the *Bulletin*. Members also get discounts on the dozens of garden courses offered.

Missouri Cooperative Extension Service

Department of Horticulture
1-40 Agriculture Building
University of Missouri—Columbia
Columbia, MO 65211

The usual strengths are represented in Missouri's catalogue of publications. Pamphlets about field crops, notably corn, may be of use to the home gardener, though they are largely geared toward farmers. The sections on insects, weeds, and soils are large and comprehensive, so if you have a specific problem, you might do well to consult the catalogue.

The Central Theme of American Agricultural History, $.20
Evaluating Missouri Soils, $7.00
Soils of the Southeast Missouri Lowlands, $1.50
Soil Testing in Missouri, $2.50

Monticello

Thomas Jefferson Memorial Foundation
PO Box 316
Charlottesville, VA 22902

■ *Historic house and gardens of Jefferson's great ferme ornée.*
■ *Tours and garden tours; plants and seeds by mail or at shop; Center for Historic Plants to coordinate educational programs beginning in 1987; 40-page The Gardens of Monticello, many color illustrations, $3.00.*

In recent years people have begun to take Jefferson's gardens as seriously as they have taken his house. In this, they are fortunate to have loads of documentation in Jefferson's own hand about the shape and contents of his ornamental and vegetable gardens and his orchards; most of these writings are published in *Thomas Jefferson's Garden Book* (see page 226). During warm seasons, it is possible to tour the gardens, which are now in the process of being restored to contain precisely what Jefferson had in them. Horticulturist Peter Hatch has gathered plants from sources around the world that fit Jefferson's original schemes, and propagator John Fitzpatrick is working to make the plants available to the public. Already, the shop offers by mail or on site a selection of the seed of roughly 40 ornamentals and vegetables that Jefferson grew, together with herb plants and fruit trees of the varieties he preferred. Among the trees are heirloom varieties of peaches, apricots, figs, and apples, including about a dozen of the last. Most plants come not only with cultural instructions but with historical information as well. This is a first-rate place to go for anyone interested in Colonial horticulture. If you can't go, or before you go, you might want to look at Peter Hatch's magnificently illustrated introduction to the gardens, also available by mail.

Mount Vernon

Mount Vernon Ladies' Association
Mount Vernon, VA 22121

■ *Restored residence and grounds owned by George Washington.*

Both the kitchen and formal gardens at Mount Vernon are kept in precisely the same form and—as far as possible—with precisely the same varieties as Washington once used. Both the heirloom gardener and the garden designer will profit from looking at them. The Ladies' Association offers a color handbook that features pictures and plans of the gardens.

Nevada Cooperative Extension Service

University of Nevada—Reno
College of Agriculture
Reno, NV 89557

The south of Nevada resembles Phoenix in climate, while the north resembles Denver, so it's a good idea to deal with a local agent for the best information for your area. The people in the south have a good sense of humor. One of their free handbooks features a drawing on the cover in which a wife shouts to her seedling-planting hubby, "Green side up!" The booklet begins by admitting, "One must learn to cope with the weather in southern Nevada," but immediately adds the upbeat side: "Southern Nevada will average around 245 days of frost-free weather." Several of the county services put out their own newsletters on gardening for their areas.

Southern:
Beginning Desert Gardening
Drought-Tolerant Low-Maintenance Plants for Southern Nevada
Ground Covers (includes many native plants suited to culture there)
Lawns for Southern Nevada

Northern:
Drought-Tolerant Trees and Shrubs for Northern Nevada: Evergreens
Drought-Tolerant Trees and Shrubs for Northern Nevada: Shrubs
Drought-Tolerant Trees and Shrubs for Northern Nevada: Trees
Fruit Trees for Northern Nevada
Vegetable Varieties and Recommended Planting Dates for Northern Nevada

New England Farm Bulletin

Box 147
Cohasset, MA 02025

■ *8-page newsletter published 24 times per year; annual subscription $12.00, two years $20.00.*

The first thing I read in this journal was a diatribe against the Massachusetts Department of Health's limits on the use of Alar, a chemical used in the apple industry. Oh boy, I thought, here's a nest of heathen polluters. Within a page and a half, however, they not only had me convinced that the department might have jumped the gun, but that they had one of the most readable periodicals in New England, despite the fact that a good half of it is devoted to classifieds, almanac information, and market prices. The readers of this witty paper must be drawn from the numbers of part-time farmers whom the editors claim are partly responsible for the fact that the number of farms has gone up by 17 percent in New England, while it has declined by 2 percent in the U.S. as a whole. There is 1 feature per issue, about anything from Alar to black-smithing to beekeeping to Emerson. The features and departments are fun, even if you aren't about to rush out and do what they suggest. In a squib on repelling deer, they suggest the use of fragrant soap bars, concluding, "Check into your local motel and enjoy a deerless weekend; the soap is in the shower." Perhaps best of all is the "Said & Done" column, offering usually caustic reviews of USDA studies and farm-and-garden books, together with useful news. Even the classifieds are fun to read, and they are a good place to buy or sell almost all farm necessaries in New England. A calendar of events gives a very good idea of what gardeners and farmers can find in the way of classes and other events, from Connecticut to Maine, for the relevant period. What a terrific newsletter—the kind of thing that makes it exciting to go to the mailbox!

PHLOX

New Hampshire Cooperative Extension Service

University of New Hampshire
Taylor Hall
Durham, NH 03824

New Hampshire doesn't go in for big publications; in fact, it doesn't even have a list of its extension publications. Nevertheless, it does offer a large number of sheets of specific interest to the state's gardeners. Check with your local agent if you have a question.

Azaleas and Rhododendrons for New Hampshire
Colonial Gardens
Extension Tips for Growing Annual Flowers in New Hampshire
Growing Indian Corn in New Hampshire
June Pink: A Hardy Native Azalea for New England
Landscaping Woodland Areas
Selected Landscape Plants for New Hampshire
Transplanting Native Trees and Shrubs
Tree Fruit Variety Guide for Home Gardens
Vegetable Variety Guide for Home and Market Gardens

New Jersey Cooperative Extension Service

Cook College
Rutgers University
PO Box 231
New Brunswick, NJ 08903

The New Jersey extension offers a varied list for home vegetable, fruit, and ornamentals growers. Pest-control titles are numerous. There are an unusual number of specific horticultural-project leaflets for 4-H clubbers. The extension also publishes a very complete list of the pick-your-own farms in the state, in case you want someone else to do the growing.

Common Forest Trees of New Jersey, $4.00
50 Small Trees for New Jersey Home Grounds
Landscaping at the Seashore, $1.00
New Jersey Apple Varieties
New Jersey Peach and Nectarine Varieties
Partial List of Small Fruit Nurseries

New Mexico Cooperative Extension Service

Box 3AI
New Mexico State University
Las Cruces, NM 88003

Robert Coughlin, an editor at the New Mexico extension, describes the state's situation very well: "New Mexico is officially classified as semiarid, but some parts of the state are pure desert. Also, the state's elevation ranges from about 3,500 feet to more than 10,000 feet, which creates a wide range of growing conditions. . . . Almost all of New Mexico's soils are classified as poor, requiring significant soil amendments to grow anything. Soils are generally calcareous with high pH levels." In short, New Mexico's gardeners can use a lot of help, and the extension provides it. Among the many home-garden titles are some directed to the planting of particularly successful native or exotic species. Send for the catalogue of publications. All pamphlets free.

Baileya in Landscape

Chile Disease Control

Evaluation of Dry Chile Varieties in New Mexico—1982

Ground Covers for New Mexico

Growing Chile in Home and Market Gardens

A Guide for Home Vegetable Gardeners (lists varieties and planting times for three regions of the state)

A History of Vegetable Crops in New Mexico

The Hopi Sweet Potato

Landscaping with Desert Willow

Making Chile Ristras

Ornamental Shrubs for New Mexico

Ornamental Trees for New Mexico

Ornamental Vines for New Mexico

Sod Lawns for New Mexico

Soils of New Mexico

Turfgrass in New Mexico

 SEMPERVIVUM TECTORUM
HOUSELEEK

Medicinal virtues: The juice is good in hot agues. It cools and restrains all violent inflammations, St. Anthony's fire, scalds and burns, shingles, fretting ulcers, cankers, tetters, ringworms and eases the pain of the gout.

The juice also takes away warts and corns in the hands or feet. Applied to the temples, it takes away headaches. The bruised leaves laid upon the crown of the head stay bleeding at the nose quickly.

—FROM *CULPEPER'S COLOR HERBAL*

New York Botanical Garden

Bronx, NY 10458

■ *Annual membership $30.00, including free subscription to bimonthly* Garden *(see page 30), library check-out privileges, discount on courses and shop goods, free admission to conservatory, limited free parking.*

The Brooklyn "Bot" has the books; the New York "Bot" in the Bronx has the courses, hundreds of them. Complete professional certification programs are offered, together with a number of courses and symposiums aimed at the serious gardener. Even professional courses are generally open to everyone, subject to minimum prerequisites and sufficient enrollment. Courses in garden design, the ornamental plants of the Northeast, and the exotics grown here are particularly good. The library is one of the finer in the East, and members are granted check-out privileges. The bookstore is a great place to find hard-to-locate books like Michael Dirr's *Manual of Woody Landscape Plants* and the complete RHS Wisley garden-guide series.

New York Cooperative Extension Service

New York State College of Agriculture and Life Sciences
7 Research Park
Cornell University
Ithaca, NY 14850

The Cornell extension service is virtually a horticultural and agricultural empire. Its publications list is too vast to summarize, including titles of both regional and national interest. The pamphlets are, generally speaking, among the finest produced by any extension service. A number of them are reviewed separately in the appropriate sections of this book.

Ohio Cooperative Extension Service

Ohio State University
216 Kottman Hall
2021 Cottey Road
Columbus, OH 43210

Home gardeners will do well to send for the separate catalogue listing 476 fact sheets for just about every problem and opportunity you might have in the garden. It's an amazing list, right down to the 9 fact sheets on different sorts of old roses like gallicas and centifolias. You can pick up individual fact sheets at county extension offices, order them in a variety of sets for different interests, or just get the whole bunch for $38.08. The general publications list is more suited to farmers and 4-H-ers, but a few titles are interesting.

Garden Calendar, $2.73 ppd.

Small Fruit Handbook, $28.27 ppd.

Tree Fruit Handbook, $28.27 ppd.

Vegetable Varieties, $.47 ppd.

Oklahoma Cooperative Extension Service

Oklahoma State University
335 Ag Hall
Stillwater, OK 74074

Oklahoma is serious about cattle and grain, and the publications list has no end of bulletins about them. 4-H-ers also get a good set of leaflets to choose from. Material for general gardeners consists of a pretty average selection, strong on specific vegetables and on pest and disease control.

Home Fruit Planning Guide
Oklahoma Garden Planning Guide
Pecan Varieties for Oklahoma (along with many other pecan bulletins)
Recommended Apple and Peach Varieties
Selecting a Lawn Grass for Oklahoma

Oregon Cooperative Extension Service

Oregon State University Extension Hall
Corvallis, OR 97331

Oregon puts out a catalogue that is fun just to leaf through, including pamphlets on everything from sexual fulfillment to "A Computer Simulation Study of Deer in Mendocino County, California." The agricultural list includes lots of single-sheet flyers on growing, fertilizing, and defending, including bugs, forage grasses, and primary commercial crops of the state; some of these sheets may be useful to the home gardener, especially the fertilizer guides, which are keyed to the different regions of Oregon. There are also a good group of "how-to-grow" fruits and vegetables sheets for the home. Except for items that are priced otherwise, the first 6 publications on the list are free to Oregon residents; after that, and for all flyers ordered by nonresidents,

each one costs $.10 plus $.25 postage.

Azaleas and Rhododendrons: Care and Culture
Control of Premature Ripening of Bartlett Pears
Cucurbit Seed Production
Growing Your Own: A Practical Guide to Gardening in Oregon
Oregon Potato Variety Trials 1979
Preparing Winter Storage for Fuchsias, Geraniums, and Tuberous Plants
Progress Report of Table Grapes in the Northern Willamette Valley
Pruning to Restore an Old, Neglected Apple Tree
Raising Forest Tree Seedlings at Home, $.25
Selecting Peach Varieties for the Willamette Valley, $.50
Sweet Cherry Varieties and Pollinators for Oregon

Pacific Horticulture

Pacific Horticultural Foundation
Hall of Flowers
PO Box 22609
San Francisco, CA 94122

■ *Quarterly magazine, many color and black-and-white illustrations, free to members of California Horticultural Society, Strybing Arboretum Society, Southern California Horticultural Institute, and Western Horticultural Society; annual nonmembers' subscription $12.00.*

Pacific Horticulture is the best magazine in the Far West for the serious ornamentals gardener; for the quality of its articles and photographs, it is among the best gardening magazines

published anywhere. I have always thought that the West is the most fertile ground in America for the graceful combination of science and art. This journal is a good example. A quarterly feature, "Laboratory Report," is written by a professor of plant pathology at UC Berkeley, yet is clear and very useful for the home gardener. A recent issue includes an article entitled "Pacific Coast Irises: A Symposium," an imposing name for an extremely attractive piece, illustrated with remarkable photographs by the magazine's editor, George Waters. In the same issue, there is an article on pebble-paving styles; a collection of uses to which children put seeds and flowers; a description of a Santa Barbara estate garden; an intelligent minihistory of the nursery trade in the Lompoc Valley; an erudite essay on marijuana as a garden plant that begins, "Here is a plant any hardworking gardener could love;" one of a quarterly series of articles on trees in the Strybing Arboretum; a wide-ranging appreciation of the penstemon; and a piece on the largest, smallest, and oldest plants that describes the 10,000-year-old creosote rings of the Sonoran desert.

Plimoth Plantation

PO Box 1620
Warren Avenue
Plymouth, MA 02360

■ *Living-history museum.*

This is a very ambitious attempt to recreate 17th-century life in Massachusetts. The Plantation appears to take research unusually seriously. A very thorough 13-page document lists the herbs and vegetables grown here, with indications of place of origin, use, and parts used. It is a particularly nice summary of 17th-century herb lore.

GINKGO LEAVES

The Prairie Garden Guild

Box 211
Saskatoon, Saskatchewan
CANADA S7H 2J3

- *Distributor of publications of the Saskatoon Horticultural Society, a nonprofit organization dedicated to gardening on the northern prairie.*
- *44-page, 5-times-yearly* Garden Clippings; *126-page annual* The Prairie Garden, *many illustrations, some color; annual membership $10.00.*

Each issue of *Garden Clippings* begins with an inspirational poem from editor Monty Zary. One is about cures for an aching back, another a memorial to a friend, another about sitting in the garden at "nite." These charming verses aside, the magazines are full of every sort of information for gardeners on the tall grass prairie of western Canada or the northern U.S. There are summaries of the latest releases from seed companies and research stations, reports of experiences with different plants and techniques on the prairie, and news of upcoming events. The annual is

DOGWOOD

more of the same, but it is longer and offers more variety. It includes a list of useful seed sources for Canadian gardeners, dozens of articles contributed by researchers and members and reprinted from specialists' publications, and more poems. The 1986 annual featured an ode to the horticultural society and a jaunty rhyme called "The Packet of Seed" that opens like this: "I paid a dime for a package of seeds/And the clerk tossed them out with a flip/'We've got 'em assorted for every man's needs.'/He said with a smile on his lips. . . ."

Rhode Island Cooperative Extension Service

University of Rhode Island
133 Woodward Hall
Kingston, RI 02881

The publications list offers a good section on growing specific ornamentals, both in the garden and as houseplants. There are 59 sheets available that tell you how to deal with every bug in the state, not to mention some slightly more ambitious bug pamphlets, such as "The Gypsy Moth: An Illustrated Biography." For trees, shrubs, fruits, and vegetables, there are individual pamphlets for certain popular genera plus the usual run of general guides.

Apples from Rhode Island, $1.00
Care and Selection of Trees in Rhode Island, $.75
Herbs for Rhode Island, $1.00
1983 New England Vegetable Production Recommendations, $2.50
Shrubs for Rhode Island, $.75
Street Trees in Southern New England, $2.50
Vegetable Varieties for the Rhode Island Gardener, $.50

Sunset New Western Garden Book

See "General Sources."

Taylor Publishing Company

1550 West Mockingbird Lane
Dallas, TX 75221

- *Publisher of regional gardening books.*

I wish there were space in this book to review all of Taylor's books separately. If you live in one of those regional climates that makes ordinary garden books frustrating to work

with, do send for their publications list. Taylor is the nation's leading publisher of books tailored for regions like Florida, Texas, the Midwest, and the Rocky Mountains.

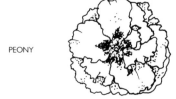

PEONY

Tennessee Cooperative Extension Service

University of Tennessee
PO Box 1071
Knoxville, TN 37901

Tennessee's publications list has good basic guides on vegetables and fruits and an unusually wide selection of pamphlets on home landscaping and ornamentals. There are fewer pest sheets and fewer sheets still about individual vegetable crops than one might expect, but, for some reason, berries are covered very well.

Azaleas in the Tennessee Landscape
The Dogwood in Tennessee
Flowering Bulbs for Tennessee Gardens
Hydrangeas—One of Tennessee's Most Colorful Flowers
Landscaping Tennessee Homes, $2.00
Selecting Lawn Grasses for Tennessee

Texas Gardener

PO Box 9005
Waco, TX 76714

- *Bimonthly magazine, many color illustrations, annual subscription $15.00; also runs Texas Gardener Press, publishing regional gardening books.*

This is a finely turned-out magazine, its articles generally written by professionals. Some features deal with ordinary subjects such as pest control, cultural techniques, and lawn care. Others are more offbeat and interesting, like one recent article on growing Texas natives as pot plants. The company runs a garden-design contest, and the winning designs appear in the magazine. Among the greatest services the magazine provides is the annual *All-Texas Selections,* an annotated selection of vegetable varieties that do very well in the Lone Star State. It appears in the January/February issue, together with a very complete planting chart for all regions of the state and a 12-month garden calendar as an insert. If the magazine is any indication, the book list should be worth checking out, too. To date, it includes *The Vegetable Book, Fresh from the Garden, The Complete Guide to Texas Lawn Care,* and *The Texas Gardener's Guide to Growing Tomatoes.*

Utah Cooperative Extension Service

UMC 5015
Logan, UT 84322

I kept being surprised by the high quality of the extension publications that many Western states offer. Utah is no exception. Along with all the usual pamphlets, it provides some really first-rate guides to the native plants of the region and to landscape selections.

Annual Flowers for the Utah Landscape $.25

Growing Trees and Shrubs in Utah, $.75

Growing Vegetables: Recommended Varieties for Utah, $.25

A Guide to Mountain Flowers, 59 pp., $1.00*

Landscape Plants from Utah's Mountains, 135 pp., $2.00*

Landscaping the Home Ground (with many suggested varieties for Utah)

Native Trees of the Intermountain Region, 82 pp., $6.00*

Ornamental and Shade Trees for Utah, 144 pp., $7.00*

> You may be sure that the soil can be improved by a thousand different means; fortunately the gardener has not usually got them at hand. In towns it is rather difficult to have at home guano, beech leaves, rotten cow-dung, old plaster, old peat, decomposed sods, weathered molehills, wood humus, river sand, moor soil, mud from a pond, soil from heaths, charcoal, wood ashes, ground bones, horn shavings, old liquid manure, horse-dung, lime, sphagnum, decayed pith from stumps, and other nutritious, lightening, and beneficial material, not counting a good dozen of nitrogenous, potash, phosphatic, and other kinds of manures.
>
> —KAREL CAPEK, FROM *THE GARDENER'S YEAR* (1929)

Vermont Cooperative Extension Service

University of Vermont
Publications Office
Morrill Hall
Burlington, VT 05405

There's a good deal of information for the beginning or part-time farmer here, with some good-looking pamphlets on maple sugaring at home and for commercial operations. Lists of leaflets about specific crops, fruit trees, ornamentals, and pests are fairly extensive.

Getting Started in Farming on a Small Scale, $.75

Growing Dry Beans: A Vermont Tradition, $.50

Landscape Plants for Vermont, $2.00

Maple Sugaring in Your Backyard

Recommended Trees for Town Plantings in Vermont, $.25

Understanding Vermont
Vermont Planting Calenda

Virginia Cooperative Extension Service

Virginia Polytechnic Institute and State University
Blacksburg, VA 24061

Virginia offers the usual selection of pamphlets about specific edibles and ornamentals, bug control, and general planting and care. The really outstanding publications from this extension—the newsletter *The Virginia Gardener* and the large book *The Virginia Master Gardener Handbook* are reviewed separately (see page 50 and following entry on this page).

Lawn Establishment in Virginia

Shade Trees for Virginia

Vegetables Recommended for Virginia

The Virginia Gardener

Virginia Cooperative Extension Service
Virginia Polytechnic Institute and State University
Blacksburg, VA 24061

- *4-page monthly newsletter, a few illustrations, annual subscription $5.00.*

This is an unusually fine newsletter, full of hands-on, up-to-date information. Articles are written by professors, grad students, and extension specialists in the state university system, so the prose can be dry, but who's complaining? The monthly notes on what to do in the garden are worth the modest cost of the newsletter in themselves, and there are articles on everything from lifting half-hardy perennials, to earthworms and pesticides, to home plant breeding, to energy-efficient landscaping. You can even find out how to tell when a watermelon is ripe.

TROWEL

Wyoming Cooperative Extension Service

University of Wyoming
University Station
Box 3354
Laramie, WY 82071

The list of bulletins is fairly brief for gardeners—unless you are growing range grass or have become an avid entomologist—but the publications include a few thorough books.

Growing Perennial Flowers in Wyoming, $1.00

Home Landscaping Kit, $2.25

Practices to Speed Vegetable Growth in Wyoming's Climate

Recommended Horticultural Plants Generally Hardy and Adaptable in the Central Great Plains Region

Recommended Tree and Shrub Varieties for Wyoming

Vegetable Gardening in Wyoming

Weeds of Wyoming, $1.55

Wildflowers of Wyoming, $2.50

Wyoming General Soil Map

Wyoming Lawn Handbook, $1.50

Wyoming Trees, $1.55

Proposed RESOLUTION FOR SQUIRREL MITIGATIONS
To Supersede 1958 Resolution
76th Annual Meeting Northern Nut Growers Association

WHEREAS: Tree squirrels, *Sciurus niger* and *S. carolinensis* were the first nut planters in North America, and

WHEREAS: Homo sapiens are Johnny-come-lately nut planters and

WHEREAS: tree squirrels continue to plant nuts, and

WHEREAS: depredations on nut tree crops can be protected with live traps and guns, and

WHEREAS: fried squirrel and hot biscuits and squirrel gravy is a culinary treat of the highest order, and

WHEREAS: nut-fed squirrels are the finest of table fare, and

WHEREAS: nut crop depredations can be alleviated or mitigated by converting squirrels to table fare, and

WHEREAS: squirrel hunters should be invited to nut orchards to harvest squirrels, and

WHEREAS: hunter invitations gain friends for nut growers,

LET IT BE KNOWN: that the Northern Nut Growers Association members will exact payment from squirrels feeding on nuts by removal of said squirrel(s) from premises with live traps or guns and where necessary, compensation be that of converting squirrel(s) to the finest of table morsels. That the Association *not* subsidize the destruction of squirrels and their habitat by bounties which bankrupt the treasury of the Association alas for naught as squirrels self generate in numbers greater than resources of the Association. That the Association accept gracefully excuses from nut growers about squirrels taking prized test nuts with tongue-in-cheek but encourage researchers to take gun in hand.

—DONALD M. CHRISTISEN, FROM *THE NUTSHELL,* NEWSLETTER OF THE NORTHERN NUT GROWERS ASSOCIATION (1986)

13 Sources of Sources

Abundant Life Seed Foundation

See "General Sources."

AgAccess

PO Box 2008
Davis, CA 95617

- *Mail-order bookseller.*
- *30-page quarterly catalogue, $8.50.*

This service is meant to keep professional agriculturalists and nurserymen up-to-date on the latest professional and popular books in their fields. It isn't necessarily a place for the average gardener to browse. You may not need a handbook on microirrigation or a complete audio course on Spanish for agricultural operations, but there are some fine books for the serious edibles gardener and for those interested in the implications of biotechnology and agricultural policy. Many of the sources come from technical publishing houses or from public governing or policy groups, so the list is indeed distinctive. Among the intriguing books included in a recent catalogue were Mas Yamaguchi's exhaustive *World Vegetables*; *Knott's Handbook for Vegetable Growers*; a whole series on integrated pest management; Westwood's *Temperate Zone Pomology*; a book devoted to Asian pear varieties, another to the pine tree, and a third to the history of edible nuts; and books on the history of American agriculture, food

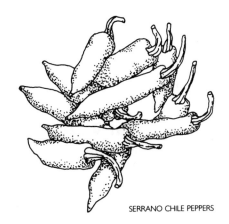

SERRANO CHILE PEPPERS

politics, and genetic diversity. Each selection is reviewed, making it easy to tell whether or not you can use it.

The American Botanist, Booksellers

PO Box 143
Brookfield, IL 60513

- *Horticultural and botanical bookseller.*
- *Variable-length catalogues issued 3–5 times per year, free.*

Proprietor Keith Crotz has built a good stock of books from the late 19th and 20th centuries. Much of what you will find here are gardening books of the last generation and more recent volumes that have gone out of print. It is therefore a good place to get that title you once saw and wished you had bought. The list of rarities is not long, but Crotz has some sought-after things like Beach's *The Apples of New York* and volumes of Andrew Jackson Downing's magazine *The Horticulturist*. Different issues of the catalogue may focus on different garden specialties, like roses or cacti.

Anchor & Dolphin Books

PO Box 823
Newport, RI 02840

- *Bookseller in garden history, landscape architecture, and early horticulture.*
- *Variable-length catalogues, published approx. 2 times per year, $1.00 each.*

There are a number of early 20th century and a few more recent books in this list, but even among these, the emphasis is on the history of landscape gardening. This is a good place to find things like original editions of books by English landscape architect William Gilpin and of parterre pattern books from 17th- and 18th-century France. There is also a good group of titles about town planning.

Warren F. Broderick— Books

695 4th Avenue
PO Box 124
Lansingburgh, NY 12182

- *Horticultural bookseller.*
- *Variable-length catalogues, $1.00 each.*

Broderick specializes in all kinds of garden and plant-lore books, some imported from England and many 20th-century American titles. He features comparatively recent books that have gone out of print, plus intriguing earlier publications, such as *Bog Trotting for Orchids* (1904).

Capability's Books

Box 114
Highway 46
Deer Park, WI 54007

- *Mail-order bookseller.*
- *67-page catalogue, free.*

Here is the best mail-order garden-book seller in the business. You will find not only a very wide choice among the currently in-print American garden titles, but a very wide selection of imported English books as well. Classics like Graham Stuart Thomas's rose books (page 158)—almost impossible to find elsewhere—are available here. Even American items from arcane sources—like the Hampton Gardener's landscaping guides (page 221)—can be ordered from Capability's.

Earthworm Buyer's Guide

by Robert F. Shields
Shields Publications
PO Box 669
Eagle River, WI 54521

- *64 pages, $3.00 pbk.*

If you want worms in a hurry, Shields tells you where to get them. Hatcheries in the U.S. and Canada are listed, so you won't have to smuggle your annelids across the border.

The Essential Whole Earth Catalogue

27 Gate Five Road
Sausalito, CA 94965

- *416 pages, many illustrations, $15.00.*

The catalogue has gotten much more businesslike over the years. Gone are oversize, newsprint pages—you won't miss them when it comes time to shelve this tome—but gone too are the running novels, the poems, and the other New Age-iana that made the thing so entertaining. I miss the latter, but I must say, I prefer the tone and selection of today's catalogue which, like its sister periodical *The Whole Earth Review* (once *Co-Evolution Quarterly*), has grown from a hey-wow publication into a very thoughtful compilation of materials for environmentally sound and human-scale alternatives. The section that relates specifically to gardening and landscape books and catalogues is comparatively small, but the selection is very well made. A number of the ecological publications I list in this book are also to be found in *Whole Earth*, but there are many more that I could not include, in such areas as field guides, urban design, ecological philosophy, general conservation, homesteading, and virtually anything else you are likely to be interested in. If I were alone on a desert isle, I would never want this to be my only book, since I'd die of wanting the things it lists; since I'm not, though, I wouldn't be without it. The catalogue has the additional advantage of keeping in stock virtually every book or catalogue it lists, so if you can't find it elsewhere, you can order it direct from Whole Earth.

Gardening by Mail

by Barbara Barton
Tusker Press
PO Box 597004
San Francisco, CA 94159

- *250 pages, $16.00 pbk.*

This is a fine and comprehensive source book to nurseries and seed companies, garden-supply houses, plant societies, libraries, magazines, and books. She lists some companies that I do not list here. Then, too, she will give you a phone number, whenever possible, for each nursery, and she lets you know such interesting facts as whether the place has a display garden. Because the book was written using a data-base program, she was limited as to how much she could say about each company, society, or publication she describes. It is sometimes difficult to judge from her entries which are the top-flight companies in a given field.

Honingklip Nurseries

13 Lady Anne Avenue
Newlands, Cape Town
SOUTH AFRICA 7700

- *Bookseller in South African flora.*
- *Variable-page list, free.*

Like it or not, many modern garden and house plants come from South Africa, including protea, some acacias, gerbera daisies, and endless succulents. Those interested in South African flora can get current, in-print titles—plus a few rare and out-of-print books—from Honingklip's book catalogue.

Hurley Books

RR 1
Box 160
Westmoreland, NH 03467

- *Bookseller in ruralia, agriculture, and horticulture.*
- *Variable-length catalogues, issued twice per year, $1.00 each.*

This is a wonderful list of ruralia just to read through. There are old nursery and seed catalogues for sale here, as well as everything from antique tractor manuals to Catharine Beecher and Harriet Beecher Stowe's *The American Woman's Home* (1869). Many important American pomological books appear, along with titles on farming. There are long lists of books by L. H. Bailey and by Andrew Jackson Downing, and volumes on silage, pastures, cooking, and even muck. I love the titles of old things like Samuel Deane's *The New England Farmer; or Georgical Dictionary: containing a compendious account of the ways and methods in which the most important art of husbandry, in all its various branches, is, or may be, practised to the greatest advantage in this country* (1790). Hurley has 4 different editions for sale.

ISBS, Inc.

5602 N.E. Hassalo Street
Suite T6
Portland, OR 97213

- *Bookseller.*
- *Variable-length catalogue, free.*

ISBS sells the books of several foreign publishers—mainly from the U.K., Australia, and South Africa—as mail-order items for North America. The firm also culls and lists selected publications from foreign and American plant societies and public organizations. The list is strong for the plants and gardening styles most popular in the aforementioned countries, and for the garden specialties of the listed societies and organizations. A good-looking title from the U.K. is Jack Harkness's *The Makers of Heavenly Roses*, a book of profiles of rose breeders (see page 160). There are also odd little books like *Earthworms for Gardeners and Fishermen*, a lively account of how to keep and propagate the useful annelids (see page 26), and how you can eat them, if you wish. In the future, the catalogue will include many more newly issued American gardening books.

SEDUM RUBROTINCTUM

Landscape Books

PO Box 483
Exeter, NH 03833

- *Bookseller specializing in landscape architecture.*
- *Periodic lists, free.*

Most of Landscape's offerings are out-of-print books from this century, including the works of prominent modern designers and garden historians. There are some interesting oddities on the list including a guide to the architecture of the Panama Pacific Exhibition (1915).

Lloyds of Kew

9 Mortlake Terrace
Kew, Richmond
Surrey, ENGLAND TW9 3DT

- *Bookseller in gardening and botany.*
- *Annual catalogue listing more than 2,000 titles, free.*

Lloyds breaks its big list down by category. Here are some of the heads: Alpine and Rock Gardens; Botany, Plant Lore, Etc.; Bulbous Plants; Cacti and Succulents; Cultivation Indoors and Under Glass; Ferns, Fungi, Etc.; Flower Decoration; Fruits and Vegetables; Garden Design and Landscape Gardening; Herbals, Etc.; Individual Flowers; Orchids; Ornamental Trees, Shrubs, and Climbers; Plant Hunting and Travel; and Roses. The lists contain mainly British titles, and though many rarities appear, the focus is on reasonably priced out-of-print and in-print books that you can actually use. The titles themselves can be charming, such as *Name That Succulent* or *The Lower Plants of the World*. There are also separate sections with volumes about British flora and about a selection of foreign floras, chiefly from countries with ties to the U.K. A few interesting American titles are mentioned, including 2 early wildflower books and Jepson's *The Silva of California*. The Garden Design section is very thorough for English gardening styles, including first and early editions of the works of such people as Gertrude Jekyll, William Robinson, and Vita Sackville-West. There is even a section of rare color-plate books, bearing prices commensurate with their scarcity. The list is immense, and almost every gardener will find material of interest.

Nursery Source Manual

See "Trees and Shrubs."

Nursery Sources: Native Plants and Wild Flowers

See "Wildflowers and Native Plants."

Orchid Species Source Book II

See "Houseplants and Exotics."

Plant Sciences Data Center

American Horticultural Society
Mount Vernon, VA 22121

- *List of 173,000 living plants, representing more than 4,000 genera.*

If you can't find that rare plant anywhere, try here. It's on microfiche, so you will have to find a library that has the book in its collection. More than 40 botanical gardens around the nation have contributed their collection lists to this work, and each entry is catalogued by scientific name and source.

Pomona Book Exchange

Highway 52
Rockton, Ontario
CANADA L0R 1X0

- *Bookseller in gardening and botany, with a specialty in pomology.*
- *Variable-length catalogues, $1.00 each.*

Pomona is the only bookseller in Canada dedicated strictly to horticulture and agriculture. It has a very strong list of works, both old and recent, about fruit growing, as well as a wide-ranging selection of botanical works, ranging from runs of important journals, to important early books on North American flora like Asa Gray's *Manual* and Michaux's *The North American Sylva*, to more recent books on flora of all sorts of places and regions. The list is extremely various, including numbers of titles on individual flower genera, some USDA agricultural yearbooks, and a 1,000-page history of gardening in the South. I was particularly intrigued by the miscellaneous list labeled "Natural History," wherein you may find a modern verse translation of Lucretius's *De rerum natura*, a book on weather vanes, another on historic houses, a treatise on mosquitos, a 19th-century history of perfumes, and a copy of Benjamin Botkin's wonderful *A Treasury of American Folklore*.

> Of course, if you wish to please your neighbour, plant melons along your fence. It once happened to me that from my neighbour's garden, on my side of the fence, a melon grew so huge, so Canaan, so record-breaking, that it caused astonishment to a whole host of publicists, poets, and even of university professors, who could not understand how a fruit so gigantic could have squeezed through the palings of the fence. After some time the melon began to look rather indecent; then we cut it, and ate it for punishment.
>
> —KAREL CAPEK, FROM *THE GARDENER'S YEAR* (1929)

Redwood City Seed Co.

See "Vegetables and Herbs."

Otto Richter and Sons Ltd.

See "Vegetables and Herbs."

Second Life Books

PO Box 242
Quarry Road
Lanesborough, MA 01237

- *Bookseller in ruralia, agriculture, and husbandry.*
- *Variable-length catalogues, $1.00 each.*

The catalogue is not so extensive as Hurley's, but it contains all sorts of fascinating stuff for students of rural life. It is perhaps stronger than Hurley in English books, particularly in a few very antique and costly ones. Here, you can get a copy of the 1690 *Theatrum Botanicum*, a very important English herb book. There are also numerous books on things like horseshoeing, laundry, cooking, and the care of chickens, and a group of broadside advertising sheets and some 19th-century George Park catalogues. Several individual titles struck my fancy: Luther Burbank's *How Plants Are Trained to Work for Man*, with an introduction by David Starr Jordan; *The Innkeeper's and Butler's Guide* (1811), an English book of recipes for wines and spirits; and Robert Manning's important *The New England Fruit Book* (1844). I even came on an anti-tobacco tract from 1861 and an early Rodale book on organic gardening (1948)!

The Seed Finder

See "Vegetables and Herbs."

Sources of Native Seeds and Plants

See "Wildflowers and Native Plants."

Jane Sutley Horticultural Books

1105 W. Cherry Street
Centralia, WA 98531

- *Bookseller.*
- *Periodic catalogues, free.*

A general list of garden books, mainly from this century, with everything from beginner's books to specialized volumes. It is a place to look for just the out-of-print title that you can't do without.

Timber Press

9999 S.W. Wilshire
Portland, OR 97225

- *Horticultural publisher.*

A number of Timber's books are reviewed separately in this volume, but I should note here that the firm is the leading horticultural publisher in the United States. An extraordinary number of what are called "garden classics" are published (or re-issued) by Timber Press. If you are a serious gardener, you will get much use out of their catalogue.

> 🌱 You can love [cacti] without touching them indecently, or kissing them, or pressing them to your breast; they don't care for any intimacies and other such frivolities; they are hard like stone, armed to the teeth, determined not to surrender; go on, pale face, or I will shoot! A small collection of cacti looks like a camp of warlike pigmies. Chop off a head or arm from that warrior and a new man in arms will grow out of it, brandishing swords and daggers. Life is war.
>
> —KAREL CAPEK, FROM *THE GARDENER'S YEAR* (1929)

Gary Wayner, Bookseller

Route 3
Box 18
Fort Payne, AL 35967

- *Bookseller in general natural history.*
- *Variable-length catalogues, free.*

What a miscellany! But it is fun to read through, even if *A Chytridi-aceious Parasite of Phytophthora* or *Vascular Plants of the Nevada Test Site* is not the first thing on your want list. Most of the books relating to the plant kingdom are field guides of flora.

Elisabeth Woodburn

Booknoll Farm
Box 398
Hopewell, NJ 08525

- *Bookseller in horticulture.*
- *Variable-length catalogues, $2.00 each.*

One of the best-established horticultural booksellers in North America, Elisabeth Woodburn has been at it for more than 40 years. She offers several catalogues, each keyed to a particular area of interest and each costing $2. She currently offers catalogues in the following areas: herbs; trees and shrubs; gardens and landscape; garden history and bibliography; travels; plant lore; fruits; vegetables; wildflowers and ferns. Each of these lists is as long and varied as the entire offerings of many booksellers.

Sources of Quotations

Page 21: Lawrence, Elizabeth. *The Little Bulbs*. Durham, North Carolina: Duke University Press.

Page 23: Capek, Karel. *The Gardener's Year*. Madison, Wisconsin: University of Wisconsin Press, 1984.

Page 24: Thacker, Christopher. *The History of Gardens*. Berkeley, California: University of California Press, 1979.

Page 26: Wilder, Louise Beebe. *The Fragrant Garden*. New York: Dover Publications, 1936.

Page 28: Warner, Charles Dudley. *My Summer in a Garden*. New York: AMS Press, repr. of 1871 ed.

Page 29: Foster, H. Lincoln. *Rock Gardening*. Portland, Oregon: Timber Press.

Page 33: *The Water Lily Journal*. Buckeystown, Maryland: The Water Lily Society.

Page 35: Lawrence, Elizabeth. *The Little Bulbs*. Durham, North Carolina: Duke University Press.

Page 37: Roses by Fred Edmunds. Wilsonville, Oregon.

Page 43: Thacker, Christopher. *The History of Gardens*. Berkeley, California: University of California Press, 1979.

Page 51: White, Katharine S. *Onward and Upward in the Garden*. New York: Farrar Straus & Giroux, 1979.

Page 52: Capek, Karel. *The Gardener's Year*. Madison, Wisconsin: University of Wisconsin Press, 1984.

Page 53: Sackville-West, Vita. *Vita Sackville-West's Garden Book*. New York: Atheneum, 1983.

Page 54: Jensen, Jens. *Siftings*. Chicago, Illinois: R. F. Seymour, 1939.

Page 57: Lawrence, Elizabeth. *The Little Bulbs*. Durham, North Carolina: Duke University Press.

Pages 61, 62: Capek, Karel. *The Gardener's Year*. Madison, Wisconsin: University of Wisconsin Press, 1984.

Page 64: American Rock Garden Society. Darien, Connecticut

Pages 67, 69: Capek, Karel. *The Gardener's Year*. Madison, Wisconsin: University of Wisconsin Press, 1984.

Page 71: North American Lily Society. Waukee, Iowa.

Page 72: Capek, Karel. *The Gardener's Year*. Madison, Wisconsin: University of Wisconsin Press, 1984.

Page 76: Oosten, Henrik van. *The Dutch Gardener*. Severinus: Boekverkopers, 1700.

Page 79: Robinson, William. *The Wild Garden*. Deerpark, Wisconsin: Capability's Books.

Page 80: Sackville-West, Vita. *Vita Sackville-West's Garden Book*. New York: Atheneum, 1983.

Page 81: *Earthworms for Gardeners and Fishermen*. Portland, Oregon: ISBS, Inc.

Page 82: *The Rock Garden*. Perthshire, Scotland: The Scottish Rock Garden Club.

Page 83: Capek, Karel. *The Gardener's Year*. Madison, Wisconsin: University of Wisconsin Press, 1984.

Page 87: Anderson, Edgar. *Plants, Man and Life*. Berkeley, California: University of California Press, 1967.

Page 89: Capek, Karel. *The Gardener's Year*. Madison, Wisconsin: University of Wisconsin Press, 1984.

Page 94: Saint-Pierre, Jacques Bernardin de, *Etudes de la Nature XIII*. Paris, France: De l'Imprimerie de Monsieur, 1789.

Page 97: Potterton, David, ed. *Culpeper's Color Herbal*. New York: Sterling Publishing Co.

Page 102: Warner, Charles Dudley. *My Summer in a Garden*. New York: AMS Press, repr. of 1871 ed.

Page 103: Potterton, David, ed. *Culpeper's Color Herbal.* New York: Sterling Publishing Co.

Page 104: Endangered Species. Tustin, California.

Page 106: *The Rock Garden.* Perthshire, Scotland: The Scottish Rock Garden Club.

Page 107: Anderson, Edgar. *Plants, Man and Life.* Berkeley, California: University of California Press, 1967.

Page 108: Potterton, David, ed. *Culpeper's Color Herbal.* New York: Sterling Publishing Co.

Page 111: Baer, Reverend Urban. *Baer's Agriculture Almanac.* Sparta, Wisconsin: Monroe Publishing Co., 1939.

Page 116: Lindsay, Nicholas Vachel. *Adventures While Preaching the Gospel of Beauty.* New York, New York: M. Kennerley, 1914.

Page 123: *Gleanings in Bee Culture.* Medina, Ohio: A. I. Root Co.

Page 125: Capek, Karel. *The Gardener's Year.* Madison, Wisconsin: University of Wisconsin Press, 1984.

Page 126: Northern Greenhouse Sales. Neche, North Dakota.

Page 127: Baer, Reverend Urban. *Baer's Agriculture Almanac.* Sparta, Wisconsin: Monroe Publishing Co., 1939.

Page 147: Capek, Karel. *The Gardener's Year.* Madison, Wisconsin: University of Wisconsin Press, 1984.

Page 154: *Cactus and Succulent Journal.* Arcadia, California: The Cactus & Succulent Society of America.

Page 154: Capek, Karel. *The Gardener's Year.* Madison, Wisconsin: University of Wisconsin Press, 1984.

Page 155: Peterson, Roger Tory and McKenny, Margaret. *A Field Guide to Wildflowers of Northeastern and North Central North America.* New York: Alfred Knopf, 1968.

Pages 158, 159: *The Rose.* St. Albans, Herts., England: Royal National Rose Society.

Page 160: Capek, Karel. *The Gardener's Year.* Madison, Wisconsin: University of Wisconsin Press, 1984.

Page 163: Roses of Yesterday and Today. Watsonville, California.

Page 163: Phillips, Henry, *Pomarium Britannicum.* London, England: H. Colburn & Co., 1828.

Page 166: Peterson, Roger Tory and McKenny, Margaret. *A Field Guide to Wildflowers of Northeastern and North Central North America.* New York: Alfred Knopf, 1968.

Page 170: Gerarde, John. *Gerarde's Herball.* Londini: Ex officina R. Robinson, 1596.

Page 173: Thacker, Christopher. *The History of Gardens.* Berkeley, California: University of California Press, 1979.

Page 174: Roberts' Gesneriads. Baltimore, Maryland.

Page 181: Faulkner, Herbert Waldron, *The Mysteries of the Flowers.* New York, New York: F. A. Stokes, Co., 1917.

Page 183: Walter F. Nicke. *Garden Talk.* Hudson, New York.

Page 187: Baer, Reverend Urban. *Baer's Agriculture Almanac.* Sparta, Wisconsin: Monroe Publishing Co., 1939.

Page 188: Wescott, Cynthia. *The Gardener's Bug Book.* New York: Doubleday & Co.

Page 192: Mantis Manufacturing Co. Huntingdon Valley, Pennsylvania.

Pages 195, 199: Capek, Karel. *The Gardener's Year.* Madison, Wisconsin: University of Wisconsin Press, 1984.

Page 200: Druce, Robert. *Journal of Garden History.* Basingstoke, Hants, England: Taylor & Francis.

Pages 203, 207: Thacker, Christopher. *The History of Gardens.* Berkeley, California: University of California Press, 1979.

Page 212: Druce, Robert. *Journal of Garden History.* Basingstoke, Hants, England: Taylor & Francis.

Page 215: Capek, Karel. *The Gardener's Year.* Madison, Wisconsin: University of Wisconsin Press, 1984.

Page 216: Thacker, Christopher. *The History of Gardens.* Berkeley, California: University of California Press, 1979.

Page 219: Capek, Karel. *The Gardener's Year.* Madison, Wisconsin: University of Wisconsin Press, 1984.

Page 221: McHarg, Ian. *Design with Nature.* New York: Doubleday & Co., 1971.

Page 224: Tewes, Michael and Sharp, Geoffrey. *The Almanac of Wit* (1779).

Page 229: Jekyll, Gertrude. *Wood and Garden* (1899). Woodbridge, Suffolk, England: Antique Collector's Guide.

Page 233: Sackville-West, Vita. *Vita Sackville-West's Garden Book.* New York: Atheneum, 1983.

Pages 235: Anderson, Edgar. *Plants, Man and Life.* Berkeley, California: University of California Press, 1967.

Page 237: Capek, Karel. *The Gardener's Year.* Madison, Wisconsin: University of Wisconsin Press, 1984.

Page 239: *The Rock Garden.* Perthshire, Scotland: The Scottish Rock Garden Club.

Page 240: *The Gloxinian.* St. Louis, Missouri: American Gloxinian and Gesneriad Society.

Page 244: Potterton, David, ed. *Culpeper's Color Herbal.* New York: Sterling Publishing Co.

Page 247: Capek, Karel. *The Gardener's Year.* Madison, Wisconsin: University of Wisconsin Press, 1984.

Page 248: Christensen, Donald M. Hamden, Connecticut: Northern Nut Growers Association.

Pages 252, 253: Capek, Karel. *The Gardener's Year.* Madison, Wisconsin: University of Wisconsin Press, 1984.

Book Publishers

Addison-Wesley Publishing Co. Inc.
One Jacob Way
Reading, MA 01867

Atheneum Publishers
866 Third Avenue
New York, NY 10022

AVI Publishing Co.
Box 831
250 Post Road East
Westport, CT 06881

George Braziller Inc.
60 Madison Avenue
New York, NY 10010

Cambridge University Press
32 East 57 Street
New York, NY 10022

Crown Publishers Inc.
225 Park Avenue South
New York, NY 10003

Da Capo Press Inc.
233 Spring Street
New York, NY 10013

Doubleday & Co. Inc.
245 Park Avenue
New York, NY 10167

Dover Publications Inc.
31 East Second Street
Mineola, NY 11501

Duke University Press
Box 6697
College Station
Durham, NC 27708

Facts on File Inc.
460 Park Avenue South
New York, NY 10016

Farrar Straus & Giroux
19 Union Square West
New York, NY 10003

W. H. Freeman & Co. Publishers
41 Madison Avenue
New York, NY 10010

Garden Way Publishing
Schoolhouse Road
Pownal, VT 05261

David R. Godine, Publisher, Inc.
Horticultural Hall
300 Massachusetts Avenue
Boston, MA 02115

Grosset & Dunlap Inc
51 Madison Avenue
New York, NY 10010

Harper & Row Publishers Inc.
10 East 53 Street
New York, NY 10022

Harvard University Press
79 Garden Street
Cambridge, MA 02138

Heyday Books
Box 9145
Berkeley, CA 94709

Henry Holt & Co.
521 Fifth Avenue
New York, NY 10175

Houghton Mifflin Co.
One Beacon Street
Boston, MA 02108

Alfred A. Knopf
201 East 50 Street
New York, NY 10022

Kodansha International USA Ltd.
10 East 53 Street
New York, NY 10022

Lane Publishing Co.
80 Willow Road
Menlo Park, CA 94025

Little, Brown & Co. Inc.
34 Beacon Street
Boston, MA 02108

Macmillan Publishing Company
866 Third Avenue
New York, NY 10022

McGraw-Hill Inc.
1221 Avenue of the Americas
New York, NY 10020

William Morrow & Co. Inc.
105 Madison Avenue
New York, NY 10016

W. W. Norton & Co. Inc
500 Fifth Avenue
New York, NY 10110

Oxford University Press Inc.
200 Madison Avenue
New York, NY 10016

Plenum Publishing Corp.
233 Spring Street
New York, NY 10013

Random House Inc.
201 East 50 Street
New York, NY 10022

Reader's Digest General Books
750 Third Avenue
New York, NY 10017

Rizzoli International Publications Inc.
597 Fifth Avenue
New York, NY 10017

Rodale Press Inc.
33 East Minor Street
Emmaus, PA 18049

Running Press Book Publishers
125 South 22 Street
Philadelphia, PA 19103

Charles Scribner's Sons
115 Fifth Avenue
New York, NY 10003

Sierra Club Books
730 Polk Street
San Francisco, CA 94109

Simon & Schuster Inc.
1230 Avenue of the Americas
New York, NY 10020

Smithsonian Institution Press
955 L'Enfant Plaza
Room 2100
Washington, DC 20560

Sterling Publishing Co. Inc.
2 Park Avenue
New York, NY 10016

Taylor Publishing Company
1550 West Mockingbird Lane
Dallas, TX 75221

Ten Speed Press
Box 7123
Berkeley, CA 94707

Texas Monthly Press Inc.
Box 1569
Austin, TX 78767

Thames & Hudson Inc.
500 Fifth Avenue
New York, NY 10110

Timber Press Inc.
9999 SW Wilshire
Portland, OR 97225

University of California Press
2120 Berkeley Way
Berkeley, CA 94720

University of Massachusetts Press
Box 429
Amherst, MA 01004

University of Minnesota Press
2037 University Avenue SE
Minneapolis, MN 55414

University of Nebraska Press
901 N. 17 Street
Lincoln, NE 68588

University of North Carolina Press
Box 2288
Chapel Hill, NC 27514

University of Oklahoma Press
1005 Asp Avenue
Norman, OK 73019

University of Wisconsin Press
114 N. Murray Street
Madison, WI 53715

University Press of New England
3 Lebanon Street
Hanover, NH 03755

Van Nostrand Reinhold Co. Inc.
115 Fifth Avenue
New York, NY 10003

Viking Penguin Inc.
40 West 23 Street
New York, NY 10010

Weatherhill
157 East 69 Street
New York, NY 10021

John Wiley & Sons Inc.
605 Third Avenue
New York, NY 10158

Worth Publishers Inc.
33 Irving Place
New York, NY 10003

Yale University Press
302 Temple Street
New Haven, CT 06520

Yankee Books
Main Street
Dublin, NH 03444

Index of Sources